BUILT FROM THE FIRE

BUILT
THE F...

 RANDOM HOUSE NEW YORK

FROM
FIRE

THE EPIC STORY OF TULSA'S GREENWOOD DISTRICT, AMERICA'S BLACK WALL STREET

ONE HUNDRED YEARS IN THE NEIGHBORHOOD THAT REFUSED TO BE ERASED

VICTOR LUCKERSON

Published in the United States by Random House, an imprint and division of Penguin Random House LLC, New York.

RANDOM HOUSE and the HOUSE colophon are registered trademarks of Penguin Random House LLC.

LIBRARY OF CONGRESS CATALOGING-IN-PUBLICATION DATA
Names: Luckerson, Victor, author.
Title: Built from the fire: the epic story of Tulsa's Greenwood district, America's Black Wall Street: one hundred years in the neighborhood that refused to be erased / Victor Luckerson.
Other titles: Epic story of Tulsa's Greenwood district, America's Black Wall Street
Description: New York: Random House, [2023] |
Includes bibliographical references and index.
Identifiers: LCCN 2022055077 (print) | LCCN 2022055078 (ebook) |
ISBN 9780593134375 (hardback) | ISBN 9780593134382 (ebook)
Subjects: LCSH: Greenwood (Tulsa, Okla.)—Race relations—History. |
Tulsa (Okla.)—Race relations—History. | Tulsa Race Massacre, Tulsa, Okla.,1921. | Goodwin family. | Urban renewal—Oklahoma—Tulsa—History. |African Americans—Oklahoma—Tulsa—Social conditions. | African Americans—Oklahoma—Tulsa—Biography. | Greenwood (Tulsa, Okla.)—Biography. | Tulsa (Okla.)—Biography.
Classification: LCC F704.T92 L84 2023 (print) |
LCC F704.T92 (ebook) | DDC 976.6/8600496073—dc23/eng/20221214
LC record available at https://lccn.loc.gov/2022055077
LC ebook record available at https://lccn.loc.gov/2022055078

Printed in the United States of America on acid-free paper

randomhousebooks.com

9 8 7 6 5 4 3 2 1

FIRST EDITION

Book design by Simon M. Sullivan

For Mommom, who taught me that words have power

CONTENTS

PART **|||**

PROLOGUE

J im Goodwin remembers the symphony of the old Greenwood well. The blues mingling with smoke as it wafted out of hazy juke joints, the sizzle of beef on the open grill at hamburger stands, the seductive murmurs of hustlers in back alleys peddling their pocket addictions, the *click-clack* of women's heels on the sidewalk when all the maids crowded the street on their Thursday nights off. Greenwood was loud. Boisterous. It was a ritual of improvised celebration and emotional release, the same kind black people had carved out in shacks, shotgun houses, and white-picket-fence homes across this nation since our involuntary arrival on the eastern shores.

For generations, Greenwood was something more than a collection of black-owned homes and businesses just north of downtown Tulsa. Perhaps it started that way, in 1905, when Emma and O. W. Gurley first opened a grocery store north of the Frisco Railroad tracks on land once owned by the Creek Nation.[1] But as the number of people living, loving, toiling, and thriving in the neighborhood grew, so did its mystique. George Washington Carver[2] and W.E.B. Du Bois visited Greenwood early on, when it was, in Du Bois's words, "impudent and noisy."[3] When the neon signs adorning all the cafés, nightclubs, and stately churches were lit up on warm summer evenings, folks would say it looked like a fairyland. By the time Jim was roaming the street in the 1940s, the neighborhood chamber of commerce described Greenwood as more than an avenue—"It is an institution."[4]

In the daily symphony, Jim had contributed his own instrument. Standing at the corner of Greenwood Avenue and Archer Street as a young boy, clutching a stack of newspapers, he would yell out his sales pitch: "The *Oklahoma Eagle*! Only five cents!" It was the paper his father, Edward Goodwin, Sr., purchased in 1937, just two years before he was born; Ed Sr. let him keep the money from each sale.[5]

Jim and his siblings took on dozens of roles over the years to get the paper out the door each week. Edwyna was the first woman to serve as managing editor. Jo Ann proofread pages.[6] Ed Jr. understood the intricacies of the printing press like no other.[7] Daughter Jeanne penned the fiery columns quoting Du Bois and Malcolm X that reminded their father every day that he had raised black children. The Goodwins had their own internal orchestra going, anchored by the whirring of a clamorous press, one of the few in the whole country owned by a black family.

By January 2020, though, the rhythms of Greenwood have changed. Cars and semis barrel over the neighborhood on an interstate overpass that has cleaved the community in half since 1967. The monotonous clanging of bolts driving into steel beams marks the steady rise of luxury apartments occupying more and more of the area. These days Greenwood Avenue comes alive only when the Tulsa Drillers, a minor league baseball team, takes the field on land once owned by black people—some of it once owned by the Goodwins themselves, in fact. Suburbanites from Broken Arrow and Jenks drive across the roaring highway for a pleasant night out in downtown Tulsa, not even realizing they are in Greenwood. They don't think too much about who or what might have been there before.

There are a handful of squat brick buildings from old Greenwood left standing, lined up on both sides of Greenwood Avenue as luxury towers and stadiums sprout up around them like weeds. These are managed by the Greenwood Chamber of Commerce; one other building on the south side of Archer Street is owned by Jim Goodwin and his family. There the *Oklahoma Eagle* continues to publish a weekly newspaper. Neither Jim nor his children have ever taken stock of how many *Eagle* editions the family has published, but an issue every week for eighty-three years equals about 4,316 newspapers. *Jet* and *Ebony* and the *Tulsa Tribune* didn't last as long, and most of the publications that did were acquired by corporations with headquarters far removed from the communities they covered. By holding on for so long, the *Eagle* has become one of the ten oldest black-owned newspapers in the United States.

Keeping the business afloat wasn't easy. A series of articles outlining the newspaper's 1996 bankruptcy are framed in an office hallway labeled the "Wall of Faith." But the *Eagle* had no intention of selling out or closing down. It was entrenched on a literal cornerstone of black history. Jim often recalled a conversation he had with his father when he was still a young lawyer. "Always keep this newspaper," Ed Sr. told him. "It will be a source of influence."[8]

And so the *Eagle* continues to sit there, in a refurbished auto garage just off the main drag of Greenwood Avenue.[9] Wandering its halls feels a bit like exploring the underbelly of an old church, where the gloss of the transcendent sanctuary gives way to the weary world of daily human toil. The weathered white tile floors have faded to gray. In the cavernous room, big enough to house a printing press, reams of unsold *Eagle* issues and abandoned newspaper racks occupy every crevice, and stains from a weathered roof are splotched across the pockmarked ceiling.

The building has seen better days, but those days are preserved, like amber, everywhere you look. In the lobby, behind the reception desk, four large framed pictures trace the paper's history under the Goodwins. In a bright watercolor painting, Ed Goodwin, Sr., wears a warm grin, his brightly jeweled hand covering a Bible. The jovial pose belies the many traumas he witnessed in life. His wife Jeanne, in a brown blazer, looks off frame with a sly smile, contemplating some secret she might tell you if you gain her trust. Ed Jr., Jim's older brother and former *Eagle* co-publisher, wears a black leather jacket with fur lining and a brown fedora; he was always young at heart. Jim, the adult in the room since he was a child, smiles the least in his picture.

He works in an office in the back of the building, concerned more with his law practice than with the daily operations of the paper.[10] The space certainly looks the part—plush red carpet, mahogany furniture, plaques and community awards occupying every shelf. On his desk are a brown accordion folder stuffed with case files, a Catholic pamphlet titled *Cathedral News,* a bronze statue of a blind angel balancing the scales of justice, and a funeral program for Luther Elliot, Jr., an old friend who has just recently died.

Jim clacks away at emails on his computer, facing out toward Greenwood Avenue, while a West Highland white terrier named Annie scurries around his feet. He is wearing a pair of thin-framed glasses while another pair dangle from the V in his gray polo shirt. It is lunchtime. Besides the two of us, the building seems to be empty.

Shortly after I arrive, he slides a recent issue of the *Eagle* across his desk. On the front page is a picture of the block outside his window, targeted in the scope of a sniper rifle. IS GREENWOOD AT THE CROSSROADS OR CROSSHAIRS? wonders a headline streaming clean across the width of the paper. The opening paragraph is as blunt as the illustration: "Presently, in some Tulsa boardrooms and offices, individuals are quietly discussing further development plans for the strategic gentrification but 'legal' usurpation of the Greenwood District."[11]

It is one of the rare editorials in the paper Jim actually wrote himself. He once told me he was ambivalent about the changes descending upon Greenwood[12]—he'd seen so many changes already—but the years of disregard for what neighborhood folks actually wanted wore on him. "Millions of dollars have been spent in planning of this community by residents of this community," he says, "only to be mothballed and forgotten with the passage of each of the political influences that are in vogue at the time."[13]

As he is discussing how Greenwood's story represents "quintessential Americana," his phone rings. It's a reporter for the *Washington Post*. Earlier in the week, Jim recorded a podcast with another journalist. He'd spent decades discussing the history of his hometown for authors and documentary crews, but the interview requests are increasing now with each passing month. Over time he developed certain pithy adages that distilled his views on Tulsa, Greenwood, and race relations into fantastic quotes. The old Greenwood was a place where "on one end of the street you get heroin and on the other end of the street, you get the Holy Ghost."[14] Segregation was a legal and moral scourge, but it also created the underpinnings of black economic self-sufficiency—or as Jim likes to say, "What man intends for evil, God intends for good."

Still, there are some words he does not repeat so readily. "My paper, as a graduating senior at the University of Notre Dame, I wrote about the Tulsa problem," he says early in our conversation. "Have I discussed that with you?"[15]

Jim became one of the first black students at Notre Dame in 1957,[16] when the train route between South Bend and Tulsa was still full of segregated restaurants.[17] He studied *Ulysses* and Dante's *Inferno* and mostly ignored football. With his credentials and his sense of adventure—his office is dotted with photos of him riding horses through the Oklahoma prairies—he could have found success anywhere in the United States after graduating. But he came home to join his father's law practice instead, because the Tulsa problem was never far from his mind.

He reaches down to a desk drawer on his left and pulls out a bundle of papers, the pages turned yellow with age. SENIOR ESSAY, JAMES O. GOODWIN, JUNE 1961, is written in typescript on the front. As he begins to read, the cacophony of the new Greenwood outside slowly fades away.

"On a hillside several decades ago stood a burning cross. Hundreds of jubilant men, all members of the Ku Klux Klan had gathered around it. Two days earlier, they had mercilessly plundered and destroyed 50 percent of the Negro community. Now they converged upon a burning cross in celebration of victory. Behind them was a trail of blood and two million dollars in property damage. The alleged assault of a white girl by a negro man had been thoroughly avenged. This hillside rendezvous was a tribute to their triumph and their expression of their gluttonous success. The burning cross symbolized all their hatred for the negro and emblemized the white supremacist doctrine. It so controlled them that as the flame grew into one massive blaze, also the single taunts of hate blended into the thunderous roar of a mob."[18]

Before the history books and documentaries and HBO adaptations, Jim described, in vivid detail, the events of May 31 and June 1, 1921, in Tulsa, Oklahoma. After a shoeshine boy named Dick Rowland was arrested on a false rape allegation, armed black men from Greenwood drove to the courthouse to defend him from a potential lynching. The confrontation escalated into an armed shoot-out between black and white men in the streets of downtown Tulsa. After the shoot-out, in order to reassert white dominance, thousands of whites crossed the railroad tracks that segregated the city to loot and set fire to everything black Tulsans had built. More than twelve hundred houses were leveled, nearly every business was burned to the ground, and an unknown number of people—estimates reach as high as three hundred—were killed.[19]

Jim grew up referring to this dark history as a *riot*. More recently the term *massacre* has come into favor. But when he stops to reflect on the magnitude of the destruction, and the dark motivation at the heart of it, he thinks *pogrom*—an organized massacre of a particular ethnic group—may be the most apt description.

He looks up from his essay. Surrounding him are photos of his father and grandfather, survivors of Greenwood's destruction, as well as people who arrived in the reborn neighborhood and helped build it anew, like his mother. They are all gone now, in flesh and in some cases nearly in memory. In the one fading photograph of Jim's grandfather, James Henri Goodwin, the man's face is nearly blotted out with age.

Jim's words arc far back into the past, but they also stretch into the future. They warn against the vagaries of mob violence and white supremacy, of actions and ideologies that Americans want to bury in the past but that have metastasized in recent years, like a resurgent cancer. "Here I am now, from age twenty to age eighty," Jim says, "grappling with the same issue."

He leans back in his chair and strokes his white, closely cropped beard. He can hardly believe he is eighty years old. At his age, the future is no longer a mystery; he can hear the echoes of the past in today's news clarions, see the well-worn currents of history in the chaotic stream of current events. The United States feels more bound to its history than it ever has before. At the beginning of 2020, it is a nation on the cusp of a once-in-a-century pandemic, a summer of racial protest four hundred years in the making, and a siege of the U.S. Capitol claiming a warped allegiance to the revolution of 1776.

America's darkest memories and its most inspiring mythologies both route their way down Greenwood Avenue, through the very land Jim Goodwin has always called home. But this is a city and a country all too eager to bury its past, to drown out the story of what happened here with interstate traffic, construction crews, and the din of an easygoing day at the ballpark. The whispers of the departed grow fainter with each passing day, as the arbiters of so-called justice patiently eye the hourglass. But an untreated wound does not heal as the years go by; it festers. An unpaid debt is not wiped from the books; it accrues interest. Greenwood's ancestors, the ones who witnessed its creation and its cataclysm, must all eventually go silent. Yet their souls still stir in the voices of their descendants—and finally, people are listening. "I'm saying to the mayor and everyone else, you cannot pave over history," Jim says. "No matter what you do, the history of Greenwood will be forever known."[20]

PART I

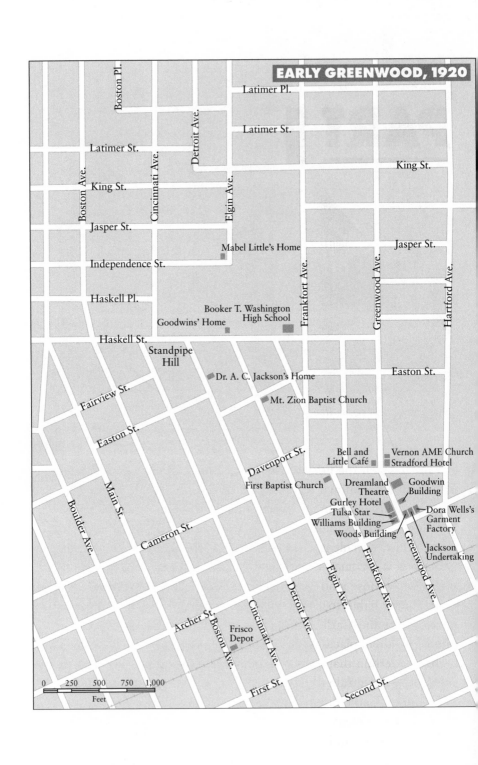

EARLY GREENWOOD, 1920

Boston Pl.

Latimer Pl.

Latimer St.

Detroit Ave.

Latimer St.

King St.

Latimer St.

Boston Ave.

Cincinnati Ave.

King St.

Elgin Ave.

Jasper St.

Independence St.

Mabel Little's Home

Jasper St.

Frankfort Ave.

Greenwood Ave.

Hartford Ave.

Haskell Pl.

Booker T. Washington
High School

Goodwins' Home

Haskell St.

Standpipe
Hill

Dr. A. C. Jackson's Home

Easton St.

Fairview St.

Mt. Zion Baptist Church

Easton St.

Davenport St.

Bell and
Little Café

Vernon AME Church

Stradford Hotel

First Baptist Church

Dreamland
Theatre

Goodwin
Building

Main St.

Gurley Hotel

Tulsa Star

Dora Wells's
Garment
Factory

Boulder Ave.

Cameron St.

Williams Building

Woods Building

Greenwood Ave.

Jackson
Undertaking

Frankfort Ave.

Elgin Ave.

Detroit Ave.

Archer St.

Cincinnati Ave.

Boston Ave.

Frisco
Depot

First St.

Second St.

0   250   500   750   1,000

Feet

CHAPTER 1

DO NOT HESITATE, BUT COME

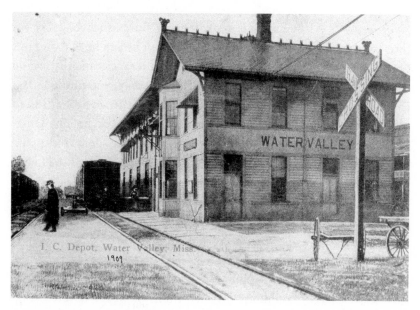

A postcard depicting the Illinois Central Railroad depot in Water Valley

They called it the Eden of the West.[1] When boosters crafted tales of the land known as the Creek Nation, Indian Territory, and eventually Oklahoma, they wrote of fertile soil that could grow any crop, yielding shoulder-high acres of wheat and melons ready to burst in their succulent ripeness.[2] They described a righteous realm where any newcomer would have "equal chances with the white man," while those who remained in the old world, the Deep South, were "slaves liable to be killed at any time."[3] Most important to James Henri and Carlie Goodwin, they spoke of good schools for colored children, places where the seeds of prosperity could be sown in the one terrain that could not be burned, stolen, or erased by an interloper—the terrain of the mind.

James and Carlie did not decide to move to Oklahoma spontaneously, for spontaneity was not a luxury that black people could afford. James was a quiet, deliberate man who sought success with a patient vigor. In the early 1900's, he and his wife lived on a segregated street in a small town in Mississippi called Water Valley, along with their four children: Lucille, James Jr., Anna, and the baby, Edward.[4] Though they were Mississippi natives, the Goodwins read about life out west for years through a black newspaper called the *Oklahoma Safeguard*. C. A. Buchanan, the *Safeguard*'s publisher, had been a thriving newspaper owner in rural Mississippi before he was run out of the state by the white folks for his "racial utterances and disturbing effusions" (he'd denigrated a group of whites-only restaurants).[5] Buchanan relaunched the *Safeguard* in Oklahoma in 1905 and hired sales agents to keep distributing the newspaper back home.[6] James and Carlie's names appeared in brief *Safeguard* news items recapping sick lists and social events in Water Valley,[7] but the bulk of the newspaper was dedicated to describing, in vivid terms, the boundless opportunities Buchanan had discovered in Oklahoma.

Here was a place where three-quarters of black farmers owned their acreage and more than 80 percent of black people could read—a higher literacy rate than any state in the South.[8] Between 1900 and 1920, Oklahoma's black population tripled as people trekked to the state however they could, on crowded trains or weary covered wagons.[9] A few even arrived on foot.[10] Keep coming, Buchanan implored his Mississippi readers. "Now is the time for the progressive negro to come west to seek a home. . . . It is superior to any other section of the United States."[11]

Mississippi residents wrote back to Buchanan in turn, cursing the dark clouds gathering over the world he had left behind. After holding three congressional seats in the state during the era of Reconstruction, black people had effectively been disenfranchised.[12] Lynchings were a threat as perennial as the thunderstorms that rattled shacks and flooded the great river.[13] "A copy of your paper came to my home and it was like the bright sunshine of the morning of May," one *Safeguard* subscriber wrote after reading about life in Oklahoma. "You are where you can have free speech and privilege to act as a man without being molested."[14]

That's what James Goodwin wanted more than anything. Growing up in Water Valley in the decades after the Civil War, he had brokered an uneasy détente with the white power structure that controlled the town, the state, and the Deep South. At first, he worked for the white folks directly, earning a job as a twelve-year-old callboy on the Illinois Central Railroad.[15] Every morning James roamed Water Valley's dirt roads,[16] banging the bedroom windows of engineers trying to shirk work[17] or luring drunk firemen from the local saloon to the railroad station.[18]

When he became a man, he was promoted to brakeman.[19] His job was to climb atop the locomotive as the train approached each town's railroad depot and engage the brake at the sound of a steam whistle.[20] It was dangerous, dirty work, for which James could expect to earn less money than his white peers, while working longer hours.[21] But in 1890 there were fewer than 2,800 black men working the railroads in the entire state, out of almost two hundred thousand black male laborers.[22] Even if he was making less than the employee average of forty-five dollars per month, it was still more than the legions of colored farmers sweating in the fields under the predatory terms of a sharecropping contract.[23] It was a start. James rode up and down the Illinois Central constantly, past the cattle ranches and strawberry farms of Yalobusha County.[24] He grew accustomed to movement and to change.

James used the money he earned working for the Illinois Central to open a grocery store by the Presbyterian church on Main Street—that is to say, in the white part of town.[25] James was fair-skinned enough to be mistaken for white, wearing his dark hair slicked back with a part.[26] The origins of his complexion were a mystery to his grandchildren, who would later learn the family history only through wisps of breakfast table conversations with the man they called Papa and from nearly forgotten revelations tucked inside his funeral program. A family story persisted that James's father was a Jewish bridge builder named Henri Goodwin and his mother, Sallie, a former slave.[27] When a census taker came to the Goodwin home on Cemetery Street, he must have been confused about how to categorize their wide mix of complexions. He listed the family as an alternating racial patchwork, from James on down to young Edward: mulatto, black, mulatto, black, mulatto, black.[28]

James's wife Carlie, meanwhile, had a wide, brown face, hair in bouncing black curls, and a natural adroitness with land transactions, though the census would never list her with any formal occupation. Instead of marrying a dark-skinned woman like Carlie, James could have moved to a different town and blended into white society, a common turn-of-the-century practice known as *passing*. One light-skinned woman who watched both friends and family disappear into the white world wondered, "How would anybody know who they were without their people?"[29] But James was strategic about when he chose to pass. While traveling around the state with his youngest son Edward, he often brought the child with him into segregated stores and restaurants, declaring to any suspicious eye, "That's my boy." He meant that Ed was his son but allowed the assumption that he was a servant to hang in the air.[30] It was a bleak compromise with bigotry, but also a clever one. Such tactics exposed the color line for the arbitrary and cruel barrier that it was, as Langston Hughes once pointed out. "There's no harm in fooling the devil is there?" he wrote in an impish essay on passing. "Most colored folks think that as long as white folks remain foolish, prejudiced, and racially selfish, they deserve to be fooled."[31]

However James's appearance came to be, it opened worlds to him that were not available to his wife or children. His Main Street store,

J. H. and Carlie Goodwin in Water Valley with their four children (left to right) Edward, Anna, Lucille, and James

wedged between a dry cleaners and a vacant storefront in a modest wooden building, was hardly Water Valley's marquee enterprise.[32] But James was successful. So long as he was selling white people confectioneries and canned goods, they were happy to have him serve their needs. In 1906, when he enlarged his store, the *Water Valley Progress,* a white newspaper, deemed it a cause for celebration. "His white friends as well as the colored rejoice in these evidences of his prosperity."[33]

Over the next few years, James's fortunes continued to rise. He opened a funeral home above a livery stable in 1910, cementing his climb into the black elite.[34] The Goodwins were among the 17 percent of black families in Mississippi who owned their homes, and they soon purchased several additional pieces of property in town.[35] James and Carlie became officers in the Knights of Pythias, a black fraternal organization that doubled as an essential professional network.[36] He began going by "J.H." in public, so that white men would not disrespect him by using his first name—or worse, calling him "boy."[37]

But J.H. was butting up against the limits of his narrow privileges. While he gained some benefits from appearing white, his children felt only the harsh constraints of being born black in the Deep South. Mississippi's public school system had been segregated since its inception in 1870.[38] For every dollar the state spent educating a white student, it spent nineteen cents on a black student.[39] Black teachers in Water Valley earned half as much as white ones, a disparity that steadily increased throughout the state as Reconstruction slipped further into the haze of the past.[40]

A person did not have to summon facts and figures to understand that inequality ran rampant—they needed only to wander through town. White students in Water Valley were taught in a large three-story brick schoolhouse with steam heating and electric lights. Black students like the Goodwin children attended school in a pair of small single-floor wooden buildings, one barely bigger than a living room, that lacked heat or electricity.[41] No matter a black child's individual ambitions, their schooling ended at the start of their teenage years—the only colored high school in all of Mississippi was in Yazoo City, 120 miles away.[42] White leaders wanted to keep it that way. "Literary education—the knowledge of books—does not seem to produce any good substantial results with the Negro," Mississippi governor James

Vardaman said in 1904, "but serves to sharpen his cunning, breeds hopes that cannot be fulfilled, inspires aspirations that cannot be gratified."[43]

The Goodwins also had to contend with the constant threat of racial violence. After the Civil War, Water Valley residents who resented the Union's victory became early and eager members of the Ku Klux Klan. Between 1867 and 1875, local Klan posses rode to the homes of black families to whip victims who had crossed them. Klan members pelted groups of black men they deemed rowdy with hollowed-out ears of corn filled with explosive gunpowder. A rumor persisted into J.H.'s adulthood that the Klan had murdered John Scurlock, a charismatic local black leader who ran for the state legislature in 1872. Water Valley's Klan cyclops, the former Confederate colonel M.D.L. Stephens, said another black killing had been committed not by any individual murderer but by "public sentiment." In 1876 supporters of the Klan-aligned Democratic Party rode through the streets of Water Valley before the presidential election, carrying banners that read WHITE MAN'S COUNTY, WHITE MAN'S RULE.[44]

After the Klan faded from the public eye, these men and their children melted back into their roles as powerful civic leaders, taking over judgeships and launching businesses.[45] Even as they made small allowances for black independence, like letting a light-skinned Negro own a store on Main Street, they remained deeply devoted to white supremacy. If J.H. or any other black man saw a white man approaching on the sidewalk, he was expected to tip his hat and step aside, scurrying into a gutter if need be. Those who didn't comply risked beatings or worse.[46] His son Edward chose never to wear a hat in public because he so deeply resented the ritual.[47]

Decades later, when J.H. told his progeny about life in the Jim Crow South, he didn't talk about the success of his grocery store or the polite praise he received in the white press. He talked about the run-ins on the sidewalk. "He did not want to be in a place where the safety of a black man could be so lightly treated," his grandson Jim explained. "He didn't want his kids exposed to that."[48]

Perhaps, following one of these humiliating encounters, Mississippi's intricate latticework of hateful mores became too much for J.H. and his family to bear. No one living today can say for sure. But deciding how to navigate the daily vagaries of racism—how to literally maneuver around them on the street—was an "all-absorbing, burning question" among the thousands of black families who contemplated leaving the Jim Crow South in the early 1900s, according to a survey by a black field investigator for the Department of Labor. Conversations that J.H. and Carlie were having at neighborhood parties, inside their funeral parlor, and during Knights of Pythias meetings must have inevitably drifted toward what the surveyor found was being whispered all across the land: "some discussion of their treatment at the hands of white people."[49]

J.H. attained only a fifth-grade education.[50] Carlie made it to the eighth grade. They knew their children deserved better than what little had been possible in the hardscrabble aftermath of Reconstruction. But when the couple looked out beyond their daily efforts to build a decent life for their family, they did not see much of a future. "They were concerned about our having academic foundations at least through high school," their son Ed recalled later. "His ambition [was] to see to it that we would have a better education than he had."[51]

By the fall of 1913, the Goodwins knew it was time to make a change. As the sparks of the Great Migration were just beginning to ignite, and the bone-deep conviction to live life unmolested was spreading from soul to soul in the Deep South like wildfire, J.H. boarded a train owned by his former employer. He was no longer an underpaid brakeman but a passenger. He had decided to leave Water Valley forever.

The plan was to go to Iowa. At the northern end of the Illinois Central lay a city called Waterloo, where the railroad company was recruiting black men to disrupt a shopmen's strike. About a third of the hundreds of new black transplants hailed from Mississippi, and many came from Water Valley.[52] J.H.'s railroad days were behind him, but a growing black enclave of southern transplants presented all kinds of business opportunities for a burgeoning entrepreneur. He decided to go investigate the town for himself.

His route to Waterloo took him through St. Louis, where the sprawling Union Station was a nexus for nationwide travel.[53] As J.H. walked into the bustling facility, he looked upon the stained glass

A.G.W. Sango

windows lining the station's walls and the sculptures of women perched in rooftop corners cradling orbs of light. Above him, a gleaming chandelier hung from the sixty-five-foot ceiling, adorned with 350 lightbulbs.[54] But what must have caught his eye most of all was something he hadn't been expecting to see: a lavish train car chartered by a black man.[55]

He had a regal name: Alexander George Washington Sango. He claimed to be a descendant of African royalty,[56] but now he ruled the city of Muskogee, Oklahoma, through his money and political back-channeling. A burly, dark-skinned lawyer and real estate investor, Sango often dressed in fine suits and bow ties, puffing on a thick cigar.[57] He had a booming voice that he enjoyed using every chance he got,[58] soliciting black votes for the Republican Party at election time and seizing leadership roles in the city's multiracial Republican caucus. "My hair may be wooly and my skin black, but you have a square deal in the selection of Sango for chairman," he said after one successful election.[59] The daily newspapers followed his every move and christened him, with some mixture of bafflement and frustration, the "King of Muskogee—black Muskogee, that is."[60]

Sango's wealth came from the land. Though he was of African heritage, he was also a tribal citizen of the Creek Nation.[61] His mother Phyllis was among the first black people to settle in what would one day be Oklahoma, arriving with the Creeks and other Native American tribes in the 1830s during the brutal forced exodus known as the Trail of Tears.[62] Black people like Phyllis weren't tribal citizens then; Native Americans, just like whites, enslaved blacks in the Deep South and continued the practice when they arrived in the eastern half of Oklahoma, which was then known as Indian Territory. The Five Tribes—the Creeks, Cherokees, Choctaws, Chickasaws, and Seminoles—even formally sided with the Confederacy in the Civil War, though there was much dissension on the matter within their ranks.[63] The slaves' allegiances were less ambiguous; they refused to remain in bondage. Sango's father Scipio fought for the Union Army in 1863 after being freed by the famed Creek chief Opothleyahola.[64]

While the tribes were formally aligned with the white planters of the South, the two groups diverged in their treatment of blacks after the war. As part of their treaties with the Union, most of the tribes granted formerly enslaved people citizenship, autonomy, and a level of respect unheard of in the post-Reconstruction South.[65] Black and indigenous people farmed together on communally owned land. They served side by side in tribal governments.[66] Alexander Sango himself was elected to the Creeks' House of Warriors, a legislative body similar to the U.S. House of Representatives.[67] Collectively, the black members of the Native tribes came to be known as "freedmen." By the turn of the twentieth century, there were twenty-three thousand of them throughout the Five Tribes.[68]

But both freedmen and Native Americans saw their way of life transformed—a few for the better, many for the worse—by the intrusion of the federal government in Indian Territory. In 1893 former U.S. senator Henry Dawes spearheaded a federal commission aimed at converting the tribes' 19.5 million acres of collectively owned land into individual property allotments.[69] Dawes called himself a "friend of the Indians,"[70] but his vision of helping them hinged on their assimilation into white America's cultural and economic systems. He was mystified by the tribes' capacity to share resources without trying to exploit them for personal profit. It seemed downright un-American. "There is no selfishness, which is at the bottom of civilization," Dawes remarked. "Till this people will consent to give up their lands, and divide them among their citizens . . . they will not make much more progress."[71]

After signing another series of treaties under intense federal pressure, the Five Tribes saw their homeland opened up to one of the nation's most ruthless conquerors: the free market. Fields, prairies, marshes, and valleys that had been "beneficently provided by the Great Spirit for the free use and support of his children," as a group of Creeks put it in 1908, were divided into standardized parcels and appraised at an average value of $6.50 per acre.[72] Progress quite literally came at a cost.

Many freedmen and Native Americans quickly sold their land for little money or lost it as victims of fraudulent schemes. But those who held on to it, like Sango, became fantastically rich. Freedmen were granted about 2 million acres of Oklahoma land, the largest transfer of property wealth to black people in the history of the United States.[73] It was the promise of forty acres and a mule, which Union general William Sherman had negotiated with a group of black Savannah ministers at the end of the Civil War, finally made real.[74] As a member of the Creek tribe, Sango was granted 160 acres, including forty acres only a few miles south of Tulsa.[75] He was proud to be able to say, as an adult, that he still owned the acreage where he was born.

Some freedmen saw black newcomers to Oklahoma as no different from the white intruders who had dismantled the old ways of life. The freedmen called the new black migrants "state Negroes" (or sometimes "Watchina," a word for "white man's Negro").[76] But Sango, who was heavily into real estate, saw new residents as a business opportunity. He liked to charter private Pullman cars to nearby cities such as Dallas and St. Louis—sometimes for joyrides with his friends, other times as part of boosterism trips to market the brand-new state of Oklahoma.[77] A Muskogee entourage even traveled to Washington, D.C., to celebrate Theodore Roosevelt's inauguration in 1905, sipping artesian water and laughing at the chagrined whites they saw when they stopped for supper in Arkansas.[78] The opulent Pullman car provided a compelling visual for Sango's sales pitch on the limitless potential of his homeland.

"This is the last chance for the Negro to acquire good farming property and a comfortable fortune without desperately struggling to obtain it," read a real estate guide in the *Enterprise,* Sango's aptly named newspaper. He promised the same things C. A. Buchanan had teased in the *Safeguard:* bountiful farmland, modern homes, and good schools. Like many black boosters, Sango specifically targeted "thrifty, law-abiding colored people" as good candidates for the move out west. What the Oklahoma boosters wanted was not to save the black masses from the vise of white bigotry, but to establish a haven for the burgeoning black middle class separate from it, a place where land could still be claimed, wealth still built, political power still secured, even as the nation turned its back on the bloody freedoms brokered during the Civil War. Theirs would be a new kind of state. "Now is your opportunity," Sango's *Enterprise* implored. "Do not hesitate, but come."[79]

J.H. knew about the promise of Oklahoma in theory. He'd no doubt read about its abundance in publications like the *Oklahoma Safeguard*. But meeting Sango must have made it real. This man, and the world he hailed from, were a universe apart from sleepy little Water Valley, and far beyond what J.H. dreamed of finding in Waterloo. In the *Enterprise,* Sango listed several Oklahoma locales where he felt blacks could find "wealth, happiness and freedom." One was a booming oil town called Tulsa. J.H. decided he would have to take a detour.

"So, my daddy came through Oklahoma," his son Ed recalled decades later, "and he decided that this is the place that he wanted us to live."[80]

The route to Oklahoma on the St. Louis–San Francisco Railway hugs the northern spine of the Ozarks, slicing through the forested hills of the Salem Plateau.[81] In 1913 many of the trains did not bother stopping anywhere in Missouri until they reached Springfield, in the southwestern corner of the state; Oklahoma was where the action was.[82] People hopped on and off the train in oil towns like Chelsea,[83] which had sprung up overnight to serve the towering timber derricks pulsing with black gold. Tulsa became one such town in 1901, when a drilling expedition in nearby Red Fork unleashed a thirty-foot gusher on a Creek citizen's land allotment.[84] Four years later an even larger oil reserve was discovered about ten miles from the first one, and Tulsa evolved into something more than yet another tar-drenched outpost. It was Magic City, the Many-Millionaire City, the Oil Capital of the World.[85] It didn't matter that the nicknames weren't altogether true, seeing as every drop of oil was actually found well outside the city limits; what mattered was how often the city's savvy boosters repeated each moniker. Tulsa soon became the financial center for oil prospecting and land leasing deals across the entire region.[86]

When J.H. rode into Oklahoma on Sango's private Pullman car, the trip felt like a vacation unto itself. The specialized cars featured dark walnut walls and plush upholstery, along with chandeliers that cast a warm glow on every inch of brass metalwork.[87] Luxury train wheels, which used compressed paper rather than wood at their center, glided along the railroad tracks to ensure a quieter ride.[88] Black people who could afford to charter these majestic trains—bankers, factory owners, politicians[89]—had ambitions far beyond opening a neighborhood grocery store. J.H. and his gregarious recruiter may have sat knee to knee as they coasted through the verdant countryside, while Sango, plucking the thick cigar from his mouth, bragged about how he planned to launch an oil drilling company himself, just like the white men whom the newspapers celebrated as moguls and pioneers.[90]

Exactly when J.H. took his luxurious tour of the state with Sango, the records do not say. But what is known is that the Mississippi native pulled into the downtown Tulsa railroad depot on the Frisco line in early December 1913. J.H. was on a scouting mission. He needed to see for himself whether this was a suitable town for a black man to open a business and provide a quality education for his children. He was almost certainly wearing a gray or brown suit—his grandchildren would later say they never saw him without one—and an overcoat to protect himself from the first chills of Tulsa's harsh winters.[91]

Standing on the train platform, J.H. could gaze up and see the epicenter of the city's wealth just three blocks south. The Hotel Tulsa, twelve stories tall and half a block wide, was the largest new downtown skyscraper, the place where oil barons brokered all their million-dollar leases. Lounging in the decadent hotel lobby, these men pored over table-size maps that lent cold authority to their contractual conquests. If this city was indeed magic, these men believed they had the monopoly on it. But J.H. turned his back to the hotel and walked north, across the Frisco tracks. That was where he would have to build his future.

Just north of the train station was the first sign that Tulsa had something to offer him that Water Valley didn't. Amid a small strip of black-owned businesses—a barbershop, a tailor, a restaurant—was a pool hall in a narrow brick building. It was owned by a black man named J. B. Stradford, who was a Tulsa city father as much as the white men whose names dominated all the street signs.[92] Stradford had arrived in the city in 1905, before statehood and the oil boom. At one point, before the degradations of Jim Crow had fully calcified out west, he'd even mulled a run for city council.[93] The white press and police did not like the way he carried himself, so they cast him as a creature of the underworld. In 1912 he was found guilty of operating a dice game out of his pool hall and was labeled a "professional gambler and booze dispenser" by the *Tulsa Democrat,* one of the city's two white dailies.[94] But Stradford, a graduate of Oberlin College and the Indianapolis College of Law, defended himself in court on the dice game charge.[95] His focus was not petty gambling; he had recently hosted an evening of music at the opera house to fundraise for a colored library. Soon he intended to use his new real estate firm, the Oklahoma Realty and Investment Company, as a vehicle to put his people "upon the road to wealth and honor."[96] He was impressed by what the white folks had accomplished with the nearby Hotel Tulsa, but he was convinced black people could build something just as spectacular if they worked together.

Stradford's pool hall was at the western border of Tulsa's black neighborhood. Once J.H. walked five blocks east, he would have come upon the thoroughfare that was drawing more and more attention from Negroes desperate to leave the Deep South. That was where he first set his eyes upon Greenwood Avenue.

It wasn't much to look at. The avenue was unpaved, with uneven sidewalks that were set below the street in places. On a dry, sunny day, the road might be clouded by a haze of dirt; on a rainy one, it became a muddy impasse so waterlogged that one observer called it "a splendid opportunity for some mariner to put in a ferry."[97] Underground, there were no pipes to provide most residents with clean water in their homes; up above, there were no streetlights to offer comfort and safety outside them.[98]

But J.H. recognized that a spirit was germinating on this street that went beyond its humble appearance. He saw a two-story brick building anchored by a grocery store like the one he'd operated in Water Valley.[99] The People's Grocery Store, chock full of meats and country produce, had been the very first business opened on this stretch of low-lying land back in 1905 by O.W. and Emma Gurley, Greenwood's first entrepreneurs.[100] Emma soon launched a twenty-five-room hotel on the second floor,[101] while O.W. spearheaded the creation of a new housing development. Located north of the new businesses, the

Gurley-Hill Addition offered 3,200-square-foot residential lots for as low as $150, paid in whatever monthly installments the new home-owners could manage. In advertisements, Gurley noted that the land was specifically "set apart for colored residences."[102]

Just steps away from the People's Grocery was the most impressive structure on the block, the three-story Williams Building.[103] Inside, Loula Williams sold fruits and fountain drinks in her popular confectionery on the building's first floor. With her loose curls pinned neatly at the nape of her neck, she maintained pristine storefront windows despite the clouds of dust kicked up by the Model T's and Norwalks trundling down the dirt road.[104] The previous spring she had started serving ice cream; soon she planned to add tile flooring.[105] Instead of renting the storefront from one of the wealthy white oilmen downtown, as so many black merchants in Detroit and Harlem did, she owned the building outright.[106]

Greenwood Avenue in the 1910s

Loula's husband John, a tall man with a stern face, was another everyday fixture on the block, always head-down under the hood of a car. He repaired the vehicles of black and white Tulsans alike at the auto garage he owned at the Greenwood-Archer intersection.[107] Opposite the Williams Building on the south side of Archer Street was the office of Dr. A. C. Jackson. The young physician cared for new-born babies, ailing grandparents, and everyone in between, even as black Tulsans were excluded from the city's all-white hospitals.[108] The Memphis native had trained at the famed Mayo Clinic, where founders Will and Charlie Mayo reportedly declared him "the most able Negro surgeon in America."[109]

A few doors north, brothers Jim and William Cherry owned a pool hall, where men went to drink, shoot dice, and tell lies.[110] A new croquet garden on Archer Street offered "first class" recreation, while homegrown chefs sold plates of chitterlings and pigs' feet out of make-do restaurants down the block.[111] The owner of the Crystal Café blared his wailing electric piano around the clock—even on Sundays—as the violin teacher at the Tulsa Colored School of Music pleaded with his neighbors to "learn real music and not be carried away in that idle ragtime."[112] On side streets, women did hair in their kitchens and men bankrolled gambling dens outside the eyes of the law. All of it was run by a population of roughly five thousand black people, a community of kin on a scale J.H. had never witnessed in tiny Water Valley.[113] The sidewalks were not filled with white men who demanded black people simper in their presence; they were filled with black men, women, and children, shuffling in and out of all those storefronts, all the time, walking tall and proud.

Five blocks north of the Greenwood-Archer intersection, another large two-story brick building dominated the landscape. Inside the cavernous Cleaver & Cherry Hall, Andrew Jackson Smitherman was busy articulating the promise and peril of life as a black person in Oklahoma better than anyone else.[114] Each week his newspaper, the *Tulsa Star* offered a mix of crusading journalism and vital neighborhood bulletins. Readers thumbed through its pages to see who had the newest business on Greenwood and what new schemes white folks were drafting to make life that much more difficult. The newspaper served not only as the chronicle of an ambitious neighborhood's rise but as an active defender of its readers' human rights—a role that black media in Greenwood would continue to embrace for generations.

Smitherman and J. H. Goodwin were both newcomers to Tulsa and Knights of Pythias members. The two men formed a fast friendship.[115] Smitherman reported on J.H.'s December sojourn to Tulsa with a short three-line item on the front page of the *Star*.[116] Above the brief article the newspaper proudly brandished its new slogan: "A Fearless Exponent of Right and Justice."

J.H. liked what he found in Tulsa. He decided to buy a house on a hill on Elgin Avenue, only a short walk from the bustle of the business district.[117] He sent a telegram home to Water Valley instructing his wife to pack their things; he had found the family a new home. Carlie and the four children soon piled into a train in Water Valley on their own western sojourn, routing through Memphis rather than St. Louis.[118] For them, there was no luxurious ride on a Pullman car; compartments on the standard Frisco Railroad were segregated by race, and the cars for black passengers featured rigid seats and smoke-filled air that could get "as hot as the hinges of the lower regions," according to one rider to Tulsa.[119] Despite the poor conditions, the trip was one of wonder for the children, especially young Edward. Carlie brought blankets for him to snuggle under during the long ride, along with fried chicken and ham sandwiches tucked into old shoeboxes. As their train approached its final destination, the porter, a towering black man, bellowed out each locale. Young Edward's world grew with every stop.

"Jonesboro, Arkansas! Jonesboro, Arkansas!"

"Monett! Monett! Monett!"

"Afton! Afton! Afton, Oklahoma!"

And finally: "Tulsey, Tulsey, Tulsey Town! Tulsey Town, the Tush-Hog town!"[120]

J.H. was waiting for them just off the train platform with a horse-drawn cab and a heart full of ambition.[121] The journey of Carlie and the kids was also covered in the *Tulsa Star,* with the newspaper anticipating their arrival on March 23, 1914. "Mr. Goodwin is a successful businessman in his hometown in Mississippi and will embark on business in Tulsa," the *Star* reported.[122]

Greenwood, of course, was much more than just a business venture for J.H. The Goodwins had sold off their property and trekked to an unknown land for the sake of their children. Edward, the baby of the family at eleven years old, would get to spend the most time in Tulsa's superior schools. He, more than any other Goodwin, would know what it meant to live in a place where every black person seemed to be striving for something greater. It would spark a drive in him that was never extinguished. "There was this outstanding and remarkable showing of energy," he reflected, decades later, on those early years of Greenwood. "They were creating their own way of life for themselves."[123]

CHAPTER 2

AND SOMETIMES BETTER, BESIDES

A souvenir mirror depicting Loula Williams's Dreamland Theatre

eering out of the window of his family's house on Elgin Avenue, perched on a grassy knoll known as Brickyard Hill, young Ed Goodwin could survey every inch of his new neighborhood.[1] To the north were endless farms and the wilderness of the Cherokee Nation, where developers were just beginning to transform rugged countryside into symmetrical lots for sale.[2] To the west was the great firewall of the Greenwood border on Detroit Avenue, where white people lived on one side of the street and black people lived on the other.[3] Close and distant at the same time. The neighborhood's most prominent homeowners all resided on Detroit and Elgin—J. B. Stradford with his two-story brick estate, local dry cleaner H. A. Caver in the manse fronted by the fine Roman columns.[4] Out beyond that pocket of affluence, though, Greenwood was a sea of frame buildings, shacks, tents, and rickety outhouses, stitched together by a braid of dirt roads largely traversed by foot or squeaky horse-drawn wagon.[5] But in the distance, less than a mile away, Ed could see the pride of all the neighborhood, the business district, where each new brick build-ing was a sign of the neighborhood's progress.

They called the commercial district the "East End," though later generations would christen it "Deep Greenwood."[6] Ed's father J.H. was always down there, wearing a crisp dark suit with a cigarette tucked behind his ear.[7] J.H. was a serial entrepreneur, and much of his energy was focused on building up the burgeoning Deep Greenwood skyline. In October 1915, J.H. began work on the Goodwin Building at 123 North Greenwood and opened a new grocery store there.[8] The next year he was hired as the business manager for the *Tulsa Star*, not long before the publication expanded from a weekly print schedule to a daily one, a rarity for black-owned newspapers of any era.[9] Soon he became a partner in a new undertaking business with a young Green-wood mortician named S. M. Jackson, a fellow Mississippi native who had migrated to Tulsa not long after the Goodwins.[10] With its silk plush caskets and brand-new family car, the funeral home was one of the best equipped in the region.[11]

Ed was expected to help out with the growing family businesses and one day, perhaps, take them over. Inside the Jackson and Good-win funeral home on Archer Street, he was sometimes tasked with helping to embalm bodies. A corpse would be loaded onto a special table, and the blood and other fluids released during the embalming process would drip through a drainage hole into a bucket on the floor. Ed's unfortunate job was to dispose of the bucket. His stomach turned when he smelled the odors of former neighbors as their fluids sloshed around—it was likely enough for him to know that undertaking wasn't the business line for him.[12]

Deep Greenwood also had plenty of entertainment to keep a teen-age boy busy. He could flirt with girls at one of the marble-top tables in Loula Williams's confectionery alongside her son Willie, or spend time in J. B. Stradford's neighborhood library with his sister Anna. (Her hobby in the class yearbook was listed as "books.")[13] He could venture with Willie to the Palm Garden Athletic Club, a boxing arena a few doors north of the confectionery where owner and fight pro-moter Billy McClain offered sparring lessons to youngsters, though he wouldn't let them set foot in the speakeasy on the same property.[14]

Every day was a new adventure for Ed in these thirty-five square blocks of land because the neighborhood was evolving so quickly.[15] In Greenwood, men in suits and bowler hats developed grand visions for the future of the Negro race, while others crept into the nearby "Choc Alley" for a taste of a cloudy beer that was one of Oklahoma's most intoxicating innovations.[16] More than a few straddled both worlds. In Deep Greenwood, a young boy like Ed would be exposed to many different notions of what it meant to become a responsible citizen, an entrepreneur, and a race man.

"Greenwood proper was a street of cigar stores, shining parlors, cafés and dance halls where phonographs blared away the blues in the wee hours of the morning and painted sirens plied their trade among a floating population which came to the Oil Capital," an anonymous "Old Timer" wrote decades later. "North Tulsa was a lively Negro community. Something was always going on."[17]

As the summer of 1914 melted into fall, Loula Williams set her sights on a new challenge. Her Deep Greenwood confectionery, five years old by that time, was flourishing.[18] Children had to be pried out of the storefront parlor, which was anchored by a twelve-foot soda fountain and an endless array of candy jars. She had seized a market opening by giving the gruff oil town of Tulsa something it lacked: a space for families. The Williams Confectionery was known as the only place on the block you could get a drink besides bootleg whiskey.[19]

Now Loula and her husband John were making a bet that motion pictures could become Greenwood's next marquee attraction.[20] They heard about a failed movie house in Oklahoma City that was selling off all its equipment and made the hundred-mile trek to the theater to haul the machinery back home.[21] On a large Greenwood Avenue plot that the couple jointly owned,[22] they built an 850-seat auditorium, complete with eight coal and gas stoves, a pair of pianos, and a piercingly bright stage spotlight.[23] The Williams Dreamland Theatre opened its doors in September 1914 to thrilled crowds[24] who soon became loyal patrons. Wilhelmina Guess Howell, a young girl at the time, loved the Friday night serials the most. "It was hard for us to wait a whole week to find out what had happened to Hands Up or Elmo the Mighty," she said later.[25]

The Dreamland soon earned effusive praise in the press. A. J. Smitherman's *Tulsa Star* called it the finest venue of its kind in the Southwest,[26] and the *Tulsa World* labeled John Williams, who was still running his popular auto shop, "the Negro Rockefeller." But in telling the story of the theater, the male journalists failed to mention Loula at all.[27]

Women of the era were used to being rendered invisible, but Loula thought it important to set the record straight. Before all this talk of Rockefellers, she had purchased the land where the confectionery stood for $742—under her maiden name, Loula Cotton, in fact.[28] She had raised much of the money herself from her wages as a rural teacher in the nearby town of Fisher, then quit her job and made the hold-your-breath leap into entrepreneurship.[29] True, the couple bought the Dreamland property together, but John transferred his one-half stake to Loula in April 1915.[30] While he helped out with the theater,[31] Loula was the one acquiring the best films from major Hollywood studios like Fox and Universal.[32] It was truly her baby. In 1919 she took a trip to the county court-house to clear up any lingering confusion.

Loula Williams

In a signed affidavit, she declared herself "the owner of all the seats, pianos, picture machinery, curtains, box scenery, desk, stoves, rugs, and all fixtures and furniture" in the Dreamland. She outlined a similarly specific claim to the confectionery. Her husband separately owned his auto garage, but as to her businesses, she stated that he "has absolutely no right, title, or interest therein or to."[33]

All the while, Loula kept building. In 1918 she assembled a team of black contractors to give the Dreamland a $10,000 renovation, transforming it into what she called a "strictly modern play house."[34] The grand reopening was anchored by *Cleopatra,* a glitzy 1917 silent film starring Theda Bara. It was one of the most expensive movies in Hollywood history—chic, refined, and ambitious, just like Loula.[35] On *Cleopatra's* opening night, she no doubt looked as elegant as her newly upgraded playhouse, with glittering rings likely adorning her fingers and her favorite leopard print coat draped across her shoulders.

Across town in white Tulsa that season, the Majestic Theater chose to screen *Birth of a Nation,* the Hollywood blockbuster glorifying the Ku Klux Klan.[36] The racist spectacle achieved record crowds in Tulsa; the *World* called it "the greatest attraction ever produced in moving pictures."[37] Greenwood leaders, including A. J. Smitherman, petitioned the city commission to ban the film.[38] But Loula could control only what was within the four walls of her theater, so she focused on excellence. "The very best that money can secure will be the motto of the Dreamland," she promised.[39]

While Loula bragged that her business was the "only colored theater in the city," she did not have a captive audience.[40] Around the time of the theater renovations, a white man named William Redfearn opened a competing picture house, the Dixie, directly across the street.[41] Both theaters screened Hollywood hits and booked live black performers.[42] But many in Greenwood viewed a Dreamland ticket stub as a symbol of race pride, proof that a community operated by and for black people could succeed just as much as one controlled by whites.[43] When the writer and sociologist W.E.B. Du Bois visited Greenwood during one of his speaking tours, he noted the curious dynamic of two theaters—one white, one black—squaring off for customers on the same block. "The colored theatre is always full. The white theatre is very poorly patronized," Du Bois observed in a travel diary. "The colored people are using the boycott and race economic solidarity in Tulsa to an extent which I had never before witnessed."[44]

The Dreamland quickly became a neighborhood nerve center. High school graduation ceremonies were hosted on the theater stage.[45] In back offices, men like J. B. Stradford and Ernest Cotton, Loula's brother, strategized to topple Jim Crow.[46] Sometimes the Dreamland seats were filled by black protesters and activists who transformed the stage into a bully pulpit. "Don't let any white man run over you," leaders declared, "but fight."[47]

On many nights, when the Dreamland marquee shone like a beacon on Greenwood Avenue, Loula quietly slipped into a seat in her theater, soaking up the opinions of her customers in silence. Then, too eager to wait until the next day, she'd meet with the Dreamland's manager to brainstorm long into the night about how to make the next show even better. "To what do I owe my success?" she mused. "The employment of competent help and my ability to please the public [and] give them what they want when they want it."[48]

Loula eventually got her due in the press, when a front-page feature in the *Topeka Plaindealer* named her the "Amusement Queen" and cheekily cast John and Willie as her "staff of able assistants." In the illustration that the *Plaindealer* published next to the article, all the family's businesses were listed under the umbrella of "Williams Enterprises." Loula's face was at the very top.[49]

Mabel Bonner came to Tulsa looking for a job—any job. She was only seventeen years old when she arrived on the Frisco Railroad in 1913 with $1.25 in her purse. Mabel believed the best path to a prosperous life routed through Langston University, Oklahoma's only black college. But she knew she needed to work in order to pay for her tuition, so it was only natural for her to take a detour to the big city. Mabel needed money, and every black person in Oklahoma knew Greenwood was the place to make it.[50]

After she pulled into the Frisco Depot on a cloudy Monday afternoon, she set off for the neighborhood she'd heard so many wonderful things about.[51] But Greenwood, she quickly realized, wasn't like her old home. Mabel hailed from the all-black town of Boley, one of dozens scattered across Oklahoma during the early twentieth century.[52] In these enclaves, black people operated everything from the bank to the police department—Boley, among the largest of the towns, even included a thriving cotton gin that was patronized by white farmers.[53] Because of its origins, Boley had a certain sobriety about its mission of black uplift; the people who built the town had sought "law-abiding, industrious negroes," according to one city father.[54] Greenwood was scrappier, less a carefully planned community than a mirror image of the unruly oil boomtown to which it was attached, full of raucous dance halls and a rebellious spirit. "It was a little on the wild side," one early resident acknowledged.[55]

Mabel was not pleased with what she found. She did not approve of the lecherous dancing, and she was shocked by the women stalking the street in the red-light district just west of the more upstanding businesses, along with the pimps strutting in silk shirts and socks.[56] None of it seemed very Christian-like to her, and much more than getting rich, Mabel cared about being faithful to God. But she was here now and needed to find a good church and good employment first and foremost.

The job would have to come south of the railroad tracks. Though affluent entrepreneurs like Loula Williams spent much of their time in Greenwood, most black people worked for white employers downtown or in South Tulsa. Many worked as live-in maids in garages appended to white people's homes.[57] For those who didn't, each day required a march across the Frisco tracks and into the white world,[58] where they were expected to be prim and polite at all times, a grinning shadow of their full selves.

Mabel was hired at the Brady Hotel, earning twenty dollars per month and regular hot meals.[59] While she and other black laborers kept the business running, the hotel was strictly for white customers.[60] Its owner was a real estate magnate named Tate Brady, whose name adorned Tulsa streets as a prominent city father.[61] As she cleaned floors and washed linens, Mabel dreamed of a job away from the white-controlled world. Each month she spent ten dollars of her salary on rent and six dollars on other life essentials. The last four dollars she saved as she built a ladder up and out of service work.[62]

Though Mabel came to Tulsa wary of cunning strangers in the big city, she met a man without really meaning to on her very first day in town. His name was Pressley Little, and she was charmed as much by his compassion as by his looks.[63] Their courtship included breezy Saturday morning rides on the streetcar to the park in Sand Springs, where the cozy teahouses on the newly manicured grass seemed built just for them.[64] Within a year and a half, the two were married.[65] Scraping together Mabel's savings as a maid and Pressley's as a waiter and shoeshiner, they managed to buy a three-room shotgun house on Independence Street for $150.[66] In that area, several blocks north of Deep Greenwood, modest frame houses like the Littles' often doubled as storefronts. Pressley opened a shoeshine parlor in one room of their home, and Mabel a beauty salon in another, offering her services at fifty cents per head.[67]

Business boomed almost immediately. Mabel didn't even need to advertise in the *Tulsa Star;* "Go to Miss Little's house" became the co-sign that granted her dozens, and eventually hundreds, of clients.[68] When their popularity exceeded the capacity of their tiny home, the Littles relocated their businesses to the East End, eventually settling on the first floor of the Woods Building, at the corner of Greenwood Avenue and Archer Street.[69] When that too became cramped—Mabel later claimed to have six hundred customers from as far away as Muskogee—she opened a larger salon on the second floor, hiring three additional hairdressers.[70]

A dollar that Mabel earned doing hair was almost certain to be reinvested back into the Greenwood community. In an era of increasingly rigid Jim Crow segregation, money recirculated within black neighborhoods multiple times. Mabel's dollar might go to pay the rent at the Woods Building, which was owned by a black pastor who lived nearby on Archer Street.[71] It might go to the Dreamland Theatre for a screening of *Runaway June* during a date with Pressley, or to J. H. Goodwin's new grocery store when she picked up a sack of potatoes for dinner on the walk home.[72] The dollar might pass into the hands of one of the hairdressers she hired to work at her salon, or be stuffed into the tithing box on Sunday at her beloved new church, Mt. Zion Baptist. "Back then, everybody tried to help one another, to patronize and encourage one another," Mabel recalled decades later.[73]

More than the money she was earning, Mabel came to enjoy the company of all the people she met while perched on Greenwood Avenue every day. Women of every stripe sat in her styling chair to have their hair washed and straightened. Singers passing through town to perform at the Dreamland. Young girls who did not squeal under her touch because she was dexterous enough to wield a curling iron without burning their scalps.[74] She even had a few male customers, who believed she held the secret to reversing their thinning hairlines.[75]

Mabel still didn't approve of the lifestyles of the "hijacking women and prostitutes" in the red-light district, as she called them, but she came to understand their struggles.[76] Many, like her, had migrated to Tulsa from smaller Oklahoma towns, and all they wanted was a chance at a comfortable life.[77] Those women proved to be some of her most loyal customers. "Working on people's heads you learn so much about life," Mabel reflected.[78] Greenwood was not the oasis she had expected, but she found pleasure even in its imperfections. She took comfort in her burgeoning business, her devoted husband, and, most important, her faith.

───────

On Sunday evenings, Rev. R. A. Whitaker marched into the heart of Deep Greenwood to bring the word of God to people who never once attended church. With members of his congregation like Mabel at his side, he held revival right there on the dusty street, reminding everyone whose day it really was.[79] Some nights, after proselytizing on Greenwood, he walked over to the pool halls on Cincinnati Avenue, a notorious drag where salvation for most men came at the bottom of a cloudy glass of beer. Whitaker preached there too, to men whose lives as day laborers were far removed from the glamour of the *Cleopatra* screening at the Dreamland. Most probably ignored him. But every year the congregation of Mt. Zion Baptist Church got a little bit bigger, and Whitaker's dream of building the ultimate house of God drew a little closer to reality.[80]

Before black people in Tulsa had their own beauty salons, movie theaters, and newspapers, they had their own churches. In 1899 about ten residents began meeting informally for prayer and fellowship, and they formed what would eventually become First Baptist Church on Archer Street.[81] Others soon built Vernon African Methodist Episcopal Church on Greenwood Avenue.[82] There were more than fifteen Greenwood churches in all, with names familiar to black neighborhoods across the nation: Mount Olive, Morning Star, Paradise.[83] "You can not turn without addressing someone as Reverend," one observer joked.[84] No matter which house of worship they chose, all of Greenwood's churchgoers were seeking the same thing on Sundays—a sanctuary where, as the novelist Richard Wright later wrote, "in our collective outpourings of song and prayer, the fluid emotions of others make us feel the strength in ourselves."[85]

Mt. Zion, an offshoot of First Baptist, was formed in 1909 in a repurposed wooden school building on Hartford Street.[86] It took years for the church's congregants to find a true home. They floated from the schoolhouse to a former dance hall on Greenwood Avenue, praying in one of the dens of carousing that Mabel so detested.[87] In 1913, Mt. Zion's then-pastor, Rev. F. K. White, purchased a seven-thousand-square foot lot on Elgin Avenue, just northwest of the business district.[88] But in April 1914, Reverend White grew sick and left Oklahoma for the cleaner air of California.[89] It was the forty-year-old Reverend Whitaker, a newcomer to Tulsa from Georgia, who then accepted the challenge of building Greenwood's largest temple.[90]

The vision was a grand one: a church made of seventy-five thousand bricks featuring a dining room, operatic gallery seating, and a mirror set above the baptism pool that would allow members to view the ritual up close, as if standing in a river over a new child of God.[91] Progress came slowly, so the congregation cherished small victories. When the initial $450 loan for the land was paid off, church members turned their financial burden to ash at a mortgage-burning party.[92] The youth choir sang on street corners in concerts that doubled as fundraisers.[93] Greenwood Avenue's Bell and Little Café, operated by Mabel Little's husband Pressley and his sister Susie Bell, donated the proceeds from its Sunday dinners to cover construction costs.[94] As they struggled to raise funds, the congregation met in a wooden frame building that they dubbed the Tabernacle, reading scripture by gas lamps.[95] "We had to build up a credit, and work by chances," Reverend Whitaker recalled. "We had plenty of knockers, but we soon found that every knock was a boost."[96]

As the years dragged on, and the cost of the project ballooned, it became clear that Greenwood could not build Mt. Zion alone. In 1919 the church's board of trustees took out a $37,500 loan with

Rev. R. A. Whitaker

a Tennessee-based construction company.[97] When even that proved insufficient, according to oral history, a white businessman offered a $50,000 unsecured loan to see the project through to completion.[98] Mt. Zion was suddenly swimming in debt, but the congregation had faith that God would lead the way to another successful mortgage-burning party one day soon. "I believe that is why Mt. Zion became the center of black community church life," Mabel Little reflected later. "Rev. Whitaker gave us a purpose."[99]

The Goodwins and their wealthy neighbors symbolized the impressive progress toward economic independence that black people had achieved only fifty years removed from enslavement. Black Oklahomans' hard work and by-your-bootstraps entrepreneurship made Booker T. Washington an early and ardent admirer. "The westward movement of the negro people has brought into these new lands, not a helpless and ignorant horde of black people, but land-seekers and home builders, men who have come prepared to build up the country," he said in 1908.[100] In a post-Reconstruction era where blacks were being shut out of political life, Washington believed the black business person would become the representative of the race in the public sphere. He insisted that American capitalism would reward black people in a way that American democracy had not.

To focus only on tales of black success, though, was to obscure the obstacles black people continued to face. Greenwood was hardly an economic paradise, as Ed Goodwin would later candidly recall. The neighborhood harbored poverty and prosperity in equal measure. While Ed's family owned their home, along with 30 percent of black Tulsans, most residents did not.[101] Derelict outhouses standing on worn-out stilts contributed to a sanitation problem and disease outbreaks.[102] Before the Goodwins' home had running water, Ed would douse the family's outdoor privy in lye and bathe in a No. 2 tin bathtub, like many of his neighbors who also lacked basic utilities that the city of Tulsa failed to provide.[103] For many living in tiny two-room homes, the only protection from the brutal Oklahoma winters were the worn-out quilts used to line the walls.[104] "In this whole area, we had no paved streets back then," Ed said years later. "We had no sewers. The blacks just built shanties."[105]

No matter a black person's economic station, living in Greenwood presented a set of grim day-to-day challenges because the city of Tulsa refused to invest in the community. Greenwood lacked a hospital, and the few black patients allowed in white facilities were rushed out immediately after sugery.[106] When a black hospital was finally built in 1917, the city refused to support it with public funding.[107] These policies led to widespread death by medical neglect, which even the white newspapers in Tulsa acknowledged.[108] "Black people who needed operations were especially susceptible," said Charles Bate, a doctor who worked in Greenwood in later decades. "They were operated on in their own homes in unsterile, inadequate surroundings. . . . It is no wonder that so many of them hemorrhaged and died."[109] At the onset of the Spanish flu epidemic in 1918, Ed later recalled, he and other funeral home staff picked up seventeen dead bodies in a single day, as his neighbors' home remedies did little to stem the deadly disease outbreak.[110]

No amount of business acumen could solve these problems alone, since white people consistently cut black people off from economic resources. Though Tulsa was an oil town, working-class black men were systematically excluded from participating directly in the oil boom; in 1920 there were nearly twenty thousand white oil well workers in Oklahoma, compared with only about one hundred black ones.[111] Black people were banned from using white taxis, and the city's streetcar service did not extend to Greenwood, making daily commutes more challenging.[112] When Greenwood leaders came to a city board meeting seeking improvements for their neighborhood park, the board told them to raise the money on their own.[113] Private institutions could be just as discriminatory as public ones; one Greenwood woman who owned a popular hotel reported that a downtown bank refused to accept her deposit because "colored people's money was not wanted."[114]

Crime was another problem that touched many Greenwood residents, exacerbated in a "wide open" oil town like Tulsa.[115] Though prohibition was enshrined in Oklahoma's state constitution, alcohol was easy to come by. Opium dens were tucked away in some of the second-floor apartments above Greenwood streets, their scent masked by hanging oil-soaked sponges from the ceiling to absorb the incriminating odor.[116] Many nights in Greenwood ended with a knife fight, a shoot-out, or a duel with smashed whiskey bottles.[117]

Such violence put a strain on the neighborhood's unspoken class distinctions. "There should be a line—a big heavy line—between the classes," the *Tulsa Star* declared after a "woman of the underworld" shot another woman on the street. "Good women cannot associate with bad women without losing the respect they should have from the general public."[118] In reality, though, there was no line in social status that determined who in Greenwood might dabble in vice. Barney

Cleaver, the Tulsa Police Department's first black officer, once accused O. W. and Emma Gurley of operating a "dope joint" out of their hotel.[119] At the northern edge of the neighborhood, choc and corn whiskey flowed amply at Pretty Belle's Place, where woozy teenagers both black and white danced together on the front porch, and fine private cars parked outside proved that it wasn't a hangout just for the working class.[120]

For teenage boys like Ed Goodwin and his friends, this world of vice and violence was almost as intoxicating as the substances people were imbibing, especially filtered through the romantic prism of nostalgia. "It was exciting!" recalled Henry Whitlow, a longtime Tulsa educator. "You could stand around and watch people fight, cut, get drunk, and the like. You would call it, in some people's minds, a rough time in Tulsa. But they were only bothering themselves."[121]

Ed Goodwin's parents did everything in their power to make sure their son did not become a morbid headline in the *Tulsa Star*—or worse, fodder for another diatribe about Negro criminality in one of the white dailies. They could be harsh disciplinarians—Ed recalled his father whipping him with a horse harness, his head trapped between the old man's legs, while his mother sometimes locked him in a closet as punishment. But Ed had a fierce independent streak. Fed up with the whippings, he stole $300 from J.H. when he was about fifteen years old and slipped onto a train headed east. He was quickly reminded that the world outside Greenwood was not a welcoming one—when he stepped off the train in Monet, Missouri, he saw a sign that said "No niggers after dark" and promptly hopped back on. He ultimately wound up at the home of an aunt in Pittsburgh, Pennsylvania, where he worked at a printing press and a shoe store to earn money. With his first paycheck, he bought a green and pink suit out of a local department store, and a lifelong taste for the finer things was born. "I put that on, and I began to feel like I'd become a man," he recalled.[122]

When Carlie called him, imploring him to come home and finish his schooling, Ed relented and made his way back to Tulsa, enrolling back at Booker T. Washington High School. Out of Tulsa's eight hundred or so high-school-age black children, Ed and his sister Anna were among the roughly 120 who attended Booker T in 1920.[123] There were only twelve students in their graduating class, but these select young people found they had an entire community eager to pour their energies and ambitions into the next generation.

Greenwood's residents both rich and poor faced challenges every day that a just society would not have laid on their doorstep. But each year brought greater wealth and prosperity to the community. As more businesses opened, more students graduated from high school, and more people poured into the once-tiny frontier town, their collective confidence grew. Whether they were forced to contend with white Tulsans south of the railroad tracks every day, or had the privilege of spending all their time in their city within a city, all of them recognized that they had the ability to build a community just as thriving as any other, if given the resources. They increasingly saw this confidence reflected back at them in the faces of their neighbors, the timbre of their pastors, the opulence of their theaters, and the fearless front page of their neighborhood newspaper. Above the fold in a 1915 edition of the *Tulsa Star*, A. J. Smitherman printed a poem called "The Negro's Challenge" by an Indiana woman named Carrie Parker Taylor. It could have doubled as the mantra for all of Greenwood for the rest of the decade:

> *You complain, my brother, my lily white brother*
> *Of our poor race now and then,*
> *Yet you never have said what we should do*
> *To prove to you that we're men. . . .*
>
> *In fact, I don't know anything that you've done,*
> *When you've given us a chance and we've tried,*
> *That we haven't done as well as you could,*
> *And sometimes better, besides.*[124]

CHAPTER 3

BLACK CAPITAL

A souvenir program for the 1914 meeting of the National Negro Business League

" f there is any place where the Negro has a chance to show his mettle, it is right here in the United States. For this reason, as well as for the sake of ourselves, it is a matter of extreme importance that we not disappoint ourselves nor those who are studying and observing us. Within the fifty years of our freedom, and even before physical freedom came, great and almost marvelous progress has been made, but we must not rest upon the past; we must continue to go forward."[1]

The crowd of eight thousand sat in rapt attention, J. H. Goodwin and A. J. Smitherman among them, as Booker T. Washington lit the torchlights of a path ahead for black America.[2] For Greenwood's leading entrepreneurs, few moments in those early years of the neighborhood were as pivotal as the journey to Muskogee, Oklahoma, to see the most famous Negro in the United States. It was a suffocatingly hot evening in August 1914, and Washington's voice filled every crevice of the packed Convention Hall, as audience members dabbed their sweaty brows with handkerchiefs.[3] The Wizard of Tuskegee, as his admirers called him, was delivering the keynote speech for the annual meeting of the National Negro Business League.[4]

J. H. Goodwin listened intently. From the moment he and his family moved to Greenwood, the neighborhood had been abuzz about the annual Business League meeting. Every year Washington and a cadre of the nation's most successful black entrepreneurs met in a different city for a three-day cornucopia of racial uplift and pageantry, celebrating both their collective progress and their own professional accomplishments. For the first time since Washington founded the Business League in 1900,[5] Oklahoma would be in the spotlight. Though the 1914 meeting took place in Muskogee, Greenwood entrepreneurs saw it as a coming-out party for themselves as well. Many were convinced that Greenwood was destined to eclipse Muskogee in stature, if it hadn't already. "We must impress our visitors with the great opportunity we have in the growing new state," A. J. Smitherman wrote in a *Tulsa Star* editorial. "We must make the Muskogee meeting a success—a grand success—a howling success."[6]

Several weeks before the event, Smitherman approached J.H. with a proposition. He needed help putting together a special "booster edition" of the *Tulsa Star,* which he planned to distribute to thousands of people in Muskogee during the event.[7] Across twenty pages, Smitherman would profile farmers and merchants from every corner of the state, highlighting the unheralded success stories of black Oklahoma (with a particular emphasis on Greenwood, of course).[8] Smitherman was as ambitious as he was assertive, and though J.H. was a quieter soul, Smitherman saw him as a strong potential ally. "Goodwin is a real homebuilder—a booster from the word 'go,'" the *Star* declared later.[9]

The two men lighted out on their promotional tour around the Fourth of July, and they had a wide choice of thriving black enclaves to visit. Black Oklahoma's success stretched far beyond Greenwood, or even Boley, where Mabel Little hailed from. In majority-white towns like Bristow and Luther, black people owned ice cream parlors and sprawling farms.[10] In the all-black towns similar to Boley, they took the land that had been ceded to freedmen through tribal allotments or purchased by migrant black homesteaders and formed new communities on the open prairies. All-black Langston was home to the state's only black college. Other towns incubated a canning factory and an oil drilling company.[11] Greenwood was surrounded by a constellation of black success, creating an ecosystem where goods as well as talent were eagerly traded.

J.H. and Smitherman crisscrossed the state to visit some of these locales, gathering tales of black prosperity and persuading rural farmers and merchants to attend the Muskogee meeting in person.[12] They played at least some small part in recruiting the audience that now sat before Washington in the Muskogee Convention Hall.

"I believe that the time has come when we as a race should begin preparing to enter upon a new policy and a new program," Washington continued in his staccato cadence. "We should get off the defensive in things that concern our present and future."[13]

The league president began ticking off statistics about crop yields and landownership rates in Oklahoma, extolling the opportunities for the Negro farmer out west. He had long been fascinated by the state's unusual streak of black independence, ever since he first rode a train through the Muskogee countryside and learned that nearly all the land before his eyes was owned by black freedmen.[14] Washington was more professor than preacher, but if he sermonized on anything, it was the gospel of wealth. He often instructed his people to focus on lifting themselves up and over the walls erected by racism through economic progress, rather than wasting their energy trying to tear those walls down through protests and activism.

"Let us get off the defensive," he repeated. "Let us, in the future, spend less time talking about the part of the city that we cannot live in, and more time in making the part of the city that we can live in beautiful and attractive. . . . Let us make such progress in these directions that the other fellow will be kept so busy talking about our progress that he will have no time to abuse us. Let us acquire wealth and intelligence so fast that the world will forget our poverty and ignorance."[15]

Washington believed black people could outrun the hate in a white man's heart, outwork it, outsmart it. The white industrialist would see black men who had once been slaves wearing double-breasted suits as they discussed crop yields and best accounting practices, and he would say, "*Now* you are men." Even if the society whites had crafted was rotten, Washington believed their economic system was a rational one. If the Wizard of Tuskegee had a blind spot, it was his assumption that the people who offered the key to his race's salvation were the ones who had built their cage in the first place.

―――――――

Sitting in the audience, A. J. Smitherman may have felt conflicted as he mulled Washington's words. He knew the leader's biography well and deeply respected all he had accomplished—teaching himself to read in the aftermath of the Civil War, journeying hundreds of miles from rural West Virginia to earn a college education at Hampton Institute, and eventually leading his own college in Tuskegee, Alabama, where he now taught fifteen hundred young black people valuable vocational skills each year.[16] But Washington was more than a neatly packaged Horatio Alger story; he was a savvy political figure in an era when blacks were systematically excluded from political office. President Theodore Roosevelt invited him to be the first black visitor to dine at the White House; nine years later Washington recruited the president to speak at a Business League meeting, where Roosevelt praised the league for "[teaching] you not to whine or cry about privileges you have not got."[17] Beginning in 1905, Andrew Carnegie donated an annual gift of $2,700 to the Business League, while also praising Washington's "wise policy" of not pushing for "the free and unrestricted vote immediately."[18] Washington ingratiated himself to white progressives by telling them largely what they wanted to hear: that vocational training, not civil rights, was the most urgent need of a people only one generation removed from enslavement. "There is no special color line in stock and poultry raising," he said in his Muskogee speech.[19]

For Smitherman, though, the color line was not so easily ignored. As a native of northern Alabama, he, like Washington and J. H. Goodwin, knew the vagaries of the Jim Crow South all too well. When he was a boy, his family moved to Indian Territory, where his father worked as a coal mine pit boss in a rural corner of the Choctaw

Nation. One of Smitherman's first jobs was working alongside his father in the mines—the hardest work he ever did in his life, he'd later say.[20] Smitherman quickly decided he'd rather ply a trade with his mind than with his hands. In the early 1900s, he enrolled at the University of Kansas and later Northwestern University, taking an interest in journalism.[21]

When he returned to Oklahoma around 1909, he settled in Muskogee, which was then the most vibrant community in the state for black people. Much of the property that had been allotted to freedmen during the breaking up of the Five Tribes' land now bubbled with oil, and the riches of newly minted black millionaires flowed freely through Muskogee's economy.[22]

Living in Muskogee, Smitherman quickly discovered the *Cimeter,* a high-spirited weekly newspaper housed in a two-room shack on Second Street.[23] The operation was headed by an accomplished lawyer named W. H. Twine, a pugnacious man with a thick mustache that reached down to frame his square jaw. Twine's vocal defense of black constitutional rights earned him the nickname "the Black Tiger," but Smitherman was able to charm the intense attorney with his ambition and work ethic.[24] He swept the floors of the dilapidated old office and eventually convinced his boss to tear down "de ole shack," as they called it, and erect a two-story brick building. Soon Smitherman was reporting on Muskogee events, writing *Cimeter* editorials, and managing the new building's tenants. He felt so inspired, he even began writing poetry; a proud Twine had one of the works framed.[25] "Life now had a real purpose for me," Smitherman later recalled. "I wanted to make good and I visualized success."[26]

Smitherman was not yet thirty years old as his journalism career began to blossom. But he quickly found himself in an ideological conflict with his mentor. Twine, like Booker T. Washington and nearly every politically active black man of the era, was a staunch Republican, owing to Abraham Lincoln's emancipation of the slaves during the Civil War. But Smitherman's faith in the party was shaken when Republicans in Oklahoma supported a voter disenfranchisement law known as the grandfather clause. The law circumvented federal voter rights protections by instituting a literacy test on any person whose ancestors had not been allowed to vote before 1866. Naturally, that included all descendants of slaves.[27] Once the Party of Lincoln, the

GOP was seized by a faction known as the "Lily Whites," who saw that racism played well among white voters and campaigned aggressively to remove black leaders from Republican tickets. Though it was still typically Democrats who introduced the most odious Jim Crow laws, the Lily Whites backed them full-throatedly, and even moderate Republicans often offered implicit endorsement through their silence.[28]

Because black voters were so loyally Republican, white leaders in both parties ignored their concerns. "There was no meaningful purpose for my voting," Smitherman reflected later. "I had been a simpleton, a 'yes' man, a 'rubber-stamp' individual."[29] After the grandfather clause vote, Smitherman became convinced that black survival depended on huge numbers of Negroes switching allegiance to the Democratic Party. A politically diverse voting bloc would be harder for either party to ignore. But when he floated his theory to Twine, the elder newspaperman warned him that switching his allegiance to Democrats—and worse, trying to convince other blacks to do so— "will be your Waterloo."[30]

Smitherman, though, held on to nothing else in life as tightly as his moral convictions. He resolved that his family would be the guinea pigs in a bold new political experiment. In 1912 he parted ways with his mentor and launched a new Democratic newspaper, the *Muskogee Star*.[31] Within a few months, seeking to create more distance from Twine, Smitherman made the move to Tulsa, along with his wife Ollie and their two children. There, he rebranded his newspaper the *Tulsa Star*.[32]

It was a difficult transition. Far from starting among Greenwood's high-flying black elite, the Smitherman family moved into the home of Barney Cleaver, a black Tulsa police officer. They later rented, rather than owned, a house on one of Greenwood's wealthiest residential streets.[33] With just four dollars in initial capital, Smitherman was able to buy the Star printing press only because the previous owner of the equipment let him pay for it in installments.[34] But the young journalist had what he wanted: the space and influence to say what he really thought.

Now it was barely a year later, and another leader of the race was espousing a worldview that Smitherman couldn't quite abide. Even as he was doing all he could to support the mission of the National Negro Business League, the newspaper publisher pursued a more radical politics than Booker T. Washington. Smitherman brandished his pen like a saber, and he wasn't afraid to point it at any white person who threatened his people. "The white man has partially subdued and enslaved the negro, but there has never been a time when the

The first issue of the Tulsa Star, *April 1913*

negro would not fight him," he wrote.[35] He would not be asked to wait his turn for dignity—not even by black leaders he admired, such as Booker T. Washington.

While the *Star* editor unsheathed a muscular form of black self-defense, Washington was convinced that simmering tensions between blacks and whites would soon be resolved peacefully. As he concluded his keynote speech in Muskogee, he told the audience not to worry about racial conditions in the country. "Perhaps nowhere else in the world can be found so many white people living side by side with so many of dark skin in so much of peace and harmony as in the United States," Washington said.[36]

In covering Washington's speech, the *Tulsa Star* declared him a "Master Mind" and called the Business League "the World's Greatest Negro Organization." The newspaper published Washington's insights on agricultural advancement word for word. But the reprint of his speech was edited; much of Washington's talk of getting off the defensive, ignoring white enemies, and celebrating a lasting racial harmony was left out.[37]

While Washington's keynote was the marquee event of the Business League meeting, attendees also heard from dozens of the leading black entrepreneurs of the era. As league president, Washington served as the master of ceremonies for all the major speakers at the meeting, conducting cordial but carefully controlled interviews that emphasized the benefits of black entrepreneurship. There were sessions on hat making, oyster packing, architecture, rural banking, poultry raising, the business side of fraternal orders, and buying and selling mules.[38] Washington even persuaded a reluctant Madam C. J. Walker onto the stage, where the cosmetics titan half-jokingly chided the largely male audience. "If the truth were known," she said, "there are many women who are responsible for the success of *you men*."[39]

Washington was all smiles as he guided speakers through their presentations on the Convention Hall stage, but he was a strict censor. He dictated who would be allowed to present, with little input from the league's executive committee, and he was careful to avoid anyone who might veer into what he called a "political harangue"—a man like Smitherman had no chance of landing on the agenda.[40] Largely, speakers' advice mirrored Washington's. The word *progress* was on nearly every presenter's lips.

The perspective of Washington—and by proxy, the Business League—was often used by whites as a stand-in for the entire black race, which by the mid-1910s had grown to frustrate a number of other black leaders. Perhaps no one was more opposed to Washington's rhetoric than the sociologist and activist W.E.B. Du Bois. Though Du Bois grew up in a starkly different environment from Washington, in a free northern family attending largely white schools, the two men's early professional years were similar. Du Bois, too, praised the enterprising nature of black Oklahomans.[41] He had edited a study called *The Negro in Business* eight years before Washington published a book with the same name. He had even proposed a national "Negro Business Men League" in 1899, though he envisioned a coalition of autonomous local leagues, while Washington devised a top-down structure that centralized power in Tuskegee. (At least one black leader of the era accused Washington of stealing Du Bois's idea.)[42]

Despite his support of black business, Du Bois was skeptical that entrepreneurship could be a cure-all to the variety of social ills facing the race. He predicted that the rise of monopolies and large corporations would decimate black small business owners, who would not be able to compete given their shallow pocketbooks and minimal formal training. When going to work for larger companies, these onetime entrepreneurs would have their leadership skills dismissed and be placed in subservient roles to white managers. The free market would become a new kind of imprisonment. "A Negro can to-day run a small corner grocery with considerable success," he wrote in 1899. "Tomorrow, however, he cannot be head of the grocery department of the department store which forces him out of business."[43]

Du Bois also worried that the extravagant Business League meetings, with their stately dinners and elaborate parades, were teaching black people the wrong lessons about the value of entrepreneurship. He feared the meetings opened a doorway toward boasting, exaggeration, and "individual selfishness" rather than collective uplift through co-ops and other collaborative forms of enterprise. "We need a strong economic foundation," he wrote before the Muskogee meeting, "but we do not need to reproduce among ourselves in the twentieth century the lying, stealing, and grafting which characterized the white race in the nineteenth century."[44]

Du Bois argued that the push for economic independence had to evolve in lockstep with the push for social equality. Black people had to be able to shape the laws that controlled the economy, rather than relying on market forces to one day elevate them. He believed the few blacks who had received high levels of education had a moral responsibility to fight fiercely to expand opportunity for the entire race. He called for rallying a "Talented Tenth," exceptional men (they were almost always men, in both Washington's and Du Bois's formulations) who would use liberal arts training to become worldly citizens, then fight ardently for civil rights. The fact that Washington was willing to cede democratic power to whites—while retaining a large amount of shrouded political power for himself—seemed to Du Bois like an abdication of his duty as a black leader. "Unless [the black man] has political rights and righteously guarded civic status, he will still remain the poverty-stricken and ignorant plaything of rascals," he argued in his seminal "Talented Tenth" essay in 1903.[45]

By the mid-1910s, Du Bois was leading a concerted fight against the Washington school of thought, as a co-founder of the National Association for the Advancement of Colored People and the editor of its swashbuckling magazine, the *Crisis*. Privately, Washington fretted that the *Crisis* was eclipsing the *New York Age*, the black newspaper that he partially owned and controlled.[46] Even as he spread the gospel of black capitalism in Muskogee, Washington could likely feel his influence waning.

For the people of Greenwood, there was no simple path toward progress. Was it better to follow Booker T. Washington's advice to focus on agriculture, vocational skills, and the symbolic success of black capitalism? Or should they adopt the more combative worldview of Du Bois, who argued that a black man without political rights was the "plaything of rascals"? The debate simmered in people's minds even when they weren't explicitly talking politics; when the neighborhood high school was named after Booker T. Washington, some resi-

W.E.B. Du Bois and Booker T. Washington

dents griped that it should have been called "Du Bois High School" instead.[47] But both men's agendas placed a responsibility for solving the race's problems on the black elite: Washington wanted them to serve as symbols of success, while Du Bois wanted the "Talented Tenth" to fight for civil rights.

The Goodwins took lessons from both Washington and Du Bois. J. H. and Carlie Goodwin lived a classic by-your-bootstraps American mythology, rising from Deep South Reconstruction to own a grocery store, a funeral home, and more than twenty real estate properties in one of the most dynamic black communities in the United States.[48] Their success was bound to the world they were forced to navigate and the privileges J.H.'s light complexion afforded him inside it. They profited handsomely from the closed-group dynamics of Jim Crow segregation, while many families merely scraped by.

But they also worked to build a better environment for themselves and all their neighbors. In November 1914, when Tulsa's own local business league reconvened, members sought solutions to community problems rather than boasting of their own success. J.H. joined a committee that lobbied the city to install a proper sewage system in Greenwood.[49] The next year he was elected president of the local chapter and made bridging the gaps between the business class and the general public a priority.[50] In 1917 he served on the board of the first neighborhood hospital.[51] "The only way to make a community progressive is by contributing something to it," he wrote later. "What a community contributes to you can be measured only in terms of what you give to that community."[52]

The people of Greenwood could not structure their lives around the ideologies of any one black leader; they charted their own paths, mixing individual achievement with collective action as they saw fit. More than a century after J. H. Goodwin went to hear Washington speak, his grandson Jim would reflect on the two famous black ideologies: "BTW's progress of mankind is we go from bottom up. Du Bois is, 'No, our progress is [horizontal] from here to there. The truth of the matter is human progress, from my perspective, is on the hypotenuse of a right triangle. We do both.' "[53]

While the early years of Greenwood were defined by the pursuit of financial and industrial success, as the 1910s came to a close, the neighborhood and its leaders soon found themselves fighting for their civil rights as well. The community's most successful entrepreneurs had to juggle these two sometimes conflicting priorities. While Washington thought economic progress would make white people more amenable to their black neighbors, Du Bois feared a much different outcome. "In Oklahoma there is a thrifty and intelligent colored populace," he wrote, "and yet Oklahoma seems to be a hot-bed of anti-Negro sentiment."[54]

CHAPTER 4

FALSE PROMISES

Oklahoma Constitutional Convention, Guthrie, 1907

The Dreamland Theatre was packed. Six hundred people were crammed into the venue as J. B. Stradford, the real estate developer and former pool hall owner, mulled the best way to galvanize his neighbors to action.[1] It was August 1916, two years after the National Negro Business League conference in Muskogee. Booker T. Washington had passed away the previous fall, and the argument in favor of accommodating white racism was buried alongside him. Black people could no longer assume that achieving economic success or patiently waiting for white views to evolve would grant them racial equality. They would have to demand it.

J. B. Stradford had no problem being a demanding man. He bore a thick chin and dark, arched eyebrows that made him look angry even when he was perfectly calm. Given all the injustices he had witnessed in his life, ever since being born the son of a Kentucky slave in 1861, a bit of rage might have always been roiling inside him.[2] He was known for his fiery temper and brooked no disrespect; he once punched a white delivery man in the jaw in the middle of Greenwood Avenue after the man tried to swing on him during an argument.[3] But he became a romantic whenever he spoke of the American project in its most noble form; on a trip to Washington, D.C., he marveled at the majesty of the U.S. Capitol and the democratic ideals it represented. "Had I the power of language to express the beauty, the sublimity and grandeur of that building and its arts, I could make you laugh," he wrote to his friend A. J. Smitherman. "I could make you weep."[4] When the ideals espoused in Washington clashed with his own tumultuous life as a black man on the frontier, though, Stradford's anger knew no bounds.

Standing before the crowd at the Dreamland Theatre, he had new reason to clench his jaw. "I tell you, gentlemen," he began, "it is time that we took some formal notice of the calumnies that are being heaped upon us in unbearable quantities by this present Republican city administration."[5]

All summer white Tulsans had been grumbling about the changing color of their neighborhoods. More and more black people were living in and around the servants' quarters behind white homes, whether they were actually servants or not, because the number of houses in Greenwood wasn't keeping up with the city's booming population. The *Tulsa Democrat* called it an "indignity" to force white people to live beside black neighbors. (In the same article, the newspaper described an interracial baseball game in which the black team drubbed the white one as "evil.")[6] On August 4, Tulsa's city commission—the predecessor to the modern city council—passed an ordinance banning black people from residing in mostly white neighborhoods unless they were domestic staff. Whites were also banned from black residential blocks, but that was a hollow gesture toward equal treatment meant to stave off legal challenges to the new law.[7]

The city chose a delicate moment to expand Jim Crow. The U.S. Supreme Court had recently declared Oklahoma's grandfather clause unconstitutional, ruling that the law violated the Fifteenth Amendment because it prevented descendants of slaves from voting.[8] But many white leaders saw segregation not as a violation of civil rights but as the natural order of things—divine right, just about. Hometown judges often agreed; a housing ordinance similar to Tulsa's was upheld by the Kentucky state supreme court in 1915, which gave local officials the confidence to press forward with their plan.[9]

The ordinance was passed on a Friday. News of it swept through Greenwood over the weekend, plastered on the front page of the Saturday edition of the *Tulsa Star*. On Sunday after church, hundreds of residents gathered at the Dreamland to strategize a response. Stradford, as one of the most outspoken people in the neighborhood, naturally took on the role of protest organizer. "We have a set of city officials in power now who will not be guided by our wishes," he told the crowd. "They seem to think that they can get along without the negro. This is impossible, they just don't know it."[10]

Stradford knew he needed to get in a room with Tulsa mayor John Simmons and explain why the new ordinance could not stand. The mayor had ridden into office in a landslide victory that April, in part on the back of the black vote—on the back of Stradford, in fact, who was the Republican committeeman in the mostly black tenth precinct.[11] Simmons was well aware he owed a debt to Greenwood and had promised to serve all of Tulsa "without regard to political beliefs, religion, or previous condition of servitude."[12] But now, to Stradford's growing frustration, the new mayor and the city commissioners refused to schedule a meeting with Greenwood leaders. "They are so far above our heads that we can't reach them with a balloon," Stradford said.[13]

If black people wanted to live among themselves, Stradford believed, it had to be on their own terms. He was a major proponent of building communal wealth, but the notion that his people would not be allowed to live where they pleased was unconscionable. At the meeting, the group drafted a resolution proclaiming that the ordinance cast "a stigma upon the colored race in the eyes of the world." They selected three men, Stradford among them, to hand-deliver the message to city hall on Monday.[14]

Maybe black people were doing themselves a disservice by aligning with a political party that not only took them for granted but was now actively working against their interests, Stradford thought. He was coming around to the worldview of his younger friend, A. J. Smitherman, who had been pushing him to switch political parties since the day the two men met.[15] "They say that Republicans will get our vote anyway and they want to demonstrate to the white people that they are not 'nigger lovers,'" Stradford said. "But we will show them."[16]

Stradford was not the first black Oklahoman who challenged the spread of Jim Crow, nor was he the first to feel the sting of betrayal from a seeming political ally as he did so. He followed a long lineage of activists who had seen the promise of equality in the Indian Territory, only to watch it wither and die as American racism became a primary import to a contested land.

In its pre-statehood days, Oklahoma was an unusually egalitarian place. When the population was still tiny, it was common for white, black, and Native American children to attend the same schools.[17] Black politicians held public office not only as freedmen in the tribal governments of Indian Territory but also in Oklahoma Territory, the modern-day western half of the state.[18] In the early days of Tulsa, black entrepreneurs like Stradford owned businesses in the predominantly white downtown district.[19] Some even had white employees.[20]

But as more white settlers from the Deep South poured into the region, they brought the mores of Jim Crow along with them. A 1910 law in Oklahoma Territory excluded blacks from white schools.[21] Black political aspirations dimmed as many Republican "Lily Whites" boxed them out to appease racist voters. Boosters who had once crowed that Oklahoma offered "equal chances with the white man" retreated to anxiety and anger. "Some cusses who do business here are putting in Jim Crow quarters for Negroes," reported W. H. Twine's Muskogee newspaper, the *Cimeter,* in 1905. "We shall see that the public are made acquainted with the prejudiced devils who inaugurate this kind of business."[22]

The ultimate test of Oklahoma's vision for the future came in the battle over statehood, a bellwether for how legally sanctioned racism would be tolerated in the United States at the dawn of a new century.

Since the 1890s, settlers in both Oklahoma Territory and Indian Territory had advocated statehood to legitimize their encroachment on indigenous land that wasn't theirs. As the white population of the region grew, so did their influence, while the political power of both black and indigenous people waned. In 1905 Congress denied an effort by the Five Tribes to get Indian Territory accepted into the Union as a state on its own, governed by Native Americans.[23] Another group of more traditional indigenous people demanded that the federal government restore its original treaties with the Five Tribes and revert the territory from individual land allotments back to communal ownership.[24] They too were ignored. In 1906, though, Congress approved a constitutional convention spearheaded by white leaders that sought to unify Indian Territory and Oklahoma Territory into a single new state called Oklahoma.[25] Delegates from every corner of both territories traveled to the city of Guthrie to draft the tenets of their fledgling society. While some white men who had married into the Five Tribes were present, along with a few men who were part-white and part-indigenous, full-blooded Native Americans were largely absent, and not a single black delegate was elected to attend.[26]

The convention was chaired by William Murray, a brash Texan who had married into the Chickasaw tribe and curried favor among many white leaders, as well as some Native ones. Murray effused a folksy charm as a defender of rural agriculture, earning the nickname "Alfalfa Bill" for his farmer-friendly agenda.[27] But he had a curdling disdain for black people, and he was determined to turn it into government policy.

"As a rule [Negroes] are failures as lawyers, doctors, and in other professions," Murray said in his inaugural speech at the convention.[28] He stood at a podium on the second floor of Guthrie's city hall, in an assembly room packed with more than one hundred white delegates.[29] An American flag, then with just forty-five stars, hung high on the wall above the chamber entrance, next to a balcony where the few black onlookers squeezed into a small corner of segregated seats.[30] "It is an entirely false notion that the negro can rise to the equal of a white man," Murray continued. He openly called for separate schools, separate train cars, and a ban on interracial marriage.[31]

Despite Murray's bluster, black people refused to cede their civil rights. While the constitutional convention was happening in Guthrie in December 1906, W. H. Twine and A.G.W. Sango helped organize nearly three hundred black leaders in a protest convention in Muskogee. Their group, which called itself the Negro Protective League, implored the constitutional delegates to preserve equal rights for "white man, red man, and black man." They warned that a constitution burdened with Jim Crow discrimination would be "a disgrace to our western civilization" and "the forerunner of other vicious legislation that would cause endless strife, racial discord, tumult and race disturbances."[32] The Negro Protective League spent months building a grassroots campaign opposing the constitution, urging black people in every town and hamlet to vote against its passage.[33] But they were wildly outnumbered; in September 1907, the constitution was put to a public vote and passed with 71 percent approval.[34]

Black leaders still believed the federal government might step in and stop the constitution from being enacted. Congress had opened the path for Oklahoma's constitutional convention through its 1906 Enabling Act, but no one could predict the reaction of President Theodore Roosevelt, who held veto power over the new state's founding documents. As the leader of the Republican Party, Roosevelt was known to be a fair-weather friend of black people. White leaders feared—and black leaders hoped—he might oppose a constitution that was too explicitly racist.[35] While the Enabling Act allowed for segregated schools in the new state, it also required that Oklahoma's constitution "make no distinction in civil or political rights on account of race or color."[36] To ensure smooth passage into statehood, the convention delegates stripped some Jim Crow measures from the document, well aware they could pass them as soon as their first legislature convened.[37] Murray and his allies understood how to follow the letter of the law while trampling over the spirit of it.

In a last-ditch effort, Twine, Sango, and a handful of other Protective League members decided to board a train for Washington, D.C. They would force a face-to-face meeting with President Roosevelt to convince him to reject the constitution and prevent Jim Crow from being cemented out west.[38]

As their train wound its way toward the nation's capital, Twine, a diehard Republican, felt confident his president and his party would do the right thing and reject the constitution. Just two years earlier he had joined Sango on the chartered car for Roosevelt's inauguration.

He remembered watching with pride as the heroic Buffalo Soldiers, the all-black regiment that had fought alongside Roosevelt in the Spanish-American War, marched in the inaugural parade.[39] "President Roosevelt is a Republican," an article in the *Cimeter* reasoned. "We believe he will give the black men of the new state a square deal and will see to it that the door of hope is not closed against them."[40]

Over the course of a few days, the delegation met with the U.S. attorney general, the secretary of the interior, and the register of the treasury, the most senior black member of the Roosevelt administration.[41] Finally, the group ventured to the White House's newly constructed West Wing to talk to the president himself. When they finally

Theodore Roosevelt speaks at the National Negro Business League meeting, New York, 1910

met Roosevelt in person, the group must have told him how Oklahoma legislators planned to institutionalize segregation on an unprecedented scale. While the constitution would segregate only schools, legislators had plans to segregate train cars, libraries, even phone booths, just as soon as they were free of federal oversight.[42] Surely, Twine and his cadre hoped, the president would not be party to this sham version of democracy.

But Roosevelt had seemingly already made up his mind. He shook Twine's hand and politely told him and the other delegates to take up their issue with the Justice Department. According to one report, he told the assembled men, "Please do not ask me to not sign it."[43]

On November 16, 1907, Roosevelt signed the proclamation turning Indian Territory and Oklahoma Territory into the forty-sixth U.S. state, Oklahoma.[44]

As blacks had feared, the very first law enacted by the state legislature a few weeks later called for segregated train cars.[45] Soon the grandfather clause was on the books. Ultimately the legislature would pass more than a dozen statutes aimed at dividing public life by race, and what wasn't required by law would soon be accepted as custom. Though Indian Territory and Oklahoma Territory had briefly nurtured a unique spirit of racial tolerance, the new state of Oklahoma would be no such place. Given the chance to construct a new foundation of equality for the twentieth century, Oklahoma instead chose to rebuild the rickety edifice of Jim Crow, statute by statute.

Senate Bill 1, the law that segregated trains, had roiled J. B. Stradford. The legislature wanted to cram black travelers into waiting rooms littered with broken whiskey bottles and onto fusty train cars that carried the permanent stench of human waste—to remind them, at every possible interval, that whites thought them a low and dirty race.[46] But Stradford refused to be boxed in. In January 1909, on a train ride from Kansas to Tulsa, he dared to sit in a car occupied by white people. When a porter ordered him to move, Stradford snapped, "It's not your business to tell me where to ride."[47]

Stradford was eventually forced to move by the train's conductor, but the encounter wasn't over.[48] When he disembarked in a nearby town, Stradford was arrested for his perceived insubordination and forced to pay a twenty-five-dollar cash bond to escape jail time. He sued the Midland Valley Railroad over the whole ordeal, arguing that state segregation laws didn't apply to interstate travel. The case wound its way to the state supreme court, but a judge ultimately ruled against him in 1912. The conductor, the judge reasoned, was merely following the rules.[49]

Four years later, in Tulsa, Stradford was once again leading a charge against an unjust law. Two days after the mass meeting at the Dreamland, he and a delegation of Greenwood leaders marched downtown to confront Mayor Simmons with the letter they had drafted. Simmons knew Stradford well as an organ of the Republican Party, but that hardly mattered to the mayor as the men strode into the city commission's assembly room at City Hall. When they approached the elected officials, Simmons told the group to offer their remarks but warned that the commissioners had important work to attend to.[50]

R. T. Bridgewater, a prominent Greenwood doctor, spoke first, making an ardent plea for justice. A man named J. H. Roberts read a long, dramatic eulogy for the Negro race. While they were speaking, commissioners read over paperwork. The mayor himself hardly looked up.

Then Stradford stepped forward. "I would like to say a few words," he began, "and won't be long."

The mayor could no longer feign indifference. "Be brief," he said. "I can tell you now that we have already carefully considered this matter and there is no need of any other discussion."

Stradford bottled up his frustration and continued. "You white Republicans asked my help in the last city campaign and you will be wanting aid this fall," he said. "I lined the colored vote up for both Mayor Simmons and Commissioner Funk. The mayor himself solicited my assistance and I delivered the goods. Now that we helped elect you we are insulted by your attempt to segregate us.

"The negroes have the right to live anywhere in Tulsa that they choose," Stradford concluded.

The mayor looked up and briefly weighed the man standing before him. But he could not even dignify a black man with a proper rebuttal. He turned to his fellow commissioners. "Let's approve these bills."[51]

When Stradford burst out of city hall, he must have been seething. How could Oklahoma, once so limitless in possibility, have wound up in the bosom of Jim Crow? For all the talk by Booker T. Washington and his followers of how far black people had come since slavery—Stradford knew the journey quite well—these days progress often seemed to be moving backward, not forward.

On Monday, August 14, as the ordinance went into effect, police began doing sweeps of every street and alley in South Tulsa. Black residents who weren't servants were instructed to vacate their homes immediately; those who refused were arrested on sight.[52] Over one hundred families were forced out of their homes during the first few weeks of enforcement. City officials knew housing in Greenwood was limited but continued with the sweeps anyway. "Negro families are doubling up in houses," the *Tulsa Democrat* reported. "In some instances three and four families are living in one house."[53] In 1917 the U.S. Supreme Court ruled that segregated housing ordinances violated the rights of property owners.[54] But the Tulsa law remained on the books for decades longer, and into the 1930s black people reported being arrested for living in white districts.[55]

White Tulsans also had less publicized legal tools to enforce segregation. Many land deeds in the city included clauses that specifically banned homeowners from selling their property to a black person. These rules, known as restrictive housing covenants, were present in Tulsa as early as 1909 and formed the bedrock of many of the city's wealthiest neighborhoods.[56] Maple Ridge, a tony area just south of downtown, had land deeds stipulating "no part of the lot . . . shall ever be sold, or rented to, or occupied by, any person of African descent." As with the ordinance, though, whites included a carve-out for the only type of black person they could tolerate: servants.[57]

While Stradford felt personally wounded by his Republican allies, their actions only reaffirmed A. J. Smitherman's suspicions about the party. The newspaper editor called the segregation ordinance "an odious insult to the race" and cast it as a climax of Republican failure, after the party had already nixed funding for the Greenwood library that Democrats had previously backed. He urged blacks to reject the "false promises" of Republicans by voting straight Democrat in the next election.[58]

But Smitherman's party would soon find its own way to disappoint Greenwood residents. In November 1916, a few months after the segregation ordinance was passed, the Democratic Party held an orgiastic parade in downtown Tulsa to celebrate the reelection of President Woodrow Wilson. Brass bands blared, revelers waved Roman candles, and donkeys strung up with decorative lights sauntered past Convention Hall. Tate Brady, the prominent real estate developer, led the parade on a large white Missouri mule.[59] Behind him, marchers waved the flag of the Confederacy—or as Brady referred to it, the "Lost Cause."[60]

Brady, along with another Tulsa realtor named Merritt J. Glass, was a leader of Tulsa's popular chapter of the Sons of Confederate Veterans.[61] When parade onlookers complained that waving the Confederate flag through city streets was unpatriotic, Brady and Glass bemoaned that Tulsa was infected with "the same spirit of the carpetbagger government of the south, which openly boasted of its intention and purpose to put the white man's neck under the black man's heel." They recalled the early days of Oklahoma politics—when black

Letterhead stationery of the Tulsa reunion of the United Confederate Veterans, organized by Tate Brady and Merritt J. Glass

people were elected to office, attended integrated schools, and sat on train cars where they wished—with rueful disdain. They pined with a knowing nostalgia for those dark years in the South that J. B. Stradford no doubt remembered, when "an all-wise Providence sent the Army of the Invisible Empire (the Ku-Klux Klan) to the rescue of the stricken Southland."[62] Their actions were a reminder that both Democrats and Republicans trafficked in racism when it suited them.

Greenwood leaders came to realize that black people would truly have to go it alone in building up their community. All they could do was draw collective strength to meet the challenge. "While other races are trying to segregate us," read an August 1916 *Star* editorial, "let us strive the harder to build more brick buildings, own more fine homes, plant more flowers in the front yards, open more business enterprises, erect more colleges, and build finer edifices and segregation with its hellish intent will be a failure."[63] But as all of Greenwood would soon find out, black people, even when left to their own devices, could not escape the wrath of white vengeance.

The residents of Greenwood bore the burden of living in two Americas at once, the idealized version imagined in the minds of white slaveholders in 1776, and the more brutal reality that black Tulsans and their ancestors bore witness to long before and after that year. Their very names often carried the weight of this contradiction: *Andrew Jackson* Smitherman, Alexander *George Washington* Sango.[64] They were bound to an American mythology, even as they saw its noblest promises crumble around them.

To observe the evolution of Oklahoma, as men like J. B. Stradford and A. J. Smitherman had, was to see the entire American myth replayed in fast forward—the "discovery" of new lands already long inhabited by a native people, the brief celebration of egalitarian ideals, the betrayal of those ideals to appease white prejudice and greed. At the core of the rot in the new state was not just Jim Crow but also the worship of the settler, the oilman, and the divine right of the free market. White real estate men hoping to strike oil hoovered up thousands of acres of tribal land allotments through fraudulent schemes, sometimes swindling landowners out of their property for less than a dollar an acre.[65] The practice was called grafting. They did this with patriotic vigor, just as William Murray had cast black people as an inferior race with the president of the United States' signature.

When a Muskogee grafter named Cass Bradley addressed a congressional panel in Muskogee about defrauding "niggers and [Native American] half bloods" out of their land so that it could be resold to white farmers, he spoke of what he did with pride. "We did the country a service," he told the senators. "If this business that I am in is a grafting game, then there is not a business in the world that is not a graft."[66] The senators viewed his testimony with bemusement and curiosity rather than outrage.[67]

Greenwood leaders opposed economic injustice just as fiercely as they fought segregation. Around 1910, while still living in Muskogee,

A. J. Smitherman partnered with a Creek freedman named Warrior Rentie to form the Negro Guardianship League, an organization that provided legal aid to tribal members whose land was at risk of being seized by white grafters. When tribal members became rich with oil, Oklahoma district judges assigned legal guardians to young freedmen and Native Americans, ostensibly as a way to protect them from financial predators.[68] Often the role was filled by white lawyers who had turned guardianship into a lucrative profession, taking on dozens of wards and becoming predators themselves. Edith Durant, a young black freedman who owned oil-rich land just outside Tulsa, was conned by her white guardian out of $43,000 (about $1.2 million in 2021 dollars).[69]

Rather than letting young freedmen be saddled with duplicitous white attorneys, the Guardianship League vetted black and Native professionals who it hoped would treat their wards more fairly. Smitherman began the initiative in Muskogee and later brought it to Tulsa as well, taking on cases all across eastern Oklahoma.[70] "It was the irony of fate that the same government which bequeathed this inheritance to these Indians and freedmen provided the machinery for their disinheritance," he wrote in his autobiography.[71]

Stradford, meanwhile, kept up his dogged opposition to Jim Crow. He lived in many places during his life—Reconstruction-era Kentucky, the progressive college town of Oberlin, Ohio, a rowdy natural gas boomtown in Indiana—but it was in Oklahoma that he observed the core hypocrisies of American dogma laid bare in the starkest of terms.[72] In the *Tulsa Star,* he penned articles about the injustices his race suffered just as often as he planned protests to thwart them.[73] His dark brow was no doubt furrowed in each instance. "Freedom of thought, freedom of speech, freedom of press, freedom of locomotion, and freedom to act as you please so long as you do not abridge the rights of others," he wrote in one column. "This is the freedom which is delegated to the white man in Oklahoma, and denied to the black man. What can I do, in Oklahoma, that my life long hope may be realized?"[74]

A newspaper front page depicting the East St. Louis riot, 1917

About forty miles east of Greenwood, Marie Scott sat alone in the Wagoner County Jail. It was 1914, and Scott, just seventeen years old, was a new arrival in the town's black neighborhood, which local white newspapers derisively called "the Bottoms." Her life and her world were usually invisible to the white people of Wagoner County, but a young white man named Lem Peace had been killed during a trip to her neighborhood. Scott was accused of his murder.[1]

The details of Marie Scott's encounter with Lem Peace were murky. Initial reports in the white press said she approached Peace on the road and stabbed him without warning.[2] According to a report in the NAACP's *Crisis* magazine, Peace came into Scott's home and raped her, then was killed by her older brother.[3] Whatever the truth, the white newspapers that described Scott's behavior in the most vicious and irrational terms expressed the most admiration for what happened next.

On March 31, at about one a.m. at the jail, a group of masked white men armed with revolvers overpowered the lone guard. They pulled Scott from her cell and cast a rope around her neck.[4] When she struggled, someone bashed her head with a six-shooter.[5] Then they marched her toward the corner of First and Main Street, right by the new Stockton Grocery store.[6] The men hanged her there from a telephone pole, leaving her body for the town undertaker to retrieve about an hour later.[7]

In nearby Tulsa, the lynching was not covered in the *Tulsa World*, and it received a short, terse treatment in the *Tulsa Democrat*.[8] The *Wagoner County Courier* praised the violent verdict of the mob, declaring, "There are conditions and circumstances sometimes that give even a lynching a peaceful and helpful appearance."[9] This vindictive writing was common in white journalism of the era, dulling a community's collective conscience with every disparaging word.

Only A. J. Smitherman and his *Tulsa Star* denounced the attack on Marie Scott. Smitherman despised mob law and defended the victims of its excesses, no matter their race, class, or circumstance. "These conditions are becoming very alarming and a serious calamity is sure to follow if something is not done to force all citizens to respect the law," he wrote.[10] Smitherman understood that the elimination of even the pretense of justice would ultimately prove disastrous for black people.

Four months later Crockett Williams, a black man in Eufaula, was accused of murdering a well-known Creek resident named Johnson King. A group of as many as 150 masked men broke into the jail where Williams was being held. The mob hanged him from a tree in the middle of a cornfield, his body swaying in the wind as his lynchers hid amid rustling stalks. Officials promised an investigation, but in the same breath, they confessed it was likely to yield no arrests.[11]

Smitherman's outcry shifted to a higher register. "Any man has a right to resort to arms to defend the law, or to protect a citizen from violence," his *Tulsa Star* argued. "It's up to us to act. We must have justice!"[12]

The Crockett Williams killing was front-page news in August 1914 under the blood-boiling headline ANOTHER MAN LYNCHED: AND THE

MURDERERS, AS USUAL, GO UNPUNISHED. Next to the article was a report on a continent-spanning conflict embroiling Britain, Russia, Germany, Austria, and France. GENERAL WAR IS NOW ON, the *Tulsa Star* announced.[13] A great war was brewing overseas, but for black Americans, an even more urgent battle was unfolding at home.

The onset of World War I thrust black people into an increasingly familiar contradiction. They were asked to accept the solemn duties of patriotism without reaping even the most basic benefits of democracy. Smitherman identified this hypocrisy as the war escalated. "It's not an equal chance to fight in the U.S. army that we want. It's an equal chance at our rights as private American citizens," read a 1915 *Star* editorial. "The time is near at hand when they will be anxious to form Colored companies of militia in every state in the union. Let us now demand the other essential things."[14]

Despite their misgivings, Smitherman and the rest of Greenwood did their part in the war effort. In early 1918, about a year after the United States formally entered the conflict, the newspaper publisher and J. H. Goodwin helped organize Liberty Bond drives in black Tulsa. (Smitherman later claimed that black Oklahomans raised $200,000 overall.)[15] In May, residents held a farewell party for black draftees at Cleaver-Cherry Hall, serving the boys cake and ice cream as a traveling black musical company led dancing long into the night.[16] At the start of September, a crowd of thousands gathered on Greenwood Avenue for a "community singing," a patriotic pep rally that was common across the nation during the war years. As dusk cast a soft glow on their proud brick buildings, the men and women of Greenwood surrounded an organ mounted atop a flatbed truck. The notes of "The Star-Spangled Banner" and "Keep the Home Fires Burning" floated into the evening sky as they sang, *Though your lads are far away, they dream of home.*[17]

During the nineteen months when the United States was directly involved in World War I, 5,694 black Oklahomans were drafted into service. It was a tiny fraction of the 367,000 blacks conscripted nationally, but it still meant every Greenwood family knew someone who was off at war.[18] A. J. Smitherman's younger brother Willie was sent to training camp in April 1918, then shipped to the trenches of

An injured black army soldier, a white woman, and a white navy serviceman stand in front of the War Savings Stamps Bank *in Tulsa*

French battlefields on the USS *Northern Pacific* later that year.[19] J. H. and Carlie Goodwin's eldest daughter Lucille married a successful young dentist named Plato Travis in July 1917;[20] four months later he was drafted into the army's dental reserve and ordered to training camp at Fort Des Moines.[21]

During training, many black soldiers were automatically shuttled into menial labor rather than physical fitness exercises and weapons practice. At segregated army bases, blacks were denied the basic tools of success, such as warm clothes for the winter months and school lessons offered to white draftees.[22] Some Greenwood soldiers brought *Star* subscriptions with them to camp to remind them of home. Private Norman Higgs had been a laborer in the home of a prominent bank president south of downtown Tulsa.[23] When he was drafted and sent to Camp Dodge near Des Moines, Iowa, he saw that Oklahoma's increasingly virulent racism wasn't unique. Des Moines restaurants refused to serve black customers, and theaters seated them only in the back.[24] White and black privates rarely interacted while on base.[25]

And Camp Dodge, just like rural Oklahoma, was haunted by brutal acts of so-called justice. In July 1918 three black men were hanged on the base after they were found guilty of raping a white woman during a rushed trial. Every soldier at the camp was forced to watch; black soldiers wept and fainted before the gruesome and eerily familiar display.[26]

Living in the segregated Negro barracks wedged into the southern corner of the camp,[27] Higgs could feel the burden of the American contradiction festering inside him. When he could no longer bear its weight, he found a scrap of paper and mailed his worries back home. "I have been wondering and thinking if I go to France and get back, will things be better?" he asked in a letter to the *Tulsa Star*. "If I go over and lick twenty-five huns and should I die before I get back, will my poor old mother be Jim-Crowed because she is black?"[28]

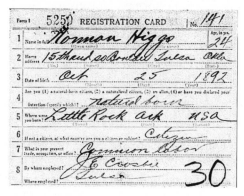

World War I draft registration card for Norman Higgs

When black soldiers left training camp and went to fight in France, though, they came to understand freedom in a different light. French soldiers respected them, French citizens appreciated them, and French women courted them. There were no WHITES ONLY signs hanging on storefronts, and no invisible jurisdictions where being black on a railroad car suddenly became a crime.[29] The black men who were fluent in French—some were graduates of elite colleges like Howard University—took up the country's national anthem as a rallying cry.[30] "There is an air of liberty, equality, and fraternity here which do not blow in the black man's face [in] liberty loving, democratic America," one soldier wrote from the port city of Le Havre.[31]

But the U.S. military's leadership insisted on exporting its racism abroad. In France, white presiding officers issued a series of orders that mimicked Jim Crow mores, preventing black soldiers from entering hotels or fraternizing with white women.[32] Violations of military doctrine could result in arrest or even execution, and multiple black soldiers testified to being dragged before tribunal courts for being caught in public with Frenchwomen.[33] This racism went further than what was even officially on the books; a secret memo by French colonel J.L.A. Linard, which was obtained and published by the *Crisis,* advised French officers to discriminate against black soldiers in order to maintain diplomatic relations with the United States. "American opinion is unanimous upon the Negro question and does not admit of discussion," the memo stated. "They fear that contact with the French will fill American Negroes with ideas which the whites consider intolerable."[34]

Many black soldiers performed bravely on the battlefield. The 369th Infantry Regiment, nicknamed the Harlem Hellfighters, earned 170 citations of the Croix de Guerre, a French medal for valor.[35] But black accomplishments in battle were often ignored by American military leaders, while missteps cast a pall on the entire race. Brigadier General William Atterbury, for example, said that many blacks were "lazy" and only suited to "road or quarry work."[36] This harsh stereotyping explains in part why prominent black intellectuals like W.E.B. Du Bois ultimately swallowed their critiques of American empire and preached utter black devotion to the war effort. In his famous "Close Ranks" editorial in July 1918, Du Bois argued, "Let us, while this war lasts, forget our special grievances and close our ranks shoulder to shoulder with our own white fellow citizens and the allied nations that are fighting for democracy."[37]

The hope from the moment the first shot was fired was that black courage and loyalty would prove to white America that black people were deserving of equal rights. Du Bois desperately wished this to be true. But black soldiers themselves, who watched Jim Crow stalk them across the Atlantic Ocean, remained skeptical. Norman Higgs concluded his letter to the *Tulsa Star* with a question to which he already seemed to know the answer: "If I go over and help give the kaiser hell . . . will I see at night in a vision the sparks going up from my old home that southern ruffians are burning?"[38]

Even before black soldiers were shipped overseas, the demand for equality at home was growing louder, resulting in an escalation of racial violence that wracked the entire nation. The peak of the unrest would come in 1919, so bloody a season that it would later be called the Red Summer. But the hate-fueled chaos began years before that time, and it would persist long afterward.

On July 2, 1917, a white mob paraded through the streets of downtown East St. Louis, Illinois, looking for black people to kill. The violence had been preceded by months of simmering tension between black and white metalworkers over a limited number of jobs, then was ignited by the killing of two plainclothes police detectives by a group of armed blacks on the night of July 1. The black group had likely mistaken the officers for a group of white attackers, after reports earlier in the night that drunken white men had assaulted a black woman in the street and fired on black homes. On July 2, the white mob made no distinction in who they targeted for their revenge. They dragged black residents from streetcars and shot others at point-blank range. Eventually they fanned farther north, torching buildings in black neighborhoods. Murder became a blood sport—cries of "Get a nigger!" were followed by "Get another!" By the next morning, at least forty-eight people had been killed, thirty-nine of them black, and more than 240 buildings were destroyed.[39]

The following month a black army unit, the Third Battalion of the 24th Infantry, was stationed in Houston, Texas, to guard a World War I military camp called Camp Logan. The soldiers, who had previously served in the Philippines and Mexico, were subject to physical and verbal abuse from white police officers and chafed at the segregation of streetcars and water fountains.[40] One night a false rumor spread through their barracks that one of their fellow soldiers had been arrested and killed by local police. That was followed by a false report that an attack by a white mob against the camp was imminent. Fueled by both panic and anger, a group of about one hundred black soldiers mutinied in the streets of Houston, shooting white police officers, civilians, and National Guard members. In the ensuing chaos, fifteen whites, one Mexican-American, and four blacks were killed.[41]

One hundred and ten soldiers in Houston were found guilty of serious crimes, and fifty-three received life sentences in prison. Nineteen were hanged,[42] thirteen of them before their sentences could be reviewed by the U.S. War Department.[43] Black newspapers across the nation, including the *Tulsa Star,* promoted petitions demanding President Woodrow Wilson commute some of the death sentences.[44] Meanwhile, although roughly 20 whites were imprisoned for their role in the East St. Louis riots (along with more than a dozen blacks), none faced capital punishment.[45] An effort by Missouri congressman Leonidas Dyer to introduce an anti-lynching bill, which would have made it a felony when a state or local official failed to protect citizens from riotous mobs, died in the halls of Congress.[46]

Racial tensions continued to mount following these events, right at home in Oklahoma. In August 1918, the black barber Aaron Wordlaw in the town of Dewey shot and killed the town's police chief during a botched arrest attempt. He was quickly jailed, but sensing that a mob might try to lynch him, police sent him to a neighboring county for his protection. The maneuver only made the mob more angry. White residents went on a rampage in the town's black district, burning down roughly twenty black homes, as well as two churches and a school.[47] Within days two hundred black residents had abandoned the town, after someone—newspaper accounts don't say who—warned them to get out, or else.[48] The intimidation mirrored successful efforts to remove blacks from so-called sundown towns across the state, including Norman, Madill, and Shroud.[49] But even by the standards of Oklahoma lawlessness, the scale of the Dewey violence was shocking.

A. J. Smitherman traveled to Dewey to survey the carnage for himself.[50] He had recently been appointed a justice of the peace, granting him the ability to issue court judgments on low-level civil and criminal offenses.[51] Though Smitherman's jurisdiction included only Tulsa, he had dedicated himself to curtailing the lawlessness that was spiraling out of control across the state. Smitherman sent an urgent telegram to Oklahoma governor Robert L. Williams, calling on him to bring the Dewey mob to justice. "At this time of our national crisis, while our black boys, along side of our white boys, are fighting, bleeding and dying on the shell-plowed battle fields of France for the principles of democracy," he wrote, "surely we will not desecrate the cause for which they are giving their life blood by permitting the mob rule."[52]

Smitherman traveled to the state capital to urge the governor further, and Williams promised to pursue prosecutions vigorously.[53] Eventually a special grand jury indicted eighteen people with race riot crimes in Dewey, including the town's mayor (though he was later exonerated).[54] It was a rare example of the justice system trying to curtail mob rule, fueled in part by pressure from the black citizenry. Smitherman earned praise from black leaders around the state for his efforts. "Go on my boy! You are on the right track," W. H. Twine wrote in a letter to his former protégé. "We must keep matters moving and put an end to mob violence."[55]

But just two months after the Dewey attack, Smitherman's very public activism began to seriously rile white authorities. In October 1918 the newspaper publisher confronted a white man, Charles H. Kretz, on his doorstep in South Tulsa, after hearing rumors that a black maid was being mistreated in the Kretz home. In a front-page article proclaiming "Whites Adopted Slavery Methods," Smitherman reported that the maid, Mary Johnson, had been denied her meager wage of two dollars per week and been whipped for talking to other black women in the neighborhood. He called Kretz a "cowardly Hun," an insulting word for Germans during the war.[56] Kretz was actually a leader of Tulsa's draft exemption board and a powerful member of the city's white elite.[57] Within days of publishing his article, Smitherman was dragged before the Tulsa County Council of Defense to answer for himself.[58]

The Council of Defense was part of a nationwide network of state and local wartime agencies created to coordinate with a new federal defense council "for the general good of the nation."[59] Ostensibly, the councils were supposed to maintain domestic morale and run savings bond campaigns; in reality, they used censorship, coercion, and carefully orchestrated acts of violence to enact their will, often for ends that had nothing to do with the war effort.[60] Council members openly advocated the lynching of their political enemies in the pages of the *Tulsa World*. A vigilante offshoot of the council, known as the Knights of Liberty, once tarred and feathered a group of oil industry unionists that they deemed to be meddlesome, forcing their victims to flee Tulsa forever.[61] The council's tactics were as ruthless as they were widely known. And the membership of both the public-facing group and its shadowy vigilante appendage reached to white Tulsa's highest ranks, including *Tulsa World* managing editor Glenn Condon, police chief Ed Lucas, and real estate mogul Tate Brady.[62]

These were the men Smitherman had crossed by exposing Charles H. Kretz. The Council of Defense threatened to confiscate his printing press,[63] but Smitherman ultimately avoided punishment. Though he conceded that he may have been wrong to call Kretz a Hun, he did not even entertain the idea that he would be silenced going forward. "We do not think it disloyal to oppose injustice and mistreatment of our people, or any other people for that matter," he wrote after his hearing.[64] Elsewhere in the pages of the *Star* that fall, he was more blunt: "The Colored man must start to fighting the devil with fire, and when cheap White men start their Ku Klux Klan methods pump hot lead into them."[65]

While the council was ostensibly a wartime emergency organization, the influence of its leaders would not wane when the group formally disbanded after the war. Thanks to his courage and activism, Smitherman was making powerful and permanent white enemies.

Nineteen-nineteen should have been a year of celebration as World War I came to an end. But for black soldiers, the long shadow of violence was impossible to escape. In the months after the armistice, black units were forced to bury tens of thousands of corpses in the French countryside while white battalions enjoyed lavish victory parades.[66] When black soldiers did make it home, many units were celebrated only grudgingly by the nation they had defended. In Tulsa, homecoming events for returning soldiers were segregated, and black veterans organized their own victory celebrations.[67]

The mounting tension went far beyond rituals. After risking their lives and losing their innocence, black soldiers returning home bore no more patience for Jim Crow discrimination and violent white coercion. But standing up for themselves was dangerous. If a black veteran brushed a white man on the sidewalk and refused to apologize, white people might assault him in his military uniform. Daniel Mack suffered such a fate after a white man stumbled into him on a sidewalk in Sylvester, Georgia. A scuffle ensued, but only Mack was arrested. Nine days later four white men removed him from his jail cell, beat him with clubs and ax handles, and left him for dead outside of town. Mack survived and fled the area.[68]

Such actions were widely publicized in newspapers like the *Chicago Defender,* angering black people nationwide and laying the groundwork for a new, more militant breed of activism.[69] White mobs had attacked black communities before World War I—in Wilmington, North Carolina, in 1898, Atlanta, Georgia, in 1906, and Springfield, Illinois, in 1908.[70] But the war marked a sea change in how black men viewed their own citizenship. They sincerely desired to apply the heroism they had mustered on the western front to protect their own people. And even among those who had not been off to war, calls for armed resistance against white incursions became common among black writers and activists. "For three centuries we have suffered and cowered," W.E.B. Du Bois wrote in September 1919. "Today we raise the terrible weapon of Self-Defense."[71]

Over the course of 1919, riots in more than thirty U.S. cities, from New York City to Bisbee, Arizona, seized the country.[72] In Chicago, the stoning of a black teenager sparked a week of mob violence between the races.[73] In Washington, D.C., after a black man suspected of assaulting a white woman was released for lack of evidence, white instigators began beating black passersby on sidewalks and hauling them from streetcars. Attacks stretched from black neighborhoods to the shadow of the White House.[74] In Elaine, Arkansas, an estimated two hundred black people were killed by white vigilantes who falsely believed that black sharecroppers were staging a violent uprising.[75] Overall, hundreds of people were killed, and thousands of homes and businesses were damaged or destroyed.

There were broader contextual reasons that racial conflicts escalated in this period. For instance, the Great Migration was causing northern cities to swell with black workers competing with white laborers for jobs. But at their core, the conflicts reflected a raw, and overtly masculine, power struggle. Black men refused to accommodate racist terrorism and ambient subjugation any longer. White men took any display of force by blacks as a provocation and as justification for unchecked retaliatory violence, no matter how extreme.

The rampaging racists could not execute a reign of terror alone. White moderates accepted the violence even if they didn't explicitly participate in it, often literally watching from the sidelines as blacks were attacked. The white press blamed blacks and outside agitators for the violence, offering the white establishment reassurances that their society was functioning just fine.[76] "All is quiet again," an *Atlanta Constitution* journalist wrote after an April 1919 riot in rural Georgia. "The innocent will have nothing to fear."[77] Government officials blamed far-left socialists and union organizers for planting radical ideas in black people's minds.[78] Efforts to address the actual issue at hand—black people being murdered with hardly any intervention by the state—gained little traction at the federal level. Dyer's antilynching bill continued to languish in Congress, and while President Woodrow Wilson called mob law "a disgraceful evil," he did not endorse Dyer's bill or any other specific policy that might stop the killings.[79] America had ostensibly entered the Great War to make the world safe for democracy, but the world of black Americans was being torn asunder.

Not only men were critiquing the rise of mob vigilantes. Greenwood resident Daisy Scott, the wife of boxer Jack Scott, was hired in 1920 as the *Tulsa Star*'s first regular cartoonist.[80] Her sketches pilloried ineffective Republican politicians and the unwillingness of any-

"The Future," a political cartoon in the Tulsa Star *by artist Daisy Scott*

one in power to put a stop to the age of mob rule. In one Scott drawing, a pair of young black children were pursued by a mob that included one man with a billy club, one with a lynch rope, and a third clutching a WHITES ONLY sign. "Shall these horrors await our future generations?" the *Star* asked in a caption.[81]

The end of summer brought more violence, as two men were lynched in Oklahoma in a single weekend during August 1920. In Oklahoma City, a black man named Claude Chandler had been arrested after being accused of killing two police officers during a shootout at his family's bootlegging still. He was taken from his jail cell and hanged from a tree.[82] Smitherman chastised the black men of Oklahoma City for not coming to Chandler's defense before it was too late.[83] What happened in Tulsa that weekend gave him even more reason to worry. A young white man, Roy Belton, was in the downtown jail, accused of murdering a white taxi driver. In the middle of the night, he was taken from his cell at the top of the courthouse, driven out of town by a caravan of cars, and hanged from a billboard. A mob of dozens ripped the clothes from Belton's body as souvenirs, while police officers directed traffic.[84] Tulsa County sheriff James Woolley called the mob attack under his watch "more beneficial than a death sentence pronounced by the courts,"[85] while the *Tulsa World* called it a "righteous protest."[86] Only Smitherman rang alarm bells about the collapse of the rule of law. "There is no crime, however atrocious, that justifies mob violence," he wrote in a letter to Oklahoma governor James B. A. Robertson.[87] He received anonymous death threats for speaking out.[88]

In November 1920, as alarm rose that the racial violence of the Red Summer was subsuming the state, black leaders organized an Inter-Racial Conference seeking a path toward peace.[89] Hundreds of such organizations had been mustered by southern white liberals, in conjunction with conservative blacks of the Booker T. Washington school of thought, in a response to the nationwide crisis.[90] Meeting in the chamber of the House of Representatives at the state capitol in Oklahoma City, hundreds gathered to discuss their demands for civil rights and how to defuse the intoxicating power of mob law. A. J. Smitherman looked on as Governor Robertson addressed the group. "A lyncher is a worse menace to a democratic form of government than a bolshevist who goes about waving a red flag and throwing bombs," the governor said. His words were powerful, but he brought them to the wrong audience. As the *Tulsa Star* noted, "Fully fifty counties were represented in the conference by over five hundred well known colored men, but sad to relate, the white citizenry was largely conspicuous by its absence."[91]

All these arguments were bandied among the black upper class—in newspaper pages, courtrooms, and legislative chambers. But a parallel conversation was unfolding among Greenwood's working class. Black people in Tulsa began refusing to get up from their seats when a white person stepped onto a crowded streetcar. They brushed past white people on the sidewalk without breaking stride.[92] They challenged police directly, their guns at the ready, when they saw officers making arrests in Greenwood.[93] Most of the men who had been shipped off to France philosophized at the barbershop rather than in audience with the governor of Oklahoma. Robert Fairchild, a teenager in 1920s Greenwood, worked in shoeshine parlors and snuck into pool halls, where he often paid more attention to what adults were saying than he let on. Looking back, Fairchild realized that every new atrocity—in Wagoner, Eufaula, and right at home in Tulsa—was strengthening their collective resolve to protect their own. "Associating with the hustlers and what have you, I often heard them say, 'They better not ever try to lynch a Negro in Tulsa. 'Cause if they do, we gon' be in the middle of it.' "[94]

Even as death and destruction swirled outside the neighborhood, life in Greenwood went on. In May of 1919, J. B. Stradford achieved his life's dream, opening a high-end hotel for black customers he had spent years trying to erect.[95] He took on roughly $30,000 in debt to fund the project, even risking his marriage when his wife initially refused to co-sign his increasingly risky loans.[96] But when the Stradford Hotel finally opened, it drew elegant crowds and national coverage in the *Chicago Defender*. Featuring sixty-eight high-end guest rooms, a dance hall, and a saloon,[97] the hotel was the largest and finest in the United States owned by a black person, Stradford proclaimed.[98] He proudly employed black carpenters, plumbers, and other artisans in its construction.[99]

Days after the hotel opened, Stradford organized a grand banquet with some of Tulsa's political leaders. The city's Democratic mayor C. H. Hubbard and his wife were the most prominent guests. The *Tulsa Star* reported that the event was the first interracial formal dinner in the city's history.[100] For Stradford, it must have felt like a triumph. It had been only three years since the previous mayor ignored and humiliated him at city hall; now, in the spacious dining room of a black man's independently owned hotel, the new mayor felt the need to pay homage to him and the rest of the Greenwood elite under the glint of newly installed chandeliers.[101] The next year Stradford would run for city commission.[102] The political ambitions he had harbored since first arriving in Tulsa were finally being realized.

For A. J. Smitherman, the political winds also seemed to be turning in his favor. In addition to being appointed justice of the peace, he had successfully lobbied the city to create a separate precinct for Greenwood, then used the *Star* to help push that new precinct to vote solidly Democratic. (His loyal friend J. H. Goodwin helped rally neighbors to their cause.)[103] He was disappointed when Tulsa again voted in a Republican mayor in 1920, but he was also encouraged by the fact that the black vote remained solidly Democratic.[104] Switching parties had not been his Waterloo, as W. H. Twine predicted; it made him a harbinger of a political sea change that would come soon enough to all of black America.

After successfully renovating the Dreamland in 1918, Loula Williams's ambitions continued to grow every year. She wanted to launch a neighborhood bank, rather than seeing her theater's take—$3,000 after a good weekend—shuttled off to a white Tulsa bank every week.[105] And she wasn't satisfied with just one theater—she wanted to own a whole nebula of Dreamlands, glittering across Oklahoma and beyond. When she and John purchased two more theaters in the late 1910s, Loula became the only black woman in America who operated three picture houses.[106] In her son Willie's high school yearbook, she placed an ad thanking all the customers who had helped her accomplish so much. "Your good will during the past years is warmly appreciated," Loula wrote. In the photograph of the remodeled Dreamland Theatre in the yearbook, a glowing two-sided marquee hung above the entrance and an American flag waved atop the crown jewel of Greenwood nightlife.[107]

The doors of Reverend Whitaker's new Mt. Zion Baptist Church finally opened in April 1921, eight years after members purchased the initial plot of land on Elgin Avenue.[108] It was two stories of gleaming red brick, with a bell tower that pointed toward the heavens.[109] On that first Sunday of a new era, Mabel Little was no doubt sitting in the pews of the church whose providence she'd prayed for so often. That first service would always mean something special for members like Mabel, who recalled the days studying the Lord's word atop the sawdust-covered floors of the old wooden Tabernacle. "That Mount Zion Church meant everything to us," Mabel said later. "No big I's and little you's in God's church. We're all just God's little children."[110]

At the end of May 1921, Ed Goodwin and his sister Anna were finishing up at Booker T. Washington High School. Ed was a star player on the school football team; Anna dazzled audiences with her sprightly soprano.[111] In the pages of their senior yearbook, they performed all the solemn duties of upperclassmen, from explaining the intricacies of true love ("a pleasant pain") to mocking their younger peers ("Ignorance—a freshman quality"). They were already wistful over a childhood innocence that was slipping through their fingers like sand, but just as excited about what the future might hold. The class voted Ed, whose ambition even then was apparent, Most Likely to Succeed.[112]

These were the people who had seen Greenwood through its humble origins and helped nurture it through its awkward adolescence. By 1921, Greenwood had matured into a proud, independent community. It was a district of roughly eleven thousand people, filled with landmarks that told their own stories: the hospital J.H. worked to erect, the theater Loula fought to own for herself, the public library Stradford offered to the neighborhood children, the daily newspaper A. J. Smitherman used to wage rhetorical war against every unjust cause. Across thirty-five square blocks, there were at least a dozen churches, three fraternal lodges, fifteen doctors, seven lawyers, and a garment factory—not to mention the rotating cast of more than fifty restaurants, grocery stores, and corner dives.[113] Greenwood was finally bigger than black Muskogee and the many all-black towns that dotted the state.[114] It was the anchor point of Oklahoma's black independence.

People from across the nation now desired to call Greenwood home. In 1918, Mary E. Jones Parrish, a typing teacher from Rochester, New York, visited the community, attracted by the friendly faces and collaborative enterprises. She felt a thrill the first time she stepped off the Frisco Railroad and into a world of black-owned businesses and well-kept homes, just as J.H. had felt in 1913. She soon settled there permanently, moving into an apartment right on Greenwood Avenue.[115]

Greenwood was becoming synonymous with black wealth, and Parrish recognized what an impetus money could be for people to pack up their bags and head west for a better life. She may well have been the first person to bestow on Greenwood its now iconic nick-

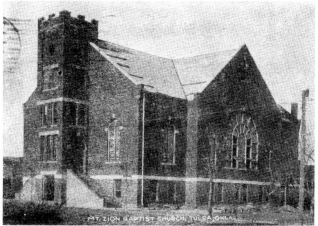

Greenwood institutions that were thriving in the spring of 1921 included the Stradford Hotel (top) and Mt. Zion Baptist Church.

name in print when she called the neighborhood "the Negro's Wall Street." But there was something else about Greenwood that Parrish truly cherished, something that couldn't be labeled with a price tag: "the wonderful co-operation I observed among our people."[116]

She would be forced to recall this vivid feeling with an almost aching nostalgia after everything about the world these families had worked so hard to build was ruthlessly torn apart. "After spending years of struggling and sacrifice, the people had begun to look upon Tulsa as the Negro Metropolis of the Southwest," she reflected later. "Then the devastating Tulsa Disaster burst upon us."[117]

CHAPTER 6

"GET A GUN AND GET BUSY"

*An armed young white man poses for the camera on
Greenwood Avenue on June 1, 1921, holding a gun
in each hand and smoking a cigar*

E d Goodwin and his classmates were excited for what tomorrow
would bring. By the end of May, the Booker T. Washington High
School Class of 1921 had survived four grueling years of economics, chemistry, typewriting, and algebra. Like most teenagers,
they carried the confidence of world conquerors. "We have attained
the dignity of Seniors," they declared in their school yearbook, "and
we wear our dignity well." They named the book *Excelsior*—Latin
for "ever upward."[1]

All that was left for them to do was graduate. On the night of
May 31, the final preparations were set. Loula Williams's son Willie
and many of his classmates were decorating for the junior-senior prom
at an event hall on Archer Street—they'd even recruited a live band.[2]
Ed Goodwin, meanwhile, was with a group at the Dixie Theater on

Greenwood Avenue. They were performing *The Sweet Girl Gradu-ates,* a school play about the theatrical pomp of commencement cer-emonies.[3] Ed's sister Anna was cast in the leading role, while Ed played her doting father.*

Elsewhere in Greenwood that evening, Mabel Little thumbed through the pages of her Bible as she settled in for women's night at the new Mt. Zion Baptist Church.[4] Mary Jones Parrish taught a type-writing class at her School of Natural Education.[5] A few doors down, the operator at the Dreamland Theatre loaded a fresh reel of film into one of Loula Williams's $475 projectors as patrons clutching candy and buttered popcorn found their seats.[6] J. B. Stradford and his wife Augusta retired early to their apartment inside the Stradford Hotel.[7] Delivery boys rode their bicycles through the dusty streets to bring groceries to mothers preparing dinner, while little girls played jacks in side alleys.[8] Men sat on their porches puffing cigars as the last vestiges of dusk got swallowed up by the night.

Around eight-thirty p.m., a young boy dashed into the Dixie The-ater, nearly out of breath. "They are trying to lynch a colored man downtown!" the boy exclaimed. "And the colored people are going down to prevent it." The news punctured the tranquility of the eve-ning like a tornado siren; teachers quickly sent all the students home as a precaution. When the high schoolers wandered out of the theater, Greenwood Avenue was thronged with people. Men with pistols and Winchester rifles were everywhere, bringing the coarse, drunken talk of the pool hall to the wealthiest part of the business district. Smoke clouded the darkening sky as men fired rounds toward the heavens, testing their weapons and their nerves at the same time. "Don't be wasting your bullets like that!" one man roaming the street said. "You might need them later."[9]

A curious child with fine bows in her pigtails was attracted by all the noise. From the second-story window of the Woods Building, lo-cated at the intersection of Archer Street and Greenwood Avenue,

---

* Some Booker T. high school students have said that a graduation rehearsal was happening at the Dixie at this time, but Ed recalled performing a play that night. These events may have been one and the same and have been condensed for narrative clarity.

seven-year-old Florence Mary Parrish watched the growing commo-
tion.

"Mother," she said, "I see men with guns."

Mary Jones Parrish ran to the window and gazed over the crowded
street, where she saw the armed men grouped off into little squads
and talking excitedly. She dashed down the stairs and out into the
humid night to find out exactly what was going on.[10]

These were the facts that had wound their way to the residents of
Greenwood through newspaper reports, whisper networks, and an
anonymous phone call to the Dreamland Theatre:[11] A black teenager
named Dick Rowland sat in the courthouse jail. He'd been arrested
on a charge of trying to "assault" an unnamed white girl, according
to a front-page article in the *Tulsa Tribune* (formerly the *Tulsa Democrat*). The incident was cast as an attempted rape.[12] After the lynching
of Marie Scott in Wagoner, Claude Chandler in Oklahoma City, and
Roy Belton right there in Tulsa, everyone knew that the accusation
alone could be a death sentence, especially for a black man. Rumor
was, a white lynch mob planned to execute Rowland before the night
was done.[13] After years of lynch law reigning supreme in Oklahoma,
that was something that simply could not stand in Greenwood.

Over at the dance hall, Willie Williams and his classmates received
the same warning that Ed's group did. As Willie walked out into the
night toward the crowd at the intersection of Greenwood and Archer
Street, his only concern was checking on his mother at the Dreamland
Theatre. He wanted to protect Loula—and while he might not have
admitted it at age sixteen, he also wanted to protect himself.[14]

On the way to the Dreamland, Willie walked by the Gurley Hotel,
where armed men stood outside and debated what should be done.
O. W. Gurley, the Greenwood pioneer who had opened the district's
very first business in 1905, preached calm.[15] He had never been on
board with the militant turn black America was taking following
World War I. At a city commission meeting in 1919, during the Red
Summer, he warned that more and more of his neighbors were carrying guns at all hours of day and night, challenging what they viewed
as unlawful arrests. All it would take was one errant gunshot for rising racial tensions to spill over into a full-blown riot. He called for
more police, white or colored, to keep the peace in Tulsa before it was

too late. "There are those who are agitating trouble in the section now," he complained. "I tell them that they wouldn't last as long as a snowball in hell, if they started any trouble."[16]

After learning of Dick Rowland's arrest earlier in the day on May 31, Gurley had spent the afternoon trying to get to the bottom of the lynching rumors, traveling between Greenwood and the county court-house about a mile away. Greenwood's black deputy sheriff, Barney Cleaver, assured Gurley that Rowland was safe. So did William McCul-lough, the white county sheriff. Because Gurley was one of the richest men in Greenwood, Tulsa's white leaders viewed him as a spokesman for the entire race.[17] "If you keep your folks away from here, there won't be any trouble," McCullough advised him.[18]

But when Gurley related the promises of police to the men gathered in front of his hotel, they grew suspicious. Many had fought for free-dom in France, only to come home and face the old endless cycles of racist violence. They didn't trust the white man's word or its mes-senger.

"You are a damned liar," one man said to Gurley, squeezing his Winchester rifle.

"Fellow you ought to be put in jail now," Gurley snapped back. These men on Greenwood Avenue might have seen themselves as lib-erators, but to Gurley, they just seemed reckless.

The man leveled his rifle and pointed it squarely at the hotel owner. Gurley might have become the first casualty of the night, but another man quickly stepped in and defused the situation.[19]

Over at the Dreamland, Willie still needed to find his mother. When he stepped inside, the dark theater was packed as a film flashed across the silver screen. The mass of untroubled customers must have been a jarring sight, considering the tensions that were boiling over outside. But the theater's cocoon of calm didn't last. Suddenly a man clam-bered onto the Dreamland stage. "We're not gonna let 'em lynch him," he announced. "Close this place down. We're going to go to town and stop 'em." The crowd of hundreds began streaming out of the front entrance, while a group of men began grabbing guns that had been placed by a side door. Just in case.[20]

Willie soon found Loula. He told his mother he wanted to go with his father, John Williams, and the other men who were headed to the courthouse to protect Dick Rowland. "I wasn't afraid," he insisted

Willie Williams (top left) and Ed Goodwin (top middle)
with their high school classmates in early 1921

decades later. But Loula wouldn't hear of it. She and her only boy were going back to their apartment in the Williams Building, above her confectionery, where they would wait for all this violent business to calm down.[21]

At the new office of the *Tulsa Star,* across the street from the Dreamland, more men were meeting to discuss a real plan of action. There was "turbulent" talk of violence, according to O. W. Gurley, backed by the rhythmic clatter of rifle cartridges being loaded into empty chambers.[22]* A. J. Smitherman weighed the group's options carefully. He too had spoken to the sheriff, but he was less confident the boy would be protected than Gurley was.[23] The newspaper editor had a complicated relationship with violence. Smitherman had been an official justice of the peace, and he believed in the rule of law, so long as he saw it being administered fairly. But he also encouraged black people to uphold their own form of justice when the law refused to do so. "The proper time to afford protection to any prisoner is BEFORE and DURING the time he is being lynched," Smitherman had written after the murder of Claude Chandler in Oklahoma City.[24] Now the threat he'd been challenging across Oklahoma for years was at his neighborhood's doorstep.

---

* John Smitherman, brother of A. J. Smitherman and a Tulsa County deputy sheriff, later denied that blacks armed themselves at the *Star* office. See "Grand Jurors' Probe Takes a New Angle," *Tulsa Tribune,* June 13, 1921, 1.

As debates continued over what to do, J. B. Stradford strode into the *Star* office. He rushed there first thing after hearing the rumors of a lynching.[25] He'd been a mentor to Smitherman ever since the young journalist first arrived in Tulsa in 1913, but the stakes of his advice had never been higher.

Stradford was torn over the best strategy. He was fifty-nine years old, two generations removed from the young war veterans who viewed protecting their neighbors as part of their sacred duty as "race men." If an effort to rescue Rowland went awry, Stradford stood to lose as much as Gurley, perhaps more. His new $50,000 hotel was just two years old. "I hesitated at first, for the situation was a very perilous one," he later recalled. "I advised the boys to be sober and wait until the sheriff called for us."[26]

But while Stradford knew caution was wise, he also held a deep conviction that Greenwood had to look out for its own. Protecting a neighbor in peril was the ultimate expression of self-reliance in the community he'd been working to build for fifteen years. How could there be any other response to an outside world that had undermined their freedom at every step? When he found the words to speak, his frustration at a lifetime of injustice reverberated in the crowded office. "If I can't get anyone to go with me," he told the men, "I will go single-handed and empty my automatic into the mob and then resign myself to my fate."[27]

After it was all over, no one could ever say anything very definitive about who Dick Rowland really was. His teenage peers—people like Willie Williams and Robert Fairchild—claimed to know him best. Willie said they were classmates at Booker T. Washington.[28] Fairchild said he was handsome, a ladies' man.[29] Rowland likely worked a job shining shoes in downtown Tulsa, earning generous tips from oilmen and bankers who had more cash than they knew how to spend.[30] Somewhere along the way he earned the nickname "Diamond Dick," perhaps a reference to a taste for flashy clothes and jewelry.[31] Like many black people in Greenwood who were not in the entrepreneurial class, he floated outside recorded history, until he walked into an elevator in downtown Tulsa on May 30, 1921.

The incident occurred in the Drexel Building, a four-story office tower on Main Street, in the heart of white Tulsa's business district. In one common telling, Rowland needed to go to the bathroom, and the Drexel Building offered one of the few toilets open to black people downtown. The bathroom was accessible via a halting elevator operated by an attendant, a white teenager named Sarah Page. She, too, lived an unrecorded life that snapped into focus during this single chance encounter.[32]

Sometime after Dick Rowland boarded the elevator and the doors slid closed, Sarah Page screamed. No one can say exactly why. Rowland may have grabbed her arm or stepped on her foot after the elevator lurched unexpectedly.[33] It was probably an accident. But Page screamed all the same—a black man had touched her.

Hearing Page's scream, a white clerk from Renberg's, a department store in the building, came to the elevator to investigate. Dick Rowland was immediately guilty of disrupting the racial tranquility of white Tulsa; now there was a witness. He had committed a grave social transgression. It would be easy to drum up a criminal accusation to go alongside it.

And so as the Renberg's employee approached, Dick Rowland ran.[34]

He was arrested the next morning in Greenwood by a pair of police officers and taken to the city jail at the police station downtown.* There he maintained his innocence. Few in Tulsa knew the incident had even occurred. But sometime before three p.m. on Tuesday, May 31, the *Tulsa Tribune* published a front-page article about Rowland's arrest with a salacious headline: NAB NEGRO FOR ATTACKING GIRL IN ELEVATOR.[35]

While the *Tulsa World* laundered its racism through a veneer of civic propriety, the *Tribune* was the more sensational of the city's two white daily newspapers. Under the leadership of sanctimonious publisher Richard Lloyd Jones, the paper had become increasingly fixated on race intermixing as a serious outrage in Tulsa.[36] In the summer of 1920, a *Tribune* editor warned, "Here's a short creed for the negro who honestly wishes to do his part in preventing mob law and lynch-

* According to Police Chief John Gustafson, Rowland was arrested the day of the elevator incident and detained overnight. See John Gustafson, testimony, 7, *State of Oklahoma v. John A. Gustafson,* No. 1062 (Tulsa County District Court, 1921), Box 25, Record Group 1–2, Oklahoma State Archives, Oklahoma City.

ings: Keep away, far away, from white women and girls."[37] By 1921, the newspaper's prurience had become a moral panic that paved the way for government intervention. That April, an Oklahoma assistant attorney general visited Tulsa to investigate claims that white women were participating in dances in the "Negro quarter."[38] At a city commission inquiry on local police corruption, just two weeks before Rowland's arrest, citizens brought lurid details of bootlegging, prostitution, and "young white girls . . . dancing while negroes played the piano."[39]

The *Tribune* piece on Rowland tapped directly into this growing paranoia, conjuring a hedonistic nightmare of the mythical black brute. Rowland had been scoping out the hallway "as if to see if there was anyone in sight" before boarding the elevator. He had scratched Page's hands and face. He tore at her clothes. And the police had already removed him from the streets, implicitly corroborating the newspaper's exaggerated account. It was a guilty verdict rendered in newsprint, advancing a narrative that even the *Tribune*'s own managing editor would admit in the coming days was largely untrue.[40]

The explosive article was circulating in both black and white Tulsa by midafternoon. Shortly after three p.m., Tulsa police commissioner J. M. Adkison said he received an anonymous phone call.

"We are going to lynch that negro tonight."[41]

Tulsa police chief John Gustafson, who reported to Adkison, said he received a call with a similar warning around 3:30. Gustafson quickly ordered that Rowland be moved from the police station for his protection.[42] The teenager was taken to the jail at the county courthouse, a stone-faced, fortress-like brick building that occupied a quarter of a city block at the corner of Sixth Street and Boulder Avenue. Less than a mile southwest of Greenwood, the courthouse jail was supposed to be the most secure location for prisoners in the city; the jail itself was on the top floor of the massive structure.[43] But the previous summer a mob had snatched Roy Belton from that very place with ease. Locks and steel bars could not prevent a murder if law enforcement condoned it.

Around four p.m., as rumors of a planned lynching swirled, Adkison recommended moving Rowland out of town completely.[44] But when Rowland was transferred to the county jail, his fate fell into the hands of William McCullough, the county sheriff. The proud lawman was determined to prove that he could stand up to any mob. "I would rather die than give up a prisoner of mine," he told the officers in his department that day.[45]

By seven p.m., as the sun slid toward the horizon, white people had started gathering around the courthouse—a few, then dozens, and finally hundreds. Police Commissioner Adkison described them as a peaceful crowd who were there "purely out of curiosity."[46] But in a private memo to federal investigators days later, Tulsa County district judge Redmond S. Cole identified E. S. Maqueen and Claud "Yellow Hammer" Cranfield as likely leaders among more than a dozen "roughnecks and hoodlums" who came out that night to conduct a replay of the Roy Belton lynching.[47] Cranfield and his older brother William, in fact, had been identified in a state investigation as ringleaders of the Belton attack.[48] "It was known throughout town what they expected to do," the judge wrote.[49]

Shortly after eight p.m., three suspicious white men entered the courthouse, but McCullough turned them back. The men continued loitering outside, ginning up the ever-growing crowd.[50] City police were conspicuously absent; officials would later blame an end-of-the-month shift rescheduling for leaving a gap on the evening of May 31 when many officers were at home asleep.[51] But when Gustafson later faced an indictment for dereliction of duty, state prosecutors argued he failed to "disarm the various parties assembled in a riotous and tumultuous manner, and did not make a reasonable effort to do so."[52]

It was 8:30 by now, not quite dark yet. There was still time to ferry Rowland to safety outside of town. But McCullough seemed to view retreating as another form of surrender. Instead, he instructed eight of his deputies to stop the courthouse elevator on the top floor, barricade themselves in the jail, and guard the steel door to the narrow stairwell, which would be a mob's only point of entry.[53]

With Rowland seemingly secured, McCullough stepped outside to face the crowd directly. "Boys, there isn't going to be any lynching here tonight if that's what you're looking for," he said. "You just as well go on home. Get away from here and stop this excitement."[54]

He was met with boos and jeers from the crowd of men, women, and children. "You must be a nigger lover!" someone yelled.[55]

McCullough's patience wore thin. He threatened to kill the next man who tried to enter the courthouse. Still, the group refused to disperse.[56] They could not countenance leaving Dick Rowland's fate to the sheriff or the courts. Whether they'd come with rope in hand or not, everyone seemed to be waiting for something dramatic to happen.

And finally, something did.

Marching down Boulder Avenue came a group of about twenty-five armed black men bearing a precision that indicated military training.[57] Among their ranks were Greenwood men familiar with combat in one way or another: Obie Mann, a popular grocery store owner and World War I veteran; Jack Scott, a welterweight boxer; and John Williams, an avid hunter.[58] Despite his earlier pronouncement, J. B. Stradford ultimately did not join the group; he later said that A. J. Smitherman offered to go in his stead.[59] But many of the men were likely members of Greenwood's working class, just like Dick Rowland. Men whose names never graced the pages of the *Tulsa Star*.

This show of force shocked the white people of Tulsa. "We had no intimation whatever of the negroes taking any part in this matter until they arrived on the scene," Police Chief Gustafson said later. "Our only information in the beginning was that a white mob was to take the negro out and lynch him."[60]

Sheriff McCullough sensed that he was losing control of the situation. He dispatched Barney Cleaver, his black deputy sheriff, to attempt to turn back the Greenwood residents. Cleaver was widely respected among black folks—everyone knew his word was his bond.[61] But no one had yet been able to appease the Greenwood men.

"Boys, where are you going?" Cleaver asked as he approached the group.

"We came to see about the lynching," one man responded.

"This boy is upstairs and the cage is locked," Cleaver said. "There is no way anyone can get to him. Go back."[62]

Far outnumbered, the black men turned and headed back up Boulder Avenue toward Greenwood. But their arrival sent an electric current through the white crowd. Some men scrambled back home for their guns.[63] Others trekked nine blocks east to attempt to raid a National Guard armory that had a weapons stockpile. When a Guardsman approached, he saw a mob of as many as four hundred whites swarming the building; a few were trying to pull the bars off a side window. He held the mass of people back at gunpoint, but he did not have the authority to clear the streets unless his bosses sought approval from the governor. None of Tulsa's leading law enforcement officials seemed to recognize how quickly the night was unraveling.[64]

The armed black men, meanwhile, only became more incensed when they returned to Greenwood. A rumor reached them that the white mob was now storming the courthouse.[65] Within the hour, a larger group of armed Greenwood men—estimates range between seventy-five and two hundred—were once again at the courthouse steps.[66] Some of them came in touring cars, packed together on the sideboards. Others again marched across white Tulsa's streets with rifles slung across their shoulders, like soldiers in the Argonne forests.[67] They demanded the release of Dick Rowland. McCullough refused.[68] By this time, there were upward of one thousand white people around the courthouse, many of them also now armed and enraged by this black show of force.[69]

Accounts differ on what happened next. Someone—perhaps a police officer, perhaps just a white man who thought these black men needed to be put in their place—began trying to disarm the Greenwood soldiers. One black man refused to give up his weapon. A tussle ensued between the two men, one white and one black—they struggled over a gun but also over who had the right to live free in the city of Tulsa, in the state of Oklahoma, in the United States of America. And then like a thunderclap overhead, a gunshot rang out.[70]

Laurel Buck was east of the courthouse when he heard the *bang*, followed by several more. The twenty-six-year-old white bricklayer had watched the armed black men marching around the courthouse and, sensing trouble, had moved to safer territory a block away. After he heard the gunshots, he headed for the police station just four blocks north on Second Street. He wanted a weapon and the legal sanction to apprehend or kill black people as he saw fit.[71] When he arrived, the station was already swarming with people from every corner of white Tulsa, from teenage boys in white flannel shirts to businessmen in Palm Beach suits.[72] On the first floor of the building, Buck found an officer who was deputizing citizens and offered to help quell the disorder that was mushrooming outside. The officer gave Buck all the license he needed: "Get a gun and get busy, and try to get a nigger."[73]

Nearby, the sound of shattering glass cracked the night air as white rioters broke into a pair of hardware stores. They picked the shelves clean, stealing shotguns, flashlights, and pocketknives.[74] According to one of the store's owners, a police captain named George Blaine helped hand out the choicest weapons.[75] Once the men were armed, police instructed them to devise ad hoc patrol routes as they plotted against a suspected Negro insurrection (even as armed white men on the streets vastly outnumbered their black counterparts). Eventually one hundred such patrols roamed Tulsa, with as many as a half dozen men cramming into each open-top vehicle.[76] "In many cases, prominent business and professional men remained at the wheel and piloted the armed men about the city," the *Tulsa World* reported.[77]

Laurel Buck assigned himself a post guarding Third Street. He waited for the black invasion to arrive, for carloads of armed black men to come storming out of Greenwood. But as he looked around, all he saw were hundreds of armed white men whipping themselves up into an excited fury. "There were people shooting out of cars," he recalled later. "Shooting just to hear the gun go off."[78]

It was after ten p.m. Back around the courthouse, the scene was even more chaotic. Several people, both black and white, lay dead or wounded on the ground after a burst of gunfire that followed the first, accidental gunshot.[79] The group of armed black men had broken off in different directions, slipping into dark alleys and hoping to find their way back to Greenwood alive.[80] Some people took pleasure in the anarchy. Cars of young men of both races drove through the dark streets, firing indiscriminately at buildings and forcing people to cower behind whatever protection they could find.[81] At the corner of Cincinnati and Second Street, closer to Greenwood, a firefight between black and white combatants left at least one white bystander dead.[82]

But black casualties quickly outnumbered white ones. Black people caught downtown were dragged behind cars with ropes and shot as they darted out of alleys.[83] When one black man ran out onto Third Street, he was shot in the face and chest by a drive-by assailant in a Cadillac. A crowd gathered to watch him bleed out in the street. Soon an ambulance arrived. But when the paramedics tried to reach the victim to take him to a hospital, the crowd closed ranks. "Don't touch him," one man reportedly said, "because he is a nigger and was up here hunting trouble." As the paramedics retreated, the mob brandished knives and closed in on the wounded black man to finish what the drive-by had started.[84]

The police made little attempt to put the savagery to an end. Eyewitnesses said that about a dozen officers spent much of the night on downtown rooftops rather than directly in the line of fire. At least one officer assigned to patrol downtown, William Maudlin, went home to change into plainclothes with the intention of later invading Greenwood.[85] Police Chief Gustafson could have asked the governor to activate all of the state's National Guard units, which would have allowed hundreds of troops from Oklahoma City to come help restore order. But at 10:30 p.m., Gustafson told Governor Robertson that Tulsa had the situation under control.[86] Meanwhile, Sheriff McCullough remained inside his courthouse fortress, concerned only with proving he was man enough to protect Rowland. "We believe we have the situation well in hand without further help," he told a newspaper reporter from the jail, even after multiple people had been killed and downtown stores had been looted.[87]

All the while, the crowds on the streets kept getting bigger as word swept through all of white Tulsa: "Get your guns! Get your guns! The niggers are coming!"[88]

After midnight, the black people who survived were driven back toward Greenwood, and they hunkered down for a pitched battle to protect their business district. The Frisco Depot and nearby railway yard, near the intersection of Boston Avenue and Archer Street, became a choke point for fending off entry into the neighborhood.[89] Armed blacks scaled the buildings they had long called home for a higher-ground advantage, while whites crawled on their bellies toward the railroad tracks and used the boxcars scattered nearby as cover.[90]

The battle unfolded about four blocks west of the Greenwood Avenue–Archer Street intersection, where Mary Jones Parrish stayed awake for hours, listening as the gunshots crept closer and closer to her home. She sent Florence to bed for a time, but as the danger approached—she could see a pinprick of fire devouring the nearby Midway Hotel from her window—Parrish realized they needed to be ready to flee at any moment. She took Florence in her arms and read

Mary Jones Parrish

chapters from the Psalms of David: *O Lord, how many are my foes! Many are rising against me.*[91]

Just a block north of Parrish, J. B. Stradford returned to his hotel after the meeting at the *Tulsa Star* to find the entire building shrouded in darkness. His wife Augusta had turned all the lights out, hoping any mob would float past a seemingly empty building. She and the hotel's guests, who had only hours earlier been lounging in black luxury, now sat anxiously in a tense late-night gloom. But Stradford couldn't spend the night cowering in darkness. He flipped on the lights and began rummaging for weapons, handing a Winchester shotgun to one companion and a .45-caliber Colt pistol to another. He stomped up the stairs to the second floor, where he would guard the building and the people inside it with his life, if need be.[92]

Farther North, at Mt. Zion Baptist Church, Mabel Little was still at her women's night services when her husband Pressley burst into the sanctuary sweating and harried, a look of terror on his face that she'd never seen before. They needed to get home immediately, he told her, then ushered her into their Model T. As Pressley explained to Mabel about the effort to protect Dick Rowland and how it had all gone so wrong, she saw people running helter-skelter through the streets. "Everybody was nearly scared to death, some near hysteria, because all around us there was shooting, and people couldn't find out why," she wrote later.[93]

Ed and Anna Goodwin made it back to the family's home at 401 East Haskell Street. J.H. and Carlie ushered their children into the place that would have to become their fortress for the night. The couple had been in the process of building a spacious new brick home near the one-and-a-half-story frame house they'd moved into when they arrived in Greenwood seven years before.[94] But now they couldn't be sure either structure would be standing by morning. Not knowing how else to protect himself, Ed climbed into a bathtub. *If they shoot through the house,* he thought, *they probably won't hit me in the tub.*[95]

All around Greenwood, people who had gone to bed on a warm spring evening were roused in the middle of the night by the sounds of gunfire and the confused cries of neighbors. But there would soon be something else in the air as well: the acrid smell of thick, suffocating smoke.

Law enforcement officials had a decision to make. Tulsa had spiraled out of control because police failed to confront the armed shooters downtown and initially refused to call for backup. No help would be arriving from out of town anytime soon. (McCullough and Gustafson finally requested that the governor send in more National Guard troops at 1:46 a.m., roughly four hours after the courthouse shootout.)[96] Even as the pitched battle across the Frisco Depot finally calmed down, white people began to set fire to black-occupied buildings at the intersection of Archer Street and Boston Avenue, likely to smoke out the black shooters.[97] City firemen who tried to stop the burning were run off by armed assailants, forced to abandon their water hoses in the streets.[98] Given limited manpower, the police and National Guard might be able to neutralize the white people who were terrorizing Greenwood, or they could stamp out the supposed black insurrection that some were still convinced was coming. But they could not do both.

For law enforcement, the choice was easy.

"All our men were kept busy going from one place to the other to prevent the negroes from getting back into the business and residence district of the white people," John A. Gustafson testified later in court. "We armed during the night probably two hundred fifty citizens who assisted the police department in trying to quell the mob." He continued: "There were many [more] men than that were armed; most of them irresponsible whites who picked up what arms they had and jumped into the scrap."[99]

Gustafson elided the police's role in empowering these "irresponsible whites," but Police Commissioner Adkison was more direct. He placed the number of deputized men higher, at about four hundred, and noted that many were handed old police stars to serve as talismans of their assumed authority. He admitted he did not even know the names of all the newly deputized officers. "I usually talked to the men and those I thought would remain cool-headed I commissioned. But some of those might have lost their heads—they might have applied the torch."[100]

Even the local members of the National Guard, who tried to project cool neutrality in their detailed reports on the night's events, clearly prioritized quelling what Guardsmen referred to as a "Negro Uprising."[101] The Guard instructed some of the auto patrols to gather maids and butlers from the servants' quarters in South Tulsa. "I thought some of the bad negroes may set fires to homes of white people," Major C. W. Daley, a National Guard member and Tulsa assistant police chief, wrote later.[102]

Around 2:30 a.m., not long after the first fires were being set in Greenwood, rumors indicated that a trainload of armed blacks were on the way from the nearby city of Muskogee.[103] A black witness would later say that J. B. Stradford bragged about calling in the cavalry from the nearby town, though Stradford, in his own recollections, denied ever asking for their help.[104] The National Guard gathered up about a hundred white patrolmen and sent them to intercept the possible black detachment at the railway station. Deputized men lined both sides of the track, guns cocked at the ready. Finally, the train rolled into Tulsa.

It was just a normal freight train on the Midland Valley line. There were no black gunmen on it.[105]

Meanwhile, around 1:00 a.m., a machine gun that had been mysteriously "dug up" by the Tulsa Police Department was mounted on a truck and paraded through town to intimidate armed blacks.[106] National Guardsmen placed the weapon on top of Sunset Hill, which abutted the wealthiest homes in the community and provided an ideal vantage point from which to shoot down on Greenwood. (A National Guardsman would later claim the gun barely functioned and fired only twenty rounds that night.)[107]

As the police and National Guard assumed a military posture against the so-called Negro uprising, more and more everyday white people were crowding the downtown streets, attracted by the violence and mayhem of the moment. They were desperate for a way to take part. Many wore the khaki uniforms they'd donned during World War I. Others had likely been members of the Home Guard, which served as the enforcement arm of the wartime Tulsa Council of De-

National Guard members man a machine gun on a Tulsa street

fense. Tulsa's white leaders were more than accustomed to punishing their local enemies through intimidation and violence.[108] On the night of May 31, though, vigilantism mixed with formal military training as it never had before.

William "Choc" Phillips, a white Tulsa teenager who spent the entire night roaming the city, watched the mood darken as the evening wore on. "Instead of the crowds on the streets diminishing as the hours passed, they grew larger," he wrote in a memoir titled *Murder in the Streets*. "A great many of these persons lining the sidewalks were holding a rifle or shotgun in one hand and grasping the neck of a liquor bottle with the other."[109]

Overnight, according to Phillips, at least six hundred whites gathered east of Greenwood at the intersection of Second Street and Lewis Avenue. Ammunition was distributed to any who requested it. A man stood up in an open car and began barking out instructions. "Meetings like this are taking place all over town and across the river in West Tulsa," the man said. "Be ready to go at daybreak."[110]

As dawn approached on June 1, the shooting upon Greenwood near the Frisco Depot finally ceased.[111] Some residents were even able to fall back into a fitful sleep as the sounds of war faded.[112] South of the tracks, though, a snarl of more than sixty haphazardly parked cars was growing larger as more and more white men streamed toward the railroad depot.[113] They clutched rifles, pistols, cans of kerosene, and matches.[114] The air was thick with tobacco smoke, and in the haze the only light anyone could make out came from the ends of their thick cigars.[115] They were not somber. Many of them were not even especially angry. The night was drunk and festive. They were going to enjoy this.

The National Guard dispatched about twenty volunteer riflemen to protect Greenwood from the group amassing at the Frisco railroad tracks, which may have numbered more than a thousand. But when Guardsman Charles Daley returned at the scene around 5:30 a.m., he found that his small contingent of Guards had been "submerged" by the "out of control" mob.[116] The commanding officer of the Tulsa National Guard later estimated that the crowds across the city had grown so large and unruly, it would have taken as many as one thousand men to bring Tulsa back to order.[117]

"The leaders of the mob were egging them to start burning and shooting and they were just about ready to cut loose," Daley reported. He tried to talk the mob down. They didn't listen. He called for police backup. No one came. He drew his weapon to threaten them, but the police department and the National Guard itself had already granted the mob all the weapons and authority it needed to rule Tulsa as it saw fit. It was their city to destroy now. "The crowd kept getting larger and larger," Daley said, "until finally the mob burst past me and ran for the business blocks cross the tracks."[118]

CHAPTER 7

THE MASSACRE

Large plumes of smoke subsume Greenwood

Willie Williams awoke to the sound of gunfire. It was just past dawn as he walked to a western-facing window in his family's Greenwood Avenue apartment and peered outside. The white men who had breached the Frisco Depot were inching eastward along the railroad tracks. Armed with rifles, they trained their guns toward Deep Greenwood as the night gave way to a dull morning gloom.

Willie's father John perched himself in the family's corner bathroom, aiming his .30 Savage rifle out of a window facing southwest. John knew the trouble that was coming; he was among the men who had gone to the courthouse to guard Dick Rowland and witnessed the chaos that erupted downtown. Poking the barrel of the gun out the window, he sniped at would-be assailants whenever they stepped out into clear view and gave him a clean shot. If anyone managed to enter the Williams Building, he also had a repeating shotgun at his side that would dispatch them in close quarters. John had the upper hand for a time—the invading gunmen couldn't tell where his shots were coming from. But eventually they recognized that the gunfire was erupting from the second floor of the Williams Building and opened a fusillade onto the family's home. The bathroom window shattered as a hail of gunshots blasted the structure.

"We're gonna have to get out of here," John said.[1]

John, Loula, and Willie dashed out of the apartment, clattering down the stairs as more windowpanes exploded around them. When they stepped outside, they saw their neighbors fleeing in all directions. Some bolted east down Archer Street, away from the railroad depot where the whites had amassed; others ran north up Greenwood Avenue. Women carried babies in their arms; a few nestled little ones in their wombs.[2]

Crouching low, the Williams family crept up Greenwood, past A. F. Bryant's drugstore, C. L. Netherland's barbershop, and the old Gurley Building. They found safety in an old funeral parlor halfway up the block, where about ten other men had already gathered. As the group caught their breath, Loula decided she was going to go check on her mother, who lived on Detroit Avenue at the western edge of the neighborhood. Always a self-possessed woman, she journeyed there without her husband's protection. This was still her neighborhood, and she would not be intimidated.[3]

Across the street from the Williams family, Mary Jones Parrish was trying to cocoon her daughter Florence in the cushion of a duofold sofa, hoping that the furniture would shield her from a stray bullet. She likened the mob to a group of bloodthirsty wolves salivating over a carcass—staying where she was as the hungry invaders approached would be suicide. Looking out a south-facing window of the Woods Building, she could see white men firing their rifles from atop the Middle State Mill on First Street, across the railroad tracks. They had even hauled a machine gun up there. When she heard a lull in the gunfire, she took Florence's small hand and guided her out of their apartment.[4]

Mother and daughter ran northward toward Standpipe Hill, another knoll topped by a large water tower that marked the western boundary of Greenwood.[5] Parrish hoped a friend who lived in the area would take them in. But as soon as they approached the intersection of Easton Street and Detroit Avenue, she stopped. Many of the Craftsman-style homes that lined the street were already on fire, with families' personal effects strewn across their yards.[6] Towering above the homes on the hill was another machine gun manned by several white soldiers.[7]

Greenwood was surrounded.

Evading the gaze of the weapon, Parrish and her daughter ran farther north. They eventually hitched a ride on the truck of another family escaping town.[8] As their home faded into the distance, fires belched out black smoke, and turbid clouds drifted out in every direction. Parrish held her daughter close. She had read about the racial violence in Chicago and Washington, D.C., in 1919, but never thought something similar—no, something worse—could happen in Tulsa.[9] As the truck trundled eastward and the acrid taste of smoke began to leave her tongue, Parrish cast her eyes on a new horror. White men with rifles were climbing into planes at the airfield just outside town. Their sights were set on Greenwood.[10]

The fires were set systematically, like this: A team of white men, some of them deputized by police, entered a chosen home, blowing the lock off the door if necessary. They then smashed the valuables inside,

Houses burn in Greenwood on the morning of June 1, 1921

wrenching open dresser drawers and tearing down window drapes. After gathering the bedding, wooden furniture, and other flammable items into the center of a room, the men doused the objects in kerosene. Then they lit a match. Each blaze conjured in the twilight carried its own awful story.[11]

George Monroe was a five-year-old boy living in a house on the same block as Mt. Zion Baptist Church. His father owned a nearby skating rink. That morning Monroe watched four white men wielding torches burst into his family's home, march directly to the windows, and set the curtains aflame. Monroe and his three siblings hid underneath a bed as the men strode past them, watching in terrified silence as their feet scraped across the floor. When one of the men stepped on Monroe's finger, his older sister clasped a hand over his mouth to prevent him from screaming. "Everything was burning around us," Monroe recalled.[12]

J. C. Latimer, a Greenwood architect, was at a friend's house on Detroit Avenue, where he'd decided to spend the night after learning about the trouble at the courthouse. As dawn crested across the neighborhood, he saw through a back window that several nearby houses were already on fire. It was shocking how quickly a wooden structure could succumb to the flames. Outside the front door, Latimer heard a call. "Come out!" a white man clutching a rifle yelled. "We are not going to hurt you."

Latimer didn't move. He would not let himself be arrested simply for living in Greenwood. But then the mob began shooting into the building, breaking windows and blasting holes through doors with their gunfire. "After seeing most of the property that was near me burned, I surrendered," Latimer said later. He was marched outside at gunpoint, hands up. As he stood amid the burning homes, one of the white men reared back and punched him square in the jaw. Then he was shoved into a line of other black detainees, loaded onto a truck, and hauled away from his home. His hands remained in the air the entire time.[13]

Back on Greenwood Avenue, J. B. Stradford had no intention of succumbing to the unruly mob. He and the men he had armed effectively guarded the hotel throughout the night and were digging in to continue their defense—if this was their last stand, so be it. But their armed protection faltered when, according to Stradford's memoirs, an airplane swooped low, looking like a great mechanical bird, and shot through the hotel windows.[14]

This was likely one of the Curtiss Jenny biplanes that Parrish had seen north of town as they took off from an airfield owned by the Curtiss-Southwest Airplane Company.[15] Police would later claim the planes were used for reconnaissance to spot refugees and ongoing fires,[16] but eyewitnesses said they were used to shoot at fleeing residents from the air and drop explosives on Greenwood.[17] Though aerial bombing was a new wartime strategy, there was evidence it was feasible in Tulsa. A few weeks before the massacre, a local pilot had successfully transported highly explosive nitroglycerine via airplane.[18] The previous year, amid the nationwide anti-Communist panic during the Red Scare, the mayor had sworn in three pilots as "heavily armed" special officers to scour the city for "radicals and for evidence of sabotage."[19] Though conclusive evidence of bombing would never emerge, these factors made a well-coordinated aerial attack on Greenwood—perhaps adapted from a plan to stop an imagined Bolshevist invasion—entirely plausible. What was true without doubt was that planes terrorized Greenwood residents on the morning of June 1, adding to the nightmarish scenario.

After the planes attacked the Stradford Hotel, the guests lost their nerve and streamed out of the building and into the hands of waiting soldiers. Stradford eventually agreed to go himself, but only on the condition that his sturdy hotel be used as a place of refuge for Greenwood residents. As he was being shuttled out of Greenwood by the soldiers, though, he saw his rooming houses on Easton Street in flames and knew he had made a mistake. The Stradford Hotel would soon follow, reduced to charred rubble within hours.[20]

By daylight, multiple members of the Tulsa Police Department had fully abdicated their duty and become members of the mob. Irish Bullard, a motorcycle officer, was seen shooting into stores on Lansing Avenue, a second black business enclave north of Deep Greenwood. Officer William Maudlin led white looters into black people's homes. I. S. Pittman, a traffic officer, reportedly drove black deputy sheriff V. B. Bostic from his own home, forcing Bostic's children outside in their nightclothes before burning the house to the ground.[21] (In a

1978 interview, Pittman said he "patrolled the streets" on the night of May 31 and that no police officers engaged in violence, but he did admit to being a longtime member of the Ku Klux Klan.)[22]

By Detroit Avenue, a white former police commissioner named John Oliphant spent all morning calling for officer protection. Detroit, which was all-white on one side of the avenue and all-black on the other, was the one place where white people risked being subsumed by the mob too. Oliphant saw some members of the mob dressed in khaki military fatigues, like World War I soldiers. Others appeared to be police officers. "They had stars, they had badges on," he recalled later. "They went in and when they came out the houses were burning."[23]

Eventually the mob came upon 523 North Detroit Avenue, the home of Dr. A. C. Jackson, the prominent Greenwood physician.[24] Jackson was a respected figure throughout Tulsa, delivering babies in his neighbors' homes and caring for the elderly when they grew sick. He had an eight a.m. appointment with a patient that morning.[25] But after years dedicating himself to the cause of preserving life, he was now witnessing the wanton destruction of it.

The doctor appeared in the doorway. He stepped out into his front yard with his hands in the air, doing his best to comply with the mob's vicious demands. Oliphant, the white neighbor, watched from a distance. "That is Dr. Jackson," he said. "Don't hurt him."[26]

A teenager wearing a white shirt and cap fired two rounds of buckshot into Jackson. He fell on the second shot. Then his house, like all the rest on the black side of the street, was burned to the ground. He died later that day.[27]

A. C. Jackson became the most famous casualty of the day's violence, but thousands of Greenwood residents were forced to flee, fight, or face death in the chaotic twelve to fifteen hours after the courthouse encounter over Dick Rowland. People hid in outhouses and underneath porches, hoping not to be burned alive.[28] Others fled into the woods north of town, where the smoke from the neighborhood's destruction sifted through the trees.[29] Some mounted impassioned last stands; when about ten blacks holed themselves up in a concrete building, firing upon both white mobsters and National Guard troops who approached, a long bloody shoot-out left both black and white gunmen dead.[30] Those who did not run were captured or killed, eventually.

All the while, the burning never stopped. Entire houses were devoured by flames, leaving only warped bedframes as discernible landmarks. The angry black smoke clouds gave way to a toxic haze that settled just above the ground.[31] Everything, everywhere, was hot. As survivor Alice Andrews later put it, "It looked like the world was on fire."[32]

As midday of June 1 approached, Willie Williams thought he had escaped the worst of the mob. After Loula left to see after her mother, Willie and his father took refuge on the top floor of a nearby pool hall, where another man was picking off white assailants. Willie served as an assistant gunner, handing the man new rifle cartridges or shotgun shells whenever he ran out of ammo. When the pool hall, too, seemed destined for the torch, Willie and his father decided to split up. John followed a set of railroad tracks toward Pine Street, the northern border of the Greenwood district, while Willie ducked into an alley behind the Dreamland Theatre. Before he could decide where to head next, he ran straight into three armed white men.[33]

"Where's your gun, nigger?" one of the men asked when they spotted him.

Willie had just tossed the last of his shotgun shells before being caught by the men. He told them he was unarmed.

One of the men patted the boy down, then looked him over. "Hold your hands up."[34]

The white men marched Willie to a larger group of about fifty detained blacks back on Greenwood Avenue.[35] The community was in full retreat, and the invasion by white Tulsa had transformed into a wholesale pillaging. White mobsters stuffed silk handkerchiefs down their shirts and sprayed bottles of perfume across their necks.[36] Larger valuables were carted onto trucks that they wheeled into the neighborhood.[37] They cracked open safes stuffed with life savings and plucked family heirlooms nestled in jewelry boxes; they stole cars from driveways and pianos from living rooms; they pilfered Bibles under the eyes of God.[38] Men, women, and children all took part.

"Some were running Victrolas, some dancing a jig and just having a rollicking easy good time," observed John Oliphant, the former police commissioner.[39] As Willie was marched right past his own family's home by his captors, he saw a white man coming out of the building carrying his mother's handbag. Dangling from the bag, he saw the strap of a familiar piece of clothing; it was Loula Williams's favorite leopard-print coat.[40]

Willie and his neighbors were paraded through the streets of downtown Tulsa to an internment camp that city officials had quickly set up at Convention Hall.[41] While the white press referred to the black captives as refugees,[42] Willie felt more like a prisoner.[43] Greenwood residents were marched into confinement at gunpoint while white Tulsans in summer dresses and blazers thronged the streets and laughed from the sidewalks.[44] The trip was humiliating. Law enforcement officials—or their deputized mobsters—patted down black men's pants and rifled through women's purses for weapons.[45] Every black person was considered a threat, from an old woman clinging to her Bible to a little girl clutching her favorite wax doll.[46] Every white man, meanwhile, became an infallible arbiter of the law. "Many of the most active in dragging these inoffensive people from their homes were real leaders in the frenzied mob," Oklahoma National Guard adjutant general Charles Barrett said later.[47]

Blacks who resisted arrest risked immediate execution. Not far from the Convention Hall entrance, an unconscious black man, likely dead, lay sprawled on a flatbed truck owned by a local oil company, perhaps as some kind of warning to all who approached.[48] Willie watched as another black man under mob custody was struck with the barrel of a rifle. When the man began fighting back, he was shot at point-blank range. *Are they going to let us live,* Willie thought to himself, *or shoot us all?*[49]

Inside the Convention Hall, more than two thousand displaced black Tulsans stood under armed guard.[50] Even more people were being detained at the local fairground, located east of Greenwood, and at McNulty Ballpark, located south.[51] All were dour scenes. Some people sobbed openly; others wandered to nowhere in a listless, stunned daze.[52] Many fainted due to a mix of intense stress and heat exhaustion.[53] At least one girl was sent to the hospital after suffering an epileptic seizure.[54] Some women were provided cots to sleep on, but men and children slept on floors, benches, and at the fairground, in stables meant for animals.[55]

Watching a man get shot shook Willie to his core. The night before, he had put on a brave face when the men were boasting about going to the courthouse, but he could no longer deny the fear bubbling up inside him.[56] He had no idea whether anyone he cared about was still alive: his friends, his teachers, his parents. He didn't know when he'd get to go home, since captives were not allowed to leave the Convention Hall unless a white Tulsan, often their employer, came and vouched for their character.[57] And if he did get out, Willie had no idea what kind of home he'd have to return to.

Convention Hall was used as an internment camp to hold Greenwood residents captive

So he felt an overwhelming sense of relief when he looked across the Convention Hall and saw some familiar faces. Several of his teammates from the Booker T. Washington High School football team had somehow found each other, along with their head coach, Seymour Williams. Willie bounded over to his coach and teammates excitedly. For a little while at least, the boys got to talk about something besides their current predicament: depth charts, cross-routes, and their rivalry with Muskogee. If they thought only about football, the future still looked promising. "This'll be over," one of Willie's teammates assured him. "What a good team we're gonna have."[58]

Later that day, the Dreamland Theatre's white projectionist came to the Convention Hall to free Willie. The teenager spent the night at the man's house in West Tulsa, still unsure of where his parents were.[59] The entire city, meanwhile, had been placed under martial law for the first time in its history after National Guard reinforcements finally arrived from Oklahoma City. The *Tulsa World* reported that the city was "quiet as a tomb" as armed soldiers occupied every corner.[60] Tulsa was placed under a seven p.m. curfew, but the restrictions placed on blacks by city leaders were more onerous.[61] Every Greenwood resident had to obtain a police-issued identification card that listed their name, address, and occupation, along with an employer's signature. Blacks found without a card, or with one that had expired (unemployed blacks had to renew their cards every day), were subject to arrest.[62] These cards governed black Tulsans' freedom for at least a month.[63]

On the morning of June 2, Willie returned downtown to look for his family. He slipped into a diner and agreed to wash a tub full of dishes in exchange for lunch. When he stepped outside later, he stumbled upon her almost by accident. She was standing at the corner of Third and Main Street. Loula.

"Mama!" Willie screamed.[64]

He sprinted down the street to embrace his mother. They hugged and kissed as if they'd been separated for years. It was the first step in a long and brutal road to rebuilding their lives.

Willie quickly learned that his always purposeful mother had been downtown for a reason. As he recalled later, "She was on the way to the lawyer's office."[65]

———

The Jackson-Goodwin funeral parlor on Archer Street was burned and pillaged along with most everything else in Greenwood. A known white huckster named Collins loaded much of the parlor's equipment onto his wagon full of pilfered goods.[66] An employee trying to save the brand-new ambulance was shot in the hand by white sharpshooters perched atop the flour mill across the railroad tracks.[67] The greatest loss, though, was the bodies. Samuel Malone Jackson had four of the deceased in his parlor on the day of May 31, three of which burned up in the fire.[68] But his workload, he soon realized, was about to increase exponentially.

Samuel had grown up wanting to be a doctor in rural Mississippi, where his father made a living selling herbs and earning the reputation of a great healer. But in a family of fifteen children, money was short, and Samuel found that undertaking was the next best thing to medical school.[69] He learned the craft at Cincinnati's School of Embalming, then moved to Tulsa to launch his own funeral home; J. H. Goodwin joined as a business partner around 1918.[70] Business was good, if morbid. The truly tragic cases, burying children and infants, came in small doses. Though Samuel was accustomed to death, nothing had prepared him for what was unfolding in Greenwood now.

Samuel Malone Jackson

Unsure what he could do to help, he decided to do the thing he understood best: care for the departed. The city quickly contracted Stanley & McCune, a white undertaking business with a parlor downtown, to start removing bodies from the streets;[71] June 1 was a hot day, and bodies would soon begin bloating in the pounding heat. Stanley & McCune enlisted Jackson to help, and so Samuel climbed into a truck with several white men and began collecting corpses.[72] Many of them were gathered around the Frisco Depot, where the brunt of the shooting had taken place the night before. One man with a thick mustache lay by the train tracks stiff-backed in a loose-fitting jacket, with his left hand gingerly draped across his stomach. Another man lay in the street with a newspaper covering his face. An older gentleman, gray hair carefully cropped, lay in a suit by a telegraph pole, his hat just askew from his head.[73] Before Samuel could get to them, several men's corpses were captured in photographs and turned into postcards, which some white Tulsans would quietly keep in their possession for decades.[74] In a few of the images, white men leered over the dead bodies.

By the time Samuel and his crew finished roaming the streets of downtown Tulsa and Greenwood, roughly twenty bodies—all black—were stacked in the truck. At some point they stopped at the McNulty

Baseball Park, which had been turned into another internment camp. The frantic cries of babies who didn't understand what was happening were mixed with the plaintive moans of aged women who understood it all too well. Inside the park, a woman had fainted, and the white authorities demanded the assistance of a "nigger doctor." Samuel was as close as they were going to get.

"Take care of this nigger wench, and get her back on her feet," a white man instructed.

Samuel collected some water and towels, and with the same care he used when tending to the deceased, he was able to revive the woman.[75]

They soon returned to the Stanley & McCune Funeral Home on Boulder Avenue, just steps away from the county courthouse.[76] All the black bodies were unloaded, and Samuel set to doing what he did best. Most of the people set before him, he didn't recognize—he couldn't know everyone in a community of more than ten thousand—but at least one person must have given him pause when he was placed onto the embalming table.

Men in a flatbed truck pick up dead bodies following the burning of Greenwood

It was Dr. A. C. Jackson. An old acquaintance. The physician who had been living out Samuel's dream of saving the living rather than salvaging the remains of the dead.

Samuel took extra care on him.

He was paid per body and housed in the servants' quarters, where the maid lived. At least eighteen people—all black—came under Samuel's delicate hand. Two people, including Dr. Jackson, were claimed by family members, embalmed, and transported out of town. The other sixteen, Tulsa County decided, needed to be buried as fast as possible. Some were burned beyond recognition but others possibly could have been identified by a loved one. Instead they were each placed in plain wooden coffins and buried in Oaklawn Cemetery, just east of downtown. Only two of their graves were marked. "So many of them were not embalmed," Samuel recalled decades later. "I don't know who they were."[77]

Samuel, like many in Tulsa, believed there could be scores or perhaps even hundreds of bodies that were never given even a rudimentary burial. Eyewitnesses both black and white recalled seeing black bodies stacked on trucks and train cars—"like cordwood," in one witness's words—but no one knew for sure where the bodies were taken.[78] Dumped in the Arkansas River, perhaps, or hastily tossed into a mass grave on the outskirts of town.[79] Early on, even members of the National Guard themselves said this was likely; Maj. Charles Daley estimated that as many as 175 people, mostly black, were killed.[80] But as national scrutiny swiveled to the horrors of Tulsa and the legal ramifications of the attack started to become clear, officials quickly dialed down their estimates. Within days the National Guard tallied just thirty-five dead, twenty-six black and nine white.[81]

Samuel had touched nearly that many black souls himself. After witnessing the scorched-earth razing of Greenwood personally, and seeing bodies too burned for even him to preserve, he seemed to suspect the figure could be much higher, even if the identities of many victims were destined to be lost forever.

The destruction of Greenwood was too wide and deep to truly calculate. It spread far across the nation with the mass of refugees who would never set foot in Tulsa again, the men, women, and children who trooped north until they hit Kansas City, who wound their way to Chicago, who slept in a park in Bartlesville under a sprawling night sky.[82] So many of them walked away from Greenwood in the chaotic aftermath, they looked to one survivor like a line of ants marching on the train tracks.[83] Dick Rowland himself was among the Tulsa refugees. He was spirited away from the city by Sheriff McCullough on the morning of June 1 and slipped back out of the historical record; the assault charge against him was formally dropped in September.[84]

The event burrowed deep into the psyches of each individual who would bear the burden of an unspeakable trauma for the rest of their lives. They would refuse to sleep in beds, jolt at the sound of fireworks, never fly on airplanes.[85] There was no way to quantify what had happened to them, despite the death tolls and dollar figures in damages that dominated newspaper headlines across the state for weeks. But for what can be quantified, the calculations, approximate as they are, go something like this.

Greenwood lost 1,256 houses to burning and another 215 to looting.[86] It lost the entirety of the business district, which had been anchored by top-end establishments like the Stradford Hotel and the Dreamland Theatre but buttressed by the financial and spiritual aspirations of dozens of ambitious black entrepreneurs.[87] According to one estimate, more than 150 businesses were burned to ash in the attack.[88]

Greenwood lost much of the social and civic infrastructure that had given the community strength. There could not have been a worse moment for the neighborhood's only black hospital to go up in flames; the Red Cross was forced to convert Booker T. Washington High School, one of the only large buildings left standing, into the equivalent of a wartime field hospital. "There were men wounded in every conceivable way, like soldiers after a big battle. Some with amputated limbs, burned faces, others minus an eye or with heads bandaged," Mary Jones Parrish reported after visiting the transformed facility. "There were women who were nervous wrecks, and some confinement cases. Was I in a hospital in France? No, in Tulsa."[89]

So many churches were lost too—ten burned in all.[90] To see the newly opened Mt. Zion destroyed was particularly devastating. "There were other nice church buildings, but Mt. Zion was our temple, and they knew it," Mabel Little reflected decades later. "That's why they came to destroy it."[91]

Greenwood lost the ability to be self-sufficient. The cash residents had hidden under mattresses, inside shoeboxes, beneath loose floorboards was all burned up or stolen. The loans they had taken out to

The people of Greenwood

Greenwood Avenue smolders

pursue their dreams were suddenly huge liabilities. They had been chasing the American myth of by-your-own-bootstraps success, and they had hoped their country would reward them for playing by the rules. Instead, at least 8,624 of them were suddenly in need of humanitarian relief, whether it was food, clothing, or shelter.[92] When Mary Jones Parrish and her daughter were forced to get in a line for clothes at a Red Cross station, she felt a mix of frustration and shame—"wormwood and gall," she called it. "But what could I do?"[93]

Greenwood lost an unknown number of fathers, mothers, brothers, sisters, and neighbors. While the Oklahoma Department of Health settled on a confirmed death count of thirty-six, historians generally agree that the number is higher, with evidence for estimates up to three hundred.[94] A precise fatality count will never be determined, but one devastating number will always stand out. Greenwood lost eight babies who were born prematurely, forced into the world and taken out of it before they knew what it meant to be loved.[95] Many who died on May 31 and June 1, 1921, would see their names lost to time as their individual hopes, dreams, frustrations, schemes, passions, and rivalries, became subsumed by the legacy of the Tulsa Race Massacre, just as their homes had been devoured by the flames of the event itself. But those eight little ones never had the dignity of being named at all.

Greenwood lost its past. Greenwood lost its future.

A CONSPIRACY IN PLAIN SIGHT

Armed white men, including a National Guardsman, watch Greenwood burn.

When the families who had built Greenwood Avenue made their way back to the neighborhood in the days after the massacre, it looked like a bombed-out war zone. Jagged remnants of brick walls jutted out from piles of rubble, half-sketched silhouettes of what had once been thriving businesses.[1] The Dream-land Theatre's electric marquee dangled by a pair of metal fasteners over the building's charred entryway, swinging in the wind above downed electrical wires.[2] The grocery and meat market housed in the Goodwin Building was reduced to ruins.[3] So was the once-lively office of the *Tulsa Star*, now a jumble of exposed pipes and ink rollers strewn across the ground.[4] When Mary Jones Parrish came upon the shell of the Woods Building, where she had been teaching typewriting at the start of the week, she expected to weep. But the tears did not come. Instead she bowed her head and walked noiselessly through the debris-covered streets.[5]

All across Greenwood, acres of land had been burned bare, the trees stripped of their foliage. Canvas tents were propped up amid the rubble of destroyed houses.[6] Everyone wore badges that said POLICE PROTECTION or carried cards signed by white employers.[7] Over at the fairground, which had become the primary internment camp, captives who could find no white signatory were put to work, picking up debris or digging latrines for twenty-five cents per hour.[8] Though summer was still ahead, people were already starting to worry about the coming winter, when the newly homeless population would be ravaged not by fire but by ice.[9]

The plight of Greenwood had already captured the attention of the nation. The June 2 edition of the *New York Times* carried the "Tulsa Riots" as its biggest front-page story, while that week's *Chicago Defender* told of bombs hurled from airplanes upon Greenwood.[10] In Oklahoma City, at the state capitol, Governor Robertson had instructed the state attorney general to begin collecting evidence for a grand jury probe to see the "guilty parties brought to justice."[11] Even in Washington, D.C., news of the Tulsa outrage swept through congressional cloak rooms and White House hallways.[12] President Warren G. Harding, who sometimes advocated for black political rights, offered a measured opposition to the burning when he prayed that "we never see another spectacle like it."[13]

On the morning of June 3, as entrepreneurs like Loula Williams and Carlie Goodwin were picking through the wreckage of Deep Greenwood, they might have noticed something they'd never seen before the neighborhood burned: a group of professional-looking white men surveying the street. The men set up a tent directly across from the husk of the Dreamland.[14] They must have looked similar to the men who went to the police station in suits and ties on the night of May 31 to begin their night of exuberant brutality. Perhaps those men from the chaotic night and these men looking friendly in the bright spring morning were one and the same. They certainly weren't going to say so. But the white men insisted they had not come to add to Greenwood's misery. They were here to help with matters concerning insurance, property appraisal, and landownership. No need to hire a meddlesome attorney—their services were free of charge. When a dazed, homeless resident wandered into the tent, the men handed them a form where they could write down their name, former address, and mortgage encumbrances. Only after gathering all this vital information could the men offer the very best assistance.[15]

These men were some of the wealthiest and most powerful in the city.[16] They claimed a noble mission: "Developing a greater Tulsa."[17]

⸻

The day before the white men set up their tent on Greenwood Avenue, they laid out, with startling efficiency, a comprehensive plan for a takeover of Tulsa's once-thriving black neighborhood.

At a June 2 meeting with city leaders, as Greenwood still smoldered, an association of the city's top realty developers called the Tulsa Real Estate Exchange proposed to buy out all the area landowners and build an industrial site there. Under the pretense of fire safety, they suggested a city ordinance that would ban new wooden houses in the district. The new rule would make rebuilding prohibitively expensive and force black Tulsans to move to the vacant land far north of Deep Greenwood, where a new neighborhood would be built and equipped—so the Real Estate Exchange claimed—with sewage and electric lines. Keeping the races more strictly segregated would benefit everyone, the group argued in its written proposal. "The two races being divided by an industrial section will . . . eliminate the intermingling of the lower elements of the two races, which in our opinion is the root of the evil."[18]

The face of the gambit was Merritt J. Glass, the Real Estate Exchange's president. An Alabama native, Glass resented the political gains black people had achieved in early Oklahoma.[19] He had openly endorsed the Ku Klux Klan alongside Tate Brady after the 1916 election parade that had featured Confederate flags—in fact, Glass was later identified as a member of the Klan himself.[20] The hate group was active in Tulsa at the time of the massacre but not yet at its full strength;[21] Glass may have played a role in helping it take root among Tulsa's white elite. His proposal to relocate Greenwood would satisfy his racist agenda and line his pockets at the same time.

Glass was hardly alone in his views. The Real Estate Exchange's plan put into action an idea that was being widely circulated by many white Tulsans after the massacre: that Greenwood, the "Negro's Wall

Street," was of little economic or cultural value and was in fact a nuisance to the city's future development. "Little Africa was one of the blackest spots in Oklahoma," Methodist bishop Ed D. Mouzon said in a Sunday sermon days after the massacre.[22] The *Tulsa Tribune* was even more blunt in a June 4 editorial: "Such a district as the old 'Niggertown' must never be allowed in Tulsa again."[23]

But the Real Estate Exchange couldn't execute its plan to oust Greenwood residents alone. It would need buy-in from three groups: a newly created Public Welfare Board, the city commission, and black landowners in Greenwood.

The Public Welfare Board helped first. A group of white businessmen and civic leaders, the Welfare Board was formed spontaneously the day after the massacre as a rebuke of the city government's failure to control the white mob. The group's chairman, a former judge named Loyal Martin, declared that "the city and county is legally liable for every dollar of the damage which has been done."[24] The board quickly pledged to raise an initial $100,000 to help Greenwood rebuild.[25] But hubris, and a fixation on Tulsa's public image, served to undercut any initial good intentions. Across the country, sympathetic Americans of all races wanted to help Greenwood's newly destitute. But Martin turned their vital dollars away, arguing that a thousand

The Public Welfare Board was established to respond to the massacre

Tulsa businessmen would open their wallets instead.[26] "I received telegrams from most all of the large cities in the United States offering to open up subscriptions for us," he wrote later. "I telegraphed back that this was our trouble; that we were to blame for it; and that we would take care of it."[27] He even went so far as to mail a $1,000 check from the *Chicago Tribune* back to the sender.[28]

Martin's vanity cost Greenwood dearly. Tulsans donated less than $25,000 to the relief effort, far short of the amount the welfare board expected to raise.[29] It was an embarrassing turn in a city that prided itself on obscene oil wealth. The state government was of no help either; Governor Robertson announced on June 3 that Greenwood residents would not receive a dime of support from state coffers, citing the huge sums he expected Tulsans to donate to the cause.[30]

As the Public Welfare Board's donation drive sputtered, the city commission unleashed a novel tool to pressure black people out of Greenwood. On Tuesday, June 7, they adopted one of Merritt Glass's ideas and passed a city ordinance banning new wooden structures in the neighborhood. The measure expanded the zone requiring fireproof buildings, which had previously applied downtown, all the way north to the Goodwins' house on Haskell Street, capturing more than twenty blocks of the Greenwood district.[31] Families whose frame houses had been burned by the mob would be forced to find the funds to rebuild more expensive homes using brick or concrete—this after the city had actively turned away vital donations that could help with the effort.

Glass's plan gained more momentum when Mayor T. D. Evans ousted the Public Welfare Board, which had at least gestured toward doing right by black Tulsans. The mayor likely resented the fact that Loyal Martin and the unelected board blamed city officials for the destruction of Greenwood and publicly stated that Tulsa should be "legally liable" for what had happened.[32] At a June 14 city commission meeting, Mayor Evans set up the need for a new board with a sensationalized account of the attack on Greenwood. The "negro uprising," as the mayor termed it, had been entirely the fault of blacks. Evans praised the behavior of the National Guard and the "good citizens" of the mob who he said had defended the city. He thanked the police for ensuring that downtown Tulsa did not suffer "a dollar's loss of property by fire." He had scant sympathy for the thousands who were suddenly homeless. "The fortunes of war fall upon the innocent along with the guilty," he said. "Think what would have happened had the Allies marched to Berlin."[33]

The mayor then proposed that a "Reconstruction Committee" replace the Public Welfare Board.[34] This new committee was a more craven group of land developers who could help hasten the efforts to convert Greenwood into an industrial site or train depot.[35] Among the members of the new committee was Tate Brady, Merritt Glass's close ally and a Klan member, who referred to Greenwood as a "disgraceful shacktown."[36] The city commission approved the Reconstruction Committee by a unanimous vote.[37] The Public Welfare Board resigned the following day.[38] Soon the new committee was building political will for emptying out Greenwood among all of white Tulsa's business class, after issuing a resolution stating, "The recent fire in the northeast portion of the city has made available a thoroughly feasible and practicable site for the union station."[39]

In just the two weeks after the massacre, white Tulsa had cut off outside aid, enacted an ordinance that made rebuilding prohibitively expensive, and installed a committee of craven capitalists to oversee Greenwood's redevelopment. Given the sheer speed and scale of the scheme, there was already speculation across the state that the fiery destruction had been part of the land grab, planned out beforehand by leading city officials.[40] While some people in later decades would attempt to blame any planned conspiracy on the Ku Klux Klan, Tulsa already had experience developing vigilante networks among the city's business elite through the World War I Council of Defense, the Home Guard, and rogue groups like the Knights of Liberty that often worked closely with police. The violence these groups organized was about politics and economics as much as it was about enforcing a white supremacist, puritanically Christian social order.[41] Applying their methods to mobilize violence against Greenwood would have come naturally, especially given growing white paranoia about an imminent "Negro uprising." (Police Commissioner Adkison reported on June 2 that Greenwood residents had been making plans for "war" for months.)[42]

"Prominent business men of Tulsa today stated that there was definite organized effort to displace the Negroes from the south portion of Greenwood because of developmental possibilities," University of Oklahoma graduate student Francis Burke asserted in a 1936 thesis about the neighborhood, citing four informants. Burke's research melded academic sociological study of both black and white Tulsans with his experience as an in-the-field social services director. He was well placed to glean an inside look at the city's white elite. "On the night of the riot a number of businessmen participating in this plan actually did much to stimulate the rioters to destroy completely the community," Burke wrote.[43]

Greenwood residents had no way of knowing the nexus of these machinations, but they knew they had the ability to put a stop to it. Because at the point when black people actually entered the equation, the city of Tulsa's scheme began to fall apart.

Four days after Mayor Evans installed his Reconstruction Committee, the leaders of Greenwood who had not been killed, arrested, or run out of town held an emergency meeting at First Baptist Church. J. H. Goodwin was in attendance. So was O. W. Gurley, the Greenwood founder and hotelier; Rev. R. A. Whitaker, the pastor at Mt. Zion Baptist Church; and Dimple Bush, a secretary and teacher.[44] First Baptist, located at the eastern edge of the neighborhood on Archer Street, had been spared because the mob considered it to be in a white district.[45] Inside, the 4,500-square-foot sanctuary retained its pipe organ, weathered Bibles, and sturdy wooden pews.[46] Outside, though, Greenwood still resembled a war zone.

The drumbeat of white pressure urging property owners to sell was intense. In the chaotic days right after the massacre, some despondent blacks considered offloading their land to unscrupulous white real estate men, but National Guard adjutant general Charles Barrett briefly halted all property transfers in the area.[47] Merritt Glass, meanwhile, was carefully crafting a narrative that cast blacks as willing partners in the seizure of their own land. He told the press that black leaders were already on board with the Real Estate Exchange's plans for "developing a greater Tulsa." Glass claimed that R. T. Bridgewater, a prominent black doctor, had taken the lead in urging black people to sell.[48] But when Bridgewater later attended a meeting with the Real Estate Exchange, he demanded answers about whether blacks would be able to collect on their insurance claims or receive favorable long-term loans to rebuild in a new area.[49] The *Tribune* reported that prominent Greenwood leaders such as Barney Cleaver were willing to sell, but it did not quote the men directly, and the newspaper had already publicly declared its agenda to see that "Niggertown" was never rebuilt.[50] It was hardly an objective source.

At the First Baptist meeting, black landowners made their intentions clear. "Almost to a man," Oklahoma City's *Black Dispatch* reported, "the Negroes on Greenwood street propose to hold their property and rebuild on their land." The gathered leaders adopted a slogan by J. W. Hughes, principal of the destroyed elementary school, in negotiations with the Reconstruction Committee: "I'm going to hold what I have until I get what I've lost."[51]

The people at the First Baptist meeting formed the nexus of the Colored Citizens' Relief Committee, a neighborhood counteroffensive to white Tulsa's encroachment. O. W. Gurley served as chairman of the committee, while J. H. Goodwin was vice-chair. The group began arguing its case throughout the neighborhood. It held mass meetings in Greenwood urging black residents to hold on to their property.[52] The group also placed calls to action in black newspapers around the country, soliciting donations that would help Greenwood residents gain a financial foothold in uncertain times.[53] Slowly, the desire to sell abated. Staying in Greenwood became a symbol of race pride and economic solidarity, just as buying a Dreamland ticket had been in simpler times.[54]

While A. J. Smitherman's *Tulsa Star* was now an ashen heap on Greenwood Avenue, another black newspaper stepped in to play a key role in refastening the community ties that both the mob and real estate developers were so bent on tearing apart. The *Oklahoma Sun*, led by former *Tulsa Star* managing editor Theodore Baughman, had launched about a year before the massacre as a Republican counterweight to the Democratic-leaning *Star*. (Smitherman had cordially welcomed the competition, encouraging black readers to show race pride by subscribing to either paper.)[55] After the attack, Baughman went right back to work, posting lists of missing persons around the neighborhood and connecting Greenwood residents to relief efforts through daily news bulletins.[56] Like the *Star,* the *Sun* believed that community solidarity should extend to economics. "In the midst of our dilemma, loan sharks and conniving persons will suggest that you sell out and leave," the newspaper warned. "Such persons should be spurned for they are not your friends. They will profit through your temporary embarrassment and misfortune."[57]

B. C. Franklin and I. H. Spears in their tent law office, days after the massacre

As J. H. Goodwin's group and others were warding off the buyout efforts, Greenwood lawyers were launching a legal battle against the city commission's fire ordinance. Leading the charge was B. C. Franklin, a prominent attorney and Choctaw freedman who had moved to Greenwood from the all-black town of Rentiesville just a few months before the massacre.[58] With a tall, slender frame and a distinguished demeanor—he wore long overcoats and stylish spectacles—Franklin knew how to counter the shrewdness of the white schemers with his own clever strategy.[59] He suspected that the ordinance was unconstitutional, violating property rights protections in the Fifth and Fourteenth Amendments.[60] Though Franklin did not know to what extent the destruction of Greenwood was pre-planned, he had no doubt that the effort to defraud black landowners afterward was intentional and well coordinated. "To enforce such an ordinance . . . would make the city a party to a conspiracy," Franklin argued later.[61] He and his law partners, I. H. Spears and P. A. Chappelle, decided to file an injunction.

The lawyers took on the case of Joe Lockard, a homeowner whose one-story frame house on Frankfort Avenue was burned to the ground during the massacre. They argued that the ordinance had been passed without proper public notification and that enacting it so soon after the devastation, while Lockard and thousands of others had been rendered destitute, imperiled their very lives by denying them shelter. "The passage and enforcement of this purported ordinance . . . is oppressive, unreasonable, and discriminatory and is tantamount to the confiscation of the property," the lawsuit read.[62]

A trio of judges initially overturned the ordinance on a technicality, but they left the city commission an opening to pass it again with appropriate public notice.[63] When the commission again approved the measure a day later, a white lawyer named Mather Eakes filed a suit for a different group of Greenwood residents.[64] It was ultimately Eakes's case that went to trial, using arguments similar to the ones advanced by the black lawyers.[65] After just a few hours of testimony, the same three judges ruled in favor of the Greenwood landowners. The fire ordinance was invalidated.[66]

The day after the court ruling, Mayor T. D. Evans and his Reconstruction Committee finally gave up on the idea of an industrial site.[67] Thanks to the efforts of the Colored Citizens' Relief Committee, the neighborhood attorneys, and residents who refused to be moved, Greenwood would remain in black hands. "These men worked faithfully and have fought many battles for their fellow man," Mary Jones

Members of the Colored Citizens' Relief Committee come together amid the wreckage

Parrish reflected on the efforts of the Relief Committee.[68] Greenwood's defiant stand became a rallying point for black economic solidarity nationwide. "Black Tulsa fights!" the NAACP magazine the *Crisis* declared. "It fights mobs with firearms and it fights economic oppression with co-operation."[69]

The battles in the courtroom and in real estate negotiations over the summer had staved off further catastrophe. But even as Greenwood banded together, the community suffered from the loss of some of its most vocal and passionate defenders.

The same week Greenwood leaders met to strategize at First Baptist Church, Oklahoma attorney general S. P. Freeling traveled to Topeka, Kansas, in pursuit of J. B. Stradford. It was the night of June 15.[70] Just hours earlier Freeling had secured a grand jury indictment of Stradford and fifty-five other black men for "riotously and feloniously" assembling in the streets, wielding rifles, and disturbing the peace. (About a dozen white men were indicted later in the week.)[71] Stradford's alleged crimes included murder, robbery, and arson; per Oklahoma law, he now faced a criminal trial and could be held responsible for all the events that transpired after the encounter at the courthouse, including the destruction of Greenwood.[72]

After briefly being detained at Convention Hall, the hotel owner had slipped out of Tulsa to stay with his brother in Independence, Kansas. On June 3 he was arrested at his brother's home at the urging of Tulsa authorities.[73] Oklahoma law enforcement wanted him extradited immediately, but Kansas governor Henry Allen wasn't convinced.[74] The governor had previously declined to send a black man back to Arkansas after officials there argued the man was responsible for inciting the violence in Elaine during the Red Summer of 1919.[75] With the indictment in hand, though, Attorney General Freeling planned to meet with the governor and convince him that Stradford would receive a fair trial in the city that had just burned down an entire black community.[76]

The governor arranged a hearing on the matter in Topeka.[77] A large group of blacks came to protest the attempt to ship Stradford back to Oklahoma. The man himself was set to appear by noon. But

Stradford never showed up.[78] While in Independence, he'd sent an urgent wire to his son Cornelius in Chicago. Cornelius traveled south immediately to rescue his father and posted his $500 bond. The two returned to Chicago before anyone was the wiser.[79] J. B. Stradford would never set foot in Tulsa again, and an open warrant for his arrest would follow him for the rest of his life.[80]

Back in Tulsa, the city's efforts to prosecute other Greenwood men were faltering. Of the roughly seventy-five black men indicted on riot charges, only a handful were arrested during the month of June—most had disappeared from the city.[81] But Stradford had been subjected to particularly dogged pursuit because of his status as a political leader willing to defy white supremacy with his fists as well as his intellect. In his memoir, he recalled learning that a pair of white politicians were talking about giving him a "necktie party" (a lynching) because he "taught the niggers that they are as good as white people."[82] The only other indicted man who invited such vehement rage from white Tulsa was Stradford's young, rebellious ally, A. J. Smitherman.

Like Stradford, Smitherman quickly left Tulsa with his wife Ollie and their five children. Oklahoma officials tried to pursue him across the nation, tracking him in at least three different states.[83] When a leader from the NAACP inquired to the *Tulsa Tribune* about exactly why Smitherman had been indicted, editor Richard Lloyd Jones responded in a telegram, "Smitherman fugitive from justice. Extradition papers granted by three governors. Bad actor."[84]

All around the nation Freeling and other powerful whites in Oklahoma were simultaneously arguing that the black men who had fled Tulsa were extremely dangerous and that they would receive fair treatment back in their home state. "There is no prejudice in Tulsa County," Freeling said in one extradition letter to officials in Minnesota.[85] But the outcome of the grand jury proceedings, which Freeling had spearheaded, showed his claim to be a farce. The grand jury was all white,[86] as were most of the witnesses who testified. When Greenwood residents lined the corridors of the Tulsa County Courthouse, hoping to offer their own testimonies, Freeling ignored them.[87] Instead, he favored accounts of police officers, select Greenwood residents familiar to Tulsa's white elite, and handpicked white citizens,

Ku Klux Klan members among them.[88] When the grand jury issued its final report, it went further than just calling for the arrest of some seventy-five black men for a specific incident. It blamed "agitation among Negroes for social equality" as a leading cause of the violence and argued that going forward, Greenwood should be permanently monitored by an all-white police force.[89]

Smitherman had no intention of facing a justice system that could render such a verdict, but he also didn't intend to spend the rest of his days lurking in the shadows. His family relocated to Roxbury, a diverse Boston enclave that was quickly becoming a hotbed of civil rights advocacy. On Christmas Day 1921, he wrote a letter to NAACP assistant secretary Walter White, who was helping him fend off extradition charges from Freeling in Oklahoma. (White, a crusading journalist in his own right, had ventured to Tulsa just after Greenwood burned and written a harrowing account in the *Nation*.)[90] "I have decided to come out of hiding and do whatever I may to add to the splendid work you have already done to expose the atrocities of the Tulsa riot and massacre," Smitherman wrote. "I plan to tell the story here and elsewhere in New England first to our own people, then to the general public."[91] At a March 1922 event honoring the role of black Bostonian Crispus Attucks in the American Revolution, Smitherman submitted a "prayer to Congress," which he hoped would compel the U.S. Senate to pass anti-lynching legislation.[92] He began writing about the massacre in both black newspapers like the Oklahoma City *Black Dispatch* and white-owned outlets like the *Boston Herald*.[93] By 1924 he was editing his third newspaper, the *New World*, in the Massachusetts city of Springfield.[94]

Smitherman and his family developed a ritual as they spread knowledge of Greenwood's horrors around the Northeast. At lecture events, he would first offer a speech about his experiences. Then his family would recite a poem he had written in the chaotic aftermath of the attack.[95] A lifelong devotee of Shakespeare,[96] Smitherman gave the events of May 31 and June 1 the sweep of an epic tragedy: the rallying in Greenwood to defend Dick Rowland, the march to the courthouse, the initial gunshot, the retreat back to Greenwood, the fight across the railroad tracks, the invasion, the burning, the airplanes, the machine guns, the fire, the death. Across sixty-one stanzas, A. J. Smitherman articulated a key distinction about the series of events that white newspapers, grand juries, and law enforcement officials had tried to elide. While the violence at the courthouse may have indeed been a race riot, the looting, burning, and mass killing that occurred in Greenwood on the morning of June 1 was something else entirely. It was a massacre.[97]

Smitherman would never again reside in Tulsa. But even in exile, he remained a loud and defiant defender of his people, at any cost.

<hr />

Loula Williams had lost everything: the ticket machine housed in its plate-glass booth, the pair of film projectors, the six buzz fans that kept the theater cool in the summer, and the five gas stoves that offered warmth in the winter. She'd lost the dozen chairs for the dressing rooms, the 850 seats in the main theater hall, even the spotlight that shone down every time a live performer took the Dreamland stage. It was more than $10,000 worth of destroyed equipment in all, to say nothing of the $42,000 lost in the ravaged building itself.[98] The nearby Williams Building, with its confectionery and rented offices, represented another $32,000 in losses.[99] And that tally did not even include any personal effects from the family's apartment, like her burned-up beds, pilfered rings, and stolen leopard-print coat.[100]

She had prepared for such a disastrous occasion as much as anyone possibly could. Before the massacre, Loula bought eight policies from three insurance firms, paying a total of about $860 in premiums. She was guaranteed a payout of roughly $32,000 in the event her properties were destroyed by fire.[101] On June 1, 1921, they were.

Loula continued following the rules. The majority of her coverage was provided by Kansas-based Central States Fire Insurance Company, so she contacted her insurer and filled out the necessary paperwork to prove her losses. (Even this was a challenge because her copies of the policy claims had been burned up along with the rest of her possessions.)[102] But Central States Fire Insurance refused to pay. The company cited an exclusion clause in its contract that absolved it of legal liability if a fire occurred in the course of a riot.[103]

On May 31, 1922, a year after her home and her businesses were destroyed at the same time, Loula filed a lawsuit against Central

States Fire Insurance Company. Greenwood property owners filed lawsuits against more than thirty insurance companies—some of which would remain in business a century later, such as the Hartford Financial Services Group and the Great American Insurance Group.[104]

The insurance companies had developed boilerplate arguments against paying out claims to customers facing utter disaster. In a legal brief responding to Loula's suit, Central States Fire Insurance cast the Tulsa "race riot" as an evenhanded battle between black and white foes: "hundreds of persons of both said races . . . [were] armed with fire arms and other weapons, and supplied with matches and other materials for setting fire to and burning property."[105] The company claimed that these opposing factions both operated "without authority of law," a key factor in Oklahoma's legal definition of a riot.[106]

In fact, many of the white people who invaded Greenwood had been deputized by police—Police Commissioner Adkison himself admitted that some of the deputized men "might have applied the torch."[107] According to eyewitness accounts from both blacks and whites, uniformed officers had broken into buildings and started fires themselves.[108] This could potentially nullify an insurance company's riot-exclusion clause, according to legal precedent. In Kentucky a few years earlier, a U.S. marshal set a lumber building on fire in the midst of a riot. A state court later found that the insurance company would have to cover the fire damage. Once law enforcement officials began actively destroying private property, it became harder to describe their actions as "beyond the control of the police department" as Central States Fire Insurance asserted.[109]

Loula was hardly the only person in Greenwood seeking justice through the courts. Carlie Goodwin filed her own suit against the city of Tulsa in June 1923.[110] The family had lost not only the Goodwin office building, a one-story brick structure located a couple of doors down from the Dreamland, but also the home they owned at 401 East Haskell Street. A piano, ten feather pillows, a couple dozen quilts, and an entire library's worth of books had all been swallowed by the flames. In addition, the Goodwins had lost about a dozen other properties they owned, ranging from a three-room frame house to a nine-room, two-story home reinforced by plaster. All burned. In their suit, the family claimed that the mayor, the police chief, and others had not only failed to protect Greenwood but had launched a pre-planned conspiracy to destroy the community. The Goodwins sought $76,000 in damages.[111]

Loula's and Carlie's lawsuits were just two of the more than 190 lawsuits filed against insurance companies and city officials following the massacre.[112] Many of the suits were brought by wealthy black families like the Williamses and the Goodwins, but others came from lesser-known Greenwood figures like Mabel Allen, who worked as a maid for white people in South Tulsa but also owned a modest rental property in Greenwood.[113] Allen sought a $750 payout on a $21 premium, but even that small claim was not honored by her insurer, the New York–based Continental Insurance Company.[114]

The volume of the lawsuits, many filed by B. C. Franklin and his partners,[115] conveyed both the scale of the massacre's destruction and the confidence that Greenwood residents still wanted to hold in the courts. For a long time, black people had thought of the law as a final refuge from the daily vagaries of racism. Changing the feeling inside a white man's heart was an impossible task. But gaining protection from a law? Or even changing one? That could be done. In Oklahoma's brief history as a state, black people had already challenged Jim Crow cars on railways, segregated housing ordinances, and voter disenfranchisement laws. Because the most educated and successful blacks had come so far since laws freed them from slavery, they retained a deep faith that institutional power could, in the long run, be a force for good. B. C. Franklin later recalled how deeply he equated law with justice as a child, when he would read newspaper accounts of convicted criminals being hanged and wished he could go witness the executions. "I thought every outlaw was, indeed, guilty!" he wrote. "The fact that some of them might be innocent of murder never entered my mind."[116]

But the execution of justice in the aftermath of the massacre would shake this belief to its very core. Loula, Carlie, and the vast majority of Greenwood residents never even got their day in court. More than fifty of the lawsuits were summarily dismissed on the same day in 1937 after languishing for years.[117] However, William Redfearn, the white entrepreneur who owned the movie theater across from the Dreamland, was granted a trial. In *Redfearn v. American Central Insurance Company*, the Oklahoma Supreme Court acknowledged that "evidence shows that a great number of men engaged in arresting the negroes found in the negro section wore police badges, or badges indicating they were deputy sheriffs, and in some instances were dressed in soldier's clothes." However, the court doubted whether these men were actually police officials. Moreover, if they detained black people while functioning as deputized police, and later returned to burn Greenwood as rogue rioters, then an insurance company could still claim the burning wasn't a state act. Redfearn, a prominent white businessman, lost his case; his black peers never had a chance.[118]

Carlie Goodwin could not wait for a lawsuit ruling to move forward with her life. Though the family had been financially devastated, she kept a rainy day fund that she did not tell even her husband about.[119] In late July, before the fire ordinance had been defeated and while white real estate grafters were still trying to buy out Greenwood, Carlie secured a construction permit to begin repairs on the family property at 123 North Greenwood Avenue.[120] It was time to rebuild.

Absent local aid, the people of Greenwood got creative in order to reopen their businesses. The barber and preacher C. L. Netherland took a chair out to the burned-out district and planted it right in the center of Greenwood Avenue as the rubble still smoldered, offering to cut hair.[121] The Dreamland, for a time, became a makeshift amphitheater, showing films in the open air on muggy summer nights.[122] B. C. Franklin and his team fended off white legal incursions from a tent they set up on Archer Street, armed with a lone wooden desk, a few salvaged law books, and a single typewriter.[123]

Black organizations also helped to get the wheels of the Greenwood economy in motion again, after some residents reported having trouble securing loans from Tulsa's white banks.[124] The NAACP, whose co-founder W.E.B. Du Bois had visited Tulsa just three months before the massacre, donated $3,500.[125] When a leader of the Supreme Camp of the American Woodmen, a black fraternal organization, visited Greenwood in late 1921, he vowed to start issuing loans to business owners there to help them rebuild.[126] Loula Williams secured one such loan, an $11,000 mortgage that aided in the reconstruction of the Dreamland.[127] "The thing on everybody's mind was struggling trying to get back to the status quo," Loula's son Willie said later. "Trying to get back in business. Trying to get back to the way it used to be."[128]

The only white-led institution that understood the race massacre as an actual humanitarian crisis was the Red Cross. Arriving in Tulsa two days after the city burned, Red Cross relief operations director Maurice Willows ultimately spent the rest of the year in Greenwood, aiding black residents and sparring with city leaders on their behalf.[129] When massacre victims' meager tents flooded that summer, the Red Cross provided shelter at Booker T. Washington High School, which would serve as a hospital and headquarters until the fall.[130] At a late June city commission meeting, Mayor T. D. Evans wanted to spend over $20,000 in emergency funds earmarked for relief work on expanding the police force and buying twenty brand-new machine guns. Willows had to fight to convince the city to use the money to aid Greenwood instead.[131] Mary Jones Parrish, along with many of her neighbors, celebrated the Red Cross workers as "angels of mercy."[132]

At the same time businesses were being salvaged, homes were slowly being built. It was a race against time since the brutal Oklahoma winter would arrive before anyone was quite ready. First came the tents, around four hundred of which were furnished by the Red Cross.[133] Some had wooden siding and flooring, but others were little more than a shield from the rain as residents slept in the dirt. "I didn't ever get used to it," recalled Essie Lee Johnson Beck, who was only six at the time.[134]

As winter approached, 225 of the Red Cross tents were converted into one- or two-room wooden houses, dotting the still-desolate landscape with the first visual signs of recovery.[135] But while the Red Cross could offer temporary shelter, Greenwood residents had to build true homes for themselves. J. C. Latimer and his brother William took on contracting work constructing many new long-term houses in the community.[136] The Colored Citizens' Relief Committee paid for the installation of new roofs by black carpenters, while also helping to pay the attorney fees of the many property owners filing lawsuits.[137] Mabel and Pressley Little built a modest three-room house at the corner of Marshall Place and Greenwood Avenue, farther north than their old, destroyed property.[138]

The Red Cross's greatest long-term contribution to Greenwood

Temporary housing was constructed in Greenwood with aid from the Red Cross

was help in constructing a new hospital. The classrooms where Ed Goodwin had learned Latin and physics were for months a gruesome intensive care unit, where doctors tended to burn victims and amputees.[139] The school needed to be turned back over to the children, and Greenwood needed a new space for health care. The Red Cross's temporary headquarters, located on Hartford Street, was chosen as the appropriate site. There the Red Cross, partnering with the Colored Citizens' Relief Committee, gathered the funds and manpower to build a nine-room hospital building valued at $65,000.[140] Greenwood residents chose to name the space after Maurice Willows, who they called "an apostle of the square deal for every man, regardless of race or color."[141]

The new facility, run by all-black doctors and nurses, was governed by a group of black business leaders called the Tulsa Colored Hospital Association. On the incorporation documents outlining the group's commitment to building a space for the "housing, feeding, and treating [of] sick persons," J. H. Goodwin's name was listed first.[142]

By Christmas 1921, Greenwood had rebuilt 180 frame shacks, 584 larger frame buildings, and fifty-four brick or cement structures, including a large brick church.[143] The Goodwin Building was back up and temporarily housing the undertaking parlor that J. H. Goodwin and S. M. Jackson operated together.[144] The Dreamland Theater didn't have a roof, and many of its 850 elegant opera seats had been replaced by wooden plank benches, but it was screening films all the same.[145] "The rapidity with which business buildings and residences are being rebuilt, in most instances, better than before is proof in wood and brick and in stone of the black man's ability to make progress against the most cunningly planned and powerfully organized opposition," the relief committee declared.[146] A visitor put it much more simply: "They have the victory in STAYING."[147]

But some things would never be the same. The Stradford Hotel property had fallen into the hands of a white real estate man named J. W. Hamel; Stradford would try to wrestle back ownership for years but would never receive it.[148] The congregants of Mt. Zion Baptist Church, with $50,000 in debt and a ravaged house of worship, voted to rebuild from their dirt-floor basement on up, but it would take decades for the church to fully reopen its doors.[149] The *Tulsa Star* would never print another issue. Under the leadership of Theodore Baughman, however, the *Oklahoma Sun* took up its mantle advocating for black Americans. In the fall of 1922, Baughman left the *Sun* and launched a new newspaper, the *Oklahoma Eagle,* to chronicle life in Greenwood after the devastation. A Kansas journalist predicted that the *Eagle* would "soar over the Southwest."[150]

Young Ed Goodwin observed many of these changes from a distance. He and his senior classmates had survived one of the worst incidents of racial terrorism in U.S. history. Like the leaders who were banished as fugitives, the neighbors who marched north on the railroad tracks, and the unknown number of souls discarded without a proper burial, Ed Goodwin left Tulsa, heading off for college in 1922.[151] But unlike all of those people, when he finished his studies at Fisk University, he would have the choice to come back. He would have to decide for himself if Tulsa was really a place where a black person could thrive—whether the promise of Oklahoma that his parents had sought when they journeyed from Water Valley, Mississippi, could still, somehow, be realized.

Just before the massacre, as he was contemplating life away from

his family, his friends, and his neighborhood for the first time, he offered a clue about his mindset in his chosen senior quote for the
Booker T. Washington High School yearbook:

> *I know not where my life shall lead me*
> *When death shall as His own,*
> *But this I know—He shall not find me*
> *Unprepared without a "Home."*[152]

PART II

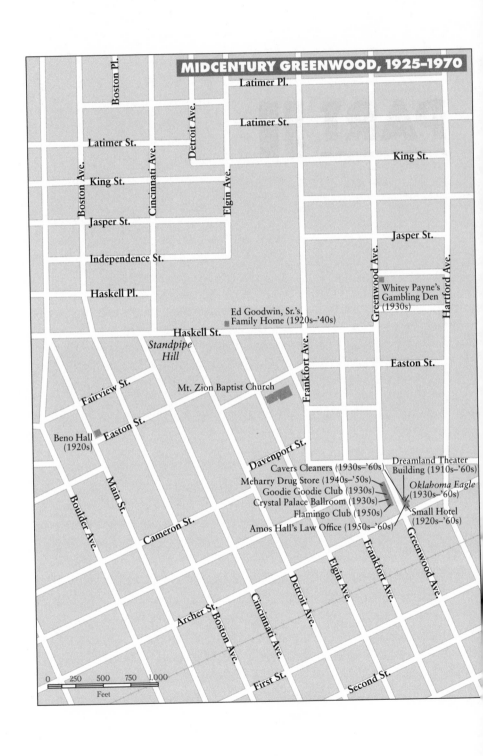

MIDCENTURY GREENWOOD, 1925–1970

Boston Pl.

Latimer Pl.

Latimer St.

Detroit Ave.

Latimer St.

King St.

Cincinnati Ave.

Latimer St.

Boston Ave.

King St.

Elgin Ave.

Jasper St.

Jasper St.

Greenwood Ave.

Independence St.

Hartford Ave.

Haskell Pl.

Whitey Payne's
Gambling Den
(1930s)

Ed Goodwin, Sr.'s,
Family Home (1920s–'40s)

Haskell St.

Standpipe
Hill

Frankfort Ave.

Easton St.

Fairview St.

Mt. Zion Baptist Church

Easton St.

Beno Hall
(1920s)

Easton St.

Davenport St.

Dreamland Theater
Building (1910s–'60s)

Cavers Cleaners (1930s–'60s)

Meharry Drug Store (1940s–'50s)

Oklahoma Eagle
(1930s–'60s)

Goodie Goodie Club (1930s)

Main St.

Crystal Palace Ballroom (1930s)

Flamingo Club (1950s)

Small Hotel
(1920s–'60s)

Amos Hall's Law Office (1950s–'60s)

Boulder Ave.

Cameron St.

Frankfort Ave.

Greenwood Ave.

Elgin Ave.

Detroit Ave.

Archer St.

Cincinnati Ave.

Boston Ave.

First St.

Second St.

0   250   500   750 1,000
Feet

CHAPTER 9

FAR FROM HOME

Fisk University students gather for prayer in the early 1900s

Ed and Anna Goodwin stood in stiff silence as "The Star-Spangled Banner" blared from a lone cornet, plaintive in the warm autumn air. Looking up, they could see a soloist standing in the white-columned tower of Jubilee Hall, the most ornate and lavish building on the Fisk University campus. Inching slowly up a pole planted atop the tower, an American flag billowed in the wind.[1]

The siblings, born thirteen months apart and both just out of adolescence, may have fidgeted in their mandatory formal clothes.[2] Ed wore a crisp white shirt and a dark tie; Anna donned a white dress with modest frills and sensible low-heeled shoes.[3] They were surrounded by more than three hundred other students representing thirty stars on that American flag, from tiny southern hamlets like

Biscoe, Arkansas, major northern cities like Chicago, and western outposts like Los Angeles.[4] But only Ed and Anna had survived Tulsa.

After the flag-raising ceremony, the band of students, excited about their new lives as college men and women, trooped south down the tree-lined streets of the campus.[5] They walked by the Memorial Chapel, where Booker T. Washington had regaled students in earlier years,[6] and passed the library where former president William H. Taft had laid the cornerstone in 1908.[7] Fisk commanded an ample forty acres in Nashville, Tennessee, dotted by roughly twenty school buildings.[8] An agent from the federal Bureau of Education described the campus as "well-kept and of unusual beauty."[9] But Fisk's appearance was less important than its founding mission: to prove that black students could be the intellectual equals of white ones, if given the opportunity.[10] The school had recently become the first Negro college in the country to earn the endorsement of the Carnegie Foundation, the leading accreditor of universities at the time.[11] The *New York Age,* a black newspaper, called Fisk "our greatest seat of higher education," while the *Nashville Banner,* a white one, called it "the greatest Negro educational institution in the south."[12]

The students filed into Livingstone Hall, the administrative building that also doubled as Ed's new dormitory.[13] In the building's chapel, Fisk's president was preparing to deliver his annual opening address.[14] Fayette McKenzie was a former sociology professor at Ohio State University who had arrived at Fisk in 1915, convinced he knew precisely the instruction, rigor, and discipline that colored children needed in order to become productive citizens.[15] He was also a white man, like all the school's leaders dating back to its origins as a missionary college in 1866.[16]

While Fisk had long offered its students the kind of liberal arts education often associated with elite white schools,[17] the college faced pressure to incorporate the industrial education that Booker T. Washington had advocated at Tuskegee at the start of the twentieth century.[18] The white philanthropists who financially backed both Fisk and Tuskegee had a single end goal: creating a class of dutiful black workers and professionals who would fit into the Jim Crow regime of the Deep South or assimilate into the less visible racial hierarchies of the industrial North. They soon found a useful mouthpiece in McKenzie. The Fisk president ostensibly championed the liberal arts but believed black intellectual freedom screeched to a halt as soon as it conflicted with white interests.[19] In a 1918 speech, he compared Fisk's focus on "unremitting toil" and "complete obedience" to that of a military institution.[20]

Sitting in Livingstone Hall for the first time, Ed knew little about the political agendas that would shape his college experience. As McKenzie droned on about the duties and privileges of being a Fiskite during his opening address, Ed could crane his neck around the chapel and get a look at all his new classmates. Among them were Yolande Du Bois, the daughter of one of the school's most prominent alumni, W.E.B. Du Bois.[21] Also present was Jimmie Lunceford, a saxophone player from Denver who would go on to become a popular jazz bandleader.[22] Many Fiskites were already famous or would be one day soon. With parents who had never even attended high school, though, Ed and Anna would have to chart their own futures.

Anna planned to study vocal training at Fisk's highly selective music school, which made her the equivalent of a star athlete.[23] Fisk was widely considered to have the best music department of any black college in the nation.[24] The school's sterling reputation had been seeded by a group of early students, many of them former slaves, who translated the spirituals of the antebellum cotton fields into stirring choral arrangements. They took the name the Jubilee Singers and became worldwide stars—everyone from Mark Twain to Great Britain's Queen Victoria watched them perform.[25] By the time Anna was a student in the 1920s, the original singers had been memorialized in a massive life-size painting commissioned by the Queen of England that hung in Jubilee Hall, which also served as the girls' dormitories.[26] Anna hoped to one day join the elite group.

It wasn't quite so obvious where Ed would fit in at Fisk. At Booker T. Washington High School, he'd been voted most likely to succeed, but succeed *at what* exactly, no one could say for sure. As a natural charmer who could create his own luck in any situation, business suited him well. He was sometimes seen around the Fisk campus wearing a white doctor's coat—not as part of his coursework but to trick girls into thinking he was an aspiring doctor at Meharry College, the local black medical school. On campus, folks liked to call him "Sugar Man"—he was sweet when he needed to be.[27]

Ed soon decided he wanted to become an entrepreneur, following

Ed Goodwin at Fisk University

the path his father had taken decades earlier in Water Valley, Mississippi. But he would not be the same kind of man as J. H. Goodwin. J.H. kept a low profile, working behind the scenes to build community institutions such as Greenwood's first hospital. Like Booker T. Washington, he had faith that business success could chart a path toward black social equality. "With a background of thriving businesses, our people can demand a place in the social and economic structures in our country," he once wrote.[28] But Ed, a young man both outspoken and quick to anger, was not so patient. With his whole life ahead of him, he did not want to waste time walking a slow and arduous path toward racial equality, or endure violent detours like the one he and his neighbors had suffered in Greenwood. He wanted freedom now.

The philosopher Alain Locke, the first black Rhodes scholar and a key chronicler of the Harlem Renaissance, classified young black people of Ed's age group and temperament as the "New Negro."[29] It was this cohort who Locke expected to pursue self-expression and independence at all costs, even in the face of white resistance. College campuses would serve as a key incubator for their activism. "The present generation of young Negroes is in the process of moulting the psychology of dependence and subserviency," Locke wrote.[30]

On campus, he quickly discovered there were communities like Greenwood all across the country. In Richmond, Virginia, financier Maggie Walker became the first black woman in the country to operate her own bank.[31] Out of Durham, the black-owned North Carolina Mutual Life Insurance Company managed a staff of eleven hundred people selling policies in twelve states, including Oklahoma.[32] Right there in Nashville there were fifty black doctors, thirty social clubs, and two hospitals, anchored around a thriving business thoroughfare called Jefferson Street.[33] Fisk students hailed from these locales and many more, pockets of black autonomy thriving from coast to coast.

Some of the students from these places would become Ed's lifelong friends. But none captured his attention more than a young woman from the Midwest who started life at Fisk on the same day as he did. Her name was Jeanne Belle Osby.

———

She grew up in the land of Lincoln, just a few blocks from the president's grave site in Springfield, Illinois.[34] On Sundays she sang "Lift Every Voice and Sing" at all-black Union Baptist Church, while on weekdays she attended desegregated public schools, sometimes as the only black girl in her class. She lived in an interracial, working-class neighborhood called Enos Park, with immigrant neighbors from Germany, Italy, and Ireland. Jeanne herself had an Irish grandmother on her mother's side, and at least one slave master ancestor on her father's side.[35] She was light-skinned, but black according to all the laws and mores of society.

Jeanne's father, James Osby, was a former janitor at the county courthouse who wanted much more for himself and his children.[36] In 1909, around age forty, he began selling real estate and was soon celebrated as one of the most prominent black businessmen in the region.[37] Later he was elected assistant supervisor of Springfield's Capital Township and served as an alternate delegate at the 1912 Republican National Convention.[38] Like W. H. Twine out in Oklahoma, he said he was an ironclad Republican because Lincoln had freed his mother from bondage.[39] Jeanne's mother, Minnie, was the first woman to register to vote in their precinct, following the passage of the Nineteenth Amendment in 1920.[40] While the Osbys became well versed in finance and politics, they, like the Goodwins, valued education first and foremost. "Clothes wear out. Money is spent," James Osby once told his daughter. "But if you get knowledge, it will stay with you."[41]

In some ways, Jeanne grew up living in the egalitarian version of America that the nation had long aspired to be, the kind of place that Oklahoma had briefly been in the era before statehood. But even when equality was promised by law, it could still be a fiction in practice. "We didn't have what we now call segregated schools but the colored students had to be twice as good," Jeanne said later. "We had to work for any honors we won."[42] And just like Ed, Jeanne was exposed to the nation's most violent forms of racism.

In August 1908, when Jeanne was five years old,[43] a white mob in

Springfield sought to lynch two black men who were being held at the local jail. One man was charged with murdering a white man; the other was accused of attempting to rape a white woman in a separate incident. Police ferried the two prisoners out of town after hearing rumors of the planned lynching. In an act of furious retaliation, a mob of at least one thousand whites descended on a poor black neighborhood, derisively referred to as "the Badlands," and burned more than forty families' homes. Scott Burton, a black barber who lived in the neighborhood, was shot four times and hanged in front of his shop. Later that night the mob seized eighty-year-old William Donegan, slashed his throat, and hanged him from a nearby tree. Neither man had any connection to the murder or rape accusations. Burton

Jeanne Osby, right, at Fisk University

had defended himself with a gun when the mob approached his home, and Donegan had committed the crime of being married to a white woman for thirty years.[44]

Jeanne's family lived about a mile and a half northwest from the nexus of the violence, but her parents recognized that no black person was safe with the mob on the loose.[45] They shuttled Jeanne and her four siblings to her grandfather's farm outside town. "My father was afraid the bloodshed might spread," Jeanne recalled later.[46]

The massacre in Springfield shocked the nation, particularly white liberals who had convinced themselves that racial violence was a problem only in the Deep South.[47] A multiracial coalition assembled in New York the following year to protest racial terror and ongoing discrimination against blacks. Their members included the outspoken intellectual W.E.B. Du Bois, the anti-lynching crusader Ida B. Wells, and the pioneering black activist Mary Church Terrell. The group came to be called the National Association for the Advancement of Colored People.[48] Du Bois's name in particular soon became synonymous with the NAACP.

While some wanted to view the Springfield massacre as a disturbing outlier at the turn of the century, mob violence outside the Deep South became common in the ensuing decades: in East St. Louis in 1917, during the Red Summer of 1919, and most devastatingly in Tulsa in 1921. Ed and Jeanne grew up in different parts of the country under polar-opposite racial customs, but they bore unnervingly similar scars.

Ed and Jeanne had a natural chemistry, but under the many mandates of Fisk, they could do little more than flirt at a distance. All dancing was forbidden at student socials, as were "party dresses" that lacked sleeves or modest necklines.[49] Playing ragtime music on university pianos was banned, and school professors derided the emergent new genre as "cheap vulgarity."[50] Even walking across the quad with a member of the opposite sex required teacher approval. "The rules of Fisk are many, and by far not all printed in the catalogue," one professor remarked. "A young lady may be sent home for casting a smile from a window to a youth below."[51]

Fisk had always been a strict environment guided by white leaders with puritanical principles—students were sometimes referred to half-mockingly as Black Puritans or "Afro-Saxons."[52] But by the 1920s, money played a bigger role in shaping campus policies than religion. In order to survive, Fisk and every other black college in the United States became beholden to a handful of powerful, business-minded philanthropists who supplanted progressive missionaries as their key bankrollers. These donors sought to shape young black minds into useful tools for white society as much as they sought to educate them.[53] Much of Fisk's funding came from the General Education Board (GEB), a nonprofit seeded by John D. Rockefeller to spread industrial training programs across the nation. The organization was explicit in its desire to make Fisk a cultivating ground for "the right type of colored leaders," people who would conform to white control rather than embrace the freethinking ideals of the New Negro movement.[54] "Due to various experiences since the World War, there is a growing disposition among the Negroes to suspect all white men and their motives and therefore to break all contact with them and go it alone," read a GEB memo about a Fisk endowment campaign. "This very real menace to the public welfare makes the strengthening of school facilities for Negroes a matter of national significance."[55]

President McKenzie, who was laser-focused on improving Fisk's shaky financial standing, became the perfect vessel for executing the GEB's goals and building a class of black graduates who could be cogs in the machinery of the southern economy. There was little space for individuality at Fisk and even less for criticism of those in power. When a group of students refused to attend a study hall in 1918, McKenzie denounced them as Bolshevists.[56] He shut down the school's student newspaper and student council, and he thwarted attempts to form a campus chapter of the NAACP.[57] At one point, he directed the campus librarian to remove all material deemed radical from the library's copies of the *Crisis*, the NAACP magazine edited by Fisk alum W.E.B. Du Bois.[58] "I am increasingly convinced," McKenzie said, "that fidelity to school and college youth requires unfailing and constant supervision."[59]

Black youth at Fisk were being held to a different standard from their white counterparts at other universities. On the other side of Nashville at Vanderbilt, white students enjoyed a student council, a campus newspaper, and a robust Greek system.[60] As elite white colleges trained their students to be freethinking intellectuals, Fisk obsessed over the notion that blacks might give themselves over to vice, laziness, or violence if they were not excessively punished for misbehavior. In fact, the college recruited donors based on that paranoia. "Fisk stands in the heart of the Great Black Belt facing this Crisis of the Black man," read a fundraising letter drafted during McKenzie's tenure, "striving to convert a National Menace into an Asset and a Blessing."[61] McKenzie's primary constituents were not his students; they were his donors. Seeking to appease them, he maintained the school's long-standing tradition of segregated seating for black and white audiences at public events.[62]

Students like Ed were not privy to McKenzie's dealings with donors, but they knew they were being treated unfairly. Their simmering frustration with McKenzie burst into public view in 1924, when W.E.B. Du Bois was invited to give a speech as part of the commencement activities. Du Bois was, at the peak of his fame and influence, and he had started paying more attention to his alma mater when his daughter Yolande enrolled. On visits to campus, he began hearing horror stories from students about their rights being trampled upon. And so in June, with Fayette McKenzie sitting in one of the front rows, and Ed, Anna, and Yolande likely peering down from the gallery, Fisk's most famous alum strode to the stage at the Memorial Chapel and took the school to task.[63] "I have never known an institution whose alumni on the whole are more bitter and disgusted with the present situation in this university than the alumni of Fisk University today," he said.

"You cannot surrender freedom and remain an institution of learning. You cannot have an institution of learning where there is no real chance at self expression," Du Bois continued. "With these things gone . . . a so-called institution of learning remains a farce and a lie.

"Is the present Fisk University the institution that it used to be?" he wondered. "And if it is not, what are we going to do about it?"[64]

A shocked McKenzie called the speech sneering and sarcastic.[65] But when students returned to campus in the fall, the groundswell of dissatisfaction fomented by Du Bois's words began to take more formal shape. Ed and Anna became leaders in a series of protests and petitions aimed at changing the school's policies.[66] Ed didn't like being forced to wash windows if he missed a meal in the cafeteria, or the fact that the baseball team had been disbanded against the will of the students.[67] But the issues went beyond day-to-day grievances. He saw plainly that there was a growing chasm between the needs of students and the goals of the institution's "controlling forces." Something had to be done.

Ed knew Anna had become friends with Du Bois's daughter, Yolande.[68] That might be what gave him the confidence to pen an article that he hoped Du Bois would publish in his alumni newsletter. "Ed Goodwin, brother of Anna," he scribbled across the top of a piece of wide-ruled paper, perhaps to ensure his missive wouldn't be tossed into a trash bin. Then he began in earnest:

Reasons Why We as Students Dislike Fisk

> *To begin with the above subject with our very preliminary discussion,*
> *I would say that we as students dislike Fisk for the following reasons:*
> *First, we as students feel that the element of oppression is being*
> *handed down upon us by the "Head" of the institution, i.e. we feel*
> *that the "Head" of Fisk practices autocracy; consequently we feel*
> *that there is no democracy. For this reason we feel that we as*
> *students are being oppressed.*

He listed eight issues in all, carefully outlining many of the complaints that had dogged McKenzie since the time he arrived on campus. "The heads of the institution are not willing for us to think and form our own opinion," Ed wrote. "We want to be treated as men and women, and not as children. . . . We feel the element of white supremacy."[69]

While Du Bois may have given the issues at Fisk a national spotlight, the students experienced life at the school every day. They would be the catalyst for any change.

A few months after Du Bois's address, a white professor stood on the same stage in the Memorial Chapel and told black students they would have to wait hundreds of years for equality. "I urge Fisk University to be patient with the frailties of the white race and to have faith in education," H. A. Miller, a sociology professor at Ohio State, said in a thinly veiled response to Du Bois. "It will take centuries to bring about race justice."[70]

It was Founders Day Weekend, and the Fisk board of trustees had descended on campus to celebrate the school's successful fundraising campaign. Fisk had just achieved its goal of building a $1 million endowment, with half the money coming directly from the General Education Board. (Nashville's white business leaders also chipped in $50,000, confident that McKenzie would continue to maintain "proper relations between the races.")[71] Students were expected to be on their best behavior, singing church hymns for white guests and accepting the handed-down wisdom of men like H. A. Miller. The scene was similar to the opening chapters of Oklahoma native Ralph Ellison's novel *Invisible Man*, where the titular character finds himself pandering to white megadonors at a fictional black college during their annual visit. "*You* are important," one donor tells the narrator, "because if you fail *I* have failed by one individual, one defective cog."[72]

An endless carousel of songs and speeches was planned for Founders Day, but Ed and other young Fiskites saw the weekend as an opportunity for protest rather than pageantry. Amid all the back-slapping, Fisk's leaders were set to have their regular board of trustees meeting. The student body elected fourteen of their peers, Ed and Anna both among them, to present their grievances to the trustees at the meeting.[73]

Facing the board must have been nerve-wracking—the group included the son of one of the school's founders and an executive at the investment bank Goldman Sachs.[74] But the students were resolute in their demands. Their eleven grievances were the same issues students had been concerned about for years: no student government, no student newspaper, no way to dispute unfair punishments doled out by faculty. This time, though, the list came with an ultimatum. "Give us the milk of human kindness and we shall never bite the maternal breast," the students wrote. "Feed us the venom of distrust—our very KISSES shall be poison."[75]

While the trustees were willing to concede to some student demands, McKenzie hardly budged. On February 4, 1925, at a speech to students in Livingstone Hall, he doubled down on Fisk's harsh policies, arguing that discipline was necessary to control the students.[76]

Late that night, around one hundred male students left their dorm rooms and descended on the chapel in Livingstone Hall. They smashed furniture and shattered windows.[77] Then they began marching toward the athletic field, banging on pans in the cool night air. Their song echoed across campus.

"Before I'd be a slave, I'd be buried in my grave!"[78]

The New Negro had fully arrived at Fisk.

Within about an hour, the protest petered out, and the students began to march back to their dorms for bed. But McKenzie, incensed at the most blatant challenge to his authority yet, called for more police. Newspapers would later report the students fired gunshots, but the students claimed it was actually a pair of police officers on motorcycles who fired at them.[79]

After midnight, at least fifty officers armed with riot guns swarmed the men's dormitory, bursting down doors and pointing weapons in students' faces. Two students said they were clubbed in the resultant chaos.[80] The police's riot team apprehended five students who McKenzie claimed were ringleaders of the protest. In a dark echo of what had happened in Greenwood, Ed Goodwin found himself being marched out of his home under the armed control of white law enforcement.[81]

Ed and the other young men were taken to the local jail and detained overnight. The next afternoon a hearing was held at the courthouse, where the five students stood accused of inciting a riot.[82] McKenzie seemed intent on making them examples. "Open rebellion and public riot cannot be the agency for the redress of grievances," he said in a statement to the *Nashville Banner*.[83] He also pulled dozens of other students into his office and demanded that they either sign a document condemning the protest or withdraw from school and leave Nashville.[84]

At the hearing, though, it became clear that McKenzie did not have concrete evidence proving Ed Goodwin and the others had actually led the protest, let alone incited a riot. He had simply targeted the activist students who had been agitating for change all year.[85] The charges were eventually dropped,[86] but the repercussions were not over. On February 5, Ed Goodwin and three of the other students were suspended from Fisk University indefinitely.[87]

Ed, though, wasn't finished fighting. That day he sent an urgent telegram home to his father, J.H. "No evidence on his side," Ed wrote of McKenzie. "City of Nashville behind us. Students are packing, ready to leave at any moment."[88]

The protest at Fisk was not the climax of years of student frustration. It was the beginning of a movement. Two days after the protest, four hundred students marched out of a morning chapel meeting, refusing to go to lessons until Ed and his suspended classmates were reinstated.[89] Many threatened to transfer to Howard University in Washington, D.C.[90] At a community rally featuring the suspended students, a crowd of more than a thousand black Nashville residents demanded the president be removed.[91]

Du Bois, living in New York at the time, doubted the accounts of the controversy he was reading in the white press. He had been corresponding with leaders of the protest throughout the school year, and more missives poured into his office after their arrest.[92] He soon took the battle to the pages of his *Crisis* magazine, calling for McKenzie's ouster. "Shall we surrender all control over the education of our children to those who despise Negroes and seek to hold them down by caste, or shall we drive this man and his methods from Fisk?" he asked in a biting essay. "Do the benefactors of Negro education want their money used to humiliate and degrade us or to make us men?"[93]

McKenzie refused to back down. He had the full support of Nashville's white business interests,[94] and the board of trustees said they supported his "unflinching stand for law and order." A subset of the black community also backed him, with a local black doctor dismissing the student protesters as arrogant "smart alecks."[95]

But the students were not swayed. At the start of March, nearly half of Fisk's students were still not reporting to class.[96] Jeanne Osby was among them. Though she was a regular babysitter for McKenzie's children, she said later that she couldn't abide the way he was treating his black students. She went to McKenzie's home and told him directly that she too was leaving.[97]

The racial harmony that Fisk had projected to wealthy white outsiders was shattered, and the students remained in open revolt. In April, with roughly a third of the student body still gone, Fayette McKenzie resigned as president of Fisk.[98]

In the *Crisis,* Du Bois praised the student leaders who had galvanized the campus toward action—first at the trustees' meeting, then with the nighttime protest, and finally with the large-scale walkout. He put photos of six of the young men in his magazine, referring to them as "Martyrs at Fisk." Peering directly at the camera, with wide-open eyes and a stoic face, was Ed Goodwin.

"I thank God the younger generation of black students have the guts to yell and fight when their noses are rubbed in the mud," Du Bois wrote. "At last we have real radicalism of the young—radicalism that costs, that is not mere words and foam. . . . Here is the real radical, the man who hits power in high places, white power, power backed by unlimited wealth; hits it and hits it openly between the eyes.

"The fight at Fisk," Du Bois concluded, "is a fateful step in the development of the American Negro."[99]

Ed was eventually reinstated at Fisk. He, Anna, and Jeanne all graduated in 1926, a year after the fallout from the protest had settled.[100] The General Education Board temporarily withheld its endowment pledge after McKenzie's ouster, a behind-the-scenes rebuke of student activism.[101] But under new presidential leadership, student life began to change. The school newspaper was revived, and fraternities and sororities were finally allowed.[102] Jeanne became one of the five founding members of the campus chapter of Delta Sigma Theta. She'd remain a devoted Delta for the rest of her life.[103]

After leaving college, Jeanne journeyed to Georgia to work at the Atlanta School of Social Work under the famed young sociologist E. Franklin Frazier. There she lived in the Sweet Auburn neighborhood, just a few doors down from the birthplace of Martin Luther King, Jr.[104] "Everything is new to me and some things seem strange," she wrote to her father James just after moving. "I have had absolutely no contact with white people yet."[105] Though she had majored in sociology at Fisk, she soon found that teaching was her true calling.

Ed, meanwhile, took his economics degree to St. Louis, where he decided to try running a business for the first time, a shoe store on Market Street.[106] He and Jeanne had dated off and on in college—he sang to her beneath her window at Jubilee Hall—but between the chaos of the protests and careers that took them in opposite directions after Fisk, they'd never forged a permanent connection. Jeanne's parents, by then firmly in the black upper crust in Springfield, didn't like the rabble-rouser who caused so much of an uproar while Jeanne was in school. She became engaged to another man, a classmate from New Orleans.[107]

Ed, though, tended to get what he wanted.

The finer details of Ed and Jeanne's courtship took on the haze of mythology over the years, but one of their children later told of Ed journeying to Springfield, grabbing Jeanne by the hand, and taking her all the way to Missouri, so they could elope.[108] He was theatrical and, when he wanted to be, more than a little manipulative. "I induced her and inveighed her into marrying me," Ed said simply of their courtship, "and she did."[109]

Jeanne saw his persistence, mostly, as a strength. She said he had a "football personality"—always barreling toward the goalpost. "Although our backgrounds were somewhat different, Ed and I grew up in a dog-eat-dog world," she reflected later. "I think this is one reason he couldn't stand the thought of any of his children being what he considered second rate or deprived."[110]

Edward Lawrence Goodwin and Jeanne Belle Osby were married on September 3, 1927, at the courthouse in Clayton, Missouri, the county seat on the outskirts of St. Louis.[111] Neither of them had a family member within a hundred miles of the place where they pledged themselves to each other forever. The couple could have built a new world for themselves there in St. Louis, or in Springfield, or in Atlanta. There were countless American cities they'd learned so much about, while fighting for equality with all the bright minds at Fisk. But despite the dark memories that lurked back in Oklahoma, Ed wanted to return to Tulsa.

Though Greenwood had suffered bruises, it was still a young community—younger than Ed, even. After the catastrophe, the neighborhood and its people insisted on redefining themselves on their own terms. The most powerful white men in America, the ones who controlled the purse strings of places like Fisk, believed that black people's disposition to "go it alone" was a "menace to the public welfare." But Greenwood defied their dictums. What the community began rebuilding in June 1921—and would continue to build for decades—was a place where self-sufficiency was valued but community support was also indispensable. Where direct political power was circumscribed by the walls of Jim Crow and so had to be seized through other avenues—the newspaper front page, the church pulpit, even the gambling hall. Where entrepreneurship—the thing that would always be bound up in the mythos of Black Wall Street—was about independence from white control more than about profit, and the ability to leave a meaningful legacy for one's children. "Scars are there, but the city is impudent and noisy," Du Bois said after one postmassacre visit. "It believes in itself."[112] Those scars would never go away—not in a city where white leaders refused to offer even the mildest balm—but Greenwood's story wasn't over. It was just beginning.

CHAPTER 10

THE MYTH OF AN IMPERVIOUS PEOPLE

*A young girl holds her baby brother
during the rebuilding of Greenwood.*

After the massacre, Loula Williams quickly regained her signature confidence, at least as far as the outside world could tell. The new and improved Dreamland featured modern electrical light fixtures and the latest box-office hits from the Fox Film Corporation.[1] The Williams Building was back, too, once again the tallest building in Deep Greenwood. Willie was sent off to school at Hampton Institute, a well-regarded college for black students in Virginia, while Loula planned more theater renovations and a new balcony for 1924.[2] In a memo to her customers, she promised high-class films, courteous treatment, and a state-of-the-art viewing experience. The *Cleopatra* opening back in the Dreamland's early years would be a trifle compared to what she had in mind. "We court constructive criticism; we welcome suggestions," she wrote in her announcement. "We ask your patronage of a Race enterprise not because of its identity but because of its service."[3]

Despite the outward appearance of normalcy, nothing had really gone right for Loula since the white mob chased her out of her home. The aggressive reopening timeline of the Dreamland threw the family deep into debt. The loan they secured from the Supreme Camp of American Woodmen, the black fraternal organization, was a vital lifeline, but it still had to be repaid within three years at 6 percent interest.[4] Loula and John borrowed another $6,000 from local white real estate men who charged 10 percent.[5] Many of their neighbors were paying rates as high as 20 percent.[6] Even if Tulsa's white businessmen couldn't buy up Greenwood outright, they found methods to profit off the neighborhood's misfortune, one way or another.

The Dreamland Theatre under reconstruction following the massacre

Williams Enterprises became tougher and tougher to manage. The theater the family owned in Muskogee was seized when they fell behind on rental payments.[7] At their Okmulgee location, they stopped paying property taxes.[8] With their debt ballooning, Loula and John scaled back their ambitions and focused on staying financially afloat in Greenwood. The vision of operating a nebula of Dreamlands was over.

Meanwhile, Loula no longer felt quite like herself. The problem was hard to articulate at first—a little more trouble remembering last month's financials, perhaps, or a tighter grip on the railing when walking up the stairs. Unusual ailments for a woman in her early forties. Dr. Joseph J. McKeever, her brother-in-law, observed the changes first, just three months after the massacre. "I noticed it as early as September '21," he said later. "[She's] been gradually going down since that time."[9]

In private, Loula exchanged frequent, weary letters with her son Willie while he was away at college. Mostly they talked about money. "We are all doing nicely, having some good shows and good pictures," she wrote in a letter around Christmas 1923. "I owe all the help back salary."[10]

Business was no better at her confectionery. "We are not making a thing in the store," she warned the next month. She had just agreed to cut the rent of Lucille Travis, daughter of J. H. and Carlie Goodwin, who owned a struggling hat store in the Dreamland building. "The whole town has a slump," Loula wrote.[11]

The slump never let up. Loula lost an employee to the rival Dixie Theater across the street.[12] She spent more hours manning the confectionery since it was harder to afford staff.[13] Before 1921, she had cherished sitting in the back of the Dreamland and seeing the joy her movies brought to her patrons; after 1921, she stood outside in the cold taking tickets.[14] "I am too proud to ask anybody to help, thinking business would get better," she wrote to Willie. "Your mother is trying to stay up until you get here. Then I will have rest."[15]

Willie felt his own financial strains at Hampton, where tuition and housing were nearly $300 per year.[16] While playing two sports and keeping up his grades, he also found jobs as a waiter at a white country club and as a steward on the SS *Cherokee*, a luxury steamship that traveled along the East Coast.[17] Still, money was tight. "I was put in an awful fix trying to graduate this year because money is the biggest thing that one needs around here," he wrote to Loula. "Only forty more dollars and I shall ask for no more. I have borrowed the rest."[18]

"You know I love you dearly," she responded. "I wish I had money to send you."[19]

Loula wanted to instill in Willie the boundless ambition she had felt in her early years in Greenwood, when the *Tulsa Star* celebrated her as "the foremost business woman of the state."[20] But with each letter to her son, the reality of her financial troubles crept closer to the center of their conversations.

"I'm doing fine, doing just like every body is that's paying nothing on my debts," she wrote in January 1924. "I hope we will all pick up."[21]

And in February: "I came through school hard up, never did I think you would have to come up that way."[22]

With each letter that arrived from Tulsa, Willie noticed that his mother's handwriting was getting less and less legible. In the fall of 1924, he took time off from school to come care for Loula and help out with the family businesses.[23] The financial pressures on Williams Enterprises were growing more relentless. In 1925 the Williamses took out an $18,000 loan with the Tulsa Building and Loan Association, requiring a $262 monthly mortgage.[24] They hardly had the money to pay it. Each month at least $100 of the rent they collected from their tenants was already going to a separate group of lenders.[25] With money so tight, it was getting harder to keep up with repairs at the theater and compete with the Dixie.[26] "My business hasn't gone down from that house across the street in five or six years," bragged William Redfearn, the Dixie's white owner.[27]

Every day, Loula found it a little bit harder to focus. She used to spend hours poring over every aspect of her business, engaging with customers, and feeling pride in her family enterprise. But the days grew dimmer. Her grip on the past was fading. Her mind became a cursed sieve as her memories slowly leaked out of it. "She was an excellent business woman," Dr. McKeever said. "But now she is physically and mentally weak. Nervous. Walks with great effort."[28] In 1924, the year she had planned for her triumphant comeback, Loula Williams stopped managing the Dreamland Theatre.[29]

"I am just tired out," she wrote to Willie. "Let me go off and rest."[30]

A jubilant procession marched past the Dreamland, stretching for a mile down Greenwood Avenue.[31] Cowboys sauntered through the streets on horses, military units marched in formation with rifles slung over their shoulders, and cars were covered hood to bumper in colorful flowers.[32] Miss Oklahoma and her regal court waved to a crowd of onlookers on an elaborate float drawn by a team of four horses.[33] Behind them came the boom of bass drums from the twenty-six-piece band of the Tenth Cavalry, a battalion descended from the famed Buffalo Soldiers.[34] American banners hung from flagpoles and car windows, as Greenwood's residents celebrated their return to the national stage.[35] The "Negro's Wall Street," as Mary Jones Parrish had once called it, was back.

For the first time ever, in August 1925, the annual National Negro Business League conference was being held in Tulsa.[36] Greenwood leaders wanted to prove that their neighborhood had fully recovered from its destruction, so planning for the event became a massive team effort. J. H. Goodwin, who had been active in the league ever since arriving in Oklahoma, continued to serve as an officer. He was joined by B. C. Franklin, the attorney who had defended black Tulsans' property rights, and Dimple Bush, the league's first female vice president. Theodore Baughman, the editor of the *Oklahoma Eagle,* became the league's chief publicist, reprising A. J. Smitherman's role as a major booster.[37] A.G.W. Sango, the Creek freedman who had helped recruit J.H. to Oklahoma, had recently moved from Muskogee to Tulsa as well, as clear a sign as any that the center of gravity in the state's black economy had shifted to Greenwood.[38] Naturally, he served as chairman of the entertainment committee.[39]

The week of festivities was a spectacle. In addition to recruiting the Tenth Cavalry Band, J.H. and Sango organized a series of Negro League baseball games between the Chicago American Giants and the Kansas City Monarchs.[40] James and Henry Nails, who owned a shoe shop and record store on Greenwood Avenue, hosted a dance party for all the new visitors at their Nails Brothers Pavilion.[41] Newcomers to Tulsa, some of whom had been nervous about setting foot in the town, couldn't help but be impressed. "[On] the main business thoroughfare of the colored section, are pool rooms, barbecue stands, drug stores, theaters, garages, news-stands," reported Albon Holsey, the executive secretary for the Negro Business League. "And one orange juice booth where the delicious fruit juice is served by an attractive colored girl in uniform."[42]

For many visitors the highlight of the trip was a joyride in the airplane owned by Simon Berry, Greenwood's informal transportation czar.[43] Since arriving in Tulsa in 1915, he'd worked his way up from driving a cab to later operating a rollicking jitney service with a fleet of Model-Ts and finally owning a bus line by the mid-1920s.[44] His latest venture was a charter flight service.[45] He took league members on aerial tours of Tulsa in his dual-cockpit plane, soaring over the newly built Mayo Hotel and the reconstructed brick buildings of Deep Greenwood. He gained mastery of the same machinery the white mob had used to terrorize his people.

Tulsa's white leaders also made a pointed effort to put on a good show. Many of them attended the Business League meeting's opening ceremony at Convention Hall, the same location that had served as a detention camp during the massacre.[46] Tulsa mayor Herman Newblock, a former city commissioner who had approved the fire ordinance that nearly prevented Greenwood's reconstruction, was one of the event's keynote speakers.[47] He was also later identified as a member of the Ku Klux Klan, but when well-to-do outsiders poured into town, he preached the gospel of racial harmony. "There will never be any more racial friction in Tulsa," he assured black visitors.[48]

In a special booster edition of the *Oklahoma Eagle*, Theodore Baughman effusively praised Mayor Newblock, as well as the new county sheriff and county attorney.[49] A large man who was part black and part German, Baughman was known to avoid controversy when he could help it—he preferred to pen articles that reflected "credit upon the race," his staff later wrote.[50] In the *Eagle*'s special edition, the destruction of Greenwood was barely mentioned, referenced obliquely as "the trouble here."[51] The focus was on the bright future to come. "No law abiding citizen, regardless of color, need fear to come to Tulsa," the newspaper wrote, "as you will find the best of feeling existing between races."[52]

The Business League attendees danced and laughed and ate long into the night. It was almost as if the massacre had not happened at all.

When black people in Oklahoma got sick—the kind of sick that medicine couldn't solve—they were often sent to Dr. H. W. Conrad's Park

Sanitarium.[53] Situated next to the Cottonwood River in Guthrie, Oklahoma, the facility mixed natural remedies with the recuperative benefits of the outdoors. The sanitarium had the capacity to treat roughly forty patients for ailments such as rheumatism, insomnia, and neurasthenia, a vaguely defined condition characterized by fatigue and depression.[54] If the local emergency room was for sudden physical traumas of the body, Dr. Conrad's Park was for those injuries that burrowed deep into the soul. It was there, in the lonely woods of Guthrie, that theater magnate Loula Williams spent much of 1925.[55]

No one knew how to help Loula. Her husband John had placed her in the Guthrie sanitarium, which brought the family another bill of $25 per week.[56] But the facility's signature remedies, mineral water and therapeutic Turkish baths, did nothing for her.[57] Soon another relative, a physician in Jefferson, Texas, took her in for several months, but he could find no effective treatment either.[58] In 1926 Loula returned to Greenwood and moved in with her sister and brother-in-law, Myrtle and Joseph J. McKeever. She tried to stay abreast of the business, but she could no longer hold a conversation that lasted even three minutes.[59] "She thinks about what she used to do, but she can't talk any business straight along," her husband John said. "She can't talk anything straight along."[60]

The bank neither knew nor cared about Loula's troubles; the mortgage was still due every month. Growing increasingly desperate, John entered into an agreement to sell a half-stake of the Dreamland to J. W. Cotter, a white former Warner Bros. employee who was buying up movie theaters across the state.[61] In exchange, Cotter agreed to take on the Dreamland's daily operations and pay off its debts, including the monthly mortgage. After signing the agreement, the Williams family were allowed to use only two upstairs apartments in the building they themselves had erected in 1914.[62]

The arrangement only mired the Williamses further in debt. Cotter initially honored the contract and paid the monthly mortgage,[63] but he seemed uninterested in protecting the Dreamland's long-term future. Within seven months, he offloaded the Dreamland to a white couple, Charles and Helen Deal.[64] The Deals refused to make the mortgage payments.[65] John often approached Charles Deal at the theater, demanding that he keep up his end of the agreement, and Deal always assured him that he'd make the delinquent payments soon.[66] But that day never came. "Not a dime, not a penny or anything" was paid toward the Dreamland's outstanding debt, John said.[67]

In April 1927, John and Loula sued the Deals and the Cotters in hopes of reclaiming ownership of their family business. The case dragged on for years. One of the leading lawyers for the Deals, Wash Hudson, was a former state senator and a leader of the Ku Klux Klan.[68] The initial trial judge was yet another Klan member, who issued an order requiring the Williams family to pay the Deals more than $7,000 to proceed with the case. (The order was later vacated.)[69] The Oklahoma Supreme Court eventually upheld a ruling that the Deals had violated their contract, but the Williamses were still required to pay more than $3,000 in reimbursements to them.[70] "The effect of the judgments and of its affirmation is to reward a man for his wrongs," the Williamses' attorney argued.[71] The family got their property back, but only after years lost to courtroom litigation and untold dollars eaten up by lawyer fees. The mortgage was still far from being paid off. The Dreamland would ultimately fall into foreclosure, be seized by the sheriff's office, and be sold to white people in the 1930s.[72]

Loula likely knew little of the legal proceedings. By the time of the lawsuit, she could barely walk across a room; she had almost no memory of the time before the massacre.[73] Her mind had fractured into a thousand shards.

What she did recall with eerie regularity was a set of rings she believed she had lost. They became a fixation. Several times a day she would start searching frantically for her jewelry, sure that her home had been robbed. Then Dr. McKeever would gingerly tell her the rings were right there on her fingers. Relief would wash over her. But soon enough McKeever's words would slip through the cursed sieve. Her feelings of safety and protection would dissolve. The rings would be lost again, as the mob pillaged Loula Williams's mind once more.[74]

⸻

Greenwood carried the triumphs of the Business League and the burdens of Loula Williams at the same time—during the same celebratory weekend, in fact. But leaders both black and white were interested in highlighting only one type of experience. "We are indestructible," a *Chicago Defender* columnist boasted during the Business League meeting. "We say to Tulsa white people and white people throughout the world that we will not be crushed!"[75] Even before the meeting was over, the unyielding resilience of Greenwood was being celebrated and mythologized. It was a common refrain of the era, and of later ones, as black people tried to excise past horrors from their minds, to cauterize the deepest wounds before they could become infected and cover the resultant scars with glittering, impenetrable armor. But the idea that Greenwood was impervious—to fire, to violence, to racism—was never the whole story.

The survivors had to pour all their energy into rebuilding because white city leaders were so eager to seize black land. That focus robbed residents of the space and time to process the horrors they had witnessed. For the rest of her life, Mabel Little would recall her husband Pressley on the verge of tears the day after the massacre. As they faced an unknown future, Mabel had told him not to worry. "I promise I won't," he responded. But he didn't look at her when he said it.

"He grieved our loss to such a degree, I could never quite understand it," Mabel reflected later. "He just couldn't seem to snap out of it."[76]

Pressley had owned a shoe shop and a restaurant before the massacre, both of which were destroyed.[77] In need of more money afterward, he was forced to become a day laborer for at least three years, cleaning up debris in his destroyed neighborhood and later taking on construction jobs. The dirty, exhausting labor made him vulnerable to the flu. The flu turned into tuberculosis. "You could see the terror and misery in his eyes as they slowly began to sink into their sockets," Mabel recalled. After years of being bedridden at home, he too was placed in a sanitarium, this one in Clinton, Oklahoma, nearly two hundred miles from Tulsa. Suddenly Mabel was juggling the costs of Pressley's medical care and her own living expenses, as she trekked across the state as often as she could to care for the man she loved most in the world. About three months after he went to the sanitarium, Pressley Little died in 1927. He was thirty-three years old.[78]

"In every block of Greenwood today," the local social worker Francis Burke observed in the 1930s, "some family can be found who lost a son or father in the race riot."[79] But a shroud of silence was already being pulled over the massacre, casting it as a shadowy aberration that had no long-term effects.

For white Tulsans, the incentive for this kind of historical erasure was obvious. Tulsa was angling to grow into one of America's great cities, and the stigma associated with mob lawlessness did civic and business leaders no favors. While Greenwood lay in ruins, police issued an order banning photographs of the burned-out district, fearing that the images would be used as "propaganda" by black journalists.[80] The local white press covered the aftermath of the massacre intensely for about a year, then began scrubbing the event from their own institutional memories. In 1923, when Greenwood property owners filed roughly 125 massacre lawsuits against the city of Tulsa in a single week, the *Tribune* did not consider it news.[81]

A group of Klansmen hoist an American flag. Tulsa County sheriff William McCullough is present.

Some of the leaders who stifled the massacre's memory were members of the Ku Klux Klan,[82] which exploded in popularity in Tulsa after the burning of Greenwood. In an August 1921 speech at Convention Hall, Caleb Ridley, the national chaplain for the Klan, declared that "every Klansman is ready to fight" to stop racial equality. Twenty-five hundred white Tulsans attended the event.[83] The group also built a three-thousand-seat auditorium just west of Greenwood on property owned by Klan member Tate Brady. The facility was known as Beno Hall, a reference to a Klan business front called the

Tulsa Benevolent Association. But the name's other meaning was well known in all corners of town: "Be no Catholic, be no nigger, be no Jew."[84]

For black people, the treatment of the massacre was more complex. Tulsa's racist reputation hurt them as well as whites. "Negroes from Tulsa traveling elsewhere or abroad were taunted and ridiculed about what had taken place," attorney B. C. Franklin recalled in his autobiography. "People everywhere of all races thought Tulsa was an unsafe place in which to locate and do business."[85] Those who had stayed, rebuilt, and hoped to keep growing their enterprises had an incentive to downplay the racial hostility present in the city. It wasn't only Baughman and the *Oklahoma Eagle* that did so—Roscoe Dunjee's *Black Dispatch* in Oklahoma City touted the state's "liberal atmosphere of freedom and tolerance" even as it published harrowing images of the burned-out Greenwood district in the very same issue.[86]

The minimizing of the massacre was not merely an economic calculation. In 1925 black Americans had just survived a yearslong, nationwide wave of white supremacist violence, suffering hundreds of deaths in the process. Entire communities had been wiped off the map. In 1923 a small black enclave in central Florida called Rosewood was burned to the ground after a white woman in a nearby town claimed an escaped black convict attempted to rape her. Over the course of a week, a white mob of about one hundred destroyed most of the homes in the 120-person town and killed at least six people. The lynching of one black man, witnessed by dozens of onlookers and the county deputy sheriff, was ruled by the coroner as "death by unknown hands." After the killing and burning was over, a grand jury returned no indictments.[87]

Because of horrors like the destruction of Greenwood and Rosewood, black people of the era realized they had no recourse in the face of white violence—courts rationalized the killings away, the federal government ignored calls for anti-lynching legislation, and local police were often in on the act. With the Klan at the peak of its political power, a truce with white people—even one that delayed civil rights victories for a generation more—might have felt necessary to ensure black residents' safety. Robert Moton, the successor to Booker T. Washington as president of both Tuskegee and the Negro Business League, emphasized the point during his speech in Tulsa. "The intelligent negroes are not agitating for so-called social equality," Moton said. "White people and members of our race have their own social spheres within which they must restrict themselves if they are to live in the same communities harmoniously."[88]

On a personal level, people feared not only what a Klansman might do in the dead of night if word of the massacre were uttered, but how their own souls might fracture if they allowed themselves to think too long on it. "I never have been angry . . . 'cause nothing you can do about it," Mabel Little said decades later. "If I would have had a bad feeling I believe I would have gone nuts. Just crazy. Because I couldn't have turned it loose."[89]

One survivor dived directly into documenting the massacre and its traumatic aftermath, well aware that what she had survived was of historical significance. On the night of May 31, 1921, Mary Jones Parrish had lingered in her apartment even as the fires began to rage because she was "seized with an uncontrollable desire to see the outcome of the fray."[90] A few days later she was approached by a black leader of the Inter-Racial Commission, the group that had held a conference on racial cooperation at the state capitol in 1920. The commission wanted her to interview other survivors and compile their testimonials.[91] Parrish spent weeks collecting first-person accounts from about twenty massacre survivors, including J. C. Latimer and Dimple Bush.[92] The work was gut-wrenching but, in its own way, therapeutic. "It helped me to forget my trouble in sympathy for the people with whom I daily came in contact," she wrote.[93]

Parrish published her interviews, along with her own harrowing firsthand account, in a book called *Events of the Tulsa Disaster.* Greenwood residents raised $900 to help cover the printing costs.[94] Published around 1923, the book was no bestseller—according to one source, fewer than two dozen copies were initially distributed.[95] But the reporting Parrish had assembled was invaluable. She and her subjects captured every major phase of the attack and challenged some of the city's prevailing narratives about what had happened. Her book cited witnesses who saw men with rifles climb aboard aircraft and fire down on Greenwood residents, while police insisted that the planes were used only for reconnaissance.[96] Parrish recognized that the violence in Tulsa fit a broad pattern, and she connected it to the Red Summer attacks on black communities in Chicago and

Washington, D.C.[97] Her work placed her in the tradition of other pioneering black female journalists, including Ida B. Wells, who exposed the scourge of lynching, and Mary Church Terrell, who criticized the convict-lease system prevalent in the Deep South. "Just as this horde of evil men swept down on the Colored section of Tulsa," Parrish predicted, "so will they, some future day, sweep down on the homes and business places of their own race."

With a striking fire-alarm-red cover, *Events of the Tulsa Disaster* stood out on any bookshelf. But the book was greeted with little fanfare and was ignored in the local white press. Parrish, perhaps disillusioned by the city's unwillingness to reckon with what had happened, left Tulsa for Muskogee around the time of the book's release.[98] Her work, however, long outlived her as the first and most visceral longform account of how Greenwood residents experienced their community's destruction. It would become a crucial primary source in later decades as the massacre became more widely remembered and analyzed.

Though Greenwood residents suffered many slow-rolling tragedies in the years after the massacre, the 1925 Negro Business League meeting brought its own shocking act of violence that compounded those troubles. It struck the Goodwin family in particular with the force of an earthquake.

Lucille Travis, J.H. and Carlie's eldest daughter, attended formals and traveled with ease through the social circles of high black society.[99] She had also picked up her father's entrepreneurial habit early, working as a clerk at his grocery store during her summers home from Fisk in the 1910s.[100] Though she married Plato Travis, a prominent dentist and war veteran, she remained an independent woman. She spent much of her time at her Parisienne Hat Shop inside the Dreamland building and made a point of retaining the G—for Goodwin—in her business name.[101]

As the Negro Business League meeting was wrapping up, a friend of Lucille's named Carrie Person, the future musical director for Booker T. Washington High School, hosted a party at her apartment on Greenwood Avenue. Black entrepreneurs from around the country gathered to relax and reflect on the successful week in Tulsa.[102]

At some point, Plato Travis called, asking after Lucille.[103] The couple, like everyone else in Greenwood, had weathered a stressful few years. Their $5,000 residence had been destroyed during the massacre, as had Travis's dental office in Deep Greenwood.[104] They got nothing from their lawsuit and were forced to live with Lucille's parents for years following the attack.[105] It was hardly the future they'd envisioned for themselves when they wed during World War I. By the time of the Business League meeting, the couple had been estranged for several months, according to Travis, and Lucille was planning to file for divorce.[106] Unable to protect his house, his business, or his community, Travis may have been trying to assert his masculine dominance over the one thing in the world he still felt he had a right to possess: his wife.

After calling Lucille, Travis walked over to the party. When he arrived, he said he saw Lucille sitting next to another man who he had "warned her" not to associate with.[107] He became incensed and demanded that Lucille come outside. Witnesses said he was bleary-eyed and drunk. "I was insanely jealous," Travis later admitted.[108]

Finally, Lucille relented. When they walked into the hallway, Plato Travis pulled out a gun. He shot his wife four times and, in a moment of bracing clarity over the horror of what he had done, turned the gun on himself next.

Lucille Travis, née Goodwin, died hours later at Maurice Willows Hospital. Travis suffered only a flesh wound.[109]

The grisly killing was front-page news as far away as Chicago.[110] The fact that Lucille was young, well-heeled, light-skinned—a "prominent society woman," as one article put it—attracted morbid curiosity about her misfortune.[111] Accounts of the shooting differed, but all of them placed other Goodwin women shockingly close to the violence. An article in the *Chicago Defender* said that Anna Goodwin had been with her older sister just before she was killed.[112] During court proceedings, Carlie Goodwin testified that she had been walking over to the party and watched the murder with her own eyes.[113]

Plato Travis was quickly convicted of first-degree murder and sentenced to life in prison. A plea of insanity—he attributed his brutal murder of his wife to a "temporary brainstorm"—saved him from the electric chair.[114] By the early 1940s, though, he was out on parole and back in Greenwood.[115] He returned to the property where he and

Lucille had lived when they were first married, just down the street from the Goodwin family home.[116] In the coming years, Ed Goodwin's children would see him when they roamed the neighborhood.

"When you get to that white house, you cross the street," Ed warned his kids.

"We never knew why we had to do that," Jo Ann Gilford, Ed's second-oldest daughter, recalled decades later. "I didn't find out until I was grown that my aunt had been murdered."[117]

Greenwood was a community with a proud history, but it was also one with closely held secrets. To many people, the violent disruptions that had shaped the neighborhood's landscape were best kept quiet. The people who had lived through Greenwood's darkest times did not want to pass that burden on to their children. They did not want to make rage and trauma an inheritance. "We were a family that lived through tragedy," Jo Ann reflected later, "but in a humble way. We accepted tragedy as we did success."[118]

And yet the elders all seemed to know that a time would come to tell the entire truth, when the world would be ready for it. And so Ed Goodwin explained, in his own time, why he never wanted his children going anywhere near Plato Travis. The Goodwin family kept a copy of Mary Jones Parrish's little red book in a small cabinet under lock and key, dug out on occasion as evidence of what had happened to them in 1921.[119] Willie Williams held on to his mother's letters for the rest of his long life.

On September 13, 1927, Willie was working once again on a steamship, this time aboard the SS *Mohawk*.[120] The crew was docked in New York, and he'd soon be returning to Hampton to begin his senior year. He had been named captain of the football team, just like back at Booker T.[121]

At 10:42 p.m., he received an urgent telegram from Aunt Myrtle and Uncle Joseph McKeever in Tulsa. "Your mother passed away Tuesday afternoon. She took suddenly ill Sunday morning. Wire us when to expect you. Our hearts go out to you in sadness."[122]

Loula Williams died at Tulsa's St. John's Hospital after a six-year struggle with physical and mental illness. John had done his best to keep the devastating details of her decline from their only son—and for a time, from the entire community—but her death sent Greenwood into mourning. The impacts of 1921 could no longer be ignored. "The passing of Mrs. Loula T. Williams . . . removes from our ranks one of the most ambitious women we had," the *Oklahoma Eagle* reported in a long, despairing obituary. "Since the riot here, she has been sick, and death ultimately relieved her of her sufferings this week."[123]

While the *Eagle* had been careful to avoid even naming the massacre while promoting the Business League, the obituary laid the blame for her death squarely where it belonged. "After years of toil and sacrificing, and seeing it all destroyed in the twinkling of an eye, so to speak, it greatly affected her and hastened her to her grave."[124]

Willie, who went by W.D. after he left school, spoke openly about his own memories of the massacre, but he never said much publicly about Loula's death. "I don't feel unduly bitter," he revealed decades later, "but it left a heck of an impression on my mother who died in 1927 at the age of 47."[125]

With his mother gone so young, W.D. became an avid chronicler of his family history. He kept the *Eagle* obituary and the telegram announcing Loula's death in a scrapbook documenting his time in college, paged between football scores and old cruise line ID cards[126]—the

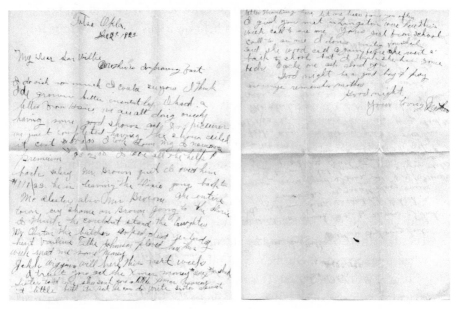

A letter from Loula Williams to W. D. Williams, 1923

triumphs and tragedies of a young life unspooling like a reel loaded into a film projector.

The scrapbook was eventually donated by his daughter to the Smithsonian Institution.[127] But the family held on to some of Loula's letters.[128] W.D. cherished those last vestiges of her—the real her—that he found in all those missives that he and his mother had exchanged. Behind the anxious musings and the wandering sentences and, eventually, the drooping script, there was ambition and tenacity and love. And it was those words he wanted to share with his children, and their children, and on and on, so that generations could know the owner of the Dreamland Theatre as he had known her—not as a symbol but as a woman striving to improve her lot and live in a dishonest world with a bit of dignity.

"Do your best," Loula instructed her son.

"Try to help yourself all you can."

"And pray always remember mother."[129]

CHAPTER 11

SUGAR MAN

Ed Goodwin, Sr., in his first haberdashery on Greenwood Avenue in the 1930s

E d Goodwin enjoyed making money almost as much as he liked spending it. While living in St. Louis, he once lost $1,200 during a heady night playing craps. The next morning he sold off his entire shoe store's inventory to a salesman for several thousand dollars, then spent every cent of his windfall on freewheeling indulgences that included a jaunt to New York City. "I was a single man at the time," he said later, "playing and having a lot of fun."[1]

Marrying Jeanne Osby steadied him. Not long after tying the knot in 1927, the couple moved to Tulsa and lived with Ed's parents at the new family home on Haskell Street, just steps away from the house where he'd grown up.[2] Ed entered their relationship with traditional views about matrimony: he would bring home the money, she would raise the children and take them to church every Sunday.[3] But Jeanne had other ambitions as well. "I was restless," she said later. "There was nothing to do but housework and that didn't suit me very well."[4] When Ed declined to take a job offer as a teacher, Jeanne applied for the role instead.[5]

Jeanne worked at the elementary school adjoining Booker T. Washington High School, a block and a half from her new home.[6] She taught lessons that went far beyond any board-issued curriculum. Each morning her young pupils recited both the Pledge of Allegiance and "Lift Every Voice and Sing," widely known then as the Negro National Anthem. They learned black history alongside the standard American history in their schoolbooks. When a young educator named Lorenzo Greene visited Greenwood on behalf of the famed black historian Carter G. Woodson, Jeanne invited him to speak to one of her classes about African mythology. He was impressed by the students' attentive questions and by Jeanne's empowering teaching style. "She has the children instruct themselves, with her lead of course," Greene wrote in his diary. "It was the most interesting experiment I have ever witnessed in education."[7]

Ed, meanwhile, was still casting about for his purpose in life. His father wanted him to join the family undertaking business, but Ed wanted to find his own way. He convinced Jeanne to loan him her first eighty-dollar paycheck, then took the cash down to Deep Greenwood. There were billiards halls and boozy nightclubs where he could have easily frittered the money away, as he had in New York. Instead he bought a small shoeshine parlor, offering the owner half the cost up front, with a promise to pay the rest in thirty days (after he borrowed Jeanne's second paycheck).[8] The same year he opened the Greenwood Haberdashery in the building his parents had erected in 1915, filling the store with hats, colorful ties, and footwear sourced from the Hanover Shoe Company.[9]

At twenty-six, Ed became one of youngest entrepreneurs in Deep Greenwood—his preppy striped sweaters and boyish face made him look like he'd just walked off a college campus.[10] He was surrounded by black enterprise: barbershops, dressmakers, dental offices, and a photography studio all on that very block.[11] Just two doors down from the haberdashery was the *Oklahoma Eagle* office, where Theodore Baughman and his wife Rosalie still issued weekly dispatches on all the race men's comings and goings.[12] The streets bustled with life, and Ed lured potential customers into his storefronts by selling them apples and bananas from a nearby fruit store (at a 50 percent markup). Soon he added popcorn and peanuts to his makeshift menu. Within a year he'd made a thousand dollars shining shoes and selling snacks.[13]

Success came easily in Greenwood for the newlywed Goodwins. They had steady work and a stable support system thanks to Ed's parents. They were thinking of starting a family. But for them and everyone else in the neighborhood who was getting back on their feet after disaster, the 1930s would soon bring another financial calamity.

When the Great Depression gripped Tulsa, it squeezed Greenwood the tightest. After the stock market crash of 1929, a surplus of petroleum caused a nationwide collapse in oil prices the following year, devastating the Oil Capital of the World and its cadre of rich white bankers and business magnates.[14] As upper-class whites saw their fortunes wiped out and began reining in their lavish lifestyles, black women were especially hard hit.[15]

Most of Greenwood's female residents had jobs, and nearly all of those jobs—some 93 percent—were in domestic work in white people's homes and businesses.[16] Work became precarious during the Depression years; one survey of about sixty black female workers found that their average weekly wages plunged below five dollars.[17] Less money in maids' pocketbooks meant less money in Greenwood Avenue cash registers, since women had long been the economic engine behind Greenwood's consumer-focused economy. Thursdays were informally known as the "maid's day off," when many of the domestic workers who lived in white people's homes came to Greenwood to socialize and spend money.[18] Once a dollar entered the neighborhood, it was famous for circulating between black folks dozens of times. But the Great Depression sapped white employers' wages from the community, knocking that prosperous cycle of trade out of sync.

As joblessness and slashed paychecks cascaded, the lingering economic effects of the massacre were once again laid bare. Many black families had exhausted their savings trying to rebuild after 1921[19]—some, like John and Loula Williams, fell into further financial despair after getting ensnared by predatory lenders. "What made conditions so hard was the fact that most Negro homes had been rebuilt from the ashes of the race conflict back in the twenties," B. C. Franklin wrote.

"There were still heavy mortgages against them, with threats of fore-closure."[20]

Black workers who held on to their jobs found that their employers worked them harder than their white counterparts, almost out of in-stinct. "When we had a white maid, I was always helping her," an anonymous white woman told the Oklahoma social worker Francis Burke during the Depression. "I felt kind of sorry for her and didn't want to see her work so hard. But when we have a colored girl, I don't mind letting her do all of the work herself."[21] In interviews with Burke, some whites quoted the Book of Genesis fable about the cursed son of Ham: *And he said, Cursed be Canaan, a servant of servants shall he be unto his brethren.* It was the same biblical scripture that slaveholders had used to rationalize keeping black people in bond-age.[22]

These were not just personal prejudices. White Tulsans' racism was reflected on an institutional scale. Burke found that the largest social services agency in the city focused on family relief took on seventeen hundred cases in April 1935, but only ninety-six were black. The local Children's Service Bureau helped only two black children in dis-tress that year. The Salvation Army did not offer aid to black Tulsans at all. Among major private charities, only the Red Cross, which had played a key role in helping Greenwood rebuild after the massacre, was a reliable help to black residents. "No organizations have ever existed in Tulsa to interpret the needs of the Negro population to the white community," Burke observed.[23]

President Franklin Delano Roosevelt was promising the nation a New Deal, but when it came to government aid for black people, relief often came with a catch. Three hundred and fifty unemployed black women were given jobs at a federally sponsored sewing room down-town in late 1933, crafting work shirts and nightgowns, but the "on again, off again" jobs were soon cut.[24] Jobs offered through the Works Progress Administration provided a vital lifeline to struggling families, but federal rules stipulated that only one adult per household could get WPA wages.[25] That was largely fine for white families, where typically only the men had jobs, but it was disastrous for the two-income house-holds in Greenwood, where 57 percent of married black women were part of the labor force.[26] When women did find relief work, they were paid less than their male counterparts and often worked more sporadic hours.[27] Sometimes black women, along with poor whites, were excluded from work opportunities entirely in favor of "society women" vying for a limited number of federally subsidized jobs.[28] And though a major New Deal program sponsored by the National Recovery Administration sought to raise wages across a variety of occupations, domestic workers and farmers—overwhelmingly black jobs—were excluded from the initiative.[29]

One of the most significant forms of New Deal relief came through cheap long-term home mortgages. In 1933 the Roosevelt administration established the Home Owners Loan Corporation to rescue debt-ridden families (and the banks collapsing under the weight of unpaid loans) by buying up their mortgages and replacing them with longer, low-interest federal loans.[30] Thousands of black homeowners nationally took advantage of the program, which was especially needed in Greenwood.[31] HOLC offered a way out of the crushing debt that blacks had been saddled with after the massacre. B. C. Franklin called the program a godsend. "Here was our government fulfilling, in a commonsense, practical way, the needs of the colored people as well as of others."[32]

In January 1934, Ed and Jeanne Goodwin secured a $3,500 loan from HOLC. Their monthly payment was $27.67, a figure they could likely come close to managing on Jeanne's salary alone.[33] The couple had moved out of the home of Ed's parents and built a stucco bungalow next door, where they were raising their three-year-old daughter Edwyna and a newborn baby, Jo Ann.[34]

But even the mortgage relief initiative had racism baked into it. Greenwood residents had long prided themselves on owning their own land—they had one of the highest black homeownership rates in the nation, at roughly 33 percent.[35] But few of these homeowners were granted HOLC loans. The Goodwins were one of only 107 black families in Tulsa whose application for the relief was granted.[36] HOLC distributed only about 4.5 percent of its loans in Tulsa to black families, even though blacks comprised about 8.5 percent of the homeowning population.[37] It was the second-largest disparity between the black homeownership rate and the loan issuance rate among major U.S. cities, trailing only behind nearby Oklahoma City.[38] Loan decisions were determined at the regional and state levels, allowing localized discrimination to run rampant.[39] There was no

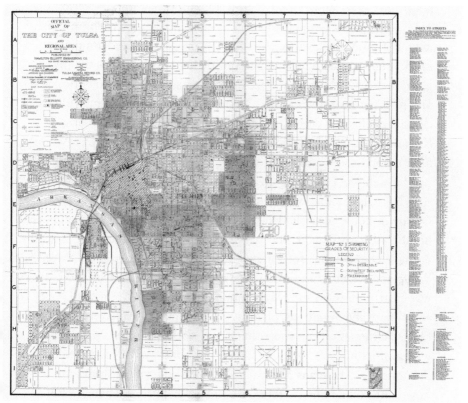

A redlining map of Tulsa by the Home Owners' Loan Corporation

federal oversight to address inequities in the system.[40] Even as the Roosevelt administration promised fairness on paper, it took no action to ensure it in practice.

Though HOLC aided about 24,000 black families nationally (roughly in proportion to their percent age of the homeowning population), it also helped engineer the policies that would make it harder for these families to secure loans in the future.[41] After issuing about 1 million loans between 1933 and 1936, HOLC set out to make detailed real estate maps of the markets where it operated, grading neighborhoods by their perceived creditworthiness.[42] A HOLC regional agent named Raymond Olson was responsible for designing the Tulsa map, and he visited the city in November 1935 to conduct his research. Per the directives from his boss at the HOLC headquarters in Washington, D.C., the map was supposed to represent "a composite opinion of competent realtors engaged in residential brokerage, good mortgage lenders and the HOLC appraisal staff."[43] Olson already had a low opinion of black communities, describing a black neighborhood in Galveston, Texas, as "very trashy" and arguing that black intermingling in white parts of the city "depreciates the [mortgage] security."[44] When he met with Tulsa's local real estate brokers and banking executives to develop his appraisals,[45] those men almost certainly reflected Olson's biases back at him. Merritt J. Glass, the Klan member who had tried to orchestrate the seizure of Greenwood after the massacre, was still a powerful figure in Tulsa real estate and had himself worked as a HOLC appraiser the previous year.[46]

When Olson's map was complete, all of Greenwood, including the Goodwin home, was shaded red with colored pencil. The neighborhood had earned a D, the worst possible rating, meaning it was deemed "hazardous" for financial institutions to issue loans there.[47] While some white neighborhoods also received D ratings, the score was nearly uniform for black communities across the nation.[48] Olson's map and hundreds of other city maps were delivered to the HOLC national office, where the agency used them to help anticipate which of its housing loans would be paid back and which would be delinquent.[49] The maps also provided a striking visual shorthand for how banks might choose to issue loans in the future. Though HOLC policy barred the sharing of the maps with private banks and real estate agents, interest in seeing them was intense, and on-the-ground agents, including Olson, sometimes handed over copies when asked.[50] The HOLC maps crystallized the economic policy that was cross-pollinating between academia, federal agencies, and local real estate firms at the time.[51] They took the sentiment that the *Tulsa Tribune* had espoused as Greenwood smoldered in 1921—"In this old nigger town there were a lot of bad niggers and a bad nigger is about the lowest thing that walks on two feet"—and gave it the official stamp of approval of the U.S. government.[52]

The practice of systematically labeling black neighborhoods as financially hazardous was eventually dubbed redlining. Though HOLC developed its redlining maps after it had already issued loans to black families like the Goodwins, the appraisal methodology the agency pursued soon became widespread in both public and private lending. The Federal Housing Administration, another New Deal agency tasked with shoring up the housing market, specifically forbade the government backing of loans for black people who were trying to move into white communities.[53] Before the 1960s, only 2 percent of the agency's insured mortgages went to nonwhites.[54]

Ed and Jeanne paid off their HOLC loan without issue in November 1944, five years before the final installment was due.[55] HOLC was confounded when it discovered that in many cities the C- and D-rated neighborhoods actually paid off loans more frequently than the higher-rated ones.[56] Ed Goodwin had no way of knowing that the federal government deemed his home a financial hazard. The HOLC maps were not discovered by academic researchers until the 1970s, and the federal government destroyed similar redlining maps developed by the FHA, in response to a racial discrimination lawsuit in the late 1960s.[57] But Ed could see with his own eyes that the Depression economy was not working in his favor. He was forced to close his businesses as the economy worsened, then briefly served as the first black social worker in the county government.[58] He tried to open a store again, but the profits just weren't there. "I did fairly well," Ed said, "but I wasn't making any money."[59]

Even as the formal Greenwood economy sputtered through the 1930s, with half-hearted help from the state and federal governments, there was a separate economy humming along quite nicely in the neighborhood. It wasn't legal, but in some ways, it was more reliable.

Every day of the Depression brought a new wave of uncertainty to Greenwood. Jobs were scarce. Government relief was subject to the whims of miserly bureaucrats. The only institution anyone could really count on, rapacious as it might have been, was gambling.

The game of choice in Greenwood was formally known as the policy wheel, but most people simply called it "the numbers." The rules were simple. A bettor would pick any three numbers between 1 and 78. Then the operators of the game would select twelve numbers from the same range. If the bettor's three picks were among the operators' twelve picks, they "hit." Winners were paid 180 times whatever they wagered.[60]

With bets starting at just five cents, anyone could participate, from deacons to deadbeats.[61] "Nearly everybody plays it," said E. K. Goldman, a black policeman of the era. "Man, woman and child, church

members and all. It doesn't cost much and very few people see anything wrong in it."[62] Each player had their own foolproof methodology for picking winning numbers. Some analyzed license plates and
stock market listings, while others used dream books to translate
their nighttime visions into winning bets.[63] There were few casino-
style antics where people shoved all their proverbial chips in at once—
most participants made small, regular bets, giving the game the
comforting rhythm of the Saturday matinee or Bible study. They
viewed the game not as a vice but as an investment in the future, not
so different from the Wall Street bankers who had gambled—and lost
badly—playing the stock market in 1929.[64]

As the numbers game grew in popularity, a financial ecosystem
emerged to support it. At the bottom of the hierarchy were the numbers runners, who collected bets from people at all the usual social
hangouts. Armed with a small record book and a friendly smile, a
runner might gather wagers at the beauty salon, in the pool hall, or at
a neighbor's apartment. Larger bets were often handled by cab drivers, but many runners were young people who couldn't find legal
work or had been denied New Deal relief for one reason or another.
Running numbers felt a bit like opening up a one-man business; the
runners were paid on commission, earning between 10 and 25 percent of each bet they recorded, as well as tips from jubilant customers
who scored a major hit.[65] "A Negro boy may be broke and hungry
and write policy to get back on his feet," observed a *Tulsa World*
columnist. "Hundreds of Negroes wrote policy to keep from starving."[66]

Once their pockets were bulging with residents' dimes and dreams,
runners would carry the bets to a policy station, an operational headquarters for the game. The station location changed frequently in
order to avoid police surveillance, but the rituals that took place inside were always the same. The mythic numbers themselves were
placed in small capsules and fished out of a pasteboard bucket by
some lieutenant in the operation. After the twelve winning figures
were scrawled on a blackboard, a lucky player might "hit" right then
and there at the policy wheel headquarters, yelping in exultation and
demanding their payout.[67] But showing your face around a policy
wheel was a dicey proposition—the game was subject to regular raids

by police and intermittently tough-on-crime mayors.[68] Most folks would wait for the runners to broadcast the winning numbers throughout the neighborhood via small sheets of paper called policy slips, which were stamped by hand with the twelve winning figures. This all happened every day, three times a day.[69]

Because the game was constantly being played and payouts were so frequent, everyone knew someone who'd just hit their number. In this one slice of black life, success seemed attainable. In reality, though, bettors rarely came out ahead. While the payout on the policy wheel seemed lucrative at 180 times the bet, the odds of winning were only 275 to 1.[70] The true winner was always the banker, who fronted the money for everything: the payouts to bettors, the commissions to runners, the bribes to politicians, and all the other expenses required to run a successful American business.[71] A big-time banker could expect to earn about $11,000 in profit in a given year (or $200,000 in 2021 dollars).[72] "The policy wheel gambling device produces perhaps more revenue for Negroes than any single business or profession in the community," wrote social worker Francis Burke.[73]

Bankers of the policy wheel tended to share similar backgrounds and aspirations. Many came from middle-class families and were college-educated or had college-educated wives.[74] They did not have prior criminal records and often owned other businesses woven deep into the community—department stores, nightclubs, even baseball teams.[75] They did not see their legal businesses as fronts for gambling; they saw gambling as one more legitimate enterprise for them to control. "Stepping out into business was just like another gamble to me," a policy operator in Washington, D.C., remarked. "I went into numbers for the same reason other people go into teaching or medicine or anything else."[76]

It was hardly surprising, then, that young Ed Goodwin—Fisk graduate, middle-class homeowner, and prolific gambler—would soon become a shrewd and influential policy operator.[77]

One day in Greenwood, when Ed was still operating one of his storefronts, a man came to him with a proposition. He wanted Ed to give him $500 to bankroll a policy game. With his other business ventures stalling out, Ed agreed. "I was back in the background," he claimed later, "and from then on I kept moving around in that area, and other peoples that I knew, I backed them."[78]

The man who approached Ed was very likely O. C. Foster, a prominent drugstore owner in Greenwood. Born in 1890 in Texas, Foster arrived in Tulsa in the 1910s and worked as a porter before opening his first neighborhood store in the mid-1920s.[79] By the 1930s, it was common knowledge that his other main business was gambling.[80] He had a penchant for the flamboyant: double-breasted blue coats and golden Buick coupes, always of the latest model.[81] "He had a fleet of 31 cars to pick up policy money and bring it to his drugstore," recalled Waldo Jones, Sr., a prominent Greenwood attorney. "He'd have maybe a thousand or two thousand dollars in his pocket, all the time."[82]

Foster's drugstore was located at 123 North Greenwood Avenue—the building owned by the Goodwin family.[83] Ed worked as a clerk for O. C. Foster in 1933, and articles in both the *Tulsa Tribune* and the *Tulsa World* identified an "Ed Goodman" as a partner in Foster's gambling operation around that time.[84] The two men were almost certainly working together in the illegal enterprise.

Before long, Ed and Foster were generating more than $1,000 per day, about three times what Burke found to be typical of local policy games of the era.[85] They probably had a diverse customer base as well—an estimated five thousand people in Tulsa played the numbers regularly, and many of them were white.[86]

Ed had stepped into quite a lucrative new profession, but it was also a dangerous one. As policy grew in economic value, white gangsters began to encroach on what had long been a black enterprise. All across the country, racial conflicts emerged in disputes over territory. In Harlem, a black Frenchwoman named Stephanie St. Clair, known as the "Queen of Policy," staged a long public battle against a white interloper named Dutch Schultz. She threatened white store owners who aided him and tried to rally black policy operators to form a larger, more powerful syndicate.[87] In Chicago, the brothers Edward, George, and McKissack Jones turned the South Side into a policy boomtown in the 1930s.[88] They were muscled out by the Outfit, the criminal gang once run by Al Capone. White gangsters kidnapped Edward and held him on $100,000 ransom; McKissack died in a car accident.[89]

In Tulsa, the policy operator Elmer "Whitey" Payne became a fierce competitor to Foster and Ed.[90] Though during the day he worked as a driller in the oil fields outside Tulsa, at night Payne operated a gambling hall on Greenwood Avenue, where he was one of the only white faces on the street.[91]

On the night of August 18, 1933, Whitey held his regular numbers drawing in a two-story building on the northern leg of Greenwood Avenue.[92] Around 10:30 p.m., after the drawing was over, he stepped outside into the muggy summer night,[93] as people sauntered down sidewalks and cars eagerly cruised to their weekend destinations.

Suddenly, two black men stepped out of a car hidden in an alley just down the street, pistols clutched at their sides. As a bus grumbled past on Greenwood Avenue, they lobbed a hail of bullets, the noise melding with the roar of the engine. The two assailants quickly dived back into their car and sped off northward, while Whitey Payne lay sprawled out in a bloody pool on the street.[94] A state prosecutor would later claim the execution was "carried out in true 'gangster' style."[95]

Within hours of Whitey Payne's killing, O. C. Foster was arrested as a prime suspect.[96] Ed was called and questioned by police.[97] Two months later Foster was indicted on a murder charge, accused of hiring three other men to carry out the attack.[98] One of the gunmen, James Hollis, flipped and turned state's witness, painting Foster as a desperate man who had paid his crew $500 to eliminate his primary competition, Whitey Payne.[99] "We will get that son-of-a-bitch tonight," Foster allegedly said on the day of the murder, "if I have to go along too."[100]

O. C. Foster categorically denied any involvement in Payne's murder. He was defended in the courtroom by B. C. Franklin, the attorney who had sued the city of Tulsa on behalf of massacre victims. Franklin dismissed Hollis's testimony as "unreasonable, preposterous, and absurd,"[101] theorizing that policy operators in Kansas City had plotted to murder Payne and frame Foster for the killing. He thought racism was clouding Tulsa County prosecutors' assessment of the facts and filed a motion in the case arguing that Foster was being discriminated against in the selection of an all-white jury for the trial.[102]

In February 1934, after nearly nine hours of deliberation, a jury acquitted O. C. Foster on the murder charge.[103] The case and Franklin's advocacy helped crack open the door for black Oklahomans to sit on juries in future trials.[104] But Foster soon left Tulsa to open a billiards parlor in Chicago—rumor had it that he tried running the numbers up north too.[105]

Ed was never arrested in the Whitey Payne investigation or implicated in Hollis's testimony. But the trial and its outcome certainly changed his life. With one policy kingpin dead and another gone from the city, it was a natural step for him to take the crown for himself.

The Depression began to feel like a distant memory as Ed lived the high life in the mid-1930s. He made an easy transition from gambling into bootlegging, which was especially lucrative in a "wide open" town like Tulsa.[106] Though prohibition was baked into the state's constitution in 1907, Ed found it easy to buy corn whiskey at a cost of six dollars per gallon and split the profits with partners who pushed it on the streets.[107] He was careful to remain a background figure, until the day beer was finally legalized in 1933. Then he bought enough cases of booze to stack shoulder-high and sold bottles for a dime each on Greenwood Avenue.[108]

In 1936 he opened a nightclub called the Goodie Goodie Club, featuring a well-stocked bar and a fleet of booths that could seat 150 people.[109] Tulsa was a regular stop on the chitlin' circuit in those years, with musicians like Cab Calloway and Count Basie visiting Tulsa to play the Crystal Palace Ballroom above the old Dixie Theater.[110] Ed's club, right next door to the Crystal Palace, was a frequent after-hours hangout for visiting musicians who wanted to take in some of the neighborhood's raucous parties—the *Black Dispatch* called the club "the most popular spot in town for the night-lifers."[111] Walter Barnes, a saxophonist and bandleader of the era, mentioned Ed's club when he chronicled a 1936 trip his band made to Greenwood, where he was impressed he could find "anything here from a shoe shine, up."[112]

Using earnings from his unlawful activities, Ed began buying real estate, as many as fifty properties in all.[113] He also became more interested in local politics. The Goodie Goodie Club served as a Greenwood voting precinct in 1937, and the *Tulsa World* described Ed as a

political "boss" of the neighborhood who curried votes and negotiated with white political leaders, just as J. B. Stradford and A.G.W.
Sango had done a generation before him.[114] The *Tribune* dubbed him
the "mayor of Greenwood" and cast his family home on Haskell
Street as something out of a mafia tale: "With 21 steps leading up
from the street . . . the windows are barred with heavy woven wire."[115]
But Ed defended his illegal and political activity in equal measure in
the local press. "Everybody knows it," he told the *Tribune* of his gambling ties in May 1937. "Why shouldn't I admit it?"[116]

A couple of months later the *Tulsa World* columnist Ralph Martin
decided to investigate the policy wheel in Greenwood more carefully.
Martin was a police reporter who used his regular column, "Hitting
the High Spots," to explain the clockwork of crime in a way that the
detached front-page headlines often missed, profiling everyone from
perennial drunks to overworked ambulance drivers.[117] He sensed that
the numbers in Greenwood were in a moment of dramatic transformation.

A new mayor, T. A. Penney, was vowing to clean up the streets on
both sides of the railroad tracks.[118] At the same time, a group of Ital-
ian mobsters from Chicago had reportedly set up shop in Tulsa in
recent months with plans to "muscle in on Greenwood's money-
drenched policy racket." These pressures, along with increasing scrutiny from the *World,* led one of the neighborhood's leading policy
operators to retire from the game—so he said, at least. Martin's three-
part series was anchored by an interview with this man, who remained
anonymous but who the journalist said "knows more that is absolutely correct about the 'numbers game' than any other man in the
city." He called him the Policy King.[119]

Martin sketched out the shadow of a biography of a young father
who had attended a Negro college, had "unusual organizational
skill," and controlled the black vote in Tulsa with the wave of his
hand.[120] Though Martin never revealed his source, it's extremely likely
that the Policy King was Ed Goodwin. Ed was a Fisk graduate with
an applied economics degree who didn't bother denying his influence
on local politics.[121] And with three young children at home (he and
Jeanne had just welcomed a baby boy, Ed Jr.), he had good reason for
wanting to exit the game.[122]

In July, Martin met the Policy King at a public-facing establishment the man operated in Greenwood.[123] Perhaps the two men slid into a booth at the back of Ed's Goodie Goodie Club. The jazz of Count Basie might have been wafting from one of Ed's new nickel-per-play jukeboxes as the buzz of Greenwood Avenue resounded, muffled but constant, through the front windows.[124] Ed knew that a white reporter would be looking for a sensational story about black criminality in Greenwood, but he had his own reasons for talking to the press.

Ralph Martin was surprised by his source's subdued demeanor. "He fails to live up to the popular perception of a gambling king or a political chieftain," Martin wrote. "He is quiet and soft spoken and, to strangers at least, perfectly expressionless in his features."

"I am no longer in the policy game," the Policy King announced to Martin. "I retired because I am a family man and your newspapers were giving me a bad reputation."

The King laid out a series of carefully selected arguments defending the policy wheel and, by association, himself. He noted that white people loved to gamble just as much as blacks—many of his clients were white, in fact. But the police crackdowns always seemed to fall on the heads of Greenwood racketeers, rather than the white men operating casinos and liquor-fueled speakeasies just a few blocks over in downtown Tulsa.[125] The King cast the policy wheel as one of the few viable entertainment options in Greenwood since neighborhood parks were scarce and Jim Crow laws meant black people were still excluded from recreational facilities anywhere else.[126] "There is nothing evil about policy," the man argued. "My people are domestics. They work all day over in your town and come back home at night and find absolutely no means of relaxation and recreation beyond our little moving picture shows. There must be some outlet and policy supplies that need."[127]

Martin seemed impressed by the Policy King's cunning and soon delivered his words to readers across the city. This mysterious man had found a way to navigate the business world, the underworld, and the white world all at once. "His control may or may not still exist without the strong trellis of policy over it to climb on," Martin wrote. "But if he has anything whatever to do with the racket still, he is doing an admirable job of keeping it quiet."[128]

Ed Goodwin needed a way to clean up his name. Whether he was Ralph Martin's Policy King or not, the issues Martin laid out aligned closely with his predicament. The numbers game was getting more dangerous, thanks to both legal pressure and the increasing threat of violence from interloping gangsters. Jeanne, a lifelong teetotaler, almost certainly disapproved of his activities. And the *World* and *Tribune* weren't helping things. "The metropolitan press here jumped on me and . . . [said] that I was dictating and running this section of the city over here because of the fact that I had become involved in all of these illegal operations," Ed complained decades later.[129]

"I thought it was a good thing for me to retaliate."[130]

Ed knew quite well the power media held in controlling narratives— his father had once worked as the business manager for A. J. Smitherman's *Tulsa Star,* and Ed himself had agitated to get a student newspaper reinstated at Fisk University during his college years. It was the sensational account of Dick Rowland and Sarah Page's encounter in the *Tulsa Tribune* that had helped light the kindling for the massacre more than a decade before. If Ed had his own media company, he realized, he could combat the negative depictions he saw of himself in the *World* and the *Tribune.*[131]

His mind fell on the old *Oklahoma Eagle,* located in the heart of Deep Greenwood just steps away from the Goodie Goodie Club.[132] The *Eagle* had been around since 1922 and was still helmed by the staid Theodore Baughman, who'd once been an editor at the *Tulsa Star* and the *Oklahoma Sun.*[133] Baughman prided himself on running a wholesome outlet that reflected positively on the black community. "A clean paper," one observer noted. "No scandal headlines."[134] But as a longtime Tulsa resident and perceptive journalist, Baughman was no doubt familiar with Ed Goodwin's many business ventures, both legal and illicit.

One day around 1936, Ed paid Baughman a visit.[135] The *Eagle* office was modest, housed in a small room at 117 Greenwood Avenue, with a weathered linotype machine and a Lee Press. It took two days to print seven hundred copies of the four-page broadsheet, operating the press by hand.[136] Baughman, a heavyset man with a jovial attitude, was approaching sixty-five years old.[137] Standing before the older man, Ed tried to channel the schoolboy charm he'd first honed at Fisk. "I'd like to buy your paper or buy an interest in the paper," he told Baughman. "I'm in a position to get you the proper equipment so you can put out a sheet."

Baughman scoffed. "Well hell, I wouldn't sell it to a racketeer," he said.

"Very well indeed, sir," Ed replied. He left, and he waited.[138]

In May 1937, Ed had a friend named Charles Roberts serve as a front man to purchase a one-half stake in the *Eagle*, with Baughman seemingly none the wiser about Ed's involvement.[139] In July 1937, Baughman died suddenly at a local hospital, after a three-day illness.[140] His death created a power vacuum at the newspaper. Ed tried to step in and seize full control, but the *Eagle*'s assistant manager, O. B. Graham, sought the paper for himself. In late 1937, Graham attempted to oust Roberts and Goodwin from the *Eagle* through a restraining order, claiming their scheme was fraudulent and Goodwin physically threatened him at the newspaper office. The gambit failed. Graham was forced to launch a short-lived rival newspaper called the *Tulsa Appeal* instead, while Ed tauntingly published a Christmas Day article in the pages of his new prize with the breaking news that Graham was "no longer involved in any capacity" with the paper.[141]

By early 1938, Ed had successfully gained complete control of the *Eagle* and begun pouring his growing wealth into improving it. He moved the newspaper's headquarters to his parents' building at 123 North Greenwood and purchased a Goss Comet printing press, which could print up to 3,500 issues per hour. He expanded the *Eagle* from four to eight pages per week and brought the size of the staff up to twelve, including an engraver and two linotype operators.[142]

More important than upgrading the equipment, Ed focused on rehabilitating his image. In 1938 he became a founding member of the Greenwood Chamber of Commerce, a group of leading black business men and women dedicated to "promoting the commercial, civic, industrial and educational interests in their community."[143] When Greenwood received a visit from Mary McLeod Bethune, the activist who worked in the Roosevelt administration to bring black people into the New Deal, Ed introduced her at a community event and chauffeured her around town.[144] He made her visit and his role as her tour guide a front-page story in the *Eagle*.[145] Rather than being vilified by the news, Ed was shaping it.

He also decided to abdicate certain bothersome titles. When Ed first gained a controlling share in the *Eagle*, he used the newspaper to coordinate an election for an actual "mayor of Greenwood," thumbing his nose at the moniker the *Tribune* had given him. Thousands of people cast votes, and in the fall of 1937 hundreds of them packed into the Crystal Palace Ballroom to celebrate the inauguration of their new mayor, real estate man T. R. Gentry. Greenwood's first official mayor sat on a purple throne as the whole neighborhood danced to swing-time music by an all-black orchestra. T. A. Penney, Tulsa's actual mayor, gave "one of the shortest speeches he has ever made" in grudging acknowledgment.[146] But his presence alone showed the new title wasn't just a gag—Greenwood's mayor would go on to appear at city commission meetings and advocate for black workers receiving municipal jobs.[147]

For Ed, purchasing the *Oklahoma Eagle* was a quick solution to an urgent problem: his need to maintain some level of respectability as he navigated legal and illicit enterprises simultaneously. "I had a selfish motive," he admitted years later.[148] But while relentlessly looking out for himself, he had constantly butted up against the edges of what black progress allowed for in the age of Jim Crow. That had given him some perspective, too. He might not have known about the official redlining policy, but he could observe how difficult it was for a black person to get a loan. He still couldn't share a meal with a friend at a downtown lunch counter.[149] His customers, whether they were lawyers seeking a shoeshine or janitors making their daily bet on the numbers, faced limited job opportunities in a city where blacks were systematically excluded from almost all well-paying jobs.[150] There were inequities everywhere he looked, and the opportunities for every person in Greenwood were hemmed in by those disparities. Instead of simply finding a way to carve his own slice of profit off a broken system, he realized he now had a weapon to combat the system itself. Sitting in the *Eagle* office decades later, he reflected on that slowly dawning revelation: "I began to realize how important a newspaper could be."[151]

CHAPTER 12

FAMILY BUSINESS

Wish You A Very Merry Christmas and
Happiness Throughout the New Year

The December 25, 1941, issue of the Oklahoma Eagle

The Christmas photo needed to be perfect. The tree in the background glistened with tinsel, its piney scent settling over every corner of the spacious living room. Everyone was wearing their holiday best—Ed in a suit and tie, Jeanne in a flowing floor-length dark dress. But the quality of the photo hinged entirely on the children. Jeanne didn't want to see Jo Ann rolling her eyes, or Ed Jr. giving his older sisters a nasty pinch, or baby Jimmy starting a fight with Betty, the pint-size family dog. The Goodwins were prepping a special holiday edition of the *Oklahoma Eagle,* and Jeanne just needed to contain this hurricane of youthful energy for the split-second *click* of the camera.[1]

Edwyna, at age eleven, sat between Ed's and Jeanne's two armchairs, wearing a well-ironed blouse and a cordial half-smile.[2] As the oldest, she had earned her parents' adoration as well as their intense expectations. (Ed had wanted a boy so desperately, he made his first daughter his namesake.)[3] She had just started at Carver Junior High School, where she became a charter member of the school's first honor society.[4] Glee club, Girl Scouts, piano lessons, after-school classes in French—for Edwyna, every afternoon was a busy one.[5] "She can cook a simple meal, sets all tables satisfactorily, keeps her share of her room presentable (at times)," Jeanne reported in an article titled "Goodwinettes Growing Rapidly."[6]

Jo Ann sat on the floor by her mother's side, with the faintest hint of preteen annoyance twitching around her lips. She was only eight but nearly as tall as Edwyna, which meant she always received her older sister's hand-me-downs. The two girls shared a bedroom adorned with Jo Ann's collection of elephant figurines and Edwyna's bottled perfumes, but they were very different young women.[7] Edwyna was polite and soft-spoken, perfect in the eyes of her younger siblings.[8] Jo Ann was louder. Sometimes she brought home crass jokes she'd heard at elementary school. ("Why did the moron cut the toilet stool in half?" "Because he heard his half-assed mama was coming to town.") Years later she tried to provoke her mother by puffing a cigarette at the dinner table, and she was the only Goodwin child willing to challenge her father's brash dictums.[9] "Jo Ann . . . is lovable, affectionate, generous to a fault," Jeanne wrote. "Outspoken. A pain to her third grade teachers no doubt."[10]

Ed Jr. stood behind his mother's armchair, his mischievous hands hidden from view. The first Goodwin boy was obsessed with blazing his bicycle through the streets of Greenwood and shooting marbles with his friends. He had a mind that raced too quickly for many of his teachers to manage. He'd started second grade at the age of five thanks to some early classes at the all-black Catholic school just thirty yards from home. Jeanne was forcing him to take piano lessons, but his general hobby was mayhem. "He is twice too full of boyish traits for his poor energyless ma," Jeanne lamented.[11]

Ed Sr. sat in the chair next to Jeanne, with the couple's youngest child Jimmy perched in his lap. Jimmy looked innocent in the photograph, wearing a striped collared shirt, shorts, and tiny dress shoes, but the feisty two-year-old was a "one-man wrecking crew," in Jeanne's words.[12] Father Ed, meanwhile, was approaching forty years old and had deftly made the transition from vilified racketeer to respected community leader. The Goodie Goodie Club had come to an inauspicious end in the summer of 1939, when police arrested thirty gamblers there during a nighttime raid and hauled in an arsenal of axes and sledgehammers to smash much of the night spot's equipment. (Ed was no longer the manager by then, though his name was still on the liquor license.)[13] Instead of mixing drinks behind the bar, he was busy attending NAACP rallies as one of the local chapter's executive board members and giving speeches to attentive white audiences on "The Progress of the Negro."[14] He had not actually given up gambling and boozing, he would later admit, but he had found a way to square the dual sides of his persona in the public eye.[15]

At the very center of the photo was Jeanne herself, wearing her usual wry smile. She was sitting in her favorite chair, the one she occupied so often that the kids swore they had been born right in that spot in the living room. They did not yet know that their mother suffered from anemia, which sapped her energy with ruthless regularity. They did not know of other agonies she'd quietly suffered—of the lifeless girl, never christened with a name, who was born before Edwyna.[16] Jeanne rarely spoke of her own troubles, as she had so much to do caring for everyone else. She quit teaching for a time in the early 1940s to raise the children and help build up the *Eagle* alongside her husband.[17] "Maybe this is corny," she later reflected, "but it is therapy for me, doing what others really want me to do."[18] Sitting in that living room, though, she was content to simply cherish the moment. Another baby was due in the spring, previewed in the *Eagle's* entertainment section as a "Coming Attraction" courtesy of "Director Stork."[19]

The quirks, passions, and foibles of each Goodwin were recorded in the Christmas edition of the *Eagle* in 1941, with the carefully choreographed family photo taking up the entire top half of the newspaper's front page. But outside that idyllic frozen frame, the world was being thrown into chaos. Three weeks before Christmas, a fleet of Japanese fighter planes bombed a U.S. naval base in Hawaii, killing more than twenty-four hundred people.[20] Pearl Harbor plunged

America into a global war once again and set the *Eagle* on a long journey advocating for black civil and economic rights both overseas and at home in Tulsa. It was an ongoing struggle that had stretched from J. H. Goodwin's childhood during Reconstruction and would reach into little baby Jimmy's elder years in the twenty-first century.

The *Eagle* became a venue to discuss both the personal and the political, to speak of what was happening on a war front half a world away and inside the festive living rooms dotting the streets of the neighborhood. The world was becoming an increasingly uncertain place—and remained, as it always had been for black people, an un-fair one—but Jeanne preferred to focus on the positive as best she could. "Despite war and pestilence, high taxes, illness and the many annoyances that pester the average family through the normal year," she wrote, "the family of E. L. Goodwin . . . are happily together."

After Pearl Harbor, the *Eagle* printed an excerpt of President Roosevelt's famous address to Congress, in which he decreed December 7 "a date which will live in infamy." But above the president's speech on the front page, the newspaper demanded that the United States treat black citizens fairly during the forthcoming war effort. "When Japan struck America, the question of red man, black man, or white man should have faded," *Eagle* editor Horace S. Hughes wrote. "The future of America depends upon a sacrifice which must not be colored with prejudice of any kind."[21]

Greenwood residents were ready to do their part to win the war. Men like George Monroe, who had been a five-year-old when the white mob invaded his family's home during the massacre, and Caesar Latimer, whose uncle J.C. had been sent to an internment camp during the burning, were deployed in the European and Pacific theaters.[22] On the home front, the *Eagle* encouraged the purchase of war bonds throughout the neighborhood—Jeanne even helped the children buy some. "In spite of discriminations and [a] weird idea of democracy on the part of some of his fellow country-men," she wrote in 1942, "Edward [Jr.] finds this the best of all possible countries in which to live."[23]

And yet those discriminations that Jeanne called out persisted. For black soldiers, not much had changed since World War I. They were still relegated to segregated combat platoons or support units tasked with menial work such as digging latrines.[24] Overseas, they were treated with respect by British citizens, while U.S. officials continued to impose Jim Crow on foreign soil.[25] Black veterans at home were once again murdered in uniform—men such as Booker T. Spicely in Durham, North Carolina, and Felix Hall near Fort Benning in Georgia.[26] "Blacks received the worst assignments, the fewest awards and honors, and were generally given the 'leftovers' that nobody else wanted," Caesar Latimer said after the war. "If we were good enough to fight and die for our country . . . then we were good enough to be treated like first-class citizens."[27]

Greenwood leaders called for better treatment of soldiers overseas and better opportunities for black workers on the home front.[28] Much of their advocacy was spearheaded by a tight partnership between the *Eagle* and the NAACP.[29] In 1938, Ed Goodwin hired Horace S. Hughes, a longtime English teacher at Booker T. Washington High School, to lead the newspaper's small editorial staff.[30] As editor-in-chief, he quickly developed a sharp pen at his publisher's behest. A few doors down from the newsroom was the law office of Amos T. Hall, the president of the local chapter of the NAACP.[31] Born in Bastrop, Louisiana, Hall moved to Tulsa shortly before the massacre, finding a job as a janitor at the all-white First Methodist Church just south of downtown.[32] In his free time, he read law books and studied legal theory. He was soon elected a justice of the peace, then admitted to the Oklahoma State Bar in 1925.[33] By the early 1940s, he was the neighborhood's most passionate civil rights advocate—and its most strategic. Coordinating across their overlapping spheres, these three men challenged the most powerful corporations in the state.

In Tulsa, a new warplanes factory promised one of the first major boosts to the local economy since the Great Depression. The Douglas Aircraft Company would put thousands of people to work building Air Force bombers with intimidating names like Dauntless, Invader, and Liberator.[34] Hopeful that black people would benefit, the *Eagle* endorsed a bond issue financing the plant's construction and published a front-page guide to landing a job on the $10 million project.[35]

But it quickly became clear that black employment in the war effort would not come easily. The construction at Douglas was managed under a "closed shop" policy, which meant that workers hired there had to be members of a labor union.[36] While national union leaders claimed racism had no place in their ranks, local union chiefs continued to exclude black workers.[37] Several black men were turned away from admission into the Tulsa chapter of the United Brotherhood of Carpenters, a large construction union that was hired to build the bomber plant.[38]

The men turned to Amos Hall for help. The NAACP chief groused in the *Eagle* about Douglas's policies and spearheaded a mass protest at Greenwood's First Baptist Church.[39] But he would soon have a new, more potent tool in his arsenal. In June 1941, President Roosevelt issued an executive order outlawing racial discrimination by government agencies and defense contractors (only after black activists, led by labor organizer A. Philip Randolph, threatened a large-scale march on Washington, D.C.). One black leader called Executive Order 8802 "the greatest thing for Negroes since the Emancipation Proclamation."[40] It brought with it a new federal oversight agency called the Fair Employment Practices Committee.[41] Hall quickly alerted the group to the discrimination occurring at the bomber plant in Tulsa. Federal officials opened an investigation. With mounting government pressure, Douglas Aircraft Company and its construction contractor agreed to hire nineteen black carpenters to help build the plant, paying them $1.25 per hour.[42] The workers appeared in a celebratory group photo on the front page of the *Eagle*—a win for them felt like a win for the whole neighborhood.[43]

These kinds of victories, measured in dollars and cents, mattered most to Ed Goodwin. While the burgeoning civil rights movement would eventually pivot aggressively to a fight over the places where blacks had the freedom to spend money, Ed wanted to open up the workplaces where they would have the opportunity to make it. "If you've read my paper, I have been advocating that equity be meted out to black people, educationally [and] economically," Ed reflected later. "I'm not too damned concerned about the social side of it."[44]

But the challenges for black people at Douglas were only beginning. Once the construction of the facility was complete and the plant actually opened, few blacks were hired to build the company's giant military airplanes. Douglas had a secret internal policy of starting all black workers out as janitors, no matter their qualifications, then promoting a few "thoughtful" blacks to higher-paying positions after

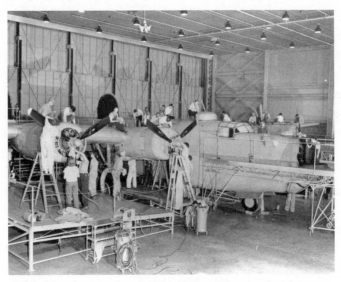

Workers at the Douglas plant building a Liberator bomber plane

white bosses could "observe their attitudes." In the fall of 1942, the fifteen-thousand-person facility employed only fourteen black workers in skilled or semiskilled positions, out of 160 black workers total.[45]

Hall, Hughes, and Goodwin again strategized to overcome corporate obstinance. Goodwin and Hall, along with Booker T. Washington High School principal E. W. Woods, met with the Tulsa school superintendent to develop a vocational training school in Greenwood.[46] When the War Department failed to provide funding for the school, Hall traveled to Washington, D.C., to lobby on Greenwood's behalf.[47] Eventually the new school opened in a repurposed garage at the corner of Archer Street and Hartford Avenue, training more than sixteen hundred black people in welding, parts fabrication, and aircraft assembly.[48] Mabel Little, the beauty salon owner, was among the many who benefited from the lessons.[49]

Even after blacks earned their credentials, though, they were still turned away outright by the Douglas bosses. Officials said they did not want to run afoul of Oklahoma's deeply entrenched Jim Crow laws by placing black and white workers shoulder to shoulder on the assembly line.[50] A black World War I veteran complained to the FEPC that when he applied for skilled work at Douglas, he was the last in a room of two hundred white applicants to be granted a job interview, then was informed there were no more jobs available. Another mixed-race worker said that the first question he was asked during his own interview was "Do you have any [black] blood in you?"[51]

With the FEPC failing to take further action, Ed decided to air Douglas's discrimination publicly in order to force change. In 1942 the *Eagle* launched a series of front-page investigative features on working conditions at the factory. Employees revealed that black janitors were being denied promotions even after they acquired the necessary trade skills. SKILLED NEGRO LABOR TABOO AT DOUGLAS BOMBER PLANT, read one headline.[52] The editorial page, meanwhile, became Horace Hughes's bully pulpit, as he complained that blacks with college degrees were being forced to porter at the bomber plant. "Unless there are some immediate changes made to bring Negroes into the scheme of things at Douglas, we shall be forced to conclude that somebody who shapes the employment of that company doesn't want an 'all-out' for Democracy," Hughes wrote.[53] Ed even visited the plant personally to lay out all of Greenwood's concerns. The plant's managers assured him that they intended to hire at least one thousand black workers, eventually.[54]

At the same time the *Eagle* was shining a light on Douglas's racism, the newspaper was exposing the plight of Greenwood residents who were deprived of well-paying jobs elsewhere in the community. The *Eagle* revealed that some maids working for white families in Tulsa were earning as little as six dollars per week.[55] At the same time, prices for food in the early 1940s were climbing nearly 20 percent per year before the United States introduced wartime rationing.[56] And New Deal relief had dried up as the government poured every dollar it had into the war.[57] "Those in the lowest bracket are finding it exceedingly difficult to obtain even the barest necessities of life," the newspaper reported.[58]

Behind the scenes, Douglas officials were trying to find a way to muzzle the *Eagle* and continue business as usual. The company claimed the *Eagle*'s insistent coverage was somehow stalling its efforts to provide jobs for black workers. A company personnel manager complained to the FEPC that "adverse publicity had been launched by a newspaper" that could "retard the program . . . for the employment of [blacks] at the Douglas plant."[59] It was telling that the company would try to persuade FEPC officials to silence the *Eagle* rather than address Greenwood's concerns directly. While black activists had initially celebrated the FEPC, the federal committee was woefully underfunded, lacked enforcement power to punish discriminatory companies, and had conflicting internal perspectives about its core purpose. The committee's white leaders were often content to let businesses determine how much—or how little—to change. "Negroes must recognize that there is no power in the world—not even in all the mechanized armies of the earth, Allies and Axis—which could force the southern white people to the abandonment of the principle of segregation," FEPC chair Mark Ethridge said in 1942.[60]

Still, the *Eagle* persisted. Between 1942 and 1943, Goodwin and Hughes published nearly twenty articles and columns on the state of the Douglas plant. Meanwhile, Amos Hall continued to criticize the aircraft maker in public speeches, while also hammering home the problem in meetings with federal officials.[61] Finally, in the spring of 1943, the FEPC took a more serious step. It contacted the procurement division of the Air Force, which controlled Douglas's lucrative federal contract for building bombers.[62] With the company's bottom line suddenly threatened, Douglas reversed course. By July, the company hired 815 skilled black workers, including fifty women.[63] When an FEPC director visited the plant the next year, a Douglas personnel manager told the official that workers would be granted jobs that matched their experience "irrespective of race, creed, or color."[64]

The years of complaints and protests by the NAACP and the *Eagle* had given the federal government the ammunition it needed to force Douglas's hand. It was a victory for Hall, Hughes, and Goodwin, but one that happened largely behind closed doors. "It did not come as the result of a letter or two," Amos Hall remarked during the campaign. "It became necessary for us to make a real fight."[65]

These men knew that Douglas could snatch back the gains they'd won as soon as the war ended and federal intervention ceased. Instead of patting themselves on the back, the *Eagle* staff threw its support behind a congressional bill that would make the FEPC and its antidiscrimination mandate permanent.[66] The law was killed by Republicans and southern Democrats, but the FEPC's antidiscrimination framework formed the basis for state legislation and the 1964 Civil Rights Act.[67]

For Ed and the *Eagle,* the work was never over. "We have opened

Horace S. Hughes and Amos Hall

up avenues that have heretofore been closed in many areas," Ed said
later. "Many doors are still opening because of what we print in this
paper concerning hate, prejudice and inequities."[68]

During the summer of 1942, as Ed was tussling with the Douglas
Aircraft Company, he took a business trip to Chicago in hopes of
expanding the *Eagle*'s influence.[69] He had recently joined the Negro
Newspaper Publishers Association, a consortium created in 1940.[70]
The group's 1942 annual meeting took place in the Bronzeville neighborhood on Chicago's South Side.[71] There Ed met with leaders from
twenty-five other newspapers scattered around the country, including
the *Chicago Defender,* the *Pittsburgh Courier,* and the *Atlanta Daily
World.*[72] Black journalists had never been more widely read—during
the war years, circulation among black newspapers tripled to more
than 1.6 million copies nationwide.[73]

Ed had chosen the perfect moment to join the media business, and
he was taking his new role seriously. In addition to the Douglas investigation, he personally visited a poorly funded state orphanage in the
all-black town of Taft and wrote on the *Eagle*'s front page about the
facility's plight; the state legislature soon opened a government probe
based on the reporting.[74] At the Chicago meeting, Ed was appointed
to a committee to oversee the operations of the Associated Negro
Press, a twenty-three-year-old national black news-gathering agency
that provided much of the copy that filled their broadsheets.[75] He was

also creating opportunities for a new generation of writers; young Beezee Littles was among the *Eagle* staffers who accompanied him on the trip. A twenty-five-year-old former Catholic schoolteacher who had been hired as the *Eagle's* society editor, Littles was thrilled to shake hands with so many newspaper veterans who knew the struggles generations of black journalists had faced.[76] "A bit of printers ink was sprinkled that is not removable," she wrote in her weekly column after the trip.[77]

But the white press was not quite as inspired. A *Time* magazine reporter who was present at the Chicago conference provided a starkly different impression of black journalism in America's most widely read newsweekly. "The smoke from big black cigars supercharged the sticky heat of the basement cafeteria in Chicago's Wabash Avenue Y.M.C.A.," the article began. "A well-dressed, pipe-smoking Negro rose to address the third annual conference of the Negro Newspaper Publishers Association. His 75 listeners, full of fried chicken and Pepsi-Cola, were still wrought up about the issue of their press and their race."[78]

The piece's condescending tone was no surprise. Black journalists rarely saw their concerns taken seriously by white government leaders or their white media peers, who helped shape national public opinion. While the white press had adopted a veneer of objectivity by the 1940s, the black press remained unapologetic about advocating for the needs of black people specifically. "If we hadn't had black newspapers, somebody to raise a little hell about what's taken place, then we would have probably still been in slavery," Ed argued later.[79]

Leading black journalists questioned how "objective" the mainstream press really was, given that it framed every issue to serve an affluent white audience. The white press's proximity to power sometimes made reporters blind to the machinations of their own government. After the United States detonated nuclear bombs over Japan, rumors swirled that people in Hiroshima and Nagasaki were dying of radiation poisoning long after the blast. As the U.S. government vehemently denied the claim and the *New York Times* parroted military talking points, black war correspondent Charles Loeb exposed "radio activity still remaining in the explosion area," becoming one of the first journalists to bring the truth of the atom bomb's devastating impact to American citizens. His work, published two months after the attack, was distributed in black newspapers across the country.[80]

"You can't distort the facts. But there's no such thing as objectivity in any newspaper," Loeb said decades later, after a long career working at the *Cleveland Call and Post*. "There's less potential for complete objectivity in the black press because how the hell can you be objective when somebody's stepping on your feet all the time? It's pretty hard to be objective when your brother just got lynched. Or the cops beat up your neighbor. . . . We don't pretend complete objectivity. We've attained it as nearly as the system permits us to."[81]

White pundits often decried black media's racial advocacy as sensational and exploitative, a continuation of the "yellow journalism" that media moguls William Randolph Hearst and Joseph Pulitzer pioneered in the early twentieth century. The loudest critic was a widely syndicated conservative columnist named Westbrook Pegler, whose musings reached 6 million readers across 116 newspapers each week. (*Time* called him "the great dissenter for the common man.")[82] In the spring of 1942, after a cursory review of the *Chicago Defender* and the *Pittsburgh Courier*, Pegler called the nation's leading black newspapers "trash" and "of lower mediocrity, at best."[83] Beyond the insulting potshots, he took issue with the black press's efforts to expose injustices that people of color faced during the war. He mocked black journalists who opposed the internment of Japanese Americans and questioned the loyalty of black soldiers who read "the race-angling of the news" being produced by outlets such as the *Eagle*.[84] "These papers bear their responsibility with much less skill and care than the average white paper," Pegler proclaimed in a June 1942 column. "On the contrary, our handling of the news in which the color question arises is done with the greatest delicacy."[85]

In Tulsa, the *Eagle* met Pegler's words with derision. "Westbrook Pegler wants the Negro press muzzled for the duration of the War," Horace Hughes wrote in an editorial. "He is one of those ardent patriots who talk about winning the war for the freedom of oppressed peoples over yonder, but he thinks this is a bad time to talk about conditions that need correcting over here."[86]

Ed no doubt agreed with his newspaper's editor, but he also encouraged debate in the *Eagle*'s pages.[87] So in June 1942, when Westbrook Pegler showed up at the *Eagle* office unannounced alongside *Tulsa Tribune* editor Jenkin Lloyd Jones, Ed welcomed him and demonstrated how their publication actually operated.[88] The three men spent an hour in Ed's private office, where Ed may have explained the issues they were having securing jobs at the Douglas bomber plant, or pointed out Greenwood's successful participation in the war bond drive, or rattled off the names of the neighborhood young men who had been shipped off to war—all issues the *Eagle* was covering without the sensationalism Pegler ascribed to the black press.[89] Beezee Littles wasn't afraid to confront Pegler directly as he walked around the office. "When asked very blankly (by me) what he really thought of Negro weeklies, he seemed to think they were OK," she wrote, "but what would you say if you were behind the eight ball?"[90]

After Pegler was gone, the paper continued to take him to task for his incendiary words. "We are still of the opinion that Pegler's outburst is mere war hysteria aggravated by a consciousness that the Negro has a lot to kick about," Hughes wrote. "It is not the facts published in Negro newspapers that have become so disturbing. It is the interpretation of those facts that has awakened the slumbering conscience of American white people."[91]

Westbrook Pegler died in 1969, bitter over the progress of the civil rights movement and blackballed from mainstream media after he compared the editorial policies of the Hearst newspaper chain to the censorship regime of Adolf Hitler.[92] The *Eagle*, ultimately, would long outlast him.

Every Saturday morning, as World War II drew to a close, the youngest employee of the *Oklahoma Eagle* took his post beside the Goss Comet printing press. He knew little of wartime struggles for jobs or squabbles with white journalists. Jimmy Goodwin simply wanted his thirty-cent salary so he could get out of that cavernous building and into the bright, bustling world of Greenwood, the only home he'd ever known.

Six-year-old Jimmy was driven to the *Eagle* office by his father every week. Even at that young age, he knew it was a time for work, not play. Ed would leave his son in the large warehouse behind the newsroom with a broom, a dustpan, and a few rags dipped in kerosene. Jimmy's first task was to crawl under the printing press and snake his small arms between the metal rollers, wiping away the ink that clung to the steel rods after the weekly printing of the newspaper. The process took hours as the rags slowly turned black. Often, he wept, because of the seeming futility of the Sisyphean task.

Once the press was clean, Jimmy grabbed the broom and began sweeping the flecks of metal that had fallen beneath the linotype machine. He could not miss a single piece. Where his father disappeared to during these laborious hours, he didn't know. But eventually, when the task was complete and his hands were slathered in ink, he would find the old boss and earn his small salary. That was enough to turn the rest of his Saturday into a fantasy.[93]

After work Jimmy and his best friend Eric Rollerson dashed from the *Eagle* office to the Dreamland Theater, a few doors down on Greenwood Avenue.[94] They ran by Cavers Cleaners, the black-owned dry cleaner that had been in business since 1913,[95] and Meharry Drug Store, where Eric's parents L.R. and Myrtle sold every kind of sandwich a hungry customer could want.[96] They passed Boulware's Food Market, where fresh slabs of meat lined the shelves, along with Otis Isaac's shoe repair shop.[97] In the alley behind the *Eagle* office, Watson's sold mouthwatering burgers with onions cooked right into the ground beef. Down at the Greenwood-Archer intersection, guests ranging from Louis Armstrong to Satchel Paige filtered in and out of the Small Hotel.[98]

The boys dodged around the legs of men wearing suits and women donning tie-neck blouses, who warned them not to run in the streets.[99] They saw teenagers only a few years their senior who already yearned for adulthood—boys smirking as they played at smoking pipes, girls bashfully fidgeting with the white pearls around their necks.[100] Sometimes a drunken reveler enjoying his weekend too much would stumble out of the Broadway Bar, introducing Jim to the odor of stale beer for the first time. Other days the whole street would roar with music, as the marching bands of Booker T. Washington High School or St. Monica Catholic School paraded down Greenwood Avenue, drum majors and baton twirlers and trombonists and majorettes all in synchronized harmony.[101]

There were plenty of smaller enterprises scattered around the neighborhood as well. On a dead-end street behind Greenwood Ave-

*The St. Monica's Catholic School band marches down Greenwood
Avenue*

nue, retired fighter Jack Scott welcomed young athletes to the makeshift boxing gym in his backyard. As teens who dreamed of becoming
Joe Louis or Sugar Ray Robinson unleashed left hooks onto his heavy
punching bag, Scott would bark questions: "What you gonna do with
your life?" "Who are your people?" Scott was not a man to brook
compromise—he had been among the armed black men who marched
to the courthouse in May 1921 to rescue Dick Rowland. The kids
didn't know that, of course; they called him "the DA" since visiting
his gym felt like being tossed into an interrogation room.[102]

A few blocks north on Independence Place, a rotating cast of neighborhood mediums communicated with the dead during the Sunday
service at the Light of Truth Spiritualist Church; some of the women
also sold homemade potions out of their kitchens.[103] Even farther
north, at a house on Kenosha Avenue,[104] cuckoo clocks of every plausible size and shape trilled at the top of each hour, led in their refrain
by the baritone gong of a large grandfather clock. Rev. W. L. Anderson was a watchmaker who converted a spare room in the house into
his workshop. Standing at a large table packed with tiny drawers, the
drawers packed with washers and screws smaller still, he guided his
callused fingers over his small gadgets, engaged in a delicate dance

with the mechanics of time.[105] Elsewhere in the community there were hatters, accountants, pharmacists, music teachers, florists, tailors, and a Wonder Bread salesman.[106] While Greenwood Avenue served as the neighborhood's main commercial artery, economic activity flowed through the residential streets as well, like capillaries branching out from a beating heart.

Young Jimmy, of course, simply wanted to reach the Dreamland. After securing a bag of popcorn and a soda from the concession stand, he and Eric filed into the auditorium.[107] At six years old, their legs still dangled in the air when they took their seats. As the room went dark, they leaned forward and traveled through a silver-screen portal into the Wild West. Lash La Rue in *Pioneer Justice*. Roy Rogers in *Lights of Old Santa Fe*. Tonto and the Lone Ranger in *Hi-Yo Silver*.[108] "That's where I got my love of cowboys," Jim recalled decades later.[109] The worlds were thrilling, the stories simple. Good always conquered evil. It was a worthy reward for a hard day's work.

While Jim was the youngest *Eagle* staffer, each Goodwin had a role to play in the family businesses. Ed Jr., Jim's older brother, also spent his early years cleaning the presses, but he eventually graduated to operating them, becoming the *Eagle*'s primary machinist. "I inherited a broom as far back as I can remember and was taught that hard work never killed anybody," he wrote later. "Although I thought I was dying every time."[110] The girls, Edwyna and Jo Ann, became deputized copy chiefs as teenagers, poring over *Eagle* proofs every week.[111] Working at the *Eagle* was as routine as doing homework or household chores. "There would be times, if we were at the table having dinner and Edward got up to go put out the paper," Jeanne recalled, "all the children would get up and follow him to the plant."[112]

Ed's father J. H. Goodwin stepped in as the official business manager of the publication, reprising his role under A. J. Smitherman at the *Tulsa Star*.[113] And while his mother Carlie had died in 1938, her presence could still be felt—the *Eagle* operated for decades out of the property on Greenwood Avenue she had purchased in her own name in 1914.[114] Jeanne, meanwhile, wore whatever hat was necessary to get the paper out, covering children's birthday parties and the minutiae of city school board meetings with equal zest, while at various times serving as managing editor and assistant proofreader.[115] For more than five decades her weekly column, "Scoopin' the Scoop," mixed

The Eagle *staff in the late 1940s*

family-oriented community news, local gossip, and promotions for the department store Froug's, which underwrote the series.[116] All her writing carried a tempered but persistent optimism that America would evolve into a better home for her black children, so long as they were willing to work hard for their success.

The *Eagle*'s most dedicated staffer outside the family was a man named James "Red" Williams. Ed and Red became boyhood friends in early Greenwood, though they hailed from opposite worlds.[117] Red grew up with little family, partial deafness, and a speech impediment that gave his words a thick, slurred cadence.[118] People thought he was stupid or dangerous—they called him "Crazy Red."[119] But Red was clever, athletic, and most of all, loyal. He ultimately worked at the

Eagle for more than fifty years, living in a small apartment at the newspaper office. Later, he was buried on the Goodwin family plot.[120]

While the *Eagle* was short-staffed during the war, readers wouldn't have known it from the volume of news it produced.[121] Ed preferred to focus on local events whenever possible, so most front pages were anchored by happenings in the Greenwood community. There were injustices like the Douglas bomber plant saga, sure, but the appointment of the first black mail carrier in 1942 was also front-page news.[122] The *Eagle* was often finding creative ways to help residents learn new skills or engage with their community, from hosting cooking classes to partnering with the Greenwood Chamber of Commerce to distribute the neighborhood's first-ever business directory.[123] What people wanted most from the paper, truth be told, was not news of the challenges they faced as black folks but information to help them strengthen their connections with their friends, their loved ones, and God. "I don't look upon myself as being a black paper, per se," Ed said. "I just look upon my paper meeting the needs of the people in this community and furnishing them with information." It was the items on the society and church pages—sick lists, fraternity and sorority updates, church auxiliaries—that kept people buying the *Eagle*.[124]

Nothing showed the *Eagle*'s commitment to the community better than its investment in the neighborhood children. The newspaper relied on a vast network of newsboys to place the paper in the hands of eager customers and collect news items to bring back to the office.[125] Dozens of children between the ages of five and sixteen, including Ed Jr. and Jim, would stake out a piece of Greenwood territory and belt out their sales pitch: "*Oklahoma Eagle!* Only five cents!"[126] On hot summer nights, when the *Eagle* was coming off the press, the boys would gather on Greenwood Avenue to eat popcorn and ice cream offered by Ed. Ever the entrepreneur, he charged the kids for the treats.[127] But each year he offered the prize of a new bicycle to the child who sold the most *Eagle*s, and all the newsboys were rewarded with regular banquets, where they dined on hot dogs, ice cream, and soda pop.[128] For many of the children, selling the *Eagle* was their introduction to the world of entrepreneurship. The newspaper issued each of them piggybanks and called them "America's future businessmen."[129]

Whether championing the welder who deserved a job at the aircraft plant or hiring an industrious eight-year-old who wanted to start selling newspapers, the *Eagle* was always trying to help black people find financial success. It was a mission that went beyond simply reporting the news or the arm's-length objectivity that white journalism of the era so often aspired to. The *Eagle* was an organ of the community that it covered, intertwined with Greenwood's fate in a way that few newspapers are. The purpose was clear from the day that Ed added a new mission statement to the front page, appearing right below the nameplate every single week: "We Make America Better When We Aid Our People."[130]

CHAPTER 13

A WORLD APART

Ed Goodwin, Sr., taking flying lessons with his trainer, Nathan Sams

From more than half a mile above Tulsa, the Arkansas River looked like a copperhead snake as it slithered its way across eastern Oklahoma, pockmarked with golden sandbanks at every curve. Ed Goodwin's hands gripped the control stick of his bright yellow Piper Cub as his eyes scanned the river's undulating path, a useful guide toward home. As he glided over an alternating pattern of farms and green forests, the land somehow seemed more vibrant than it ever did roaming the dusty earth.[1]

At intervals all too frequent, the plane shuddered violently.[2] The slightest hint of turbulence could shake the fifteen-hundred-pound vessel off course, causing an unskilled pilot to overcorrect and go tumbling out of the sky in a stall, an often fatal violation of the laws of aerodynamics.[3] Ed also had to watch out for the quick-tempered thunderheads that often gathered over the Oklahoma plains.[4] But the sense of danger was not a detriment to him. It was part of the appeal.

Ed insisted that he purchased the plane for practical reasons. In 1943 he became the business manager of the orphanage in Taft that the *Eagle* had investigated two years prior.[5] The prestigious role, a high-level political appointment for black Oklahomans, came thanks to a friendship he struck with Governor Robert Kerr, a Tulsa Democrat who had promised to aid "all the people of this state" during his campaign (along with providing the usual plum jobs for his political allies).[6] Traveling regularly between Taft and Tulsa, Ed believed he could wedge more business meetings into a day with his own wings.[7] But he also enjoyed the simple pleasure of a joyride and regularly took his sons airborne.[8]

Owning a plane was a status symbol that placed Ed in a long lineage of prominent black Oklahoma aviators. There was Simon Berry, the transportation magnate who had given aerial tours of the neighborhood for years, as well as Yancey Williams, a Booker T. Washington High School graduate who was denied a position in the Army Air Corps at the onset of World War II.[9] When Williams sued the war department with the backing of the NAACP, the Air Corps grudgingly started training black pilots at a segregated base in Tuskegee, Alabama.[10] The Tuskegee Airmen went on to become a highly decorated unit in the war,[11] dismantling white assumptions about black inferiority in the military. One of the Airmen, an Oklahoma native named Nathan Sams, became Ed's instructor when he moved back home after the war.[12] In a photo published on the front page of the *Eagle,* the two men peacocked in front of the Piper Cub, Ed's hand caressing the hull while Sams stood next to him grinning behind a pair of sunglasses.[13]

As he soared through the clouds, Ed must have recalled his brutal first encounter with airplanes. He had been hiding in a bathtub as a teenager in 1921 when terror rained down on Greenwood. So much had changed for him in the years that followed. The *Eagle*'s circulation had grown from 700 to about 5,000 in the first decade of Goodwin ownership, and advertising revenue started picking up after the war.[14] Ed owned a bevy of retail establishments in Deep Greenwood—an ice cream parlor that his daughter Jo Ann ran, a popcorn stand for Ed Jr., and the *Oklahoma Eagle* Stationery Store, where Edwyna manned the cash register.[15] Much of his income came from the dozens of residential properties he and Jeanne owned in Greenwood, including at least fourteen small shotgun houses, sequestered together on Hartford Avenue and rented out at a rate of twenty-five dollars per month.[16]

Then there were the numbers. In 1943 the *Tulsa Tribune* reported that Ed had publicly disavowed any involvement in Greenwood's underground lottery,[17] but he may have used his printing company, which operated alongside the *Eagle*, to print the paper pads numbers operators used to make policy slips.[18] When Jo Ann was in college in the early 1950s, a spiteful roommate from Oklahoma City blurted out one day that the Goodwin girl's daddy ran a policy wheel. She confronted her father immediately. "Jo Ann, I guarantee you after tonight I won't be involved in that," she remembered him promising. "My business should not affect you."[19] Perhaps that was when he finally got out. But as Jim recalled it, the reason Ed once cited for quitting the policy wheel was a federal gambling tax passed in 1951, which compelled numbers racket operators to join a public registry. That put a chill on policy games in black communities nationwide.[20] Whatever the case, Ed benefited from the numbers racket for several years, perhaps longer than a decade. It helped him to accrue a small fortune, placing the Goodwins firmly in the neighborhood's wealthiest strata. They were among the group whose political mission to dismantle Jim Crow dominated front pages across the black press, while their fashionable parties filled society pages tucked inside.

When Jo Ann was still a young girl, at their house on Haskell Street, she recalled her father telling her, "One of these days I'm gonna build a house for you, and everybody's gonna have a room."[21] The Goodwin clan was getting bigger by the year. Since the Christmas photo in 1941, the family had welcomed an inquisitive and literary daughter named Jeanne, a scientifically minded girl named Carlie, and a charismatic young orator named Bob (after Ed's powerful friend, Governor Robert Kerr).[22] The family also adopted an older girl from the Taft orphanage named Onetha Manuel, who loved children herself and looked after the youngest Goodwin siblings.[23] That made for a family of eleven—Ed and Jeanne, the eight kids, and J.H., who welcomed the lot of them into his house after Carlie passed away. They certainly could use more space than cramped quarters of Greenwood could provide, and they weren't likely to find it nearby. Bordering white enclaves refused to sell homes to black residents.[24]

In 1945, J. H. Goodwin had purchased a large plot of farmland near Alsuma, a tiny outpost twelve miles southeast of Greenwood—truly out in the country in those days.[25] About two years later he transferred the property to Ed, and Ed moved the entire family out to the new estate.[26] He expanded the modest stone house on the farmland into a nineteen-room manse, complete with six bedrooms on the first floor for the children and his father.[27] Because Ed didn't believe in stocks[28]—he may have had a lingering suspicion from the financial shell shock of the Depression—he poured his money into the things he could touch and feel. A newspaper plant, an airplane, a lavish new abode. "Daddy always pursued new projects with vim, vigor, and vitality, both financially and physically," his son Ed Jr. reflected later.[29] Most important to Ed, though, was building a foundation for his children, whom he expected to be self-sufficient after he provided them the best schooling money could buy. Beginning when Edwyna went off to Fisk in 1946, the Goodwins had a child or two in college every year for two decades.[30] "I may go down," Ed told his wife cryptically once, "but I will get my children an education."[31]

After floating far above the world, Ed pushed forward gently on the plane's control stick and used the two pedals to delicately balance the aircraft's rudders as he began his descent.[32] Coming into view was the two-story stone house with one-floor annexes flanking each side. His wheels touched down in the well-trimmed grass that surrounded the residence, just a few yards off from a large brick barn. The backyard was lined with pear and peach orchards, along with a garden for cultivating beets, corn, and other Sunday dinner staples.[33] Before stepping inside the house, Ed might check on the birds—he reared, at various times, chickens, pheasants, pigeons, and a pair of glamorous peacocks named Romeo and Juliet.[34] Out on the farmland surrounding the house, a pair of horses galloped toward the horizon, one for Jim and one for Ed Jr. They had 160 acres to roam.[35]

Ed climbed out of the cockpit and strode toward his new homestead. His children and grandchildren would refer to it as the House, though Jeanne preferred the formal name: Willow Lake Farm.[36] Here the Goodwins hosted elaborate parties for Ed's business colleagues and Easter egg hunts for the black children of Alsuma, who were still not allowed in Tulsa County parks.[37] They welcomed world-renowned black celebrities like singer Dinah Washington and pianist Teddy Wilson who, despite their fame, could not stay in a white hotel or enjoy a meal at a white restaurant.[38] Ed could not force Tulsa to open the doors of opportunity to his children and others who looked like them. But he could build his progeny a world all their own—at least, he could damn well try.

Every Wednesday evening, a little boy named Washington Rucker ventured down to Deep Greenwood with three nickels in his pocket, enough for five copies of the *Oklahoma Eagle*. Near the printing press in back of the *Eagle* offices, he saw the stoic man in a suit and closely trimmed haircut, sitting behind a table and surveying the scene. His complexion was the color of slightly weathered bronze; light-skinned, in other words, from Rucker's vantage. Without asking anyone, the boy sensed that this man commanded the operation. "Mr. Goodwin?" Rucker recalled decades later. "Oh, he was the king."[39]

Rucker waited in line among several boys, most of them not yet teenagers, and placed his change in Mr. Goodwin's large hand. Then he watched the man drop the coins with a *clink* into a bucket, on top of all the other money he'd already collected.

"Give him five papers, Red!" Mr. Goodwin bellowed. The copies clutched under his arm, Rucker dashed back out onto Greenwood Avenue, eager to sell them before the other newsboys claimed all the potential customers. Since the *Eagle* had a sticker price of five cents, Rucker stood to make a ten-cent profit for his trouble. "As poor as I was, any way you can make a penny made all the difference in the world," he said.[40]

Rucker lived at the intersection of Greenwood Avenue and Jasper Street, about half a mile north of the *Eagle* office and the neon-lit delights of Deep Greenwood.[41] His home was a "shotgun" house, like the ones Mr. Goodwin rented out on Hartford Avenue. The twelve-foot-wide structures had no hallways; instead each room was placed one behind the other, in a straight line. If you fired a shotgun through the front door, the slug would sail clean through every room and out the back.

Shotgun houses were often overcrowded, ramshackle affairs. "No electricity, no telephone, no radio, no gas," Rucker said later, ticking off the utilities missing from his childhood home.[42] He completed his homework by a gas lamp and skipped the three-cent lunches at school. He owned a single pair of shoes.[43]

Rucker's experience was not abnormal. In 1940 the U.S. Census Bureau analyzed the living conditions in 427 dwelling units surrounding Rucker's home, all on the east side of Greenwood Avenue. About two-thirds were rented, at about ten dollars per month on average. Close to 20 percent were in need of "major repair," and a similar share housed more than 1.5 people per room, a statistical measure for overcrowding. More than 70 percent lacked private indoor baths.[44] Across Tulsa, 54 percent of nonwhite homeowners had houses valued at less than $1,000, compared to just 9 percent of white homeowners.[45] Outside the pleasing symmetry of the brick buildings in the heart of Deep Greenwood, much of the neighborhood was slapdash construction, with rickety shacks and repurposed boxcars often abutting elegant middle-class homes.[46] For all the efforts by the Greenwood Chamber of Commerce to promote the neighborhood as a symbol of "racial prominence and progress," many residents lived in poverty.[47]

Some of the housing problems traced their origins to the 1921 massacre. Greenwood had rebuilt astonishingly quickly in a race to beat the arrival of winter, but many of the structures weren't made to last.[48] When Greenwood residents were denied restitution from the city and insurance companies, they were forced to rely for decades on what they had cobbled together themselves. In 1940 only about 10 percent of Greenwood homes dated back to before 1920, a clear sign of how much destruction the massacre had wrought.[49] "After the disastrous race riot . . . most of the Negroes had no resources and little credit," the National Urban League reported in a 1945 study of local living conditions. "They began to erect makeshift shacks, many of which still stand."[50]

Meanwhile between 1921 and 1945, Tulsa's black population more than doubled, to 25,000 people.[51] Due to racist housing policies, blacks were still hemmed into a five-square-mile area anchored by the original Greenwood district.[52] Just a block west of where the Goodwins grew up on Haskell Street, racial housing covenants still stipulated that homes "shall never be sold to a person of African de-

scent or a Mexican."[53] Similar legal language restricted access to upscale white neighborhoods like Maple Ridge to the south and Ashton
Heights to the north.[54] There was even a Tulsa neighborhood called
White City, supposedly named for the color of its picket fences, that
barred black residents in its founding documents.[55] These policies
were buried in legal paperwork, but they were also displayed proudly
on front lawns. In communities near Greenwood in the 1940s, residents put signs in their yards that read, RESTRICTED TO WHITE PROP-
ERTY OWNERS.[56]

In 1948 the Supreme Court deemed racial housing covenants unconstitutional, but many white people chose to ignore legal precedent.[57] The Oklahoma Supreme Court ruled in 1951 that neighbors
could sue blacks for moving into a white community, on the grounds
that their presence caused property values to fall.[58] The argument relied on a cruel circular logic: property values declined only because of
how desperately whites wanted to live far away from blacks.

As Greenwood grew more and more dense, Washington Rucker's
family grew too. But he didn't get to move to a big country farm. He
slept on a pallet in his family's living room, joined by an additional
younger sibling every year or two.[59] There were no airplanes or horse-
back rides in Rucker's version of Greenwood. Mostly, he and the
other children on his block played around a ten-foot-tall mulberry
tree planted between their homes. Climbing its sturdy branches to
taste the sweetest fruit at its heights, he came to cherish the lessons he
learned about perseverance. He called it the "Mawberry Tree," as he
and his friends worked to scale their personal Kilimanjaro.[60]

Rucker also had a rhythm inside him. Nearly since the time he
could walk, he remembered lining up on the sidewalk alongside everyone else in the neighborhood to see the Booker T. Washington
High School marching band come strutting down Greenwood Avenue. On special occasions, the band would march a nearly two-mile
lap around the neighborhood, starting at the high school and ending
at Carver Junior High, where the football stadium welcomed fans
every Friday night in the fall.[61] Leading the drum section was Red, the
janitor and handyman at the *Eagle* office. Whenever an opposing
team's band came to town, Red would be the first to square up against
their drumline, declaring, "Betcha can't play this!" before rattling off
an impossible pattern.[62]

Watching the way Red played, Rucker was inspired.[63] He soon began banging a knife and fork on the black iron skillet in his mother's small kitchen.[64] In seventh grade, while attending Carver Junior High, he decided he wanted to learn to play the drums properly and tried to join the school band. But at Carver, there were only so many instruments. Because Rucker had skin the color of dark chocolate, and a name no one in Deep Greenwood would recognize, the teacher passed him over when it came time to hand out drums. Rucker absorbed the hurt without understanding it and ultimately transferred schools.[65]

"My family was considered one of those marginal families," he said. "There was no history of my name."[66]

Within Greenwood, class lines were at once rigid and blurred. Expensive homes stood side by side with tin shacks. Teachers dated bootleggers without an ounce of shame.[67] Many of the community's most prominent businesses and civic institutions, like the *Eagle*, were run by people whose illegal endeavors were widely known, like Ed Goodwin and his (former) policy wheel. "Black life in Tulsa was a series of paradoxes," reflected Herbert Scott, a Greenwood native born in the 1940s. "There was little 'formal' class division in the community; we seemed to be thrown into this giant black cauldron in North Tulsa."[68]

Skin color, however, remained a clear demarcation of privilege, as it was throughout America. In a survey of Greenwood residents in the 1930s, social worker Francis Burke found that twenty-five out of thirty believed the "average Negro" preferred lighter-skinned black people, and more than half believed that being lighter-skinned would elevate their own social status. "It is . . . an influencing factor within already existing class groups," Burke wrote.[69] Rucker didn't need a college degree to arrive at that conclusion. He could just repeat the old adage that hovered over the neighborhood without needing to be spoken explicitly: "If you're white, you'all right. If you're brown, stick around. If you're black, get back."[70]

Rucker lived on the opposite end of the societal spectrum from the Goodwin children, whose mother Jeanne and grandfather J.H. could both have passed for white. He ultimately overcame the obstacles that class and color put before him, just as he scaled the tangled branches of the mulberry tree. Returning to Greenwood's school system as a teenager, he became a star member of the Booker T. marching band. (Red, a perennial band member for years, defended Rucker's skills to skeptics.)[71] Jim Goodwin was a couple of years behind him, playing cornet. They were acquaintances as teenagers; as adults, they became close friends. Jim admired Rucker's tenacity in overcoming adversity. Rucker respected that Jim, despite the opportunities he had to leave home, remained loyal to Greenwood and Tulsa's black community. But Rucker never forgot the yawning difference in how their lives began. "The reason he doesn't have my experience? Daddy rich, mama good looking, daddy was highly influential in town, the color of his skin and the shade of his hair," Rucker said years later. "So the total black experience, he don't know nothing about. That's not a put down, but it's just one of the dynamics."[72]

For the children, Willow Lake Farm felt like a boundless playground. They swam in the property's three large ponds and played games like follow-my-voice until the sun slipped below the horizon.[73] There were chores, of course—seemingly endless acres of grass to cut for the boys, mountains of dishes to wash for the girls (though the maids and gardeners whom Ed and Jeanne hired did much of the work).[74] The high school boys courting Jo Ann would call and teasingly ask if she had fed the cows already so she could go out.[75] But the ample space allowed each child to find fulfillment in their own way. Ed Jr. brought his Cub Scouts troop out to explore the farm, while Jim roamed for acres with his reliable brown Tennessee walking horse Star.[76] Daughter Jeanne liked clipping all her favorite articles out of the issues of *Jet* and *Ebony* magazine on display in the family living room.[77] Bob, touched by God early in life, knew he would be a preacher practically before he knew anything else; at the age of nine, he became a lay minister at the tiny Alsuma church a few blocks from the farm,

Susan Goodwin at age five

standing on a stool behind the lectern to read the Sunday scripture each week.[78]

One of the most momentous occasions was the wedding ceremony for Onetha and her husband Godfrey Goff. The couple recited their vows in the family living room before a fireplace mantel covered in ivy, surrounded by baskets full of daisies. Jo Ann sang a solo ahead of the wedding march, while Ed gave Onetha away during the ceremony. A photo of the couple slicing their wedding cake led the society page of the *Eagle* that week.[79]

On Sundays, the Goodwins would gather in their large living room, surrounding a rosewood grand piano that rested in a corner next to the adjoining sunroom.[80] Jeanne would sit at the piano, her fingers gliding effortlessly across the keys, setting the tempo for the musical number of the night.[81] Edwyna played the violin while Jo Ann would join in on the accordion, an instrument she had mastered simply because her father asked her to.[82] Ed Jr. played the clarinet and Jim took up the cornet as the younger children sometimes sang along. Ed Sr. would lead the singing in his soothing tenor, his voice reverberating off the room's polished mahogany walls.[83]

When at its most regal, Willow Lake Farm could match the grandeur of the Stradford Hotel, the Dreamland Theater, and the other treasured spaces that had defined Greenwood a generation earlier. It was, without a doubt, a symbol of black success. But in many ways, it was a sign of things to come in black America, with that success becoming decoupled from the daily rhythms of life in the heart of the black community. The Goodwins were still part of Greenwood, but they were also separate from it. Not everyone got to experience what they did. Young Carlie, who carried both an analytical mind and a big heart, was the oldest Goodwin child to grow up almost entirely on the farm, far removed from the "giant black cauldron" north of the railroad tracks. She would later spend years working in public health in inner city Boston, taking in an almost inverted version of the black experience. It made her see Willow Lake differently. "I grew up protected," she reflected later, "in a world of fantasy and idealism."[84]

———

There was one more member of the Goodwin family in Tulsa. Young Susan cherished the weekends she got to spend in Greenwood. Her mother, Doretha McMillon, lived in a two-bedroom shingle house on Seminole Street, about a mile and a half north of the business district.[85] Nearly every weekend Susan's father would come to the house to share a home-cooked meal. On long Saturday nights, when he and his friends played poker in the large living room, she played cocktail waitress, cleaning out their ashtrays for tips. Susan loved nestling in the passenger's seat of his white Chrysler as she accompanied him to run errands or simply glide through the Oklahoma countryside on afternoon drives. "I was with him all the time," Susan said. "He supported me."

When she went home to the town of Okmulgee, where she lived with her grandparents during the week, Susan brought a piece of the neighborhood back with her through the *Oklahoma Eagle*. She would take the newspaper to her elementary school teachers, her neighbors, and family friends, pocketing all the money from each sale. She imagined she might work at the *Eagle* one day, as her mother and father did.

One day, when Susan was about twelve, her father came by Doretha's home on one of his regular visits. He clutched a bundle of photographs in his hand, photographs of children with big smiles and lighter skin, riding horses and climbing into rowboats. There were so many of them, and the world they inhabited in these pictures seemed vast. All of them, in one way or another, looked like her father. This was his family, Ed Goodwin told his daughter. It was her family too.

Until that moment, Susan had thought she was an only child. The news of a huge family was thrilling. "As a kid, you know, you're real excited. You've got older sisters and brothers," she said decades later. "But it was contentious. There was some resentment, which I didn't understand at the time."[86]

Susan Goodwin was the last of Ed's nine children, born in 1950, just two years after his wife's youngest child, Bob. Her mother, Doretha McMillon, was Ed's secretary when he worked in Taft and an office manager for the *Eagle* for more than ten years afterward.[87] Ed never explained the affair in full to any of his children. He largely kept the two parts of his life separate. The children at Willow Lake Farm learned about their connection to Susan haphazardly; Bob, closest to Susan in age, did not meet her until he was a teenager.[88] There was no

The Goodwin children in the late 1940s: (back row) Onetha,
Ed Jr., Edwyna; (front row) Jim, Jo Ann, Carlie, Jeanne

family meeting or dinner table discussion about how to best integrate
her into their world. "In later years, we were told that she was our
sister," Ed's daughter Jeanne said, "but neither of them [our parents]
sat down and said, 'This is your sister and this is the story.' "[89]

Susan found that her relationships with her siblings varied drastically. She forged a close bond with Ed Jr., who taught her how to
drive a stick shift; as the firstborn son, he also navigated a complicated relationship with his father. She also grew close to Bob, who
became most familiar with intimate family dynamics as the baby of
Willow Lake. On the day they met, the two siblings marched down
Greenwood Avenue hand in hand during a religious rally.[90] Eventually she found common ground with Jo Ann too, who had to overcome her own frustrations with her father's actions in order for them
to bond. "When we did connect, she could tell the same stories," Jo
Ann recalled. "The same songs he told to us were the same songs she
knew. She had the same philosophy we had."[91]

People in the neighborhood talked, of course, but Ed never made Susan feel like a lesser child. He came to Okmulgee for her school plays and had dinner with her and Doretha at her North Tulsa home when Susan spent time in the city. He bought her the same kind of expensive gifts he showered on the women of Willow Lake. Just as he had vowed to do for the children he had with Jeanne, he paid for her college education. "It's been a challenge, but I had a really good childhood," Susan said later. "My dad did very well splitting his time. And that was probably hard on him, but he did it."[92]

In the fall of 1949, the *Tulsa Tribune* columnist and entertainer Cal Tinney visited Willow Lake Farm to write a profile of the Goodwins, whom he intended to cast as the perfect black American family. On a warm September day, Jeanne showed him their "movie-proportioned" living room with brown asphalt-tile flooring, the family Ford station wagon, and the 160 acres of land that stretched as far as the eye could see.[93] If they ventured upstairs, Tinney would have seen the library overflowing with books, the spacious master bedroom, and Jeanne's large walk-in dressing room.[94]

It was unusual for Tinney to be there in the first place, lavishing praise on a black couple for all they had achieved in more than two

The Goodwin homestead at Willow Lake Farm

decades of marriage. White media outlets rarely wrote about black people's lives or concerns, and certainly not about their accomplishments.[95] But Tinney had a clear political motive. "The Goodwin family's two story native stone home would open the eyes of Communist agitators who shout that the Negro is downtrodden in America," he wrote. "There may be Negroes doing better in Russia, but I doubt it."[96]

The column arrived as white Americans were once again questioning black people's loyalty to the United States. In the spring of that year, the entertainer and activist Paul Robeson had decried the "hysterical stupidity" of the United States for potentially engaging in a war with the Soviet Union.[97] A longtime socialist, Robeson flirted with Communist ideology as well. He had taken multiple trips to the USSR and once said that, unlike in his home country, he walked there in "full human dignity."[98] After World War II, as a new world order was split between American and Soviet interests, the United States once again began aggressively ferreting out and persecuting alleged Communists, making examples out of high-profile figures. As a black man, Robeson was particularly vulnerable. His critique of the brewing Cold War was exaggerated by the press into a declaration that blacks should refuse military service outright. The controversy over his comments led to the revocation of his passport and the cancellation of more than eighty planned concerts.[99]

Tinney wanted to show that this big black family in Tulsa, with the beautiful mother and the enterprising father and the cute cowboy kids, was nothing like Paul Robeson. The Goodwins were "hardworking" and "well-adjusted," unlike the "neurotic" leftists on the wrong side of the Cold War.[100] The binary categorization of "good" and "bad" blacks was an age-old tactic of whites seeking to use individual black success stories to distract from mistreatment of the race as a whole. The federal government was employing the very same strategy that year—Jackie Robinson, then at the peak of his fame in Major League Baseball, was brought before the House Un-American Activities Committee in Congress so that he could denounce Robeson's statement. The All-Star player and avowed anti-Communist dismissed Robeson's remarks as "silly," but he spent more time explaining that racism in America was not a figment of the "communist imagination."[101]

Like Jackie Robinson, the Goodwins walked a rhetorical tightrope. They upheld American values like democracy and equality in theory, while criticizing how unjustly they were meted out to black citizens in practice. Jeanne felt the chasm of opportunity between blacks and whites was closing, however slowly, and that she had the ability to help fill in some of that gap. In the late 1940s, she was among the women who formed a biracial board soliciting city funds to keep the Greenwood nursery open.[102] She also penned a letter to the editor of the *Tulsa Tribune* decrying the fact that black children were being denied service at white hospitals, even in cases where the hospitals claimed not to discriminate.[103] She did not want to seed resentment in the minds of her children by focusing on what black people lacked, so she emphasized what they were gaining through resilience and hard work. "Don't get bitter, get better" was the motto she passed down to them from her father.[104] But staying positive, of course, was easier for a family that already had so much.

"Our Greenwood Avenue people need parks," Jeanne told Tinney during his visit. "The children need recreational facilities. But the gains have been tremendous even in the last 10 years." Regarding Robeson and Communism, her response was simple: "America is our home and there could be none better for us."[105]

The *Eagle* soon staked out a similar position. In a 1950 front-page editorial, the newspaper argued that it was the freedom to protest in America—an activity likely to be suppressed in the Soviet Union—that black people should hold sacrosanct.[106]

The editorial criticized both Robeson and W.E.B. Du Bois; the famed intellectual had once been an admirer of Ed's when he was protesting at Fisk in 1925. Du Bois had slowly become disillusioned with the "Negro intelligentsia," of which he had long been a part, as he saw them doing little to reverse the increasingly stark class divisions among black people.[107] He wanted the "highbrow" NAACP, which he had co-founded, to become an organization for the black masses and not just the black elite.[108] When it became clear that the organization would remain geared toward the black middle and upper classes, he left and pursued more radical politics.[109] Du Bois ultimately embraced Communism as a path toward the global liberation of black people across the world. "Capitalism cannot reform itself," he famously declared when he joined the Communist Party in his twilight years. "It is doomed to self-destruction."[110] The *Eagle* disagreed, advocating reform over revolution. "Don't take Robeson and Du Bois too seriously," the newspaper's editorial read. "They are curious specimens of what American segregation and discrimination can do to brilliant minds."[111]

In the 1940s and '50s, a schism was opening up between black leaders who wanted to push for desegregation, which would radically change the lives of the rising black middle class, and those who prioritized wealth redistribution, which would impact the black working class and poor. In 1957 one of Jeanne's former bosses, the sociologist and Howard University professor E. Franklin Frazier, published the provocative book *Black Bourgeoisie,* which argued that the black middle class was in the thrall of the destructive seductions of American capitalism, such as conspicuous consumption and a poorly placed faith in free markets as a pathway toward liberation.[112] Their tendency to overinflate their own success—often mediated through glowing profiles of black entrepreneurs in the black press—only served the capital interests of white people by obscuring the financial turmoil common in black communities.[113] "The picture which white Americans wanted to present to the world was that although Negroes had been enslaved and had suffered many disabilities since Emancipation, on the whole they were well off economically, had gained civil rights, and had improved their social status," Frazier wrote. "*Black Bourgeoisie* was a refutation of this image."[114]

Much of Frazier's ire toward the black press was directed at national outlets like *Ebony,* which had been pitched from the start as affirmation for the middle class—*LIFE* magazine for black people.[115] The Goodwin family was an *Ebony* feature incarnate, with a quirky country twist, but the *Oklahoma Eagle* tried to thread the needle between celebrating the accomplishments of the black elite and supporting the black working class through efforts such as labor advocacy. "The educated or more prosperous Negro who imagines that he can get away from his ignorant and poverty stricken black brother is a bigger fool than the poor Negro who allows someone to build a wall of hate between him and the Negro who is in fairly good circumstances," *Eagle* editor Horace Hughes wrote in a 1941 editorial. "Bound together by color, we march to fate abreast."[116] Still, such soaring rhetoric never stopped Greenwood from replicating the same income inequality that gripped the United States as a whole.

To the Goodwin children, it was obvious that some people in Greenwood had more than others. Ed Jr. recalled dreading the new church suit his parents bought him each year because he knew his friends couldn't afford the same clothes. "I'd prefer to be raggedy too, as I could fit in," he wrote in an unfinished memoir. "But my mom wouldn't go for it. I stood out like a sore thumb."[117]

Jeanne wanted her children to have the very best and to reach their highest potential. It was important to her that they understood they were deserving of greatness at a time when black inferiority permeated all aspects of white American society. But she also instilled in them a sense of humility and an awareness of the duties that came with being a responsible member of society. "Of course, our people don't have as good a time of it in some parts of the United States, I don't particularly like that," she told Cal Tinney as she showed him her home. "But knowing something about the condition, I have learned to take it in my stride."[118]

As the interview was concluding, Jim, age nine, bounded into the kitchen for a sandwich. He and Ed Jr. had just been out riding their horses. "I want to be a cowboy like Roy Rogers," he announced to Tinney.[119]

But just two days later tragedy struck. When Jim and a neighborhood friend were out riding across the farmland, they decided to trade horses for fun. After they swapped, the two steeds got spooked and started racing. Soon they were barreling toward an oncoming train on the Katy Railroad line. Panicked, Jim leaped from the horse to try to escape the collision, but he landed directly on the train tracks, his head smashing the iron railing. The deafening roar of the train engine clouded out every other sound in his mind. Then everything went dark.[120]

It was a Tuesday evening.[121] The rest of the family had been preparing for dinner. When someone from Alsuma sped over to Willow Lake to deliver the news that Jim was hurt, Jeanne sprinted out of the house barefoot, desperate to reach her injured son.[122] She found a gruesome scene: the boy's right arm had gotten mangled in the undercarriage of the train as he was dragged for twenty yards, his small body bouncing off the track's crossties.[123] Jim's bones were completely crushed just above the elbow. After a pair of Good Samaritans placed him in his mother's arms, blood poured from the gash in his head and onto Jeanne's dress. The next several hours were blessedly excised from Jim's memory, but he retained a swimming image of his mother's face floating above him as his head was nestled in her lap. "She was either crying, or singing, or praying," Jim said later. "All three."[124]

The arm had to be amputated at the shoulder. Jim spent two weeks in recovery at Mercy Hospital, in the basement where all the black patients were kept.[125] There was no waiting room for black family members, but his mother was with him nearly every waking hour, while his father came whenever he got off from work.[126] Jeanne could not find the language to describe the hurt she felt for her son, but in public, she retained her unshakable optimism.[127] When Cal Tinney heard the news and reached out to learn how the family was coping, she told the reporter that every sibling would be there to help Jim make a complete recovery. "Yes, Jim lost his arm," Jeanne said, "but he has acquired 16 more."[128]

When Susan was a teenager, she finally got to see Willow Lake Farm for herself. For years, when it was time for Ed to leave Susan after a day spent together, he would tell his daughter with a bit of disarming humor that he needed to go "survey his property." Finally, he invited her to the property herself for dinner with him, his sister Anna, and his wife Jeanne.

Susan was nervous as she walked around the rippling ponds, entered the magnificent stone house, and saw the family pictures that kept accruing with each passing year. It was the mid-1960s. The older children were grown or in college, so she and the adults ate alone at the large table where the family had dined every Sunday for more than a decade. The estate was gorgeous; the dinner was uncomfortable. "I was received well," she said. "But there's nothing to draw on."

Susan would visit Willow Lake only two more times in her life: to introduce her father to the man she wanted to marry, and to mourn him after he died. Though Susan bore her father's name, and he talked openly about her presence, she still sometimes felt she was on the outside looking in on her own family, especially when she returned to

Tulsa for funerals. But she would not apologize for her existence, because her father had never once made her feel like she should have to. "That never entered my mind because he was always there," she said. "I had his name."

If there was one trait that Susan inherited from Ed, it was confidence. She stood up for herself and for the relationship they forged together. "I was his child," she said. "And I always felt that."[129]

CHAPTER 14

SEPARATE BUT EQUAL

The new Booker T. Washington High School, still segregated, opened in 1950

ven after the Goodwins left Greenwood, Jo Ann always knew she would graduate from Booker T. Washington High School. The school was one of the oldest neighborhood institutions, paying homage to the past at the same time that each class of new graduates replenished Greenwood's ingenuity and ambition for the future. Teachers stayed on for decades, mentoring their neighbors' children and sometimes their grandchildren, too.[1] To call it close-knit was almost to undersell the interweaving bonds that grew thicker with each passing year. *Don't call it Washington,* proud graduates would insist a century after the school's founding. *No, it's not BTW. The name is Booker T.*

The school was thirty-five years old by the time Jo Ann enrolled in the fall of 1948, and the list of notable alumni was already long.[2] There was John Hope Franklin, the rigorous historian and son of Greenwood lawyer B. C. Franklin. His 1947 book *From Slavery to*

Freedom chronicled the experiences of black Americans since their arrival on colonial shores and became a college classroom staple for generations.[3] George Lythcott became a physician after growing up around his father's medical practice on Archer Street. He was the first black resident physician at Boston City Hospital and later served as an assistant surgeon general under President Jimmy Carter.[4] Anita Williams, the daughter of W. D. Williams and granddaughter of Loula Williams, was the only black woman in her graduating class at the Northern Illinois College of Optometry.[5] When she returned to Tulsa after school with her husband, Charles Christopher, they opened an optometry clinic on the northern edge of Greenwood, becoming the first licensed black eye doctors in Oklahoma history.[6]

But by the time Jo Ann enrolled, Booker T.'s facilities did not match its intellectual pedigree. The campus had been built in the heart of the Greenwood district in the late 1910s, while Ed Goodwin was a student, and it was showing its age by the 1940s.[7] Gas stoves couldn't provide enough warmth during the icy winters, while the library took on an inch of water during the rainy spring. Classrooms meant for twenty students now had forty, and lessons were often taught in the poorly lit basement. "We are all interested in equal education opportunities," read an *Eagle* editorial, "but if one were to pass by the other three high schools in Tulsa and then pass the Booker Washington high school, we feel sure your head would be lowered in shame."[8] Students themselves recognized the chasm between white and black education in the city. When John Hope Franklin saw downtown's imposing Central High School for the first time, the size and grandeur of the building both awed and disappointed him. "So this is what they have, compared to what I have," he recalled thinking.[9]

When Oklahoma's legislators segregated schools in the state constitution in 1907, they decreed that a "separate school" system with "like accommodations" would be created for black students, while children of all other races would be classified as white.[10] White school districts could collect property tax revenue at a rate seven times higher than black school districts and float bonds to generate even more money. Black districts could not collect revenue from such bonds. With their limited funding, they barely had enough money to cover maintenance costs.[11] "In the matter of providing buildings, the separate schools are at a decided disadvantage," the Oklahoma Department of Education acknowledged in a 1938 report. "Improvements [are] made on a meager scale."[12]

A 1941 state law backed by longtime Booker T. Washington principal E. W. Woods finally allowed counties to issue bonds to fund new buildings for separate schools, but such measures had to be approved by three-fifths of citizens in a countywide vote.[13] The *Eagle* and Greenwood leaders were forced to conjure their own updraft of political will, separate from white schools, every time they wanted better facilities for their children.

A breakthrough came in 1945, when Tulsa County finally agreed to hold a vote on funding separate schools. The pivot was likely meant in part to stave off the growing calls to dismantle segregated schools altogether because they disadvantaged black children. Despite the cynical politics, the *Eagle* saw an opportunity to provide material gains for Greenwood's next generation. The newspaper urged Tulsa's "liberal hearted" white people to endorse the measure and told Greenwood residents, "The future of your boy, your girl, and our community depend on it."[14] The persistence paid off; Tulsa voters approved a bond for funding black schools by a wide margin, the first such effort to ever pass anywhere in the state of Oklahoma.[15] Five years later, in 1950, the new, $1.7 million Booker T. Washington High School opened its doors.[16]

That fall Jo Ann was a rising senior. She and her best friend Phyllis Madison felt like queens of the new campus as the students streamed into the sprawling new sixty-five-room facility. The new auditorium had all the lighting equipment necessary to make a sixteen-year-old feel like she was on Broadway (or Beale Street). At the indoor pool, the water was as clear as the public pools south of Greenwood, where black folks were not allowed to swim. "It was all modern," Jo Ann recalled, "and we were excited about it."[17]

Every morning Jo Ann's father drove her from Willow Lake to the school's stately entrance, where BOOKER T. WASHINGTON was written in bold block letters above the doorway. She could look up and admire the colorful mural above Washington's name, which featured a yellow bushel of corn, a towering oil rig, a black microscope, and a golden luxury train—symbols for nearly every professional aspiration. At the center of the mural was Washington himself, lifting a shroud off of a seated black man's head. It was a re-creation of a famous statue on Tuskegee's campus, depicting the school's founder as he bestowed knowledge upon a newly freed slave. "He lifted the veil of ignorance from his people," read the inscription, "and pointed the way to progress through education and industry."[18]

The Goodwins were so proud of black Tulsa's new school, the *Eagle* published a special souvenir edition in November 1950. The front page featured a photo of the new two-story building alongside an image of the tiny four-room frame structure where the first Booker T. students had learned Latin and mathematics in 1913.[19] Inside the issue, there were photos of the new high-fashion homes that surrounded the school and portraits of several of the women who had played key roles in Greenwood's growth, including Ed Sr.'s mother Carlie.[20] Articles celebrated the select black Tulsans who had crossed the color line of employment and earned stable, well-paying jobs in city government— police officers, bus drivers, mail carriers.[21] A loving remembrance honored the life of the high school's recently deceased principal, E. W. Woods, while new principal C. L. Cole wrote a column vowing to "turn out children who are able to think for themselves."[22]

One article in the special issue stood out from the rest. On the second page, stretching all the way across the top of the newspaper, was a panoramic photo of Greenwood on June 1, 1921. Smoke billowed across a landscape dotted by ravaged trees and the charred husks of former homes. The photo captured blocks and blocks of wholesale destruction.[23] Twenty-nine years after the attack, thousands of massacre survivors and descendants still lived in Greenwood, but the event was rarely recounted in the pages of the *Eagle* anymore or in public at all.

Many of the young people who'd grown up in the aftermath of 1921 had no knowledge of the year's significance, but they unknowingly saw some of the signs. One time when Jim Goodwin was playing in the weeds at the top of Standpipe Hill, he found a human skull half-buried in the dirt; it would be decades before he realized it might have been the remains of a massacre victim.[24] James Bolton, a playmate of Jim's older brother Ed Jr., often played around a large metal cylinder at the top of a hill; one day when adults came to inspect the object, they discovered it was an inert bomb with the capacity to blow up a city block. No one knew how the bomb had wound up there, but when James later learned that his neighborhood had been reduced to rubble before he was born, he had an idea.[25] Even the most innocuous pieces of city infrastructure served as silent reminders of the destruction: a burned fragment of a telephone pole near George Monroe's childhood home stood well into the 1940s and lodged itself into the back of George's mind for decades long after.[26]

But while the photo in the 1950 *Eagle* summoned a public memory of the massacre for the first time in a long while, the article was not about the attack itself. There was no recounting of Dick Rowland's arrest, of the shoot-out at the courthouse, of the ensuing arson and murder. No talk of internment camps or looted buildings or great mechanical birds in the sky. The article was about what had happened after all that. How Greenwood leaders—people like O. W. Gurley, B. C. Franklin, Dimple Bush, and J. H. Goodwin—had worked together to protect the neighborhood from the predatory financial schemes of Tulsa's white elite. The story the *Eagle* wanted to tell in 1950, as a new school rose alongside beautiful new homes, elegant churches, and the limitless promise of tomorrow, was one of resourcefulness and resilience. "A general scene of the fire-swept Greenwood area following the riot of June 1, 1921," read the understated caption by the brutal photograph. "Progress, as evaluated today, dates from this point."[27]

"Thought for the week: Seniors, only 104 days until graduation."[28]

Jo Ann always liked to sign off her *Eagle* column with the vital information her classmates needed. "Teen Tattle" was her personal mix of community journalism and tabloid gossip, tucked into the back of the newspaper on the "School News" page each week—a "Scoopin' the Scoop" for a younger generation. She began with a diligent report of the week's school assembly. Next came a recap of the latest campus news, like the election of the homecoming queen and the unveiling of a new electric scoreboard in the gym for basketball games.[29] But this was all preamble for—her words and punctuation—"the latest scoop!!"[30] Jo Ann gathered intel measuring how long Shirley Fork and Wilber Moore could be expected to remain an item, and reconnaissance revealing that Dorothy Lowery had been spotted wearing Chester Terrell's jacket.[31] "Say Ruthie Webb, do you have a crush on Edward Goodwin?" she teased in one column about her classmate and her little brother. "Or do you just like to give your friends Valentines?"[32]

Jo Ann always felt like she was getting into more trouble than the rest of her siblings. Between classes, she served as lookout for the boys who smoked cigarettes out behind the school. In biology class, she convinced a pliable friend named Janet to let her copy answers to a test one Friday. (Unfortunately, she was so thorough she also copied Janet's name at the top of her paper.) Jo Ann didn't like to lie to her parents when confronted, but she also wasn't afraid of whatever punishments they might dole out.[33] "Cowards die many times before their death," she wrote in one "Teen Tattle" sign-off.[34]

When she wasn't getting caught up in mischief, Jo Ann was learning from an accomplished group of teachers, more than two-thirds of whom had master's degrees.[35] She loved how James Ellis's passion for mathematics was infectious among the students, while she counted on C. D. Tate's hands-off approach to geometry just as much. ("Kids just ran over him," she said.) She knew Bernadine Brookens in home economics would discount the meals she cooked in class as "slop," while she didn't dare cross Gertie Crawford, the no-nonsense English teacher.[36] Whether the teachers were easygoing or strict, dynamic or didactic, they knew their students and the world they all occupied together in ways that extended far beyond the school's walls. "Principal Henry Whitlow . . . told me that his staff of teachers at BTW put their best efforts into the students and looked forward to their returning to make Tulsa a better city," said Bill Boulware, another Booker T. student in the 1950s.[37]

Among the longest-tenured teachers was W. D. Williams, Loula's son. He had been the very first alum to come back home and start teaching in 1928.[38] His days were soundtracked by the hesitant thwacks of children pecking at keys in his typing classes. Whenever he got behind the typewriter, eyeing a fresh sheet of paper behind his horn-rimmed glasses, the rat-a-tat fire of the device sounded like a toy machine gun.[39] Students were convinced he could type at least 130 words per minute.[40] "Mr. W.D.," as most kids called him, was known for a healthy sense of humor spliced with a stern command of respect.[41] He took his role seriously, so his students did too. "I wasn't the best typist he had ever taught but he made me and other students feel as though we were," Bill Boulware reflected later.[42]

W. D. Williams during his years as a typing and commerce teacher

Mr. W.D. didn't teach history, but he carried a deep passion for it. As the adviser to the school yearbook, *The Hornet,* he helped students understand that their clubs, football games, and yes, teenage gossip, were not frivolous distractions but a chronicle of the "history of community," as one student remembered him putting it.[43] At home, his devotion to chronicling the past included more personal effects. Photos of the old Greenwood District from his childhood days, when the street outside the Williams Confectionery still kicked up dirt every day. A photo of him and a young Ed Goodwin in suits, putting on their best grown-up faces for a group shot of the boys' YMCA. An oval-shaped paperweight emblazoned with a photograph of the Dreamland, declaring it "The Only Colored Theater in The City."[44] And always, those final letters from Loula.

When he introduced himself to a new group of yearbook staffers, Mr. W.D. would sometimes give an informal history of Greenwood, re-creating the world he could access only through those old artifacts. He talked about O. W. Gurley and all the land black people once owned in Oklahoma.[45] Perhaps he mentioned Loula's confectionery and John Williams's auto garage.

The lessons bored Don Ross. He was a fifteen-year-old trouble-maker who attended Booker T. in the 1950s and wound up on the yearbook staff trying to impress a crush. He had little interest in the legacy of his high school or his neighborhood. His priorities were "loafing, mischief, and girls," he later explained in his memoir.[46] In that era, the abundance of Greenwood was obvious to him—and so was the fact that everyone didn't get to enjoy it. Ross grew up in the cramped quarters of a Greenwood housing project, relying on welfare to eat.[47] But one day Mr. W.D. told him something he wasn't expecting, something besides the platitudes about black uplift that were plastered on the mural above the school's front entrance.

When Mr. W.D. was a student, he said, there had been some trouble over a white girl who accused a black boy of rape. Even bigger trouble at the old courthouse downtown. Soon a riot was on. Planes dropped bombs from the sky. Greenwood, including the old Dreamland Theatre, where the kids still went to flirt and watch movies on weekends, had been burned to the ground.

Ross refused to believe it. Like many Greenwood teenagers of the 1950s, he had never heard of any riot. "Greenwood was never burned," he told his teacher. "We're too old for fairytales."

"Sit down, fat mouth," Mr. W.D. snapped, according to Ross's recollections. The teacher had photographic evidence. The next day he brought to school a photo album filled with shocking images. Ross saw Mt. Zion Baptist Church covered in billows of smoke, and the marquee of the Dreamland collapsed in a pile of stone and mechanical wreckage. There were more photos out there, Mr. W.D. told him, gruesome ones.[48] But white people hoarded them like carnival souvenirs, then mailed them out as postcards.[49]

Don Ross was shocked. He'd never given much thought to the world that surrounded him—the wealth, the poverty, the segregation, all of it just seemed to be part of the natural architecture of the universe. But Mr. W.D. helped him see that the order of the world wasn't natural—it was shaped by the politics and machinations of human beings.[50]

At the same time Greenwood was finally reaping the benefits of a long fight for school funding, the most prominent civil rights figures in America had identified Oklahoma as the ideal launch pad for a campaign to dismantle "separate schools" altogether.

In October 1945, just two months before Tulsa voted on the $1 million bond to fund black schools, the Oklahoma state branch of the NAACP held its annual conference in the town of McAlester. The meeting included a high-wattage marquee speaker: NAACP chief counsel Thurgood Marshall.[51] The thirty-seven-year-old attorney was planning to get a black student enrolled at the University of Oklahoma, the state's all-white flagship college. "This is the easiest case to beat that ever entered the courts of Oklahoma," Marshall boasted to a cheering crowd of two hundred. "I could win this type of case even down in Mississippi."[52]

Marshall was spearheading a legal strategy, originally devised by his mentor and earlier NAACP counsel Charles Houston, to dismantle Jim Crow from the top of the education system on down. While the 1896 *Plessy v. Ferguson* ruling had allowed "separate but equal" to dictate K–12 education for decades, many states did not offer segregated schools for black students who wanted professional degrees. If these law schools or graduate schools refused to admit qualified black applicants and failed to offer a viable substitute, the NAACP could sue on the grounds that the states weren't following the letter of their own misguided laws. Court victories for black students at the graduate level, Marshall hoped, could then be leveraged as legal precedents for a more direct assault on the separate-but-equal doctrine in K–12 schools.[53]

Ada Lois Sipuel, a twenty-one-year-old Langston University graduate, became the first student in Oklahoma to test out this strategy. A native of the small, segregated town of Chickasha, she hailed from a family deeply familiar with the violent depths of white intransigence.[54] Her parents had fled Tulsa after the massacre in 1921, then reeled from the brutal 1930 murder of a black man named Henry Argo in Chickasha, the last documented lynching in the state.[55] When the NAACP offered her a chance to pick a legal fight with the University of Oklahoma, she leaped at the opportunity. "The law was wrong," she said later of her motivation. "The whole system was unfair."[56] In January 1946, Sipuel applied for admittance to the University of Oklahoma School of Law and was rejected solely on the basis of her race.[57] Three months later she stepped into the Cleveland County Courthouse in Norman to file a lawsuit against the school. Accompanying her were Roscoe Dunjee, the editor of Oklahoma City's longtime black newspaper the *Black Dispatch,* and Amos Hall, the respected Greenwood lawyer. They were the twin anchor points of the NAACP's operations in Jim Crow Oklahoma.[58]

While Thurgood Marshall brought star power and rhetorical panache to the case, Greenwood lawyer Amos Hall shepherded their carefully crafted argument from courtroom to courtroom, judge to judge. The attorneys knew that if a district court judge ruled against Sipuel, they could always appeal to the state supreme court and eventually the U.S. Supreme Court. A ruling from a higher court, in fact, could ultimately have a greater impact, and the NAACP's long-term goal was to find the perfect case to dislodge *Plessy v. Ferguson.*[59]

On July 9, 1946, Ada Sipuel and Amos Hall sat together at the plaintiff's table in a courtroom in Norman.[60] "I was scared, scared stiff," Hall admitted later.[61] Norman, like Tulsa and Chickasha, had its own brutal history of racial violence. Even into the 1940s, the city remained the state's most prominent "sundown town," meaning black people were not welcome there after dark.[62] With no lodging available to them, Hall and Sipuel were forced to sleep in the basement of a friendly Methodist church for the duration of the trial.[63]

Despite these setbacks, Hall was undeterred. In the courtroom, there was no jury to persuade, only District Judge Ben Williams. So the Greenwood lawyer addressed his oral argument to the bench. "The requirements of the Constitution cannot be set aside in the maintenance of separate schools," Hall said, as white and black onlookers listened intently. "If Ada Lois Sipuel is the only one out of the two hundred thousand Negroes of this state desirous of securing education in law, the state is required to give her that regardless of how expensive this dual system of education is."[64]

In his twenty-year legal career, Hall had already defended black Tulsa policemen in a wrongful firing case and wedged open a door for black workers at the Douglas Aircraft plant during World War II, working closely with Ed Goodwin and Horace Hughes.[65] Soon he would launch a campaign to get black teachers in Oklahoma City pay equal to that of their white counterparts.[66] He knew well how effectively people in power could twist laws promising equal treatment into policies that reinforced the opposite. He dared to say as much in his closing remarks: "I don't see any way in the world to correct these injustices unless courts have this courage."[67]

Judge Williams bristled. "This court feels he has the courage to do his duty in this or any other judicial proceeding," he said. The judge ruled against Sipuel, arguing that the court could not compel a college to violate state segregation laws. Halle quickly filed an appeal.[68]

So began a yearslong odyssey of appeals, remands, and petitions, as the University of Oklahoma did everything in its power to prevent a black woman from entering its doors. When Sipuel's case was eventually heard by the U.S. Supreme Court, the court ruled in her favor, declaring that the university had to provide Sipuel an education. But in order to evade compliance with the court ruling, university officials hastily established a sham black law school, located in a few spare rooms in the state capitol. Sipuel refused to attend.[69] Finally, in the

Thurgood Marshall (left) and Amos Hall (right) worked together on multiple school desegregation cases in Oklahoma

summer of 1949, after the NAACP had worn the school down through sheer bureaucratic exhaustion, Ada Lois Sipuel was accepted as a law student at the University of Oklahoma. She was forced to sit alone in the back row of the classroom, in a large wooden chair with a sign hanging off it that read COLORED.[70]

The Sipuel case was just the first salvo by Marshall and the NAACP against "separate but equal" in Oklahoma. In 1948 the longtime Langston University professor George McLaurin tried to enroll at OU's College of Education to earn his doctoral degree.[71] Running through a similar legal gauntlet as Sipuel, he was denied admission by the school, enrolled via court order, then was placed in an alcove in the back of an all-white classroom in order to maintain segregation.[72] But when McLaurin's case made it to the U.S. Supreme Court (Hall led the plaintiff's arguments), the high court ruled that the school's attempts to separate black students "handicapped his pursuit of effective graduate instruction." Another section of the ruling foretold the imminent future: "State imposed restrictions which produce such inequalities cannot be sustained."[73] "Separate but equal" still stood, but it had suffered a significant blow.

In Tulsa, a similar fight was unfolding at the city's most prominent private college, the University of Tulsa. In early 1950, inspired by the

Sipuel and McLaurin cases, North Tulsa resident Anita Hairston applied for admission to the school's master's program in education.[74] TU refused to allow her to attend classes on the main campus, but said it would be willing to open an "extension" campus at Carver Junior High School in Greenwood, if Hairston could find nine other students to join the classes herself.[75]

The plan was controversial among black people. Violet Bate, an *Eagle* columnist, called it an "embarrassing climax" to the effort to fully desegregate TU and warned that black students should "refuse to make it so beautifully easy for T.U. to maintain the status quo."[76]

Despite the sniping in the press, Hairston just wanted to learn. She rallied the necessary students, and the extension campus opened in Greenwood in the fall of 1950.[77] The *Eagle* helped promote the classes available in the following semesters.[78] "I am not in favor of segregation," Hairston told the newspaper, "but I see no reason why I should miss a chance to further my education simply because I am asked to sit with students of my own race."[79] She graduated with a master's degree in 1952 and attended the commencement ceremony on the main campus.[80]

The NAACP, meanwhile, was no longer brooking any compromise with white institutions that wanted to slow-walk the road to equality. In 1951 Kansas welder and pastor Oliver Brown became the lead plaintiff in the NAACP's class-action lawsuit against the Topeka school board. Brown's third-grade daughter Linda had been denied access to a nearby white elementary school. When the case reached the U.S. Supreme Court, Thurgood Marshall was finally ready to take on the "separate but equal" doctrine directly. The case that would become known as *Brown v. Board of Education* came to life.[81]

Since the Supreme Court's *Plessy v. Ferguson* ruling, "separate but equal" had kept black people in underfunded schools and dirty train cars. But for decades, black people had been chipping away at both the logic and the morality of the court's argument—refusing to give up their seats on trains, staging marches on city hall against segregated housing, and waging courtroom battles against a legal doctrine at odds with the U.S. Constitution. The first Oklahoma lawsuit opposing *Plessy* was filed not by the NAACP and Ada Lois Sipuel in 1946 but by Edward P. McCabe, the founder of the all-black town of Langston, who challenged segregated railroad cars in *McCabe v.*

Atchison, Topeka & Santa Fe Railway Co. in 1908.[82] The struggle had been a long one.

In the Supreme Court chambers, Marshall decried the separate-but-equal doctrine as a betrayal of the Constitution and an attempt to keep the descendants of slaves "as near that stage as is possible."[83] Backing up his rhetoric was a mountain of persuasive legal argument, much of which could be traced back to Greenwood. Ada Lois Sipuel, the plaintiff of one of the first NAACP cases to begin dismantling *Plessy,* was a massacre descendant. Amos Hall, who had called Tulsa home for decades, provided oral arguments on behalf of both her and George McLaurin. McLaurin's case would ultimately be cited in the *Brown* decision as a key precedent.[84] John Hope Franklin, a Booker T. graduate, spent much of the fall of 1953 in the NAACP offices in New York, working with Marshall and a team of academics to establish whether the Fourteenth Amendment had intended to eliminate segregation in public schools. "[Marshall] tolerated no speculation of how the Court might rule," Franklin recalled.[85]

On May 17, 1954, the ruling finally came. "We conclude that in the field of public education the doctrine of 'separate but equal' has no place," wrote Chief Justice Earl Warren. The decision was unanimous.

The *Oklahoma Eagle* ran a headline that streamed atop the front page: SEGREGATION RULED UNCONSTITUTIONAL.[86] In an interview, one school principal called *Brown v. Board* "the greatest and most significant decision that the court will render during the 20th century."[87] The *Eagle,* as it was wont to do, melded a stone-faced pragmatism with an undeniable optimism about what was coming next. While the front page soberly analyzed the feasibility of eradicating Jim Crow from schools across the South, the editorial page allowed for a triumphant headline: A NEW BIRTH OF FREEDOM.[88]

Inside the halls of Booker T., the reaction was more muted. Bill Boulware, a high school junior at the time, didn't like the idea of his younger siblings not getting to experience the same world of dedicated black teachers and intergenerational bonds that had so shaped his path to success. "The students of Booker T. Washington were not happy with the decision," he reflected. "The loss of Booker T. Washington to integration . . . ripped the heart out of a community that once had the pride to succeed in all aspects of a good life."[89]

Boulware's harsh reassessment of *Brown v. Board*'s impact came more than sixty years after the historic decision. At the time of the ruling, though, there was so much excitement over what Greenwood stood to gain through desegregation, there was less talk of what it might lose.

CHAPTER 15

CROSSING THE LINE

*A protest against Jim Crow at the Oklahoma Capitol
during the civil rights movement*

rown v. Board upended American education—or promised to,
at least. Less than a week after the Supreme Court ruling, leaders of seventeen state chapters of the NAACP, along with Thurgood Marshall and Walter White, met in Atlanta to strategize how to
force the integration of their local school districts.[1] Elsewhere in the
Deep South that summer, in the tiny town of Indianola, Mississippi, a
group of disgruntled whites also met, intent on preventing black children from entering white schools and neighborhoods through intimidation and worse, if need be. They called themselves the Citizens'
Council.[2] Within a year, there were hundreds of chapters scattered
across the South.

The *Eagle* methodically reported out every new development in the
emerging civil rights battle, week by week. For years before *Brown*,

the newspaper had been carefully chronicling and critiquing the Jim Crow regime that gripped Tulsa, from the whites-only sections on public buses to the upscale department store that refused to let black women try on dresses.[3] After the Supreme Court decision, the newspaper's work became even more urgent. Throughout the 1950s, Ed spent the dollars necessary to recruit out-of-town talent to help lead the *Eagle's* coverage of a tumultuous moment. He hired accomplished journalists such as Edgar T. Rouzeau, who had worked as the first black war correspondent during World War II for the *Pittsburgh Courier*.[4] Former *Eagle* newsboys who had sold papers alongside Jim and Ed Jr., like Eddie Madison, became reporters and editors as young men.[5] Ed also provided a platform for vital community leaders, like the Rev. Ben Hill, the eloquent new pastor at Vernon AME Church. In his weekly *Eagle* column, Hill wrote that Jim Crow had "shortened the lives of thousands without cause, twisted the minds of others, and divided the nation for centuries."[6] Integration, Hill and so many others hoped, would help begin to undo generations' worth of harm.[7]

But as much as the newspaper headlines cast *Brown v. Board* as a flashpoint moment, the actual pace of change on the ground in Greenwood was slower. The neighborhood didn't transform overnight, and many of the people who enjoyed its raucous nightlife and tight-knit sense of community didn't want it to. "That ruling by the Supreme Court had no effect on us in high school at the time," recalled Washington Rucker, who entered his senior year the fall after the *Brown v. Board* ruling. "We were so deeply entrenched in surviving as black people that this ruling meant something for future generations and not us."[8]

The *Eagle* was documenting a moment of rapid change, but it was also keeping a record of streetscapes, corner stores, and nighttime haunts that would begin disappearing within years. Some of Ed's key new hires captured the dual trajectories of the community in the newspaper's pages—often reporting on both in the very same issue.

One morning in August 1954, less than three months after the *Brown v. Board* decision, Luix Virgil Overbea dragged himself out of bed around seven and made his way to Booker T. Washington High School.[9] It was a new school year, but Booker T. was just as black as the day before the Supreme Court shot down "separate but equal."[10] Overbea, the newest hire at the *Oklahoma Eagle,* was supposed to be evaluating the Hornets, the most important football team in the world to every Greenwood resident. But as he hustled from his new home on Virgin Street to the football stadium, he realized practice had started at 6:30. He was already late.[11]

For Overbea, moving to Tulsa had been like stepping into an alternate universe. He grew up in Chicago, a metropolis with more than half a million black residents and no laws dictating where black people could sit on the bus.[12] He earned a journalism degree from nearby Northwestern University, which admitted its first black student before 1905, and he had been represented by a black man in Congress since 1929, when he was just six years old.[13] Meanwhile, there were barely 150,000 black folks in all of Oklahoma.[14] The state had fought school desegregation all the way to the Supreme Court, twice, and had a governor, Johnston Murray, who was the son of the state's most famous segregationist, old "Alfalfa" Bill. (The *Eagle* broke with years of precedent endorsing Democratic candidates in order to oppose Alfalfa Jr.)[15]

In Tulsa, blacks and whites seemed especially distant, by custom just as much as by law, and for darker reasons that were not discussed much in public. But Overbea, a reporter for the Associated Negro Press, wrote a boxing column that Ed Goodwin must have liked, because the *Eagle* syndicated it every week.[16] The young scribe was looking to make the leap from writing to editing, so he mailed a letter to Ed applying for a managing editor role at the *Eagle.* When Ed offered him the job, Overbea quickly packed up his life on Chicago's South Side and moved to North Tulsa. After he arrived, though, he found that his supposed new role had already been filled by Thelma Thurston Gorham, a diligent journalist from Kansas City who would one day take on editing roles at *Jet, Ebony,* and the *Crisis* magazines. Overbea was demoted to city and sports editor before he even started, but he took the confusing onboarding process in stride. If nothing else, this would be an adventure.[17]

Overbea made it to football practice around 7:30 that August morning, as the players were doing fifty-yard sprints in full uniforms and pads. Just watching those boys run made him tired. "It seems that a cardinal sin for any person here in Tulsa is to admit that he is not familiar with the Booker T. Washington High School football team," he reported after the scrimmage in his new weekly *Eagle* column, "Sportopics."[18] Practically every word he printed in the paper was laced with the same dry humor. But more than cracking jokes or re-capping box scores, Overbea wanted to document where the color line was blurring in Tulsa and where it was still frustratingly stark. At University of Tulsa football games that fall, black and white teenagers sat together in a special students' section for the first time, but at Tulsa Oilers baseball games, black fans continued to be relegated to a small Jim Crow section of the stands.[19] "Folks in North Tulsa love baseball," Overbea wrote, "but they will not pay to see it when they are segregated because of their race."[20]

Sports were just a small part of what Overbea covered at his new job. Working double duty as city editor, he quickly discovered that while Greenwood had the population of a small town, its entrepreneurs had much grander ambitions. At Mann Bros. Grocery, owner McKinley Mann told Overbea how he and his brother Obie had launched the store in 1918, back when it was just a 540-square-foot wooden building.[21] Everything, from their massive cooler to the canned blackberries, had turned to ash during the 1921 massacre.[22] Thirty years later, the family received "citywide, statewide and national attention" when they opened a new air-conditioned, seven-thousand-square-foot facility on Lansing Avenue, with 128 feet of rack space for vegetables (for the adults), and state-of-the-art freezers chock-full of ice cream (for the kids). Overbea and the *Eagle* declared the new Mann Bros. Grocery a "Tulsa landmark."[23]

Of course, there were less noble pursuits that Overbea didn't write about, even if they were common knowledge to everyone in the neighborhood. Silas Goodlet, a one-man walking meat market, roamed Greenwood Avenue in a long khaki overcoat, out of which he sold steaks and sausages. No one knew where he sourced his meat—he was caught up with the police enough to guess it was nowhere legal—but his slick talk and infectious, high-pitched laugh won him lots of customers.[24] The numbers runners also remained ever present, making sure that the policy wheel never stopped turning. They now answered to Alphonzo Williams, an enterprising cab company owner from Oklahoma City who had taken on the mantle of Policy King while launching a minor league baseball team in Greenwood, the T-Town

Clowns.[25] Like a lot of black folks, he was wary of banks, so Williams kept his money in an office back room stacked high with shoeboxes and hired teenagers such as Princetta Rudd-Newman to sort the cash by denomination.[26] Within the captive audience of a segregated community, everyone had a chance to go into business for themselves, one way or another.

Overbea celebrated the black business success that reminded him of Chicago, but he grew frustrated with how white businesses in Tulsa continued to discriminate against his race. In April 1955 the restaurant chain Howard Johnson's opened a new location on Eleventh Street, near downtown Tulsa. When several black customers tried to sit down for a meal and were denied service, they called the *Eagle* office.[27] Overbea decided to launch an investigation—the idea of new Jim Crow policies being enacted after *Brown* particularly riled him. He got a copy of the state constitution, as well as a pile of statute books, and began poring over every law that actually governed life in Oklahoma, line by line.[28] He found that the state had no legal mandates preventing black people from entering "whites only" restaurants, movie theaters, and concert halls—just business owners, politicians, and police who were trying to will their racism into having the force of statutory law.

"Why does Jim Crow continue although it is not legal? Fear, ignorance, bigotry," Overbea determined. "Most white persons in conversation will declare they are against discrimination but in action do not have the guts to do anything about it or prove they mean what they say."[29]

Overbea's boss at the *Eagle* shared similar thoughts. Thelma Thurston Gorham was the *Eagle*'s second female managing editor, taking over the top role just months before *Brown v. Board*.[30] Like Overbea, she was a well-traveled journalist who'd had a formative experience as a correspondent for the first organizing conference of the United Nations in San Francisco.[31] Perhaps it was that organization's diplomatic mission that gave Gorham some level of optimism about Tulsa's ability to bridge the divide between black and white. "Prejudices are not innate, have nothing to do with genes," she wrote in one of a series of front-page columns ruminating on race relations in the city after *Brown*. "[They] may be overcome with patient and positive effort."[32] But she also knew of Tulsa's dark history and of how the memory of the massacre left a bitter taste, "like ashes in the mouths of Negroes," among Greenwood residents. White Tulsans, meanwhile, would rather not remember the massacre at all. "It seems to be a mixture of fear and guilt feeling," Gorham wrote, "that rises like a wall between the tracks that literally and figuratively separate North Tulsans from their white brethren."[33]

While Greenwood was opposed to segregation on principle, the neighborhood found ways to flourish despite it in practice. This was most clear at night, when the issues south of Archer Street hardly mattered. Weekend revelers packed every bar and restaurant. Men who shined shoes in white country clubs by day became dance floor kings; women who spent hours tending to rich white families as maids were now queens lording over a court of would-be suitors. Bonded liquor bottles were sold discreetly out of car trunks at all the popular hangouts, then liberally applied to glasses of Coke or ginger ale to lubricate the weekly release. All of it was typical on a lively evening on "the stroll," where problems of the world could be forgotten until the sun came up.

When the neon lights of Greenwood flickered to life, Luix Overbea ventured into the neighborhood's bustling clubs to write the *Eagle*'s weekly entertainment column, "The Night Beat."[34] He got the plum assignment of covering the stars that filtered in and out of the Big Ten Ballroom, North Tulsa's marquee music venue. Opened by police officer Lonnie Williams in 1948, the Big Ten boasted a rooftop garden and a thirty-five-foot fountain near its entrance. It was billed as "the toniest nightclub this side of Harlem" by the *Tulsa Tribune*.[35] The signature feature was the huge open dance floor right below the stage, where patrons crowded shoulder to shoulder every Saturday night at 10:30 to catch the first live band, then kept the rhythm going for hours on end.[36] A night at the Big Ten was guaranteed to be a cyclone of "sweat, swelter and confusion," as Overbea put it. But, he wrote, "everybody seemed to have a great time."[37]

In 1955 the Big Ten booked a future musical icon nearly every other week—artists for whom the warping color line was a persistent concern. The ground was shifting far beyond *Brown v. Board*, in culture as well as in the classroom. In March, when a twenty-nine-year-old B. B. King showed up at the ballroom in a personalized $7,000 tour bus, he assured Overbea he would keep playing black venues as he rose in fame.[38] In April, Fats Domino brought the easygoing blues of New Orleans to the stage, then said to Overbea after the show, "White musicians always want to sit with us and catch our style."[39] In May, Willie Mae "Big Mama" Thornton rocked the audience with her back porch barnstormer "Hound Dog," which was a smash hit among black listeners. Overbea joked that the "down-with-it" single was her "favorite pet."[40] A year after she performed in Tulsa, an up-and-coming Mississippi singer named Elvis Presley recorded the same song with a pristine electric guitar lick and a clean-cut white face. It sold nearly half a million copies in its debut week and became the signature example of a white performer eclipsing a black innovator in a burgeoning new genre that white radio DJs had coined "rock and roll."[41]

The biggest show of the year came in September 1955, when several of the most popular R&B acts of the era visited the Big Ten at the same time for a nightlong musical battle called the Top Ten Revue. In "perspiration drenched dressing rooms" after the show, Overbea learned just how seriously seventeen-year-old Etta James took her growing career, playing bass and writing her own lyrics. An early song of hers, "The Wallflower," had recently been rerecorded by a white artist, transforming it from a genre track for black audiences into a "mainstream" hit. "Why is it that when we do a song it's rhythm and blues," James wondered backstage, "and when white artists take over the same it's 'pop'?"[42]

Overbea also got some time with Bo Diddley, the bespectacled, gap-toothed singer who, just like the reporter, got his creative start in Chicago. Diddley was doing things with a guitar that the Big Ten audience had never seen before. The musician's first single, the self-titled "Bo Diddley," had been released just five months before and featured a syncopated guitar riff backed by frenetic maracas and a warbling electric chord that sounded like the soundtrack for an impromptu beach party. Even at the time, the unusual melodies felt like they were ushering in a new era. "I want to bring out something different," Diddley told Overbea, "and bring out new sound and rhythms."[43] Artists ranging from Buddy Holly to Guns N' Roses would eventually borrow the "Bo Diddley beat," though it was most famously lifted for 1965's "I Want Candy" by the Strangeloves.[44] Overbea was awed by

Diddley's abilities and declared him the "new rage," but he also saw how these new rhythms fit firmly in the black musical tradition that already existed. There was a direct line from the ragtime records that had been sold on Greenwood Avenue in the 1920s to the manic melodies now bringing down the house at the Big Ten. Overbea didn't need a new phrase like "rock and roll" for it. "The sound is pulsating," he wrote. "It is 'crazy,' and it is strictly the blues."[45]

After the show at the Big Ten let out, Overbea could drive over to the Three Bears, a low-lit, upscale club where men were expected to remove their hats when they walked through the front door.[46] Every weekend at the stroke of midnight, owner Arthur Graves shoved all the tables to the far walls, creating a spur-of-the-moment dance floor. Then he'd jam a nickel into the jukebox and start to mambo, luring shy patrons to the dance floor with his swinging hips. Some nights a challenger named Al Jackson sauntered into the club—Overbea nicknamed him the "Mambo Kid"—and the two men staged an epic dance-off. Their antics helped get everyone else on their feet.[47]

The Wagon Wheel was open as late as there were hungry stomachs. There Overbea devoured juicy steaks and a new summer delicacy: frog legs served with French fries, salad, and green peas.[48] Owner Bessie Todd wanted a space in her restaurant to match her colorful personality, so she painted one of the dining rooms with bright pink and green walls, put up chartreuse plastic curtains, and accented the décor with a pair of taxidermy animal heads. A buffalo peered down from one Technicolor wall, while an antelope held court on the opposite one.[49] Overbea, who an *Eagle* gossip columnist noted was "un-spoken for and quite definitely eligible," wrote glowing profiles of all the young waitresses.[50]

By 2:30 a.m., a Saturday night in North Tulsa was still just getting going. That's when the Flamingo Club in Deep Greenwood started its weekend floor show.[51] The true night owls would come dance to local acts booked by the club's famed house guitarist, Jimmy "Cry Cry" Hawkins. Bandleaders and promoters sat in the back, gauging crowd reactions to see if there was anyone on stage worth whisking away on a nationwide tour or a Las Vegas residency. "They'd hear musicians and like 'em and take them on the road with them," recalled Washington Rucker. "That's how you left Tulsa."[52]

Rucker, the former *Eagle* newsboy who had once been turned away from the Carver Junior High band, was a teenage regular at the Flamingo and sometimes featured in the "Night Beat." His high school band, the Kings, were often the champions at the Flamingo's Monday night talent show, where local singers, dancers, musicians, and comedians all faced off.[53] From the Greenwood nightclubs, Rucker was able to travel to California, eventually touring with artists like Stevie Wonder and Nancy Wilson as an internationally recognized drummer.[54]

Overbea was also impressed by Red Williams, the *Eagle* custodian, who won several talent shows by jitterbugging and roller skating better than anyone else in Greenwood.[55] Overbea served as the master of ceremonies for the weekly affair, wearing a tie and blazer, Bermuda shorts, and knee-high socks, along with his signature thick-rimmed glasses.[56] His efforts to engage with the community he covered extended far beyond the newsroom.

Every week the "Night Beat" highlighted how people from all around the nation—Los Angeles, Chicago, Detroit—were crowding into North Tulsa's bars and restaurants to catch a whiff of the Greenwood nightlife.[57] That included local folks south of the railroad tracks too. "A lot of musicians from around Tulsa would come to North Tulsa and listen to the music and then take it back to their areas in South Tulsa," Greenwood native and longtime local musician Leon Rollerson said.[58] White teenagers crowded into the Flamingo so regularly, city police even tried to invoke segregation laws to prevent the practice.[59] "We went over there . . . a number of times and met a lot of the musicians over on the north side of town," recalled harmonica player Jimmy Markham. "My heart was always in that style of music, the R&B and the blues music."[60]

Markham and other white musicians like J. J. Cale and Rocky Frisco would later be credited with pioneering the "Tulsa Sound," an eclectic mix of blues, country, and rock that influenced megastars like Eric Clapton and Neil Young.[61] But the sound's origins wound their way back to Greenwood Avenue and some of the black musicians whose fame never extended beyond the *Eagle*'s coverage of talent night at the Flamingo.

Overbea's time in Greenwood, while energetic, was short-lived. In late 1955 he crossed the color line himself, leaving Tulsa for North

Carolina to become the sole black reporter for the *Winston-Salem Journal*.[62] *Eagle* editor Eddie Madison soon followed suit, leaving to become the first black section editor at the *Chicago Tribune*.[63] In the 1950s, the NAACP, along with many in the black middle class who took cues from the organization, saw crossing over into the white world as a paramount task for the race. It seemed critical at the time to prove that black people could excel in their arena, too. "We never stand in the way of progress," Ed Goodwin said after several of his talented staff members departed during the decade.[64] But opportunities on the other side of the tracks could also be more limited. In Winston-Salem, Overbea oversaw the "Negro Page" buried in the back of the paper. Later he would say he heard "nigger" used casually in the newsroom too many times to count.[65] Whenever any black person crossed over into the white world, the results could be volatile, sometimes in ways both quiet and explosive.

When news reached Greenwood about the boy murdered in Mississippi in August 1955, it was as if a fuse were lit in the hearts of black people. It was no longer a matter of *if* a nation that allowed fourteen-year-old Emmett Till to be beaten, shot, and dumped in the Tallahatchie River could be radically changed. It was only a matter of *when*.

For weeks, each issue of the *Eagle* updated readers on the latest developments in the grisly Till case. The boy's body had been found tangled in floating debris in the muddy waters of the river. Two white men had been arrested the day after Till's disappearance. His mother, just thirty-three years old, decided to show the world what happened to her son by insisting on an open-casket funeral.[66] She was going down to the town of Sumner, Mississippi, to testify in the trial.[67] The governor of Mississippi, an outspoken racist, promised a "complete investigation."[68]

The *Eagle* dismissed the governor's vow as empty politics, and the assessment soon proved true."[69] The two alleged white assailants, Roy Bryant and J. W. Milam, were found not guilty after a five-day trial. (Months later, in an interview with *Look* magazine, the two men freely admitted to committing the murder.)[70] After the verdict, Greenwood residents flooded the *Eagle* with angry letters of protest, unable to bear seeing the system fail black people once again. The newspaper sent a reporter out to the neighborhood streets to gather people's thoughts on the "sham trial."

"I get angry every time I read or hear about the infamous incident," said Samuel McGowan, the owner of a variety store on Greenwood Avenue.[71]

"The best example of a kangaroo court I've seen," said a staff member at the Small Hotel.

"I have three sons myself," said housewife Fannie Mae Hytche, "and I pray to God nothing ever happens to them like that."[72]

After the Till trial, a Mississippi doctor and civil rights leader named T.R.M. Howard began giving speeches in black communities around the country, carrying news of the horrors unfolding in Mississippi.[73] It wasn't just Till—antiblack violence increased around the South after *Brown v. Board,* mirroring the backlashes that had occurred against black progress during Reconstruction and after World War I.[74] When Howard's speaking tour brought him to Tulsa on a freezing day in February 1956, he called the trial "a mockery of the U.S. Judicial system."[75]

Howard warned that Till's lynching was a harbinger of a new, more violent phase of white supremacy that would reach far beyond the small town of Sumner, Mississippi. He told the audience about the white Citizens' Council, the segregationist group that was spreading from city to city and cloaking its hate in talk of tradition, safety, and civil order, much as the 1920s version of the Ku Klux Klan had done when it was first spreading across the nation. "If you look closely," Howard said, "you'll probably find some members right here in Tulsa."[76]

The white Citizens' Council was a regional network of white southern organizations bent on waging a guerrilla war against desegregation after the *Brown v. Board* ruling. Like their Klan forebears, they were often cut from upper-class cloth—they wore ties and suits and had upstanding jobs at the bank and the courthouse.[77] From their high-class positions, council members used economic and political pressure to try to keep black people in line.[78] But their so-called peaceful agitation had a habit of unspooling into violence.

Greenwood residents regularly read about councils' activities in the pages of the *Eagle*—waging legal battles against the *Brown* decision in Texas, blacklisting Negro farmers in Mississippi to ensure that white bankers wouldn't issue them loans.[79] In Little Rock, Arkansas, the Capital Citizens' Council whipped up enough political furor to convince Governor Orval Faubus to activate the National Guard and prevent nine black students from attending Central High School in 1957.[80] Hundreds of whites descended on the school and transformed into an unruly mob, hurling slurs at the students and beating black men they encountered on the streets. An Associated Press reporter on the scene was shocked at how quickly the "ordinary people," folks who looked like his own friendly white neighbors, transformed into a frenzied and violent mob—"like an explosion, a human explosion," he wrote.[81]

Ed Goodwin, whose parents had uprooted their entire family in search of better education, was especially aghast at the news. He wired Governor Faubus directly: "You as chief executive of the State of Arkansas were a party in creating this violence. . . . Because of your apparent lust for power, you would literally eradicate segments of the human race. May God have mercy upon your soul."[82]

As T.R.M. Howard predicted, the white Citizens' Council did eventually make its way to Tulsa. After Little Rock, the Tulsa council distributed flyers declaring that the violence at Central High was the fault of the NAACP and the Urban League. The group demanded that the local branch of the Urban League be cut off from city-sponsored donations. "It seems that half-truths, glittering generalities, and out-and-out lies are the chief weapons of the Tulsa Chapter of the Citizens Council of Oklahoma," the *Eagle* responded. "This campaign to stir up trouble between Negroes and whites is being led by people who actually have no real interest in any of the principles of American democracy."[83]

That same year, Thurgood Marshall stopped in Greenwood for an NAACP fundraiser. As president of the NAACP Legal Defense Fund, he was still a regular visitor to Oklahoma and keyed into the state's civil rights struggle. Addressing an audience at First Baptist Church, he too warned of the rising threat that white Citizens' Councils posed to black communities. Many of the councils insisted they were nonviolent, but Marshall saw how destructive their tactics could be. They didn't just want to slow black progress—they wanted to roll back the clock on it. "You cannot violate the law by lawful means," Marshall said, "but you can breed disrespect for the law."[84]

On the night of January 19, 1958, fourteen-year-old Peggi Gamble was in her family's new house on Young Street, trying to do her homework.[85] The block, about a mile north of Greenwood, had been all-white until 1957, when several black families began buying properties in the area. The Gambles arrived around Thanksgiving, not long after a four-foot cross was burned in the yard of the Turners, a black family who had moved in a couple of blocks away. "I'm a peaceable man," John Turner, the father of the family, told the *Eagle*. He said it multiple times. While the police blamed the burning on kids playing pranks, the intimidation tactic reminded Turner of how the Klan had run Oklahoma back in the 1920s.[86] The FBI, which was investigating racial intimidation in Tulsa, reported that the white Citizens' Council had announced plans to "scare the Negro family out of the neighborhood" before the cross-burning took place.[87] Other black families who moved into all-white neighborhoods around that time received crude and threatening anonymous letters. "Your place can be blowed up any time," read one. "Maybe this week or later on if it takes a year to do it. But it will be done."[88]

Peggi Gamble didn't know any of that when her family moved to the white neighborhood, though her parents likely did. All she noticed was that her neighbors never came over to visit with her family.[89] Some of them had signs on their windows that read WHITE CITIZENS' COUNCIL.[90]

It was a rainy Sunday evening.[91] Peggi's mother Louise was singing hymns at the nearby Church of God in Christ; her father, Johnny, was still at the filling station he owned at the northern border of Greenwood, where Peggi sometimes pumped gas and wiped windshields.[92] Peggi was sitting at the dining room table, with her back to one of the house's front-facing windows. The curtains were drawn, and her younger siblings were blissfully quiet. As she whirled away on her typewriter, the only sounds were the twin patters of her keystrokes and the raindrops on the roof.[93]

At 9:32 p.m. there was a sudden flash of light and a boom loud enough to be heard by everyone within a square mile.[94] The explosion hit 625 East Young Street with such force that it ripped the front door from its hinges and cracked the south wall of the dining room, the wall closest to Peggi. Windows shattered in five nearby houses—in one neighbor's home, a pair of pictures hanging on the wall clattered to the floor. After the concussive shock, smoke plumed out over the entire street, drifting one hundred feet into the night sky and making it hard for neighbors to make out the Gamble house in the thick haze.[95]

Peggi was sitting only a few yards from the two sticks of dynamite that had exploded in her family's front yard. The glass from the shattered dining room window could have diced across her back, but the venetian blinds and thick drapes absorbed the blow.[96] Fragments of shrapnel meant to tear through human flesh like tissue were instead lodged into the house's wooden frame.[97] Peggi was okay, physically. But as soon as she heard and felt the blast, she started screaming, and she couldn't stop. "It made me go into hysterics," she said. "You knew something really bad had happened but you couldn't really tell what it was."[98]

Police soon swarmed Young Street, along with people who lived blocks away and believed they'd heard a gas explosion. An officer told the *Tulsa World* that the bombing "possibly resulted from racial strife in the mixed neighborhood."[99] But that was more than mere possibility—the white Citizens' Council had been holding meetings at the house next to the Gambles' in the months before the bombing, as well as getting white teenagers to pass out pamphlets in the neighborhood that declared, in all capital letters, "WE WILL NOT BE INTEGRATED, EITHER SUDDENLY OR GRADUALLY."[100] Neighbors whispered that the group was responsible.[101] But after police made an initial show of investigating, the case quietly petered out. No culprit was ever found.[102]

For several weeks, Peggi, her mother, and her two younger siblings stayed at the home of a friend from church. Her father Johnny, meanwhile, spent most of the nights serving as sentry in the damaged house, cradling a shotgun in his recliner and waiting for the next potential attack. The family moved back in after about a month; the neighbors made sure the Gambles knew they would never condone such violence.[103] But within a few years, nearly every house on the block was occupied by black people. If no one was going to scare the black folks off, all the well-meaning whites quietly decided they would pack up and leave instead.

Peggi was the same age as Emmett Till the day someone attempted to kill her for violating the unstated rules of white supremacy. Years later, when she recounted the shocking details of the story, she spoke of it almost as just another childhood memory. She laughed at how terrified she'd been, so much so that she'd been rushed to a hospital for an examination. She had done what she could to rob the traumatic moment, and the anonymous bombers who caused it, of any lingering, terrorizing power it might hold over her. But she also recognized its importance. "It probably did change me," she reflected. "It took away my innocence."[104]

CHAPTER 16

YOU'LL BE A MAN, MY SON

Ed Goodwin, Sr., and his father, J. H. Goodwin, at the office of the Oklahoma Eagle

E d Goodwin Jr. arrived home from his college years eager to return to his favorite beat: covering Greenwood. After graduating from Booker T. in 1952 at just sixteen, he went to Kansas and earned a degree in printing and journalism at Kansas State Teachers College.[1] When he came back home to Tulsa, he was named vice president of the *Oklahoma Eagle* at the age of twenty-one.[2] More than any of his siblings, he saw himself as a reporter first and foremost, and while he dabbled in jobs at other outlets, it was difficult for him to imagine working at any newspaper besides his father's. "If I did anything of a creative nature, I'd much rather do it for *The Okla-*

homa Eagle," he said later. "I think that there will always be a need for a black newspaper, as long as inequities exist within the system."[3]

During school he had met a young girl from the nearby town of Cherryvale named Alquita.[4] The two were soon married and had a baby, Eric, on the way. Ed Jr. suddenly had a lot of new responsibilities to shoulder. He moved back to Tulsa in 1956 to get back to work on the paper, and his young and growing family followed from Cherryvale a few years later, eventually moving into a home in the heart of the neighborhood on Greenwood Avenue.[5]

It seemed a given that Ed Jr., who could write a breaking news story and operate a linotype machine with ease, would one day take over the family business. But despite being so devoted to the enterprise his father had built, he didn't share Ed Sr.'s fixation on wealth. "All daddy talked about was money and work, both of which never fazed me," he later wrote in an unfinished memoir. "I had always lived comfortably thanks to my parents and could do without those, I thought."[6]

Still, he enjoyed the privileges he gained simply by being the Goodwins' firstborn son (and would often joke that he was the oldest child of all, to Jo Ann's annoyance).[7] It was taken as a given in the family, as it was for so many, that the boys would be stewards of the Goodwin legacy, while the girls would play supporting roles. Edwyna (who changed the spelling of her name from the more masculine "Edwina" as a teenager) was actually the first of Ed's children to take a leadership role at the *Eagle.*[8] She served as society editor, treasurer, and president at various times.[9] But in the mid-1950s, she relocated to Flint, Michigan, her husband's hometown, eventually becoming the first black female journalist at the *Flint Journal.*[10] The younger Jeanne, Carlie, and Susan wrote columns and copy edited for the *Eagle,* but they were never offered the paper's top job.[11] In 1954, while Jo Ann was earning her degree at the same time as her younger brother, their father gifted Ed Jr. a brand-new purple Ford Thunderbird, an event all the siblings still remembered vividly decades later. "He had a convertible car, and I didn't have anything," Jo Ann recalled. "Dad would say, 'Should have been a boy.'"[12]

Though he was afforded favors his siblings weren't, Ed Jr. took his work seriously. He was rarely anywhere in the neighborhood without a camera slung over his shoulder, and when he pulled out his reporter's pad, people opened up to him naturally.[13] "Ed Jr. was a brainiac who acted common," recalled Princetta Rudd-Newman, a longtime Greenwood educator and family friend. "He was not better than anybody."[14]

One of his most significant early assignments involved Oklahoma's burgeoning civil rights movement. In August 1958, Ed Jr. traveled to Oklahoma City with *Eagle* editor Viola Sue Drew to document a sit-in at a whites-only lunch counter by a group of nearly three dozen children and teenagers.[15] The protest was organized by thirty-five-year-old high school history teacher Clara Luper, who led the students to occupy the Katz drugstore counter for three days.[16] White customers abandoned their half-eaten meals at the sight of black children and hurled obscenities at the group.[17] But after the company's national office learned of the controversy, the local management relented.[18] The day Ed Jr. and Viola Sue Drew covered the protest, thirty-three black children were served sandwiches, hamburgers, and ice cream for the first time. The *Eagle* was able to capture the children at their jubilant moment of victory. "We just want service for everyone," fifteen-year-old Barbara Posey told the newspaper. "We're planning to sit in all the public eating places that discriminate."[19]

The Oklahoma City sit-ins, launched two years before the more famous protests in Greensboro, North Carolina, were proof that collective action was a potent tool against segregation.[20] These were exactly the kind of pivotal moments of activism that Ed Jr. wanted to cover. Having been reared in a card-carrying NAACP family, he believed that the breakdown of racial barriers was key to black progress, and he wanted to be there when the foot soldiers stormed the gates. In the 1960s, he spearheaded an *Eagle* investigation into bias at the street department, where most black workers were being restricted to low-paying unskilled positions.[21] The crusade was similar to the one his father had launched against the Douglas bomber plant a generation before, when Ed Jr. was selling the *Eagle* for a nickel on the street.

Ed Jr.'s various beats touched every facet of the community. He profiled Greenwood's youngest residents while they learned potty training at a neighborhood daycare, then wrote about the communi-

Ed Goodwin, Jr., carried his camera everywhere

ty's oldest members crocheting and playing checkers at a nursing home.[22] He covered the crime beat, but he brought just as much verve to dispatches from park board meetings.[23] Like his father, he urged civic involvement. "Every week to me of the newspaper is just like a baby being born," he said later. "It's always something different, never the same, and it's always a challenge."[24]

While Ed Sr. could be didactic and domineering in his speeches and writings, Ed Jr.'s compassion came through more than anything else. In 1959 he profiled a destitute family living just off Greenwood Avenue, in conditions that were all too familiar for a large portion of the community: no electricity, little furniture, and a daily struggle to get food on the table. Joe and Earline Richardson, along with their son Willis, peered out at the world from the front page of the *Eagle*'s local section, under the headline "AM I MY BROTHER'S KEEPER?" THE ANSWER MUST BE YES.[25] By the next week, the newspaper had raised enough money to help the family buy new clothes and move into a larger home.[26] Ed Jr. collected the donations himself, putting off other assignments and classwork for a law degree to make sure the Richardsons got the help they needed.[27] "Edward had a great heart," his younger brother Jim said.[28]

The eldest Goodwin boy was getting to do what he'd always been meant to: write about the community that he loved. "I really thought I had arrived," Ed Jr. later wrote of those early years back in Tulsa. "I could control my own destiny."[29]

In the years when Ed Jr. was off at college in Kansas, his younger brother Jim didn't yet know what he wanted to do with his life. After his accident, his parents made sure he quickly regained his independence. Ed Sr. made him mow the sprawling lawn.[30] Jeanne insisted that he learn to make his bed with sheets so snug, a quarter could bounce up off the mattress. One time after he tormented his younger sister by wrinkling her bedspread, the two of them got into a physical fight. When Jeanne found out, she pulled him aside. "If you ever hit your sister again, or you hit any other woman again," she told him, "I hope you lose your other arm."[31] Jeanne sometimes played the ruthless disciplinarian, but after she demanded Jim shape up in this way or that, she would leave his room and cry outside the doorway. He didn't know of the hurt she felt, doing all she could to toughen him up, until decades later. But her severity was effective. Jim learned how to tie his shoes with one hand and how to fix his bicycle.[32] He relearned swimming and got his lifeguard's certificate.[33] And he kept on riding horses, attending rodeos with his trusty new steed Champ during his teenage years.

More than anything else, Jim loved reading and writing. The passion was bred at home, where his mother kept a complete volume of the Harvard Classics and picked off all *ain't*s and subject-verb disagreements at the dinner table.[34] His father was less formal but no less eloquent, his voice an odd mix of the Oklahoma frontiersman who had populated early Greenwood, the genteel affectations J. H. Goodwin must have put on for the white folks at his Water Valley grocery store, and somewhere deeper, the somber timbre of the plantation, where his grandmother Sally Williams had once toiled. Ed Sr. would summon these contradictory influences all at once when he began reciting poetry to Jim during his teenage years. His favorite was "If" by Rudyard Kipling. Long after Jim was grown, Ed would still regularly recite the last stanza:

If you can talk with crowds and keep your virtue,
Or walk with kings—nor lose the common touch;
If neither foes nor loving friends can hurt you;
If all men count with you, but none too much;
If you can fill the unforgiving minute
With sixty seconds' worth of distance run—
Yours is the Earth and everything that's in it,
And—which is more—you'll be a Man, my son!

"He delighted in saying that," Jim recalled, his own voice softening at the memory. "He always had a very pleasant smile on his face. And it was a warmth about him when he said it, sometimes almost as if it was a ceremony. He had that kind of gusto behind him."[35]

Jim carried his father's poetic passions with him into school. Rather than singing or dancing at a Booker T. talent show, he recited the poem "The Creation," a rumination on the Book of Genesis by the black activist James Weldon Johnson.[36] He did not know what a "man of letters" was, but it was clear to anyone who encountered him that he would become one. "Jimmy Goodwin sounded quite intellectual," the *Eagle*'s resident high school theater critic noted in a review of one of the Booker T. plays.[37]

After *Brown v. Board* was decided, Jim got his first exposure to

Young Jim Goodwin

how white students learned literature. The Goodwins were among a group of black and white families who decided to organize an informal summer school program mixing high schoolers from both sides of the railroad tracks. Ten to fifteen students met on weekends at a white family's house in South Tulsa to discuss English and other academic subjects. Sitting with white children from another school and another world, Jim for the first time felt academically outmatched. "They seemed to know so much more about literature and literary characters than I did," Jim recalled. "I thought I was getting cheated out of subjects I really wanted to know more about."[38]

It was his second interaction with whites that subtly shifted the foundation on which his world was built. Back when Jim was about thirteen, he'd been on a public bus going from the family farm to the *Eagle* office. Above the doorway of the bus were stencil letters painted on the metal frame: COLORED PASSENGERS USE REAR SEATS.[39] Jim, only dimly aware of the racial hierarchies that existed in Tulsa, found an empty seat in the middle. He did not mean it as a grand political statement. But as the bus trundled north toward Greenwood, the bus driver barked at him: "Get to the back of the bus!" Jim was old enough to know what was happening was wrong, and he considered getting off and walking the several miles left to Greenwood. But he ultimately retreated to a seat next to a black couple in the back. "To this day, I lament this fact," he said. "My dad could have bought the driver and the bus."[40]

Brushes with blustering racists were to some extent expected in a town like Tulsa; it was the interaction with those well-read white students that made Jim question his world much more. He became dissatisfied with his education at Booker T., convinced there were better schools out there somewhere across the color line. He learned that Waldo Jones, Jr., a friend and academic rival, was going to Andover, an elite boarding school in Massachusetts. Jim felt he was at *least* as smart as Waldo. And so he began an urgent campaign to convince his parents his life required a drastic change. It was clearly time for him to leave Tulsa.[41]

⸺

As much as he was determined to be his own man, Ed Jr. often felt like he was being crushed under the weight of his father's expectations. From the day he began selling copies of the *Eagle* at the age of five, Ed Sr.'s approval had meant everything to him. Just being around the old man made him nervous, as he feared that any interaction, no matter how innocuous it started, might end with his father's anger, ridicule, or disappointment. Ed Sr. was notoriously impatient, and he could wield the same eloquence he used to recite poetry to conjure words that cut like razors. Late in life, Ed Jr. could still recall with searing clarity the brutal beatings his father had given him as a boy, once for leaving the *Eagle* office unattended to go observe a passing ambulance. When Ed Jr. was a pitcher on a Little League baseball team, his father once stood behind home plate to watch him play. He was so nervous his pitches went sailing over the backstop. Daddy was always in his head.[42]

Ed Jr. wanted to be like Ed Sr. and nothing like him at the same time. "At an early age I decided to capture his good qualities according to my estimation and eliminate the bad ones," he wrote later. "However, some of the bad ones were attractive to me."[43] It was amid these swirling contradictions, with an ascendant family anchored by a father who bent both strangers and loved ones to his will, that Ed Jr. began to drink.

He was about thirteen when the habit started, stealing sips of wine when he was out with older friends. The taste was awful, but the thrill of transgression was addictive. "It made me feel grown-up," he wrote later. Soon he started coming home to the farm buzzed after nights out in Greenwood, but composed enough to avoid suspicion (or at least open acknowledgment) from his mother. He spent his allowance on booze and laughed off the hangovers. He bought a shirt that said U.S.A. OLYMPIC DRINKING TEAM. When his parents eventually found out he'd been drinking and smoking, Jeanne was furious. Ed Sr. was largely indifferent, at least at first. "My father told me I could smoke as long as I supported my own habit and said drinking was OK as long as I controlled it and didn't let it control me," Ed Jr. recalled. A man could handle it.[44]

And so Ed Jr. drank, constantly, a minimum of three or four nights a week.[45] "Edward would drink when he was successful and he would drink when he was sorrowful," Jim recalled. "That's the way he expressed himself."[46] He started getting arrested for public intoxication, driving under the influence, resisting arrest. He would pay the fines and spend the necessary nights in the drunk tank, then pick up where he left off. He crowned himself "King of the Misdemeanors." Time and money lost were part of the cost of enjoying life to the fullest.[47]

More than once he nearly died, or endangered the life of someone else. When he was still a teenager, drunk and confused on wine, he pulled a switchblade on an older girl who put her tongue down his throat, unable to process his frustration with his own sexual inexperience.[48] Another time, he and a group of drunken friends were driving down the highway when they got caught in a flash flood. His friends left him in the car to drown, but Ed Jr. managed to clamber out of the submerged vehicle. He and his group found another bar to indulge them that very night, their clothes still dripping wet.[49]

Ed's siblings did what they could to help him. His younger sister Jeanne, a social worker, attended a six-week workshop on alcoholism to see if there was some potential solution that might cure him.[50] Bob and Jim were responsible for plucking him out of the Double D and his other favorite bars when needed, or preventing him from climbing into his car after a bender. Though Ed had half a foot on Jim and an additional arm, the two men would sometimes scuffle in the street. "He was six four and I'm an amputee, but I'd tangle with him," Jim said, "trying to contain his alcoholism."[51]

Ed Sr., meanwhile, didn't understand how a boy of his could so easily succumb to temptation. "Son, you have a head shaped like mine, but I'll be damned if it thinks like mine," he would say.[52] Ed Sr. indulged in vice, yes, but he could control it—in fact, he'd profited from it, in his days running the policy wheel and the Goodie Goodie Club. He kept a fully stocked bar at Willow Lake but rarely drank at home because of how much Jeanne disapproved.[53] He had tamed his vices.

At least, that's what he told himself. Ed Sr. was also a drinker, a regular at bars like the Double D and the Pink House. Goodwin children at both the oldest and youngest end of the spectrum recalled seeing their father drunk. "If my father came home and he was a little tipsy, [Mother] would tell us to go take his shoes off," Jo Ann recalled.[54] But whatever struggles he may have had with alcohol, he did not process them with his son. As he got older, Ed Sr. became an earnest preacher of the gospel of personal responsibility. The boy needed to get his life straight, somehow. And while Ed Sr. might have had the money to look after Ed Jr.'s family and the influence to keep him out of the worst sorts of legal trouble, he lacked the language to connect with problems at the heart of his child's despair.

More than once, Ed Sr. said to his namesake, "Son, I'll be glad when you find yourself."

"Find yourself?" Ed Jr. thought. "I ain't lost nothing."[55]

The thirty-eight new streetlights lining Greenwood Avenue shone blue the first time they hummed to life on a chilly evening in January 1955.

As the mercury vapor inside the lamps heated up, the tint shifted toward white, though never quite reaching a pure hue. It didn't matter; hundreds of people crowded onto the intersection of Greenwood and Cameron Street—two blocks north of the *Eagle* office—in order to see the full length of the thoroughfare lit up for the first time. The mayor would take credit, of course, along with the streets commissioner, as if Greenwood residents hadn't been clamoring *let there be light* (and paved roads and regular trash pickup and a functioning sewer system) since the days of A. J. Smitherman's *Tulsa Star*. Greenwood had no black representatives on the city commission, on the school board, or in the state legislature, so it was the black men headlining the lighting ceremony who served as the community's de facto leaders: Amos Hall, civil rights attorney; M. M. Taylor, executive secretary of the Tulsa Urban League; and Ed Goodwin, Sr., publisher of the *Eagle*.[56]

"This is an improvement much needed in the area," Ed Sr. said to the gathered crowd. He called it "an example of progress in North Tulsa."[57] Though he was only in his early fifties, with five children still to put through college, by 1955 he was already an elder statesman of Greenwood. He regularly spoke before civic clubs, youth groups, and church congregations, articulating a vision that married the quest for equal rights with the necessity of self-help.[58]

Ed knew how to tailor his message to his audience. At a meeting of national Democratic Party leaders at Carver Junior High, he admonished Tulsa's mayor for failing to meet a campaign promise that blacks would receive 10 percent of city jobs. "You can't urge our people to vote for you when you don't give them fair employment," he said.[59] At a Juneteenth event in the all-black town of Red Bird, on the other hand, he emphasized how black people must get more involved politically in order to advance change. "The American Negro must take account of himself," Ed Sr. lectured. "He must awaken himself to a more responsible attitude toward his civic duties."[60] He wanted to wedge open the door of opportunity for his children and the millions of other black youth in America, but he also believed they'd have to walk through that open door themselves.

Like his wife Jeanne, Ed Sr. taught his children "to be always grounded, yet have a positive self-image," Jim explained.[61] But it was ultimately his boldness that would become the stuff of family legend.

Once when his daughter Jeanne was working at the *Eagle* office, an anonymous white man called and threatened to "blow off our blankity-blank heads," as Jeanne later modestly told it. She handed the phone to her father. "Come on, I'll be waiting for you," Ed Sr. said. The man never showed up—Jeanne was sure her father, who typically carried a pistol in his back pocket, would have shot him if he did.[62]

Another time, his children said, Ed Sr. was driving home to the farm in his pickup truck when a police officer stopped him on a dark, empty road. "Nigger, I'll kill you," the cop said. Ed was unfazed. "I'll be the last one you kill," he replied, and somehow drove away.[63]

In the pages of the *Eagle,* Ed Sr. was the dapper, eloquent patriarch of the Goodwin family and of Greenwood itself, often smiling wide behind black frame glasses with a blazer and bow tie. But a mythology was emerging around him even as he yet lived, of a man who should not be crossed. In Jim's mind's eye, decades later, he saw his father at a poker table—calm, collected, effortlessly in control, almost like a character from the old westerns at the Dreamland. "He'd have a stack of money on one side and a gun on the other, so nobody was going to mess with him," Jim said. "He was Mr. Goodwin."[64]

For his boys, Ed Sr.'s personality caused fear as much as it did admiration. Once when his mother Jeanne was out of town, Jim came home several hours past curfew after a night out with his girlfriend, Vivian Palm (who would soon become his wife). It was so late that the haze of early morning had settled over Willow Lake. When he opened the door and walked inside, there was his father, about to leave for the day. Ed swore every epithet in the English language, then swung on his son as hard as he could. Jim quickly dodged and saw his father's fist slam into the doorjamb. Cursing more, Ed retreated farther into the house, turning the corner toward the shotgun he had stashed in a closet. Jim dashed off the family property and into the neighboring marshes. He waited there an hour, legitimately afraid that his father might shoot him in his blind rage. He was by the very train tracks where he had lost his arm.

That evening when Ed Sr. got home from work, he acted as if the encounter had never happened. Jim wanted to move out of the house, but Jo Ann talked him out of it. It became a story the entire family could laugh at, years later, but it didn't feel that way at the time. "He had that kind of violence in him," Jim said. "Maniacal kind of temper that would diffuse itself." Ed did not bend for the world; the world bent for him.⁶⁵

But this need for dominance butted up against the realities of Jim Crow, which dictated that even a black man of Ed Sr.'s wealth and education could never be seen as a true equal in white society. His daughter Jeanne recalled a time, in the late 1950s, when she, her father, and her younger siblings stopped at a whites-only restaurant in rural Oklahoma, on their way to visit the elder Jeanne while she was sick in a hospital. The restaurant initially refused to serve them. "I'd like to feed my kids," Ed pleaded, with an inflection that young Jeanne had almost never heard her father use—humility.⁶⁶ Forty years after leaving Water Valley, Ed found himself caught in the same restrictive vise as his father J.H. when he had taken Ed into establishments as his "boy."

Perhaps it was this disconnect between Ed Sr.'s ambitions for his family and the arbitrary restrictions of a racist society, this chasm that no amount of money or British poetry could fill, that left a latent rage quietly roiling inside him, waiting to erupt. But he often channeled that frustration into a zealous fixation on progress—building up his enterprises, ensuring that his sons would continue his legacy, and breaking down racial barriers in Greenwood so other families could do the same.

In the mid-1950s, Ed Sr. enrolled at the University of Tulsa School of Law as one of its first black students.⁶⁷ He never explained to his children precisely why he shifted careers. In the more romantic accounting of family lore, he was carefully planning out the Goodwin legacy by taking up law. Jim believed that Ed had a long-standing plan to have each of his three boys pursue noble community professions that would make them respected and influential leaders: Ed Jr. would run the *Eagle,* Jim would become a lawyer, and Bob would be ordained as a minister.⁶⁸ With Ed Jr.'s future at the *Eagle* already secured, batting down the last vestiges of segregation at TU would help pave the way for Jim. Ed Sr. never laid out this vision publicly, exactly, but he did later boast, "I have a lawyer in my family, I have a preacher in my family, I have three kids with master's degrees."⁶⁹

But it was more likely that Ed Sr. simply needed the money a law practice would generate. "I was not having enough income from my activities to give my children the proper education that I had," he recalled.[70] His money issues became especially acute after he faced legal challenges in the 1950s. In 1957 Ed Sr. and Amos Hall were charged with second-degree arson in the burning of a Masonic temple in Boley, allegedly to collect the insurance payout. A former *Eagle* employee, Isaac Williams, who had been arrested on separate burglary charges, confessed to the crime and claimed that Ed had paid him $450 to burn down the building. He claimed he even drove from Tulsa to Boley in Ed's car, lighter fluid in tow.[71] Prosecutors noted that after the burning, both Hall and Goodwin had cashed checks appearing to claim some of the insurance payout and that nearly all the money was returned to the insurance company shortly after police opened an investigation.[72] The Tulsa *Tribune* and *World* covered every twist of the winding case. The *Eagle* featured it on the front page too, vehemently denying any wrongdoing by Goodwin and Hall.[73]

As the case inched along over the course of months, then years, Ed Sr. studied law at night.[74] The difficulty of the coursework humbled him ever so slightly; it was easier to bear a child bringing home a C grade when he was making those grades himself.[75]

Ed's return to school impacted his wife as well. Jeanne too crossed the color line to help with Ed's studies, joining a mostly white Law Wives Club sponsored by the University of Tulsa. The club sponsor advised the women not to be "gabby" about their husbands' work and to find a hobby outside housewifery so they could be more interesting at parties.[76] Jeanne had an encyclopedic knowledge of Greenwood history, worked as an elementary teacher in Alsuma's segregated school system, and served on the board of Greenwood's sole hospital (to say nothing of her ongoing *Eagle* column).[77] But she politely accepted the group's P.H.T. (Putting Husbands Thru) diploma and an accompanying pair of earrings.[78] Then she sat at Ed's side and helped him retain the facts he'd need to pass the bar. "Often, I'd stay up until 3 and 4 a.m. reading and rereading the case laws, trying to understand," Ed said later. "Had it not been for the patience and help of my good wife, who was a schoolteacher, I'd probably never have made it."[79]

Ed Sr. graduated in 1958.[80] The arson case against him was quietly dismissed the following year, after the prosecution could produce no direct evidence beyond Williams's testimony, and several witnesses testified that the man was lying about Ed's involvement.[81] Rumors persisted that Ed had somehow been involved in the burning, but the case faded from public memory—the *Eagle* did not even report on his acquittal. In 1960, despite a letter of protest presented to the bar association by a Greenwood resident who questioned his character, Ed obtained his license to practice law and opened a firm with another recent TU grad, Charles Owens.[82] It was front-page news in the *Eagle*, which provided a brief biographical sketch of the publisher. The Fisk protest, the numbers racket, and the arson case were no longer part of Ed's history. In fact, he said he had always wanted to practice law. "His ambitions to become a lawyer earlier were terminated when he decided to marry and raise a family," the *Eagle* recounted. "He married Jeanne Osby, of Springfield, Ill. and as he puts it, 'I've had to get out and scuffle for my family ever since.'"[83]

"There exists a disease in the heart of America more deadly than Communism ever dared to be, because this disease is bred from within. It takes on many forms and is spread nation-wide. When it attacks one America, all America is hurt. This is the problem of racial segregation."[84]

It was April 1960, and Jim had just finished polishing the opening paragraph for his latest column in *Scholastic*, the student magazine at the University of Notre Dame. So much had changed for Jim, and for the South, since he was made to walk to the back of that Tulsa bus at the age of thirteen. Protests in Montgomery, Alabama, sparked by Rosa Parks and led by Martin Luther King, Jr., had included not only a boycott of the bus system but a lawsuit challenging segregated public transit. The case traveled all the way to the Supreme Court, as so many had in the past. But this time the Supreme Court ruled that segregated buses were unconstitutional, citing *Brown v. Board* as a precedent.[85] Two months after the ruling, the Tulsa City Lines bus company began painting over the COLORED PASSENGERS USE REAR SEATS signs above its vehicles' doorways.[86]

Jim was living in Springfield, Illinois, at the time. He had successfully convinced his parents to ship him to Cathedral Boys High School, a mostly white, private school in the city where much of Jeanne's family still resided.[87] The school was not the intellectual oasis Jim dreamed of; his English professor was more concerned about the yearbook than the classics. "I didn't really get what I wanted there," he recalled of the literature program. But Jim's aunt Layle, his mother's sister, knew he could compete with anyone, white or black. She encouraged him to apply to some of the most prestigious colleges in the nation—Harvard, Marquette, and Notre Dame. He chose to attend the school where he'd be able to pursue his passion for letters and devout Catholicism at the same time. While his parents were Baptist, they encouraged their children to practice a faith of their choosing.[88]

Jim's was one of about two dozen black faces in a sea of more than six thousand young men when he enrolled in 1957.[89] Notre Dame had graduated its first black students ten years before, and at the time of Jim's arrival, the school was still more than a decade away from admitting its first woman.[90] It was a place as bound by tradition as the southern cities then convulsing under the collapse of Jim Crow.

On campus, overt discrimination was rare, but the school was not a progressive bastion. Some students tut-tutted the illegal tactics of black protesters in the South, which prompted Jim to write passionate defenses of civil rights activism in *Scholastic*.[91] In one column, Jim pointed out that a new professor recruited from Howard University had turned down Notre Dame's offer after local realtors in South Bend refused to sell him a home. "Yet, it is the Northern hypocrite who points the finger at the Southerner and accuses him of wrongdoing," Jim wrote.[92]

Race shaped his experience in more subtle ways too. There was a radio sitcom he'd loved his whole life called *Amos 'n' Andy*, about a pair of black farmers in the Deep South who move north seeking opportunity in the big city.[93] The titular characters were played by white actors with minstrel accents; the show was both popular and reviled in black communities, achieving record ratings while also being subject to intense protests by the *Pittsburgh Courier* and the NAACP.[94] For Jim, it was more of a security blanket than a social commentary on the black experience, a fragment of childhood blasting out of his dorm room radio. But if he heard a white student knock on his door, he'd instinctively cut the radio off. Back home, the caricatures had felt harmless, but in a white world, they suddenly seemed tied up in his politics, his authenticity, his "blackness." "I didn't want to be associated with it," he said later. "That's denying yourself a pleasure."[95] It was only around the handful of other black students that Jim could feel comfortable being his full self.

Jim had not traveled north to become an activist, no matter how much his roommate, a razor-sharp engineer named Percy Pierre, wanted to go investigate the segregation policies of every potentially racist restaurant in South Bend.[96] Jim wanted to study all the books he'd been craving to read since his days at Booker T. He joined the General Program, a new broad-based liberal arts major that allowed him to march through the chronology of Western thought, from the *Odyssey* to the Federalist Papers to *The Communist Manifesto*.[97] Jim read constantly. On Saturdays, when the Fighting Irish took the field as America's most famous college football team, he was often at his desk, studying, as the crowd of jubilant fans streamed past his dorm.[98]

Jim's main activity in those years, outside doing schoolwork, was writing for the *Eagle*. Each summer he returned home to Tulsa and picked up his reporter's pad, often writing front-page articles that appeared alongside ones by his older brother, Ed Jr. He covered a speech by Thurgood Marshall in Greenwood and interviewed Joe Louis at the white-owned Mayo Hotel, after black customers were finally allowed to stay there.[99] While Ed Jr. wrote heartfelt articles chronicling the stories of Greenwood's less fortunate, Jim analyzed the facts in search of big-picture solutions. He wrote a series of columns examining 1960 census data and argued that North Tulsa residents needed to channel their downtown spending into businesses that hired black workers.[100] "They come from the same school of thought, but different methods," said Jim's daughter Jeanne-Marguerite, who in later decades worked with both her father and her uncle at the *Eagle*. "We all think alike. But how we get to that point is so different."[101]

Jim's *Eagle* columns ultimately served as the basis for his senior thesis, a comprehensive plan for closing the city's racial employment gap and lifting more Greenwood residents firmly into the middle class. It was in that document, on the first few pages, that he described the massacre that his father and grandfather had survived in vivid, crushing terms. He saw a connection between the brutal violence and the economic harm the community suffered afterward. "The past must be recalled, for how else can be explained the flagrant inequities between white and Negro citizens which now exists in

Tulsa," he wrote, "except that they are explained by the still smoldering coals of the cross burned forty years ago."[102]

By the time he'd finished working on the capstone project of his college career, Jim no longer felt restricted by the career options available in Tulsa. He saw instead that he could help others attain the bountiful opportunities he'd had growing up on the privileged side of Greenwood Avenue. "Tulsa had a history of Black folks, other than the Black Wall Street crowd, in servile capacities. Maids, butlers," he said later. "I was so desperately wanting to get Black folks involved in the mainstream American life."[103]

After college, Jim could have thrived in any city he chose.[104] Many of his peers, sick of Tulsa's limited opportunities and stifling racial atmosphere, left and never really looked back. Washington Rucker was playing drums in Washington, D.C., after a stint in the navy, while Bill Boulware had left for Detroit a few months after he graduated from Booker T.[105] But Jim returned home and enrolled at the University of Tulsa School of Law, with the intention of one day joining his father's law firm. "It was natural for me," he said.[106]

Ed Jr., meanwhile, continued to throw himself into his work at the newspaper. Rifts between him and his father, spurred by his alcoholism, sometimes caused him to leave the *Eagle;* one such falling-out led him to become among the first black machinists at the *Tulsa World.*[107] But Ed Jr. always came back home. For all his personal struggles, he was beloved throughout the neighborhood, as well as by his siblings and growing family. (He and Alquita welcomed Greg, Sabrina, and Regina after their first son Eric.) He cherished the chance to chronicle the lives of his people. "He was a natural journalist," Princetta Rudd-Newman said.[108]

While Jim discussed politics and policy, Ed could rattle off long lists of the Greenwood establishments that had surrounded him in the 1930s, '40s, and '50s.[109] People called him a "walking encyclopedia," but he was also a human switchboard, using his familiarity with practically everyone in the neighborhood to help people from different corners of the community to connect. In later years he also spoke openly about his alcoholism, recounting drunken public incidents and his complex relationship with his father in a regular *Eagle* column called "The Party's Over." Ed Jr. valued honesty above all else and

wanted others to be able to learn from his mistakes. His candor sometimes shocked Jim, but it also made Jim respect his older brother even
more.

"Edward, why do you want to say that about yourself?" Jim once
asked him when he published another deeply personal column for all
the neighborhood to see.

"Well, because it happened," Ed Jr. replied. "And I'm a reporter."[110]

By 1958 James Henri Goodwin had lived for more than eighty years,
long enough to see his son reach for a law degree from a historically
white school and his grandson enroll at one of the most prestigious
colleges in America. All his grandkids, in fact, would go on to be college graduates.[111] He had left Water Valley so his children could gain
an education beyond a tiny wooden schoolhouse without heat or
lights. He had outlived two of them, and Carlie too.[112] Those were
experiences no father wanted, but the Goodwins who survived had
achieved all J.H. hoped for them and more.

Well into his eighties, he put on a suit and tie every day and car-
pooled with his son to the *Eagle,* where he still kept an office. (He
owned the building, after all.)[113] Out on Greenwood Avenue, people
called him "Mr. Goodwin," and he was always bartering. "Dear
Brother, do you have a cigarette?" he would ask. "Dear Brother, can
I get a ride?" J.H. was never not negotiating.[114]

When asked about the old days, he would get especially animated.
In 1954 Charles Loeb, the former World War II correspondent who
had exposed U.S. lies about the atomic bomb, visited Greenwood and
stopped by the *Eagle* office during his tour. He only teased the wisdom
that J.H. shared: "Colored Tulsa's most colorful character . . . still
active, still talkative, and whose exciting recollection of the bloody
race riots, which once wiped out every home here, is material for another story."[115]

J.H. had outlived almost everyone else from those early days of
Greenwood. The massacre had taken much from all of them. After
helping to protect Greenwood landowners through the Colored Citizens' Relief Committee, O. W. Gurley and his wife Emma left Tulsa in
March 1923. They traveled to California, searching for what they
had been seeking when they ventured west to Oklahoma in the first

place: "freedom and security."[116] Naturally, one of the first things he did was start selling plots of land to black people.[117] Gurley died in 1935.[118]

J. B. Stradford relocated to Chicago, where he immediately launched into plans to build a better version of the Stradford Hotel—"the finest hotel in the world owned and operated by colored people," one newspaper profile promised.[119] But the financing for the project never quite materialized, and Stradford never again reached the economic heights he'd achieved in Tulsa. Still, his passion for justice never waned. In 1935, at about seventy-five years old, he launched the Chicago Civil Rights League, an extension of the "militant attitude" he'd preserved his entire life, the *Chicago Defender* reported. He died a few months later.[120]

John Williams lived a dozen years after Loula passed. He wasn't able to keep her Dreamland, but the Williams One-Stop Garage and Service Station continued, right on Archer Street a few steps from Greenwood Avenue. Though his employee head count was decreased by more than half after the massacre, John remained one of Tulsa's premier auto mechanics until his death in January 1939.[121]

A.G.W. Sango's life never stopped being a colorful one. Before moving to Tulsa in the early 1920s, he was arrested in Arkansas on a narcotics charge and served nine months in a state prison, working as a barber behind bars.[122] After he got out, he later became, ironically enough, a justice of the peace in Greenwood.[123] He remained politically active the rest of his life and continued to identify as a Creek freedman as well as a black man.[124] The *Eagle* christened him "Last of Territorial Leaders" after he died in July 1949 at eighty-one.[125]

A few folks from the old days were still hanging on. B. C. Franklin still lived in North Tulsa. While his son John Hope Franklin was gaining national acclaim for his elegant chronicles of black history, there was no question where he got his talent. "The Negro has much to do," B. C. Franklin wrote in a 1960 *Eagle* column about the burgeoning civil rights movement. "Seek out and court the friendship of men of good will, whatever the color of their skin. . . . We should be able to make the journey—in time. After all, this struggle is not just for one race, but for all races of men."[126] Franklin died later that year.[127]

Finally, residing a thousand miles northeast of Tulsa, writing furiously every week, was A. J. Smitherman. After spending a few years in Boston following the massacre, Smitherman relocated to Buffalo and started a newspaper there, the *Empire Star,* which he operated for almost thirty years.[128]

One day in 1960, Smitherman received a surprising letter in the mail. It was from a woman who, like him, had once been a newspaper editor in Tulsa: Thelma Thurston Gorham. Gorham had left the *Eagle* around the time Luix Overbea did in 1955, to become the editor of Oklahoma City's *Black Dispatch.*[129] By 1960 she was working on a history of the Negro press and had heard much about Smitherman in her time in Tulsa. "I would like very much to have you recapitulate for me an account of that first publishing venture," she wrote, "as well as your goals and objectives."[130]

Reading her words was like being transported back in time. "I had given no thought to writing a biographical sketch of my life," Smitherman wrote. After replying to Gorham, he decided to mete out his life story in installments in his newspaper, like a Dickensian novel.[131] Every week the old Wild West of black Oklahoma got a little bit clearer as Smitherman described all that had happened out there in the years before the massacre—from meeting W. H. Twine in "de old shack" to his first time walking the streets of Greenwood. He recalled the vital mentorship of J. B. Stradford, the eagerness with which he'd launched the *Tulsa Star,* and the virulent racism that seemed so bone-deep in Oklahoma, it must have been buried in the soil. But before he could write about attending the National Negro Business League meeting in Muskogee, or the trials of World War I, or the events that banished him from Tulsa for the rest of his life, he died of a heart attack, while working at his newspaper office.[132] He didn't get to finish his final assignment, but the words of his last biography installment offered an appropriate coda to his life's work: "I have boldly preached democracy to my people."[133] A. J. Smitherman was seventy-six.[134]

At home they called J.H. Papa (except his daughter-in-law Jeanne, who preferred "Mr. Goodwin"). There he was a quiet soul, tending to his business in his room and reading his Bible each night before bed. The most the grandkids heard him talk was when he led Bible study at the one-room church in Alsuma on Sundays, and when he yelled at the TV while watching professional wrestling. Sometimes he'd walk down the hall singing song lyrics from the 1920s, strange but familiar to the children: "Some of these days, you're going to miss me, honey."

"He blended in. . . . He never was inappropriate, or angry, or mad, or ugly," said his granddaughter Jeanne. "I just adored him."[135]

One day in March 1958, when the younger Jeanne came home from high school, there was an ambulance in the driveway. Papa was sick. Arteriosclerosis, the doctors said. He did love to have a couple of eggs for breakfast every morning.[136] He died a few days later at St. John's Hospital, which still had a segregated ward for black people.[137]

Ed Sr., often louder in speeches than on the printed page, wrote a letter to his departed father. "After 55 years of your kindness and tolerance for me, you finally tired and crossed the bar. All I can say is it wasn't bad for me, and I hope it wasn't bad for you."

"One thing I know from living with you for 'lo these many years, there was no truer man or friend to me," Ed Sr. wrote. Indeed, J.H. had provided both seed money and office space for the *Eagle* and had helped Ed purchase Willow Lake Farm. According to family oral history, it was J.H. who had bailed out Ed when he was arrested for inciting a riot at Fisk. Whenever Ed was in a tight spot, J.H. had been there to help him maneuver out of it. "We both loved each other. Now that you have gone, my love will continue to abide in your spirit."

J. H. Goodwin left no diaries or personal letters, and his bylines in the *Eagle* were exceedingly rare. But the actions he took, especially in the aftermath of the massacre, would have a lasting effect. "You wrote your own history," Ed Sr. wrote. "God you and I know how precious you were." And to his father, he made a final promise: "Whatever may be said, my sons and I will be here to answer in your behalf until our Maker comes for us."

The letter ran on the front page of the *Oklahoma Eagle,* beneath an obituary and a photo of J. H. Goodwin quietly working at his desk. The headline was as straightforward as the man himself.

SO LONG, PAPA.[138]

CHAPTER 17

SOMEWHERE BETWEEN HOPE AND EXPECTATION

Martin Luther King, Jr,. at a reception during his 1960 visit to Tulsa

The motorcade at the Tulsa Municipal Airport was two hundred cars deep as Greenwood awaited the young preacher's arrival.[1] His plane skidded down on the tarmac on a late summer afternoon in July 1960.[2] The trip had been weeks in the planning by the local ministers and the *Oklahoma Eagle,* but it had been years in the dreaming as black Tulsa's leaders watched the preacher's ascent from afar.[3] He was growing more loved and loathed in the United States by the day, but by either measure he was becoming more well known. This was his time.

After he arrived at the airport, he was ushered into the motorcade's lead car and whisked through a tour of the neighborhood. He passed the stately Big Ten Ballroom, the sprawling Mann Bros. Grocery, and the colorful mural that adorned Booker T. Washington High School. Soon they reached the southern border of the neighborhood and turned right onto Archer Street, driving parallel to the railroad tracks that had once been the staging ground for a vengeful white mob. If the preacher knew what had transpired there, he, like most outsiders, never mentioned it. Finally, the motorcade made another right and drove north up Greenwood Avenue, past the *Oklahoma Eagle,* the old Dreamland Theater building, the well-kept brick houses, and the squalid wooden shacks, until they eventually arrived at First Baptist Church.

When the preacher stepped out of the car, people swarmed him as if he were Ray Charles playing the Big Ten, asking him to sign programs, parking receipts, whatever scrap of paper could be converted into a lifelong memento.[4] When he walked inside, fifteen hundred people, dressed as sharply as they would be for a Sunday revival, packed the worn wooden pews.[5] They peered down at him from the horseshoe-shaped balcony and spilled into the lobby and out onto the street, where loudspeakers were set up to blast his words for blocks and blocks.[6] That evening everyone in Greenwood needed to hear what Martin Luther King, Jr., had to say.

"We stand between two ages," King began, his fierce gaze set upon the congregation of Greenwood. "The dying old and the emerging new."

The desegregation victories of the 1950s, King argued, had ushered in a second epoch for black America. He drew a clear connective line between the dark genesis of colonial enslavement, the brutality of antebellum plantations, and the insidious legal cover for racism long provided by Jim Crow. But times were changing. The future was theirs to mold. Reminding the audience of the fifty thousand Negroes in Montgomery who believed "it was better to walk in dignity than ride in humiliation," Dr. King declared that the people must shatter the yoke of colonialism that had choked America and the world for centuries.[7]

"As we stand on the border of the promised land of integration, we can not wait for the coming new order," King said.[8] He urged more sit-ins, boycotts, and marches, like the ones that had already seized cities from Greensboro to Oklahoma City. He criticized the nation's growing Cold War military machine and called on the United States to "use our vast resources of wealth to help the underprivileged people of the world." He urged blacks to vote but to be strategic about how they cast their ballots—just before coming to Tulsa, he'd organized demonstrations at both the Democratic and the Republican national conventions. "No party has the Negro vote in its pocket," he said.

Finally, he laid out his protest strategy, which would become the dominant form of black activism in the ensuing decade: "The white man must have love in the coming new world. Until then, we will meet his physical force with our soul force; his tendency to inflict with our tendency to endure, and his hate with our love. And one day, our capacity to suffer will overcome him."[9]

The church roared again as King concluded his speech. Powerful, people called it. Hopeful. "That man could make an ant want to get up and march for freedom," Opa Cheney, a young student at the time, said later.[10]

After the event, as onlookers milled in the parking lot, Jim Goodwin walked across the street to his father's new law office. A senior at Notre Dame, Jim had helped introduce King at the start of the rally and then sat in the First Baptist pulpit as the great orator spoke. He was the youngest person invited to participate in what everyone knew was a historic moment for Greenwood. Now he was about to get the rare opportunity to talk to the civil rights leader one on one.[11]

Jim drew much of the inspiration for his own burgeoning civil rights activism—what he'd called the "struggle for freedom" in his brief remarks before the First Baptist crowd—from King.[12] He used King's evolution as a series of benchmarks for his own intellectual growth. When King invoked Socrates or Søren Kierkegaard, Jim was pleased that his Notre Dame education could help him parse the allusions.[13] What especially thrilled him was the way King had converted his voracious intellectual appetite into a fight that had real impacts on black people's lives. Jim loved to learn, but he didn't want to burrow away in an ivory tower. He wanted to touch real people, and King offered a model.[14]

Jim waited as the crowd around the church slowly thinned out. But King never showed up at the Goodwin law office.[15] By the next day, he was off to Oklahoma City to deliver a similar speech on the importance of nonviolent protest, then back to his Atlanta home to preach the Sunday sermon at Ebenezer Baptist Church ("Making the Most of a Difficult Situation").[16] He had injected a jolt of excitement into Tulsa's nascent civil rights crusade. But the nexus of King's activism would remain in the Deep South, where the racist anger that once blazed in Greenwood was burning anew in the streets of Birmingham and across a bridge in Selma.

Jim and the rest of Greenwood would have to fight their struggle for freedom by themselves. And they would soon find that while King spoke with a prophetic optimism, as though he had peered across the curve of time itself, he was no sage. He could not predict when his people would actually drink from the oasis of opportunity America had promised them time and again, rather than be forced to chase after an ever-elusive mirage.

Nine months after King's visit, in a church just a mile away from First Baptist, the black people of North Tulsa listened carefully as a white man from the downtown offices tried to sell them on a grand new vision for their community. He called it urban renewal.

The St. John's AME Church was the most popular community meeting place in Seminole Hills, a small neighborhood of about 350 families located just northeast of Greenwood.[17] Using a slide projector in the church's darkened sanctuary, a city official named Paul Chapman flashed photos of dilapidated houses occupied by black families in Little Rock, Arkansas, where he had previously worked. Through a new federal program, Chapman told the standing-room-only crowd, their neighborhood could be completely transformed. The slide projector clicked over to images of new, modern homes built for those Little Rock families with financial support from the local and federal government. "We need your help to renew your neighborhood," Chapman said.[18]

The audience had reason to be skeptical. For half a century in Tulsa, government officials had blocked black people's access to quality housing—through segregation ordinances, redlining, and in 1921, racial terror. But Chapman assured Seminole Hills residents that this federally approved transformation of their neighborhood would be in their best interest. Only "sub-standard" houses would be demolished. Everyone who moved would be going to a better home, not a worse one.[19] He spoke with a confident ease, and for good reason. There was no doubt that Tulsa would soon follow the path of Little Rock, like most every other major city in America.

The theory behind Chapman's speech was more than a decade in the making. All across the United States in the 1950s and '60s, as the civil rights movement reshaped the freedoms of black individuals, a separate but related debate was unfolding over the collective future of black and low-income communities. A new term had crawled into the government lexicon to describe the mostly black neighborhoods that abutted downtown districts across the country: the "inner city." These locales were deteriorating due to all the issues that had long plagued Greenwood: overcrowding, lack of municipal services, and a large population of poor people shut out of well-paying jobs reserved for whites. At the same time, middle- and upper-class white people were abandoning cities in droves for the suburbs, their flight fueled by favorable home loans offered through World War II's GI Bill and the Federal Housing Administration's mortgage program, both of which largely excluded black families.[20] The demographic shifts in cities alarmed mayors and business executives keen on maintaining steady tax bases and vibrant downtown districts.[21] Bipartisan interest in solving the nation's housing problems led to the passage of the Congressional Housing Act of 1949, which promised "a decent home and a suitable living environment for every American family."[22]

The new law's very first provision outlined a detailed nationwide plan for "community redevelopment," which would soon become known as "urban renewal." The federal government agreed to help cities pay for razing and redeveloping entire neighborhoods classified as "blighted." But "blighted" was a slippery term, and the solutions for removing it even more so.[23] An urban renewal project could range from rehabbed housing for a low-income community, in the most idealistic vision of the process, to a "slum clearance" plan that uprooted thousands of residents to make way for a silver-domed civic center, in the most cynical of executions.[24] In either case, it was rare for the people whose lives were being upended to have much say in the planning process, especially if they were poor.

Urban renewal arrived in Oklahoma in 1959, thanks to legislation written by state lawmakers from Tulsa.[25] While one local conservative critic warned that it was an "inroad to socialism" (never mind that the government had been subsidizing predominantly white housing since the New Deal), urban renewal was met with cautious optimism in Greenwood.[26] To neighborhood leaders, the initiative looked like a long-sought economic olive branch after decades of neglect. Charles E. Christopher, the respected local optometrist and son-in-law of W. D. Williams, was even appointed to the Tulsa Urban Renewal Authority's initial five-person board by the city's mayor.[27]

No one could deny, by the early 1960s, that Greenwood was in decline, largely because of the same city government that now promised to "renew" it. The problems dated back decades and had festered over time. Since 1924, much of Greenwood had been zoned as industrial land rather than residential, achieving at least one aim the old Tulsa Real Estate Exchange had harbored when it devised the 1921 fire ordinance to prevent the rebuilding of Greenwood. The zoning measure depressed property values and provided banks a pretext to deny loans to black homeowners in the area. The *Eagle* advocated for a change to this policy in 1951 but was ignored by city officials.[28] At the same time, the majority of blacks were still circumscribed to low-paying jobs in white Tulsa, with two-thirds of black women employed in the services sector and nearly 50 percent of black men working as service workers or common laborers.[29] Many people continued to live in slapdash homes built hastily in the aftermath of the massacre.[30] As Greenwood's decline quietly began, the *Eagle* no longer cast the community as Tulsa's thriving "Little Harlem," as it had in the 1940s.[31] "For almost a decade we've watched the properties in the Greenwood area deteriorate and go down and with it the standard and hope of a people," the newspaper lamented in a 1959 editorial. "Urban Renewal is the answer to much of this people's problem in the North Tulsa area."[32]

But there was a disconnect between how black leaders saw urban renewal—as a form of long-overdue community investment—and how white people were talking about it. A 1959 article in the *Tulsa World* called the substandard housing in North Tulsa "a rash on an otherwise clear city complexion" and recommended that the slums be replaced with "things like light industry, warehouses and clean, rot-free housing."[33] In its annual report, the Urban Renewal Authority itself called Seminole Hills a "parasite" that "drained finances from the city, but contributed little in return."[34] While the residents of Tulsa's white suburbs heard little about Greenwood's entrepreneurship, its community activities, or its proud history, they read about its crime and its poverty, and they saw the lurid images of dilapidated buildings that confirmed their worst suspicions about the people who lived there. Greenwood and neighboring black enclaves like Seminole Hills were not communities to be helped; they were a problem to be solved, in service of the greater master plan of the city of Tulsa.

From the very beginning, though, residents in many of the nation's black communities challenged these municipal master plans. When Paul Chapman stood before the expectant pews in Seminole Hills, he wasn't telling the whole story about Little Rock. Urban renewal had been deeply controversial in the city and especially disruptive in its Dunbar neighborhood, a black community that urban renewal officials had tagged for "slum clearance." More than one hundred residents signed a petition vowing not to sell their homes, and four filed a lawsuit seeking an injunction to stop the razing process. In their suit, the Dunbar residents argued that their neighborhood did not qualify as a slum—it featured paved roads, municipal services, and a sizable portion of middle-class blacks. They believed the targeting of their neighborhood was racially motivated. Courts ruled against the black residents, and all their homes were eventually seized and destroyed. A Little Rock Housing Authority official of the era later acknowledged that his agency, as part of a larger effort by the city government, "systematically worked to continue segregation."[35]

A black homeowner in Tulsa had little reason to know about an obscure court case in Arkansas. While civil rights battles over buses and lunch counters nationwide were often front-page news in the *Eagle,* urban renewal disputes outside the city were rarely covered. The national pattern hadn't yet come into clear view. In his early years as an activist, Martin Luther King rarely spoke on the subject, since the focus of the country's black leaders and institutions was elsewhere. Residents at the Seminole Hills meeting had little choice but to take the man in front of them at his word when he spoke of well-meaning investment in their community. The *Eagle* called the event "a grand success."[36]

Seminole Hills became the guinea pig neighborhood for a sweeping urban renewal program that would eventually touch many parts of the city: the derelict portions of downtown, the low-income white neighborhoods of West Tulsa, and the growing swaths of North Tulsa that were predominantly black.[37] Within months of the first meeting at St. John's AME, though, neighborhood residents were already voicing their displeasure with the plan.[38] At a public hearing in October 1962, residents complained that they were about to be removed from their neighborhood against their will. "I don't know where you get this [idea of] blight," a community grocer said at the hearing. "You're going to uproot 120 families to put in 120 more." Paul Chapman and the director of the Tulsa Urban League, both present at the meeting, ignored the complaints, and the city commission passed the plan unanimously. Chapman did offer the residents not willing to sell a reprieve until the spring, when the weather was better, for a forced buyout.[39]

With the city commission's approval and funding from the federal government, more than one hundred lots in Seminole Hills were bought and razed, replaced with housing built by white developers.[40] While the city initially offered to help low-income residents purchase the newly built homes, the plan was less successful than hoped when the Federal Housing Administration denied loans to dozens. (Local officials said the FHA was unwilling to "take a chance" on low-income families seeking to better their lives.) Instead, those homes were converted to public housing.[41] Seminole Hills went from being about a quarter renter-occupied in 1960 to half renter-occupied in 1970.[42] Black homeownership and autonomy were crippled in service of so-called progress.

Though the *Eagle* had struck a note of optimism about urban renewal early on, the newspaper's tone grew increasingly ambivalent after that first church meeting with Paul Chapman. Urban renewal "poses a multitude of problems and perhaps as many hardships and inconveniences . . . for those who have been in the section long years," the newspaper wrote in a December 1961 editorial, two years after praising the initiative. "This Urban Renewal Project, therefore, as badly as it is needed, unveils as nothing else what too long Tulsa, as a city, has either chosen to ignore or has been too complacent about—improving the job opportunities for Negroes and providing for those long denied, the chance to make a living wage."[43]

North Tulsa was changing in more ways than one. In the fall of 1961, the Tulsa Board of Education decided that Jo Ann Goodwin—by then Jo Ann Fields, after marrying the musician Ernie Fields, Jr.—would become the first black teacher at Burroughs Elementary School, located a mile and a half north of her childhood home.[44] When Jo Ann got the news, she immediately knew she didn't want to venture there alone. She was twenty-eight years old, with a three-year-old daughter (Michelle) and a newborn baby girl (Lisa), but she had never spent much time in the white parts of her hometown, outside the quietly degrading visits to downtown department stores where she wasn't allowed to try on clothes.[45] "I was kind of fearful even though I was older," she said later. So it felt only natural to call her father and ask him to drive her to her first day of school, as he had so many times when she was a student at Booker T.[46]

"Don't go on Cincinnati": that was one of Ed's cryptic edicts when Jo Ann was still a child living on Haskell Street, like the command that she not walk in front of the house of the man who murdered her aunt Lucille.[47] Burroughs was located on the west side of Cincinnati Avenue at the boundary of Reservoir Hill, one of Tulsa's many upscale white neighborhoods. Originally marketed as "Tulsa's Subdivision Deluxe," Reservoir Hill had been developed by oil magnates back in the 1920s.[48] In public advertisements, realtors touted it as a "strictly high-class residence section."[49] Privately, they embedded racial housing covenants into land deeds to ban black people from living there.[50] Jo Ann had set foot in the neighborhood only a few times, when she snuck trips to the top of the hill itself on prom night to take in the sweeping view of the city skyline.[51] Any other time she and her classmates were seen there, they felt they were likely to be arrested.[52]

Things had changed fast after *Brown v. Board*. Tulsa's school districts were rezoned based on geography rather than race, turning Burroughs into a true neighborhood school. At the same time, hundreds of black home buyers with aspirations like those of Peggi Gamble's family began pouring into the area north of Greenwood and just east of Reservoir Hill. With a white neighborhood now abutting a black one, Burroughs inadvertently became the primary social laboratory for school integration in Tulsa. Between 1956 and 1959, black enrollment at the school increased from seven pupils to almost three hundred.[53]

That moment, much like urban renewal, could have signaled transformative change for the city. Though Greenwood touted its self-reliance and successful black entrepreneurship, the broader North

Tulsa region was in fact majority-white before desegregation,[54] with white neighborhoods like Reservoir Hill and Ashton Heights flanking Greenwood to the west and north. Integrating schools and neighborhoods would be the first step to building a truly integrated economy across North Tulsa, which would open up more job opportunities for black workers and a larger customer base for black business owners. Poverty and all its attendant social ills could be curbed if white and black Tulsans worked together to solve them.

But that's not what happened in Tulsa or anywhere else in America. North Tulsa's wealthy white parents did everything they could to retain power at Burroughs Elementary, maintaining an all-white Parent-Teacher Association and voting down a proposal to allow black women to serve as homeroom mothers. When one white mom visited the school and saw that her child's class was majority black, she "went to pieces" and "became hysterical," according to a friend. Once white families realized the law prevented them from keeping blacks out, they began leaving the school en masse. School officials helped them at every step. Parents were allowed to transfer their students out of their neighborhood school for health reasons, so some proclaimed that their children were suffering "emotional health" issues at an increasingly black school. The city's desegregation plan also allowed students of the minority race at a given school to transfer to a different school at any time. When Burroughs tipped over to a majority-black student body early in the fall of 1959, the school system issued a press release providing white parents with detailed instructions on transferring their "minority" children. By the time Jo Ann arrived in 1961 to start teaching first graders, there were only twenty-eight white students out of Burroughs's entire student enrollment of 954.[55]

The *Eagle* called white Tulsa's breathtaking exit from its own school and neighborhood a form of sabotage. More than individual parents, the newspaper blamed the institutions that enabled their departure. "Just when we thought the experiment was working . . . the experiment collapsed," the *Eagle* wrote in a 1961 editorial. "We believe the experiment could have worked, if those, who by virtue of their offices, had tried to make it work rather than contribute to the panic and encourage the transfers."[56]

Despite her apprehension about working at Burroughs, Jo Ann was no stranger to white communities. In her first job out of college she taught first graders in Des Moines, Iowa, as her school's only black educator.[57] Later she lived in Heidelberg, Germany, where her husband, Ernie Fields, Jr., was stationed in the military. Things had hardly been perfect in those places. In Heidelberg, upstairs neighbors poured dirt on Jo Ann's bedsheets when she hung them outside to dry—she soon learned they were former members of the Nazi Party. She and her husband left that first apartment as soon as they could. But the line between black and white was starker in Tulsa than anywhere else in the world she had lived, including post-Nazi Germany. And white Tulsans were discovering a new set of tools besides guns and torches to fortify it.[58] "Imagine traveling around the world and being afraid to cross the street because it was like that before you left," she said later.[59]

But after she walked into Burroughs on that first day at her father's side, Jo Ann was no longer afraid of what she might face at the school. She had a mixture of white and black students that year, as she'd had in her classrooms in Germany, and she was already well versed in treating all her students with the same amount of respect.[60] Some white educators requested transfers out of Burroughs as soon as the white students were gone, but Jo Ann couldn't allow their decisions to faze her.[61] There were children to teach.

The charter bus rumbled in the St. John's AME Church parking lot on a warm Monday evening in August 1963, as Pat Lark clambered aboard for the grandest adventure of her young life. She and about forty other college-age students were embarking on a trek to Washington, D.C., where they would join a mass civil rights rally of a quarter-million people who sought the same thing Pat did from the federal government: "Action, NOW!"[62] Even as disruptive urban renewal projects spread across the country in the early 1960s, defeating segregation remained the black community's overwhelming focus, both in and outside of Tulsa.

Pat was working as a summer intern for the *Oklahoma Eagle*, content to spend afternoons writing up wedding announcements and answering phone calls.[63] One day her boss, executive secretary Doretha McMillon, gave her a much bigger job: to join the young people representing Tulsa at the March on Washington and report on their journey. Pat was intimidated by the assignment, but the task suited her. She had always loved to write, and she had a gnawing displeasure with the daily injustices that were as much a part of Tulsa's infrastructure as the roads that snaked through town.[64]

Once when Pat was in high school, a waitress at a downtown Woolworth's told her, "We don't serve colored people." Pat shot back, "Well, I don't eat 'em." Her barbed reply gave her a brief moment of satisfaction, but it didn't do much to numb the hurt of the exchange. She left the restaurant feeling defeated and angry at the same time.[65]

To Pat, the D.C. protest felt like the harbinger of a new era. The March on Washington for Jobs and Freedom, as the event was officially called, was supposed to highlight both the fight to dismantle Jim Crow in the United States and the economic struggles black people continued to face in the country. Martin Luther King, Jr., known nationwide by 1963 as an electric speaker with a legion of followers, became the face of the event. But the idea for the march originated with A. Philip Randolph, the longtime union leader and labor organizer who was laser-focused on the plight of black workers. Together they sought to pressure President John F. Kennedy to endorse the march and accelerate the passage of comprehensive civil rights legislation. They were careful to frame the event as a peaceful, multiracial act of civic engagement that showed a path toward racial harmony, even as more militant critics of the event, like Malcolm X, called it a delusional "picnic" for " 'integration'-mad Negroes."[66]

Pat Lark didn't know any of these political particulars, but she knew she wanted to hear Dr. King. She hoped that he would be able to conjure the language to right the course of history, the way her schoolbooks insisted men like Thomas Jefferson and Abraham Lincoln had. She believed words could have power. She had to.[67]

The bus ride was twelve hundred miles. Everyone was wired with excitement, singing protest songs. But a nervousness was coursing through the bus too, as Pat explained in her first dispatch for the *Eagle*. "There are those of us who, in a way, are afraid," she wrote. "Maybe they have a right to be afraid, for who but God knows what will happen next."[68] The world outside Tulsa felt frighteningly unstable at that moment. Images from Birmingham of black protesters being blasted by water hoses and attacked with vicious dogs had beamed around the country in May.[69] Rumors swirled that Nazis or the Ku Klux Klan planned to infiltrate the D.C. event.[70] Pat quietly suspected that even her own mother didn't really want her to go, out of fear she might get hurt.[71]

When the Tulsa delegation arrived in Washington around nine a.m. on Wednesday, August 28, the city was already swarming with people. Pat counted the fleets of buses that hailed from places like Birmingham, Alabama, and Greensboro, North Carolina, and suddenly felt embarrassed by the small group Tulsa had managed to bring. As the temperature crept past eighty degrees, she saw people passed out from exhaustion, others with nosebleeds. Her own feet swelled as she marched around the nation's most iconic landmarks.[72]

But as her group made their way from the Washington Monument, Pat's aches and anxieties were soon swept away by the spectacle that she was witnessing. Gazing out over the National Mall and across the reflecting pool, toward the Lincoln Memorial where King would soon speak, she saw both excited smiles and wrinkles of worry etched on people's faces, hope and doubt mingled as one. More than anything her eyes could behold, she felt a transformation in her heart as she saw this mass of strangers of all races bursting with a passion for justice. It unlocked within her a sudden and sincere belief that the future of America could in fact be better than its brutal past.[73]

As the temperature inched up to nearly eighty-five degrees, the Tulsa group found a scrap of shade beneath an American elm tree on the National Mall.[74] They were so far back they could not see the ant-sized people standing at the podium before the Lincoln Memorial.[75] But loudspeakers had been placed around the grounds; they could hear every word.[76] Up at the podium, a twenty-three-year-old John Lewis criticized the half-hearted civil rights bill that the Kennedy administration was trying to shamble through Congress and urged people to keep protesting in the streets.[77] Gospel singer Mahalia Jackson sang a fast-paced version of her hit song "How I Got Over."[78]

Finally, King took the stage. Pat watched as the entire mass of people around her surged toward him.[79] She was too far away to hear the moment around the halfway mark of his speech, when Mahalia Jackson exclaimed, "Tell them about the dream, Martin!" The preacher abandoned his prepared notes and began signifying with one of the most iconic exhortations in U.S. history.[80] As King articulated his dream, Pat stood watching in awe. "Everybody knew that he was a great orator," she reflected later, "but I think the expectation was that what he had to say was somehow going to change the fabric of our lives."[81]

Seven months after the March on Washington, black Tulsa launched a large-scale protest movement of its own. City officials were stonewalling Greenwood efforts to enact a public accommodations ordinance that would desegregate most local businesses, a policy that mirrored what King advocated for in the yet-to-be-passed federal Civil Rights Bill. Tulsa's restaurant association was the ordinance's fiercest opponent, constantly mewing about the rights of private establishments.[82] Leroy Borden, who operated a chain of whites-only cafeterias in Tulsa, opposed desegregation at both the federal and the local level. He traveled to Washington, D.C., to personally lobby Oklahoma congressmen to vote against the Civil Rights Bill, and he gathered fourteen thousand local signatures against the city ordinance, claiming that the measure would introduce "legal conflict" in Tulsa.[83] The mayor endorsed Borden's argument that a new antisegregation law wasn't necessary.[84]

Frustrated with the city's glacial pace of change, young people in Greenwood took charge. On March 30, 1964, the local NAACP Youth Council, along with white students at the University of Tulsa's Student Committee on Human Rights, planned a "Freedom Parade" calling for racial equality in the city.[85] Hundreds of Tulsans of all ages gathered in the heart of Deep Greenwood that cold spring morning, standing shoulder to shoulder across the length of the street and stretching back a city block. Like the marchers in Washington, they sang protest songs and waved signs that read "Jim Crow Must Go" as they wound from the Greenwood-Archer intersection down south toward Boulder Park, which abutted the all-white neighborhood of Maple Ridge.[86]

During their march, the protesters gained an inspiring new guest. Clara Luper, the Oklahoma City activist who had organized some of the first youth sit-ins of the civil rights movement, had spent the morning on a Greyhound bus barreling toward Tulsa with at least thirty more young people in tow.[87] Luper was no stranger to the city; she had spoken before congregations at Mt. Zion and Vernon AME, while also helping train Tulsa's youth groups on techniques of non-violent protest.[88] Rev. B. S. Roberts, a Greenwood leader who served as the youth adviser for the local NAACP chapter, liked to call Luper the city's "civil rights transfusion."[89]

At the park rally, Luper led a cadre of speakers who emphasized the importance of voting and boycotts. That was the end of the events that had been formally sanctioned by the city—the police, in fact, had escorted the activists to the park.[90] But after the speeches were over, Luper and the youthful organizers decided to have a celebratory lunch at Borden's, the notorious segregated restaurant at the heart of their grievance.[91]

When the group reached the North Tulsa location, staff immediately slammed the door in their faces. Undeterred, Luper and about twenty other protesters wound their way to the back entrance and slipped into the Borden's kitchen. They waved American flags and chanted the Twenty-third Psalm while another group of protesters recited the Pledge of Allegiance outside the front of the building. Leroy Borden locked the front and back doors to prevent any more people from getting inside, or out. Then he called the police.[92]

When Luper peered out one of the restaurant's windows, she saw a crowd of angry whites gathering outside. Likely members of the white Citizens' Council, she thought. The group, waning in influence but still active in pockets of the South, had planned a counterprotest against the young activists but had been denied a permit by the city.[93] Soon a dozen police cars and a paddy wagon surrounded the building.[94] Officers who had been ostensibly protecting black marchers not an hour earlier lined up on a nearby street, equipped with tear gas.[95]

A detective walked into the cafeteria, took Luper by the arm, and marched her to one of the police cars. She could hear the boos and slurs of white Tulsans as her face was pelted with subfreezing sleet.[96] Luper and thirty-two others—twenty-four black and eight white—were arrested and driven to the city jail (which was itself segregated). According to one protester on the scene, at least three people were injured in scuffles with the police.[97]

Though most of the protesters were charged with trespassing, Luper and the other leader of the demonstration, a white University of Tulsa student named Dan Dryz, were also charged with resisting arrest.[98] About an hour after she was detained, her attorney strode into the jailhouse: Ed Goodwin, Sr.[99] While Ed had not entered the law planning to pick up the mantle of civil rights, when he saw structural barriers to black people's dignity and prosperity, he always worked to eliminate them, even if it was behind the scenes.[100] Luper walked free that afternoon, but Tulsa's civil rights movement was just beginning.

In the weeks after the Borden's demonstration, local protests were led by Tulsa's chapter of the Congress of Racial Equality, the interracial civil rights group that organized the Freedom Rides in 1961. Activists were dragged out of a downtown Piccadilly restaurant amid driving sheets of rain. They soon returned to the scene of their first dramatic encounter at Borden's, waving picket signs that read ALL OF THE SEGREGATED CHICKEN YOU CAN EAT.[101] The protesters, many of them juveniles, were often released into the custody of Ed Sr., who became their legal bulwark during the movement.[102] Ed Jr., capturing much of the civil disobedience for the *Eagle*, was even more active in the protests, getting arrested alongside ten protesters staging a restaurant "stand-in."[103] "The only way we will ever be the great nation (we think we are) is when we learn to live together through education and association," he wrote in a front-page *Eagle* column.[104]

Finally, on June 30, after three months of agitation, the Tulsa City Commission passed an ordinance outlawing segregation in hotels, restaurants, soda fountains, movie theaters, and most other public places.[105] The ordinance preceded the signing of the federal Civil Rights Act by two days.[106] Though much work remained to be done, especially when it came to ensuring enforcement of the new law, Greenwood cautiously celebrated a hard-fought victory.[107]

It felt like Dr. King's dream was really beginning to come true. Pat Lark was off at college when Tulsa claimed its first major civil rights victory, but she was amazed to see King's rhetoric conjured to action so soon after she'd heard him speak.[108] In her *Eagle* coverage of the March on Washington, the young journalist crystallized the moment, and the era, as well as any of the hundreds of professional writers who covered the civil rights movement: "It has been said by many that no change will come as a result of this mass trek. I think differently. Certainly it is understood that this demonstration was not meant to be like Bayer Aspirin, guaranteed to give fast action; but as long as we possess strong determination, faith, and realize that in unity there is untold strength, we can doubtlessly pave the way for future genera-tions, both black and white, to live in peaceful harmony without fear of discrimination."[109]

Fifty-eight years later Pat heard those words again for the first time since she had written them. It felt odd, reacquainting herself with the young woman who had floated with such buoyant optimism during those years. The words of that moment—uttered by King, written by Pat, felt by millions—were almost painful to return to because the dream of peaceful harmony they all longed for was already collapsing by the end of the decade. "*Hopeful* is an overused word, but that's what we were," she said, looking back. "It gave us hope that maybe once these words sunk in that there would be a change, a real change, in people's attitudes, in legislation, in the justice system, in all areas of life that would propel us as a people and a nation, propel us forward. I think that was the expectation that people had."

She paused. "Somewhere between hope and expectation."[110]

Nearly every day during the long, hot summer of 1967, Ed Goodwin, Sr., saw the rubble where the *Oklahoma Eagle*'s office once stood. The Goodwin Building, at 123 North Greenwood Avenue, had been reduced to a garish jumble of lumber, bricks, and old mortar, along with the Dreamland Theater building, Amos Hall's longtime office, and about a dozen other businesses on the block.[111] If he waited long enough, with his eyes fixated on the spot where his father once sold groceries, where O. C. Foster once stashed his gambling fortune, where his son Jim once wiped the ink off the presses every Saturday morning, Ed Sr. would inevitably see a rat or cockroach scurrying over the rubble. It seemed like a cynical flex of the city's power to leave the debris out there baking in the summer sun, like a predator's discarded kill; Ed Jr., reporting on the front page of the *Eagle,* called it "an eyesore to the community."[112] This was progress, as defined by the Oklahoma State Highway Department and its newest major proj-ect, the Crosstown Expressway.

At the same time that urban renewal was beginning to dismantle black neighborhoods, another intrusive federal program was start-ing to invade, distinct but just as destructive. By the late 1960s, Tulsa, like the rest of the United States, was obsessed with cars, roads, and construction—or at least its city planners were. Local officials had been campaigning for a high-speed expressway system since the 1940s, but voters had consistently shot down the prospect at the polls.[113] In the early 1950s, residents sought court-ordered injunctions against a superhighway planned to cross the Arkansas River into South Tulsa.[114] But political opposition to highways weakened after Congress passed the Federal-Aid Highway Act of 1956, which stipulated that the federal government would provide 90 percent of the money required for a new national Interstate system.[115] That was the push the proponents needed. In 1957 Tulsa voters passed a bond issue approving a massive expressway project by large margins.[116]

Initially, as with urban renewal, the *Eagle* endorsed the measure full-throatedly, running a front-page article ahead of the vote headlined PROGRESS HINGES ON EXPRESSWAY VOTING.[117] Details of the program were vague, but the Interstate promised shorter commutes, fewer traffic fatalities, and improved gas mileage. The city's leading white businessmen were ecstatic over the vote, calling it "a victory for all Tulsa." The *Eagle* reported that five local Tulsa engineering firms would work to pinpoint exact routes.[118]

In fact, the likely path of the expressway had been determined years before, in Washington, D.C. In 1955, ahead of the congressional vote on the Interstate, the Bureau of Public Roads (now part of the Department of Transportation) published the "Yellow Book," a collection of maps of more than one hundred American cities with proposed urban freeways.[119] The Tulsa map showed what would eventually become Interstate 44, connecting Springfield, Missouri, to Tulsa and Oklahoma City, before veering south into Texas. The Interstate would split on the eastern edge of Tulsa. The southern path of I-44 would politely route around the southeastern portion of the city, where home developers were building bucolic new neighborhoods for all the white families fleeing northern enclaves surrounding Greenwood. But the northern part of the route, a bypass dubbed I-244, would not be so deferential. It would slice through the working-class neighborhoods of northeastern Tulsa, cut directly through Greenwood, then veer south through the low-income white neighborhoods located west of the Arkansas River, before reconnecting with the main route of I-44 and barreling out into the prairies toward Oklahoma City.[120] Nearly every map in the Yellow Book showed the same pattern: highway routes that avoided areas with higher home values and tore through dense urban neighborhoods. All that mattered was making suburbanites' daily commutes as direct as possible.[121]

Highway planners tended to argue that their work was apolitical or even inherently benign. "The highway is the sinew that ties the community together," read a 1961 plan for Tulsa's interstate system produced by the Oklahoma State Highway Department.[122] But highway plans changed often when powerful people demanded it. In New Orleans, Interstate 10 tore across Claiborne Avenue in the predominantly black Treme neighborhood, while residents of the French Quarter successfully blocked a similar highway from being built in their historic district.[123] In Oklahoma, state legislators passed a statute barring the highway department from using state funds on Interstate 35 unless it followed specific route guidelines dictated by the politicians.[124] And in Tulsa itself, the neighborhood association for all-white Maple Ridge managed to mothball plans for a Riverside Expressway that would have cut through their homes, in part by filing a federal lawsuit.[125] At a statewide meeting of highway planners in 1962, Oklahoma Highway Department planning engineer William Dane was more honest about his agency's role when he said, "Planning does not occur in a vacuum."[126]

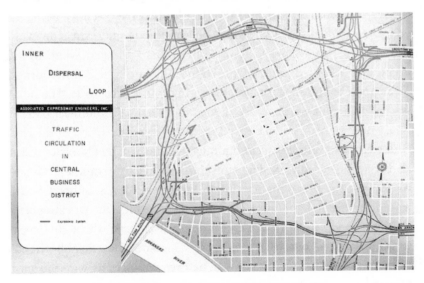

A 1961 map of Tulsa's planned Inner Dispersal Loop, which routed its way through Greenwood

Greenwood would have an uphill battle mounting such well-organized and well-resourced opposition as their southern neighbors in Maple Ridge. For the most part, each individual property owner in the path of the expressway made their own decision about what to do when an acquisition agent from the highway department came knocking. Amos Hall accepted an offer to buy his law office building on Greenwood Avenue for $24,000 without too much of a fuss, but Josefina Villareal, a Mexican immigrant who had operated a grocery store on Detroit Avenue since before the massacre, was "not too happy" when an agent offered her $12,000 for her half-acre plot, according to highway department files. She tried to negotiate for a higher sale price but ultimately settled for the initial offer.[127] For the few property owners who refused to sell at all, the highway department invoked an increasingly popular legal tool called eminent domain. The courts had long ago decided that governments reserved the right to seize private property for public use, though the Fifth Amendment of the U.S. Constitution required that landowners receive "just compensation" for their property. That's how Alex Spann, who owned Spann's Pool Hall on Greenwood Avenue, was forced to move, after a judge-appointed commission declared, "It is necessary for the Department of Highways to acquire said property."[128] Using carrots that could quickly mutate into sticks, the Oklahoma State Highway Department acquired more than forty land parcels in Greenwood to build much of the northern leg of I-244, including the *Oklahoma Eagle* building.[129]

After the land was secured, the bulldozers arrived in the spring of 1967. For all its support of civil rights, jobs for black workers, and voting, the *Eagle* staff was split as it tried to gauge how best to respond to the upheaval. In a May 1967 staff editorial called "Maybe We Need to Think South," the *Eagle* labeled Greenwood a "cubbyhole" and "concentration camp" that black people had been saddled with by Tulsa's segregation laws.[130] Escaping Greenwood, in some sense, seemed to signify escaping the racist legacy that had shaped the neighborhood's evolution at every step. The "promised land of integration" that Martin Luther King so poetically described would ultimately require leaving the segregated world of Greenwood behind.[131] The highway could also be an accelerant on the road to integration, if one squinted hard enough. "Way back in our subconscious minds we

[are] resigned to the proposition that we shall never get out of this little census tract to which we have been assigned," the editorial read. The newspaper encouraged displaced entrepreneurs to open businesses in South Tulsa and continue smashing color barriers.[132] But it also spoke to a larger argument about how the definition of black success had changed—from building up your own community in the era of Jim Crow to "getting out" to chase bigger opportunities in the formerly all-white world.

At the same time, though, the newspaper was publishing small, melancholic paeans to the old days, tucked into its back pages. Whatever challenges Greenwood faced, however much its dark past may have shaped its present, the community was theirs, and many did not want to give that up. "Have you driven down Greenwood lately. . . . It's almost like a ghost city," wrote Doretha McMillon in her weekly column. "This is progress, they say, but it sort of brings tears to the eyes of many of us who have been used to Greenwood as it is now."[133]

Both the rationalizations and the ruminations on Greenwood's state stemmed from a certain sense of powerlessness over the future of the neighborhood. Jim Goodwin, who had been so adamant in defending black people's civil rights as a college student, was head-down in his new law practice and raising three young children by 1967. The urgency of the civil rights movement, with its big, thrilling victories, clouded his awareness of the more mundane aspects of urban planning that could have more impact on people's day-to-day lives than a WHITES ONLY sign. And he wasn't alone. "There was no big protest about it coming through," he said later of the highway. "I was oblivious to the fact that they could have rerouted it . . . and was certainly not aware it was going on in other black neighborhoods and other cities."[134]

Don Thompson, who covered some of the early stages of urban renewal for the *Eagle* as a cub reporter, perceived a certain amount of futility in trying to oppose such sweeping plans with little financial or political power. "I hate what happened to this area, but what could I have done?" he wondered decades later. "Those decisions were already made. . . . You can go up and put a picket line, but if that decision has already been made, what could have been done about that?"[135]

After selling off their land, some entrepreneurs did choose to re-launch their businesses elsewhere, but many simply folded altogether. Amos Hall moved his law office several blocks north up Greenwood Avenue, but Joe Bulloch couldn't find a new place to operate his barbershop. Otis Isaacs moved his shoe repair shop ten blocks away, but W. H. Small, who had been running the Small Hotel for just about forty years, simply decided to retire. A core group of business owners who had served as a stabilizing force for Greenwood's economy and politics for generations were suddenly scattered to the winds.[136]

Ed Sr., like many, agreed to sell without triggering eminent domain proceedings and going to court.[137] Perhaps, after Amos Hall and other close allies had taken a buyout, the tides of so-called progress seemed inevitable. He was sincerely mulling taking his own newspaper's advice to "think south," in fact. Finding a location in South Tulsa would make for an easier daily commute from Willow Lake Farm and might position the *Eagle* well for the fully integrated future that some racial optimists were sure was imminent.[138] But he also already owned a parcel on the other side of Greenwood Avenue, the former site of William Redfearn's old Dixie Theater. J. H. Goodwin had acquired the property in 1945 and bequeathed it to Ed when he died.[139] It was easily big enough to fit a newsroom and a printing press, and though the original structure had been destroyed by a fire in the 1940s, Ed saw the potential for beauty on the old lot.[140]

As Ed Sr. weighed his options, part of his calculation was, of course, the pure financial upside—staying in the black part of town would be a lot cheaper than buying new property in a white area farther south.[141] But there must also have been some mix of nostalgia for the past and hope for the future that made it difficult for him to fully abandon Greenwood. Ed was often pragmatic in his descriptions of what it had really been like to live in the area—he remembered the dirt roads and outhouses better than most—but when a *Tulsa Tribune* reporter visited the ruins of the block not long after the demolition, the publisher summoned the grand old visions of the community that were beginning to feel a bit like an incantation on the lips of everyone who remembered even a glimpse of that old prosperity: Ed called it "once a Mecca for the Negro businessman—a showplace."[142]

Instead of leaving, Ed became determined to prove that Greenwood's legacy could live on. He began constructing a new *Eagle* headquarters, built directly across the street from the demolished one.[143] It

*Following the destruction caused by the highway, Ed Goodwin, Sr.,
built a garden behind the* Oklahoma Eagle *office*

was a beautiful structure—maple wood walls, a fully functioning fireplace in the publisher's office, and in the former orchestra pit, a sunken
open-air garden, complete with colorful flowers and his signature
peacocks.[144] His growing brood of grandchildren loved to gawk at the
luxurious birds through the large office windows. "Grandfather had
that design built and specced for what he wanted," one granddaughter,
Regina Goodwin, said later. "He designed every room."[145]

But it was a beautiful space on an increasingly barren block. Of
the seventeen businesses that had existed on Greenwood Avenue in
the highway's path in 1960, only Ed Sr. and the *Eagle* remained on the
block after demolition was complete in 1967.[146] Homeless people
took refuge in the abandoned buildings that flanked the new newspaper office, and prostitutes continued to ply their trade on the largely
abandoned street at night. The white press described it, in an uncomfortable echo of the language of 1921, as a veritable hell on earth. The
Negro's Wall Street, in the eyes of the *Tulsa World,* had become "symbolic of the ghetto-like cage that holds thousands of Tulsans in a sort
of captivity."[147] Most everyone, white and black, agreed that Greenwood had problems. The question was whether solutions would be
dictated by the city, state, and nation's white elite, or whether black

people would be given the time, money, and authority to chart solutions for their own community.

The Goodwins, in their own quiet way, began making an argument for the latter approach. As Deep Greenwood fell into abandonment, the *Eagle* remained. Regina made the short walk from her elementary school on Greenwood Avenue to the newspaper office every day after school. Activists and celebrities like Clara Luper and Muhammad Ali filtered through the *Eagle* office from time to time, but so did the neighborhood's homeless denizens.[148] Ed Sr.'s youngest son Bob, who became an ordained minister at the age of fifteen, invited all needy souls in for a weekly Bible study on Friday evenings. They ate spaghetti cooked by Doretha McMillon or Ed Jr.'s wife Alquita and studied scripture as the light leaked out of the new building's large street-facing windows. Most weeks Ed Sr. sat in the prayer circle alongside his son.[149]

The new *Eagle* office was stately, but it also felt like something of an anachronism, a symbol from an earlier era plopped into a new world that was becoming unrecognizable. The reporter from the *Tulsa Tribune* captured the odd image of a neighborhood in ruin guarded by a forlorn king in his new, gilded castle. "There still will be a Greenwood Avenue, but it will be a lonely, forgotten lane ducking under the shadows of a big overpass," the *Tribune* writer predicted. "The *Oklahoma Eagle* still will be there, but every forecast is that some urban renewal project will push down the buildings that have not already been torn down by the wrecking crews."

Ed Sr., like his parents before him, found himself on a block that had been completely destroyed. "There is no Negro business district anymore," he told the *Tribune*. "They might as well take down all these parking meters."[150]

On the night of April 4, 1968, Jim Goodwin sat stewing in the quiet of his law office on the northern edge of Greenwood, which had not yet been claimed by the tides of progress. Feelings of anger, despair, and disappointment competed in his mind, one devouring the next, then cycling back to the beginning. He had fallen into a similar state on the day in 1963 when he was driving to his clerkship job at the county courthouse and a bulletin had cut in on the radio announcing that the president of the United States had been murdered. For a time that day, he could not even look a white person in the eyes, so sure he was that Kennedy's death was sparked by his support of civil rights.[151]

Now he was forced once again to square in his mind a world that outwardly projected order, decorum, fairness, and opportunity but that embedded in its social contract a nullification clause that said these rights could be ripped from a black person at any moment, even if he was the most influential and righteous black man in the world. It was ironic—or perhaps simply cruel—that a man of God had been sacrificed not long before Easter Sunday, discussing one of his favorite hymns, "Precious Lord, Take My Hand," just as the sun began flirting with twilight.[152] If Rev. Martin Luther King, Jr., was dead in Memphis, the apostle of nonviolence bleeding out on the balcony of the Lorraine Motel, didn't that mean the world must be chaotic, lawless, rigged? If the social contract was null and void, then the contract should be burned, along with all that it was designed to protect. That's what the rioters in Harlem and Detroit and Washington, D.C., were arguing that night, through actions rather than words, and what the white bankers and politicians and newspaper owners in Tulsa feared most. Jim had not yet turned thirty and barely begun his legal career. He had to believe that the law could still be used as a tool of justice. But following King's assassination, there would be fewer believers than ever.

Kennedy, King. At some point during the evening, Don Ross, a recent hire as a columnist for the *Eagle,* had come over to Jim's office to commiserate. Jim looked over at his longtime friend and asked, "Who's going to be the third K?"[153]

The morning after King's death, the flags at Booker T. flew at half-mast as dazed students shuffled to their homerooms. Principal Henry C. Whitlow's voice crackled through the PA system with a solemn greeting: "This morning, I ask that we all join in a silent prayer for this nation of ours," he said, "remembering that Dr. King's way was Christ's way, through peaceful means, not violence, as the only means that we may reach men's hearts."[154]

Everywhere loomed the specter of violence, as rumors flew through the city with a speed they hadn't carried since 1921. Jim recalled an angry young man threatening to hurl a Molotov cocktail at the

Apache Circle, a North Tulsa restaurant that had been the target of antisegregation protests in 1964, but the building still stood when the sun rose.[155] "A lot of people thought that Tulsa was going to explode into a second riot," recalled Norvell Coots, whose parents were active in civil rights groups in Greenwood.[156] White people falsely believed black students were knifing their children at Roosevelt Junior High, a desegregated school near downtown.[157] In Greenwood and the surrounding black neighborhoods, men loaded their rifles and placed them near the front door, just in case wild rumors once again incited a white mob.[158]

That night Jim went to a memorial service at First Baptist Church, where he'd helped introduce King in 1960. The crowd again packed every pew, this time wrenched with anguish rather than excitement. The congregation was two-thirds black, but there were white people there too. Rev. T. Oscar Chappelle, who had invited King to make his Tulsa visit, noted that the city was slow to adopt the civil rights measures that the slain leader had so ardently fought for. Even at that moment, the city was equivocating on an ordinance that would criminalize housing discrimination in the city. "Why do we have to wait until some great tragedy strikes us to awaken our own conscience to treat other people like we wanted to be treated ourselves?" he asked the crowd. "Unless we quit waiting for Washington to issue directives about freedom of all people, we will always have problems and the dangers that lurk in our community tonight."[159]

A few days later Jim, his father, and his older brother Ed Jr. all traveled to Atlanta for King's funeral. In the Sweet Auburn neighborhood where Jeanne Goodwin had briefly lived in the 1920s, they stood outside the burnt-red brick walls of Ebenezer Baptist Church as loudspeakers beamed the funeral service to the massive crowd milling about in the morning sun.[160] They were among the hundred thousand people who marched in a brisk processional to Morehouse College, joining hands and singing "We Shall Overcome" while onlookers standing twenty people deep observed from the sidewalks.[161]

Ed Jr., as always, was on assignment. He took note of the people he saw peering down at the march from rooftops and telephone poles, and he kept a running log of all his celebrity sightings: Jackie Robinson, Jim Brown, Marlon Brando, Eartha Kitt. He caught a glimpse of Coretta Scott King leading the march directly behind her husband's body, which was carried in a painted green wagon by a pair of Georgia mules.[162]

When they got back home, it was once again time to put out the weekly paper. A photo by Ed Jr. of the funeral procession graced the front page of the Eagle, under the headline MULES SYMBOLIZE PLIGHT OF POOR: THOUSANDS ATTEND RITES FOR MARTYRED LEADER.[163] Inside the paper appeared poems mourning King's death by Ed Jr.'s two boys, sixth grader Eric ("Rev. Martin Luther King / A friend indeed. / Always trying to help / his black and white brothers in need") and fifth grader Greg ("A friend to everyone / I doubt if he owned a gun / A shot rang out like a sudden shout / And there on the tower with all his power and pride, he died").[164]

In an unsigned editorial, the Eagle pushed back against the efforts to turn King into a toothless symbol of racial harmony. The idea was already being seeded by white leaders, and it would only grow more pernicious with time. But the Eagle did not for a moment forget what his murder represented. "The fact is the greatness of America is fast fading into myth, and the reality of its corrupt and inhuman philosophy is beginning to show it up for what it is: a bastion for white bigotry," the Eagle wrote. "One thing we know is that it is the law of a moral universe that the law of retribution is as sure as death and on the basis of this premise, this nation faces a terrible judgment."[165]

The time for reconciliation, appeasement, and negotiation—the posture Greenwood had been forced to adopt in large and small ways ever since 1921—was over. It was becoming clear to everyone in Greenwood that the movement would have to move far beyond breaking color barriers. It had been clear to King before he died too. He had been in Memphis to support a sanitation workers' strike on the day he was killed, and he had spent the last year of his life advocating specifically for the impoverished across all racial lines in his Poor People's Campaign. He had also evolved into a louder critic of urban renewal and the way federal programs often steamrolled through black communities with little input from residents. Following a 1967 parade advocating citizen control of urban renewal initiatives in Washington, D.C., King invoked his most iconic phrase for a new purpose. "I still have a dream," he told the crowd. "Renewal with the people, by the people and for the people."[166]

With King gone, the way ahead was suddenly hazier than it had been in a long time. To make matters worse, the people who might do black communities harm had gotten much better at cloaking their true intent. Quite suddenly, the black people of Tulsa—and indeed, all of black America—were embroiled in fractious debate over the best path forward as a race.

CHAPTER 18

A SLOWER BURN

An official with the Tulsa Urban Renewal Authority reviews a plan for transforming Seminole Hills

When the bulldozers first started showing up, Mabel Little didn't need to get a letter in the mail from the Tulsa Urban Renewal Authority to know that her house, old as it was, would eventually become a target. She'd lived at 1231 North Greenwood Avenue for nearly fifty years, since the month after the white mob burned her former home to the ground. She and Pressley had cleared their new lot themselves, slicing down cornstalks on a third-of-an-acre parcel of farmland they purchased just six weeks before their lives were upended.[1] If there were any blessings to be salvaged from the massacre—Mabel, a devout Christian, saw blessings everywhere—one was the fact that they already owned a plot on the northern edge of Greenwood to start over.

They put up two buildings there—a three-room house for living and a second one for working, where Mabel eventually reopened her beauty parlor.[2] Pressley was sick by the time their lives regained some level of normalcy and dead by 1927. So Mabel spent most of her life in the house without the man she called "so tender."[3] She never had biological children, but she adopted a cadre of nieces and nephews and protected her community with a fierceness that could only be described as true love.[4] During the Depression she had to sell off half the property as she struggled to make ends meet, and during World War II she briefly left Tulsa to work at an aircraft plant in California, but that plot of land on Greenwood Avenue never stopped being home.[5]

Now it was a chilly spring evening in April 1970, and Mabel was on her way to a community meeting with city officials, worried that her house might soon be taken from her.[6] The Oklahoma State Highway Department had already claimed more than seven acres of land in and around Deep Greenwood, tearing down apartment buildings, hotels, cafés, and law offices to make way for the Crosstown Expressway.[7] Soon a federal program called Model Cities promised even more radical change in the neighborhood. The experimental five-year initiative was part of President Lyndon B. Johnson's sweeping War on Poverty. It was an attempt at a friendlier rebranding for urban renewal, after countless examples of black neighborhoods being torn down to make way for commercial projects turned that phrase toxic. (James Baldwin famously rechristened urban renewal as "Negro removal.")[8] Model Cities promised to marry housing needs with social services and educational programs in inner city neighborhoods, and it included a commitment to serious community engagement.[9] In order to receive federal funding for Model Cities initiatives, local governments had to incorporate "widespread citizen participation" into their planning processes.[10]

Mabel was on her way to one of these citizen meetings at Carver Junior High, just two blocks north of her longtime home.[11] Though she'd been walking those blocks for half a century, she had not seen Greenwood change so much since 1921. Some of the destroyed businesses of Deep Greenwood, like Spann's Pool Hall, had relocated to the blocks surrounding Mabel's home.[12] Amos Hall, who in 1970 became the first black judge elected to serve in Oklahoma, reopened his law office next to Ed Sr.'s in the 1400-block, near First Baptist Church.[13] Even as Deep Greenwood stagnated, there was still a buzz of activity on what people called "the shallow end" of the street.[14]

There were entirely new neighborhood institutions moving in as well, ones that put the fissures in the black community following Martin Luther King's assassination on stark display. In February 1970, the Black Panther Party opened its first Tulsa office at 1318 North Greenwood Avenue, just a block north of Mabel's home. "We don't say kill every honky you see," local party leader and Vietnam veteran Wilbert Brown said in an interview with the *Eagle*, "but we do say defend yourselves."[15] His rhetoric was a rejoinder to King's dream of reaching a "promised land of integration" through peaceful protest, and it riled the sensibilities of the older generation who had laid the groundwork for the civil rights movement. Amos Hall, who had helped clear the path for *Brown v. Board* in his days at the NAACP, came out forcefully against the burgeoning Black Power movement in 1966, when he and six other national black leaders took out a full-page ad in the *New York Times* condemning "both rioting and the demagoguery that feeds it" while re-emphasizing "the goal of integration into every aspect of the national life."[16] In a later interview with the *Eagle,* Hall alluded to the criticism he garnered in his own community for his stance. "You're called an Uncle Tom, but . . . I see no reason why those who have made monumental contribution in the past should be considered sell-outs now."[17] It was ironic that Hall and the Black Power activists were suddenly neighbors on Greenwood Avenue, and a sign that Greenwood remained a lively landscape of sometimes warring ideologies.

While some black leaders wanted to integrate the white power structure and others wanted to burn it down, a third group emerged as a bridge between the divergent factions: the Target Area Action Group. The nonprofit, comprised entirely of North Tulsa residents, functioned as the citizen-participation arm of the Model Cities program.[18] And TAAG, as the group was known, was determined to be more than a toothless government task force. It was led by Homer Johnson, a forty-one-year-old former city street sweeper who, besides leaving high school to enroll in the Army Air Corps at the end of World War II and studying zoology at Tennessee State University, had lived in North Tulsa all his life.[19] Johnson had the diplomatic skills to deal with Tulsa's white leaders but the backbone to stand up to them when needed. On the way back home from Tennessee State, he'd made a point of riding in the front of the bus despite the Jim Crow laws reigning supreme at the time. Later, he was a founding member of the local chapter of the Congress of Racial Equality, which spearheaded much of Greenwood's civil rights activism in the 1960s.[20]

The civil rights movement, Homer well knew, had never been solely a moral crusade but was also an economic one. He believed black people in Greenwood should have access to the same financial machinery that had made the Oil Capital of the World so wealthy for generations. If federal money was going to be used to revive Greenwood, the neighborhood's residents should dictate how it was to be used. Model Cities could be the spark to reinvigorate Greenwood's model of self-reliance. Homer and TAAG called for an independent school board in the Model Cities neighborhoods and pushed for programs that would promote economic self-sufficiency.[21] "All the [Model Cities] programs deal with people," he remarked shortly after TAAG's founding. "We have advocated that the people should have some say-so."[22]

But as Model Cities began to take shape, Homer became deeply skeptical of Tulsa's approach. A Greenwood redevelopment plan approved by the Urban Renewal Authority in May 1969 called for replacing many of the detached homes in the neighborhood with "medium-density apartments," a large expansion of green space for parks, and a six-block commercial thoroughfare on Greenwood Avenue.[23] It would make for a beautiful, modern neighborhood, but to Homer, it seemed to be putting the cart before the horse. Who would live in these new, more upscale apartments, and who would have the capital to maintain

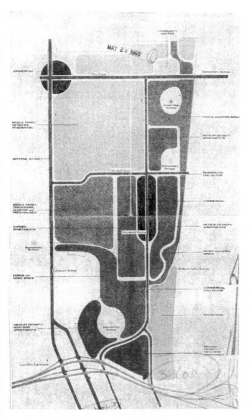

A proposed urban renewal plan for revitalizing Greenwood

storefronts in the revitalized commercial district? What black people needed first and foremost was access to well-paying jobs and money to launch and maintain businesses, but Model Cities in practice seemed mostly focused on turning the physical blight of the "slums" into less of an eyesore.[24] "Economic development must precede the physical redevelopment," he had said at an Urban Renewal Authority meeting just before the Model Cities program was approved. "Timing is a most critical issue."

"If you do this now," Homer predicted, "we won't have a chance to keep our land."[25]

Homer and TAAG did not have the final say in how any Model Cities initiative would be carried out. TAAG's official role in the program was to "review and screen planning" while the mayor and the city commission would "determine local policy."[26] The federal rules were of little help. The new U.S. Department of Housing and Urban Development oversaw Model Cities and required citizen participation in some form, but the specific guidelines for involving citizens were recommendations rather than requirements.[27] In Tulsa, TAAG was constantly trying to wrest more control over the program from the city, and it was internally divided over the line between negotiation and capitulation. "The time for shuckin' and jivin' is long past," read one internal report by TAAG's education committee, which rejected a slate of school initiatives because they did not include citizen oversight. "This committee would rather remove the veil of deceit—we would rather have nothing at all—than to have more of the same kinds of policies and programs we have had in the past."[28]

But in order to have any influence, TAAG was compelled to operate within the parameters erected for it by city officials and federal mandates, especially when it came to changing Greenwood's physical landscape. "Blight is symptomatic of economic deprivation and social degradation," read another TAAG committee report, echoing Homer's argument. "Under ideal circumstances, through the Model Cities effort, economic and social projects would be launched with sufficient lead time to allow an evaluation of the project's impact upon the people of the area . . . This ideal process is not possible at this time." Operating under the federally mandated deadlines of the five-year program, TAAG submitted to the more "practical procedure" and offered a "tentative endorsement" for the widespread demolition of homes and relocation of residents in North Tulsa, with the hope that a reborn Greenwood would benefit the neighborhood's longtime inhabitants.[29]

With TAAG's endorsement, the city quickly got to work. But perspectives on the plan began to sour as soon as it was put into action. In early 1970 the health department launched a demolition program that razed 166 dilapidated structures in the area. Hundreds more buildings were set to be destroyed in the coming months. That's why Mabel and 150 other North Tulsa residents had trooped to Carver Junior High that April night to have their voices heard.[30]

The city officials managing the Model Cities program—Mayor James Hewgley, Model Cities director Kenneth Bolton, and members of the city commission—soon found themselves squaring off against their own citizen participation group. The conflict revolved around what should stay in Greenwood and what should go. While the mayor-elect, Robert LaFortune, said the soon-to-be-razed buildings were "vermin infested and a refuge for alcoholics and winos," TAAG leaders countered that some were functioning rental properties and that the health department was being overly aggressive in what it categorized as "blighted." Though much of the meeting revolved around the largely abandoned shacks, TAAG and the residents were more concerned about what would happen next—and to whom—as urban renewal's mandate expanded.[31] According to the Tulsa Urban Renewal Authority, of the 1,943 buildings in Greenwood, 88 percent had "structural deficiencies," which made them subject to either rehabilitation or destruction.[32] In its annual reports, the agency called the neighborhood "badly blighted" and "one of the worst slum areas in the City of Tulsa."[33]

Mabel watched as, one by one, her neighbors in the "slum area" walked up to complain about the first steps in the "renewal" of Greenwood. "How can people get a portion of control?" a local minister asked. "It's a confusing and frightening program."

"I don't appreciate the mayor and commission or anybody else coming over here and telling us to tear them down," one person said to thunderous applause.

"If you want to take my house," another homeowner said, "it would be better to shoot me."

As the dissatisfaction with the razing plan became clear, TAAG leaders proposed that the group be granted final approval over Model Cities projects, rather than city officials. The city commission rejected the idea, citing stipulations from the federal Department of Housing and Urban Development. All the legalese sounded to Greenwood residents like the city simply wasn't interested in working with them in a genuine partnership. When one person asked the Model Cities director whether they could rehab neighborhood buildings rather than raze them, the director hedged. He said it was a "possibility," but the city hadn't requested such funds. One speaker strode to the mic but refused to ask the politicians and planners a question. "I'm skeptical of the answers," he said.

City leaders bristled at these challenges to their authority. "If you don't want a Model Cities program up here—forget it," Mayor Hewgley said. It was a typical example of how the city viewed citizen participation as a binary proposition—provide the rubber stamp of approval or receive nothing at all.[34]

So many different players were involved in the neighborhood's future—the Urban Renewal Authority, the health department, the city commission, the mayor, Model Cities, TAAG—that it was hard for an everyday citizen like Mabel Little to keep it all straight. But Mabel did not believe she lived in a slum. She still attended church at Mt. Zion every Sunday, even though its parking lot now abutted the droning construction of the Crosstown Expressway.[35] Though she had recently retired from hairdressing, there were more than 150 people still operating small businesses in the neighborhood—beauticians, lawyers, jewelers, grocers, and more.[36] Like other longtime residents, she saw potential in her community's future because she remembered its prosperous past.

Mabel likely knew on some level that the people in charge would do whatever they pleased in the end. If the health department wanted to raze hundreds of "blighted" Greenwood buildings, the city agency already had all the power it needed. But she still wanted to say her piece. When she finally got her chance during the meeting at Carver, she briefly recounted her early years in Tulsa—her arrival on the Frisco Railroad in 1913, the idyllic life she had built with her beloved husband, and the horror of watching it all get burned to ash on June 1, 1921. In all this talk of dilapidated homes and blighted blocks, she noticed that the event that shaped Greenwood's physical landscape hadn't been mentioned at all. "You destroyed everything we had," Mabel said, her mind floating back to that fiery hellscape. "I was here in it, and the people are suffering more now than they did then."[37]

In the same spot where the flames prowled fifty years before, devouring a house of God, a choir began to sing. They hummed a melody that every soul in the sanctuary knew, from the elders who straightened their shoulders as they joined in song, to the babes swaying almost unconsciously to a rhythm that stirred uninterpretable feelings in their hearts. The murmur of the melody grew into a rumble, the rumble into a roar, the roar louder than gunshots and cracking flames and monstrous winged machines descending from the sky. The words finally came, but the sound was so loud that it was still a sonorous wail, more feeling than language.[38]

Lift every voice and sing
Till earth and heaven ring
Ring with the harmonies
Of Liberty

Mabel sat in the pulpit as the voices rose to the rafters of Mt. Zion on June 1, 1971. She had spent weeks helping to plan this evening, along with Ed Goodwin, Sr., W. D. Williams, and a handful of other old-timers who remembered 1921 with gruesome detail. In early April, they started reaching out to people they knew carried the same dark memories they did.[39] The riot committee, as the group called itself, met often that spring, trying to determine the best way to commemorate the fiftieth anniversary of the event.[40] Though they had lived together in the same community for decades, their gatherings still had the feeling of a spiritual reunion. Sitting together for their first meeting at the *Eagle* office, some shared their stories of the night for the first time. "Started listening to all the versions," W.D. said later. "Boy I'm telling you, I said I didn't know all this happened."[41] At one of their last meetings, the group snapped a photograph together in front of the newspaper building on Greenwood Avenue, the men in broadshouldered dark suits, the women in calf-length dresses and pearls.[42]

Somehow the word *celebration* got attached to the anniversary, which some recognized as a mistake as soon as they walked through the doors of Mt. Zion and were handed a program.[43] But it was hard for the survivors to find the right language for what they were trying to accomplish. No one had done anything like this before. They were simultaneously proud of what they had built in the last fifty years and angry over what they had lost. They mourned the dead and the banished, while feeling hopeful for the next generation that descended from those who remained.

At least the story was finally being told—that was what mattered to Mabel. She was gathering information for a book that she intended to be "a memento to her race," as the *Eagle* put it.[44] It was vital to her that future generations understand what really happened. She still resented some of the rumors that had been bandied about in the immediate aftermath, like the one claiming that a cache of ammunition had been stored at Mt. Zion.[45] There had been a prevailing sense among some white Tulsans—not all, she was careful to note—that the Negroes had it coming. A postcard of Mt. Zion on fire, its belfry clouded by smoke, even carried a caption that read, "Burning of church where ammunition was stored," as if to offer a readymade justification for the horrific image.[46] Tonight, and eventually with her book, Mabel wanted to put such foolish notions to rest.

She wasn't the only one speaking about the massacre more openly. A white woman sitting among the pews of Mt. Zion was documenting this historic evening with a tape recorder. Her name was Ruth Avery, and she'd been haunted by images of black bodies stacked on flatbed trucks ever since she was a six-year-old in 1921.[47] She was working on her own book, probing the role that the Ku Klux Klan might have played in the attack. (Her tentative title was *Fear the Fifth Horseman: A Conspiracy of Silence*.)[48] Don Ross, who was well known in the neighborhood for his satirical *Eagle* column "On the Ghetto Line," was doing his own serious work to elevate the story. He had recently launched a local black magazine called *Impact*, which

Mabel Little

took a more radical view of racial politics than the newspaper. That June, Ross published an in-depth account of the riot by white journalist Ed Wheeler, after the *Tulsa World and Tribune* rejected the story.[49] PROFILE OF A RACE RIOT, read the cover, the words engulfed in angry flames.[50] For many young people in Greenwood—including some of Ed Sr.'s grandchildren—that magazine issue would mark the first time they heard about the destruction of their own community.[51]

On both sides of town, there was a burgeoning sense that the massacre could no longer be relegated to hurried asides in newspaper articles and hushed conversations out of the earshot of children. Everyone needed to know about it.

As the booming organ backing "Lift Every Voice" faded, the Mt. Zion sanctuary settled into a profound silence. W. D. Williams approached the rostrum. He had recently retired from forty-two years of teaching typing, bookkeeping, and commerce at Booker T., so it was fitting that he offered a lesson on the history of Greenwood's economic prowess.[52] "The blacks within this community had all types of businesses," he said. "They had a sort of togetherness that we've rarely ever seen since."[53]

He noted that many black people in early Greenwood had worked as maids, chauffeurs, and bricklayers—"menial tasks," he said. But when he thought of the old days, what he remembered were the nights helping out at the Dreamland and the grand aspirations of his mother to build a thriving race enterprise. He wanted to emphasize the independence that a select few Greenwood entrepreneurs had carved out in order to show the young people in the audience a path toward their own financial prosperity. "Hundreds of blacks were employed by other blacks," he told the audience.[54]

W.D. didn't want to dwell on the details of the massacre itself, though he could recall with startling clarity all that had happened to him from the moment he awoke fifty years before to the sound of gunfire. Tonight was not the night for all that. "Everything was burned by . . ."

He paused for a beat.

". . . another race. We've always felt it was out of jealousy. We were doing too well."[55]

W.D. told how everything had been replaced by 1925, when the

National Negro Business League came to town. He did not mention Loula's fatal struggles during that period or the bitter dispute over the Dreamland ownership that followed, but he summoned her memory, obliquely. He seemed to be speaking more about his own family than about Greenwood at large when he said, "We couldn't survive the race riot and a depression too. So the black community died."

The crowd was quiet. Seeking to end on a high note, he burrowed for the wellspring of optimism that black people are so often required to find. "Now it's up to these youngsters, of course, to bring it back," he concluded.[56]

As W.D. returned to his seat, the organ sprang to life again to lead the choir in a rendition of "In Times Like These," a hymn written amid the mounting casualties of World War II.

Soon it was Mabel's turn. "I'm going to give you the brief, true story of my life," she began, her words carrying the crisp diction of an English teacher. "Today I'm happy to let you know—I'm not ashamed of my age because God's been good to me—I'm seventy-four years old."

The crowd thrummed with amens.

"I'm not old, I've just been here a long time."[57]

Mabel began as she always did—at the Frisco Depot on Monday, September 22, 1913, with a dollar and twenty-five cents in her purse. She breathed life back into Pressley, he a junior deacon at this very church, she a Sunday school teacher, neither of them much older than the teenagers in the youth choir behind her. She resurrected the first beauty shop in their shotgun house on Independence Street, her bustling enterprise in the heart of Deep Greenwood, and the home they'd built for themselves in the spring of 1921. She brought forth names that had not been heard in Tulsa, in any formal setting, for a very long time: J. B. Stradford, A. J. Smitherman, Simon Berry.

"Seven years of saving and work, sacrificing to meet an objective. All spoiled by needless burning," she said.

She took a breath and began telling the story she had really gotten on stage to deliver, the story of the church that cradled them at that very moment. "We rose from a tabernacle . . . to a beautiful edifice," she said, recalling the evenings reading scripture by lamplight, the mornings of toil assembling those seventy-five thousand red bricks. Fire had once been a tool for celebration at Mt. Zion, when they burned mortgages to mark their path toward economic freedom. When the flames were under their control.[58]

She had been numb to most of the massacre destruction—still was, truth be told—but she had cried when she thought about that church on fire.[59] Tonight, though, she was on stage to deliver facts, and if her voice quavered, it was not with despair but with intensity, for she wanted more than anything else in the world for these facts to reach back across time and clear Mt. Zion's good name. "The church was destroyed on June 1, 1921, following untrue rumors," she said. "When the city cleared the ground, they did not find any ammunition."[60]

Mabel surveyed the audience. She and her fellow congregants lost something sacred that night fifty years ago, but the mob had lost something too. It was unnatural to desecrate a temple of God. Beyond all the looting and devilment that had taken place, this was a spiritual theft, and she knew deep in her heart that the Lord always collected His purloined goods—often with interest. If His will had seen right to bring cataclysm to Greenwood, so be it. But the thieves would have a greater reckoning of their own one day, too. She knew it.[61]

"God's church was destroyed," she said. "We come today just to remind you that God still lives and he loves this church."[62]

Mabel didn't like the idea of tearing down all the old buildings of Greenwood, but it was her objection to closing the neighborhood school that ultimately got her arrested.

In 1971 Tulsa was in the midst of a messy, court-mandated effort to desegregate its school system. The U.S. Department of Justice had sued the city three years earlier on the matter. Despite the mandate of *Brown v. Board* to desegregate schools nationwide with "all deliberate speed," Tulsa officials, like those in many cities, devised schemes that let them skirt around the court ruling.[63] Parents who wanted their child zoned for an all-white school rented apartments in their district of choice for a single month, or paid for their children to live on their own in the area, with the school board's implicit approval.[64] School board meetings boiled over with parental fury—at one December 1970 meeting, a white man who was incensed that his son "might not turn out the way he should" if he were rezoned for all-black Booker T. Washington High School collapsed from a heart attack and died.[65] A federal judge confirmed what the *Eagle* had been saying for years—that Tulsa schools were part of "a continuing legacy of subtle yet effective discrimination."[66]

The summer of '71 marked an urgent deadline for Tulsa public schools. The Tulsa School Board had to come up with a desegregation plan that would withstand federal scrutiny, and the solution seemed likely to involve busing.[67] In a city as residentially segregated as Tulsa, ferrying students across town every day was the most straightforward way to diversify schools. Most black parents didn't love the idea of busing, but some were willing to entertain the concept if it meant fully integrated schools and a more concerted investment in black education from the city. "We need to press for an acceptable plan of integration with all neighborhoods bearing their share of the burden," the *Eagle* argued in an editorial.[68] Even Homer Johnson, who'd been cast as a Black Panther–loving separatist by city commissioners, sent his daughter to Central High School, the most integrated high school in the city at the time.[69]

Many white parents, however, rejected the idea outright. A white group called the Association of Tulsans for Quality Education gathered more than forty thousand signatures for a petition against busing. The group hand-delivered the complaint to Oklahoma congressmen in Washington, then bragged that its lobbying spurred "behind-the-scenes efforts" by public officials to protect their interests. The group even claimed it was "strongly instrumental" in the final shape of the Tulsa School Board's desegregation plan, which was developed with input from the U.S. Justice Department. (The board denied colluding with the group.) Eugene Harris, the lone black member of the school board, was left out of the Justice Department discussions as the desegregation directive took shape.[70]

The final result was a plan that called for the closing of Carver Junior High School, the only school for seventh through ninth graders in Greenwood. At the meeting where the closure was announced, two hundred black Tulsans crowded into the school board headquarters to object to the decision. Mabel was there, and she did not mince words when it was her turn to speak. "Black folks in Tulsa never burned a school," she said, perhaps alluding to the urban riots of the era, or the fact that whites had burned Greenwood's elementary school to the ground in 1921. "But I am afraid that something will happen if you keep agitating us."[71]

Days after the meeting, roughly three hundred black Tulsans gathered in the Carver parking lot to protest and to strategize.[72] They were a sea of afros and picket signs, with many of those present young enough to be Carver students. One person in the crowd hoisted a sign that read, POWER TO THE PEOPLE. Below the platform where various community leaders were set to speak, the organizers placed a large coffin on a transport stretcher. Atop it was a sign that wondered, WILL THEY BURY US?[73]

Homer Johnson clambered up onto the stage. TAAG had offered up its Greenwood offices as an organizing place while residents decided what to do about the school closing.[74] The group, along with the NAACP Legal Defense Fund, would also soon file a federal lawsuit seeking to force the Tulsa School Board to abandon its desegregation plan.[75] Homer knew that for Greenwood, closing down Carver could be as much an economic blow as a moral one. A neighborhood without a school would be more like a husk, waiting for urban planners to hollow it out further. The plan was especially insulting because TAAG had an entire education committee that had been trying to grant Greenwood schools more independence, not less. "We expect to hold classes in the Carver building," Homer insisted. "That's our school. We paid for it with our taxes. If it's not ours, what else do we have to show for the taxes we have paid? We certainly haven't any parks or streets."

He looked down at the coffin below the platform. "If 50,000 blacks can't make an impact on this community," he said, "then we all belong inside that box."[76]

This was a younger generation of activists than Ed Sr. and Amos Hall, the men who had fought so adamantly for black people's right to enter whites-only schools, neighborhoods, and workforces. The Black Power movement, which the *Eagle* had initially dismissed as "a folly," was a rejection of that long struggle.[77] In the late 1960s and early '70s, there was a growing sense that the decades-long effort to break down the color barrier had somehow gone awry. The tumultuous violence of the civil rights movement demonstrated that white supremacists would not accept black equality, while white flight and opposition to busing showed that so-called white moderates wouldn't either. "A black man spends half of his life expectancy attempting to do what he thought was right and still is rejected by a vicious racist white society," a frustrated Ed Jr. wrote in the *Eagle* that summer. "I am convinced that blacks must seek to learn more about themselves and be reeducated."[78] His younger brother Jim echoed the sentiment. "We all know that there is a savage attack and assault being made on our community," Jim said during a panel on school integration that year, pointing out that Greenwood residents were being encircled by expressways and displaced by urban renewal.[79] Desegregation, delivered on white people's terms, increasingly felt like a hollow victory to the people of Greenwood, as their neighborhood quite literally crumbled around them.

While many older civil rights activists rejected the growing calls for black separatism, the idea made total sense to Mabel Little. She did not look the part of the young black radical, but she shared their overriding belief that black uplift and self-reliance were preferable to an integrated world that relied, ultimately, upon white benevolence. "Segregation made black folk take care of themselves," she reflected later. "Be independent. Have their own business. Train their children. Build their colleges. Build their home. Integration separated [them]."[80]

In the Carver parking lot, she was right there at the younger generation's side, nodding along as neighbors who could be her children or even her grandchildren spoke on the importance of black institutions. When she was asked to speak, she recounted the history of the building they had committed themselves to protect. She told the crowd how she had been in that very spot way back in 1929, when George Washington Carver himself came to Tulsa to dedicate the school.[81] In his characteristically gentle voice, Carver had encouraged each student to become "the architect of his own fortune, the carver of his own destiny."[82]

"When they closed the doors to George Washington Carver Junior High School, the black community grieved," Mabel recalled later. "We loved our school."[83]

After that parking lot protest, a bold plan quickly came together to save Carver: by leaving the Tulsa public schools altogether. The

A poster advertising the Carver Freedom School

people of Greenwood would open a new, independent "Freedom School" in a vacant Catholic school across the street.[84] A widely used political tool in black communities during the civil rights movement, the Freedom School would be part protest, part social experiment.[85] Every day a student stayed out of their assigned Tulsa public school, the school system lost $1.50 in state education funding.[86] A mass boycott might make the school board reconsider its decision. Opening a new school would also illustrate that an institution with black leaders, operated in a black community, could be just as good as a white one.

In September, the Freedom School opened its doors, welcoming about a third of Carver's previous students.[87] The school had seventeen instructors, twelve of them black, teaching English, social studies, math, industrial arts, and several other subjects. On the first morning, the students met in the small auditorium for their opening assembly. "All of Tulsa and the entire nation have their eyes on you today," school principal Robert Waugh, told them. "We hope they will be pleased with what they see." In the Spanish classroom, above the blackboard in bright red letters, was the phrase *Debo Ser Libre—Ahora*, "I must be free—now."[88]

Money was tight. School leaders were trying to pay for teacher salaries, classroom equipment, and facility maintenance all through community donations. After a tour of the grounds on the first day, a *Tulsa Tribune* reporter noted worn textbooks and cracked blackboards. Waugh admitted they were still trying to secure typewriters and gym equipment.[89] But the community got creative to lessen the financial pinch. Parents held a rummage sale on school grounds, while kids sold candy bars with CARVER FREEDOM SCHOOL printed on them.[90]

The *Eagle* also threw its full weight behind the Freedom School movement, as Ed Sr. and the paper's older leadership seemed to let go of their early misgivings about Black Power. The newspaper helped organize a rally that brought the famed actor Ossie Davis to Greenwood. Before a crowd of four thousand at Carver's football stadium, Davis called the Freedom School "a shining symbol of Black determination" and summoned the Afrocentrism of the times when he gave the audience a potent new slogan: "Give me back my damn Black drum."[91] Later in the fall, the *Eagle* sponsored a Battle of the Sexes contest to see whether men or women could raise more money for the school. Ed Sr. vowed to put on a dress if the men lost; in December he appeared on the front page of the newspaper wearing a knee-length corduroy ensemble.[92]

Mabel Little had no more dramatic speeches to give, but she served as a volunteer the day the Freedom School opened its doors and helped organize a twenty-four-hour prayer vigil to ensure those doors stayed open.[93] She also continued to pressure the school board directly. That was how she had her run-in with the police.

One November night, Mabel and a handful of other activists were staging the latest of many sit-ins at the school board headquarters. A court injunction banned their presence there outside office hours. When a school official tried to persuade them to leave, they went to a second-floor window to retrieve bologna sandwiches that their allies outside delivered by rope. They were settling in for the night. Incensed, school board officials called the police. Eight people—five white, three black—were arrested and jailed. Mabel, at seventy-five, was the oldest in the protest by nearly thirty years.[94]

"I was so happy in jail," Mabel said later. "Ed Goodwin found out I was in jail and came down and bailed all of us out and joined in with us."[95] Soon after being released, Mabel was right back to volunteering for the Freedom School.[96]

In February 1972, after the Freedom School protest had gone on for a full semester, the school board finally relented. Carver would be reopened the following year as a "magnet" middle school, with a re-vamped advanced curriculum meant to help attract white students. There would be no forced busing; all students would enroll on a vol-untary basis, with a racial makeup targeting 60 percent white stu-dents and 40 percent black. (Racial quotas at Tulsa's magnet schools would become a decades-long point of contention, with North Tulsa leader Julius Pegues consistently arguing to get as many black stu-dents into these black-neighborhood schools as possible.)[97] While Carver was unlikely to attract the white parents who had lobbied Congress to avoid sending their kids to black schools, other predomi-nantly white groups, like the League of Women Voters, had been pushing for integrated schools and would embrace the magnet model.[98] It wasn't a solution to solving segregation across the city of Tulsa, but it was a harbinger of the multicultural future that educa-tors in the 1970s believed they had to chart. Most important to peo-ple in Greenwood, the plan preserved a treasured cultural institution at a time when nearly every building around it was being reduced to rubble. (The original Booker T. campus, which had been turned into an elementary school in 1950, was demolished in 1983; at the time of its destruction, the *Eagle* wrote that "it was really the last historical building of any significance in North Tulsa.")[99]

On Mabel Little's seventy-fifth birthday, Principal Waugh awarded her a plaque for her dedication to the Freedom School.[100] The *Eagle* also offered its glowing praise. "In Mrs. Little we have a veteran na-tionally known leader of church women," the newspaper wrote. "Yet, she cared enough about her people in the ghetto to put her prestige, dignity and good name on the line for the good of her people. This black woman who ran a successful cosmetology business in North Tulsa for many years took her love and concern for humanity out of beautiful Mt. Zion . . . into the street and into the hearts of North Tulsans."[101]

━━━

The letter finally came on October 13, 1975, about a week after her seventy-ninth birthday. NOTICE OF INTENT TO ACQUIRE was printed in all capital letters at the top of the page, as if the point needed to be emphasized.

> *Dear Ms. Little:*
> *We wrote you advising that the above referenced parcel was being considered for acquisition by the Tulsa Urban Renewal Authority. It is now the intent of the Authority to acquire the parcel in connection with the implementation of the Neighborhood Development Program redevelopment plan.*
> *Please contact our office as soon as possible to make an appointment for the presentation of our offer.*[102]

The question was not whether Mabel would sell—the city would get the land eventually—but how difficult she would make the process for the Urban Renewal Authority and for herself. If she ignored the letter, she could expect another one in the mail in a matter of weeks, like the one the Latimer family had received after failing to accept an offer to purchase Latimer's Barbecue a couple of blocks north: "Since this property is in a clearance area and is needed by TURA to carry out the Neighborhood Development Program redevelopment plans, it is essential that we acquire the property as soon as possible. . . . We feel that we have made a diligent and conscientious effort to arrive at an equitable purchase. Unless we can obtain an agreement as to the purchase price . . . we will have no alternative but to institute condemnation proceedings."[103]

By late 1975, the Latimers and nearly every other Greenwood family surrounding Mabel had already cashed out and moved on.[104] Some took the TURA checks immediately, as many had done when the Oklahoma State Highway Department came through demanding land for the Crosstown Expressway.[105] Others went through the rigamarole of condemnation proceedings to eke out a few extra dollars.[106] But the thing they called progress was sweeping down Greenwood

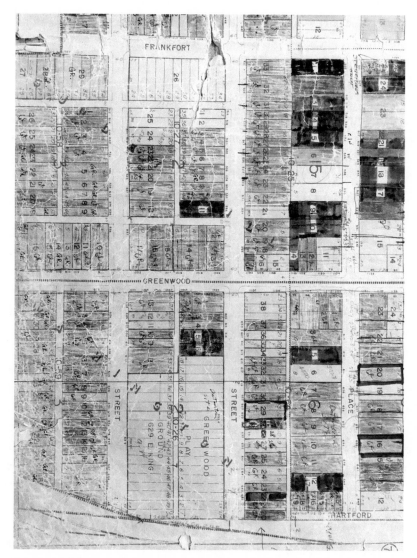

*A map of Greenwood Avenue created by the Tulsa Urban Renewal Authority,
with parcels shaded different colors based on the year the government
acquired them*

Avenue no matter what any individual property owner might think or
want. There would be no more overflowing town hall meetings or
parking lot protests. Even though the *Eagle* astutely predicted what
was coming for Greenwood in a 1971 staff editorial—"blacks will be
pushed northward to God knows where until the whites get ready for
that too"—there was not much the newspaper could do to stop it.[107]

By 1975, twenty years after the civil rights movement became an all-consuming concern in black communities, Greenwood was understandably a bit exhausted. "Nothing is good just because it's old," *Eagle* reporter David Breed reflected in one article about aged North Tulsa homes. "And, despite what many might wish, the past will never come again."[108] Following the optimism of the King era and the radicalism of the Black Power movement, a strain of nihilism was creeping into the community at its edges. Was all this really worth fighting for?

Three days after receiving her offer letter, Mabel took a trip to the urban renewal office. A relocation agent offered her $7,700 for her 5,750-square-foot parcel at the intersection of Greenwood Avenue and Marshall Place. On November 11, 1975, Mabel transferred the title to her land to the Tulsa Urban Renewal Authority.[109] Her property soon became what city leaders saw all of Greenwood to be—an inconvenient eyesore, "ravaged by more than a month of vacancy and pilfering," according to an *Eagle* article. Her house and adjacent beauty salon were demolished in early 1976.[110]

Mabel remained bitter about what happened to Greenwood for the rest of her life. "They put us out of our homes and put our black folks in apartments," she said, noting the rise of public housing projects around North Tulsa.[111] TAAG had earlier proposed spreading the projects throughout the city to avoid overconcentration of poverty in black areas, but the recommendation was ignored by city officials.[112] "You cannot raise families in apartments," Mabel wrote, echoing an argument Homer Johnson had made early in the Model Cities program. "Everybody needs a home."[113]

But it would be too simple to say that the Tulsa Urban Renewal Authority had unilaterally imposed its will on an unwitting or unaware populace. TAAG was following the Urban Renewal Authority's actions at every step, and as TURA pointed out in some of its letters to homeowners, TAAG's citizen groups voted on and approved property clearance initiatives.[114] Some of the things TAAG advocated did come to pass, including the opening of a new football stadium for the Booker T. Washington High School Hornets funded through Model Cities.[115] Some local residents who served on TAAG's citizen boards appreciated learning about the mechanics of government. "It means so much to see some of the things we planned for become a reality,"

North Tulsa resident Catherine Thomas wrote in a letter during the Model Cities program. "I have enjoyed every moment of it."[116] Others came to renewal meetings hoping they would soon get access to the federal dollars that might lift them up and out of poverty. At one meeting, Ida Kelley, who had also served on a TAAG citizens' planning team, told the city commission that she "and others have removed our shacks into decent homes" and pointed out that "others . . . are waiting anxiously to be relocated."[117]

"There are obvious benefits to urban renewal," reflected Bob Goodwin, who was closely involved in the Freedom School movement and active at the *Eagle* throughout the 1970s. He noted that a portion of Greenwood's deteriorating housing stock was eventually replaced with new middle-class housing, as urban renewal had always promised. But he also watched as the hollowed-out neighborhood soon became a shadow of its former self. "Blacks have felt that they have lost any control over how the land was to be utilized or financial benefit from that utilization," Bob said. "I think it's a mixed bag. At that time agencies like TAAG and the Urban League were trying to mitigate the negative implications and accentuate the positive implications."[118]

What people like Mabel wanted, if they couldn't hold on to their homes, was a genuine effort to revive the community-driven and entrepreneurial spirit that Greenwood had long embodied. TAAG wanted this as well—job opportunities, not urban renewal, were actually the group's first priority. But the widespread razing of North Tulsa's black neighborhoods coincided with a collapse in federal funding for Model Cities, as the Nixon administration drastically curtailed public spending on housing initiatives for the poor after his landslide reelection in 1972.[119] "The withdrawal of this assistance has left critical problems for renewal agencies and cities that want to continue improvement of their worst blighted areas," the Tulsa Urban Renewal Authority wrote in its 1975 annual report. "Without some such support, the rebuilding of cleared areas may be a long delayed dream."[120] While some detached homes were soon constructed west of Greenwood Avenue, the promised apartments, gardens, and townhouses were never built. Most devastatingly, the commercial district that had been planned for the heart of the neighborhood—a new version of Deep Greenwood—never even began construction.[121] By 1976, the Urban Renewal Authority had acquired 850 parcels in Greenwood and surrounding, predominantly black North Tulsa neighborhoods, but only about one hundred had been conveyed or sold to private parties for redevelopment.[122]

It was this failure to make good on policy promises that most roiled Jim Goodwin, whose childhood home on Haskell Street was among the seized properties. "What's the difference between going in and actively destroying land," he said, "and sitting on it to prevent development? What's the difference in terms of black progress, or lack of it? You're still an impediment. It may be by omission as opposed to commission. [But] that's still part of that lingering legacy."[123]

If urban renewal had been a failure for the community of Greenwood, however, it had been a success for the city of Tulsa. Ever since 1921, city officials had sought to relocate Greenwood residents farther north so they could use the neighborhood land for their own commercial ends. The gambit failed initially, because Greenwood property owners banded together to refuse to sell, and a court judge ruled that the city's scheme to require fireproof buildings was unconstitutional. "I'll hold what I have until I get what I lost" had been the neighborhood rallying cry then.

Everything played out differently in the 1970s. The notion of a government takeover of Greenwood was no longer a local scheme but part of a national one, implemented at scale in every major city in America with billions of dollars in federal funding.[124] Instead of stopping the seizure of land, courts made the process more efficient by processing eminent domain claims. Property owners did not put up a collective front against the effort; instead, they cashed individual checks as compensation for generations of toil. While the Colored Citizens' Relief Committee had been an oppositional force against the city after the 1921 massacre, TAAG's role was more ambiguous, as its leaders tried to oppose the worst outcomes of Model Cities even as the program paid their salaries.[125] By granting black people an illusion of control and a modicum of money, city leaders ended up more effectively controlling them.

All this was in service of what Tulsa had always cared about most: building a booming economy. With white people fleeing North Tulsa because of desegregation and downtown because of aging infrastructure, the city spent the 1970s taking dramatic steps to "save" the urban core. It was increasingly obvious that white people simply did not want to live near black people—not the poor renters in Greenwood, not the middle-class homeowners moving into neighborhoods farther north, not the black children of every economic station enrolling at formerly all-white schools. And the federal government was too scared to make them; while the original Model Cities legislation had called for using federal dollars to "counteract the segregation of housing by race or income," the provision was struck from the final version of the law.[126]

The result was that black and white neighborhoods, which had once shared geographical borders, were suddenly miles apart. "Outright abandonment of homes—new homes—has become a serious problem," the Urban Renewal Authority fretted in one early 1970s report. "At the heart of the trend is the issue of race as a market factor."[127] Any effort to "save" downtown would have to be coupled with a plan to clear out the so-called slums nearby and create a larger buffer zone between black and white Tulsa. The Crosstown Expressway did the first half of the legwork, and urban renewal and Model Cities finished it. By 1975, planners had poured $33 million into new downtown construction, hoping to encourage white people to continue living, working, and shopping there. But only $1 million had been spent on the redevelopment of Greenwood and other parts of North Tulsa, while vastly larger sums were dumped into relocating black residents farther north.[128] Fire-wielding mobsters hadn't been able to destroy Greenwood, but urban planners and real estate developers did it with ease. It was just a slower burn.

So it was at 1231 North Greenwood Avenue. Rather than being used to house new black families or incubate new black businesses, Mabel's property was transformed into an empty lot, which it would remain for the next forty-five years and counting, after being sold by the Urban Renewal Authority to the nearby First Church of God in Christ in 1976. The authority would continue to hold on to at least two hundred acres of empty land in Greenwood and surrounding areas for years afterward.[129] "We have allowed too many of our landmarks to crumble," Mabel reflected later, "while we stumble into the fields of the fatherless."[130]

After selling her home, Mabel wanted to return for a time to the blue skies of California, where she'd spent time as a factory mechanic during World War II. Before her departure, the neighborhood organized an official "Mabel Little Day" as part of her sendoff. The festivities were anchored, of course, at Mt. Zion. Ahead of the celebration, the *Eagle* christened her "The First Lady of Greenwood" in a front-page article.[131] The streets where Mabel had spent a lifetime were increasingly empty, but the spirit of the community was still alive.

In her *Eagle* profile, Mabel offered advice for city leaders to ensure a bright future for Tulsa. "Get enough of these young people together and let them speak the conviction of their conscience," she said. "Let them work out what they think is best. They'll make it."[132]

CHAPTER **19**

HANDOFFS

Ed Sr. and Jeanne take a walk at Willow Lake

"Bob, come home," Ed Sr. said to his youngest son, "or I'm going to give it away."[1]

It was the fall of 1972, and Ed was tired of running the *Oklahoma Eagle*. He was about to turn seventy and had been working on Greenwood Avenue in some form or fashion since he opened his haberdashery in 1929. Age had only brought more responsibility as he juggled his law practice with his duties as a newspaper publisher. Retirement beckoned, but Ed hoped that the *Eagle* could remain in the family.

Bob was an unlikely successor. Ed Sr.'s first choice had always been Ed Jr., the firstborn son and the most versatile *Eagle* staffer in the family. But his alcoholism continued as he approached middle age, putting his clear dedication to the paper in conflict with the unpredictability caused by his drinking. Regina, Ed Jr.'s youngest daughter, remembered sitting in the stands at Booker T. football games and watching him saunter onto the field inebriated while the band was playing, dancing in bright red pants. It was funny to the crowd but not to her. She admired her father's daring, his resourcefulness, and his humor, but she also saw all the ways his addiction put a strain on the family. "One of the most brilliant men I knew," Regina said later, "but he was also troubled and challenged with alcoholism."[2]

Jim was the next most likely to take over, but despite having a fair bit of early experience in journalism, he was busy with his law practice. In the early 1970s, he'd found himself defending the local Black Panther Wilbert Brown, who was arrested on obscenity charges for calling police "motherfucking fascist pig cops" at an anti–Vietnam War rally at the University of Tulsa.[3] Jim did not identify as a Panther—in fact, his family's newspaper had found much to critique about the group's ideology.[4] But while Jim was loyal to the *Eagle,* he was also his own man. Not long before Brown was arrested, Jim's friend Don Ross bought him a copy of *Soul on Ice,* the essay collection by Black Panther leader Eldridge Cleaver. Jim was taken by it. He began growing a thick, coarse beard in solidarity with the movement and wearing sunglasses in the courtroom. "They all thought I became a radical," he said. "Here's a Notre Damer, a guy steeped in faith, trying to defend the use of the word 'motherfucker.' "[5]

Coverage of Brown's high-profile case reached newspapers across the country.[6] Jim brought a sociologist to the witness stand who explained that *motherfucker,* while derisive, had no sexual connotation, and he had Brown take the stand to define *pig* as someone who had "no respect for human beings." Despite Jim's best efforts, Brown was found guilty after just a fifteen-minute deliberation by the jury.[7] In early 1972, Jim sent a lawyer from his firm to Washington, D.C., to petition the Supreme Court for an appeal. The Court agreed to review the case and found that Brown had used the foul language in the context of a "political meeting" and that such language could have been anticipated by the audience.[8] It wasn't obscene, by legal standards, after all. Brown's name was cleared in the summer of 1972, and Jim found he had made a small contribution to the free speech wars that were raging in the turbulent protest era following the civil rights movement. For the rest of his life, whenever Jim grew a beard, he thought of that case.[9]

Though Ed Jr. and Jim were out, plenty of women in the Goodwin family had the skills to lead the *Eagle* as well. Ed's daughters Onetha, Edwyna, Jo Ann, Jeanne, Carlie, and Susan had all written for the paper, edited articles, or sold copies at various points in their lives— Edwyna had even been president at one time. But they all ultimately adopted different professions. Edwyna became a lawyer in Michigan, Onetha and Jo Ann teachers in Tulsa, Jeanne a social worker in Nashville, Carlie a medical researcher in Boston, and Susan a human resources manager in Houston.[10] Ed Sr., a proud patriarch, seemed to believe it was men who would carry on his professional legacy, so he never seriously considered them for the job anyway.[11] "My sons and I will be here to answer in your behalf," he had written in that farewell letter to his father in 1958.

So that left Bob. He was only twenty-two years old, working on a theology degree in San Francisco, when his father called him offering him the role of publisher. Bob had little training in journalism beyond a single high school class and no background in business.[12] The youngest Goodwin man could have quite easily wanted nothing at all to do with the *Eagle*. Like his older brothers, Bob had previously withstood Ed's sudden eruptions of violence. "The first few years of my relationship with him was a one-sided affair," Bob said in a 1971 speech, "because at the sound of his voice, I trembled."[13] When he was about ten, Bob dumped a pile of his mother's discarded peach pits in the back yard. Weeks later his father ran over them with a lawn mower, damaging the mower's blades and sending the pits flying like bullets in every direction. Ed stormed into the dining room during Saturday-morning breakfast, demanding the skull of whoever had sabotaged him with the pits. When he discovered it was his youngest son, he hit him in the head with enough force to knock him into a wall.[14]

But their dynamic changed when Bob was a student at Oral Roberts University and decided, for the first time, to grow out his afro. The school was in Tulsa, but Bob lived in the dorms and embraced ideas—Christian fundamentalism, Black Power radicalism—that were largely foreign to his father. "What's wrong with your head, boy?" Ed asked him one day when Bob came home for a visit, eyeing his son's huge head of hair. He dragged Bob upstairs to the master bedroom and slathered Vaseline into his son's woolly mane. Then

Bob, shocking himself as much as his father, coolly walked to the sink and washed the grease from his head.

"Daddy, I know who I am as a person. And if I choose to wear my hair to signify my ethnic heritage, that's what I'm gonna do."

Ed Sr. clenched his fists in roiling frustration. Bob could just about see the fury vibrating off of him, like heat waves bouncing off asphalt. But Ed's anger, whose origins no one in the family could fully explain, was mellowed by age and, perhaps, wisdom. Bob suspected his father also feared the devoted relationship his son had with God. Ed's hands relaxed as the tension wound out of his body. "You can do what you want to do now," Ed said. "You're a man."[15]

Bob wasn't especially committed to the *Eagle,* but he was, despite their conflicts, committed to his father. When he got the call in San Francisco, there was only one answer. "Daddy, if you want me to come," Bob told his father, "I'll be on the next plane." *The Godfather* had recently come out, and Bob's older sister Carlie joked that he was Michael Corleone, the young, reluctant scion to an empire.

The two men ultimately decided that Bob would take over the fol-

Bob Goodwin working on an edition of
the Oklahoma Eagle

lowing summer, after he had earned his degree. He flew back into Tulsa in June 1973 and slept in his old bedroom at the farm. By then the other rooms were often occupied by his siblings' children rather than the siblings themselves. His first full day in town, his mother cooked a massive breakfast for the three of them—ham, grits, eggs, the works. Then Bob climbed into Ed's car, as he had so many times as a child, and his father drove him to the *Eagle* office.

"He gave me a set of keys and showed me what doors they opened," Bob recalled. "He gave me the combination to the wall safe. At nine o'clock when the bank opened, we went to the bank and changed the signature card so I could sign the checks. And he said, 'Adios.' "[16]

On an autumn day in November 1974, Ed Sr. took a handful of fish chow and hurled it into one of the ponds of Willow Lake. The water quivered with a thousand ripples as a sea of channel catfish swam up to devour the food.[17] Ed had turned the property's six farms into a thriving fish farm, where anglers were welcome from dawn till to dusk to take home all the fish they could catch—just one dollar per pound. Goodwin's Katt Fish Haven, as Ed rechristened Willow Lake, was a retirement gift to himself, yet another reinvention of his never-ending hustle.[18]

Manual labor suited Ed well. He rose at five, threw on a pair of loose-fitting blue overalls (he lost eighty pounds after retiring), and finished after the sun had slinked back below the horizon. He spent much of his time battling the wildlife that threatened to reclaim the farm from him, chasing turtles lurking in the grass and muskrats that burrowed deep into the dams controlling the water. "Now I don't have the other fellow's problems," he told a *World* reporter, referring to his old legal clients. "I have my own."[19]

One day, his granddaughter Regina recalled, when the two of them were standing at the water's edge, Ed eyed a snake slithering across the surface of one of the ponds. He turned to her and said, "Go run back to the house and get my shotgun." Regina was just ten years old.[20] Though she liked a long list of things that were supposedly for boys—professional wrestling, G.I. Joe action figures, Muhammad Ali—she had never held a gun before.[21]

She hesitated as her mind raced. *This man just told me to go get a shotgun*. But like everyone else in the family, Regina already knew there was no opposing Grandfather's wishes. It was perhaps a quarter-mile jog to her grandparents' home, down the wide dirt road that was often clouded with dust when cars loaded with fishing poles trundled toward their chosen ponds.[22] Often on Saturdays, Ed Jr. or Alquita would bring Regina and her three older siblings—Sabrina, Greg, and Eric—up the curved driveway to the stone home and leave them there for the day or sometimes the entire weekend. For them, Willow Lake was simply "The House." They spent hours banging discordant notes on the living room's baby grand piano and telling ghost stories in the loft of the nearby rock barn.[23] But everyone was also expected to help with chores around the property. And Regina had just earned armed duty.

As she made her way into the side door of the house and past the laundry machine, Regina saw her grandmother standing in the kitchen. Jeanne was, in Regina's eyes, the epitome of grace and civility. Hers was a world of silver serving trays and ornate spoons. If she caught any of her grandchildren roughhousing, Jeanne was liable to send them to her library, also known as the "quiet room." The only reprieve from the dreary silence were the ancient books lining the shelves, which seemed to Regina like an extension of her punishment. "I'd just sit there and be mad," she said later. There was no chance Grandmother, a woman of letters, would let a small girl run off with a loaded weapon.

But when Regina reached the kitchen and told Jeanne about Ed's request, the prim and proper grandmother suddenly turned pioneer woman. Jeanne rummaged behind a nearby door and nonchalantly handed her granddaughter the shotgun. "She didn't hesitate," Regina said years later. As she ran back out toward the lake, her ponytail bouncing behind her and the gun hoisted like a time bomb, Regina did her best to avoid pointing the long barrel of the weapon anywhere near her face. "I'm thinking all along, *This man is crazy*." Years later Regina couldn't even remember whether Grandfather killed the snake or not.[24]

Each grandchild developed their own unique relationship with Ed Sr. Regina's older brother Greg spent the most time with him, after Ed convinced him to quit his part-time job at McDonald's and start working at the catfish farm after school. "Why you working for them

Three generations of Goodwins at Willow Lake Farm in the 1970s

white folks?" Greg recalled him saying. "You think you're ever gonna own that? Well, you own the stuff I got. You need to leave them people and come work for me."[25]

Greg became Ed's official field hand ("his indentured servant"), pulling moss out of the ponds and monitoring the aerators that kept the water clean. He discovered many things about his grandfather as they worked side by side. He saw how clever Ed Sr. could be, especially when it came to negotiations. When dealing with contractors, Ed would pretend to know less than they did, letting the drawl of his elastic accent wrap him in a shroud of ignorance as he asked simple questions. Acting "country dumb," Greg called it. "He would play and use that to his advantage. He was extremely smart. He was a hustler."

Grandfather was also a coarse man at times, from his gravelly voice to his word selection. "It was 'dammit' and 'hell' mostly," Greg remembered. "But he would use the big ones as well, depending on who he was talking to."

Once, when Greg was about sixteen, while he was cleaning moss out of one of the ponds, he saw a pair of white men fishing. The men flagged him down while he worked.

"Hey, I hear an old black man owns this," one man said.

"He does," Greg acknowledged.

Then the man said to his friend, "I told you a nigger owns this place."

Greg ran off to the house to find his grandfather and tell him what he'd heard. Ed immediately drove out to the pond on his riding lawn mower, his pistol in hand. "I heard y'all said something about a nigger running this place?" he said to the men. "Well this nigger giving you five minutes to get off this property." They were gone before their time limit expired.[26]

While Greg spent long days with Ed, Regina was more often with Grandmother Jeanne. It was Jeanne who woke the children before sunrise when they spent weekends at Willow Lake and insisted they cram into Alsuma's tiny First Baptist Church on Sundays, even if they were still wearing shorts and tank tops. She scheduled staggered bedtimes based on age and assigned the children to color-coordinated rooms in which to sleep—the Red Room, the Blue Room, and so on. Hers was a regime of "loving discipline and order," Regina reflected later. It was through Jeanne that Regina learned the difference between a salad fork and a dinner fork, as well as the scourge of improper grammar. (Regina, stuck doing chores: "Where's the vacuum cleaner at?" Jeanne: "Behind that preposition.")[27]

Jeanne was soft spoken, but she wasn't soft. Regina and her sister Sabrina recalled a time Grandmother took the two girls to a shoe store in town. Jeanne could pass for white; the girls, most certainly, could not. When a store clerk's eyes glided past them to the assumed white woman, he asked her, "Can I help you?"

Jeanne responded, "You can help me when you help my granddaughter."[28]

After dark on the farm, the grandkids would crowd into Ed and Jeanne's master bedroom on the second floor for the family's most obsessive pastime, Scrabble.[29] Jeanne had picked up the game sometime around the 1960s and soon had the entire clan playing almost every night. With the deluxe wooden game board perched on a swiveling lazy Susan, one or two of the children would square off against their grandparents, while other kids spectated from an armrest or Ed and Jeanne's king-size bed.[30] Ed was fiercely competitive and always demanded a rematch if he lost, though Jeanne was far and away the best player in the family, earning the nickname "Barracuda" for her ability to devour opponents with small but lethal words.[31]

At Christmastime, most of the seventeen grandchildren were likely to be at the farm, a mishmash of wailing babies, excitable preteens, and disaffected adolescents.[32] Anna, Jim's eldest daughter, was always excited to see Grandfather. She long remembered the piggyback rides he would give her when she was a small girl, making her laugh until her stomach hurt, and how he let her wriggle the lobes of his oversize ears. "He was a boisterous man but a gentle spirit," she wrote later in reflections on her childhood. "He, I'm told, terrified his children, but he was the kindest, sweetest man to his grandchildren. We all loved him so."

Anna was younger than Greg and Regina, but she and her grandfather developed a close relationship; he treated her less like a soldier to toughen up, as he had his sons, and more like a friendly confidante, as he had his daughters. "Get an education because they can take your money and your things, but they can never take your mind," he advised her.[33]

As the 1970s wore on, more and more of Ed's friends began to pass away. Amos Hall died in 1971. His onetime colleague Thurgood Marshall, who was by then a Supreme Court justice, returned to Greenwood for his funeral. "I can't think of anything more he could have done," Marshall eulogized. "He led the fight here and around the country in the days when it was a little rough—and to say a little rough is putting it mildly."[34] Longtime *Eagle* editor Ben Hill died the same year, after serving three years as Greenwood's second-ever black legislator in the state House of Representatives.[35] Anna sometimes accompanied her grandfather to these homegoings, often elaborate affairs in Greenwood at First Baptist or even at Boston Avenue Methodist, the massive white church downtown.[36] But Ed, despite his stature in the community, didn't want such pomp and circumstance for himself. At one Greenwood funeral, he took his granddaughter aside and told her something else she'd always remember. "When I go, don't go through all that. Just put me in an old plain box and send me on my way."[37]

"I graduated from Booker T. Washington High School in 1921. I was in the play the night of May 31, 1921. The principal dismissed us by announcing that there was trouble, and that everyone was to go home. That was the night the riot began."[38]

Ed Sr. delivered the information matter-of-factly in the lavish office he'd kept for himself at the *Oklahoma Eagle*, as Ruth Avery feverishly jotted down notes. It was November 1976.[39] Jimmy Carter, who visited Greenwood's Vernon AME Church on an early presidential campaign stop, had just won the White House.[40] Ed had spent a lifetime always looking toward the future, but more and more, he found himself talking about the past.

It must have been a curious thing for him to be meeting with Avery, a white woman intent on hearing his story. Ed harbored more than half a century of knowledge about Greenwood, remembering everything from the Friday night lines at the Dreamland to the Klan marches that once snaked around the neighborhood.[41] Most of it had been reported in the *Eagle* at some point or another, but for the first time, it felt like the mainstream world—that is, the white world—was interested in hearing black stories.

The United States was undergoing a fundamental shift in how it both interpreted and popularized black history. Alex Haley's generational saga *Roots*, which had just been released in August, was climbing up the *New York Times* bestseller list every week.[42] A much-anticipated television adaptation was set to premiere in January on ABC.[43] Nineteen seventy-six marked the first year that the White House acknowledged Black History Month, which had been known as Negro History Week when Ed was a young man.[44] Meanwhile, more and more colleges were adding black studies to their curriculum, following the lead of Oklahoma native Nathan Hare, who launched the first black studies program in America at San Francisco State in 1968. (Hare was a regular visitor to Greenwood after courting and marrying a young woman from the neighborhood named Julia.)[45] It was during this period that the concept of "oral history," recollections of the past handed down through family and community narratives rather than through written documents, first gained academic legitimacy.[46] In a place like Tulsa, oral history would be the only way to get at a semblance of the truth about what happened in 1921, considering that the white press had helped spark the massacre with sensational reporting, and later tried to destroy the evidence. When researchers like Ruth Avery inspected the *Tulsa Tribune*'s archives to see how the paper had covered the massacre, they made a startling discovery. The article falsely accusing Dick Rowland of attempting to rape Sarah Page had literally been ripped from the newspaper's pages. Documenting the recollections of survivors like Ed was needed to combat a wave of lies and obfuscation.

Ed wasn't the only one in Greenwood talking. His former classmate W. D. Williams had held on to many of his childhood mementos, including a scrapbook of his college years at Hampton, photos of Greenwood Avenue from the 1910s, and a small oval paperweight perched on a credenza in the family living room, showing a stately two-story brick building with movie posters running down its walls. "The Only Colored Theatre in the City," the ornament boasted.[47]

Though W.D. occasionally brought pieces from his collection to yearbook class at Booker T. so he could school "fat mouths" like Don Ross on their own community's history, he rarely shared the meaning behind these artifacts with anyone—not even his own grandchildren. His granddaughter Marilyn Christopher recalled seeing the Dreamland paperweight at eight years old, when Grandmother Babe assigned her to clean the living room. Even before anyone explained its significance to her, she knew it was a precious thing. W.D., whom she and her siblings called Daddo, told her about how his mama once owned a majestic theater. But he never went into detail. Perhaps, in the optimistic times of desegregation, it didn't seem right to dwell on the past. Perhaps it hurt too much. "We didn't sit around the dinner table talking about the Tulsa massacre of 1921," Marilyn recalled. "Because who would?"[48]

One day, not long before Ed's sit-down with Ruth Avery, W.D. received a phone call from twenty-one-year-old white college student Scott Ellsworth. He was writing his senior thesis on the race riot. Ellsworth, who was being trained in the burgeoning field of oral history, had been trying and failing all summer to get white people to tell him about what had happened. The people who knew wouldn't talk, and the people who talked didn't know much. "All you would get in the '70s and '80s would be white middle-class families or upper-class families who would talk about how they heroically saved their servants," Ellsworth recalled. "There was no list of white rioters. . . . I could never find anybody to fess up."[49]

To Ellsworth, the riot remained a grand mystery. But the story had been swirling in Greenwood, quietly but consistently, for generations: in the *Eagle*'s special edition in 1950, in the 1971 issue of *Oklahoma Impact Magazine* published by Don Ross (which featured a lengthy Q&A with W. D. Williams in addition to Ed Wheeler's investigative feature), and during the fiftieth-anniversary commemoration at Mt. Zion in 1971. In 1975 the *Eagle* mentioned the riot in its pages at least seven times, including in a scathing review of a tourism-friendly history book published by the city that largely ignored Greenwood's legacy.[50] But students both white and black were unlikely to find much mention of the riot in their schoolbooks, and even on the black side of town, many never heard a word about it from their parents.[51]

W.D., who had recently turned seventy, agreed to meet with Ellsworth. He was an affable young man with the quasi-southern accent endemic to Tulsa, and he tried his best to charm his interview subject. But it was slow going. "He was fairly stiff," Ellsworth recalled. "I'm thinking this was a mistake. This guy doesn't know anything. He's a little suspicious of me."[52]

As the meeting dragged on, Ellsworth reached into his backpack and pulled out a three-by-two-foot map he'd acquired from the city engineer's office. It was a depiction of the original Tulsa town site, which had been drawn in 1902 to give the seizure of land from the Creek Nation an orderly legality. Between Blocks 46 and 47 in the top-right corner of the map, Greenwood Avenue bounded northward past the edge of the city limits and into the Cherokee Nation (which was also platted, appraised, and sold to outside settlers shortly after the core of Tulsa was). Ellsworth had cross-referenced the building addresses on the map with the city directory and handwritten onto each lot the person who lived or worked there circa 1921. Next to Lot 3, Block 46, he wrote "Williams Confectionery." Next to Lot 8, Block 47, he wrote "Dreamland Theater."

W.D.'s entire demeanor changed as Ellsworth unfurled the map on the kitchen table. He ran his fingers past names that had almost been lost to the haze of memory, some that had not been seen or heard in Tulsa since 1921. He saw his boyhood splayed out before him for the first time since it had been set to flame. He looked up at Ellsworth.

"Okay, so what do you want to know?"[53]

With a genial patience across multiple interviews, W.D. narrated every step of the 1921 Tulsa Race Massacre as he had experienced it, from the moment he learned that his acquaintance Dick Rowland had been falsely accused of rape. He spoke like a veteran reliving a war story, with his father John playing the role of the brave grizzled general, sniping at white assailants from the bathroom window. He sometimes used sound effects—*zoom* for the bullets that whizzed by them as they tried to escape their home. He had distanced himself from the terror, somehow, perhaps by keeping it compartmentalized in his carefully curated photo collection, which allowed him to talk about being marched to Convention Hall against his will in a matter-of-fact way: "I was afraid outside because I saw them shoot a man right on the steps of the place." While he had steeled himself against the worst parts of the night, his voice softened at the tenderest moments. He remembered being reunited with Loula the following morning, on a random street in downtown Tulsa. "I'd walked the town looking for her," he said. The warmth was palpable in his voice.[54]

W.D.'s interview became the anchor point of Ellsworth's thesis and later of his 1982 book *Death in a Promised Land*, the first book-length retelling of the massacre since Mary Jones Parrish's *Events of the Tulsa Disaster* to make extended use of black eyewitness accounts. Historian John Hope Franklin, a massacre descendant himself, called the book "as close to being *the* definitive history of the Tulsa riot as I have seen."[55] The work would go on to be cited in academic and journalistic works about the massacre for decades.

Such vital academic texts couldn't have been crafted without W.D. and other Greenwood old-timers who relived the worst experience of their lives for posterity's sake—people like Robert Fairchild, Mabel Little, and Ed Goodwin. Decades later W.D.'s recollection would form the spine of big-budget adaptations of the event that placed the Dreamland at the center of the horror, such as the HBO television shows *Watchmen* and *Lovecraft Country*. The stories that these survivors recounted in the 1970s would eventually grow into legends and, later, big business.[56]

Of course, W.D. wasn't in it for money. Throughout the 1970s, Booker T.'s longest-serving educator grew more comfortable telling the story of what had happened to him to nearly anyone who cared to listen. Back then the number was still small. But W.D was a teacher at heart, and the knowledge he shared was destined to one day reach a much larger audience. "I have lived longer than most of my friends," he told the *Eagle* in 1977, "so my community contribution is talking about black history in Tulsa."[57]

The orange glow of the *Oklahoma Eagle*'s neon sign shone alone on the avenue at night, as the rest of Deep Greenwood lay vacant and barren. The Crosstown Expressway had opened in 1973 and added the steady drone of highway traffic to the local ambiance.[58] By the end of 1978, the *Eagle* office building was the last one still open in the block and a half south of the new interstate. Harold White packed up his recreation club, decks of dominoes and all, while Georgia Ola Walker, who owned a café across the street, retired after more than sixty years in the restaurant business.[59] The rest of the buildings on the block, most of them burned-out or vandalized, were sold to urban renewal around the same time.[60] Even the men who sometimes sold Regina and her older sister Sabrina five-cent candies in the abandoned husk of the Williams Confectionery eventually disappeared.[61] "Most of the buildings are vacant awaiting demolition," read a report commissioned by the Greenwood Chamber of Commerce from the period. "Holes have been burned in the floors of several buildings by winos seeking to keep warm. Litter blows in empty streets. The bulldozer and the backhoe wait to remove the last signs of what was once a majestic place in the history of a race and a city."[62] Ed Sr. sometimes paid a landscaper to tend to the gnarly patchwork of grass and weeds where the Goodwin Building once stood, but the city had largely left the block to decay.[63]

Farther north, Greenwood Avenue was looking similarly desolate. Mabel Little's had been just one of more than nine hundred households and more than three hundred businesses forced out of Greenwood and surrounding neighborhoods.[64] Each plot of land, as it had in the destruction of the massacre, carried its own painful story. Don Thompson, the former *Eagle* reporter, had discovered that he could tell more powerful narratives with images rather than words. After watching much of Deep Greenwood be destroyed for the Crosstown Expressway in 1967, he began capturing images of the remaining Greenwood businesses before they were gone—restaurateurs, shoeshiners, and the patrons who breathed life into the neighborhood's streets every day. One day in the early 1970s, he walked into a storefront on the northern end of Greenwood, where a lone barber with a single chair was manning his property. Bulldozers were demolishing structures directly across the street. Don's journalistic instincts kicked in.

"Would you mind standing and just looking outside the window?" he asked the barber.

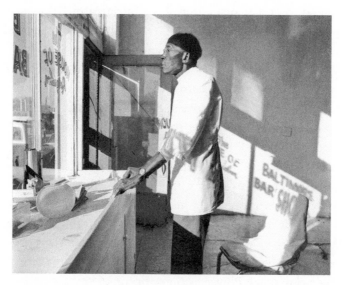

During the era of urban renewal, the owner of the Baltimore Barber Shop looks at businesses being bulldozed on Greenwood Avenue

The image Don captured of the forlorn Baltimore Barber Shop owner would eventually become the most striking visual symbol of the pain caused by urban renewal in Greenwood, capturing the tragic disruption of the initiative in a way that neither sunny brochures celebrating renewal nor newspaper editorials denouncing it really could. "I tried to show what racism looks like visually," he said later. "What this trauma was doing to them because they had to try to find a new life for themselves." Don planned to follow up with the man the next day, to learn how he planned to adapt to a world changing against his will, but when the young photographer returned to Greenwood Avenue, the Baltimore Barber Shop was already being razed. He never saw the owner again.[65]

Just a couple of blocks north of the barbershop, young Regina also felt the disruptive impact of urban renewal. Her family's three-bedroom house, located directly in front of Carver Junior High, had always been a popular hangout for the neighborhood children. Dozens of kids would cram into 1415 Greenwood Avenue every weekday morning, filing through the front door for a few precious minutes of laughter before dashing out the back when they heard Carver's five-minute warning bell.[66] Regina's mother Alquita welcomed all comers, whether they wanted to grab a snack out of the refrigerator before school or get a plate at the dinner table afterward—she made them feel so at home, some of them called her Mom too.[67] Regina's father Ed Jr., meanwhile, coached youth basketball for years at the First Baptist Church gymnasium directly across the street, providing a stabilizing force for some of the teenagers who couldn't find it at home. The kids would train with Ed Jr. during the week and worship with him on Sunday too.[68]

In the afternoons, when Regina joined Greg and the older boys playing pick-up football at Carver's athletic fields, the hose in the Goodwin family backyard became a makeshift water fountain.[69] At night, Regina could hear the roar of Booker T. Washington marching band and the cheers from the football stadium, located on the Carver campus. She'd often be at the games herself, cheering on the Hornets and throwing a tiny Black Power fist into the air.[70]

All that ended in 1974, when the Goodwins sold the house and an adjacent property to the Tulsa Urban Renewal Authority for $29,000 ($162,000 in 2021 dollars). Ed Sr., who owned the land and was always seeking the best angle, rejected the authority's initial lowball offer and triggered condemnation proceedings on the land. But he eventually sold, and the family moved, just like everyone else.[71]

Regina's parents purchased a larger two-story home in Brady Heights, the neighborhood just west of Greenwood, where Ku Klux Klansman Tate Brady built a lavish mansion at its southern entry point in 1920.[72] Just twelve years old at the time of the move, Regina was awed by the size of the new home and thrilled to have her own room. But day-to-day life was different. She could no longer walk to visit her friend Angie Dixon's house, where the girls would cook homemade Big Macs using Thousand Island dressing. She no longer heard the spectacularly loud arguments of Leon and Honey Hush, the young couple next door, or feigned terror when Honey Hush walked by and made goofy faces in the Goodwins' living room window. "We didn't have the same kind of relationships," Regina said later. Instead of feeling like the center of the universe when the children of Greenwood descended on her home every morning, she took a bus to school and was often late. The gravity of her world had shifted.[73]

While Regina's family moved west, most Greenwood residents were pushed farther north, often past the busy thoroughfare of Thirty-sixth Street. It was an area where small business owners were already facing headwinds, as their tiny shops struggled to compete with the mega-chains taking root in other parts of the city, now easily accessible thanks to all the new highways. (Tulsa's first Target opened in 1970, and its first Wal-Mart in 1983.)[74] Moton Hospital, the Greenwood facility where Regina was born, was closed in 1967.[75] Pushing black residents north only made it harder for them to receive full-access care from South Tulsa hospitals, even if segregation had technically been deemed illegal.[76]

Tulsa Public Schools, meanwhile, did not adopt the experiment in multiculturalism at Carver en masse. As white residents vacated North Tulsa, the schools in the area became increasingly black. Booker T. Washington High School was an exception—it, like Carver, became a magnet school, meant to attract white residents back to the inner city.[77] Some older alums quietly resented that the school that had produced esteemed black historians, doctors, lawyers, and newspaper publishers would now be forced to accept fewer black students each year in order to accommodate whites.[78]

Combined, these factors turned many in the Greenwood community decisively against urban renewal as the decade wore on. The effort had wrought individual successes for poor renters transported to more stable homes—more than five hundred relocated families and individuals ended up purchasing housing elsewhere—but it had failed as a community-building project.[79] Much of the property in the neighborhood remained in the indefinite possession of the Tulsa Urban Renewal Authority. People felt they had sacrificed their history and their livelihoods and gotten nothing in return. "The black community agreed to peacefully vacate the 50 acres of cleared land where they were assured that the community would have the right to participate in the ownership of the redevelopment," the *Eagle* wrote in an editorial.

"This promise of a rebirth of black economic strength was a powerful inducement to cooperate with urban renewal. Downtown Tulsa must be made to understand that this promise will not be ignored."[80]

Even some of urban renewal's biggest initial proponents turned against it. Charles Christopher had been the lone black member of the Tulsa Urban Renewal Authority board when it was formed in the late 1950s, and he used the *Eagle*'s pages to tout the program's potential to "correct substandard housing conditions."[81] But two decades of glacial progress left him bitter to any promise of redevelopment offered by the city—especially because TAAG, the citizen-participation group that at least gave residents some say in the planning decisions, had been disbanded.[82]

When the city secured a new round of federal urban renewal funding at the end of the 1970s, Christopher spoke out against the plan, which was set to engineer another round of forced relocations.[83] "Black people should be leery of public officials who come bearing gifts," he wrote. "TURA flunked-out its last effort to relocate the black people who were moved out of the Greenwood area," he continued. "They were instrumental in creating a new ghetto to the north with all of the evils and social injustices that are inferred from this action. What assurances do the people have that this will not continue for those who choose to leave the area?"[84]

Christopher was not a Tulsa native, but he had married into a family with a long history in the neighborhood. His wife Anita was the daughter of W. D. Williams and the granddaughter of Loula Williams, whose confectionery building still stood on Greenwood Avenue. WILLIAMS BUILDING, 1922 was still etched into the top of the structure, as legible as the day the family rebuilt their home and business from the ashes of the massacre. But the building fell out of family ownership around the time of Loula's death in 1927.[85] By the late 1970s, the Tulsa Urban Renewal Authority determined that the building needed to be condemned along with the rest of Deep Greenwood. In an appraisal report, an examiner suggested "demolish[ing] [the] structure for land use as open storage or parking."[86]

Ed Sr., like others in the neighborhood, saw the writing on the wall for the Williams Confectionery and other Deep Greenwood landmarks long before the bulldozers threatened to come. "This land is being acquired and then it's turned over to another power structure for little or nothing because they're using government money," he said in one 1970s speech, likely referring to the fact that a large percentage of urban renewal projects were subsidized by federal dollars. He noted that the city was pouring vast sums into redeveloping downtown, even as it spent paltry amounts on improving Greenwood, rather than emptying it out. "You better get the young people together and the old people together and begin to pile up some money to buy this land back," Ed Sr. said, "because it's going to be the most valuable land in the city of Tulsa."[87]

Perhaps that could have been Ed's last line of business—going in on a co-op with other Greenwood leaders who wanted to see the glory days reclaimed, the days of social and economic solidarity. He was a man with the foresight and strength of will to make it happen. But in January 1977, as Ed was visiting the home of a family friend, he collapsed suddenly and was rushed to Hillcrest Medical Center.[88] Greenwood Avenue was a fragile shell of its former self, and suddenly, so was its longest-serving steward.

CHAPTER 20

IN FLESH AND STONE

Ed Goodwin, Sr., tending to his garden at
Willow Lake alongside his grandson Jerry

E d Goodwin, Sr., gave countless speeches throughout his life. A
live recording of only one of them exists today.

For the fiftieth anniversary of the massacre, Ed had been asked
to give the keynote speech at Mt. Zion back in 1971. After, W. D. Williams and Mabel Little spoke of the old Greenwood, and then the choir
erupted in "Lift Every Voice and Sing," and his son Bob introduced him
as "a man that was possessed with a great deal of feverish energy," Ed's
job was to transform half a century's worth of suppressed memories
into some form of communal catharsis. Loud applause greeted Ed as
he approached the rostrum. He had drafted prepared remarks with
the help of both Bob and Ed Jr., but when he reached the center of the
stage, he knew he would speak whatever he was feeling in his heart.

"I hope I'm not too harsh this evening in what I might say," Ed Sr. began.

He turned to his son behind him in the pulpit. "But I would like to say that I'm very grateful to you, Bob, and I love *you*. I loved you when I was being a little rough. I think it made a good Christian out of you."[1]

Ed remembered the thirty-first day of May 1921, he told the crowd. He never eagerly elaborated on what he had experienced. Even his children had heard just fragments of the night. According to one story, while Ed was hiding in a bathtub, an older female neighbor yanked him out by his oversize ears to claim the most secure spot in the house.[2] There were also two narratives about what happened when the mob showed up at the Goodwins' doorstep. In one telling, J. H. Goodwin stepped outside and posed as a white man in order to steer the mob away from the family house, with an apocryphal, "They went that-a-way."[3] In another account, it was a white friend or neighbor who quelled the mob, as the white judge John Oliphant had tried and failed to do for Dr. A. C. Jackson.[4] Ed's daughter Carlie once tried to sit her father down in front of a tape recorder and get him to recount his life story, beginning to end. But the tape ran out of space long before Ed reached 1921; if he told of his experiences in detail then, the memories were lost forever.[*][5]

Standing before the Mt. Zion audience fifty years after the massacre, on a day of somber remembrance, Ed Sr. would still insist that he had not come to dwell on the past. "Somewhere in the scripture it says, 'Let the dead bury the dead,'" he said. He told the congregation he had come not with malice or hatred or envy or jealousy, but to "eliminate hate and supplement it with love."

But make no mistake: there was still a debt to be paid.

"Tulsa—America—owes you something," Ed told the audience. "And they must pay. They must pay, and they will pay because God is living. God will see to it that justice and equity will come your way."

Ed eyed the young people sprinkled throughout the crowd. It was

---

[*] Lawsuits filed by the Goodwins in 1923 and details reported in Ed Sr.'s obituary indicate that the family likely took refuge in a new brick house they were building on their property, while their original home was burned to the ground.

for them, really, that they had all gathered that evening. "We want you young people to know that there has been blood shed here in Tulsa, Oklahoma, on your behalf," he said. "We are here tonight to commemorate those stalwart blacks who stood up four-square, who died that you might live today."

"Yes, sir!" a man in the crowd called out.

"This is why I'm here."

Despite himself, despite living a life that was always barreling headfirst toward the future, Ed spoke of days gone by. He spoke of being born into a world where black people could learn only up to the eighth grade, and of a family who came to Tulsa from Mississippi but could just as well have come from Georgia or Alabama or Louisiana, for so many black souls in those places were seeking a better way of life as well. He spoke of a Greenwood Avenue that was once packed with thriving businesses, including the many he'd owned himself—the haberdashery, the Goodie Goodie Club, the little popcorn stand. (He chose not to mention the secret gambling halls where the numbers were selected each day.) He spoke of a world so vivid that he, and his children, and his grandchildren, could recite the names and locations of the dozens of businesses that inhabited it, as if reading out of a phone book, as if summoning a map that hovered right before their eyes. As if being back in the old Greenwood District.

"I do not come to talk to you too much about the past," Ed reminded himself.

And yet when he reached the spine of his speech, the part he had clearly prepared for the occasion, his remarks were framed by a simple question.

"Who were we in 1921?" he asked. "We were the blacks who were degraded by the majority white race and looked upon more or less as chattel.

"Who were we? We were the ones who were denied the right to use toilet facilities, drinking fountains and public accommodations.

"Who were we? We were the benefactors of the oppressed. Courageous black men and women who came to Tulsa from the South."

More than once, he could not help but divert from his prepared rhetorical path, to go burrowing down side alleys into digressions, historical asides, and inappropriate jokes, often all three at the same time. He told a tangentially related story about a meeting he'd once had with a racist former mayor. The man disliked the word *Negro* and clearly said *nigger* all the time outside black people's earshot. In Ed's presence, the man settled on a compromise. "He could only say, 'the Niggra,'" Ed recalled, tossing on a gruff white southern accent. "The niggra." He chuckled while he said it, and the crowd cackled in a way you're not supposed to at church.

But soon Ed returned to the central theme.

Tulsa, he said, was a city "where we were herded together like a bunch of cattle and marched to the Convention Hall, where many of us fled to outlying communities for our safety. Where lumber companies refused to sell lumber to build and we were forced to build makeshift dwellings, which were substandard and which accounts for many of the slum conditions that exist in North Tulsa today."

He spoke briefly of his own memories of the massacre, but he couldn't help cutting the tension with another slice of humor. He recalled when a group of whites came walking down Haskell Street, seeking to separate men from the rest of their families. "They herded us out of our house up here and they said, 'Come out. We don't want you, women and children.' I was nineteen years old. My mother was standing there and I said, 'Pick me up, Mama, and put me in your arms.'"

The crowd again tried to stifle their laughs, as Ed hopscotched between levity and gravity like a man who had long ago learned to walk on the moon. But there was pain hidden behind the joke. "I sure didn't want to go out there," Ed said.

He had a natural felicity with words, of course, but he urged people to take action, to demand the best education while also voting in every local election. He openly criticized the "fear from the American Tulsa white man" while also telling young black people to "climb out of the mire that you seem sometimes to think is a pleasure to wallow in." He melded self-help with civil rights, Washington with Du Bois. He straddled, as his son Jim would later put it, the hypotenuse of a triangle.

The loudest cheers of the night came when he said a simple truth that Greenwood residents had believed for a long time, one that Washington had embraced and Du Bois had ultimately left the country to escape, a truth the legacy of Greenwood, of "Black Wall Street," would forever be shaped by: "Money is what you've got to have to move up in this society!"

Ed moved on to school segregation, racial housing covenants, and other racist government policies that the *Eagle* had battled over the decades. There was no way to talk about 1921 without talking about all the injustices that had come in its wake.

After about an hour before a rapt crowd, he had tired both himself and the audience out. "I'm gonna close," he said. "I'm not gonna keep you any longer. Bob's looking over here, shaking his head, shaking his feet. He's getting uneasy, thinking I'm gonna steal his thunder by trying to preach."

In truth, Ed had more to say. He wanted to tell the youngsters about all the black history that was being left out of their state-issued textbooks and limited school curricula. He wanted to tell them about Jesse Owens, Langston Hughes, Benjamin O. Davis, Daniel Hale Williams, and George Washington Carver. ("Patriarchs" of the race, he called them, ignoring the matriarchs who existed as well.) Ed knew the obstacles black people faced every day, but he also had a bone-deep conviction that they could be overcome.

There simply wasn't enough time. "If you don't have any Negro history books, come down to the *Oklahoma Eagle*, I'll let you read plenty of 'em," he told the children of Greenwood. "It would be good for you to know something about your race."[6]

After Ed Sr. collapsed in January 1977, it was a tough year for everyone in the family as they watched dementia slowly set in. He spent more than a year floating between nursing homes, too sick for Jeanne to take care of at the house.[7] Jim, who had bounced on Ed's knee in the Christmas photo in 1941, was shocked to see his father's faculties wither to those of a baby.[8] Jo Ann would always remember one thing he said shortly before he passed, in one of those startling moments of clarity that strike people who have been betrayed by their bodies and their minds but not yet their souls. It was about Susan. "Love her," Ed said. "She's your sister, and it's not her fault."[9]

Before he got sick, Ed had rediscovered God for the first time in many years. He rarely went to church when his children were growing up and saw nothing wrong with his boozing and gambling.[10] That changed after Bob became a pastor and introduced the family to Oral Roberts, the white pastor and televangelist who developed a surprisingly deep tie to black Oklahomans and welcomed integrated congregations.[11] Before retiring, Ed had begun attending the tiny Baptist church in Alsuma more regularly, even leading Bible study from time to time.[12] The modest trappings of the small sanctuary, barely bigger than the family's living room, were in stark contrast to the lavish lifestyle he'd been aggressively pursuing since he first set foot in Greenwood as a boy and met the wealthy strivers who would one day become legends. Somehow, though, the humble surroundings suited him.

He had told his family to hold his services there when the time came.[13] So on September 14, 1978, three days after Ed's death, his wife, sister, nine children, sixteen grandchildren, and a select number of well-wishers crammed into the "stereotypical little country church," in Rev. Bob Goodwin's words. It was not even a thousand square feet in size and barely able to hold fifty people, with a two-hole outhouse in the back and large somber image of Jesus behind the pulpit.[14] "I don't even know if they had air conditioning at that time," recalled Ed's daughter Jeanne. "It was packed. People were standing outside, 'cause people admired him for what he did for them and the community."[15]

Bob sat in the pulpit, preparing to give the toughest speech of his young life. He had not yet turned thirty, had not lost a close relative since his grandfather died when he was ten, and had never delivered a eulogy for a family member before.[16] Summoning all his strength, Bob stood at the rostrum and faced the packed-in crowd. Decades before, he had stood in the same spot on a tiny stool every Sunday, reading the morning scripture as the church's youngest lay minister.[17] How he had feared his father back then, saw him as some great immovable force that changed the temperature of a room when he entered. But he was a man like any other, Bob eventually realized, one with strengths and flaws like the rest of us. When he'd introduced his father at the Mt. Zion ceremony in 1971, he said that understanding led to love.[18] That was what allowed him to swallow his anxiety and take up the impossibly difficult task of seeing Edward Lawrence Goodwin, Sr., for who he really was.

"How does one measure the life of a man like Daddy?" Bob began.

"We knew him at such different extremes. He was notorious on the one hand for his brashness, yet famous on the other for his generosity. When he was bad, he was pretty bad, but when he was good, there was none better.

"He could look at a sagging storefront and visualize a livelihood in hats, dishes, ice cream, or newspapers, God forbid. He could look at a desolate plot of ground and see a garden alive with marigolds and fountains and peacocks; or he could look in a man's eyes and see either loyalty or deceit—and once perceiving what was, move decisively and emphatically to create vitality and productivity out of vacancy and waste. . . . His offspring, not without our idiosyncrasies and shortcomings, bear the mark of his forthrightness, zeal and tenacity. And oh, was he tenacious!"

Bob told a story about a day not long before, during Ed's retirement years out at the farm. He encountered his father one day on his hands and knees, planting flowers by a fountain, even though he could have hired as much help as he wanted to complete such a task. "You're not living till you're in the dirt," he told Bob with a broad smile.

"How do you measure the life of a man like Daddy?" Bob repeated. "We will all remember him as we each knew him best. But I challenge us to measure his worth through the way we live our lives.

"Death is not extinguishing the light," Bob concluded. "It is putting out the lamp, because the dawn has come."[19]

The services were modest and brief. As the attendees marched out of the church behind the coffin, anyone thumbing through the funeral program would have found a short unattributed poem opposite the schedule of events. It was the same piece Ed had chosen for his high school yearbook. The only thing that had changed was the place he laid himself to rest.

I know not where my life shall lead me,
When death shall claim me as His own.
But this I know—He shall not find me
Unprepared without a Home.[20]

The September 14, 1978, edition of the *Oklahoma Eagle* featured a reverent obituary of Ed Goodwin, Sr., and a tranquil photo of him on his catfish farm.[21] Tucked inside the paper, though, was a short article showing that in the wake of Ed's death, things in Deep Greenwood were anything but peaceful: "Many of the structures in the 100 block are presently unoccupied and owned by the Tulsa Urban Renewal Authority. TURA has been getting increasing pressure to demolish the buildings or tighten security to prevent health and fire hazards in the area."[22]

In the summer of 1979, less than a year after Ed died, the city began moving forward with its plans to clear out the last vestiges of Deep Greenwood. A study sponsored by the Tulsa Urban Renewal Authority found that Tulsa builders had no interest in residential development north of downtown. The entire premise of razing huge portions of Greenwood to build back something even greater had apparently been forgotten. "Why should they want to look at a new area, which involves some risk," a TURA staffer mused to the *Eagle*, "when they have (southeast) areas where they know there is a market?"[23]

That market was being defined along purely racial lines. There was plenty of interest in redeveloping Greenwood among black people. At a city commission meeting in May, Greenwood residents lobbied for the next round of urban renewal to focus on rehabilitating the neighborhood's remaining houses, rather than relocating more people farther north. Residents suspected that they were being moved to foster the "stockpiling of close-in land for larger financial interest," the *Eagle* reported.[24] Homer Johnson, who had left TAAG before it shut down, wanted to build an apartment complex near the Crosstown Expressway and make sure black people were the primary investors.[25] But he didn't have the private money or city backing to see the project through to fruition. If money, mission, and motivation could not align to get a project off the ground, the city might just bulldoze all that was left of Greenwood and wait until a more lucrative use for the land arrived.

But at least one idea was gaining traction with both city officials and neighborhood residents, an initiative that might transform the intersection of Greenwood Avenue and Archer Street back into one of the liveliest blocks in the entire city: the Greenwood Market.

The market was a last-ditch effort to salvage the neighborhood's oldest structures before they were reduced to rubble. Through a process called adaptive use, the old Williams Building and its neighbors on Greenwood would be renovated for the modern age, while still keeping their historic street-facing facades.[26] Shop owners and restaurateurs would be recruited to open businesses on the first floor of the old buildings, while lawyers, doctors, and other professionals would be on the top floors, just like in the old days.[27] The project included 48,000 square feet of retail and office space in the recovered buildings, as well as another 24,000 square feet south of Archer to support a new "historically oriented" theater. The *Eagle* would also relocate to the south side of Archer, with its old space being torn down to make way for a community plaza.[28]

Fittingly, the plan to save Deep Greenwood was being spearheaded by the Greenwood Chamber of Commerce. Ed Sr. had been one of the organization's co-founders in 1938, when those blocks were at their most lively. Now, forty years later, the chamber argued that the multimillion-dollar project would spark a "renaissance" in Deep Greenwood "while preserving her built heritage."[29]

The proposal was a long shot. The city of Tulsa was in the midst of a demolition frenzy, and not just in black neighborhoods. West Tulsa, where Latinos and poor whites lived, was also hit hard by urban renewal, while some of the city's most iconic downtown buildings, including the derelict Hotel Tulsa, had been torn down recently with little fanfare.[30] Under the leadership of a new mayor, more and more investment was migrating to the area southeast of downtown. "Lack of local commitment and the shift of local redevelopment priorities may kill the project before it gets off the proverbial ground," the *Eagle* warned.[31]

But it was a legal maneuver by Ed Sr. and his son Jim that ultimately helped keep the dream of the Greenwood Market alive.

As bulldozers were sweeping through Greenwood in the late 1960s and early '70s, the Urban Renewal Authority had eyed the shotgun houses Ed long owned on Hartford Avenue. Ed agreed to sell, but he had a condition: he demanded an option to buy the western side of the one hundred block of Deep Greenwood, the block surrounding the *Eagle* office, and redevelop it himself. The arrangement was actually Jim's idea, an example of their teamwork as a father-and-son law firm.[32] Jim held on to the option for years, waiting for the political winds to blow in Greenwood's favor whenever more federal funds were available for urban renewal projects. By the end of the 1970s, the time was ripe. In a letter dated October 9, 1979, just over a year after Ed's death, Jim transferred the option to purchase the property to the Greenwood Chamber of Commerce. His professional stationery still included Ed's name in the footer right next to his own, with "1903–1978" appended below it.[33]

After the transfer, Jim became one of Greenwood Market's key backers. He pledged to pour $44,000 into a $300,000 equity fundraising campaign to get the project off the ground.[34] But progress on the market was difficult. The chamber was slow to raise the necessary funds to buy the land. As the group kept asking the city for deadline extensions, it faced growing skepticism that it could manage the project at all.[35] In the fall of 1981, a financing deal seemed close at hand when a local investment firm, First State Financial, offered to take on about a one-third ownership of the market.[36] But at the last minute, First State demanded a larger stake in the project, a gambit that was quickly supported by city officials. In order to proceed, the chamber would have to replace its president and transfer the land it had finally acquired back to the city, essentially ceding formal control over the direction of the project.[37] But Greenwood Market was conceived as an initiative to help rebuild black wealth in Tulsa first and foremost. In the hands of white developers, it would just become another extension of downtown. The chamber refused to comply, and the deal fell apart.[38]

Despite such a massive setback, Jim remained undeterred. He knew that there was no way for Greenwood, fractured now by both geography and internal politics, to salvage the project alone. He would have to bring city officials back to the bargaining table. At a city commission meeting in March 1982, he once again reminded officials why they had all embarked on the initiative in the first place. "Greenwood is not just a street crumbling, not a vestige of another proud era gone by," he said. "It symbolizes the pioneering spirit of men who dared, in spite of limited resources, and even worse, a limited market."

Jim was forty-two years old, but he could recall with great detail what that limited market had provided: a community that melded young and old, rich and poor, literate and illiterate, preacher and sinner. Unity had been easier then—required to some extent. Now he had to contend with white people who wanted to box him and the

Greenwood Chamber out of their own neighborhood project and black people who thought they were lackeys of the white power structure. Still, he and dozens of others doggedly pursued their vision— "nurtured this project, slept with it and fought over it," he told the commission.

"The spirit of Greenwood is one of unity and unity is needed now more than ever," he said. "Greenwood is still with us, patiently awaiting a reprieve. She has captivated our imagination and we seek to preserve her sense of community in flesh and stone."[39]

Regina Goodwin had walked past those decrepit old buildings on Greenwood a thousand times since she was a little girl, watched them slowly hollow out as businesses left or were demolished, one by one. But June 19, 1982, was different. On that day, Greenwood finally came alive.

In every direction she turned as she walked through Deep Greenwood, people were celebrating. It was Juneteenth, the day when many black Americans commemorated their freedom from slavery. The holiday began on June 19, 1865, when enslaved people in Galveston, Texas, were informed of their liberation by a Union general. The news came two months after the Confederate Army surrendered in Appomattox, Virginia, and two and a half years after President Abraham Lincoln signed the Emancipation Proclamation. Freedom came late then—and for generations afterward.[40]

Black Tulsans had celebrated Juneteenth at least as far back as 1913, when a man leaped from a hot-air balloon and parachuted down to the crowd in Midway Park as part of the festivities.[41] In Greenwood's heyday, a 1942 celebration saw residents crowd into Lincoln Park on the northern edge of the neighborhood for a festival that included a parade and an Emancipation Dance.[42] As the neighborhood declined, the holiday had become more muted. But a community arts activist named Maybelle Wallace was determined to revive it. Through her arts program Theatre North, she began nurturing a Juneteenth celebration in the late 1970s and decided to move it to largely abandoned Deep Greenwood in 1982—"Where there's some life, there's hope," she told the *Eagle*.[43] Her persistence paid off, and the celebration quickly grew. Now Regina was striding through a sea of thirty thousand excited faces, more than she'd ever seen in the neighborhood.[44]

She saw children devouring fried funnel cakes. Grandmothers lounging in lawn chairs. All of it before a backdrop of burned-out buildings. But even the structures themselves were transformed; teenagers sat in the empty windowsills craning to see the stage at the corner of Greenwood and Archer, where a litany of jazz and soul artists played into the night. Every square inch of that street was being put to good use.

"It moved, it swayed, it rocked," Regina and her sister Sabrina wrote in an article for the *Eagle*. "Greenwood warmly embraced its people and graciously roared, 'Welcome Home.' "[45]

It was an especially needed homecoming for Regina. She had just finished her sophomore year at the University of Kansas, where she was studying art. Her older siblings all attended HBCUs—Howard for Eric, Tennessee State for Greg and Sabrina—but Regina decided that KU offered the best opportunity to follow her creative passions, as well as a modest scholarship. Though she had attended a racially mixed high school—Booker T. was a magnet school by the time she enrolled—it was difficult to transition from the "Negro Wall Street," as the *Eagle* was now regularly calling her neighborhood, to a school where just three percent of the students were black.[46] She couldn't help comparing her school to Tennessee State, where she spent plenty of weekends hanging out with her sister. "The pride that they had in their school, the joy that they had walking on their campus, [compared to] me being all depressed at KU looking for a black face," she recalled. "Literally hoping and praying I would see another black face that day as I'm going to my classes. That was the difference."[47]

Walking the streets of Greenwood, it felt good to be back in an environment where finding common cultural ground wasn't a constant battle. Of course, the minute she stepped south of the railroad tracks, Tulsa and most of the rest of Oklahoma would offer the same type of conservative resistance she encountered in Kansas. But Greenwood was a protective haven, and for the first time in a long while, its main thoroughfare appeared joyous and lively.

"Even the heavy traffic with its unending stream of old and bright lights was exhilarating," she and Sabrina reported. "Perhaps the approval of the Greenwood Market will provide for more permanent revitalization."[48]

The day before Juneteenth, the Greenwood Chamber, the Tulsa Urban Renewal Authority, and the city commission had announced an agreement to move forward with the Greenwood Market. It was a complex financial arrangement with seven stakeholders, but it provided the project with solid financial footing and created a pathway for the Greenwood Chamber to become the largest stakeholder in the future, as well as the landowner of record.[49] Jim and everyone else who had fought for the market for years couldn't have asked for a better outcome at a better time. As Jim walked among the thirty thousand people participating in the Greenwood Jubilee, young and old, black and white, he felt nostalgia for the streets he had roamed as a child and excitement for what the future might hold. "Could history be repeating itself?" he allowed himself to wonder in an exultant column titled "The Heart of Greenwood."[50] For once in the neighborhood, that often-ominous question was a hopeful one.

Over an entire weekend, people laughed, danced, and devoured an endless buffet of delicious food, from barbecue to hot links to sweet potato pies.[51] They saw neighbors they never tired of talking to, friends they'd been meaning to catch up with, and acquaintances they'd always wanted the chance to get to know a little better. After so many years being torn apart by forces outside the community, they were reconnecting it for themselves.

Even Don Ross could find nothing to poke fun at in the festivities. "That lonely corner has stood abandoned, but hopeful," he wrote in the *Eagle*'s leading coverage of the event. "Black Wall Street . . . stood as a monument of faith—structures that refuse to fall, to deteriorate, or to become confiscated by those who have no appreciation of why they stood there so firmly."

Roaming the crowded thoroughfare, Ross encountered Curtis Lawson, Greenwood's first black representative in the state legislature. Lawson was as awed as anyone else at Greenwood's resurgence, but he felt there was one thing missing from the festivities. "If only some of the old people who made this street happen could be here," he told Ross. "As I wandered through the streets I couldn't help but feel the presence of some of the old pioneers. In my mind Ed Good-

Greenwood Avenue is thronged with people during a Juneteenth celebration in the 1980s

win, Sr., was there. He and Amos Hall were witnessing the gaiety together."[52]

Across generations, Greenwood still stood resilient, defying the doubters that said it would be reduced to rubble and replaced with a parking lot. The remaining buildings were just a small shell of what the neighborhood had once been, but they prevented a proud community with a nationally resonant legacy from being completely torn from the landscape, root to stem.

After Regina spent a few hours catching up with old friends and enjoying a band of African conga drummers, she ducked into the *Eagle* office to write her story. The newspaper would soon be moving offices once again to make way for the market remodeling. No matter, though. She was hopeful that the family business would continue to tell the neighborhood's stories for a long time to come.

"Greenwood, the keeper of a rich history and a notorious past, was never dead," she and her sister wrote. "It had just long been sleeping."[53]

PART III

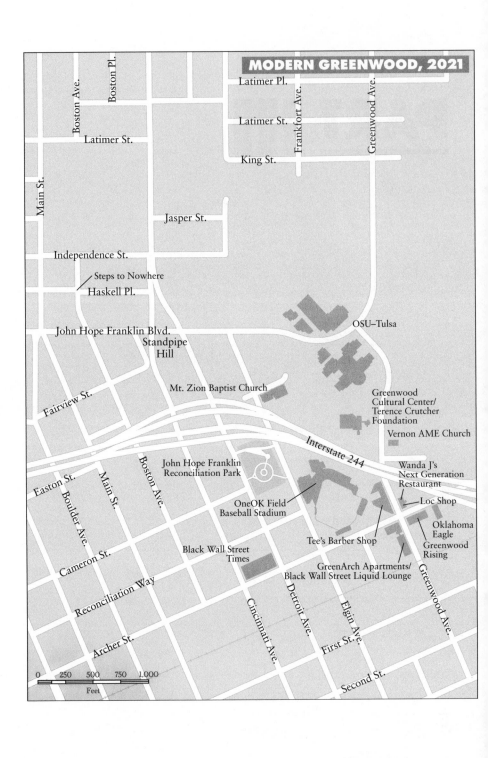

MODERN GREENWOOD, 2021

Latimer Pl.

Boston Pl.

Boston Ave.

Frankfort Ave.

Greenwood Ave.

Latimer St.

King St.

Latimer St.

Main St.

Jasper St.

Independence St.

Steps to Nowhere

Haskell Pl.

John Hope Franklin Blvd.

Standpipe Hill

OSU–Tulsa

Fairview St.

Mt. Zion Baptist Church

Greenwood Cultural Center/ Terence Crutcher Foundation

Vernon AME Church

Interstate 244

Easton St.

Boulder Ave.

Main St.

Boston Ave.

John Hope Franklin Reconciliation Park

Wanda J's Next Generation Restaurant

Loc Shop

OneOK Field Baseball Stadium

Tee's Barber Shop

Oklahoma Eagle

Greenwood Rising

Cameron St.

Black Wall Street Times

GreenArch Apartments/ Black Wall Street Liquid Lounge

Greenwood Ave.

Reconciliation Way

Detroit Ave.

Cincinnati Ave.

Elgin Ave.

Archer St.

First St.

0   250   500   750   1,000

Feet

Second St.

CHAPTER 21

RECONCILIATION DAY

Graffiti on the Crosstown Expressway overpass that cuts through Greenwood

"Don't you realize that Greenwood was Wakanda before Wakanda?"[1]

On a sweltering spring evening at the corner of Greenwood Avenue and Archer Street, local poet Phetote Mshairi performed for a crowd of about three dozen onlookers. His large black T-shirt was emblazoned with a solemn picture of Barack Obama, the monochrome illustration matching the wispy white tendrils in his dark beard. His poem, "I Am the Line," was an allusion to the nearby Frisco Railroad tracks, which by then abutted a new luxury high-rise apartment, a sports bar, and a cycling studio. It was May 31, 2018, ninety-seven years after the night that a white mob crossed the tracks and left this block and the dozens surrounding it in ruins.[2]

The multiracial crowd huddled around Mshairi on the northwest corner of the Greenwood-Archer intersection, outside the building where Loula Williams's confectionery once stood. Many of them wore purple T-shirts with the words JOHN HOPE FRANKLIN CENTER FOR RECONCILIATION printed on the front.[3] The center, named after the famed historian and Booker T. graduate John Hope Franklin, was holding its annual symposium on the anniversary of the massacre to "[create] new knowledge in areas of reconciliation to advance equality, racial justice, and social harmony."[4] Later in the evening, there would be a ceremony at John Hope Franklin Reconciliation Park, just a block north of a street that was set to be renamed Reconciliation Way.[5] May 31 had been rechristened Reconciliation Day, according to a proclamation by Mayor G. T. Bynum, though he was not present to issue the proclamation himself.[6]

Mshairi clutched a microphone next to a portable PA as the small crowd ringed around him and drank up his every word. "I am the soundwave that carried the sound of freedom ringing throughout Greenwood before it was quieted by riots, Molotov cocktails and gunshots," he said. "I'm the fading line of history that the beneficiaries of atrocities wish that we all forgot."[7]

It was just after six p.m.[8] Around that time ninety-seven years before, Mabel Little was on her way to Mt. Zion Baptist Church for Bible study, W. D. Williams was decorating for the Booker T. prom, and Ed Goodwin, Sr., was rehearsing his lines in the school play. Greenwood was blissfully tranquil. But it had been unsettled, in one way or another, every night since—especially every May 31, when the memories of what happened there were most haunting. Few people at the intersection seemed to recognize that they were standing at the site of an atrocity, though. Hundreds of Tulsans were streaming by the vigil and toward the art deco sports stadium located just west on Archer Street. The Tulsa Drillers were playing the San Antonio Missions in Double-A baseball.[9]

Greenwood changed in the thirty-five years after Jim Goodwin and the Greenwood Chamber of Commerce successfully preserved the buildings in the heart of the old business district. The two structures were occupied by black small business owners starting in 1985, when Charlie Wilson, Greenwood native and front man for the Gap Band, cut the ribbon for the new renovation project.[10] Wanda J's Next Generation Restaurant, Blow Out Hair Studio, and Tee's Barber Shop were all building tenants at various times.[11] Vernon AME and Mt. Zion re-

Plaques commemorating businesses destroyed
during the massacre abut gentrifying real estate
projects

mained in the neighborhood as well, near the roar of the Crosstown Expressway. And while the *Oklahoma Eagle* had spent a few wayward years bouncing between interim locations after the Greenwood Market renovations, the newspaper was soon back on the same block where it had originally stood, relocated to an abandoned auto garage just southeast of the Greenwood-Archer intersection.[12] Beyond those landmarks, though, most every other vestige of the old Greenwood was gone.

In 1986 the Tulsa Urban Renewal Authority gifted two hundred acres of land in and around Greenwood to the state university system toward the erection of a new college in the district. The ambitious new school would be a combined satellite campus for the University of Oklahoma, Oklahoma State University, Northeastern State University, and Langston University.[13] When Greenwood residents were originally forced out of the area in the 1970s, the Urban Renewal Authority said it planned to put high-rise apartments, parks, and a

new commercial district in the area. But those projects were abandoned due to declining federal funding and a lack of interest from
white real estate developers. Instead, the University Center at Tulsa
(UCAT), as the new mega-college was called, brought a fresh set of
promises: facilities for twenty thousand students and a greater footprint
for Langston University, Oklahoma's only historically black college.[14]

Once again neighborhood leaders tried to negotiate their way to
some benefit in a plan that was largely out of their control. "Citizens
should be given the opportunity to have some input in the process,"
repeated Homer Johnson, the disillusioned former TAAG director, at
a planning meeting for the college.[15] But UCAT soon became another
disappointment. Early plans for a hilltop mall that promised an economic boost to Greenwood were scrapped, and enrollment at the new
campus never reached far beyond three thousand students.[16] In 1999
the original college consortium was dissolved, and Oklahoma State
was given legal authority over the sprawling acreage, which had once
been occupied by streets full of houses.[17] Langston retained control of
just nineteen acres, and much of the land remained undeveloped.[18] A
set of eerie stone stairs leading to a long-ago demolished home on the
UCAT site became emblematic of urban renewal's failed promises—
people called them the Steps to Nowhere.[19]

The baseball stadium was more successful at injecting spending
dollars into Greenwood, but it was no less controversial. In January
2008 the Tulsa Development Authority agreed to sell the empty land
just west of the Deep Greenwood storefronts to the Greenwood
Chamber of Commerce to develop into a retail and residential complex named after B. C. Franklin. It seemed a fitting complement to the
John Hope Franklin park being constructed just a block away.[20] But
a few months later, Tulsa mayor Kathy Taylor abruptly announced
that the Greenwood site would instead be the home of the new Drillers stadium, after the baseball team threatened to relocate to a nearby
suburb.[21] The stadium, along with new shops and restaurants, would
be part of a coordinated local effort to "connect" Greenwood to the
industrial-chic projects that were opening in long-abandoned buildings downtown. Much of the redevelopment was being bankrolled by
nonprofit organizations.[22] The Tulsa Community Foundation, a
mega-philanthropy spearheaded by local oil billionaire George Kaiser, purchased a $25 million bond to fund construction of the sta-

dium.[23] At the same time, Kaiser's other large nonprofit, the George Kaiser Family Foundation, bought several surrounding Greenwood parcels and transferred them to a trust managing the stadium project.[24] The Kaiser Family Foundation's public mission revolved around initiatives benefiting children and families in need, and it would later make large investments in expanding black entrepreneurship in the city through programs like Build in Tulsa. But the nonprofit also counted "government sponsored life enhancement projects" as a key pillar of its activities[25]—real estate and recruitment ventures geared at boosting Tulsa's marketability to suburbanites and young, affluent transplants. Just as a college campus serving mostly white students had taken over Greenwood's former residential area, a baseball stadium for mostly white fans was set to dominate the old commercial corridor.

It all seemed a little too familiar to the Goodwins. The family newspaper was still being co-published by Jim and Ed Jr., after Bob gave up the mantle in the 1980s.[26] The two brothers bickered constantly, but they always agreed on Greenwood's right to control its own destiny. Under the mayor's plan, the *Eagle* would see its property assessment tax rise from $51 per year to more than $1,600.[27] The property might be rising in value, but the family had no intention of selling, so what was the benefit? While the stadium was the centerpiece of an aggressive effort by city officials and real estate developers to "revitalize" downtown Tulsa, there was no guarantee that Greenwood's historic black residents would benefit in any way.

"If plans are not in place for small business development, which promotes the celebration of diversity and the historical significance of the Greenwood Business district," Jim wrote in a front-page editorial, "we regard the baseball stadium as a ploy to steal home base; a trick, which failed in 1921." Next to his words were two photos: one of the Greenwood that his grandparents J.H. and Carlie had known that peaceful evening before the massacre, and another of the burned-out war zone they'd been forced to rebuild.[28]

The plan went forward anyway. The mayor quickly got most community leaders to fall in line: Greenwood's city councilor, Jack Henderson, said the ballpark was a "home run for everyone." Reuben Gant, the president of the Greenwood Chamber of Commerce, agreed to move the proposed B. C. Franklin complex across the street.[29] While some black Tulsans grumbled that Greenwood's identity was being sacrificed, Gant later defended the stadium's construction, arguing that trying to cordon off the area specifically for black people wouldn't work in modern society. "What was most important to the survival of the district? Its pedestrians," he said. "I don't see how the ballpark is bad at all. . . . We have to change with the times."[30]

Jim, too, ultimately endorsed the plan. Though he had reservations, he was persuaded by the urging of Julius Pegues, an intimate family friend and prominent North Tulsa leader who believed the stadium would help bring more exposure to the new John Hope Franklin park nearby. ("My debt to him was greater than my debt to my community," Jim admitted later.)[31] The week after the *Eagle* aired skepticism about the stadium, it shifted its stance dramatically. "Notwithstanding the broken promises of the past, the *Oklahoma Eagle* has decided to endorse the ballpark," read a staff editorial.[32]

The younger generation was less charitable toward the city's motives. Regina Goodwin, Jim's niece, protested at a city hall meeting against the ballpark's construction.[33] And his youngest son Joey wrote a bitter rebuke of the stadium right below his father's endorsement. "The baseball park, for all its good, whatever that might mean, signals in my belief the end of an era," Joey wrote. "At least someone was thoughtful enough to put a freeway close enough so I know my way out of town."[34]

Ten years later, as the massacre vigil was swarmed by oblivious Drillers fans, it was clear that Joey was right; Greenwood would never be the same. A luxury apartment complex at the Greenwood-Archer intersection called GreenArch, funded by another large local nonprofit, the Hille Foundation, ultimately replaced the Chamber of Commerce's vision for a B. C. Franklin Square.[35] Nearly every inch of land running along Archer Street had already been transformed into carefully partitioned dirt lots, fenced off and tagged with blue signs by the Ross Group, one of Tulsa's most prominent real estate developers.[36] The five-story frame of a Holiday Inn Express was rising at the corner of Detroit Avenue, and a nearby lot for The View, a soon-to-be-built luxury apartment complex, was staked out with a NOW LEASING sign. Next to the baseball stadium, an empty lot would soon be transformed into a six-story, hundred-thousand-square-foot headquarters for the Oklahoma corporation Vast Bank, complete with a high-rise sushi restaurant with striking views of the Tulsa skyline.[37] By the time Tulsa's grand revitalization was finished, there would be no way to tell where downtown Tulsa ended and Greenwood began. The only vestige of the old neighborhood beneath the glittering new structures would be small, weathered black plaques embedded in the sidewalks, which noted the locations of businesses that were burned down during the massacre.[38] GRACE JOHNSON'S RESTAURANT, read one plaque in front of the Drillers stadium. DESTROYED 1921. NOT REOPENED.

A trumpeter marches through a portion of Greenwood that was turned into a campus for Oklahoma State University–Tulsa

After Mshairi completed his poem, the small group commemorating the massacre marched north up Greenwood Avenue, retracing the route Loula Williams, Mary Jones Parrish, and so many others used to flee the white mob in 1921. No longer lined with homes and businesses, Greenwood Avenue was flanked by the brown brick buildings of Oklahoma State University, endless slabs of parking lot asphalt, and large tracts of fallow land that had not even been put to the most basic of uses. The only symbol of the old Greenwood on the campus was a beige-colored marble memorial at the site of the original Booker T. Washington High School campus, which had served as a field hospital during the massacre. As the small group walked by the marker, children in strollers among them, a forlorn trumpeter wailed into the night air.[39] In the distance, the national anthem bleated from the baseball stadium.

The group soon reached John Hope Franklin Reconciliation Park. The space featured three large bronze sculptures of famous images of the massacre: a black man with his hands in the air labeled HUMILIA-TION, a young member of the white mob with a rifle slung over his shoulder labeled HOSTILITY, and a white doctor holding a newborn black baby labeled HOPE. At the opposite end of the park, a twenty-six-foot-tall bronze sculpture sprang up out of a fountain, chronicling the history of Oklahoma since the days indigenous and black people first walked the Trail of Tears.[40] The site could be a place for somber reflection, perhaps, if not for the constant droning of the Crosstown Expressway right next to it.

On that evening, the park was being honored as a U.S. Literary Landmark, and Greenwood's elected officials were on hand to commemorate the occasion.[41] With the mayor absent, city councilor Vanessa Hall-Harper presented his Reconciliation Day proclamation in his stead. Several times, she corrected the word *riot*, in the written text she'd been given to read, to *massacre*.[42] The distinction was key to the community—the *Black Wall Street Times*, a new black-owned digital media outlet in Tulsa, had recently published a column critiquing the use of the word *riot* for the ruthless attack as "social conditioning at its finest."[43]

When Hall-Harper was finished, Regina Goodwin stepped up to the podium. The ponytail she'd had when helping her grandfather shoot snakes at Willow Lake Farm had given way to a gray coif. She clutched a formal proclamation from the Oklahoma House of Representatives celebrating John Hope Franklin.[44] Regina was in her third year representing the 73rd District, which included all of Greenwood and much of North Tulsa.[45]

"It's just a blessing to have known Dr. Franklin. He was such a fighter," she said to the crowd. "I remember him telling me on many occasions, 'You keep fighting.' We can do no less."

Evening crept closer to twilight, and the statues in the park cast elongating shadows across the ground. Another local artist, Dawn Tree, was painting an abstract depiction of the Greenwood District live on the pavement next to the podium, the blazing yellow spray paint evoking streets once lined with proverbial gold. Regina glanced down at the proclamation she was about to read, full of dependent clauses that began with *whereas* and other stuffy signifiers of ceremony. But first she had something real to say. She recited a favorite quote of hers from John Hope Franklin, as the hour drew near when the first gunshot had rung out at the Tulsa County Courthouse nearly a century before.

"I think knowing one's history leads one to act in a more enlightened fashion. I cannot imagine how knowing one's history would not urge one to be an activist."[46]

About forty years separated Regina's early runs for office, as a preteen at Carver Middle School, and her election to the Oklahoma House of Representatives. "It's Time for a Change That Only a Lady Can Arrange" was her first campaign slogan as an eleven-year-old.[47] Even as a sixth grader who enjoyed performing in school plays and squaring off against her older brother Greg in games of pick-up basketball, she understood that representing others was a serious responsibility.[48] Later, when she served as a legislative page in high school, she saw even more clearly how politics shaped the entire world around her.[49]

But becoming a politician was not Regina's dream in life, not by a

Regina Goodwin, left, works as a page for state legislator Bernard McIntyre, alongside her cousins David Goodwin and Lisa Fields.

long shot. She wanted to be an artist. After college, she moved to Chicago in the 1980s to pursue a graduate film degree specializing in animation, then began picking up freelance work on all sorts of television projects—Froot Loops commercials, Tiny Toon Adventures shorts, graphics for *The Oprah Winfrey Show*. When she wasn't drawing, she was listening to live bands at downtown jazz clubs and attending Anita Baker concerts.[50] Her small studio apartment in Hyde Park, a historic neighborhood that thrummed with the creative energy of black folks, felt a universe apart from the slow-moving world of Oklahoma. Chicago became a playground for her personal passions and ambitions. Politics hovered only in the background of her life.[51]

In 1996 she applied for a job opening at Walt Disney Animation Studios and passed a grueling animation test that involved drawing figures from *Pocahontas,* one of the studios' latest hit films. She envisioned moving to Los Angeles and working on their next iconic movie. That summer Regina packed up her life in Chicago and decided to move home to Tulsa, briefly, while the job details were finalized. She didn't even look for an apartment, instead occupying her old room in her mother's house in Brady Heights. But the job fell through. A hiring freeze, they said. When she applied for another opportunity at Hallmark, she was given the same excuse. It was a bitter disappointment for the girl who had spent her childhood scribbling cartoons.[52]

For all of the Goodwins remaining in Tulsa, the center of gravity had shifted dramatically in the years since Regina left home. Jeanne sold off Willow Lake Farm in 1982, four years after her husband's death, because the property was too sprawling for her to manage alone.[53] A suburban snarl of gas stations and strip malls soon littered the acres that had been a wonderland for two generations of children. "They'll say Negroes used to live here," Ed Sr. had predicted one day on the farm before he died. "Sure enough, that's what happened," his daughter Jo Ann reflected decades later.[54]

The *Eagle,* meanwhile, struggled as black media everywhere tried to adapt to an increasingly integrated society.[55] The company sold off its printing press—long a source of pride—in the 1980s as its profits dwindled.[56] Weekly issues shrank in length, while regional editions for nearby cities and a regular Sunday edition were scrapped entirely.[57] Jim used the earnings from his law practice to fund the struggling enterprise, but the *Eagle* was forced to file for bankruptcy twice in the late 1990s and early 2000s.[58] Still it remained in Deep Greenwood, with Jim constantly driven by words his father had told him long ago: "Always keep this newspaper. It will be a source of influence."[59]

The Goodwins were not a family to stew in resentments, and so Regina found she couldn't either as she readjusted to life in her hometown. She spent long hours with her grandmother at Jeanne's new apartment in South Tulsa, where the Goodwin matriarch continued to play countless games of Scrabble and became the last-surviving founder of the First Wednesday Reading Club, a long-standing integrated book club that she had helped launch at the peak of the civil rights movement.[60] If she could find purpose and meaning in a lifetime spent in a single place, Jeanne reasoned, so could her granddaughter. "Cast down your bucket where you are" was her constant refrain, echoing Booker T. Washington's famous command that black people should change the South rather than flee it.[61]

It was all Regina could do not to roll her eyes, at first. "All that would burn me up when she would say that," she recalled, "because I did not want to cast down my bucket in Tulsa, Oklahoma." Tulsa was small and lacked the robust arts scene of Chicago or Los Angeles. In fact, the city was offering fewer and fewer opportunities for black people, as Greenwood and the rest of North Tulsa were steadily hollowed out. While urban renewal had transformed Greenwood to suit white interests, private businesses quietly abandoned the rest of North Tulsa along with white residents. Another grocery store or shopping center seemed to close every few years;[62] once-lively entertainment venues like the Big Ten Ballroom loomed as large empty husks on the landscape.[63] White flight, along with the departure of some of the black middle class, explained much of the economic malaise; the population of North Tulsa decreased by almost 60 percent between the 1960s, when Regina was born, and the year 2000, even as the overall population of Tulsa grew by 50 percent during that period.

In 1996, at thirty-three, Regina didn't feel like Tulsa was the place for her. Many of her classmates and relatives had left and never really looked back.[64] But she made the best of things. She began designing and selling greeting cards under the brand Power Cards, while she worked as a sales clerk at a local light fixture store.[65] She tried and failed to thwart Jeanne, the "Barracuda," in Scrabble. And she began to re-engage with her community. Many of its issues hadn't changed much since she was a little girl handing out copies of the *Oklahoma Eagle* on Greenwood Avenue alongside her sister.[66]

Activism came naturally to Regina. In college, she'd led a protest at the University of Kansas to get Martin Luther King, Jr.'s birthday recognized as a federal holiday, a change that finally happened in 1983.[67] In the early 2000s, when the local school board was planning to change the admission standards at Booker T. to reduce the number of seats guaranteed to neighborhood students, she helped organize meetings at the Greenwood Cultural Center to voice the community's displeasure.[68] Later, partnering with other leaders, she successfully lobbied school officials to restore a black history course to the Tulsa high school curriculum as an elective, after it had quietly been removed. She worked to defend Greenwood's parks, its schools, and its residents' civil rights.[69]

The decision to make the leap from activist to elected official came spontaneously one day in 2015, from her family living room in Brady Heights. The local news had another segment on a problem in North Tulsa, and Regina found herself suddenly fed up. *I can just sit here and talk back to the TV out of frustration,* she thought to herself, *or I can go down to Oklahoma City, file for office, and do something about it.* Before she knew it, she was on the Turner Turnpike, slicing through the Oklahoma prairies on a spring afternoon. Regina filed to

Regina Goodwin announces her candidacy for the Oklahoma state senate

run for the state senate on the last possible day, nearly at the last possible hour.[70] But by the time of her campaign kickoff event, she had
found her voice. "Some women get lost in the fire and some . . . are
built from the fire," she said before an audience of family and longtime neighbors in Deep Greenwood. "I am that woman."[71]

Regina campaigned at the schools, churches, and community centers that had surrounded her family for generations, crafting messag-
ing centered on collective action to achieve long-sought community
goals, such as economic development and criminal justice reform.[72]
Goodwin lore also came up early and often.[73] Though Ed Sr. might
have expected one of his sons to run for office, the Goodwin women
actually entered the political arena. Regina's aunt Jo Ann had served
on the Tulsa School Board in the 1970s, and her aunt Edwyna was
elected to a community college school board in Flint, Michigan,
around the same time—both firsts for black women.[74] Carlie Goodwin, her great-grandmother, had served as Booker T. Washington's
first PTA president a century before. Regina was following in their
legacy as much as the one Ed Sr. had crafted for his boys at the *Eagle*.
"Her grandparents would be particularly proud," her uncle Jim said
at a campaign fundraiser in March 2015. "She comes from a family
who is imbued with a sense of community and the necessity for trying
to make life better in this community."[75]

In the end, though, she lost by about three hundred votes to Kevin
Matthews, a former fireman and North Tulsa native who served as
the state representative for Greenwood and was also looking to make
a leap to the state senate.[76] It was the Disney disappointment all over
again. But Regina wasn't deterred. Matthews's move to the senate
opened up his house seat in the 73rd District, and a second special
election was held in the summer. After a few more weeks of stumping,
Regina earned 35 percent of the vote in a crowded seven-way race.[77]

She became one of just a handful of black people among Oklahoma's 149 legislators, and the only black woman in its House of Representatives. Greenwood was one of the only reliably black districts in
the entire state, and Regina had ties to nearly everyone who had preceded her in her role. Before Kevin Matthews, the seat had been occupied in various eras by Bernard McIntyre, who Regina paged for as
a teen; Don Ross, the former *Eagle* columnist and editor; and Ben Hill,
the Vernon AME pastor and *Eagle* editorialist.[78] Regina had known all

of them personally, either through their work with the family paper or through their close relationships with her older relatives. She had a familial legacy to uphold, but also a community one.

As she prepped for her new role, though, she was forced to grapple with tragedy during a brutal end of the year. Her mother Alquita, a bedrock of the family, became sick just after Thanksgiving with an illness doctors couldn't diagnose.[79] Regina was forced to draft much of her legislation at her mother's hospital bedside on her phone or in hand-scrawled notes. (GOP lawmakers refused to grant her a filing extension.) After Alquita passed in December 2015, Regina penned her obituary in the *Eagle*—"people were drawn to her joyful love and wisdom," she wrote.[80] Regina's father, Ed Jr., had passed just the year before.[81] Regina missed him dearly, but she was proud that he had overcome his struggles with alcoholism and stopped drinking for the final fifteen years of his life.[82] She carried with her both her parents' ability to connect with people in the community from all walks of life, no matter their class or station.

On her first day at the capitol in February 2016, Regina came equipped with eight bills to introduce: she wanted to raise the state minimum wage, stop the practice of sending people to jail for failure to pay fines, and increase teacher salaries, among other initiatives.[83] But the Oklahoma legislature was getting redder every year, as rural districts increasingly defaulted to Republican candidates. The Democrats had lost their majority in the House in 2005, then shed another fifteen seats in the ensuing decade. The chances of her eight bills passing in a sea of 2,500 were remote.[84]

Life at the capitol in the minority party, Regina soon discovered, was a daily struggle. In a given year, Democrats might author and successfully pass fewer than forty bills, compared to more than 350 Republican bills that became law.[85] Committee chairs had total discretion to decide which bills would be heard, and all of them were Republican.[86] Regina didn't understand all these dynamics at first, but she learned quickly. "People say when you first come to the capitol, it's like drinking out of a firehose," she said. "Comes on full blast."[87]

She knew that being the lone black woman on the House floor also made her job harder. Many Republican legislators were opposed to her agenda ideologically, but they were also regularly rude and dismissive to her personally. When she grilled Republican lawmakers on the House floor, anonymous legislators would sometimes yell "Debate!" in the middle of her questioning, an interruption meant to mock Regina for making a statement instead of asking a question.[88] The interruptions became so frequent that one day Regina turned to the sea of white faces on the House floor behind her and demanded, "Please be big enough and bold enough and brave enough to stand up and tell me who it was." She was met with silence. A press release sent out by the Democratic Party decried racism and sexism on the House floor, while a hashtag #IStandWithRegina briefly gained traction on Twitter and Facebook.[89] But Regina had no interest in letting that incident define her role in the capitol. "Somehow I'll get pigeonholed into, 'Regina Goodwin is the race baiter,'" she told the Oklahoma journalism outlet *Nondoc* later that day. "'Regina Goodwin tried to play the race card. Regina Goodwin's always talking about race.'"[90]

Despite the challenges, Regina found that her job gave her a new perspective on Greenwood and a new voice within it.

One day in the summer of 2017, not long after the "debate" incident, a woman named D'Marria Monday approached Regina at a neighborhood block party.[91] Monday was a budding community activist and aspiring businesswoman who was working hard on a bachelor's degree in entrepreneurship from Oklahoma State University–Tulsa.[92] Before that, she had served more than seven years in prison on a nonviolent drug charge, incarcerated just months after the birth of her first child. She was trying to find purpose in that pain, and one horrific experience among inmates stuck with her: pregnant women in prison had been chained to their beds during childbirth.

Regina was in near disbelief when Monday told her of the practice. "This happens?" she said. "It's so barbaric."[93] Monday introduced Regina to a woman who had been chained; then the pair began researching and finding others. Regina recorded one mother's account on video. The women's stories were consistent—right ankle, right wrist—and stretched back more than a decade.[94] "Just to know that happens, to hear another woman's pain, and to think about how our ancestors were shackled and chained on the slave ships," Monday said on the radio program *Focus: Black Oklahoma*. "I felt compelled to do something."[95]

With Monday's support, Regina authored House Bill 3393, a measure that would ban the use of restraints on imprisoned women during childbirth, while also allowing them to have a family member, friend, or doula present during birth.[96] Much of the language was modeled on similar laws that had been enacted in more than twenty states.[97] Still, getting it passed felt like an uphill battle. At the time, Oklahoma led the nation in incarceration across multiple grim categories—out of every hundred thousand people in the state, more than one thousand were behind bars, the highest rate in the nation.[98] Oklahoma also led the United States in the rate of incarcerating women.[99] It was a uniquely punitive state in a uniquely punitive country.

But Regina whipped up the support for the bill she needed, shepherding it through committee deliberations and legislative floor votes. She even brought some of the women who had been shackled to the capitol to meet legislators in person.[100] "She was very tenacious in the fight to get it passed," Monday recalled. On May 10, 2018, Oklahoma governor Mary Fallin signed HB 3393 into law; the next day Regina and Monday held a victorious press conference at the *Eagle* office. The measure, Regina said, would provide "dignity for women who, incarcerated or not, are of worth and entitled to humane treatment."[101]

Though many fights took longer than she wanted, Regina had managed to effectively enact laws on behalf of the folks back in Greenwood. The year before the anti-shackling bill was passed, Regina had earned a smaller victory with a bill that expanded workshops for caregivers and made it easier for them to access government vouchers.[102] The year after the anti-shackling bill, she authored a law that clarified the voting eligibility of people convicted of felonies, making it clear they could cast ballots after serving their time.[103] A nationwide analysis of state legislators by the Center for Effective Lawmaking found that Regina was the third-most effective Democrat in the Oklahoma House in 2017 and 2018, meaning she was among the most adept at getting her bills through committees and onto the governor's desk. She even ranked ahead of nearly thirty Republicans, who all had many structural advantages as members of the majority party.[104]

Regina also successfully drafted legislation for a Black Wall Street–themed license plate tag, meant to raise funds for Greenwood's annual Juneteenth celebration.[105] When she got the special tag on her car, she added a custom license plate number as well: PAY BWS. In other words: Pay Black Wall Street.

"On historic Greenwood, my grandfather was one of the youngest entrepreneurs. He had a haberdashery. [Like] all of the entrepreneurs he stood on the shoulders of, we can only do our best when we collaborate."[106]

On June 1, 2018, the day after the Reconciliation Day march, Regina spoke before another modest audience inside one of the few successful projects from the urban renewal era, the Greenwood Cultural Center.[107] The facility was part museum, part event space, anchored by a sunlit atrium. Lining the walls were framed exhibits detailing the rise, destruction, and rebirth of Greenwood in measured and patient prose. (Don Ross championed the creation of the Cultural Center in the legislature and wrote the historical accounts that formed the basis of the exhibit.)[108] A framed display on the western wall recounted the Goodwin story; there were photos of J.H. working at his desk, a young Ed Sr. standing dapper in his Depression-era haberdashery, and the elder statesman version of Ed Sr. grinning in front of the *Eagle* office.[109]

The crowd had gathered to commemorate a new mural being dedicated on the wall of the Crosstown Expressway that bordered the Cultural Center parking lot. There had already been several attempts to beautify this concrete intrusion on Greenwood's peace—a large image of a jazz saxophonist was painted beneath the overpass, between two wide murals that spelled out WELCOME TO GREENWOOD in large white letters. On a concrete wall at the edge of the overpass, the words 1921 TULSA RACE RIOT CENTENNIAL COMMISSION were painted in a playful white font. Someone had crossed out the word RIOT and replaced it with a blood-red MASSACRE.

The new mural spelled out BLACK WALL ST in a thick, graffiti-like font on a black background, with each letter representing a different piece of Greenwood history: the Dreamland, the *Eagle*, and so on.[110] A ribbon-cutting ceremony in front of the mural was accompanied by polite applause, competing with the buzz of cars whizzing by at seventy miles per hour just a few feet above. Dozens of people snapped photos of the colorful project; officials said they hoped it would become a popular Instagram attraction.[111]

One woman at the ceremony quietly wondered when Tulsa would do more. She was from the neighborhood too, had gone to Carver and Booker T. in the decades after Greenwood had been emptied out and the legend of "Black Wall Street" largely lay dormant. She had a measured intensity when she spoke, her thoughts flowing sharp and fully formed.

"That same culture that burned down Black Wall Street is the same culture that killed my brother," Tiffany Crutcher said, as the photo ops unfolded around her. "They shot innocent people with their hands in the air. They left them on the ground to die. Some of the first aid and ambulance workers were threatened saying don't you dare touch them. That same thing happened to my brother. My brother had his hands in the air. He was shot. They left him on the pavement to die. Didn't render first aid. And now, guess what? My family, we're still fighting for justice, and we're still fighting for reparations, just like the survivors. Just like our community. The parallels are stark, and the culture is the same."[112]

Two years earlier Tiffany's twin brother Terence was shot and killed by a Tulsa police officer in the middle of a road while unarmed. Since then, even though she lived in Montgomery, Alabama, Tiffany had become a fixture at community town halls and street protests in Tulsa.[113] Her family had filed a civil wrongful death lawsuit against the city as she pursued a broad range of police reform policies.[114] On the day the mayor decreed Reconciliation Day, she was a co-signer of a letter from the NAACP Legal Defense Fund to Mayor Bynum demanding the establishment of an independent agency to investigate lethal encounters with police, commonly known as an office of the independent monitor.[115] Such an agency would be able to immediately inspect a crime scene where an officer fired a weapon, re-examine evidence and witnesses, and recommend discipline for police misconduct.[116]

The mural before her was amazing, Tiffany said. She found it encouraging that the story of Greenwood and the massacre was finally, slowly reaching more minds and hearts. But she believed a long road still lay ahead. "We can no longer sing kumbaya," she said. "We have to really press for policy change. We have to press for new laws as it relates to police accountability."[117]

Back inside the Cultural Center, after the ribbon-cutting ceremony, Regina sat down at a long foldout table in the Goodwin/Chappelle Gallery, named in part after her grandfather. Surrounding her were stately black-and-white photographs of massacre survivors, men and women with vintage names like Harold and Blanche. Each photo subject had formed a different relationship with the camera. Some were smiling broadly, looking directly at the lens. Others were staring off, lost in an excavated memory. Each had a grim story to tell, captured in excerpts of interviews conducted by local historian Eddie Faye Gates.

Portraits of massacre survivors (clockwise from top left): Samuel Walker, Joyce Walker Hill, Leanna Johnson Lewis, Eldoris Mae Ector, Ophelia J. Richardson, Vera Ingram, Hazel Delores Smith Jones, and Wordie Peaches Miller Cooper

Joe Burns: "I remember running with my parents, siblings and other fleeing blacks. I will never forget how cold and scared I was that night."

Johnnie L. Grayson Brown: "Some of the riot survivors my age remember a lot about the riot. But I just can't remember much about it. I guess it was so horrible that my mind just blotted it out."

Otis Grandville Clark: "We ran for our lives. We never saw my stepfather again, nor our little pet bulldog, Bob."

Ernestine Gibbs: "Going back to Greenwood was like entering a war zone. Everything was gone! People were moaning and weeping when they looked at where their homes and businesses once stood."

Thelma Thurman Knight: "My mother lost everything she owned. It might not have been a whole lot, but it was hers!"

Leroy Leon Hatcher: "I believe my father was killed in the riot. I just wish I knew where he is buried."[118]

"There are folks who have received reparations," Regina said, referencing Japanese Americans who were interned during World War II. "So it should not have been any different for all of these beautiful black faces you see on this wall. But it was."[119]

Many of these survivors, along with more than one hundred others, sued the city of Tulsa in a federal civil rights lawsuit in 2003. Johnnie Cochran and Charles Ogletree, the famed Harvard Law School professor, were among the star attorneys on the case.[120] Jim Goodwin served as local counsel, while his mother Jeanne was among the named plaintiffs, representing the departed Ed Sr.[121] But the city fought the case aggressively, and it was ultimately thrown out in federal district court because the two-year statute of limitations on civil cases in Oklahoma had expired in 1923.[122] The only gesture toward recompense that the aging survivors received during those years was a set of commemorative medals from the state legislature.[123]

Regina had followed the lawsuit closely, attending town hall meetings and spending personal time with Ogletree and John Hope Franklin, who testified on behalf of massacre survivors and descendants. She was as disappointed as anyone when restitution was delayed once more.[124] But more than a decade later, she had to believe that the law could still offer some pathway toward justice—especially now that she had the power to shape laws herself. The question was not whether Regina had the conviction to pursue justice but whether her fellow Oklahomans did.

CHAPTER 22

"TRUST THE SYSTEM"

Tiffany Crutcher leads a march through Greenwood after the killing of her twin brother Terence Crutcher

erence Crutcher loved to sing. When he and Tiffany were children, they developed a mutual love of music—she played the viola, he the cello. Though they lived far apart as adults, Terence in Tulsa and Tiffany in Montgomery, the pair always celebrated their birthday together with a phone call. On their fortieth, in August 2016, they spoke of their hopes and dreams for the second half of their lives. Tiffany, who held a clinical doctorate in physical rehabilitation and served a mostly black region of rural Alabama, wanted to launch a wellness company that would marry health and financial literacy. Terence, still a musician at heart, planned to one day open a music production studio. Like many folks with deep Greenwood ties—their great-grandmother Rebecca Crutcher was a massacre survivor who had owned a barbecue pit on Greenwood Avenue[1]—entrepreneurship was in their blood.[2]

Terence's life had taken him in wayward directions. In the early

2010s, he spent four years in an Oklahoma prison on drug-trafficking charges.[3] But as he entered a fifth decade of life, he had a renewed sense of purpose and focus. In just a few weeks, he was planning to begin work on a music degree at Tulsa Community College. "I'm going to make you proud," he told Tiffany.[4]

A month later Tiffany sat in her clinic on a Friday evening, feeling sick. Not physically ill, but still unsettlingly off. She thought of her twin and all they'd been through together—the shared rooms on field trips, the afternoons practicing jump rope, and always the Sundays at church.[5] Their father, Joey Crutcher, was one of the most renowned ministers in North Tulsa and an accomplished musician;[6] their mother Leanna was a beloved music teacher.[7]

Tiffany and Terence Crutcher

Tiffany pulled up a picture on her computer of her and her brother at Reverend Crutcher's church—Terence smiling slyly behind a pair of sunglasses, Tiffany throwing up deuces while grinning as his arm wrapped around her. The odd sickness left her for a bit.

Then her phone rang. It was a cousin from Tulsa. "You need to call home."

"Why?" Tiffany wanted to know. The dead air caused her body to deflate.

The cousin didn't want to say, but eventually Tiffany got it out of her, a rumor too awful to believe. It couldn't be true—as long as she didn't call home, it wouldn't be. She could remain separated from the awful news by seven hundred miles. She drove through the streets of Montgomery, her body numb but her hands trembling on the steering wheel. Unknown numbers with a 918 area code—that meant Tulsa—kept her phone vibrating constantly. She ignored them and drove to a friend's house to pray. Eventually, the Caller ID showed a name she could not ignore: *Daddy*.

Joey Crutcher raised his voice to the heavens every Sunday, amplifying the spirit across his sanctuary. But when Tiffany answered the phone, her father's voice was louder and more desperate than she'd ever heard it before. "They killed my son!" he said. "They killed my son!"[8]

On the evening of September 16, 2016, Terence Crutcher left his SUV idling in the middle of a North Tulsa road. He had recently finished his music appreciation class for the day at Tulsa Community College.[9] Terence abandoned the vehicle and was behaving erratically, according to eyewitness accounts.[10] One witness said his wife saw a distressed man walking down the road and thought he was in need of medical attention. She wanted to help him, but the couple were afraid to approach Terence. Instead, they called 911.

Terence's next encounter was with a Tulsa Police Department officer named Betty Shelby.[11]

Aerial footage from a police helicopter showed Terence walking toward his vehicle with his hands up as Shelby walked behind him, gun drawn. "That looks like a bad dude. Could be on something," the helicopter's pilot, Michael Richert, says in the video clip.[12] More officers arrived at the scene. Soon three of them were pointing weapons at Terence. As he stood by the driver's-side door of his vehicle, Shelby fired a gunshot into his chest, while the officer next to her fired a Taser. Terence immediately crumpled to the ground. Shelby would later claim that he was reaching into his car window, potentially for a weapon, but Terence was unarmed, and police found no weapons in his vehicle.[13] He was pronounced dead at a nearby hospital that night.[14]

Tiffany was in Tulsa the next day, returning to the home where she and Terence had grown up just north of Greenwood. For years she had been closely following the ever-growing list of black people killed by police or in their custody: Michael Brown, Philando Castile, Alton Sterling, Sandra Bland. She had thought about booking a ticket to Baltimore after Freddie Gray died in the back of a police van and the city erupted in protest. "I always wanted to speak up for the voiceless," she said. "I never thought I would be on that other side."[15]

The relationship between Tulsa police and the black residents they were bound to protect had been poisoned in 1921, when Greenwood burned under police watch. But the mistreatment had continued long afterward. In 1936 the social worker Francis Burke reported that black people in white neighborhoods after dark were regularly "picked up" for arbitrary reasons, leading to inflated statistics about black criminality.[16] The *Oklahoma Eagle* had chronicled a steady drumbeat of police brutality cases for its entire existence. "Those who cry that protecting the rights of the criminal is a sign of weakness side with the cop who thinks that the night stick is a substitute for brains," the newspaper wrote in 1971.[17] The *Eagle* and groups like TAAG had often argued that increasing the number of black officers could be part of the solution, but those officers met with discrimination themselves.[18] In a 1994 lawsuit, black officers said they were often denied backup from their white colleagues and were routinely deprived of raises and promotions. (The suit was settled in 2002, with the department agreeing to multiple reforms.)[19]

Beyond the cases of police violence that garnered headlines, there was a constant hum of physical confrontation. A study released by the city of Tulsa and the Rockefeller Foundation in 2018, the Equality Indicators Report, found that black residents were more than twice as likely as white ones to experience the use of force from police officers.[20] The Terence Crutcher case became a focal point of all these pressures and, coming amid the growing Black Lives Matter movement, exploded to receive worldwide attention.

Days after Terence's death, Tiffany marched through Greenwood locking arms with Rev. Al Sharpton and Ben Crump, the prominent civil rights attorney who had previously represented the families of Michael Brown, Trayvon Martin, and Tamir Rice. Hundreds of protesters, mostly black, marched behind them, chanting "No Justice, No Peace!" as they walked toward city hall.[21] "Whether it's in Tulsa, whether it's in Ferguson, Staten Island, Cleveland, Charlotte, wherever, people are standing up because they have tension inside their soul," Crump said of the case.[22]

Shelby was arrested six days after killing Terence and charged with first-degree manslaughter.[23] She chose to stage an unusually public defense. In an interview with *60 Minutes* before her trial, she said that Terence had caused his own death. "I saw a threat, and I used the force I felt necessary to stop a threat," she said. Tiffany, who had always shared in her twin brother's pain, became Terence's public advocate. "She wasn't called to the scene because Terence was committing a crime," Tiffany said on *60 Minutes*. "She just noticed a car in the middle of the road, and the outcome was my brother was murdered."[24]

Shelby's legal defense built on the arguments she had laid out on television. At her trial, in May 2017, she said that Terence had refused to comply with her repeated orders to stop and get on his knees, and that she had feared for her life because of his behavior. While she described him as "very big" and looking like a "zombie," she overestimated his height by three inches and his weight by forty-six pounds.[25] Defense lawyers outlined portions of his criminal record during the trial and hinged much of their argument on a toxicology report that revealed that PCP, a hallucinogenic drug, had been in Terence's system at the time of his death.[26] No one claimed that Terence had behaved in an aggressive or violent manner.[27] The perceived threat of violence, Shelby and her lawyers said, had been enough.[28]

The trial lasted eight days.[29] On the night of May 17, 2017, a packed courtroom awaited the jury's verdict. Shelby sat at the counsel table with a few family members in the row behind her, while Tiffany and dozens of members of Terence's extended family and community occupied nearly half the courtroom. More Crutcher family members lingered in the hallway, and outside on the courthouse steps, supporters of both Shelby and Terence waited to see what form justice might take. "I'm asking you to trust the system," District Judge Doug Drummond said before the verdict was read.[30]

"Not guilty," the jury foreman announced.

Shelby was acquitted of all charges by a jury of nine white and three black people.[31] As the verdict was read, jurors openly wept—in an interview after the trial, one regretted not forcing a hung jury, believing Shelby could have been found guilty if the state had argued its case more effectively.[32] Shelby was whisked out of the courtroom within moments of the announcement of the verdict, while a devastated Tiffany, standing with her father before the news cameras in the courthouse, expressed her shock and disappointment at a verdict she could never accept.[33] "Betty Shelby was the aggressor," she said. "Betty Shelby had the gun. Betty Shelby was following him with his hands up. Betty Shelby murdered my brother."[34]

Her grief soon transformed into conviction. "I'm going to make sure that I don't rest until we get reform for this police department in Tulsa, Oklahoma."[35]

It was a monumental task. But Tiffany hoped to build a coalition of residents and community leaders who could reverse these trends and halt the tragedies. In 2017 she and her parents co-founded the Terence Crutcher Foundation, a nonprofit that used grassroots organizing to advocate for criminal justice reform, lead community service projects, and honor victims of racial violence.[36]

She had an immediate ally in Regina Goodwin. Regina had been a fixture at the protests throughout the Crutcher case, marching with Crump and Sharpton and helping keep attention on the issue after the national leaders had left.[37] In 2017 she and state senator Kevin Matthews issued a state citation honoring Terence's legacy and the work of the Terence Crutcher Foundation, despite protests from some police officers that Terence's criminal past made him unworthy of remembrance. "He had dignity in his life, he should certainly have it in his death," Regina said in response.[38]

Regina was also one of the most vocal critics of the way the police closed ranks around Shelby after her acquittal. After resigning from the Tulsa Police Department, Shelby was hired by the Rogers County Sheriff's Office, just thirty miles from Tulsa, and taught a class to other officers on "surviving the aftermath" of shooting someone while in uniform. "Folks are talking about there's a scab on the wound,"

Regina Goodwin, with Terence Crutcher's parents Joey and Leanna Crutcher, speaks at a protest outside the Tulsa County Sheriff's office

Regina said at a 2018 protest over Shelby's new job. "There's no scab because there's been no healing."[39]

It made sense that Terence Crutcher's name was never far from Regina's mind. Since her first year in office, much of her proposed legislation had focused on reining in the violence and punitiveness of the criminal justice system, burdens that fell disproportionately on black people. She wanted to remove the financial burdens that the state places on citizens: forcing people to pay down interest rather than principal on late child-support payments, using civil forfeiture to bankroll sheriff's departments, and throwing people into jail for failing to pay back court fees.[40] She believed there had to be strategies to curb the reckless violence that officers sometimes engaged in, almost always without consequence. While her colleagues across the aisle preached the gospel of personal responsibility, Regina was more interested in using the law to shape institutional responsibility, to focus more on protecting people rather than punishing them.

Regina and Tiffany both agreed on one way to introduce institutional responsibility into the Tulsa Police Department: establishing an office of the independent monitor. In earlier eras, city officials had tried to assuage black Tulsans' concerns by creating "liaisons" between citizens and police, but these workers typically answered to the police chief; they were officers by another name. Instead, reformers looked to the independent monitor's office in Denver as a model. It had a staff of twelve attorneys, policy analysts, and community-outreach managers. In 2017 the Denver monitor challenged the police department's lax use-of-force standards, prompting a more stringent policy. The office also successfully advocated for the suspension of officers who inappropriately discharged their guns. "Any time a Denver officer fires his or her weapon, I get called by dispatch," said Nick Mitchell, the attorney who served as Denver's lead independent monitor. "We can walk in there and pick up any investigation."[41]

A monitor as powerful as Denver's was rare. Among the eighteen thousand police departments in the United States, less than 1 percent had oversight agencies, and few of those agencies could conduct independent investigations of police conduct.[42] With that kind of institutional structure, though, the internal investigation of the Betty Shelby case might have gone differently. Shelby, for instance, was not interviewed by police until three days after the shooting, and she was allowed to view a video of the encounter before being questioned.[43] "It's not ideal," Mitchell said. "I want people's native recollections of what they remember unaltered by extraneous information."[44]

Mayor Bynum took office after Terence was killed, and despite his party, he seemed to be an early advocate for police reform.[45] The thirty-nine-year-old conservative leader styled himself as a policy wonk who was too data-driven to play politics—in 2017 he gave a TED Talk entitled "A Republican Mayor's Plan to Replace Partisanship with Policy."[46] Like Tiffany and Regina, his familial legacy was bound up in Tulsa's history. Bynum's uncle served as mayor in the 2000s, his grandfather was elected in the 1970s, and his great-great-grandfather became the city's second mayor in 1899.[47] From the very start of his term, he knew that reckoning with Tulsa's dark past, and the ways that past continued to reverberate, would be a cornerstone of his time in office. In 2018, following urging by city councilor Vanessa Hall-Harper and a viral *Washington Post* article about the race massacre, he announced that the city would launch a search for long-rumored mass graves of massacre victims.[48]

Bynum's candid talk about race, and his commitment to closing the city's horrific life expectancy gap—children in some parts of North Tulsa could expect to live twelve years less than their South Tulsa counterparts[49]—helped him build a diverse and capable staff when he first came into office. In January 2019 he visited Denver's office of the independent monitor to learn more about implementation strategies and to speak to staffers, community activists, and the local police chief.[50] Later that month Bynum announced that Tulsa would have its own independent monitor.[51] "Internal Affairs investigations are conducted confidentially, and citizens don't have a means of verifying results," Bynum said at the time. "I think we owe it to the citizens and to the officers to do better."[52]

Tiffany allowed herself some cautious optimism.[53] More than two years after Terence's death, this could be a first step toward preventing another black man from facing such a nightmare in the city. But even then she knew that powerful forces in the world of Oklahoma politics would do all they could to prevent any sort of police oversight from happening.

The Oklahoma capitol is a massive structure, looming as one drives across the winding statehouse grounds. A $21 million dome, which gives the structure an air of Greco-Roman antiquity, was actually added in 2002, with the names of million-dollar donors—Halliburton, Hobby Lobby, General Motors—etched into its base in six-inch gold letters.[54] A functioning oil rig in front of the building pays homage to the state's most valuable natural resource.[55]

When the House of Representatives first assembled, in Oklahoma's initial capital of Guthrie, there was a lone black legislator. A. C. Hamlin represented a predominantly black district in Logan County, where Guthrie was located. But he lost his reelection bid in 1910, after Oklahoma passed the "grandfather clause," the early voter suppression tactic that excluded blacks from the ballot box.[56] The legislature would remain all white until 1964, when the U.S. Supreme Court ruled that state legislative districts must be based on population, and three African Americans took seats in the capitol.[57] Regina kept a small photo of Hamlin next to the doorway of her office.

As Tiffany worked on police reform in Tulsa, Regina was making a similar push for accountability throughout the state. More and more of the people she represented were coming to her with accounts of negative police run-ins. During the summer of 2019, a constituent named Chris Brown had called her with a harrowing story. He had been riding his motorcycle in North Tulsa when he saw police officers conducting a traffic stop. He observed from a distance to ensure that the stop was being handled properly. As he began to leave, at the nearest intersection, an officer roughly ripped him from his motorcycle, hurled profanities at him, and placed him in handcuffs. No arrest was made because the man had committed no crime. But Brown's motorcycle was damaged, and he was left with bruises, internal and external.[58]

Regina wanted to see video footage of the event, to get a full picture of what happened, but police evaded her request for months. The department's response was typical. "I'm not surprised when police say, 'Oh, I just forgot to turn on my body cam. Oh, I left my body cam at the office,'" she said one evening in her living room. "You have corrupt folks that are in these agencies. You have folks that continue to get away with doing wrong."[59]

In 2020 Regina drafted a bill that would make camera enforcement more stringent. The measure would bar police officers from deleting body camera footage and charge them with a misdemeanor if they purposefully turned off their cameras, while on patrol, in an effort to obstruct justice.[60] To her, the logic was simple: cops needed strict laws in place in order to control their behavior, just like everybody else.

But the backlash was swift. "When you put a law in place that says you can now be criminally liable, because of that little object you attach to your chest, you're going to make agencies want to shy away from [using cameras]," TPD Lieutenant Shane Tuell told a local news station.[61] "There's no need to record your coffee break at the Quik-Trip," sniped Jerad Lindsey, the chairman of Tulsa's Fraternal Order of Police.[62]

In February, Justin Humphrey, the Republican chair of the Public Safety Committee in the House of Representatives, agreed to let Regina's bill be heard and put up to a vote. But the committee was filled with eleven Republicans and only two Democrats, and a few members had recently accepted campaign contributions from police unions.[63] Humphrey, the committee chair, had also accepted a $2,500 donation from the Geo Group, one of the largest owners of private prisons in the United States.[64] (Regina accepted a $250 donation from the Tulsa Fraternal Order of Police during her first year in the legislature; "I didn't solicit it," she said later. "I think they didn't write me any more checks because they didn't like what I was saying.")[65]

Even before the vote happened, Regina knew the likely outcome. "I have had to fight lies just to get the bill heard," she wrote in a 1:30 a.m. text message the night before the committee meeting. "If this goes down, which all indications say so, this will be my first bill in five years to die in committee. God bless us all."[66]

The next day, a conference room on the third floor of the capitol was filled to capacity, with the members of the Public Safety Committee sitting at a U-shaped table. About thirty onlookers stood just behind them on three sides, and an overflow room was filled with dozens more citizens. A man wearing a white cowboy hat sat at the far end of the room, watching the crowd filter in. As the committee chair, Justin Humphrey ultimately had final say over which bills would even have a chance to be approved and sent to the House floor for a vote. Regina had spent weeks cajoling him into considering her bill just to get to this moment.

Humphrey leaned toward his mic and quieted the undercurrent of chatter. "There's a lot of people in here. We've got 30 cases going today," he said. "Some of these will be very emotional to lots of people in the room. . . . If you're emotional, go out in the hall."[67]

This was, in effect, the day Democrats and Republicans would hash out competing visions over who had the right to protection in Oklahoma—those who were armed or those who weren't. Regina's bill had been all over the news, but so had a bill authored by Rep. Jason Lowe, a Democrat, that would have repealed a law allowing Oklahomans to carry guns without background checks. Meanwhile a Republican, Kevin West, was presenting a bill that would strengthen the state's stand-your-ground law, placing the burden on prosecutors to prove that a person who shot and killed someone else wasn't responding to a threat.[68]

As each lawmaker stood up to present their legislation, a television monitor behind Humphrey served as an electronic scoreboard, with committee members' names listed in white. As they voted on each bill, the names would shift in color. A name turning green meant a yes vote; red meant a no. Lowe's bill was voted down with little discussion. West's was passed with just as little fanfare. Then it was Regina's turn to step forward.

Though she'd expressed cynicism about the bill's chances beforehand, it was clear as she began to speak that she wanted to get it over the finish line. "What this bill is is an accountability bill," she said. She pointed to a situation in Jackson County, Florida, where the state department of law enforcement found that an officer had been routinely turning off his body camera during traffic stops and planting drugs in the vehicles of innocent people. "This is a common sense bill," she concluded. "I think we're going to see all green lights up there because I know we're trying to pursue justice and we want to do the right thing."[69]

As the members locked in their votes, the names flickered one by one: red, red, red again. The bill failed 12–1.[70]

Regina left before the committee meeting ended. Enacting change in the legislature was getting harder, not easier, for her side of the aisle as the years wore on. She'd known the bill had no shot before she walked into the room, but she insisted on proposing policies she knew would benefit the people back home.[71]

Outside the conference room, a group of four young people approached her in the hallway. They were students at Rose State College, a school near Oklahoma City.[72] Adriana Laws, a black woman with thick black-rimmed glasses, introduced herself first. "Some of us have projects where we're following legislative bills," Adriana said. "I'm following your bill 3548." That was Regina's bill about ending the jailing of people who fail to pay court fees, which she had been trying to get passed since her first year in office.[73]

The legislator looked at the students around her and smiled. Then she cocked an eyebrow. "Were you in there at all? Was that interesting? Did you notice all the Democrats go down in flames? And all the Republicans, their stuff gets voted on."

Adriana nodded. "I've been following you around for a couple of weeks now," she said, laughing.

Regina jerked her head back. "You didn't even introduce yourself!"

"You're busy!" Adriana replied. "You're always in meetings so I just kind of show up and see what you have to say."

Regina began to explain exactly the kind of problem HB 3548 was written to address. A constituent of hers who had previously been incarcerated was behind on his legal fees. His failure to pay prompted a warrant for his arrest. When he didn't show up for court, he was put in jail, missing a shift at his job on a Monday morning. He was quickly fired, making it even less likely he would ever manage to pay off his fees. "It's no good for us to get money out of folks that don't have it," she said. "The whole concept is wrong and it's been wrong for a long time."

Regina looked around at the group. "Y'all are college students. Do you know what that is when folks are put in prison because they can't pay fines?"

"Debtor's prison," one of the students said.

"Yeah. That's illegal," Regina said. "You cannot put people in prison because they cannot afford to pay.

"Y'all walk with me," Regina continued, and began heading toward her office two floors above. The students followed, with Adriana leading the pack.[74]

"I completely understand," Adriana said.[75] She'd spent the previous semester working in a public administration internship in the town of Spencer and observing the mundane injustice of government bureaucracy up close.[76] "I'm watching him every Tuesday we have court, putting people in jail because they can't afford to pay their fines. When I saw your bill, a light bulb went off in my head. Like, 'I've gotta meet her.'"[77]

For Adriana, the measure was even more personal. Earlier that year, when leaving school late at night, she'd gotten a traffic citation. Her infant daughter had been crying in the back seat as the officer handed her a pair of tickets totaling more than $700. She didn't have the money, so she entered into a time payment agreement that would allow her to pay the fees in installments—and potentially face jail time if she failed to do so. "I can go to jail and end up ruining my college career, ruining my political career, I could get my child taken away," she said later. "Maybe that's why it sits so personal with me."[78]

The group approached Regina's office. The representative still had a million things to do that day, so she and Adriana agreed to meet later in the legislative session. Afterward, in the basement cafeteria, the students reflected on all they'd seen so far in the capitol. They were a diverse group—two black, two white, at least one conservative—but they'd all been shocked to see just how impossible it was to pass legislation that could help vulnerable people. "It's a cycle," Adriana said. "And as we apparently just heard today, not too many people are trying to fix that cycle."[79]

In Tulsa, just a few weeks after Regina's body cam bill failed, the city council had its own decision to make about installing an office of the independent monitor. The initial optimism that activists and the mayor had expressed about the office had stalled, after the Tulsa Fraternal Order of Police issued a letter to Mayor Bynum threatening to sue the city if a monitor was established without first negotiating with them.[80] Such tactics are common among police unions, which are nearly always opposed to outside oversight.[81]

Months passed as the city searched for a solution that would satisfy community leaders without inviting the wrath of the union. Details of the monitor's role finally emerged in the summer of 2019, as a city council ordinance. But the monitor that the mayor and council were proposing was not as independent as Tiffany Crutcher and other activists had hoped. Instead of being an investigator like the monitor in Denver, who could roam a crime scene, question police, and launch investigations at the public's behest, the Tulsa monitor would act more like an auditor, reviewing internal affairs investigations after the fact and offering policy recommendations.[82] The mayor later said that he hoped to increase the monitor's power through collective bargaining with the union.[83] Tiffany called the new role toothless. "It was watered down, it didn't have any power, and it wouldn't prevent what happened to Terence from happening again," she said.[84] She and other activists pulled their support for the ordinance, as did some city council members, forcing the mayor to withdraw it.[85]

In February 2020, Vanessa Hall-Harper, the city councilor who represented the Greenwood district, argued that Tulsa citizens should decide on the issue themselves. She proposed putting the establishment of a monitor up to a public vote in August.[86]

Behind the scenes, the Fraternal Order of Police launched a strategy to kill the vote. The police union was a big spender in local politics, having donated to four out of the nine sitting council members during their 2018 and 2020 campaigns.[87] Lindsey, the union chair, approached councilors who didn't want FOP money with physical checks written out directly to them rather than to their campaign committees.[88]

The effort went further than trying to sway councilors. The FOP mobilized Tulsa residents to send thousands of emails and phone calls to city council members opposing the monitor vote. Union members even showed up at residents' houses to argue their case.[89] While Hall-Harper's measure initially had the support of a majority of the council, most members ended up voting against it, citing opposition from their constituents.[90]

Three and a half years after Terence Crutcher's death, Tulsa's police department continued to police itself. The fight for change had come to consume Tiffany's life—in December 2018, she moved back to Tulsa to pursue activism full-time.[91] But for most Tulsans, the debate over policing played out quietly, in newspaper articles that they didn't read, city council meetings they didn't attend, and legislative committee votes they never heard about. Even in one of the reddest states in

America, though, the summer of 2020 would change all that. "People automatically assume that all police officers are good, maybe the victim did something wrong," Tiffany said. "They toil, they go back and forth between what's right and what's wrong and what was or what wasn't. But this time I think the light bulb finally came on."[92]

CHAPTER 23

THIS IS OUR TIME

Greg Robinson leads a protest against police brutality in midtown Tulsa

Tiffany was at home on her sofa on May 25, 2020, when she saw the picture of a police officer in Minneapolis with his knee on a black man's neck. She felt nauseated. She watched a short video clip of George Floyd calling out for his mother as the life was choked out of him. She felt angry. Soon a cascade of messages flooded her phone, her email, and her Facebook account, as friends and online followers turned to her to make sense of things. Whenever a black man died at the hands of police, people seemed to think Tiffany had to bear witness.[1]

Over the next few days, a cruel cocktail of emotions familiar to far too many black people—rage, fear, sadness—made it difficult for Tiffany to sleep. "It was almost as if Terence had died all over again," she recalled.[2] On Facebook, she encouraged people to call leaders in Minneapolis and demand justice for Floyd. She used all the familiar hashtags: #blacklivesmatter, #icantbreathe, #policereformNOW.[3]

The national response to George Floyd's death, however, expanded rapidly beyond what had occurred in the aftermath of the killing of Michael Brown or Terence Crutcher. By late May 2020, the world had been eerily still for more than two months due to shelter-in-place orders issued to stop the spread of Covid-19. But suddenly, there was motion. On Tuesday, May 26, protests erupted in Minneapolis near where Floyd was killed. People marched through the streets during the day and squared off against police in riot gear at night.[4] On Wednesday, the white-hot rage spread to other cities—big ones like Chicago and Los Angeles and small ones like Brunswick, Georgia, where a black man named Ahmaud Arbery had been followed and killed by a pair of white men while out jogging.[5] In Louisville, protesters were demanding justice for Floyd and for Breonna Taylor, a twenty-six-year-old black woman killed in her own home by city police in March.[6]

Tulsa remained quiet, as it so often had since 1921. Unlike many places, the city had not witnessed civil unrest when Martin Luther King, Jr., died in the 1960s.[7] In 2016, President Obama called Dewey Bartlett, then Tulsa's mayor, to praise his handling of the Crutcher case and the fact that protests had not turned violent.[8] And yet it was clear that somehow, this moment could be different.

On Thursday, three days after Floyd was killed, several black ministers and community leaders held a press conference at a church just north of Greenwood. When Tiffany stepped up to the podium, wearing a black face mask as a precaution against Covid-19, she spoke with a halting exhaustion that carried the weight of much more than the past few days' events. "Here we are, yet again, angry and devastated at the killing of another unarmed black man by law enforcement," she said, in front of a phalanx of impassive cameras. "The compounded trauma that my family, that our community, that we endure is real."[9]

She had exchanged so many words over the years in city council meetings, social media posts, town halls, and press conferences. Now, for the first time, she felt hopeless. The rituals of outrage felt like pantomiming solutions that didn't seem to be moving the criminal justice system far enough or fast enough. *Is this going to help anything?* she thought. *They're not hearing us.*[10]

Nehemiah Frank felt the same. The thirty-six-year-old entrepreneur and journalist ran a digital news outlet for Tulsa's black community called the *Black Wall Street Times* and had dedicated much of his life to organized civil engagement. He sat on a community advisory board for the *Tulsa World* and had nudged the newspaper to officially refer to the events of 1921 as a massacre instead of a riot.[11] He was a Tulsa native whose great-great-grandfather, Jim Cherry, had lost at least $50,000 worth of property ($760,000 in 2021 dollars) in the blaze.[12] He too was tired of incremental change and had observed Tulsa's eagerness to ignore its own history when at all possible—he'd been present at the 2018 anniversary vigil and taken the somber walk down Greenwood while hundreds of people streamed into the baseball stadium.[13] It wasn't lost on him or anyone else in Tulsa's black community that the weekend after Floyd's killing would also be the ninety-ninth anniversary of the massacre.

That night, the *Black Wall Street Times* posted an event on Facebook slated for Saturday, May 30: "We Can't Breathe—Peaceful Protest." While previous Tulsa protests regarding policing had taken place in Greenwood or at city hall, the location listed for the event was the corner of 34th Street and Peoria Avenue.[14] That was Brookside, a posh leisure district filled with upscale restaurants and boutiques, south of downtown Tulsa. "We have to disrupt commerce," Tiffany recalled thinking. "When people's money is affected, that's when they listen."[15] It wasn't far from where Clara Luper and other activists had marched during their protest against racist accommodations policies in 1964.

Tiffany was quiet as the protest began that Saturday afternoon. The crowd was larger than she'd expected, as several hundred people milled in front of Brookside's many restaurants and boutiques. Protesters were initially contained to the sidewalks, but they eventually streamed out onto the streets and staged a "die-in" in front of an Urban Outfitters store. They chanted Terence Crutcher's name and those of black men in Oklahoma who had been killed in Tulsa after him, such as Joshua Harvey and Joshua Barre. From the roof of the Brook, a popular sports bar, Tulsa police officers peered down in silence.[16]

Tiffany paced among the bodies splayed out on the sweltering as-

A die-in during the George Floyd protests in Tulsa

phalt, recording everything with her phone for Facebook Live.[17] She spoke only briefly at the start of the march, asking the crowd to acknowledge Terence's three daughters, who were accompanying her and wearing #JUSTICE 4 CRUTCH T-shirts. Then she directed everyone to start marching.

The crowd was energized, rapidly growing, and surprisingly white. People held signs with jolts of moral clarity that had suddenly become accepted by a wide audience: BLACK LIVES MATTER, WHITE SILENCE IS VIOLENCE, TERENCE CRUTCHER SHOULD BE ALIVE![18]

Farther ahead in the procession, Greg Robinson, a community organizer and Terence Crutcher Foundation board member, wielded a bullhorn like a drum major's mace.[19] "Dr. Tiffany Crutcher and the Crutcher family have done everything they could for this city!" he shouted. "They've talked to the mayor! They've researched for the mayor! They've sung for the mayor! They've laid Terence Crutcher's bloody clothes down at city hall for the mayor! And what were they asking for?"

The crowd roared back, "Justice!"

"And yet justice has still not been served."[20]

Robinson hailed from a family where community meant everything. His father, Greg Robinson, Sr., had been a North Tulsa nonprofit leader and civil rights activist for decades, working to provide financial assistance to low-income residents. He'd brought his son and namesake to city council meetings, petition drives, and public protests nearly from the moment little Greg could walk.[21] The elder Greg died when his son was only thirteen, but an internal fire to fight for change only grew stronger in the younger Robinson as he aged.[22] Greg worked on the presidential campaigns of Barack Obama and Hillary Clinton, but after Terence Crutcher was killed, he felt a duty to return to Tulsa. Working for national leaders, he learned that politics and community organizing were two sides of the same coin. "Both are motivated a lot of times by a hopeful anger," Greg said later. "Anybody can get somebody to protest, but it's going from the protest to the policy side that requires the strategy and the organization."[23]

The crowd grew quiet and formed a natural circle around the die-in. Greg continued through his bullhorn: "We have four simple demands." He listed them, one by one. They wanted an independent monitor, which Tiffany Crutcher, Regina Goodwin, and a cadre of community leaders had first called for in 2018. They wanted some of the city budget to be divested from the Tulsa Police Department and invested in mental health services. They wanted the city to settle pending litigation with the Crutcher family, who had filed a wrongful death lawsuit against Tulsa in 2018. And they wanted the mayor to cancel the city's contract with *Live PD,* a *Cops*-like reality show on A&E that shadowed police officers performing arrests and that many Tulsans decried as racist.[24]

The protesters marched on. As the demonstration swelled to more than a thousand people, Tiffany noticed that police had successfully guessed the route of the march and diverted traffic as the protesters walked. They were, in essence, serving as escorts.[25] She thought of Martin Luther King, Jr.'s Albany Movement, of the early 1960s, in which an effort to gain attention for the black struggle for desegregation in Georgia had been thwarted because Albany's savvy police chief chose not to brutalize black protesters while cameras were present.[26] And right there at home in Tulsa, the very first protest of the civil rights movement had featured the guardrails of police "protection," until Clara Luper shifted tactics and dared to enter the segregated Borden's restaurant unannounced. Change, quite often, was bred by disruption.

"Let's take the highway," Tiffany said on her livestream. "We need the mayor to hear us."[27]

Protesters streamed onto the exit ramp of Interstate 44, darting between idling vehicles and scrambling over a concrete barrier. One protester was injured as a truck accelerated along the left shoulder lane and struck him.[28] But soon enough protesters had overtaken both sides of the highway. It would remain closed for at least half an hour. Standing near the interstate median, Greg repeated the group's demands on his bullhorn as Tiffany strafed him with her phone, continuing to broadcast the demonstration live.[29]

The march then turned toward the mayor's house, located in a wealthy neighborhood not far from Brookside. Hundreds of people chanted "Black Lives Matter!" as they passed leafy mansions tucked behind stone walls. Under the direction of police, Bynum, along with his wife and children, left their home when he found out marchers were headed in their direction.[30] In a Facebook post that night, the mayor wrote, "Change occurs in Tulsa through collaboration, deliberation and thoughtful action—not through attempts at intimidation."[31]

The march wound its way back to Brookside, and the massive crowd encircled Tiffany in front of the Urban Outfitters store. If she had begun the week feeling hopeless, the presence of so many passionate Tulsans gave her the fuel she needed to keep going. Energized once again, she grabbed hold of the bullhorn. But even without it, her voice would have been louder than it had been in any public setting since George Floyd's death.

"Since we are actually encroaching on the ninety-ninth anniversary of the massacre, I need y'all to do just one more chant for me. Just one more chant for the ancestors."

The call and response was deafening.

"Justice for Greenwood!"

"Justice for Crutch!"

"Reparations Now!"[32]

If Tulsa seemed slow to react to Floyd's death initially, everything lurched into fast-forward after the Saturday protest. On Sunday,

Tiffany Crutcher leads a chant of "Justice for Greenwood"
at the conclusion of a protest in midtown Tulsa

May 31, the ninety-ninth anniversary of the race massacre, an even larger demonstration was organized in Greenwood. People chanted the names of George Floyd and Breonna Taylor, but they also held a long moment of silence for the victims of the 1921 attack. Families and teenagers crowded onto a field across from the Greenwood Cultural Center, then marched right past, for once, the Drillers stadium. For the first time in Tulsa's history, more than a thousand people, many of them white, came to Greenwood to remember the horrors that had happened there.[33]

The demonstration eventually wound its way back over to Brookside. As the night stretched on, the protesters grew restless, and so did the police. After midnight, officers fired pepper spray balls into the crowd, sending everyone scattering to the sidewalks. People doused their eyes in milk as the pain from tear gas—a burning sensation that grows worse with each sputtering cough—became seared into their brains.[34] The windows of a few businesses were smashed in, and a more militant group of protesters made another failed attempt to visit the mayor's house.[35]

Still, even after the Sunday night conflict, Tulsa's week in the wake of George Floyd's murder had hardly been among the most chaotic in the country. In Seattle, police cars burned as the governor of Washington deployed the National Guard.[36] In Minneapolis, the police's Third Precinct, whose jurisdiction included the block where Floyd was killed, was set on fire, and days later a semi truck plowed through a group of protesters.[37] In Washington, D.C., protesters outside the White House were tear-gassed so that President Donald Trump could take a photo in front of St. John's Church.[38] In nearby Oklahoma City, at a night of protests that Adriana Laws attended, three of the people arrested were charged with committing acts of terrorism.[39]

The heat that was spreading around the nation felt like it was closing in on the city. On Monday morning, Tiffany, Greg, Regina, and several other community members assembled in front of city hall, calling on Mayor Bynum to meet with them and address the demands they'd laid out during the weekend protest. After a few minutes, word came that the mayor was granting them an audience.

The group filed into city hall, a glittering fifteen-story glass structure with blue-tinted, floor-length windows.[40] More than a hundred years before, J. B. Stradford had made a city hall visit to lobby the mayor to change Tulsa's racist segregation ordinance. Now, in the center of a cavernous conference room, about two dozen chairs were placed in a large circle.

Mayor Bynum was waiting. "I heard about 10:30 this morning that you all were going to be here at city hall and cleared my schedule," he began. "We can visit as long as you would like."

Everyone had a lot to say. Regina emphasized how important it was to bring longtime community leaders into meetings about shaping city policy, even if those conversations were not always pleasant. "This is not gonna be happy talk," she said early in the meeting. "It's not going to be something that we're always gonna agree on. But I guarantee you people wouldn't take the time to come here if we didn't want what was best for Tulsa."

The meeting lasted more than three hours—part candid discussion, part strategic negotiation, part personal confessional. The mayor's statement that the effort to march to his house had been a form of intimidation hung heavy in the room. "I've been a tall, imposing-looking black man since I was fifteen years old. I cannot tell you the number of times that just by me entering a room, people clutch their bags," said Robert Turner, the pastor of Greenwood's Vernon AME Church, who'd been one of the leaders of the Saturday march. "The fact that now that I'm in the ministry and exercising my right to assemble, that I hear my mayor that I respect . . . say that he felt that we tried to intimidate him? That hurt me to my core."

Bynum was firm in his opposition to how the protest had evolved. "You're good people . . . but you were with a group that had just shut down an interstate highway," he said. "I had to go and tell my thirteen-year-old son and ten-year-old daughter that they had to go get in the car and leave their own house. I know that wasn't the intent, to make us feel intimidated, but my kids are terrified of their own house right now."

As Bynum and Reverend Turner bickered over the appropriate boundaries of decorum, Greg interjected. "We can play politics in here and pick out what people have said and what people have done and how we've been rubbed the wrong way," he said. "Everybody in here can do that. That would be about us. And that would be a mistake."[41]

The tenor shifted. Bynum agreed that an office of an independent monitor was still worth fighting for and committed to taking on the police union in order to do it. His deputy mayor reminded the group that the city was soon launching a pilot program for an around-the-clock psychological emergency room, where police officers could take people who were experiencing mental distress rather than throwing them in jail. Bynum also agreed to end the contract with *Live PD*. (The show would be canceled nationally within days.)[42]

The meeting was a breakthrough that seemed to prove that protesting worked, but so did open dialogue. "What happened today—work, three hours sitting in a room, two sides, coming together to find a middle ground to move our city forward—is what this is about," Greg said as he stood next to Bynum and Tiffany after the long discussion. Tears ran down his cheeks.[43]

The change that Tiffany, Greg, and so many others had been fighting for seemed within reach. But the following Sunday Tiffany found herself once again defending her brother on national television. In a *CBS Morning News* segment on Tulsa's history of racial violence, Mayor Bynum said he didn't believe that Betty Shelby's killing of Terence Crutcher had anything to do with the fact that Terence was black. "It is more about the really insidious nature of drug utilization than it is about race," the mayor said. Crutcher was also interviewed for the segment, but she focused on policy. "The use-of-force standard has to be changed," she said. "He could then finally rest in peace."[44] Bynum later walked back his comments in a Facebook post, calling them dumb and simplistic.[45]

Days later the actions of three Tulsa police officers escalated tensions. On June 8, Travis Yates, a major in the Tulsa Police Department, said on a conservative radio show, "We're shooting African-Americans about twenty-four per cent less than we probably ought to be, based on the crimes being committed," citing specious research. The major's comments sparked condemnation from the mayor and the Black Officers Coalition.[46] That same day Tulsa police released body cam footage of two officers accosting a pair of black teenagers and forcing them to the ground, ostensibly for jaywalking. That encounter was placed under internal investigation. Since Tulsa had no independent monitor, the exact nature of the investigation remained opaque.[47]

After a long and anxious few days spent trying to determine the appropriate way to respond to all that had happened in Tulsa since George Floyd was killed—really, since Terence Crutcher was killed—Tiffany and Greg decided to take political matters in the city into their own hands. On the blustery morning of June 10, they met at the Tulsa County Election Board. Robinson had exchanged his LEGALIZE BEING BLACK T-shirt for a charcoal suit. Rather than a bullhorn, Tiffany carried a fifty-dollar check, made out to the city of Tulsa. The pair announced that Greg would be running for mayor in the August 2020 election. Tiffany would be his senior campaign adviser.

At thirty, Greg would be the youngest mayor in Tulsa's history and the first black one. "I have to tell you that I'm scared," he said at the start of his speech announcing his candidacy. "I'm scared to stand up and say this is what the time has called for, and that I'm the person that's called for it. But what I'm more scared of is continuing to live in a city where we're not doing right by all of the citizens of Tulsa."[48]

Tiffany nodded in quiet agreement. If Greg hadn't been able or willing to run, she would have run herself. "This is really a form of protest for us," she said later.[49]

Just a few hours after Greg announced his candidacy, Tulsa became the center of the political universe. At a June 10 meeting at the White House, President Donald Trump announced that he would be holding his first rally since March in the city.[50]

The world had changed drastically in the three months since Trump had been on the campaign trail. More than one hundred thousand Americans had died from the coronavirus.[51] Vast portions of the economy had shut down indefinitely. Widespread protests against police brutality had erupted in thousands of U.S. cities and towns.[52]

Trump planned to arrive on June 19—Juneteenth, the most important holiday in Greenwood. Many white Americans were oblivious to the celebration, including Trump himself. He and many on his staff reportedly learned about the holiday and the Tulsa Race Massacre only after they had picked the date and place for Trump's return, though from the beginning one high-ranking Republican official had told Trump that it was a bad idea.[53] No one in Greenwood knew of these internal deliberations in Washington, but given the president's regular antagonism toward black people during his presidency—he defended white supremacists, disparaged black athletes, and pursued a policy agenda that limited oversight of police departments—it was easy for many to assume that returning to the campaign trail on that day was a deliberate provocation.[54] With a force as chaotic as the president in town, Tulsa risked becoming another Charlottesville, where a white supremacist rally in 2017 had culminated in a terrorist attack that left a woman dead.[55] Some feared the city might even roll back the clock to 1921, with thousands of agitated and potentially armed Trump supporters descending on Greenwood. After huge public blowback, Trump made a rare concession by delaying his rally to June 20, but that did little to quell the feeling in North Tulsa that a weekend long treasured by the community would be fraught with danger.

Tiffany saw no upside to direct conflict. The goal had to be to protect Greenwood at all costs. "I had to figure out how can we bring everyone together to channel the anxiety," she said, "and drown out hate, and drown out rhetoric, and try to prevent history from repeating itself."[56]

Many Juneteenth events had been canceled due to Covid, but Trump's arrival changed the Greenwood community's calculus.[57] With little more than a week to plan, the community began organizing. Sherry Gamble Smith, who had led the resurgence of Juneteenth celebrations in the 2010s, began working her logistical magic to plan space for vendors and artists. Fire in Little Africa, a music collective of young black Oklahoma singers and rappers, prepped for a free concert in the grassy field across the street from the Greenwood Cultural Center. Both the *Oklahoma Eagle* and the *Black Wall Street Times* began laying out special editions that would be handed out over the weekend. This would not be a counterprotest against Trump but rather a reaffirmation of what Greenwood had always stood for. "Coalition building and having a collective group of people to pull off movements like this is so important," Tiffany said. "You don't want to go to war alone."[58]

The morning of Juneteenth was quiet, dreary, and anxious, except for the burst of canary-yellow paint on Greenwood Avenue that spilled across the asphalt in loud, bright, and confident letters—BLACK LIVES MATTER.[59] A group of fifty-six artists had painted overnight, risking arrest to mimic the identical installations that had already sprung up in Washington, San Francisco, and Birmingham, Alabama.[60]

"I love it," Regina Woods said as she eyed the street art in front of her newly opened hair salon. The Loc Shop, the latest enterprise to open in the Greenwood Market buildings, abutted the first letter *L* in the mural. "We've seen that to some people our lives don't matter. Sometimes it's sad that they have to be reminded. But if that's what it takes, that's what it takes."[61]

Kitty-corner to the Loc Shop stood a recently opened sneaker store called Silhouette Sneakers & Art, run by black Oklahoma native Venita Cooper. She would welcome customers all day to try on the newest Jordans or purchase a redesigned city flag with its central star replaced by a Black Lives Matter fist. Farther north on the block, Wanda J's Soul Food Restaurant had closed its dining area due to Covid-19 but was still serving pork chops and chicken dinners in takeout boxes.

Just north of the Crosstown Expressway, streetside vendors set up tents where they'd sell jewelry, cosmetics, and art—much of it venerating Black Wall Street—all weekend long.

Outside at the corner of Greenwood and Archer, Nehemiah Frank waited nervously. He had entered into a business partnership with a man he'd never met, Ryan Fitzgibbon, to create the first-ever print edition of the *Black Wall Street Times* for the occasion. Soon he saw Fitzgibbon walking north up Greenwood by the railroad tracks—the same tracks the white mob had crossed before the burning began ninety-nine years before.[62] Fitzgibbon handed Nehemiah the bundle of pristine white newsprint, with simple declarations of black existence— HANDS UP! I CAN'T BREATHE! I AM!—sprawled across the front page.[63] The *Times* suddenly felt more real than it ever had in its four years of digital operation. Nehemiah knelt down next to the massive Black Lives Matter mural and wept.[64]

It was not only an emotional day for locals. Nationally, as protests over the murder of George Floyd spread, Black Wall Street was a commonly invoked symbol of black people's inability to pursue common pleasures that white people take for granted. Trump's announcement galvanized hundreds of African Americans to make the pilgrimage to a mecca of black entrepreneurship. "The callousness with which that officer killed George Floyd, that eight minutes did something to people," said Erik Byrd, who had driven more than twenty hours with a lifelong friend to participate in the Juneteenth festivities and see Greenwood for himself. A native of Los Angeles, Byrd had seen the way violence transforms communities. He had watched the 1965 Watts riots from his roof as an eight-year-old child, and he had participated in the 1992 unrest that followed the acquittal of four Los Angeles Police Department officers who were videotaped beating Rodney King. He said he saw the Floyd protests bringing change faster than the L.A. uprisings did, because of who was involved. "This is the first time I've seen much participation of the white people in the protest," Byrd said. "Everybody has some humanity in them, and I think that's what's bringing out these younger white folks."[65]

Visitors drew power both from the legacy of the local community and from the energy of the current moment. At a free-form art station on Greenwood Avenue, where passersby were encouraged to pick up a piece of chalk and write what they felt, Cherrelle Swain inscribed the phrase "Black Girls Heal" in a declarative font similar to the letters that had transformed the street overnight. "When I started walking down this street in particular, it gave me goosebumps," said Swain, a documentary filmmaker from Washington, D.C. "On the plaque out there, it says $2.7 million that was never recuperated, no reparations. You just think about the generational gaps in wealth between black families and white families. To me, it gives me momentum to make sure that we continue that fight for liberation."[66]

As evening approached, the holiday activities turned explicitly political. For most of the day, President Trump had gone unmentioned. But on a platform in a grassy field flanked by two Jumbotron screens, Al Sharpton strode onto the stage as the marquee speaker of the event. He criticized the president's recent executive order that encouraged but did not mandate police reform. "Come here to Tulsa tomorrow night and announce something concrete or don't say anything at all," Sharpton said to a roaring crowd.[67]

Greg Robinson, in his first major speech as a mayoral candidate, excoriated Bynum, who had turned from a collaborator to a political opponent in a matter of weeks. Bynum would soon welcome the president at the airport, despite the fact that a large indoor rally had high potential to be a super-spreader event for the coronavirus. (The mayor later said that stopping Trump's rally would have required a citywide ban on public events and that delaying it "[was] not in my power.")[68] His handling of Trump's visit became a microcosm of his increasingly tenuous ability to strike a middle ground between Tulsa's opposing sides. "He made a choice to stand with Donald Trump instead of Greenwood," Greg said.[69]

Early on June 20, when Adriana Laws stepped into the lobby of the Ramada just off Route 66, she could feel dozens of pairs of eyes swivel toward her. The college student who had been shadowing Regina Goodwin before the coronavirus wore a black T-shirt that read BLACK LIVES MATTER with a large clenched fist; most of the lobby dwellers wore MAKE AMERICA GREAT AGAIN hats, shirts bearing American flags, and lots and lots of Trump paraphernalia. It felt like she was stepping into foreign territory in her home state. But from the moment Donald Trump had announced he intended to hold his first rally since the onset of the pandemic in Tulsa, on Juneteenth of all weekends, she knew she had to be there.[70]

Trump had galvanized both sides of a city, a state, and a nation that felt like it was in the middle of a fundamental reconstruction. People from across the country had come to Greenwood on Juneteenth to pay homage to the legacy of Black Wall Street. Adriana arrived with a similar righteousness but a different purpose—she felt she had to signal directly to Trump that she didn't agree with his hateful rhetoric, and she wanted to directly confront his followers. As she'd ridden along the empty Turner Turnpike that separates Oklahoma City and Tulsa the night before, she didn't know what that confrontation might look like. She'd brought the statistics and talking points that she hoped could change hearts and minds, but she'd also brought extra ammunition for her 9-millimeter handgun. A litany of death and rape threats online—some anonymous, some not—had put her on edge.[71] The president's violent bluster didn't help. "Any protesters, anarchists, agitators, looters or lowlifes who are going to Oklahoma please understand, you will not be treated like you have been in New York, Seattle, or Minneapolis," Trump tweeted on the morning of Juneteenth. "It will be a much different scene!"[72]

Shortly before noon, Adriana and eighteen-year-old Sincere Terry, a friend she'd arrived with, walked past the MAGA supporters in the lobby and climbed into Sincere's Chevy Malibu. Adriana pulled out her cell phone and started playing "Fuck Donald Trump" by YG and Nipsey Hussle as they pulled onto the interstate and Tulsa's downtown skyline came into view. They soon parked as close as they could to the BOK Center, where Trump would be speaking that evening. Though the president wasn't scheduled to arrive for several hours, the sidewalks were already filling with navy blue flags and bright red hats.[73]

Adriana and Sincere began searching for fellow protesters. They came across a small group from Oklahoma City, then picked up a set of rental scooters and began cruising through the streets, surveying the scene and looking for a demonstration they could join. That's when Adriana noticed a man wearing a bright red shirt that said, in all caps, WHERE IS THE OUTRAGE WHEN BLACKS MURDER EACH OTHER?[74]

She stopped so abruptly that the person behind her nearly crashed into her. "Our outrage is the same place it is when white people kill each other!" she yelled across the street at the man. She started walking toward him.

The Trump supporter seemed oblivious, as if he had forgotten the provocative question his own shirt was posing. But he was game for an argument. Black people kill each other more than white people, so there was no reason to be getting angry at whites, he said. There is no such thing as "black on black crime," Adriana countered—white people are also mostly responsible for white killings. As they went back and forth, a crowd began to gather around them—Trump backers, Black Lives Matter supporters, and lots of television cameras. Suddenly, Adriana realized, she and Sincere had found the protest. They *were* the protest.[75]

In Greenwood, the goal was to ignore Trump and his followers, not argue with them. The heart of Black Wall Street was less than a mile from the BOK Center, and the arena itself was not far from the site of the old courthouse where the armed altercation over Dick Rowland's life had erupted so many years ago. The idea that 1921 could repeat itself felt all too real. "We want to let everyone know that any counter-Trump protest in the name of black lives, we do not condone that," Tiffany said at a press conference in front of the Greenwood Cultural Center. "We're going to continue to encourage citizens, if this Trump rally persists, that you all stay home and stay away from hate because love is so much stronger."[76]

Rumors swirled all afternoon that Mike Pence, who would be introducing the president at his rally, was planning to visit Greenwood Avenue. The idea that he might leverage Greenwood's history for a photo op roiled community leaders.

But Nehemiah had an idea—why not deny him the photo?[77] After the press conference, Tulsa residents covered the Black Wall Street memorial, which served as the centerpiece for remembrance of the 1921 race massacre, with a large blue tarp. They taped sheets of paper with hand-scrawled demands onto the covering: "$2,719,745.61 of unpaid claims remain UNPAID!" "REPARATIONS NOW!" "THIS IS SACRED GROUND!" The lawn around the memorial was also littered with pro-black slogans. If Pence wouldn't say "Black Lives Matter," the people of Greenwood dared him to take a picture that visually endorsed those words.[78] Tyrance Billingsley, an entrepreneur and North Tulsa native, was one of the young men who physically cast the tarp over the cool black marble of the memorial. "It felt kind of invigorating, taking a stand against the president of the United States like that," he said later, "and protecting my local history."[79]

Tulsa residents covered the Black Wall Street memorial with a tarp ahead of President Trump's visit

Pence, ultimately, did not come to Greenwood. Whether the threat of protest deterred him was unknown, but that small act of resistance had opened up a sense of agency over the area that would serve the community well going forward. "We have given too much," Greg Robinson said that day, sitting under the awning of Vernon AME Church. "We have allowed for our communities to be bastardized. We've allowed for our stories to be bastardized. We've allowed for our oppression to be bastardized. No more." He personally rejected an invitation to meet with Pence, instead spending the afternoon helping to guard Greenwood.[80]

Down the street, at the *Oklahoma Eagle* office, Regina and her uncle Jim were fielding interviews from national media outlets that were giving Tulsa around-the-clock news coverage.[81] Jim, who had recently turned eighty, saw a tragic beauty in the summer of racial reckoning. "The world looked at George Floyd, and they saw a man," he reflected later. "They didn't see a black man. They looked at his humanity. There was outpouring of compassion and empathy."[82]

Regina, ever the pragmatist, remained skeptical about the nation's appetite for institutional change. "I've been living a little bit," she said. "Right now everybody's in this feel-good moment. And folks are donating money to this cause and that cause, and throwing money at the situation. But we're not getting to the systemic issues, the structural issues that are in place, and I don't see anybody addressing that." Her own struggles in the statehouse showed what a tough road that was to walk.

Rather than talking about Trump, she preferred to talk about the Medicaid expansion that Oklahoma voters would be considering at the polls at the end of the month. But when forced to address the president and the specter of violence he'd brought with him to Tulsa, her response was simple: "That is a question for his base. Might take your cameras over there and ask them what they plan to do tonight."[83]

Near the Trump rally, the day got louder and angrier as it dragged on. Police and members of the National Guard had cordoned off several blocks near the BOK Center. A street lined on both sides by Trump tailgate tents—a kind of Trump bazaar—was blocked off by concrete

Donald Trump supporters before his rally in Tulsa

barriers.[84] Around midafternoon, Adriana and Sincere led a large group of protesters through the space, blaring "No Trump! No Pence!" through a bullhorn. They eventually squared off against a group of Trump supporters, led by an older white man carrying a Trump-Pence flag.[85] The mass of people lurched to and fro around the narrow street, the barriers making it impossible to fan out. Within the tight confines of the area, there was no physical space for a neutral observer, let alone rhetorical space.[86]

Trump supporters brandished Confederate flags, FAKE NEWS signs, and middle fingers.[87] They carted a bronze Trump statue through the downtown streets in a small truck and waved an American flag that was emblazoned with an image of the president giving a thumbs-up sign.[88]

It was a day of small spasms of violence, extinguished before they could grow into raging fires. Adriana spent half her time arguing with Trump supporters and the other half breaking up shouting matches that risked devolving to physical blows.[89]

But as the rally drew closer, the number of anti-Trump protesters grew. About an hour before Trump was scheduled to speak, a group of about fifty protesters marched across downtown's Boulder Avenue, wielding three massive sixteen-foot papier-mâché puppets. One represented a police officer with a pig face, another a Klansman wearing a cop badge, and the third was Trump himself, sprouting devil horns and holding an upside-down Bible. Adriana's group cheered the new arrivals when they joined with the larger protest. "Everyone rejoiced, and then kind of ran toward each other in solidarity and union," Yatika Fields, an indigenous Tulsa artist who helped design the puppets, recalled later. "It was the most beautiful thing."[90]

Tyrance spent the entire day in Greenwood, waiting in case something, anything, went wrong. But slowly, the tight ball of tension that had been inside him since Trump first announced he was coming to Tulsa began to loosen its grip.[91] Neither Trump nor Pence was coming to Greenwood. Though the depths of the Trump rally zone felt like hell, shockingly few people had actually come to cheer the president, barely more than six thousand.[92] No troublemakers had wandered over to Greenwood, and no organized MAGA protest seemed headed their way.

Something else was happening too. Black Tulsans were coming out to Greenwood Avenue to enjoy their Juneteenth weekend—not in the ritualized way of watching political speeches and listening to gospel singers as they had on Friday, but in the relaxed, casual, familial way they did every year. Lawn chairs began lining the streets.[93] Young black men popped wheelies on motorcycles up and down the avenue.[94] Soon someone was serving margaritas out of a plastic bag.[95] "Everything went beautiful," Tyrance said.[96]

He, Tiffany, Greg, and several others filed into Vernon AME, Robert Turner's church, to decompress. It felt like a crisis had been narrowly averted. They were standing in the church's kitchen when Turner looked around at them and said with a knowing smile, "I got something real special to show y'all," he said. "First time in the history of Vernon."

They walked outside to the southern side of the church, standing on the patch of grass that had once housed the Stradford Hotel. Turner told everyone to stare down Greenwood Avenue, away from the church. "Keep your eyes straight," he warned.

They waited for what felt like ages but couldn't have been more than sixty seconds. "Look," Turner finally said.

When Tyrance turned around, he couldn't believe it. Taking up nearly the entire southern wall of Greenwood's oldest surviving church were the towering letters of BLACK LIVES MATTER and a massive clenched fist. It was one of those perfect moments. "Everybody was just laughing and joking," Tyrance recalled later. "I was like, 'This is who we are. This is Tulsa.'"[97]

Adriana didn't know exactly what to expect as she and hundreds of other protesters marched toward Greenwood. It had been a long and exhausting day, but predictions of widespread violence had not come to pass. The president's speech had been as disjointed and rambling as ever, and he didn't bother to mention Greenwood or its history.[98] His supporters, seemingly shaken by the low turnout, had thought it better to head home rather than linger all night in the city. A political reporter for ABC would later call Trump's Tulsa rally "the worst day of his entire campaign."[99]

As Adriana walked down Archer, no longer leading the march but simply experiencing it, she heard the song "Savage" by Megan Thee Stallion and Beyoncé blasting out of a group of teenagers' speakers just west of the Greenwood-Archer intersection. The vibe was shifting. As they got closer to Deep Greenwood, the crowd grew thicker, the bass louder.[100]

Just south of the highway overpass on Greenwood Avenue, a man gripping a microphone stood atop a loudspeaker. Next to him, a DJ bobbed his head as his fingers flitted across his console. "Thank you, protesters. You might as well dance your way through," yelled Neil McDonald, the emcee with the microphone. "This is a block party!"[101]

As the protesters wove between honking cars on one of the most historic thoroughfares in America, the DJ blasted Bruno Mars, then "Changes" by Tupac Shakur. All the anxiety of the previous week was deafened by the boom of the speakers, drowned in the slosh of red Solo cups, crushed by buoyant feet that danced across the pavement for hours and hours. "It was just such good energy. So wholesome," Adriana recalled. "That was just such a perfect, peaceful, ideal night."

The impromptu celebration unfolded beneath the overpass that had divided Greenwood more than fifty years before. On one side, new businesses like Silhouette and the Loc Shop were exposed to a crush of customers due to the international attention on Tulsa. On the other side, the Black Power fist projected on the wall of Vernon AME seemed to be lighting up every inch of the neighborhood. If one strand of history was fading with the small turnout at Trump's rally, another was shining brighter than ever.[102]

The block party raged on long into the night, but Tyrance, Greg, Tiffany, and many others were dead tired from such a harrowing week. Still, they carried a different kind of energy inside them. As Tyrance and Greg walked from Greenwood to a nearby street to hail an Uber, they allowed themselves to dream—really dream—about Greg as the leader of Tulsa. Mayor Robinson. He'd take the coronavirus more seriously, introduce the police reforms Mayor Bynum claimed to advocate for, and begin the work of building a pathway to reparations for massacre victims—those few who yet lived, and their legion of descendants, who were defending Greenwood's soul that

*Black Lives Matter is projected on the side of Vernon AME
Church as a fleet of Cadillacs line Greenwood Avenue*

very night. "We were excited about how different we could govern if
we got in there," Tyrance said.[103]

The two took a ride to the house of Vanessa Hall-Harper, the city
councilor, where many local political movements had been hashed
out over beer and brisket.[104] The living room television was turned to
CNN, and they saw the scene they had just left: hundreds of people
dancing, smiling, celebrating Juneteenth with a spotlight they had
never before had. "We were just there drinking, eating our food, and
chilling," Tyrance said later. "I remember Greg posted, 'Greenwood
has risen.' And I posted, 'This is our time.'"[105]

CHAPTER 24

DISSOLUTION

The Oklahoma Eagle *office and the new Greenwood Rising history center sit side by side in Deep Greenwood*

wo months after the Greenwood block party, on a cleared-out patch of dirt next to the *Oklahoma Eagle* office, a crowd of seventy-five people gathered in a massive tent under the baking August sun to witness the groundbreaking for Greenwood Rising, Tulsa's largest and most expensive effort ever to commemorate the race massacre.[1]

The lot would soon hold a $19 million facility that promised to feature rare historical artifacts and a model Greenwood barbershop with period-appropriate hologram stylists.[2] The eleven-thousand-square-foot history center would be wedged between the *Eagle* headquarters and a new five-story office building called 21 North Greenwood, under construction at the same time.[3] The Hille Foundation, another Tulsa nonprofit whose heritage tracked back to oil riches, was building 21 North Greenwood to accompany its GreenArch apartment complex, both of which loomed larger over the neighborhood than Loula Williams' three-story office building ever had.

A fence separating Greenwood Rising and 21 North Greenwood advertised class A office, restaurant, and retail space in the new highrise, which the Hille Foundation promised would "bring professional services back to the historic Greenwood District" (an overwhelmingly white law firm would soon be named as the first major tenant). The commercial space in the office building would soon abut brutal depictions of violence and racial terror in the history center. Every year the streets of Deep Greenwood had to serve more and more agendas. But the landscape itself revealed priorities better than any ceremony could; when Greenwood Rising was complete, the *Oklahoma Eagle* office would quite literally be in its shadow.

As the centennial of Tulsa's darkest day approached, city and state leaders knew they needed to prepare for an onslaught of national attention, as well as potential scrutiny. Greenwood Rising was the centerpiece of their plan. The history center was the primary project of the 1921 Tulsa Race Massacre Centennial Commission, a government-backed organization whose mission was to educate the public about Greenwood and make the neighborhood a nexus of "heritage tourism" to spark economic growth.[4] The idea for the commission was first pitched by state senator Kevin Matthews. He saw entrepreneurship as key to reviving Greenwood's former success and believed luring tourists would help small businesses there thrive.[5]

But many figures in Tulsa more powerful than Matthews were also keen on the idea of "heritage tourism" for their own interests. From the very beginning, George Kaiser's twin philanthropic ventures, the George Kaiser Family Foundation and the Tulsa Community Foundation, played an instrumental role in shaping the centennial commission and Greenwood Rising. The Kaiser Family Foundation had already spearheaded the creation of downtown museums dedicated to folk singers Woody Guthrie and Bob Dylan in recent years; a Greenwood museum would continue to build the city's tourism engine. Ken Levit, the executive director of the George Kaiser Family Foundation, was an inaugural member of the centennial commission's board.[6] Another high-ranking GKFF staffer led the commission's capital campaign.[7] In 2020, when plans to house the history center on the property of the

Greenwood Cultural Center fell through, the Hille Foundation donated a small piece of the land parcel for their office building to serve as a new, more high-profile site for the museum.[8] The Tulsa Community Foundation then entered into a development agreement with the Hille Foundation to construct the new center, utilizing funds raised in the capital campaign (Tulsa Community Foundation president Phil Lakin said in an email interview that the Foundation has never owned the Greenwood Rising property and that after being incubated with help from the Foundation, Greenwood Rising became "self-sustaining and independent"; the history center registered as its own federally tax-exempt nonprofit before opening).[9]

Thanks to the Kaiser Foundation's powerful fundraising machine, the centennial commission was able to raise more than $30 million in less than three years, including donations of $250,000 or more from Boeing, JPMorgan Chase, and Bank of America.[10] The state legislature also allocated $1.5 million to support the commission's work.[11] It was the largest sum of money ever amassed in response to the massacre, dwarfing the $25,000 ($380,000 in 2021 dollars) that white city leaders raised in their meager fundraising campaign as Greenwood still smoldered in 1921. But the commission's plans for how to allocate the money proved controversial. While approximately $1 million of the money raised was pledged to aid black business development, and smaller sums were handed out to a few legacy Greenwood institutions like the Vernon AME Church, most of the money was poured into building Greenwood Rising.[12] And while the organization's rhetoric was lofty—"dedicated to a vision of a stronger and more just Tulsa"—it did not directly advocate for reparations for massacre survivors and descendants.[13]

Phil Armstrong, who served as the first executive director of Greenwood Rising, said he personally supported reparations but that it was not the role of a history center to engage in direct political advocacy. He argued that by telling the true story of Greenwood and the massacre in an accessible way, Greenwood Rising could be part of a hearts-and-minds campaign to get more people personally invested in the community's quest for restitution. "It will organically build an incredible coalition of people from all over the world to put pressure and say, 'Tulsa, what the hell have you been doing for the last twenty years? You owe this to these people. Do it.'"[14]

But some members of the new commission explicitly opposed reparations, including Mayor Bynum. Shortly before the centennial, he told the *Tulsa World*, "Direct cash payments do not solve problems of inequity in this city."[15] George Kaiser, who was not a member of the centennial commission but employed people who were, told *Air Mail* that he believed in reparations in the "broader sense" for people denied equal opportunity, but not "just to compensate for one unspeakably evil event."[16]

This stance was at odds with an earlier commission on the massacre that had been backed by the state government. In the 1990s, Greenwood legislators Don Ross and Maxine Horner organized the Tulsa Race Riot Commission, which was much more aggressive in its calls for justice. The group issued a two-hundred-page report outlining all the known facts about the massacre, which forced state and city officials to formally acknowledge the role their agencies played in the neighborhood's destruction. The earlier commission also recommended reparations in a variety of forms, including scholarships for massacre descendants and direct cash payments for survivors.[17]

Armstrong said the centennial commission's remit never included exploring reparations because it did not want to retrace the steps that had already been taken in the 1990s and early 2000s. But the disconnect between the old commission and the new one rankled many in Greenwood with long memories, including Regina Goodwin. "The profits that come from that, they're really not considering the descendants," she said.[18] Though Regina was named a member of the commission when it launched, she stopped attending meetings as she grasped the commission's direction and resigned in early 2020 before the groundbreaking ceremony.[19]

On hand for the event, though, were many of the people who were gaining more and more control over Greenwood's land, as well as its narrative. One by one, they stepped up to the podium to talk about what a powerful symbol Greenwood Rising would soon become.

"Not only did black lives matter in Greenwood then, but they will matter always," said Maggie Yar, a board member of the Hille Foundation, the nonprofit that helped finance the GreenArch development shortly after the construction of the baseball stadium.[20] She was also a member of the centennial commission's steering committee, as well as a board member for the upcoming history center.[21] Her husband

Kajeer Yar was developing the office complex right behind the new structure.[22]

"This has to be about the people that were impacted," Mayor Bynum said. "About being able to tell their stories, to do right by them, to honor them."[23] Though he referred to unnamed attackers murdering Greenwood residents and the dangers of "hate," he failed to acknowledge that his predecessor, Mayor T. D. Evans, helped lead the effort to seize black-owned land from Greenwood residents after the massacre.[24]

"We're going to tell the world this story," said Matt Pinnell, Oklahoma's lieutenant governor and the secretary of tourism in the state. He did not mention that in the days after the massacre, the governor specifically declined to offer aid to victims. But he was clear in his assessment of the money to be made in Greenwood one hundred years later. "It will be one of the premier locations in this country," Pinnell said, "and one of the foundational blocks of the tourism department in the state of Oklahoma when it is built."[25]

Black history was becoming big business—bigger than anything survivors like Mabel Little and Ed Goodwin, Sr., could have envisioned when they told their story to curious academics in the 1970s. Greenwood and Black Wall Street had transformed into totems of inspiration for millions of black Americans, but they also became effective marketing slogans. In 2020 a Stradford & Smitherman clothing line was launched in Tulsa, but it wasn't owned by the two families' descendants.[26] In Atlanta, a new online bank fronted by the rapper Killer Mike adopted the name Greenwood without adopting a physical presence in the neighborhood.[27] Greenwood was no longer just a place—it was a brand.

The people who most acutely felt this tension between commemoration and commercialization were the descendants of the neighborhood's most ardent teacher of its history: W. D. Williams.

In October 2019, months before Trump's arrival in Tulsa, HBO exposed millions of people to the story of the race massacre for the first time through its sci-fi television show Watchmen. The reboot of Alan Moore's iconic graphic novel, created by television auteur Damon Lindelof, had been kept tightly under wraps during its two years of production in order to preserve the shock of its grand reveal: instead of being set in New York, like the original story, the new *Watchmen* took place in a Tulsa shrouded in the century-long shadow of the race massacre. And it opened with a seven-minute reenactment of the brutal attack itself, anchored by a black family who owned a Greenwood movie theater called the Dreamland.

Marilyn Christopher, a granddaughter of W. D. Williams, tuned in to the *Watchmen* premiere expecting to be transported by a sci-fi yarn—she'd grown up devouring *Star Wars* and Robert Heinlein novels in North Tulsa. But she instantly recognized the broken theater marquee, the neighborhood on fire, and the boy caught amid the chaos on her television set. Marilyn watched as anonymous black people, their faces barely visible, were gunned down by airplanes and shot in the back as they tried to escape a white mob. The destruction of her hometown had never been brought to life on screen with such gruesome glamour. *That's Tulsa,* she thought. *That could be my grandfather. That's the Tulsa race riot!*[28]

W.D.'s full name was William Danforth Williams—the *Watchmen* boy went by Will Williams, though he changes his last name to Reeves later in the series. As the people on TV fled for their lives, Marilyn saw another of her family's businesses flash on the screen: Williams Auto Repair, which John Williams had owned a century before. The biographies of the real Williams and the on-screen family diverged in key places—the boy on the show was younger than W.D., and his father, unlike John Williams, was a war veteran—but the similarities were stark. Even some of the sequence's smallest details, like a brief shot of a white man brandishing a stolen leopard coat, appeared to be taken from oral histories that had traveled from W.D.'s lips to academic books to popular culture.[29]

It was all a little too real. After the opening spectacle, Marilyn turned the show off and had little motivation to revisit it. "Once I saw dead black bodies, I said, 'I don't want to watch this,'" she recalled later. "I know that I should appreciate this, but I guess I didn't."[30]

Watchmen went on to be viewed by eight million people and to win eleven Emmy Awards, including the award for Outstanding Limited Series.[31] Implicit in the widespread praise for the show was the righteousness of its mission in bringing a long-buried story of racial terrorism to a wide audience. "I have a pretty large megaphone that these people [HBO] are willing to give me," Lindelof recalled thinking as he first developed the show. "Maybe I can use popular culture as a way of transmitting the Tulsa massacre in a way that it will stick."[32]

But Lindelof and his team did not reach out to the descendants of Loula and W. D. Williams, or of any other families, before lifting elements of their legacies to translate them into a sci-fi fantasy. When he and his writing team decided to tell the story of the massacre through the eyes of a single family, the couple onscreen were composite characters whose backstories melded details from John and Loula, the Greenwood entrepreneur O. B. Mann, and other Black Wall Street historical figures. The writers decided that the Williams Dreamland Theatre's marquee should be presented exactly as it had existed historically, in order to lend the scene more authenticity.

"If we actually felt like we were using the family as those characters, the real Williams family, then it would have been incumbent upon us to reach out and include them," Lindelof said. "It didn't feel like it was appropriation. It felt like we were telling history."[33]

But that history rang hollow to some of John, Loula, and W.D.'s descendants. Jan Christopher, Marilyn's younger sister, didn't like how the show leveraged the Williams family's story through their businesses without making her ancestors into fully developed characters. The approach showed an interest in telling "their story in our place, not our story in our place," she said. "Loula Williams should be a character in Black history. They should probably go ahead and talk to us and actually incorporate her as a real figure instead of trying to get around it just by what they're seeing on the Internet."[34]

However positive Lindelof's creative intentions, *Watchmen* was as much commerce as art, a big-budget product of HBO, a subsidiary of Warner Media and the telecom giant AT&T. While entertainment conglomerates ferociously guard their intellectual property (the characters in HBO's *Watchmen* will be protected by copyright for generations), regular people are often told that seeing their stories come to light should be payment enough. And when money does flow, it tends to go to institutions rather than to individuals. Lindelof and HBO both made donations to Greenwood Rising after *Watchmen* premiered.[35] Black people are always expected to welcome an ever-expanding tent of newcomers to learn about their triumphs and traumas, even if they're not earning a dime for having their stories reproduced as mass entertainment.

For people who have lived with the weight of what happened in Greenwood for generations, though, it can be frustrating to watch ancestors they knew and admired seep into the public consciousness as silhouettes of their actual selves. "Our legacy—I don't think it's perceived as something that's ours," Marilyn said. "If you have passion and a desire to share and illuminate this point of time in history, that can be taken advantage of, if you're not careful."[36]

On the ground in Tulsa, Greenwood leaders were trying to channel the national attention on their neighborhood, sparked by *Watchmen* and Trump's visit, into momentum for change. Greg Robinson's mayoral campaign began with a burst of enthusiasm, quickly amassing a volunteer base of thirteen hundred people and raising nearly $250,000 in campaign funds, including more than two thousand small donations of fifty dollars or less.[37] Greenwood Avenue saw an uptick in visitors as people came to take photos against the backdrop of the vibrant Black Lives Matter mural.[38] Regina began planning a new slate of criminal justice reform bills, which she hoped would be buoyed by the national focus on the problems with policing.[39]

But at the same time, a national backlash to the George Floyd protests was brewing, and it would be expressed especially virulently in Oklahoma.

In the August mayoral race, Greg lost with 29 percent of the vote, just shy of the share needed to knock Bynum below 50 percent and force a runoff. Though he won the mostly black North Tulsa precincts and even managed to claim much of Tulsa's young, mostly white downtown core, his lack of experience as an elected leader hurt him, and the complications caused by the pandemic made it harder to persuade skeptical voters with face-to-face canvassing.[40] His campaign platform went far beyond police reform—he wanted to introduce a participatory budget, a process that allows citizens to devise plans for allocating a portion of the city's annual funds.[41] Under his plan, residents would have more of a say over their own communities than they ever had in the days of Model Cities. He also supported reparations for massacre victims, saying that survivors and descendants must be given the opportunity to determine the appropriate form of recompense. "I'm not going to sit here and tell someone else what justice looks like for them," Greg said. "What this is about is providing justice to people who have not had any."[42]

Bynum preferred placing citizens on advisory councils rather than giving them direct authority.[43] He pitched himself as the "CEO of one of the largest organizations in Tulsa" and indeed had the support of most of the city's business class, including the executive director of the George Kaiser Family Foundation. (Bynum had been a congressional lobbyist for the foundation before entering politics.)[44] Bynum's campaign ultimately outspent Greg's two to one.[45] After his victory, he stopped talking about his commitment to installing an office of the independent monitor to oversee the Tulsa Police Department.[46] Instead, he vowed to work on improving his relationships with Republican voters rather than focusing on Democrats and independents.[47]

Before dawn one morning, a few weeks after the election, a city grounds crew arrived on Greenwood Avenue to remove the Black Lives Matter mural.[48] The city viewed the unauthorized street art as a point of controversy, though business owners in Greenwood expressed admiration for it. The issue came to a head when the chair of the Tulsa County Republican Party, along with members of a pro-police Facebook group, said that they wanted to paint a Back the Blue mural just south of where President Trump had held his rally, as a rejoinder to the mural on Greenwood Avenue. Rather than picking a side, the city council decided to wash the street clean. Other cities preserved their Black Lives Matter murals by endorsing the art as government-backed speech, but a Tulsa city councilor warned that such an action would be the same as endorsing a "criminal offense." Tori Tyson, a business owner on Greenwood, watched from her beauty salon as the yellow-specked gravel of the mural was poured into a dump truck. "I was not surprised in Tulsa but hurt, because the world is watching us," Tyson said later. "It's embarrassing." Tulsa became the first major city to wipe the words *Black Lives Matter* from its memory.[49]

Despite these setbacks, Greenwood leaders were still devising new strategies to pull the levers of government to serve their needs. At a September press conference inside the Greenwood Cultural Center, local attorney Damario Solomon-Simmons announced that he was filing a lawsuit on behalf of massacre survivors and descendants.[50] The new lawsuit charged the city of Tulsa, the chamber of commerce, the Tulsa County sheriff, and several other government agencies with exacerbating "the damage and suffering of the Greenwood residents" in the days, years, and decades after the massacre. Among the plaintiffs were descendants of J. B. Stradford, A. J. Smitherman, and Dick Rowland, along with a small handful of massacre survivors who were still living.[51] "We must have repair. We must have reparations. And we must have respect," Solomon-Simmons said.[52]

Solomon-Simmons was a North Tulsa native who had served as a law clerk on the legal team for the failed reparations lawsuit in the early 2000s.[53] He'd been inspired to revisit the effort around the time that Congress held a 2019 hearing on HR 40, a long-standing bill that sought to establish a commission to study the impacts of slavery and racial discrimination across the United States.[54] One of the attorneys from the first Greenwood case, Eric Miller, had appeared at the hearing, and both he and the writer Ta-Nehisi Coates had invoked Black Wall Street during their testimony.[55] Solomon-Simmons knew there would likely never be a better time to make one more big push for justice in Tulsa. The limited time the survivors had left gave urgency to his cause—one planned plaintiff on the suit, Hal Singer, died at the age of one hundred just days before the case was filed.[56]

Solomon-Simmons and his legal team were testing a novel use of Oklahoma's public nuisance law, which states that a business or government entity can be held liable for actions that endanger the health or safety of a community. Critically, the law puts no time limit on bringing a suit against a public nuisance, as long as the nuisance is ongoing.[57] An Oklahoma court had recently ruled that Johnson & Johnson caused a public nuisance due to its deceptive marketing of opioids, which contributed to an ongoing crisis in the state.[58] Solomon-Simmons saw parallels to what had happened in Greenwood; he often compared the city's actions to the type of corporate malfeasance that wrecked natural environments, like an oil spill.[59]

The lawsuit went far beyond the impacts of the massacre itself. It included the Tulsa Development Authority (previously the Tulsa Urban Renewal Authority) as a defendant, arguing that its urban renewal policies led to "further fragmentation of the Greenwood community" and deepened wealth, educational, and health divides between

North and South Tulsa. The suit also took a hard stance against the organizational structure of Greenwood Rising. The plaintiffs alleged that the city was enriching itself by leveraging Greenwood's history for tourism dollars without sharing the bounty with massacre survivors and their descendants. Solomon-Simmons requested a court injunction that would prevent the city from using massacre victims' likenesses in promotions or earning revenue from Greenwood Rising without paying victims' descendants or placing money in a group compensation fund.

"The problem is not that the Defendants want to increase the attraction to Tulsa," the suit claimed. "It is that they are doing so on the backs of the people they destroyed."[60]

In October 2020, Regina hosted a legislative hearing on policing, explaining to her fellow lawmakers how criminal justice reform would curb police transgressions against black and brown Oklahomans. Tiffany Crutcher and former Tulsa police chief Drew Diamond, the rare high-level police official who supported large-scale reforms, were among the featured speakers, showing that people both inside and outside police departments could advocate for change.[61] But for the next legislative session, Republicans had a very different political agenda in mind. When Regina returned to the capitol at the start of 2021, she found herself trying to stave off a wide-ranging GOP effort to ensure that protests like the ones in 2020 would never happen again.

One controversial Republican bill made obstructing a highway during a protest punishable by up to a year in jail. Even more alarmingly, it granted motorists permission to run over and kill pedestrians while "fleeing from a riot." (The bill essentially made the 1910 riot law that had been used to charge J. B. Stradford and A. J. Smitherman in 1921 even more punitive.)[62] "It's these kind of bills that encourage folks to go ahead and take their cars and plow through the crowd," Regina said on the House floor.[63]

Soon after the protest bill came HB 1775, which sought to control how schools teach lessons about race and history. The bill, introduced by Republican Kevin West, banned schools from teaching that any race was superior to another, or that any individual was "inher-

Regina deliberates on the floor of the Oklahoma House of Representatives

ently racist, sexist or oppressive" due to their race. It also stipulated that students should not be made to feel discomfort or guilt over their race or sex, but it didn't specify who got to determine what qualified as "discomfort."[64] While the bill's language was race-neutral, and its white author at one point claimed to be "multicultural," its intent was made clear in deliberations on the House floor. "Under the current swing of the pendulum, I would be made to feel guilty for things that had happened in the past," West argued.[65]

While the bill was couched in terms of protecting the emotional state of children, it was as much about preserving key American myths: that people begin life on an equal playing field and that the nation's past shouldn't define its present. But Regina challenged these myths directly; if any state should be having a reckoning with its past, it was Oklahoma. "Do you understand that while you say you don't need to be held accountable, while you say you don't need to feel guilty, do you understand that you are a beneficiary of racism?" she asked West during a round of pointed questioning. "Hundreds of years later, as you stand here today on the floor, claiming that you're not a white man, which I imagine you might have put that on your census, do you understand that you're a beneficiary? That that's why there's a difference in median income, there's a difference in job employment, there's a difference in health care?"

"What I do understand is that with this language, an individual would not be made to feel personally responsible for these actions that had happened before," West insisted.[66] The bill passed easily along party lines. The ACLU, which sued to block the law on free speech grounds, warned of a chilling effect on what teachers would feel comfortable saying in the classroom.[67] Some Oklahoma educators spoke of fears of getting fired for doing their jobs. Similar bills, generally grouped together as a rebuke of "critical race theory," soon passed in more than fifteen states.[68] These laws were used around the country to ban books in schools about police brutality, homosexuality, and the Holocaust.[69]

With many Oklahoma Republicans pursuing increasingly radical politics, the vision of bipartisan reconciliation advanced by the centennial commission began to look more like a fantasy. Oklahoma governor Kevin Stitt was removed from the commission on May 14 and Republican senator James Lankford resigned two weeks later, as controversies surrounding critical race theory and the U.S. Capitol riots of January 6, 2021, swirled. (Lankford was challenging the 2020 election results at the Senate dais at the moment the mob breached the Capitol.)[70] As the hundred-year anniversary of the race massacre inched closer, Tulsa's favorite catchphrase—"reconciliation"—seemed ever more distant. While a full-page ad in *USA Today* claimed Tulsa was "leading America's journey in racial healing," the city's shaky projection of unity was cracking apart in public.[71]

But no matter how disjointed Tulsa's politics had become, the centennial would arrive all the same. Amid a deeply fractured political environment, thousands of massacre descendants and others with ties to Tulsa would soon begin arriving in the city. The families of Greenwood would be forced to find meaning and community not through formal government support or televised commemorations but the way they always had: together.

CHAPTER 25

THE RITUALS OF REMEMBRANCE

Jars of soil collected in Greenwood represent the unknown black residents who were murdered during the massacre

On the afternoon of May 27, 2021, the *Oklahoma Eagle*'s small staff was racing to meet its weekly print deadline for the most important issue of the year. Jim Goodwin's son David, his daughter Jeanne-Marguerite, and page designer Sam Levrault could no longer measure how long they'd been laying out spreads, brainstorming headlines, and writing captions. As they gathered on a group video call, they were finally reviewing the last proofs of the paper's three-section special edition, set to welcome visitors to the city for the somber weekend of the massacre centennial.

The *Oklahoma Eagle*'s origin story was bound up in what had transpired in Greenwood one hundred years before. Theodore Baughman, the newspaper's founding publisher, had been a managing editor at A. J. Smitherman's *Tulsa Star* before 1921 and had just launched his own black newspaper when Greenwood was destroyed. The mas-

sacre upended both men's plans. Smitherman was forced to flee the
state as a fugitive, while Baughman picked up his former boss's mantle. In those first days after the attack, he posted vital updates about
missing persons at the Red Cross headquarters. By August, Greenwood once again had a print newspaper.[1] "The *Oklahoma Eagle* was
born in a tent," a Baughman obituary later proclaimed.[2]

"There's no jubilation to celebrate your beginning when it came
at such a horrific chapter in humanity," David said. "The best way,
we thought, was to revisit the narratives that told the race massacre
story."[3]

While Jeanne-Marguerite and Sam were working from Tulsa,
David was at his home office in Liberty Township, a suburb of Cincinnati, where he squeezed in editing duties at the *Eagle* around his full-
time job as an editor for a chain of Ohio newspapers. Like everyone
else in the Goodwin family, he had grown up immersed in the world
of the *Eagle*—spending afternoons in the office after school, writing
articles for the front page, and of course, managing his very own
paper route. "The paper needs me, and I need it," he once wrote as a
teenager.[4] But he had come of age not in Greenwood's midcentury
heyday, as his parents had, but in its nadir, when the *Eagle* was the
only business left in the old business district and black newspapers
around the country were struggling to adapt to a newly desegregated
world. When David decided to become a professional journalist, he
started comparing the *Eagle* to other, larger papers around the country. His ambition colored his view of what his family had built. In a
college essay, he critiqued the *Eagle* harshly, saying that the newspaper lacked quality photographs, was saddled with "lazy" writing, and
relied too much on articles submitted by readers. "Hopefully this
paper will get its act together before it is too late," the young David
warned.[5]

"My position of course was one of arrogance," he said, looking
back. He didn't know what he or his neighborhood really had back
then—a dedicated team of reporters covering the community day in
and day out for little pay, and a space for everyday people to have
their voices heard. "Right in my face was a good example of solid
journalism," he said. "Our narrative is being written every single
day."[6]

The *Eagle* had struggled in the decades since David left Tulsa. Two bankruptcies in the 1990s and early 2000s led to the newspaper nearly being bought out. Like many other publications, it was slow to adapt to the rise of digital media. But the centennial and the onslaught of national attention on Greenwood was raising the *Eagle*'s profile. The Oklahoma Historical Society sought to digitize its archives so they could be used for academic study.[7] The insurance company Liberty Mutual sponsored a ten-part feature series on the history of Greenwood in the *Eagle*'s pages.[8] The paper was also in the midst of redesigning its print edition, revamping its website, and expanding its multimedia presence. "People still believe that there's value in what the *Eagle* stands for," David said. New readers were regularly emailing him out of the blue from different corners of the country, asking how to buy a subscription.[9]

Around three p.m. the team submitted the last of the issue's pages to their printer. Jeanne-Marguerite was exhausted, having stayed up until 3:30 a.m. the previous night editing, then waking up at five to continue the work. She was the fourth of Jim's children to take on a leadership role at the paper, but she had always been the least likely candidate. As a child in a newspaper family, she had avoided journalism as best she could, feeling intimidated by her relatives' writing skills. In college, she majored in electrical engineering specifically because it was so far afield of the news business, then got a job as a patent consultant in Washington, D.C. "I told my dad today I didn't even know how to spell engineering when I applied," she said on the drive to the printer. But she too was eventually pulled back home to the *Eagle*. Her formal title was editor, but she was also the receptionist, the ad manager, the newspaper distributor, and on certain days, the janitor.[10]

The race massacre centennial edition of the Oklahoma Eagle *is printed in May 2021*

By the time Jeanne-Marguerite arrived at the printer just outside Tulsa, the first section of the paper had already come off the press. Endless copies of the *Eagle* were stacked on metal carts, wooden tables, and giant rolls of newsprint shaped like hay bales. She started rifling through an issue, looking for errors in the color images, and with some help from the printing press staff, she began tucking the B and C sections inside the front section by hand, just as she and all her siblings and cousins had done when they were children.

The next morning Jeanne took some copies to the post office to mail to subscribers. Others went to the last remaining barbershop in Deep Greenwood, or the barbecue spot farther north, places that continued to sell the *Eagle* on newsstands every week.[11] Thousands of copies would soon be handed out on the streets of Greenwood to the large crowds who were beginning to stream into town. The sticker price of each issue was $1, but most people would get this special edition for free. "We didn't hang on to the paper for money," Jeanne-Marguerite said. "Speaking the truth is more important than making a dollar."[12]

The cover of the special centennial section was a full-page image of a rickety elevator, like the one Dick Rowland and Sarah Page had shared a century before.[13] Inside, readers would find a reprint of the 1971 *Oklahoma Impact Magazine* article that had first laid out the details of the massacre in brutal terms.[14] To highlight the community's resilience, the *Eagle* also reprinted the article from its 1950 special edition that outlined the efforts of J. H. Goodwin and the Colored Citizens' Relief Committee to defend the neighborhood's land.[15]

The issue, though, was not only about Greenwood's past. On the opinion page, an editorial called for continued efforts at police reform a year after George Floyd's murder.[16] In the news section, Kavin Ross, son of former state legislator and *Eagle* editor Don Ross, gave an update on a city-sponsored search for mass graves of massacre victims.[17] And just as it had since its earliest days, the *Eagle* published a list of church items in its back pages.[18] Collectively, these calls for justice, historic chronicles, and helpful daily information formed the heartbeat of a community that sought justice but also connection— a place that deserved it.

Above the newspaper's nameplate was the same slogan Ed Goodwin, Sr., had appended to the *Eagle*'s front page more than eighty years before: "We Make America Better When We Aid Our People."[19]

"Every week, we put it on," David said of the tagline. "That's why people come to the *Eagle*. Because we have a soul."[20]

Instead of fire, May 31, 2021, threatened rain. The morning began dour and gray, but a burst of color in Greenwood punctured the gloom that had settled over Tulsa. At the base of Standpipe Hill, where the National Guard had trained a machine gun down on the neighborhood a century earlier, one thousand flowers were arranged in a twelve-foot-tall archway, flanked by two hedges just as lush with cream-colored garden roses and pink peonies. Standpipe Hill was usually a desolate and unsettling landmark, where young black children were long warned not to play in the years before Greenwood's buried past was excavated with plaques and landmarks. But the blossoms were quietly restorative.[21]

One hundred years before, when the temperature reached well above eighty degrees, the roses would have wilted, and the leaves would have grown raw and brittle under the burning sun. But the moisture that suffused the air cradled the petals in a nourishing hydrochamber. They grew strong in the mist; they thrived in a world that looked inhospitable. The Wild Mother, the black-owned floral company that had trimmed and arranged every bloom, called the installation "The Covering."[22]

"You are standing on sacred ground. Take in the energy of this space," said Kristi Williams, chair of the Greater Tulsa African American Affairs Commission. She stood at a podium beneath the grand archway, surrounded by roughly one hundred people. A few sat in simple folding chairs, while more crowded shoulder to shoulder behind them. Others dotted the infamous hill behind the flowers that stretched up toward the gray sky.[23]

Kristi was a massacre descendant. Her great-aunt Janie had been enjoying a movie at the Dreamland Theatre when news of the trouble at the courthouse first reached Greenwood.[24] "I also call this the valley of the dry bones, and these bones have been speaking out for a very long time," Kristi said. "Today, we're going to honor them."[25]

In front of The Covering was a long table dotted with pink roses the size of clementines, arranged around five empty glass jars. Each was emblazoned with the same words:

Unknown

Tulsa, Oklahoma
May 31–June 1, 1921

After Kristi's introduction, a man in flowing white robes approached the podium. He had sharp eyes and a big warm smile. Chief Egunwale Amusan, like Kristi, was a massacre descendant. For decades he had been spearheading the Black Wall Street Memorial March through the streets of Greenwood, honoring massacre survivors and descendants long before the city did much to mark the anniversary. "This is a sacred mound where those who should have never been left behind were left behind," Chief said as his eyes scanned the crowd. "Those whose names were forgotten, those whose blood fertilizes this very hill we stand on."

Chief Egunwale Amusan at the soil collection ceremony on the centennial of the race massacre

Iba Se Egungun, Chief said in Yoruba, a West African language. "Honor and praise to the ancestors."[26]

Beneath the empty jars were two flower beds filled with rich soil. Soon the gathered crowd would fill the jars, handful by handful. For two years, the Tulsa Community Remembrance Coalition, a group of about a dozen community members organized by Tiffany Crutcher, had been conducting soil collection ceremonies around Greenwood at sites where black people were killed during the massacre. The ritual was modeled after a program launched by the Equal Justice Initiative to collect soil samples from lynching sites across the United States.[27] Local high school students, church members, and everyday citizens had been invited to participate in ceremonies outside Vernon AME Church and on the very ground where Greenwood Rising was being built.[28] But today's ceremony would be different. This was the first time participants would include some of the massacre's survivors.

Viola Ford Fletcher and Hughes Van Ellis—often referred to in Tulsa as Mother Fletcher and Uncle Red—sat in the front row before The Covering. They were two of three known massacre survivors, along with Lessie Benningfield Randle, still living one hundred years after the attack. Van Ellis, 100, had been a newborn baby in May 1921, but Fletcher, 106, could remember more details than she'd like. She still recalled being woken up by her parents in the middle of the night in their modest home on the northern edge of Greenwood. After someone warned everyone to get out of town because black people were being killed in the streets, she and her five siblings, including her younger brother Van Ellis, were shuttled out of town by their parents on a covered wagon. They relocated to the nearby town of Claremore, leaving all their belongings to be burned or stolen.[29] Fletcher said she saw neighbors' bodies in the streets, smelled the smoke pouring from burning houses, and heard the roar of airplanes overhead.[30] She never slept quite as soundly afterward. "It kind of still bothers me," she said in an interview a few days before the centennial. "Seems like when I can't go to sleep, that comes across my mind."[31]

Relatives carefully pushed Fletcher and Van Ellis in their wheelchairs up to the flower beds. Each grasped a spade filled with soil. Tiffany tilted the jars so they could reach. After the survivors had completed the ritual, Tiffany returned to the podium and looked out over the large audience, the biggest they'd ever had for a soil collection ceremony. "If everyone would come and partake and put your hands in the soil," she said. "Help us collect the soil from the very ground our ancestors were lynched. Everyone, just come."[32]

As they lined up, one by one, to fill the jars, a drum circle behind The Covering began playing a soothing rhythm. Some people plunged the spades deep into the soft soil. Others cupped their hands together and dived forward into the earth, then were careful to dust every grain of soil from their fingers into an open jar. People of all ages and all races joined together in a way that Tulsans rarely do.

It was not just a local moment but a national one. Sheila Jackson Lee, a congresswoman from Houston, made the trip to Tulsa for the centennial. She had sponsored the major reparations bill HR 40 in Congress.[33] "Do not deny us, do not diminish us, do not leave us," she intoned after the soil collection was complete. During her speech, she looked over at Regina Goodwin, who was standing in the front of the crowd. "Listen to the stories told by Representative Goodwin's family newspaper. Because they hold the stories unheard."[34]

After Lee returned to her seat, a towering black man in a crisp blue military uniform approached the podium. The badges dotting his coat were the brightest objects on the scene besides the flowers. Michael Thompson was the first black adjutant general of the National Guard in the history of Oklahoma. One hundred years before, his predecessor, Adjutant General Charles F. Barrett, had arrived in Tulsa at about nine a.m. on June 1, after much of Greenwood had been burned and some members of the National Guard, by their own admission, had fired on Greenwood residents protecting their neighborhood.

Thompson spoke of how inspired he'd been to see Mother Fletcher coming up the sidewalk to participate in the ceremony at 106 years old. He spoke of how amazing it was that black people had gone from being considered property in 1865 to owning much of it in Greenwood only fifty years later. He spoke of the heartbreak in seeing all that progress wiped away in a single night.

Then he paused. "I probably could get away without saying this, but I think it would be disingenuous," he said. He looked to Fletcher and Van Ellis. "We can debate what the Guard did a hundred years ago, but there's no room for debate about what the Guard didn't do. And what the Guard didn't do is protect this community. What the Guard didn't do is save your house from being burned to the ground. What the Guard didn't do is save businesses from being ruined. We didn't stop you from fleeing here for your life, and some people never returned. So because I am the adjutant general today . . . and you are here as representatives of that horrific event, I want to give you my

Race massacre survivors Viola Fletcher and Hughes Van Ellis were honored at the soil collection ceremony

most heartfelt and sincere apology for our unwillingness to do the right thing a hundred years ago."[35]

Eight miles north of Standpipe Hill, as the soil collection ceremony was under way, Leslie Christopher carefully placed a copper vase on the center of W. D. Williams's grave. The flat marble tombstone was marked WILLIAMS in plain font, as weeds crept along its edges. A small plaque at the top right corner of the tombstone memorialized W.D.'s wife, Babe: "Mary S., 1906–1970." But the plaque in the top left for W.D.—the man Leslie and her siblings called Daddo—was missing; the family assumed it had been stolen sometime since their last journey to the cemetery.

"Usually they have this place a little more manicured," Charles Christopher II said a little sheepishly as they approached. Every Memorial Day morning since Charles could remember, he had accompanied his grandfather Daddo to the Crown Hill Cemetery, north of Greenwood, to tend to the family graves. At first W.D. had come to pay respects to his father, John Wesley; then his aunt and uncle, Joseph and Myrtle McKeever.[36] Later his wife Babe became one of the souls receiving flowers rather than placing them.[37] When W.D. died, he was buried right next to her. But even after Daddo was gone, the ritual continued, and the Williams plot continued to grow. Charles would spend his adult years tending to the graves of his ancestors, now including his mother Anita and his father, Charles Christopher, Sr., a military veteran whose headstone was adorned with a tiny American flag.[38]

"From the time I was a kid until Daddo died, we would come out here every year to do the same thing we're doing now," Charles said. "To honor these people."[39]

The cemetery was dreary and not especially well kept. But everyone pitched in to get the Williams family graves back into pristine shape. Leslie plucked away the troublesome weeds. Karen Robinson and Brendan O'Toole, children of W.D.'s son David, used dust rags to polish the tombstones' gray marble. Two small girls in pink and purple hoodies—W.D.'s great-grandchildren—placed white, blue, and red roses in the vase Leslie had secured back atop W.D.'s grave. The colorful bouquet popped against the wet, oversaturated grass.

Allyn Bacchus looked over W.D.'s plot, feeling a special kinship with his great-grandfather. Like W.D., he was a schoolteacher who loved diving into history and sharing stories of Greenwood, the Dreamland, and the massacre with his students. "I say, for my African American students, that you may not be able to connect to Ellis Island. You may not even be able to connect to a home country, because of our history," he said. "But you can still trace a few generations and see where your family came from."[40]

As the two young girls delicately adjusted their flower arrangements, Charles's wife Cassandra approached them. "We're going to have to take some of y'all's flowers," she said. "We have to take some to another cemetery."

The Williams descendants drove twenty-five miles south to Rolling Oaks, a cemetery on the opposite end of the city. They turned onto a web of neatly paved roads surrounded by freshly cut grass; white people were buried here. But Rolling Oaks had once been known as Booker T. Washington Cemetery, a popular resting place for Greenwood residents.[41] Here, on a somber day in 1927, Loula Williams had been laid to rest.

As the family walked toward her plot, Charles saw the rolling hills leading deeper into the graveyard where he used to run with his relatives as a child. Back then the old-timers would say, "We think the bodies are buried on across the hill." Mass graves of massacre dead. The city was investigating the matter, Leslie told her out-of-town cousins. They had plans to scan the grounds for "anomalies."[42]

Loula had not been buried so carelessly—she had a fittingly elegant tombstone. Like the unnamed bodies lost in mass graves, she had never been counted in any official tally of the lives snatched by the white mob. But the *Oklahoma Eagle* had not shied from the truth when it reported in her obituary that the vicious destruction of her livelihood "hastened her to her grave."[43]

Standing at Loula's plot, Charles climbed down onto his knees behind the tombstone and began tending to the earth with a hand rake. His two young cousins placed the last of their flowers at the front of the tomb. The first raindrops began to fall from the skies.

Charles Christopher and two of his young cousins tend the grave site of Loula Williams

Byron Crenshaw, one of Leslie's sons, stepped forward and took the rake from his uncle. He had been coming to these graves every few years with his family since he was a small boy. He learned about the Dreamland around the time he started elementary school, but only in his teenage years did he grasp the full scope and scale of the massacre.[44] No one in the family talked much about what happened to Loula afterward. There were always new layers to unpeel in the family history, some of them hopeful, others harrowing. When he discovered the article in the *Topeka Plaindealer* that had dubbed Loula the

"Amusement Queen," he wanted to turn it into a family T-shirt.[45] But he was also frustrated when he saw people leveraging the Dreamland name without involving his relatives. He was proud and angry thinking about the life of his great-great-grandmother, sometimes both at once. "Grieving is so nonlinear," he said later. "Especially when it's a collective loss."[46]

Byron stepped back and eyed the grave up and down. Loula was buried alongside her mother, Sallie Cotten, and the two women shared a joint tombstone. He noticed, for the first time, the dates of their deaths. Loula died on September 13, 1927, Sallie on January 9, 1936.

"I didn't realize her mother passed after her," Byron said.

"The race riot took Loula out," Charles replied. "It took a toll on her."[47]

According to lawsuits filed by Loula herself, the Williams family is owed $1.2 million from destroyed property alone, in 2021 dollars. Near her gravestone, family members mulled the form justice should take for their ancestor's life-shattering loss.

Charles Christopher III, a teenager, said he believed massacre descendants were owed reparations and that Greenwood should be rebuilt. "All the other ethnicity groups have gotten reparations," he said, noting that the government had offered restitution to both Japanese Americans and Native Americans. "The whites, whenever the slaves were released, they got reparations for that, too. We're the only ones that haven't."[48]

Allyn said he would like to see a Greenwood scholarship targeting students who planned to attend business school, one that could be endowed and replenished every year.[49] Milton Washington, another son of Leslie's, said he wanted to see black ownership in the Greenwood district.[50]

Byron supported cash payments for survivors and descendants. "There's that saying of money can't buy happiness," he said. "It's more than just money that we're talking about. It's opportunity, and it's time, and it's the gift of leisure. Since we have so much trauma, not only in the black community but specifically in our family around this event, I think that it's imperative that we, as a family, do whatever we can and take all the time that we need to exorcise this trauma."[51]

The rain grew more insistent. Soon the family was on their way back to Greenwood. They reconvened at the Black Wall Street Liquid

Lounge, a new black-owned coffee shop across Archer Street from the old Williams Building, still standing after Loula and John rebuilt it in 1922. Inside the new space, nearly every chair, couch seat, and barstool was occupied as people laughed and traded jokes and knowledge. Loula's confectionery must have felt the same one hundred years before.

On the walls of the back room were several large three-dimensional renderings of chic, modern-looking arenas. All had the same title: *Williams Dreamland Theater.* They had been designed by college students as part of an architecture class at Ball State University, led by Greenwood native and architecture professor Olon Dotson.

But this wasn't just an academic exercise. Charles was seeking funding to turn one of the designs into an actual venue. His family wanted to use some of the large empty acreage of Greenwood controlled by the city of Tulsa and the Tulsa Development Authority to build a new open-air amphitheater. The concerts that typically happened on a grassy field near Vernon AME Church could be infused with a bit of the Dreamland's old splendor. With so many people claiming to care about the Dreamland, and so much money swirling around the Greenwood story, why not build something the community could actually make use of?

"My goal is to have this monument dedicated to this black woman

An architect's rendering of a new Dreamland Amphitheater, based in part on the work of Ball State University student Kiona Casarez

who was, one hundred years ago, doing big things," Charles said. The project would be an expensive one, but he felt confident he could turn Loula's fallen dream back into a reality.[52]

———

The Williams family descendants and thousands of others had planned to attend the centennial commission's nationally televised concert on the afternoon of May 31, featuring John Legend and Stacey Abrams. It was to be the anchor event for the city's official commemoration efforts. But earlier in the week, the concert had been abruptly canceled with no public explanation. Visitors pieced together what had happened through rumors and tidbits meted out in news articles over the weekend. The leaders of the centennial commission and the representatives of the massacre survivors had spent days negotiating over how much money the commission would be willing to raise to aid massacre survivors and descendants directly. Figures ranged from $100,000 for each of three known survivors on the low end, up to $1 million for each, along with a $50 million reparations fund for massacre descendants. When the two sides reached an impasse, and it became clear the survivors would not participate in any of the official centennial commission activities, Abrams and Legend quickly backed out.[53] The optics were embarrassing for the city. "I think there were missteps made by both sides," Phil Armstrong, the Greenwood Rising director, said later of the failed negotiations.

But massacre descendants did not need a televised ceremony to find ways to reconnect with the past. Visiting the city for the very first time for the anniversary was Anneliese Bruner, a great-granddaughter of *Events of the Tulsa Disaster* author Mary Jones Parrish. While Parrish's book had long undergirded academic texts about the massacre, the woman herself was relegated to the footnotes of history. Bruner had been seeking to change that ever since her father gave her a copy of Parrish's book in 1994 and told her, "Now you're the matriarch of the family." Days before the centennial, she'd republished her ancestor's seminal work under a new name borrowed from the text: *The Nation Must Awake*. She spent her days in Tulsa reciting her great-grandmother's words at public readings and connecting the issue of mob violence in 1921 to the uncomfortable echoes a century later. The fire-alarm-red cover had been replaced with a regal illustration of

Parrish herself. "It's convenient to use her work, but not to mag-
nify and amplify her person," Bruner said. "Here is my opportunity
to reiterate what my great-grandmother has said, to resurrect her
memory."[54]

Bruner brought her son and daughter, Kevin and Portia Hurtt, on
the trip to Tulsa. For all of them, it felt like a pilgrimage. But the family sensed that Tulsa's racial issues were roiling beneath a still surface,
that the spatial segregation entrenched by urban renewal so many
decades ago had created a yawning chasm between black and white.
The geography of Greenwood itself told the tale; the irony wasn't lost
on them, as first-time visitors, that the ceremony meant to honor
Greenwood's past had been set to take place in the sports stadium
that had redirected the neighborhood's future. "It's hallowed ground
for us, and they are here enjoying a baseball game," Portia said.[55]

For at least this one weekend, though, the sliver of Greenwood that
remained would be given proper reverence. Around ten p.m. on
May 31, after the gray of the evening finally faded to black, a crowd
began to gather at the corner of Greenwood and Archer Street for a
candlelight vigil. At about that time one hundred years before, the
avenue had been thronged with people debating what to do about
Dick Rowland's arrest and possible lynching. A group of men at the
Tulsa Star office steeled themselves for the march downtown to the
courthouse. Anxiety, adrenaline, courage, fear, and dread had all
mingled on the streets of Greenwood that night. Conflicting emotions
swirled a century later, too, given the controversies that surrounded
the day's disrupted events. But the brutal reality of what had transpired back then, discussed and documented and dramatized so much
in recent years, snapped into focus, and the weight of the anniversary
forced every person, at least for a brief moment, to feel transported
back to a cataclysm.

The energy at the vigil was peculiar. There was no orator to list the
names of lives lost or property destroyed, nor anyone to provide a
historical account of exactly what had happened on that street a century earlier. The long-planned magnitude for marking this moment
seemed to have dissipated in the confusion over the canceled remembrance ceremony. Eventually, a woman standing in the middle of the

crowd started singing "Hallelujah" as attendees murmured in chorus and tried to protect their candles from the rain. The chant soon morphed into a call of "Greenwood Rising"—the name of the new history center just down the street.

The patter of rain that had soundtracked the day grew into a roaring, torrential downpour. It would last for much of the night. There were no flames of terror on the anniversary of the Tulsa Race Massacre, but in a city still groping its way toward justice, the water could not bring absolution either.

The following day, June 1, Lauren Usher was nervous as she stood before the crowd of roughly two hundred in the banquet hall of the Greenwood Cultural Center.[56] A row of American flags flanked the makeshift stage, and the podium on which she tidily arranged her notes bore the presidential seal. Cameras from CNN, ABC, and a raft of other television networks were trained on her as the room settled into an expectant silence.

"When I enrolled as an undergraduate at the University of Pennsylvania, my grandmother gave me a manuscript written by her great-grandfather, J. B. Stradford," Lauren began. "It was a memoir that began with J.B.'s father buying his own freedom from enslavement in Versailles, Kentucky, and continued through J.B.'s life as a successful business owner and hotelier in Tulsa, Oklahoma. It was by reading this memoir that I understood a part of the family history that had only been spoken about in whispers—the Tulsa Race Massacre destroyed our family business and criminalized our patriarch."[57]

Lauren explained how the Stradford Hotel would be worth more than $2 million in 2021 dollars, to say nothing of the compound interest and real estate equity that Stradford himself would have accrued. She said she was thankful to have access to her ancestor's memoirs, which traced the family lineage from Congo to Tulsa and on to Chicago, where Stradford had been forced to relocate after being falsely accused of inciting a riot in Greenwood. "But as thankful as I am to know my history, I understand that history has no firm line to divide it from the present," she said.

"Today we welcome President Joe Biden here, to stand beside us as we continue the fight for justice for the survivors and the descendants of the Tulsa Race Massacre."[58]

The crowd burst into applause as Lauren took the president's hand, and he leaned into her ear to whisper encouragement. She smiled, then walked off the stage.

That day Biden became the first sitting president to walk the streets of Greenwood.[59] He toured the Greenwood Cultural Center and met privately with the massacre survivors.[60] And on that stage, before a national audience, he became the first president to speak candidly about what had happened there. "For much too long, the history of what took place here was told in silence, cloaked in darkness," he said. "But just because history is silent, it doesn't mean that it did not take place."

Biden did not speak only on the massacre. He also discussed the devastating impact of urban renewal on Greenwood. "A highway was built right through the heart of the community," he said, "cutting off black families and businesses from jobs and opportunity."

President Joe Biden speaks at the Greenwood Cultural Center

The president announced plans to increase federal contracts for minority-owned businesses and to try to curb racist housing appraisals, but the word *reparations* was nowhere in his speech. Still, for people who had lived with the hidden story of the massacre for generations, it was a step forward to hear the most powerful man in the world say plainly what had resisted acknowledgment in Tulsa for so long.[61]

Lauren watched from just offstage. It seemed natural to her to start her speech where her knowledge of the race massacre had begun—with Stradford's memoirs. The family had long hoped to publish or adapt the work. But more important was that each Stradford descendant got to read their ancestor's words for themselves. Lauren's grandmother had made sure every branch of the family tree got a digital copy of the memoir before she died in 2016.[62]

After Biden's speech, Lauren and her mother Karen went for a celebratory meal at Wanda J's, the only soul food restaurant left in Deep Greenwood. The Stradford descendants had no home to return to in the neighborhood, so they then retreated to the lobby of the Hyatt Hotel downtown—a chain founded about forty years after the Stradford Hotel.[63]

Their brief time in Tulsa had been bittersweet. "Everyone looks like family," Lauren said. "And in some cases, they have been, honestly."

But there was no mistaking the loss the Stradford descendants had suffered. Before the president's arrival, Lauren and Karen visited the site where the Stradford Hotel had once stood, now a vacant lot next to Vernon AME Church. A sidewalk plaque marked his former enterprise, but it was being covered by a street vendor selling BLACK WALL STREET T-shirts. Karen had to ask him to move so they could crawl under the table and take a picture.

The entire ordeal depressed her. "That plaque, to me, it doesn't represent him," she said. "You go to a cemetery, and you see those plaques, those tombstones. I thought about that, and I was like, 'What is this? This is the death of J. B. Stradford right here.'"

But Lauren retained some sliver of optimism in the fact that Stradford's name had been etched into the street he once walked. "It's important to know what was, because at the end of the day they didn't even want us to know that," she said. "They didn't even want us to know that we were capable enough and strong enough and important enough to have businesses and community and wealth. They wanted to erase us from the face of time." Her voice thickened with the weight of that harsh reality.

Both women agreed that commemoration was not enough. "I want to see cash reparations. I want to see land reparations," Karen said. "I want that educational piece to be passed on."

"Money is key," Lauren said. "I'm not here for the paternalism of 'We know what to do better with your money than you do.' Start with the money. Start with the money and the land." She supported a provision in the Greenwood lawsuit that would waive local taxes for massacre survivors and descendants for one hundred years. And she, like others, wondered why black Tulsans weren't offered free tuition to OSU-Tulsa, the school that had been built atop Greenwood land.

Their flight home to New Orleans was in just a few hours. Neither woman knew the next time they'd be back in Tulsa. But seeing their family's home for the first time had rejuvenated them. And if introducing the president mattered, it was only because it might help nudge him and other powerful politicians to finally do right by Greenwood.

"The average black person is not going to stand up there and talk to the president," Karen said. "That's why I say you have to be humble, 'cause all you are is a vessel."

"It's not on me to center myself in this," Lauren agreed, "but center my ancestors in the fight for justice."[64]

The floral arrangers at the Wild Mother had expected to remove the installation at the base of Standpipe Hill the day after the massacre anniversary. They did not want to watch the flowers wither and die under a brutal June sun. But the overcast clouds hung over Tulsa for days. The air remained wet. The flowers stayed in full, powerful bloom.

Whenever Wild Mother co-founder Lauren Palmer came by to check on the installation, something unexpected would happen. A Greenwood resident would ask her to keep the flowers up just one more day, because they were so beautiful. An anonymous soul would leave a coin or a small bouquet at the base of the installation. To Lauren, who is black, indigenous, and Mexican, the gifts reminded her of an *ofrenda*, a home altar that Mexican families build for their ancestors during the Día de Los Muertos. The word is Spanish for "offering." The purpose of the *ofrenda* is not only to mourn the dead, but to honor them.[65]

CHAPTER 26

BEYOND CEREMONY

A sign hanging on the fence of OneOK Field during the race massacre centennial commemoration

Tulsa was still covered in a blanket of snow from a February blizzard as Regina rushed out of her longtime family home and climbed into her old gray Lexus. It was just after nine a.m. on the first day of the 2022 legislative session, and Greenwood's House representative was running late.

"My clock should be ten minutes fast," she said hopefully as she backed out of her driveway, patting down a few unruly strands in her gray coif as she consulted the rearview mirror.[1] Oklahoma City was 104 miles away—not too far to make her 10:30 Democratic caucus meeting if she hurried. It was a cold but almost garishly beautiful morning. The sky was a pure and brilliant blue, flecked with wispy streaks of clouds that reminded Regina of brushstrokes on a boundless canvas. "It looks like God painted this sky," she said, peering up over her steering wheel.[2]

The Turner Turnpike, the eighty-eight-mile asphalt ribbon that connects Tulsa to Oklahoma City, was nearly empty, as always.[3] As quickly as the car was racing, her mind was running even faster. She was expecting the most hostile environment yet for Democrats in her seven years as a lawmaker.[4] But she was also planning to introduce her most ambitious legislative agenda, including several bills that would provide tangible restitution for the wrongs Greenwood had suffered over the previous century.

The most ambitious gambit was a $300 million victims' compensation fund for survivors of the race massacre and their descendants.[5] The figure was eye-popping to some folks across the aisle, but for Regina, the math added up. Greenwood residents had claimed about $1.8 million in damages in their lawsuits after the massacre, or about $30 million in 2022 dollars.[6] But that figure accounted only for residents who had the wherewithal to hire lawyers and go to court. Take the 1,256 homes that were destroyed during the burning of Greenwood, and multiply them by the $200,000 median home selling price in Tulsa in 2022 and you reached $250 million, not far from her figure.[7] That didn't take into account the losses incurred from the destruction of the business district, the opportunity cost from thousands of disrupted lives, or the lasting psychological traumas of the event. If anything, Regina argued, $300 million was an undercount.[8] And thanks to recent increases in taxes on the oil industry, the state had $2.5 billion in savings reserves, which meant that funding the effort wouldn't require raising taxes or taking money from other programs.[9]

Regina wanted to address the impacts of urban renewal and highway construction as well. She proposed a state-funded study on potentially removing the northern leg of the Crosstown Expressway, which led to the destruction of Greenwood homes and businesses in 1967.[10] Regina hoped that by making a legislative commitment, Tulsa would be in a better position to attract federal grants. Joe Biden's infrastructure plan had set aside $1 billion for reconnecting neighborhoods that were destroyed by federal highways around the nation during that era.[11] She had hosted a legislative hearing to study the subject in the fall, recruiting urban planners from around the country to discuss the positive economic impacts that highway removal brought to cities like Milwaukee and Rochester.[12] With the right backing from local and state leaders, it could be done in Tulsa too.

Both bills were long shots. Twenty years prior, when Democrats controlled the legislature, Don Ross hadn't been able to get any kind of comprehensive reparations legislation passed.[13] Since then Democratic power in the statehouse had waned every year, and Republicans were growing less and less willing to even hear Democratic bills in committee or on the chamber floor.[14] Regina expected to largely be playing defense against increasingly extreme Republican legislation, as she had during the 2021 session. Several GOP bills sought to further control school curriculums, including one that would ban books on gay and trans experiences from schools and another that banned the teaching of the *New York Times*'s 1619 Project, a series of essays arguing that slavery was as core to the United States' origin story as independence.[15] Ahead of a polarizing Supreme Court ruling on *Roe v. Wade*, the legislature introduced a bill that would ban abortions after six weeks of pregnancy, creating one of the strictest cutoffs in the nation.[16] Regina actually considered herself conservative in some respects—"I'm a Christian, I don't drink, I don't smoke"—but she didn't want to get in the business of limiting other people's rights and freedoms.[17]

She still had one other Greenwood bill that she thought had a legitimate shot at becoming law: expanding a long-neglected scholarship fund set up for massacre descendants. The Tulsa Education and Reconciliation Scholarship Trust, first devised by former representative Don Ross in 2001, was the one tangible way the government had ever attempted to atone for the massacre. Up to three hundred Tulsa students could qualify every year for money to pay tuition at public colleges in Oklahoma. But when Regina started digging into the details of the rarely discussed initiative, she was shocked to find that in the eighteen years since the program started, only 172 scholarships had been issued—about nine per year. The state government was providing only $1,000 to each student, even though the law said the scholarships could cover full tuition, and no one was tracking whether the money actually went to massacre descendants—it wasn't even a question on the scholarship application form.[18] Florida had developed a more robust scholarship for descendants of the 1923 Rosewood Massacre, in which a white mob destroyed about a dozen homes, compared to more than a thousand in Greenwood.[19]

Regina thought the program needed an overhaul. Her bill called for injecting $1.5 million into the scholarship trust, which was then hovering around $800,000. (Earnings on the corpus of the trust were used to pay for the scholarships.) She also wanted to raise the maximum qualifying family income from $70,000 to $120,000, to account for cost-of-living increases and the fact that poverty had not been a prerequisite when the mob burned Greenwood. Most important, she wanted to change the language of the bill to ensure that massacre descendants were being considered for aid first and foremost.[20] She was positive there were more than nine students in Tulsa who could use help attending college. She'd round them up herself if she had to.[21]

"It's been on the books for twenty years. It's just a matter of amending it and making sure that more people can benefit," she said as she drove. "No one has denied that the state was culpable and complicit in the destruction of Greenwood, like the city and the county were."[22]

Regina's phone rang. It was Sabrina. The sisters talked every day, often more than once. Regina gave Sabrina a quick rundown of her itinerary for the day: she would attend a Democratic caucus meeting, do a quick interview on a local black radio station about her agenda for the year, then watch Governor Stitt's annual State of the State address from her office. (Most legislators refused to wear masks on the chamber floor, but Regina was still taking Covid-19 seriously.) Sometime during the day she would need to chase down one of the legislative attorneys to adjust the language in her highway bill. She knew her opponents would be looking for any excuse to discard her legislation on a technicality.

"Watch your speed limit," Sabrina warned her younger sister. "Take your time. Have a good session. I love you."

Regina eased back a bit on the gas. "I love you too," she said.

It was almost 10:30. Regina pulled off the highway into Oklahoma City. The sky was still a brilliant blue as the capitol grew larger and larger in Regina's field of vision down Lincoln Boulevard.

"I never tire of that image," she said as she pulled into the capitol's south-side parking lot. "It's a privilege just to be driving here and seeing the big capitol building and, with God's will, really trying to represent folks in the right way. Having a voice that's not often expressed here."

But she couldn't deny that opposition to her agenda had grown more and more vitriolic in the years since she announced her candidacy at the Greenwood Cultural Center. Early on, she worked to find Republican co-sponsors for her bills, like the anti-shackling measure, and even attended Bible study with some colleagues across the aisle. Those kinds of interactions were over. "The climate has changed," she said. "There's a lot of wickedness and wicked bills. You have to prepare yourself and prepare your mind."

But she had to keep the faith. "This is not about me," she said before stepping out of the car. "This is about ancestors. This is about people right now that I am representing. This is beyond me."[23]

As expected, most of Regina's bills were ignored by the House committee chairs who decided which bills got heard and which didn't. But in late February, she got word that HB 4154, the scholarship bill, was going to be heard before a subcommittee of the Appropriations and Budget Committee. If she could convince seven out of thirteen legislators (ten of them Republican) to support her initiative, the bill would advance—though there would still be a long path from a House subcommittee to the governor's desk.[24]

On the morning of February 21, Regina took a seat at the far end of one table in the committee room, eyeing the legislators who slowly filtered inside. She took out a pen and began scribbling notes into the margin of one of her bill printouts. Scholarship dollar amounts, references to old bill numbers, turns of phrase that might catch a bored legislator's ear. In the right margin, she jotted down the names of massacre victims, one below the next:

Smitherman
Stradford
Williams
Mary E. Parrish.

Just before nine a.m., a man wearing a lavender blazer and with a thick, droopy mustache entered the room. Regina knew Mark McBride, the chair of the committee, didn't like her bill—he'd told her as much directly when she was trying to convince him to put it up for a vote.[25] But she'd been hustling the last few days to get every other committee member she could on her side. When Regina was pushing to get her bills heard, Republican legislators often ignored her phone calls and emails, but over the years she had become adept at tracking them down in person—meeting them face-to-face in their offices, as they stepped onto elevators, or in the parking lot as they climbed into their pickup trucks.[26] Whatever it took to get the job done. "This is the one tangible thing that we can point to that the legislature has done that is good as it relates to the race massacre," she said to each lawmaker. "This is too important for people to take lightly." Many seemed receptive; a few said outright that they planned to vote in her favor.[27] But that meant little until the names on the vote-tracking monitor flicked from white to green or red.

When it was her turn to present, Regina walked over to the microphone on the opposite side of the room from McBride. She laid out the terms of the bill as clearly and simply as possible: the legislation would prioritize massacre descendants for scholarship awards, raise the family income limit, and streamline the financial forms families used to report their income.[28] But she did not mention the $1.5 million in additional funding she was seeking; Republican leaders had convinced her to remove the language from the bill in order to make its passage more likely. They committed to negotiating to include the funds in the state budget before the legislative session was complete.

"I certainly ask for your support and all yes votes," Regina concluded.

Committee members peppered her with questions. How was she going to make more students aware of the scholarship? Why increase the income threshold? Shouldn't government money be going to people who were truly in need?[29]

The legislator least happy with the bill was the committee chair himself.

"When Rep. Goodwin came to me, I didn't really care for it," McBride said of the legislation. "But I do care for what she's trying to do." He said he had offered to add between $250,000 and $1 million to the massacre scholarship fund if Regina dropped her legislation.

State representative Regina Goodwin presents her race massacre
scholarship bill before a legislative committee

"You chose to go this route instead of taking money that would fund way more people than you have applying for the scholarships."

Regina was shocked by the accusation. "I didn't say I wanted one or the other, I said I wanted both," she said.

"You know that I made you an offer," McBride replied, "and you don't want the money, evidently."[30]

It was already documented that Regina did, in fact, want the money—her original draft of the bill had included the $1.5 million appropriation.[31] "That is absolutely and patently false," she said. "We have never had that conversation where I told you that."[32]

Finally, McBride dropped the argument. "Please open the queue," he said.[33] Regina looked up at the television monitor behind McBride's head to watch the names of each legislator as they weighed their votes. She braced herself as she saw three names, McBride's included, quickly flash red. *Okay,* she thought, *this is going to crash and burn.*[34] But to her surprise, every other name turned green. The bill passed 10–3.

"Thank you Mr. Chair," Regina said. "I look forward to working with you in the future."[35]

Regina breathed a sigh of relief but also one of exhaustion. Just making incremental changes to a scholarship law already on the books had taken her months of research, several meetings with state education leaders, her personal cajoling of thirteen legislators, and an acrimonious grilling that lasted more than twenty minutes. Before it became law, she would still have to win four more legislative votes, and get the governor's signature, while also ensuring that the potential $1.5 million appropriation didn't get sidelined. The bill that followed hers, an initiative about requiring Holocaust education in schools that was co-sponsored by McBride, passed unanimously in ninety seconds.[36]

"Oh, Lord," Regina said when she got back to her office. "This is gonna be a long slog."[37]

The courtroom on the sixth floor of the Tulsa County Courthouse was thronged with people on the afternoon of Monday, May 2. Every bench in the gallery was full, and dozens more people lined the walls, their faces etched with anxiety. They were there to witness the latest legal attempt by the massacre survivors and descendants to achieve justice.[38]

By May 2022, the massacre lawsuit filed by Damario Solomon-Simmons had been inching through the Tulsa County court system for nearly two years. The plaintiffs had been sparring with the city, the chamber of commerce, and other local agencies in back-and-forth legal briefs, even as Tulsa was welcoming massacre descendants to town and selling them on the idea of reconciliation. When Judge Caroline Wall announced that the case was advancing to a hearing where she would consider the city's motion to dismiss the lawsuit outright, that was actually a victory for Greenwood. The night before the hearing, community members gathered at Mt. Zion Church for a prayer rally, but even more people were now crammed into the courtroom, eager to see exactly how the courts would define justice more than a century after the massacre.[39]

During his oral argument, Damario Solomon-Simmons, wearing a trim black suit with a purple tie, summoned dramatic images to illustrate the public nuisance his legal team alleged the city had created in 1921. On a television set on one wall of the courtroom, photographs of dead massacre victims, some burned beyond recognition, flashed on the screen as Solomon-Simmons recited the criminal codes for murder, arson, and other brutal acts from the Oklahoma lawbooks. In a crowd peppered with massacre descendants, some wept openly as the photos were displayed. "Your Honor, what could be more offensive than destroying an entire neighborhood?" Solomon-Simmons asked the judge.[40]

Solomon-Simmons walked through evidence that had long been buried in lawsuit trial transcripts, newspaper articles, and National Guard reports, but had never been collected and recounted before a Tulsa County judge until this case. Government officials had played an undeniable role in turning the assault on Greenwood into one of the worst acts of racial terror in the history of the United States. The police chief at the time openly acknowledged that he deputized members of the white mob without collecting their names and that some of these men "might have applied the torch" to Greenwood. Tulsa mayor T. D. Evans said that the mob members who attacked Greenwood were "good citizens," and an all-white grand jury ruled that black residents were responsible for their neighborhood's own destruction. After the attack, city officials installed a Reconstruction Committee tasked with removing black landowners from their burned-out property in order to pursue commercial development near downtown. The chamber of commerce, meanwhile, reneged on an initial promise to enact a "plan of reparation" for the black community. With little financial aid from the city, Greenwood rebuilt haphazardly, and substandard housing remained an ongoing issue in the neighborhood in the ensuing decades.[41]

The defense, represented by Tulsa Chamber of Commerce attorney John Tucker, argued that the massacre was too far in the past to litigate. Tucker attempted to walk a rhetorical tightrope by acknowledging that the massacre was "a really bad deal" but denying that the city of Tulsa and other government agencies could be held responsible for it a century later.[42] He argued that the various issues that the plaintiffs claimed to stem from the massacre—racial disparities, economic inequalities, and psychological trauma—constituted a set of "social ills" that were too broad to be addressed through the courts. He suggested they try their luck in the legislature, where Regina was struggling to get the small reparations scholarship expanded. "However grave the problem is of discrimination in Tulsa," Tucker said, "public nuisance law does not provide the remedy for the harm."[43]

Much of the legal wrangling during the three-hour hearing centered on the importance of a recent high-profile decision regarding public nuisance law and the opioid crisis. In 2019 an Oklahoma district court judge ruled that Johnson & Johnson was liable for nearly half a billion dollars in damages for its aggressive and misleading marketing of deadly painkillers in the state. But in November 2021, the Oklahoma Supreme Court ruled that the pharmaceutical company's actions were outside the scope of public nuisance law, which the court said applied primarily to "criminal or property-based conflict" and "discrete, localized problems, not policy problems."[44]

Solomon-Simmons argued that the Johnson & Johnson ruling actually bolstered the survivors' case, since the race massacre involved the destruction of property in a discrete local area. But Tucker seized on another portion of the opinion that said that expanding the circumstances that are classified as public nuisances would leave the law "impermissibly vague."[45] The outcome of the massacre lawsuit would hinge on specificity—whether Solomon-Simmons and his team could convince Judge Wall that the precise problems the massacre caused for Greenwood residents persisted into the present and were the fault of government agencies.

Around 4:30 p.m., the judge called a brief recess. Many in the crowd expected that she might be preparing to adjourn the court with no decision, as she had after a previous hearing. So it was a shock when she returned to her bench and began reading her verdict.

Judge Wall announced that she "granted in part and denied in part" the city's motion to dismiss, stating that details of the ruling would be issued at a later date. There was a brief moment of confusion in the gallery following the judge's split decision, but when Solomon-Simmons embraced one of his team's lawyers in a triumphant hug, it was clear to everyone that the massacre survivors and their representatives were claiming the ruling as a victory. Cheers erupted in the courtroom, and some onlookers leaped up onto their seats.

"History was made today," Solomon-Simmons said at a press conference after the hearing. "We all stood on the shoulders of the ancestors who started fighting for Greenwood on May 31, 1921."[46]

Both sides would have to wait months for Judge Wall's written order, which clarified which portions of the case could move forward. If the massacre survivors and descendants were victorious, the court

Damario Solomon-Simmons, Congresswoman Sheila Jackson Lee, and supporters of the race massacre survivors celebrate the judge's May 2022 ruling to let the case proceed

would determine the appropriate method to rid Greenwood of the harms caused by the massacre and subsequent government-sponsored programs like urban renewal. The plaintiffs proposed a relief plan that included a victims' compensation fund, a community land trust, a new hospital in Greenwood, and a scholarship program for massacre descendants.[47]

Previous efforts to seek financial restitution for massacre survivors had all failed. But by framing his argument around Oklahoma's public nuisance law, Solomon-Simmons seemed to have wedged open a legal door that had long been thought closed. Once the case went to a formal trial, legal teams on both sides would have the opportunity to uncover more evidence, which might reveal unknown truths about the massacre. "There's never been a judicial account of exactly what happened with this massacre," Solomon-Simmons said. "We want to know. We're going to find out."[48]

In the weeks after the scholarship bill's contentious vote in the House subcommittee, Regina continued working to get the proposal across the finish line. Her legislation hopped every hurdle it met, passing by a comfortable margin on the House floor and unanimously in three more House and Senate committees.[49] Even McBride voted for the bill when he was forced to reconsider it.[50] After a rocky start, the bill seemed destined for the governor's desk. All Regina needed to do was win the vote on the Senate floor.

But during the last regular days of the legislative session, she hit a roadblock. The Senate and the House were sparring over their competing education agendas, with the Senate threatening not to hear any more education bills unless the House heard a charter school bill.[51] When that bill was finally passed on the House floor on the second-to-last day of the session, Regina believed her scholarship bill was safe. But at nine p.m. that night, when she was sent the readout of the final day's bills in the Senate, she saw that HB 4154 was not on it.

She got to the capitol early the next morning to ask Senate leadership why her bill wasn't being heard. But she couldn't get a straight answer. Regina hoped that George Young, her Senate co-author on the bill, might be able to convince Senate leaders to put the legislation up for an honest vote, but at 11:23 in the morning he sent her a devastating text message: "I was just told that the bill will not be heard. No reason and no excuse."[52]

Regina's bill was killed without ever being considered by the full Senate. She didn't even get to argue it on the merits. It only rubbed salt in the wound that Mark McBride's scholarship bill, aimed at recruiting teachers to Oklahoma, passed at the end of the legislative session with little trouble.[53]

On the way back home to Tulsa that night, Regina got a flat tire. The Turner Turnpike was nearly empty, and sitting alone, she risked being swallowed up by the Oklahoma night. She had little to do but reflect on how difficult it was to make change in her hometown and home state.

Disappointment wasn't the right word for how she felt. Every day she stepped into the capitol, she knew someone might try to undermine her. Over seven years, she had witnessed many of the arbitrary and vindictive aspects of governance that don't get taught in civics books. The fact that a community's needs could be circumvented by the whims of a single person—a committee chair who didn't want to hear a bill, a legislative floor leader who thought it best not to let the entire chamber vote on a measure—illustrated that democracy was not always as representative as it seemed outside the capitol walls. With so many obstacles placed before her, she risked having her core of optimism extinguished—a feeling that so many in Greenwood had been forced to endure before her.

But Regina allowed such doubts to enter her mind only briefly. "I'm gonna hold on to my integrity and to my soul," she said on the turnpike. "My soul is intact. You can take the bills, you can take away the victories, you can take away all of that, but you ain't gonna take away my spirit."[54]

The next week Regina got back to work. The $1.5 million scholarship appropriation was still on the table. She consulted regularly with House Republican Kevin Wallace, chair of the appropriations and budget committee, to ensure he would include the money in the state budget. She knew there was no guarantee, and she was concerned that if she voted against the Republican budget, they might remove her line item as punishment. Sticking to her principles, she voted no anyway. She was surprised when Wallace came to her desk after the vote and gave her a conciliatory fist bump.[55] He kept his word on the scholarship money, and by June, an additional $1.5 million had been allocated to the fund, bringing its total corpus to $2.3 million.[56]

The scholarship requirements were still much too narrow for Regina's liking. The family income limit remained at $70,000, and the language of the fund's original governing law still said that prioritizing massacre descendants was completely optional, rather than mandatory. It also applied only to Tulsa high schools.[57] In Regina's ideal vision, the fund would pay for students' full tuition and be made available to any Tulsa Race Massacre descendant in the country who wanted to go to school in Oklahoma.[58] The fund could help atone for the past and build a more prosperous future for the state at the same time.

But what she'd accomplished was more than the local, state, or federal government had ever committed to before in providing money that could directly benefit Tulsa's massacre descendants. It was a start. In the 2022–23 school year, the state planned to award twenty-three scholarships instead of nine, with awards of $2,000 instead of $1,000.[59] Regina intended to push for more changes in the future, to make the program more in line with the sweeping reparations program Don Ross had originally envisioned. Her agenda was "an effort to keep this issue alive and to show we're not going anywhere," she said just before the legislative session. "Whether I live to be a hundred or tonight is my last moment, there's gonna be a generation after me. And as long as folks are being born, we have to make sure people understand what we've got to fight for and why we have to press onward."[60]

In a state and a nation first scaffolded by laws meant to dehumanize black people, Regina insisted on using those very same legal tools to build bridges to opportunity for her community. If the bridge was out, she'd find a detour, and light a lantern for those who came after her. For the people of Greenwood, for black Oklahomans, for black Americans, strategy never stopped.

Tiffany Crutcher, even as her stature rose, knew her work went beyond public protests. It was about building the infrastructure to sustain a self-sufficient community, like the historic Greenwood district whose story the entire world now knew.

In September 2021, at a North Tulsa event center far from where news cameras gathered during the centennial, she marked the fifth anniversary of her brother's death with a day of service. The Terence Crutcher Foundation, the organization she and her parents launched a year to the day after her brother's killing, had grown to a staff of roughly ten and a volunteer crew numbering in the hundreds. The organization continued to push for the reforms she had hashed out with Mayor Bynum in the aftermath of George Floyd's murder, such as the office of the independent monitor and increased investment in mental health services rather than sprawling police budgets. But the foundation also funded scholarships for underprivileged North Tulsa students and summer programs for neighborhood youth, focusing, too, on change it could make in the immediate present.[61] And on this unseasonably hot September Saturday, Tiffany was trying to empower smaller local organizations as well by distributing $1,000 grants in Terence's honor.[62]

"We're going to make sure that we get back to where we were one hundred years ago," Tiffany said on a small makeshift platform, "going back to when Black Wall Street was prosperous."[63] Flanking

Tiffany Crutcher, Joey Crutcher, Terence Crutcher, Jr., and community supporters mark the fifth anniversary of Terence Crutcher's death with a day of service

her on the stage were many of her regular allies—Kristi Williams, Greg Robinson, and Regina Goodwin.

The grant recipients included entrepreneurs, ministers, and artists. Tyrance Billingsley offered a huge smile when he stepped up to accept his grant for Black Tech Street, his initiative to build a pipeline of technology jobs for black Tulsans. "I love everybody on this stage," he declared, "not only because of how they protect us, but how they also hold us accountable when we need that."[64] These recipients were the kind of people who were best equipped to devise North Tulsa's solutions, in Tiffany's mind. They were the ones who lived every day so close to its problems. "Service comes in many different forms," she told the crowd. "You don't have to just be at city hall, protesting or pushing for policy reform. You don't have to be at Capitol Hill like I am all the time. But service comes through art. It comes through music, it comes through technology, it comes through mentorship."[65]

As much as Tiffany was regaining her roots in Tulsa, she was also becoming an increasingly prominent national activist. In some ways, the police reform movement had lost ground since the explosion of grassroots energy in the summer of 2020. A nationwide spike in crime during the disruptions of Covid, and according to some, an intentional work slowdown by police departments, had caused many citizens to turn away from radical reform ideas. Voters in Minneapolis, for instance, rejected a ballot initiative to replace the police department with a department of public safety oriented around public health.[66] City council members in Tulsa continued to block more modest reforms, like the proposed office of the independent monitor.[67] By the summer of 2022, Mayor Bynum seemed to be signaling he had backed away from the OIM idea and pivoted to the concept of an "external police liaison."[68] How independent this person would be from the police department, or how representative they would be of the people most adamant about police oversight, was unknown. (Bynum declined a request for an interview.)

But there were also signs of progress—or at least greater accountability. In April 2021, Minneapolis police officer Derek Chauvin was convicted of murder for causing George Floyd's death.[69] It was not a sign that the system worked—the police had reported Floyd's death as a blameless "medical incident" before cell phone video emerged—but that the system could at least be swayed under intense public pressure.[70] About a year later, on the second anniversary of Floyd's death, Tiffany was in the audience at the White House as the president signed a new executive order that banned the use of chokeholds, mandated body-worn cameras, and set up a database of police misconduct among federal officers.[71] Biden's order could only set standards for federal agencies, but the White House hoped it would be a model that states and cities might adopt. The *New York Times* called the effort a "centrist position" that represented a walkback from the revolutionary rhetoric of 2020.[72]

With more than five years of organizing under her belt via the Terence Crutcher Foundation, Tiffany said her priorities were shifting as she thought about how to tackle the problems with policing. She wanted to spend less time trying to negotiate with people already in power, many of whom were skeptical of her proposed policies, and more time talking to regular citizens about their needs. By building a base of political power at the ground level, she hoped to be able to flip city council seats and increase civic engagement overall. Even if protesters were no longer swarming brunch districts and shutting down highways, the work remained the same. "My priorities haven't changed," she said. "I have a duty and a responsibility to continue to hold the elected officials accountable . . . and the fact that they've moved on? There are thousands of families who haven't."[73]

It's a brilliant Saturday afternoon on Greenwood Avenue in June, and North Tulsa native Kode Ransom is leading a pair of newcomers to the city on one of his regular walking tours. Each tour begins in the largest room of the Black Wall Street Liquid Lounge. On the back wall a local artist has painted a mural featuring five Greenwood pioneers carved into a mountain: A. C. Jackson, Loula Williams, J. B. Strad-ford, O. W. Gurley, and Mabel Little. "These five people are on the Mount Rushmore of Greenwood because they were all pivotal for this area at some point in time," Kode says.[74]

Though Greenwood Rising is now the largest attraction on the block, a number of local tour guides are regularly roaming the streets. Chief Amusan's tour is the most spiritual; he honors the ancestors and focuses more on Greenwood's history of cooperative economics than the legends about the community's wealth. Terry Baccus likes to talk about Greenwood's underworld: the numbers runners, bootleggers, and hustlers who formed the backbone of the old neighborhood econ-omy (and sometimes financed its most storied institutions). Princetta Rudd-Newman, seasoned enough to remember the heyday before urban renewal, is all about the surprising facts—did you know, she'll ask with a sly smile, that Greenwood had a black women's softball team in the 1930s? Kode, at thirty-three, is the youngest regular guide. He likes to make Greenwood relatable to people of all ages.

As they walk up to the Greenwood-Archer intersection, he recounts the locations of lost landmarks: the Dreamland Theater, the Stradford Hotel. And he makes sure to note the ones that remain. "The Good-wins are the oldest family still here, as far as owning," he tells his small delegation. "The *Oklahoma Eagle* newspaper is still a function-ing newspaper, and it's the only piece of black land we got left."[75]

Elsewhere on the block, young children dash down the sidewalk with Popsicles from the neighborhood Frio Gourmet Pops. Tee's Bar-ber Shop is open for whoever needs a trim; so is Regina Woods's Loc Shop, on the opposite side of the street. Some of the retail space in the buildings Jim Goodwin once helped preserve is vacant, awaiting new tenants. But it's a given that they'll be filled eventually. Someone is always trying to make it on Greenwood Avenue.

Just north of the Crosstown Expressway overpass, Regina Goodwin, Tiffany Crutcher, and Chief Amusan are chatting in front of the Greenwood Cultural Center. Chief notices a family wander out of the Cultural Center and senses, somehow, that he should connect with them. He introduces himself as a tour guide and massacre descendant, then leads them over to the grand marble Black Wall Street memorial. There he provides the best rundown of the neighborhood's sprawling history he can in twenty minutes, free of charge. "I have this policy— you never charge starving people to eat. Those people looked like they were really hungry," Chief says. "I just said, let me give them a piece of the gift. Because that's what it is. The fact that we even know, at this point, is a gift. . . . and I pay it forward when I can."[76]

Tiffany has just stopped by the Terence Crutcher Foundation offices, located in the Greenwood Cultural Center, after spending the day leading one of the organization's summer youth programs. It's been another busy week for her, having organized the second annual Legacy Fest during the weekend of the race massacre anniversary. The keynote event on the night of May 31 was a talk by 1619 Project creator Nikole Hannah-Jones before a crowd of hundreds at the historic Booker T. Washington High School.[77] Just an hour after the Hannah-Jones event, the centennial commission organized another vigil in front of Greenwood Rising, but not even two dozen people came.[78] The mayor, once again, was absent, along with Senator Kevin Matthews, who spearheaded the commission in the first place.

"Last year was very performative," Tiffany says. "But our plight, and our efforts and our energy hasn't shifted one iota. . . . We were able to continue on, but I think it's going to be hyperlocal. We're gonna have to keep pushing this story ourselves and not depend on national media to do it all." Outside the blip of attention caused by *Watchmen* and *Lovecraft Country,* television documentaries and magazine articles, the intrusion of a sitting president and the welcoming of another, focusing on the hyperlocal is what Greenwood had always done. "Our motive is simply to get restitution and atonement for what happened here a little bit over one hundred years ago," she says. "That fuel is never going to stop burning because it's a part of us. This is our story."[79]

Regina has spent much of the afternoon on the block, working and strategizing. Earlier that day she provided a preliminary tour to an official from the U.S. Department of Transportation, ahead of a planned trip by Deputy Transportation Secretary Polly Trottenberg. Though Regina's bill to study removing the Crosstown Expressway was never heard in the legislature, she intends to continue pressing the issue, in part by enlisting federal support. "Everybody thinks it's crazy," Regina would later say of the removal plan. "This big piece of concrete, that's all folks have known all their lives. But if you constructed it, you can deconstruct it."[80]

Everyone here is still on a mission, but the day feels relaxing for once. Leisurely. As Tiffany and Regina sit inside the open trunk of Tiffany's SUV, another visiting family approaches them, a trio from Sacramento, California. Ahrray Young is an eighteen-year-old basketball recruit who will soon be starting her freshman year at the University of Tulsa. Tiffany and Regina smile when they learn she's an athlete; both women hooped in high school, and they joke about who might win in a game of pick-up today. But they also share with Ahrray those facts about the community that don't get discussed on plaques and monuments—about the impact of the highway that roars above their conversation, about the politics that quietly shape what narratives are placed before tourists' eyes. Both women have accrued generations' worth of knowledge about how Greenwood actually came to be the place it is now. "We're both descendants of race massacre survivors," Regina says, "so this is part of who we are."

This is Ahrray's very first weekend as a resident of Tulsa. She'd visited on a recruiting trip in September and seen Greenwood for the first time then. "It brought tears to my eyes just thinking that there were people just like me growing up, eighteen years old, trying to figure out what they want to do with the next fifteen or twenty years of their lives and having to go through that," she says. "And it made me mad just because it's not talked about enough." Ahrray learned about Greenwood from her father, not her schoolbooks.[81]

As the family prepare to leave, Regina pulls out her cell phone and offers to exchange numbers with Tulsa's newest young resident. "I know what it was like when you don't know anybody in the city you're moving to," she says. "It's always good to have a contact."

It doesn't matter whether Ahrray will wind up living in Regina's legislative district or not. What matters is that the newest person who has been touched by the story of Greenwood will feel, whenever she walks the streets in pride or in protest, that she is at home. "I don't care where you're from," Regina says to the young woman. "We all have a shared history."

Greenwood Avenue circa 2021

" Right is slow and tardy, while wrong is aggressive," attorney and race massacre survivor B. C. Franklin wrote in his autobiography. "That's the only way it can survive."[1]

For more than a century, Greenwood has been grappling with wrong in all its combative forms. Wickedness flamed white-hot in 1921, but the embers continued to burn long after: In relief aid withheld during the Great Depression. In wartime jobs denied during World War II. In discrimination proclaimed loudly on WHITES ONLY signs and quietly in land deeds barring residence by people of African descent. In urban planning brochures featuring smiling black faces and words laden with double meaning—*blight, renewal, progress.*

What happened in Tulsa at each historical juncture was not unique, but it was uniquely well documented. For all the talk of a conspiracy of silence hanging over the massacre, there are a shocking number of images of the event—more than a hundred photographs of houses aflame, black victims lying dead in the street, white Tulsans admiring their gruesome handiwork. That was the mob's catalog of events. But Greenwood residents kept their own ledger too, captured in interviews conducted by Mary Jones Parrish; oral histories passed down by W. D. Williams and Mabel Little; poetry written by A. J. Smitherman; and historical accounts reprinted decade after decade by the *Oklahoma Eagle.*

Tulsa wanted badly to forget, but Greenwood demanded the city remember. "They must pay, and they will pay," Ed Goodwin, Sr., said from the pulpit of Mt. Zion in 1971, when the number of massacre survivors still totaled in the thousands. "Restitution is still due," his granddaughter Regina Goodwin echoed fifty years later.[2] By then, there were only three known living people who had witnessed the attack with their own eyes, but the legions of departed survivors had told their story enough times—to grandchildren, neighbors, historians, and journalists—that the memory of the massacre transformed from a private burden to a collective one. First the city, then the state, and finally the nation recognized that what happened in Tulsa was not a bizarre outlier in the inevitable arc of history toward justice; it was a warning buried in the past that any society, no matter how noble it purports to be, can be wracked by hate and violence that destroys people's lives and livelihoods, then see it rationalized from the highest seats of power. Wrong is aggressive.

Tulsa can no longer forget, but remembrance is not the same as compensation. In the wake of the massacre centennial, the city grappled with some attempts at uncovering its true history but rejected others, leaving the people here to sift between symbolism and material gains.

The most public attempt to reckon with the history of what happened in Greenwood has been a yearslong search for mass graves of massacre victims. Relaunched in the fall of 2018 by Mayor G. T. Bynum, after city councilor Vanessa Hall-Harper advocated for such a search in a viral *Washington Post* article, the effort began with lofty expectations to honor the massacre dead and provide forensic evidence for mass killings that some recalcitrant white Tulsans still reject as mere rumor.[3] Bynum reiterated again and again that the search for mass graves was a "homicide investigation," and he promised that an oversight committee of North Tulsa stakeholders would help ensure community trust. Across three separate digs at Oaklawn Cemetery, a downtown graveyard where funeral records already document eighteen massacre victims, archaeologists and excavation crews hired by the city uncovered more than sixty bodies in mostly unmarked graves—including at least two with gunshot wounds and several infants.[4] About two dozen of the bodies were exhumed for further analysis, a sign that they could potentially be massacre victims. Kristi Williams was among the massacre descendants who helped carry an infant's remains from the mass grave to a forensics trailer on site. "It just hurt my soul," she reflected in *Oaklawn*, a locally produced documentary about the dig.[5]

But over the years, transparency around the search process dwindled. An effort that began with monthly in-person meetings between leading city officials and the public oversight committee at open community venues devolved to private video conference calls once per quarter. (The city declined to return to an in-person format after the impacts of Covid-19 waned.)[6] The Public Oversight Committee also saw its authority reduced, after a summer 2021 dig, when the city overruled its call to keep exhumed bodies above ground. The decision led to a despairing scene at Oaklawn of black North Tulsa residents angrily pleading with city leaders not to rebury potential massacre victims in the same hole where they were long ago discarded.[7] In the fall of 2022, the dig at Oaklawn continued.[8] But the process of analyzing remains to determine their ties to the massacre, connecting them to the DNA of descendants, and potentially searching for more potential mass grave sites will take years more, if the city chooses to keep funding the search.[9]

In the courts, Tulsa County district judge Caroline Wall clipped Damario Solomon-Simmons's sweeping effort to force the city to offer restitution for a hundred years of black mistreatment in Tulsa. In August 2022, Wall ruled that the public nuisance case could proceed but on narrower ground. The three living survivors could argue their claim, but descendants of massacre victims like J. B. Stradford and A. J. Smitherman could not. Even entities that had existed in Tulsa at the time of the massacre, like Vernon AME Church, were dismissed from the case because their modern incorporation filings differ from those the church possessed in 1921.[10] Once again in Greenwood, the limits of the law were constricting the clearest pathways toward justice.

No matter its ultimate outcome, the case, and the inspiring presence of the three living survivors, played a significant role in raising awareness of the massacre during the centennial. The three centenarians have at least found some financial comfort in their twilight years thanks to a deluge of donations from people around the country, totaling more than half a million dollars for each survivor.[11] And the lawsuit, which hinges on proving that the massacre caused a public nuisance in Greenwood that persists today, could still play a pivotal role in establishing a blueprint for addressing injustices of the past, if the narrower case succeeds.[12]

There are also ongoing efforts to change Greenwood's physical landscape. In August 2022, Secretary of Transportation Pete Buttigieg visited the neighborhood during a multistate tour of federal infrastructure projects. He and his department hold the keys to the $1 billion federal Reconnecting Communities initiative, aimed at undoing some of the damage caused nationwide to urban communities by the construction of the interstate system. Regina Goodwin led Buttigieg around neighborhood landmarks and made sure to impart the importance of bringing down the highway that looms over Greenwood and getting the federal government to help. Buttigieg acknowledged that both the massacre in 1921 and the highway construction fifty years later had scarred the community. "There's stories all over the country," he said, "but Greenwood is a very unique place."[13]

In October 2022, Regina Goodwin led the drafting of an application for federal funding to remove a portion of the northern leg of I-244, diverting the traffic to existing alternative routes. Such a removal would free up about thirty acres of land in and around Greenwood that could be used for commercial and residential development benefiting the community's historic residents. The application received letters of support from the Greenwood Cultural Center, Mt. Zion Baptist Church, the Terence Crutcher Foundation, and multiple Greenwood Avenue businesses, among others.[14] But the Oklahoma Department of Transportation filed a competing application for the same federal funds, presenting a plan that would see the highway remain in place and instead focus on beautification projects and expanded sidewalks. The highway already has a Black Wall Street mural on one wall and a photo exhibit called *Pathway to Hope* on the other. While the Department of Transportation did not rule out the possibility of removing the highway, in its proposal the agency projected the process would take thirty or more years. In the 1950s and '60s, it took ten years to go from public approval of the highway plan to the destruction of Greenwood businesses; now, tearing down the highway to let those businesses flourish once more would span at least another generation. Supporting the ODOT proposal were the George Kaiser Family Foundation, Greenwood Rising, state senator Kevin Matthews, and the city of Tulsa.[15]

But in February 2023 came a major surprise: The federal Department of Transportation selected Regina's proposal over the one put forth by the Oklahoma Department of Transportation. With a $1.6 million grant for an initial study, she and the grassroots organizations that backed the plan will have about two years to devise feasible ways to remove a mile of the expressway and eventually place the newly opened area into a community land trust. Federal officials said Regina's proposal stood out because of the details she and her partners were able to summon about the interstate's disruptive impact half a century ago.[16] The careful efforts to document Greenwood's past had paved the way for an alternative future. "Not only was it our family that was affected, but I thought about all the other families," she said. "We were touched by two waves of destruction. And to be able to show documents in that application, to point to dates and times—that put a human face on this whole highway construction story." Getting the grant for the study is only the first step in a long and complex process that will require buy-in from other local and state officials. But Regina's strain of optimism shone through when she got the good news. She now measures the timeline for interstate removal in years rather than decades.[17]

Even as efforts to uncover the truth about the past have brought unprecedented attention to Greenwood, Oklahoma lawmakers have gotten more aggressive in their efforts to whitewash history. Following the passage of HB 1775, the state law meant to curtail classroom discussions involving race, sex, and gender, Tulsa Public Schools received a warning against their accreditation status after a local high school teacher complained about being forced to watch a training video on implicit bias.[18] The state board of education voted to reprimand the school district without actually watching the video, with one board member saying it was important to "send a message."[19] The message has been received around the state. Because of HB 1775, one high school teacher in northeast Oklahoma has declined to assign her students *Killers of the Flower Moon,* a nonfiction 2017 book about brutal murders of indigenous people in the Osage Nation. Another teacher in Oklahoma City has removed real-world statistics from her math classes meant to help students engage more effectively with the lesson material.[20] Ryan Walters, the new state superintendent, has promised to go further to enforce the new law, railing against the "left wing indoctrination" of Oklahoma students.[21] While Walters and other proponents of HB 1775 have insisted that it will not curtail teaching about the Tulsa Race Massacre or the Trail of Tears, parents have already railed against classics such as *A Raisin in the Sun, Narrative of the Life of Frederick Douglass,* and *I Know Why the Caged Bird Sings.* A chilling effect sweeps through Oklahoma classrooms and the spark of knowledge every educator hopes to ignite in their students grows dimmer.[22] "It's not about parents' rights, it's not about liberty," Regina said at the meeting where the state board voted to punish Tulsa schools. "This is not the time to go along with this national agenda, to not do right by all of our children. They need to see themselves in our history."[23]

B. C. Franklin had another penetrating insight in his autobiography: "Most great issues are moral, not political." For all the legal hurdles to reparations put up by the justice system, the state legislature, and the federal government, nothing is stopping the city of Tulsa and its most influential power brokers from offering material support to massacre survivors and their descendants today.

Tourism is the third-largest contributor to Oklahoma's economy, after energy and agriculture, with Tulsa alone estimated to bring in $240 million from visitors in 2022.[24] The Greenwood Rising History Center is attracting 4,500 visitors per month, and as many as 8,000 during the summer.[25] The history center could divert some portion of its fifteen-dollar ticket price to a fund that benefits massacre descendants; hotels and restaurants in and near Greenwood that are benefiting from Black Wall Street's global appeal could also contribute, diverting a percentage of sales to the fund. Artists, writers, and filmmakers from outside Tulsa who are capturing the story of Greenwood—I include myself in this group—also have a responsibility to make sure that any work they do tangibly benefits the people and institutions that have been here for generations. And they must push their corporate backers to offer that kind of support as well. More than once, when the city was ready to bulldoze this history off the map, black people preserved it, yet North Tulsa residents continue to suffer disparate outcomes compared to residents of South Tulsa across too many quality-of-life measures. They deserve to participate in the financial bounty of Black Wall Street beyond plaques embedded in the sidewalks and real estate developers' vague promises to honor the neighborhood history.

There is plenty of precedent for such arrangements, both within and outside the context of reparations. In Alaska, every resident receives a check in the mail each year from the Permanent Fund Dividend, a government-run investment fund seeded by profits from an oil pipeline built in the 1970s.[26] Today black culture—black music, black food, black history—is one of our nation's most lucrative exports, and the people who nurture it should benefit as it skyrockets in value. A roster of massacre descendants, derived from research completed by the 2001 Tulsa Race Riot Commission, could receive an annual dividend from a fund, or be granted financial assistance for college tuition or small business loans.

There are already both public and private examples of entities taking responsibility for the violent traumas they heaped upon black people in the past. The trend has increased in recent years. Some offer money—in Evanston, Illinois, black families who were impacted by redlining are being granted $25,000 to pay off their mortgages or to complete house repairs.[27] Some offer land—in California, the state government ceded Bruce's Beach, an idyllic waterfront property that had been seized by city officials using eminent domain in the 1920s, back to the descendants of the Bruce family in 2021.[28] And some offer knowledge: the Middleton plantation, a site of brutal enslavement in antebellum South Carolina, now gives scholarships to the descendants of the slaves who once toiled on the plantation's soil.[29]

Tulsa has its pick of models to choose from. But any effort must be guided by the wishes of massacre survivors and descendants. Any pathway toward racial reconciliation, as Tulsa leaders profess to so ardently want, should adopt the principles of transitional justice, a framework developed by the United Nations to address international human rights abuses. Under the model of transitional justice, the perpetrator of an abuse should "[recognize] the centrality of victims and their special status in the design and implementation of transitional justice processes" while also striving for a "comprehensive approach" to addressing the harm. The United Nations applies transitional justice to societies that have been physically devastated by conflict, that lack resources, and that harbor a divided population.[30] It is an ongoing stain on this city that these descriptors could apply to Tulsa 102 years after the massacre.

Whether or not Tulsa ever does right by the people of Greenwood and North Tulsa, they will continue to do what they've always done: build.

Old institutions that fostered community bonds are being rebuilt, such as the Big Ten Ballroom. For decades the once-lively dance floor stood vacant. Now it is being remodeled by Lester Shaw and his nonprofit, A Pocket Full of Hope, which provides arts programs for North Tulsa youth. The descendants of Loula Williams hope to orchestrate a similar revival of the Dreamland Theater, on some of the acres of property owned by the Tulsa Development Authority.

New ventures are also being built from the ground up. The Terence Crutcher Foundation purchased a 5.8-acre former business center just north of Greenwood in December 2022; foundation board member Greg Robinson said the facility will be "a center of economic vitality and one of the centerpieces of a growing north Tulsa."[31] The *Black Wall Street Times* now has a physical office on Archer Street, where its staff of local journalists publish stories for the entire world to see. Just a couple of blocks away at the Greenwood-Archer intersection is the Black Wall Street Liquid Lounge; farther north is Fulton Street Coffee and Books. Both serve a diverse pool of customers, but they especially attract the young black clientele who once filled places like Loula Williams's confectionery. One was opened by a Tulsa native, the other by a transplant. Both types of Tulsans have a role to play in restoring economic vibrancy to North Tulsa.

And then there are the institutions that never left. Willie Sells, of Tee's Barber Shop, has been cutting hair on Greenwood Avenue since before the highway went up.[32] Princetta Rudd-Newman, a former educator, began giving tours on the block for decades, since the phrase "Black Wall Street" was just coming into popular use.[33] All around North Tulsa, plumbers, electricians, handymen, and carpenters have been patiently plying their trade for decades, tending to the homes and lives that those south of the railroad tracks have so long ignored.

Longest-running among these enterprises is the *Oklahoma Eagle,* which marked its one-hundredth birthday in 2022.[34] The newspaper has put a renewed focus on its digital presence and expanded its coverage of local events. The *Eagle* recently launched a nonprofit, the Greenwood Institute for Media and Strategic Communications, which seeks to preserve the long legacy of the black press in the United States by focusing on the impact it has had and continues to have in Tulsa. During the summer of 2022, the nonprofit organized a class curriculum in which college students at the University of Maryland and the University of Wisconsin got the chance to write about Greenwood's history in the *Eagle*'s pages, covering topics like the legacy of Booker T.

Washington High School.[35] The news organization is expanding its digital footprint by joining URL Media, a multiplatform collective of black- and brown-centered media outlets. And the *Eagle* hopes to one day bring some of its training opportunities into its physical property in the heart of Greenwood Avenue—just steps away from the site of J. H. and Carlie Goodwin's first commercial property in Deep Greenwood. The Goodwin family wants to have a space that both honors the past and looks toward the future, as the *Eagle* itself does every week.

Jim Goodwin, in his forty-second year as the *Eagle*'s publisher, is excited to see the paper persist for another century. So is his son David, the president of the new nonprofit. "Being able to maintain this legacy through four generations is a blessing, but the ownership is not mine. It's not the Goodwin family's," David said. "The ownership really is the community's, and I just want to make sure that whatever we do as we move forward, this is an institution that the community owns."[36]

ACKNOWLEDGMENTS

want to thank those writers who came before me. Many of the black people who have studied and written about Oklahoma were not given the platform I have been granted to tell their community's story, but their names deserve to ring out beyond the footnotes. I am indebted to authors such as Mary Jones Parrish, Mabel Little, Dottie Reed, B. C. Franklin, John Hope Franklin, Eddie Faye Gates, and Hannibal Johnson. I build on the work of earlier journalists who captured Greenwood's story in the *Tulsa Star* and the *Oklahoma Eagle*: A. J. Smitherman, Theodore Baughman, Horace Hughes, Thelma Thurston Gorham, Viola Bate, Luix Overbea, Ben Hill, Doretha McMillon, Eddie Madison, Jr., Don Ross, and Carmen Fields, among so many others. Today many local black writers, artists, and researchers continue to lift up Greenwood and the wider North Tulsa community: Chief Amusan, Gary Lee, Dreisen Heath, Mike Creef, Deon Osborne, Alicia Odewale, Quraysh Ali Lansana, Phetote Mshairi, and Kendrick Marshall. The story of Greenwood would not be so widely known, and its world could not be rendered so richly, without their persistence.

My agent, Elias Altman, saw the potential for this generational tale to be a book before I saw it so clearly myself; I owe him a debt of gratitude for guiding me through the proposal process and providing valuable feedback with each successive draft. I also could not have corralled more than one hundred years of history without the astute and timely feedback of my editor, Molly Turpin, who helped me figure out how to shape a long list of facts into a coherent narrative and build a scaffolding to guide readers through the decades, so they could become as excited about this world as I was. The entire Random House team—Greg Kubie, Michael Hoak, Ada Maduka, Janet Biehl, Tom Perry—worked tirelessly to get this book in the best possible shape, as did my publicist, Whitney Peeling. Thank you to each of you.

Much of this project was incubated in public, through feature articles I wrote about Tulsa across several different publications. Thanks to Sean Fennessey at *The Ringer* for sending me on my first reporting trip to Greenwood and to Bill Simmons for cultivating a workplace where such passion projects were encouraged. Thanks to Arik Gabbai at *Smithsonian* magazine and Lucas Wittman at *Time* for giving me the runway to explore hidden byways in our nation's history tied up deeply with this book's themes. I owe David Rohde at the *New Yorker* a beer or three for his thoughtful editing of my many dispatches from Tulsa. He offered care and precision on the page during tumultuous times and never tried to dilute my voice.

To the friends who held me down while I spent years secluded halfway across the country, thank you. Your calls, texts, and spontaneous Venmo and Uber Eats gifts helped me feel remembered during an isolating time. Thanks to Gabi Baetti, Connor Fox, Sarah Hughes, Seema Kumar, Mark Mayfield, Austen Parrish, Daniel Roth, R. J. Rico, Cheikh Robertson, Jake Smith, and Alexandra Tucci, who all celebrated my tiny victories and listened to my gnawing anxieties. Thank you to Wil Haygood for the kind words you wrote about this book before publication and your insight on navigating the whirlwind world of publishing. Thanks especially to Will Tucker, who read pages, bounced themes back and forth with me, and offered his skills as an investigative journalist when I was trying to crack some mysteries seemingly lost to time. Our Sunday Zoom calls were a highlight of these years.

The mountain of research summoned for this work would not have been possible without the aid of dozens of researchers, curators, and library staffers. Thank you to the staff at Oklahoma State University–Tulsa library, in particular Sheena Perez and Lynn Wallace, who wheeled out archives for me to review dozens of times over the years. The staff at the main branch of the Tulsa City–County Public Library were similarly patient. At the Tulsa Historical Society, I appreciated Michelle Place offering any and all aid early in the project, and Luke Williams diligently helping me secure photos and archival documents. At the Oklahoma Historical Society, Larry O'Dell shared his vital research on Greenwood insurance claims and property destruction, while Chad Williams graciously digitized obscure newspapers for me and allowed me to use OHS images to enhance my newsletter. I owe the world to Michelle Brown-Brudex and Frances Jordan at the Greenwood Cultural Center, who shared historic photos of Greenwood and helped me understand the community's history when I was first learning about it. An extra thanks to Ms. Frances for being a responsive and gracious landlord during my Oklahoma adventure, despite the multiple possum invasions.

I also owe so much to the people who helped me access vital government documents. Thank you to Holly Hosenfratz and the staff at the Oklahoma Department of Libraries, who helped me access court transcripts and highway archives; T. J. Gerlach at the Oklahoma Department of Transportation, who promptly provided responses to my open records requests; Carol Young and Nicole Travis at the Tulsa Development Authority; Kitsy Wyrick at the Tulsa County microfilm and records department, and the entire staff of the real estate services division of the Tulsa County Clerk's office, who provided me a crash course on analyzing historic land records.

I owe a special thanks to Scott Ellsworth, who shared with me his 1970s interviews with massacre survivors such as W. D. Williams, material that proved foundational to my retelling of 1921. Scott was gracious as I followed in his footsteps and encouraged me at every juncture. Thanks for both the big suggestions and the small ones.

Outside of Oklahoma, so many curators, archivists, and academics were essential for my research: Johanna Obenda and Paul Gardullo at the Smithsonian National Museum of African American History and Culture; Robert Spinelli at the special collections library of Fisk University; Joe Smith at the Notre Dame Archives; Louisa Hoffman at the Oberlin College Archives; Jack Gurner and Calvin Hawkins in Water Valley, Mississippi; the special collections staff of the Buffalo & Erie County Public Library; Julius J. Machnikowski at the Cook County Circuit Court Archives in Illinois; and Kristin Butler and Cameo George, who allowed me to review interview transcripts conducted for the 1993 PBS documentary *Goin' Back to T-Town* with Greenwood luminaries such as Mabel Little. I also received valuable insight on the history of redlining and HOLC Loans from Todd Michney and Thomas Storrs; on the numbers game from Matthew Vaz; on the mechanics of 1940s aerial flight from Kim Jones; on 1940s Oklahoma topography from Leah Jackson and the Oklahoma Geological Survey; on modern Oklahoma political trends from Keith Gaddie, Michael Crespin, and Craig Volden; and on urban renewal policies in Little Rock from Acadia Roher.

I enlisted my own small army of researchers to plow through a century of black history alongside me over the course of three years. Thank you so much to Aubrey Wilborn, Keely Brewer, Nkem Ike, Rachel Parker, Baylor Freeman, and Izz LaMagdeleine. Your efforts transcribing interviews, analyzing newspaper archives, summarizing key historical texts, and even conducting an interview or two made this project manageable for me. Also thank you to my excellent fact-checkers Gillian Brassil and Kellen Becoats, who were pivotal in the home stretch. An especially big thank you to David Spindle, who stuck with me on this project for more than two years, contributed a large amount of original research (shout out A.G.W. Sango), and helped me out with fact-checking when I was in a real bind. I owe you and your family so much for helping me keep the progress on this book steady through the ups and downs. Thank you to Debra Spindle and Angela Jerome Spindle as well.

It was a pleasure working with local photographers to capture Greenwood as it is today. Thanks to Joe Rushmore, Rico Green, and Chris Creese for agreeing to have your work showcased in this book. And a special thanks to Don Thompson for sharing your memories of urban renewal along with one of your most powerful images with readers in this venue.

My very first hire to work on this book was my younger cousin Stanley. He was thirteen when I asked him if he wanted to be my research assistant; a few days before my book was published, he graduated high school. Jacks, I hope you learned something about our people, and I only wish we'd gotten a chance to talk more about all you were absorbing. Keep writing.

I owe much to others who were not in my employ but still generous with the research they unearthed about Greenwood. Thanks to Carlos Moreno, one of the first to welcome me to Tulsa, for being generous with both your documentary evidence and your insight. Randy Krehbiel, who has been writing about Greenwood for decades, shared essential *Tulsa World* archives and his own well-informed takes on some of the narratives I was crafting. Larry Phillips offered his father Choc's firsthand account of the massacre from a white perspective, a rare and important document. Tara Brooke-Watkins connected me with longtime Greenwood residents early in my research. Thanks to Rob Harvilla, who didn't know much about Greenwood but signed up for a Cleveland Public Library card just so I could get access to some essential archives. Patrick McNicholas shared his amazing visual research into both the massacre and urban renewal. Arley Ward did incomparable work on the role of the *Eagle* fighting for Greenwood jobs during World War II. Thank you as well to University of Tulsa College of Law students Jack Schaefer and Connor Doyle and Urban Institute research assistant Elizabeth Burton. Your investigations into urban renewal policies in Greenwood were invaluable to me. To Jeff Martin and the staff at the Philbrook Museum, I appreciate you offering me a space to write and reflect on the beautiful garden grounds and the cozy cabin.

No amount of facts, figures, and historical research can replace lived experience, so the most precious thank-yous of all must go to the people of Greenwood. Thank you to those who welcomed me into their homes and told me their stories: Daisy Rogers, who showed me her grandmother and namesake Daisy Scott's *Tulsa Star* cartoons; Francine Campbell, who let me review her father Homer Johnson's TAAG files in his old house; and Princetta Rudd-Newman, who painted the old Greenwood nightlife with only slightly self-incriminating clarity. And I so appreciate those who no longer live in Tulsa but brought their childhood visions of Greenwood to life over the phone: Peggi Morrison, Elizabeth Early, Herbert Scott, James Bolton, Bill Boulware, Pat Bell, and Norvell Coots. A special thanks to Washington Rucker, who connected me with his old high school classmates and whose invocation that I "keep pushing" helped fuel my journey.

Greenwood's legacy lives on through many of the community leaders who continue to fight for it today, and so many of them were generous with their time over the years. Thank you to Dr. Tiffany Crutcher, who always found time for another interview with me amid her packed schedule; your clarity of vision is an inspiration. Thanks as well to Greg Robinson, Nehemiah Frank, Dr. Stevie Johnson, Therese Alduni, Onikah Asamoa-Caesar, Guy Troupe, and Tyrance Billingsley. All the time each of you took to either share your experiences with me or help amplify my work was so appreciated.

I owe a great deal to the descendants of many of the families whose stories arc across the generations in this book. To the descendants of Loula, John, and W. D. Williams—Marilyn Christopher, Gloria Christopher, Jan Christopher, Leslie Christopher, Charles Christopher II, and Karen Robinson—thank you for trusting me with your family's story and allowing me to depict some of Loula's most intimate moments. Jan once said that Loula deserves to be a prominent figure in black history, and hopefully this book can contribute some small part to that goal.

Thank you to Anneliese Bruner for helping me flesh out my understanding of Mary Jones Parrish and for working to ensure her words resonate a century after they were written.

This book is anchored by the legacy of the longest-surviving Greenwood family, the Goodwins. Capturing their triumphs and tribulations would not have been possible without the exhaustive, decades-long archival work of Jeanne Arradondo, daughter of Ed Goodwin, Sr., and Jeanne Goodwin. The Jeanne Osby Goodwin Arradondo Family Collection, housed in Jeanne's Nashville home, contains a treasure trove of materials including videos, letters, books, newspaper articles, citations, audio tapes, and photos spanning over a century—enough to fill an entire attic and then some. Family members have supported Jeanne with memorabilia and phone calls for more than seventy years. She and I are both grateful to her departed forebears who helped build and archive such a powerful family legacy, including her mother, Jeanne Goodwin, her grandfather J. H. Goodwin (or "Papa"), her grandmother Minnie Osby (or "Nannie"), her cousin Jewel Hines, her older sister Edwyna Anderson, her older brother Edward Goodwin, Jr., her niece Kathie Dones-Carson, and her aunts Georgia, Ethel, Layle, and Mayme. We also wanted to thank her son, Michael Arradondo, for his efforts in maintaining and digitizing the archive for its future preservation. And I must thank Jeanne once again for patiently walking me through her knowledge of the family across our weekly hour-long phone calls. You helped me find a phone number for practically any Greenwood native I could think of, and allowed me to publish so many treasured family photos in this book. This project would not have been the same without your tireless efforts.

In addition to Jeanne Arradondo, the four other living children of Ed Goodwin, Sr., showed a boundless generosity with their time and their stories. Thanks to Jo Ann for making me ham-and-turkey sandwiches while we discussed your memories of Booker T., thanks to Susan for your honesty and encouragement as I burrowed deeper into the family history, and thanks to Bob for offering the kind of clear-eyed clarity on what made his father tick that only a baby brother can provide. I'd also like to thank Jim, the first of Ed and Jeanne's children I got to meet, who accepted every one of my interview requests and threw his support behind my project before he knew what shape it would fully take. When you told me you were proud of me for what I was trying to do, before I had written a single word of this manuscript, it felt like someone else saw the ambition burning inside me to create something that could outlast all of us. I thank you for that.

I also owe so much to the following generations of Goodwins, who helped me find my way on this project from its first steps. Thanks to Greg and Sabrina for sharing memories of The House and 1415 North Greenwood (sorry about the "biscuits" line!), to Jerry for connecting me with valuable sources, and to Jeanne-Marguerite for letting me shadow you on *Eagle* delivery runs. Thanks to Sydnee for your help digitizing documents in Nashville and helping me understand how a younger generation interprets family legacy. Thank you to David and Angela for welcoming me into your home in Ohio, and to David in particular for supporting this project from our very first phone call, when I was still working on my proposal. You always put others before yourself in service of supporting the community that reared you, which is an admirable model to follow, both as a journalist and as a man.

By following Regina Goodwin for years in my reporting, I learned she does so much to help people that does not get reported in the news or on the House floor. Thank you for helping me find somewhere to live in Tulsa, for making sure I had something to eat on Thanksgivings spent working alone, and for being an advocate for my work before you'd laid a single eye on it. There are not that many real people in the world; you are one of them (or as your Daddy would say, you "tell it like it IZZ"). I'm so glad we met and consider you my lifelong lifeline in Tulsa.

Finally, I'm so thankful for the support of my family, who have nurtured my love of writing since I was a boy tooling around on my parents' typewriter. Thank you to Mommom, who taught me how to read, and to Grandma, who taught me how to be disciplined. Thank you to my cousins Monique and Anthony who were always big-upping my work (when they weren't bullying me). Thank you to my aunt Pat for passing down a literary spirit, which I admire more in you each year. Thank you to all my cousins, aunts, and uncles who have already assured me they plan to make sure *everybody* hears about this book. And to my brother Kevin: I hope you read this and know that you were the first person in my life I felt could accomplish anything. Thanks for making me believe in myself.

When I first started on this project, I was lucky to meet a woman who was beautiful, compassionate, and driven. A woman who had her own accolades and aspirations (and an encyclopedic knowledge of female rappers), but who also wanted the best for me, wherever that might take me. Ariel, I'm so glad we got to spend this time growing into each other even across distance. When we were apart, you shrank the miles with your wit and warmth over text messages and video calls. And every time we were united, amid a world that was unraveling, I was at peace. I love you and I can't wait for the next steps of our adventure, together.

I would not be a writer without all my parents did for me. Dad taught me how to think and to see the simple answers to complex questions. Whatever clarity I was able to bring to this book, I owe to you. Mom talked through every twist of this thrilling and harrowing process with me, from the day we were at the Fried Tomato Buffet and I said I might quit my job to write a book. You once told me writing was my gift from the Lord, but the sacred gift has been having a person whose love and support is unconditional for every day of my life. Thank you for willing my dreams to come true with your optimism, your sacrifice, and your love.

NOTES

PROLOGUE

1. "Peoples Grocery Store," *Tulsa World,* July 28, 1905, 5.
2. Peter Duncan Burchard, *Carver: A Great Soul* (Fairfax, Calif.: Serpent Wise, 1998), 7.
3. Hannibal Johnson, *Black Wall Street: From Riot to Renaissance in Tulsa's Historic Greenwood District* (Fort Worth, Tex.: Eakin Press 1998), 141.
4. Greenwood Chamber of Commerce, *Business Directory of North Tulsa, Oklahoma,* 3.
5. Jim Goodwin, conversation with the author, December 13, 2018.
6. Jo Ann Gilford, conversation with the author, September 11, 2019.
7. Regina Goodwin, conversation with the author, August 14, 2020.
8. J. Goodwin conversation.
9. Ibid.
10. Ibid.
11. "Is Greenwood at the Crossroads or Crosshairs?" *Oklahoma Eagle,* June 20, 2019, 1.
12. J. Goodwin conversation.
13. Jim Goodwin, conversation with the author, January 23, 2020.
14. J. Goodwin conversation, December 13, 2018.
15. J. Goodwin conversation, January 23, 2020.
16. Margaret Fosmoe, "A Voice for All the People of Tulsa," *Notre Dame Magazine,* Winter 2020–21, https://magazine.nd.edu/stories/a-voice-for-all-the-people-of-tulsa.
17. J. Goodwin conversation, December 13, 2018.
18. J. Goodwin conversation, January 23, 2020.
19. *Tulsa Race Riot: A Report by the Oklahoma Commission to Study the Tulsa Race Riot of 1921* (Oklahoma City: Commission, 2001), https://www.okhistory.org/research/forms/freport.pdf.
20. J. Goodwin conversation, January 23, 2020.

CHAPTER 1: DO NOT HESITATE, BUT COME

1. "Unequaled Advantages in the B.I.T.," *Muskogee Comet,* June 23 1904, 2.
2. "Homeseeker's Guide: A Word of Information Concerning Oklahoma," *Enterprise,* May 12, 1910, 1.
3. Arthur Tolson, "A History of Langston, Oklahoma, 1890–1950," master's thesis, Oklahoma Agricultural and Mechanical College, 1952, 69.
4. 1910 U.S. Census, Yalobusha County, Miss., pop. sch., ED 117, sheet 9B, dwell. 33, fam. 42, James H. Goodwin.
5. "Race Question Will Not Down in Mississippi," *St. Louis Post-Dispatch,* Sep-

tember 18, 1904, 1; " 'Nigger, Be Good,' " *St. Louis Palladium*, October 8, 1904, 1.

6. "Water Valley, Miss.," *Oklahoma Safeguard*, April 27, 1905, 1.

7. "Water Valley, Mississippi," *Oklahoma Safeguard*, March 9, 1905, 4; "Water Valley, Miss.," *Oklahoma Safeguard*, February 1, 1906, 6.

8. U.S. Census Bureau, *Statistics for Oklahoma* (Washington, D.C.: Government Printing Office, 1913), 623, 597; U.S. Census Bureau, *1910 Census: Abstract of the Census: Statistics of Population, Agriculture, Manufactures, and Mining for the United States, the States, and Principal Cities* (Washington, D.C.: Government Printing Office, 1913), 245.

9. 1920 U.S. Census, *State Compendium: Oklahoma* (Washington, D.C.: Government Printing Office, 1924), 28.

10. Homer D. Woods, "A Brief Biography of Ellis Walker Woods," February 11, 2021, Ellis Walker Woods Memorial, Oklahoma State University–Tulsa, https://tulsa.okstate.edu/ewwoods/biography.

11. *Oklahoma Safeguard*, February 2, 1905, 1.

12. "Black-American Members by State and Territory, 1870–Present," History, Art & Archives of the U.S. House of Representatives (website), https://history .house.gov/Exhibitions-and-Publications/BAIC/Historical-Data/Black -American-Representatives-and-Senators-by-State-and-Territory/.

13. Monroe and Florence Work Today, Auut Studio, 2016, https://plaintalkhistory .com/monroeandflorencework/.

14. "Down in Dixie: A Revolution Is Coming," *Oklahoma Safeguard*, March 9, 1905, 4.

15. J. H. Goodwin funeral program, March 1958, Jeanne Osby Goodwin Arra- dondo Family Collection, Nashville, Tenn.

16. *Water Valley, Yalobusha County, Mississippi,* map (Sanborn Map Co., May 1893), Image 1, Library of Congress.

17. Jack Gurner (curator, Water Valley Casey Jones Railroad Museum) to David Spindle (author's research assistant), January 22, 2021.

18. Rudolph L. Daniels, *Trains Across the Continent: North American Railroad History* (Bloomington: Indiana University Press, 2000), 30.

19. 1900 U.S. Census, Yalobusha County, Miss., pop. sch., ED 102, sheet 6B, dwell. 127, fam. 42, James Goodwin.

20. Daniels, *Trains Across the Continent,* 69; Michigan Central Railroad Com- pany, *Rules for the Government of the Conducting Transportation Depart- ment* (Cleveland: W.S. Gilkey, 1916), 114.

21. Eric Arnesen, *Brotherhoods of Color: Black Railroad Workers and the Strug- gle for Equality* (Cambridge, Mass.: Harvard University Press, 2002), 25.

22. Wharton Vernon Lane, *The Negro in Mississippi 1865–1890* (1945; reprint New York: Harper Torchbooks, 1967), 126; 1890 U.S. Census, *Report on the Population of the United States,* part 2 (Washington, D.C.: Government Print- ing Office, 1895), 348.

23. John F. Stover, *History of the Illinois Central Railroad* (New York: Macmillan, 1975), 215.

24. 1910 U.S. Census, *Statistics for Mississippi* (Washington, D.C.: Government Printing Office, 1913), 633; Franklin L. Riley, ed., *Publications of the Missis-*

sippi Historical Society (University: Mississippi Historical Society, 1912), 11:217.

25. "J. S. Goodwin, Dealer in Fancy Groceiries [*sic*], Confections, Can Goods," *Water Valley Progress,* November 5, 1904, 8; Jack Gurner, conversation with the author, November 2, 2022.

26. "A Man Full of Push," *Tulsa Star,* November 23, 1918, 2.

27. J. H. Goodwin funeral program; Jeanne Arradondo, conversation with the author, August 3, 2020.

28. 1910 U.S. Census, Yalobusha County, Miss., pop. sch., ED 117, sheet 9B, dwell. 33, fam. 42, James H. Goodwin.

29. Allyson Hobbs, *A Chosen Exile: A History of Racial Passing in American Life* (Cambridge, Mass.: Harvard University Press, 2014), 156.

30. E. L. Goodwin, Jr., *There Must Be a God Somewhere* (unpublished, n.d.).

31. Langston Hughes, "Fooling Our White Folks," *Negro Digest,* April 1950, 38–41.

32. *Water Valley, Yalobusha County, Mississippi,* map (Sanborn Map Co., September 1910), Image 4, Library of Congress.

33. *Water Valley Progress,* June 16, 1906, 5.

34. *City Itemizer,* April 7, 1910, 2; Suzanne E. Smith, *To Serve the Living: Funeral Directors and the African American Way of Death* (Cambridge, Mass.: Belknap Press, 2010), 8.

35. U.S. Census Bureau, *Negro Population, 1790–1915* (Washington, D.C.: Government Printing Office, 1918), 465; Yalobusha County, Miss., Deed Book S, 207, Sally Williams and J. H. Goodwin, September 25, 1908; Deed Book S, 352, J. H. Goodwin and H. R. Sanders, April 8, 1910; Pearl and John Whickum and J. H. Goodwin, September 16, 1910; Deed Book T, 96, J. H. and Carlie Goodwin and Sam and Lizzie Wheelis, August 18, 1913.

36. *Water Valley Progress,* July 19, 1902, 5; Thomas Bell, "D.C. Knights of Pythias Hope to Eliminate Color Barrier," *Washington Post,* February 22, 1990, https://www.washingtonpost.com/archive/local/1990/02/22/dc-knights -of-pythias-hope-to-eliminate-color-barrier/8be38101-6d31-4696-a1ea -2f015a940f9a/.

37. Arradondo conversation, August 3, 2020.

38. Charles C. Bolton, *The Hardest Deal of All: The Battle Over School Integration in Mississippi, 1870–1980* (Jackson: University Press of Mississippi, 2007), 8.

39. Ibid., 21.

40. *Biennial Report and Recommendations of the State Superintendent of Public Education to the Legislature of Mississippi for the Scholastic Years 1911–12 and 1912–13* (Nashville: Brandon Printing Co., 1913), 117; Lane, *Negro in Mississippi,* 248–49.

41. *Water Valley, Yalobusha County, Mississippi,* map (Sanborn Map Co., September 1910), Images 2–3, Library of Congress; *City Itemizer,* November 12, 1914, 10.

42. Department of the Interior Bureau of Education, *Negro Education: A Study of the Higher Schools for Colored People in the United States* (Washington, D.C.: Government Printing Office, 1917), 2:336.

43. Stuart Grayson Noble, *Forty Years of the Public Schools in Mississippi* (New York: Teachers College, Columbia University, 1918), 111.

44. Riley, *Publications of the Mississippi Historical Society*, 227–52.

45. J. C. Hathorn, *A History of Grenada County* (Self-published, ca. 1970), 131, 96.

46. Lane, *Negro in Mississippi*, 232.

47. E. L. Goodwin, Jr., "The Party Is Over . . . Same Old Soup Warmed Over," *Oklahoma Eagle*, January 9, 1986, 16.

48. Jim Goodwin, conversation with the author, January 15, 2021.

49. Neil McMillen, *Dark Journey: Black Mississippians in the Age of Jim Crow* (Urbana: University of Illinois Press, 1990), 264.

50. 1940 U.S. Census, Tulsa County, Okla., pop. schedule, James H. Goodwin.

51. Ed Goodwin, Sr., interview by Henry G. La Brie III, August 12, 1971, transcript, 1, Black Journalists Oral History Collection, Columbia University.

52. Zantel Nichols and Jim Stanton, "African-American Residents Followed Tracks to Waterloo," *Waterloo-Cedar Falls Courier*, June 30, 1996, 132; Kenneth Pins, "New Generations Leave the Iowa of Their Ancestors," *Des Moines Register*, February 14, 1999, 4.

53. Ed Sr. interview by La Brie, 1.

54. "How a St. Louis Icon Keeps Reinventing Itself," *St. Louis Union Station*, https://www.stlouisunionstation.com/story; State Historical Society of Missouri, "St. Louis Union Station," National Register of Historic Places Nomination Form (Washington, D.C.: U.S. Department of the Interior, National Park Service, 1968).

55. Ed Sr. interview by La Brie, 2.

56. *Topeka Plaindealer*, April 24, 1903, 1.

57. Red Bird Investment Company, *Red Bird, Creek Nation, I.T.* (Fort Smith, Ark., 1905), 5; "T. H. Martin Is the Standard Bearer," *Muskogee Times-Democrat*, March 21, 1907, 1.

58. Jo O. Ferguson, "In the Cool o' the Evening," *Pawnee Chief*, December 6, 1962, 2.

59. "Thugs, City Officials and Paving Men Run Caucuses," *Muskogee Times-Democrat*, February 28, 1908, 4.

60. *Muskogee Times-Democrat*, March 13, 1909, 4.

61. Alex Sango, Enrollment Jacket, Applications for Allotment, compiled 1899–1907, Office of Indian Affairs, Record Group 75, National Archives.

62. "Mrs. Phyllis Sango Is Dead," *Muskogee Evening Times*, January 25, 1902, 4.

63. Murray Wickett, *Contested Territory: Whites, Native Americans and African Americans in Oklahoma, 1865–1907* (Baton Rouge: Louisiana State University Press, 2000), 8.

64. Scipio Sancho, Claim 204, Records Relating to Loyal Creek Claims, 1869–1870, Office of Indian Affairs, Record Group 75, National Archives.

65. Wickett, *Contested Territory*, 7–13.

66. David A. Chang, *The Color of the Land* (Chapel Hill: University of North Carolina Press, 2010), 49; Wickett, *Contested Territory*, 172.

67. A.G.W. Sango to Booker T. Washington, December 2, 1905, Black Economic Empowerment: National Negro Business League Collection, Library of Congress.

68. Angie Debo, *And Still the Waters Run* (1940; reprint Norman: University of Oklahoma Press, 1989), 47.

69. Kent Carter, "Dawes Commission," *Encyclopedia of Oklahoma History and Culture*, https://www.okhistory.org/publications/enc/entry.php?entry=DA018.

70. Francis Paul Prucha, ed, *Americanizing the American Indian* (Cambridge, Mass.: Harvard University Press, 2013), 1.

71. James Wilson, *The Earth Shall Weep: A History of Native America* (New York: Atlantic Monthly Press, 1998), 300.

72. *An Act to Ratify and Confirm an Agreement with the Muscogee or Creek Tribe of Indians, and for Other Purposes,* Public Law 676, *U.S. Statutes at Large* 31 (1901): 862; Gary Zellar, *African Creeks: Estelvste and the Creek Nation* (Norman: University of Oklahoma Press, 2007), 253–54.

73. Calculations made by the author based on figures provided in Debo, *And Still the Waters Run,* 47–51.

74. Henry Louis Gates, Jr., "The Truth Behind '40 Acres and a Mule,'" PBS/African Americans, n.d., https://www.pbs.org/wnet/african-americans-many-rivers-to-cross/history/the-truth-behind-40-acres-and-a-mule/.

75. Alex Sango, Applications for Allotment, July 1, 1901, Office of Indian Affairs, Five Civilized Tribes Agency, Department of the Interior; *Hastain's Township Plats of the Creek Nation* (Muskogee, Okla.: Model Printing Co., 1910), 160.

76. Wickett, *Contested Territory,* 31.

77. Lester A. Walton, "Using 'Oil' as a Stepping Stone to Power and Wealth, Oklahoma 'The Boomer State' Boasts Many Race Millionaire Families," *Pittsburgh Courier,* September 19, 1925, 9.

78. "On the Wing," *Muskogee Cimeter,* March 2, 1905, 1.

79. "Homeseekers' Guide: A Word of Information Concerning Oklahoma," *Enterprise,* May 12, 1910, 1.

80. Ed Sr. interview by La Brie, 2.

81. John Bradbury, "St. Louis–San Francisco Railway Company," *Missouri Encyclopedia,* https://missouriencyclopedia.org/groups-orgs/st-louis-san-francisco-railway-company; Thomas Foti, "Ozark Mountains," *Arkansas Encyclopedia,* https://encyclopediaofarkansas.net/entries/ozark-mountains-440.

82. St. Louis–San Francisco Railway Co., Public Time Table (August 1913), 20.

83. "Making Hole-Drilling Technology," American Oil and Gas Historical Society, https://aoghs.org/technology/oil-well-drilling-technology; Donna Casity McSpadden, "Chelsea," *Encyclopedia of Oklahoma History and Culture,* https://www.okhistory.org/publications/enc/entry?entry=CH013.

84. Bobby D. Weaver, "Red Fork Field," *Encyclopedia of Oklahoma History and Culture,* https://www.okhistory.org/publications/enc/entry.php?entry=RE004.

85. *Tulsa World,* November 16, 1912, 6; Clarence B. Douglas, "Tells Truths About Teeming Tulsa in 'The Tulsa Spirit,'" *Tulsa Democrat,* May 26, 1918, 1; "We Believe!" *Tulsa World,* December 19, 1918, 9.

86. Bobby D. Weaver, "Glenn Pool Field," *Encyclopedia of Oklahoma History and Culture,* https://www.okhistory.org/publications/enc/entry.php?entry= GL007.

87. Jimmy Stamp, "Traveling in Style and Comfort: The Pullman Sleeping Car," *Smithsonian Magazine,* December 11, 2013, https://www.smithsonianmag .com/arts-culture/traveling-style-and-comfort-pullman-sleeping-car -180949300/; Arnesen, *Brotherhoods of Color,* 16.

88. H. Roger Green, *The Railroad: The Life and Story of a Technology* (Westport, Conn.: Greenwood Press, 2005), 54.

89. Melissa Stuckey, "All Men Up: Race, Rights, and Power in the All-Black Town of Boley, Oklahoma, 1903–1939," Ph.D. diss., Yale University: 2009, 133–34.

90. "New Charters," *Tulsa Daily Legal News,* December 3, 1917, 1.

91. J. Goodwin interview, January 15, 2021; Arradondo conversation, August 3, 2020.

92. *Tulsa City Directory, 1913,* 419; *Tulsa, Tulsa County, Oklahoma,* map (Sanborn Map Co., 1915), Image 15, Library of Congress.

93. "City News Briefs," *Coffeyville Daily Journal,* August 19, 1905, 1; "Politics Warms with Spring Time," *Tulsa Democrat,* March 9, 1906, 1.

94. "Lawyer's Game Gets into Court," *Tulsa Democrat,* October 14, 1912, 2.

95. Ibid.; "J. B. Stradford Civil Leader Is Taken in Death," *Chicago Defender,* January 4, 1936, 4: "McKinney Law Alumnus J. B. Stradford Was Prominent on Black Wall Street," Pride of IU Stories, February 22, 2022, https://www.myiu .org/stories/pride-and-tradition/mckinney-law-alumnus-j-b-stradford-was -prominent-on-black-wall-street/.

96. "Colored Reading Room," *Tulsa Star,* April 18, 1913, 1; "Annual Address of President Stradford," *Tulsa Star,* February 14, 1914, 1.

97. "Will Pave Greenwood," *Tulsa Democrat,* September 2, 1914, 2; *Tulsa Star,* September 5, 1914, 4; "The Bright Side of Oklahoma," *Topeka Plaindealer,* June 15, 1917, 1.

98. *Tulsa, Tulsa County, Oklahoma,* map (Sanborn Map Co., 1915), Image 4, Library of Congress; "News Around Town," *Tulsa Star,* May 29, 1915, 4.

99. "Tulsa, Okla.," *Topeka Plaindealer,* June 5, 1908, 7.

100. *Tulsa Democrat,* July 28, 1905, 5; *Tulsa Star,* August 19, 1914, 17.

101. *Tulsa City Directory, 1913,* 452; "Keep Clean," *Tulsa Star,* September 19, 1913, 6; Theodore Baughman, "Progress of the Race in Our Sister State," *Topeka Plaindealer,* April 14, 1916, 2.

102. "Business and Social Life in Oklahoma," *Topeka Plaindealer,* March 10, 1911, 1; *Topeka Plaindealer,* May 12, 1911, 3.

103. "Mrs. Lulu T. 'Cotton' Williams: Williams Confectionery," *Tulsa Star,* August 19, 1914, 10.

104. "Business Professional Directory," *Tulsa Star,* April 3, 1915, 4.

105. "Locals," *Tulsa Star,* April 18, 1913, 1; "A Cozy Store," *Tulsa Star,* April 4, 1914, 4.

106. Tulsa County, Okla., Deed Book 127, 356, J. H. Hill and Lula Cotton, December 4, 1912.

107. W. D. Williams, interview by Ruth Sigler Avery, November 29, 1970, tran-

script, Box 7, Ruth Sigler Avery Collection, Oklahoma State University–Tulsa; *Tulsa City Directory, 1914*, 527.

108. J. S. Kirby, "News Around Town," *Tulsa Star,* January 24, 1914, 4; "What's Doing in Town?" *Tulsa Star,* April 6, 1918, 4.

109. Walter F. White, "The Eruption of Tulsa," *Nation,* June 29, 1921.

110. *Tulsa City Directory, 1913,* 452; *Tulsa Star,* August 19, 1914, 15.

111. *Tulsa Star,* July 18, 1913, 5; "The Bright Side of Oklahoma," *Topeka Plaindealer,* June 15, 1917, 1.

112. "Editor Threatened with Violence," *Tulsa Star,* August 1, 1913, 1; *Tulsa Star,* August 1, 1913, 4.

113. "Tulsa as the Leading City," *Tulsa Star,* August 19, 1914, 1.

114. *Tulsa City Directory, 1914,* 528; Theodore Baughman, "Oklahoma: A Squint at Negro Enterprise in That Land of Promise," *Topeka Plaindealer,* May 28, 1915, 7; *Tulsa, Tulsa County, Oklahoma,* map (Sanborn Map Co., 1915), Image 36, Library of Congress; A. J. Smitherman, "Autobiography: Launching the *Tulsa Star,*" *Empire Star,* March 25, 1961, 10; Andrew Jackson Smitherman registration, Tulsa County, Okla., "U.S., World War I Draft Registration Cards, 1917–1918," https://www.ancestry.com/search/collections/6482/.

115. *Tulsa Star,* January 24, 1914, 4.

116. "Local News," *Tulsa Star,* December 13, 1913, 1.

117. Tulsa County, Okla., Deed Book 161, 392, G. B. Littlejohn and J. H. Goodwin, February 18, 1914.

118. Ed Goodwin, Sr., interview by Carlie Goodwin, ca. 1970s, Jeanne Osby Goodwin Arradondo Family Collection, Nashville, Tenn.

119. "In the 'Jim Crow Coach' Ahead," *Tulsa Star,* April 7, 1917, 1; "Subscribe Complains of Frisco Train Service," *Tulsa Star,* December 11, 1915, 1.

120. Ed Sr. interview by Carlie Goodwin.

121. Ibid.

122. "News Around the City," *Tulsa Star,* March 14, 1914, 5.

123. Ed Goodwin, Sr., interview by Ruth Sigler Avery, November 21, 1976, transcript, Box 2, Ruth Sigler Avery Collection, Oklahoma State University–Tulsa.

CHAPTER 2: AND SOMETIMES BETTER, BESIDES

1. *Tulsa, Tulsa County, Oklahoma,* map (Sanborn Map Co., 1915), Image 4, Library of Congress; David M. Breed, "A Look at the Life of E. L. Goodwin, Sr.," *Oklahoma Eagle,* September 14, 1978, 10.

2. Cherokee Nation, Cherokee Nation Reservation Map, https://vmgis4.cherokee .org/portal/apps/webappviewer/index.html?id= d890e55c04c04c31a658301f9d020521.

3. *Tulsa City Directory, 1918* (Polk-Hoffhine Directory Co.), 730–31.

4. *Tulsa Star,* August 19, 1914, 17.

5. Mabel Little, *Fire on Mount Zion: My Life and History as a Black Woman in America* (Wilmington, Del.: Black Think Tank, 1992), 32.

6. *Tulsa Star,* September 5, 1914, 4.

7. Jim Goodwin, conversation with the author, January 15, 2021.

8. "New Building in E. End," *Tulsa Star,* October 30, 1915, 1; *Tulsa Star,* November 11, 1916, 4.

9. "Goodwin on the Staff," *Tulsa Star,* January 15, 1916, 1; "Notice to Subscribers," *Tulsa Star,* June 12, 1916, 1.

10. Samuel Malone Jackson, draft registration card, serial no. U3304, World War II Draft Registration Cards, 1942, National Archives.

11. Mary Jones Parrish, *Events of the Tulsa Disaster* (Tulsa, ca. 1922), 89–90.

12. Jeanne Arradondo, conversation with the author, August 10, 2020; Ed Goodwin, Sr., interview by Carlie Goodwin, ca. 1970s, Jeanne Osby Goodwin Arradondo Family Collection, Nashville, Tenn.

13. Booker T. Washington High School Yearbook, 1921, National Museum of African American History and Culture, Smithsonian, Washington, D.C., https:// collections.si.edu/search/record/edanmdm:nmaahc_2011.175.18

14. David M. Breed, "Little Africa," *Oklahoma Eagle,* November 2, 1978, C12; *Tulsa City Directory, 1918,* 495.

15. Don Ross, prologue to *Tulsa Race Riot: A Report by the Oklahoma Commission to Study the Tulsa Race Riot of 1921* (Oklahoma City: Commission, 2001), iv, https://www.okhistory.org/research/forms/freport.pdf.

16. "Convict Negress of Manslaughter," *Tulsa World,* May 12, 1916, 1.

17. "Before the Riot," *Oklahoma Eagle,* November 2, 1950, 10.

18. "Race Woman Theatrical Magnate," *Topeka Plaindealer,* November 28, 1919, 1.

19. W. D. Williams, interview by Scott Ellsworth, June 7, 1978 (recording), Tulsa Race Massacre of 1921 Archive, University of Tulsa.

20. Daniel Czitrom, "Movies as Popular Culture," in Kathleen Franz and Susan Smulyan, eds., *Major Problems in American Popular Culture* (Boston: Wadsworth, 2012), 170.

21. Williams interview by Ellsworth.

22. Tulsa County, Okla., Deed Book 157, 435, Elias Rambo and J. W. and Lula Williams, May 15, 1914; Tulsa County Clerk, *Original Townsite, Tulsa, Okla.* (map) (Tulsa: County Clerk, 1920).

23. Exhibit A, *Loula T. Williams v. Central States Fire Co. Insurance Dept.,* Case No. 19248 (Tulsa County District Court, 1922).

24. "New Theatre Draws the Crowd," *Tulsa Star,* September 5, 1914, 4.

25. Ann E. Weisman, "Greenwood: Tulsa's Phoenix," *American Visions,* August 1987, 35.

26. "New Theatre Draws the Crowd."

27. "Dark-Skinned Inhabitants of 'Little Africa' Doing Well in the Light of White Metropolitan Improvements," *Tulsa World,* July 4, 1915, Sunday features section, 1.

28. Tulsa County, Okla., Deed Book 127, 356, J. H. Hill and Lula Cotton, December 4, 1912.

29. "Mrs. Lulu T. 'Cotton' Williams: Williams Confectionery," *Tulsa Star,* August 19, 1914, 10.

30. Tulsa County, Okla., Deed Book 140, 258, J. W. Williams and Loula T. Williams, April 3, 1915.

31. " 'Battling Jim' Johnson," *Tulsa Democrat,* January 20, 1916, 6.

32. "Race Woman Theatrical Magnate," *Topeka Plaindealer*, November 28, 1919, 1.

33. Tulsa County, Okla., Deed Book 262, 541, Loula Williams Affidavit, June 24, 1919.

34. "Popular Play House," *Tulsa Star*, September 14, 1918, 2; *Tulsa Star*, September 7, 1918, 8.

35. Richard L. Stokes, "Cleopatra Movie Lavish Waste of Resources," *St. Louis Post-Dispatch*, December 24, 1917, 3.

36. " 'The Birth of a Nation' at the Majestic Theater," *Tulsa Democrat*, September 25, 1918, 10.

37. "Majestic," *Tulsa World*, September 27, 1918, 10.

38. "Mayor and Commissioners Oppose 'Birth of a Nation,' " *Tulsa Star*, September 28, 1918, 4.

39. *Tulsa Star*, September 7, 1918, 8.

40. *The Road West: The Steve Turner Collection of African Americana*, lot 196, Cowan's Auctions.

41. *Tulsa City Directory, 1920*, 594.

42. "Next Week's Attractions at the Dixie Theater," *Tulsa Star*, December 11, 1920, 8; "Irving C. Miller's Company Captivates Tulsa," *Tulsa Star*, December 11, 1920, 1.

43. "Race Woman Theatrical Magnate."

44. W.E.B. Du Bois, "Diary of Journey" (typescript notes), ca. 1921, 32, MS 312, Du Bois Papers, Special Collections and University Archives, University of Massachusetts Amherst Libraries.

45. "Three Dunbar Graduates," *Tulsa Democrat*, May 29, 1916, 3.

46. Henry Sowders deposition, *J. B. Stradford v. American Central Ins. Co.*, Case No. 370,274 (Cook County Superior Court, 1921), 6; "Negroes Protest Segregation Law," *Tulsa World*, August 8, 1916, 1.

47. Sowders deposition, 6, in *Stradford v. American Central*; "Negroes Protest Segregation Law."

48. "Race Woman Theatrical Magnate."

49. Ibid.

50. Little, *Fire on Mount Zion*, 26–28.

51. Mabel Little, in *Goin' Back to T-Town*, PBS/American Experience, March 1, 1993; "The Weather," *Tulsa World*, September 21, 1913, 1.

52. Larry O'Dell, "All-Black Towns," *Encyclopedia of Oklahoma History and Culture*, https://www.okhistory.org/publications/enc/entry?entry=AL009.

53. Melissa N. Stuckey, "Boley, Indian Territory: Exercising Freedom in the All-Black Town," *Journal of African American History* 102, no. 4 (Fall 2017): 503.

54. Melissa Stuckey, " 'All Men Up': Race, Rights, and Power in the All Black Town of Boley, Oklahoma, 1903–1939," Ph.D. diss., Yale University, 2007, 49.

55. Eunice Cloman Jackson, in Eddie Faye Gates, *They Came Searching: How Blacks Sought the Promised Land in Oklahoma* (Austin, Tex.: Eakin Press, 1997), 118.

56. Little, *Fire on Mount Zion,* 31; "The Bright Side of Oklahoma," *Topeka Plaindealer,* June 15, 1917, 1.

57. Elsie Gubser, interview by Ruth Sigler Avery, March 1, 1971, transcript, Box 2, Ruth Sigler Avery Collection, Oklahoma State University–Tulsa; hereafter Avery Collection.

58. Alice Andrews, in Gates, *They Came Searching,* 41.

59. Mabel Little, interview by Ruth Sigler Avery, May 24, 1971, transcript, Box 4, Avery Collection.

60. W. D. Williams, interview by Ruth Sigler Avery, November 29, 1970, transcript, 116, Box 7, Avery Collection; *Tulsa City Directory, 1914,* 527.

61. Paul S. Vickery, "Brady, Wyatt Tate (1870–1925)," *Encyclopedia of Oklahoma History and Culture,* https://www.okhistory.org/publications/enc/entry ?entry=BR002.

62. "A Conspiracy of Silence," National Public Radio, n.d., transcript, Box 2, Avery Collection.

63. Little, *Fire on Mount Zion,* 28.

64. Ibid., 43; "New Colored Park," *Sand Springs Review,* July 10, 1914, 1.

65. Little, *Fire on Mount Zion,* 32.

66. Ibid., 43; "Conspiracy of Silence."

67. Little, *Fire on Mount Zion,* 43; Mabel Little, in *Goin' Back to T-Town;* D. Elaine Fowler, "Mabel Little in Business Forty-One Yrs," *Oklahoma Eagle,* October 15, 1953, 1.

68. Little, *Fire on Mount Zion,* 34.

69. Fowler, "Mabel Little in Business."

70. Little, *Fire on Mount Zion,* 33.

71. Tulsa County, Okla., Deed Book 68, 227, Elias Rambo Hill and W. H. and Eliza O. Woods, July 1910; *Tulsa City Directory, 1917,* 503.

72. Rob L. Edwards, "In the Social Circle," *Tulsa Star,* June 5, 1915, 5.

73. Little, *Fire on Mount Zion,* 74.

74. Ibid., 35.

75. Mabel Little, in *Goin' Back to T-Town,* 8.

76. Little, *Fire on Mount Zion,* 34.

77. Shelly Lynn Lemons, "Down on First Street, Prostitution in Tulsa, Oklahoma 1900–1925," Ph.D. diss., Oklahoma State University, 2004, 90.

78. Little, *Fire on Mount Zion,* 34.

79. Mabel Little, in *Goin' Back to T-Town,* 21.

80. "Church Holds Street Meetings," *Tulsa Star,* November 13, 1915, 1; "34 Baptised at Mt. Zion," *Tulsa Star,* February 20, 1915, 8.

81. "History," First Baptist Church North Tulsa, https://fbcnt.org/members -guests/history/.

82. Leroy Alfred et al., *National Register of Historic Places Nomination, Vernon A.M.E. Church, Tulsa County, Okla.,* ed. Lynda Ozan (Tulsa: Vernon AME Historical Preservation Committee, 2018), 11.

83. D. Jackson, S. Wiley, J. Simmons, and M. Jackson, "Faith Still Standing (100 Years Later)," May 31, 2022.

84. "Bright Side of Oklahoma."

85. Richard Wright, *12 Million Black Voices* (New York: Macmillan, 1941), 131.

86. Cathy Ambler, *National Register of Historic Places Nomination, Mount Zion Baptist Church, Tulsa County, Okla.* (Tulsa: Preservation Oklahoma, 2008), 7.

87. Parrish, *Events of the Tulsa Disaster,* 55.

88. Tulsa County, Okla., Deed Book 151, 90–91, Susan Querry and A. W. Anderson and F. K. White, May 21, 1913.

89. "A Good Man Gone," *Tulsa Star,* April 25, 1914, 4.

90. Robert Whitaker, 1910, Census Place, Oklahoma City Ward 6, Oklahoma, Oklahoma, Roll T624_1266, p. 32B, Enumeration District 0227, FHL microfilm 1375279.

91. *Tulsa Star,* June 19, 1915, 1; F. K. White, "Address of Dr. F. K. White," *Tulsa Star,* February 14, 1914, 8.

92. Tulsa County, Okla., Deed Book 121, 226, Susan Querry and A. W. Anderson and F. K. White, June 21, 1913; *Tulsa Star,* June 19, 1915, 1.

93. *Tulsa World,* June 15, 1918, 2.

94. "To Aid Mt. Zion Church," *Tulsa Star,* October 30, 1920, 11.

95. *Tulsa, Tulsa County, Oklahoma,* map (Sanborn Map Co., 1915), Image 4, Library of Congress; *Tulsa Star,* June 19, 1915, 1.

96. Parrish, *Events of the Tulsa Disaster,* 55.

97. Tulsa County, Okla., Deed Book 262, 360, Trustees of Mt. Zion Baptist Church and Tri-State Construction Company, July 17, 1919; "Members of Negro Baptist Church to Build Handsome Edifice in Tulsa Shortly," *Tulsa Democrat,* March 16, 1919, 9.

98. Hannibal B. Johnson, *Black Wall Street: From Riot to Renaissance in Tulsa's Historic Greenwood District* (Forth Worth, Tex.: Eakin Press, 1998), 84.

99. Little, *Fire on Mount Zion,* 53.

100. Quintard Taylor, *In Search of the Racial Frontier: African Americans in the West 1528–1990* (New York: W.W. Norton, 1998), 151.

101. Alex Albright et al., "After the Burning: The Economic Effects of the 1921 Tulsa Race Massacre," National Bureau of Economic Research, Working Paper No. 28985, 4, https://www.nber.org/papers/w28985.

102. Don Ross, "From the Ghetto Line," *Oklahoma Eagle,* September 19, 1968, 8; "Typhoid Is Reported in Extreme East End," *Tulsa World,* June 13, 1911, 5.

103. Ed Goodwin, Sr., interview by Ruth Sigler Avery, November 21, 1976, transcript, Box 2, Avery Collection; Ed Goodwin, Sr., interview by Carlie Goodwin.

104. "Blacks Making Good in Oklahoma!," *Topeka Plaindealer,* May 13, 1910, 1.

105. Ed Goodwin, Sr., interview by Avery.

106. "Negro Hospital a Certainty Now," *Tulsa World,* July 29, 1916, 3.

107. "Application for a 'Y' Gets Approval," *Tulsa Democrat,* August 29, 1918, 3.

108. "$8,000 Subscribed for Tulsa Negro Hospital," *Tulsa Democrat,* August 5, 1916, 5.

109. Dr. Charles Bate, in Gates, *They Came Searching,* 46.

110. Ed Goodwin, Sr., interview by Carlie Goodwin.

111. U.S. Bureau of the Census, "State Compendium: Oklahoma," Table 25, *Fourteenth Census of the United States* (Washington, D.C.: Government Printing Office, 1924).

112. Little, *Fire on Mount Zion,* 32, 42.

113. "Front Foot Tax for Boulevard System," *Tulsa Democrat,* September 25, 1917, 1.

114. "First National Bank Draws Color Line!," *Tulsa Star,* January 9, 1915, 1.

115. "Jurors Fail to Back City in a Cleanup," *Tulsa Democrat,* February 11, 1913, 1.

116. "Opium Scent Led to a Well-Fitted Den," *Tulsa World,* December 7, 1913, 6.

117. Lemons, "Down on First Street," 86.

118. "Another Murder for Tulsa," *Tulsa Star,* March 9, 1918, 2.

119. Barney Cleaver, statement, in *State of Oklahoma v. John A. Gustafson,* Civil Case No. 1062 (Tulsa County District Court, 1921), Box 25, Record Group 1–2, Oklahoma State Archives, Oklahoma City.

120. Report on Vice Conditions in Tulsa, May 18, 1921, ibid., 5.

121. Henry Whitlow, interview by OETA, 1980, Box 2, Avery Collection.

122. Ed Goodwin, Sr., interview by Carlie Goodwin.

123. U.S. Bureau of the Census, "State Compendium: Oklahoma," Table 8, *Fourteenth Census of the United States* (Washington, D.C.: Government Printing Office, 1924); Booker T. Washington High School Yearbook.

124. Carrie Parker Taylor, "The Negro's Challenge," *Tulsa Star,* October 8, 1915, 1.

CHAPTER 3: BLACK CAPITAL

1. William H. Davis, *Annual Report of the Fifteenth Annual Convention, National Negro Business League* (Washington, D.C., 1914), 79.

2. "Dr. Booker T. Washington Delivers Master Mind Address," *Tulsa Star,* August 29, 1914, 1.

3. *Observations: Muskogee, Oklahoma* (Asheville, N.C.: U.S. Dept. of Commerce, National Oceanic and Atmospheric Administration, National Environmental Satellite, Data, and Information Service, National Climatic Data Center, Climate Services Division, Satellite Services Branch), https://www.nesdis.noaa.gov/; Davis, *Annual Report,* 205.

4. "Washington Tells Muskogee Negroes to Beautify Homes," *Muskogee Daily Phoenix,* August 20, 1914, 1.

5. Robert C. Kenzer, "National Negro Business League," *Encyclopedia of North Carolina,* https://www.ncpedia.org/national-negro-business-league.

6. Editorial, *Tulsa Star,* August 19, 1914, 8.

7. "Facts About the Colored People of Tulsa," *Tulsa Star,* August 29, 1914, 4.

8. *Tulsa Star,* August 19, 1914.

9. *Tulsa Star,* August 27, 1915, 4.

10. *Tulsa Star,* August 19, 1914, 10; "J. T. Armstrong," *Tulsa Star,* August 19, 1914, 11.

11. "Stradford Notes," *Tulsa Star,* October 30, 1915, 4; "Black Cow Oil and Gas Company Plan for Big Expansions," *Tulsa Star,* February 2, 1918, 1.

12. "The Editor Touring the State," *Tulsa Star,* July 4, 1914, 1; "Little 'Big Men' Among Negro Leaders," *Tulsa Star,* August 29, 1914, 4.

13. Davis, *Annual Report,* 80.

14. Booker T. Washington, *The Negro in Business* (Atlanta: Hertel, Jenkins, & Co., 1907), 210.

15. Davis, *Annual Report*, 81–82.

16. Booker T. Washington, *Up from Slavery: An Autobiography* (1901; Project Gutenberg, 2008), https://www.gutenberg.org/files/2376/2376-h/2376-h.htm; "Tuskegee and Hampton," *Southern Workman* 43, no. 11 (November 1914): 593.

17. Jill Watts, *The Black Cabinet: The Untold Story of African Americans and Politics During the Age of Roosevelt* (New York: Grove Press, 2020), 13–14; John Howard Burrows, *The Necessity of Myth: A History of the National Negro Business League, 1900–1945* (Auburn, Ala.: Hickory Hill Press, 1988), 68, 112; "Roosevelt Urges Negroes to Work," *New York Times*, August 20, 1910, 2.

18. Burrows, *Necessity of Myth*, 86, 112–13.

19. Davis, *Annual Report*, 81.

20. A. J. Smitherman, "A Biography: Introduction," *Empire Star*, September 3, 1960, 8.

21. A. J. Smitherman, "A Biography: The Beginning of My Fight for Citizenship Rights," *Empire Star*, September 17, 1960; "Publisher of Nation's First Negro Daily Paper Is Dead," *Buffalo Evening News*, June 22, 1961, 38.

22. *Hastain's Township Plats of the Creek Nation* (Muskogee, Okla.: Model Printing Co., 1910), 285; A. J. Smitherman, "Autobiography," *Empire Star*, October 15, 1960.

23. Smitherman, "Beginning of My Fight."

24. Art T. Burton, *Black Gun, Silver Star: The Life and Legend of Frontier Marshal Bass Reeves* (Lincoln: University of Nebraska Press, 2006), 293.

25. A. J. Smitherman, "Autobiography: De Ole Shack," *Empire Star*, October 8, 1960.

26. Smitherman, "Beginning of My Fight."

27. A. J. Smitherman, "A Biography: The Grandfather Clause," *Empire Star*, October 1, 1960.

28. Murray Wickett, *Contested Territory: Whites, Native Americans and African Americans in Oklahoma, 1865–1907* (Baton Rouge: Louisiana State University Press, 2000), 184–86.

29. Smitherman, "A Biography: The Grandfather Clause."

30. A. J. Smitherman, "Autobiography: Twine's Gloomy Prophecy," *Empire Star*, February 11, 1961, 10.

31. A. J. Smitherman, "The *Star* Is Launched," *Muskogee Star*, July 12, 1912, 1.

32. A. J. Smitherman, "Salutation," *Tulsa Star*, April 11, 1913, 1.

33. A. J. Smitherman, "Autobiography: The *Star*'s Reception," *Empire Star*, April 1, 1961; 1920 U.S. Census, Tulsa County, Okla., pop. sch., ED 222, sheet 10B, dwell. 122, fam. 247, A. J. Smitherman.

34. A. J. Smitherman, "Autobiography: Launching the *Tulsa Star*," *Empire Star*, March 25, 1961.

35. "Negro Answers Well Known Tulsa Pastor," *Tulsa World*, July 14, 1914, 3.

36. Davis, *Annual Report*, 84.

37. "Dr. Booker T. Washington Delivers Master Mind Address"; "World's Greatest Negro Organization Comes to Oklahoma This Week," *Tulsa Star,* August 19, 1914, 1.

38. National Negro Business League, Program, 15th Annual Session, 1914, Black Economic Empowerment: The National Negro Business League, Cleveland Public Library.

39. Davis, *Annual Report,* 150–52.

40. Burrows, *Necessity of Myth,* 77.

41. "Schools in South Worse Than They Were Ten Years Ago," *Afro-American,* June 25, 1910, 4.

42. Burrows, *Necessity of Myth,* 23, 36–37.

43. W.E.B. DuBois, ed., *The Negro in Business: Report of a Social Study Made Under the Direction of Atlanta University* (Atlanta: Atlanta University Publications, 1899), 25.

44. "The Business League," *Crisis,* October 1913, 290.

45. W.E.B. Du Bois, "The Talented Tenth," in Booker T. Washington, ed., *The Negro Problem* (New York: James Pott, 1903), 33.

46. Louis R. Halen, *Booker T. Washington: The Wizard of Tuskegee, 1901–1915* (New York: Oxford University Press, 1983), 321, 365.

47. "Booker T," Booker T. Washington High School Yearbook, 1941, 18, Williams Dreamland LLC Collection.

48. Author's analysis of Tulsa County Deed Books, 1914–1923, Tulsa County Clerk Official Records, Tulsa, http://www.countyclerk.tulsacounty.org/Home/Land.

49. "Local League Holds Meeting," *Tulsa Star,* November 7, 1914, 1.

50. "The Local Business League Elects New Officers," *Tulsa Star,* November 13, 1915, 1.

51. Booker Washington Hospital Articles of Incorporation, May 7, 1917, Oklahoma Secretary of State, Oklahoma City.

52. J. H. Goodwin, "Why Not Use Your GI Rights?" *Oklahoma Eagle,* August 11, 1945, 8.

53. Jim Goodwin, conversation with the author, December 13, 2018.

54. "Schools in the South Worse Than They Were Ten Years Ago."

CHAPTER 4: FALSE PROMISES

1. "Negroes Will Storm the City Hall Tuesday Morn," *Tulsa Democrat,* August 7, 1916, 1.

2. "J. B. Stradford Dies," *California Eagle,* January 3, 1936, 10; "Oklahoma Clears Black in Deadly 1921 Race Riot," *New York Times,* October 26, 1996, https://www.nytimes.com/1996/10/26/us/oklahoma-clears-black-in-deadly-1921-race-riot.html.

3. J. B. Stradford, "Memoir" (unpublished ms., ca. 1935), 190, Reel OHS-202, Tulsa Race Riot Commission Collection, Oklahoma Historical Society.

4. J. B. Stradford, "Stradford Continues Journey Through East," *Tulsa Star,* June 26, 1915, 1.

5. "Negroes Will Storm the City Hall."

6. "Caucasian and Ethiopian," *Tulsa Democrat,* June 6, 1916, 4.

7. Frank Newkirk and John R. Woodard, *City of Tulsa, Oklahoma: Compiled Ordinances of Tulsa* (Tulsa: Democrat Job Printing Co., 1917), 519; "Four Good Ordinances," *Tulsa Democrat,* August 5, 1916, 4.

8. Alfred L. Brophy, *"Guinn v. United States* (1915)," *Encyclopedia of Oklahoma History and Culture,* https://www.okhistory.org/publications/enc/entry?entry=GU001.

9. "Segregation Passes City Council," *Tulsa Star,* August 5, 1916, 1; George C. Wright, "The NAACP and Residential Segregation in Louisville, Kentucky, 1914–1917," *Register of the Kentucky Historical Society* 78, no. 1 (Winter 1980): 48.

10. "Negroes Protest Segregation Law," *Tulsa World,* August 8, 1916, 5.

11. "All Hail to Latest Republican Leader," *Tulsa Democrat,* February 29, 1916, 1.

12. "Simmons Elected by the Biggest Majority Ever Received by a Candidate," *Tulsa World,* April 5, 1916, 1.

13. "Negroes Will Storm the City Hall."

14. Petition by Greenwood Residents Against Segregation Ordinance, J. B. Stradford Folder, Box 2, Jewel LaFontant-Mankarious Collection, Oberlin College Archives.

15. A. J. Smitherman, "Autobiography: Launching the *Tulsa Star,*" *Empire Star,* March 25, 1961, 10.

16. "Negroes Will Storm the City Hall."

17. Murray Wickett, *Contested Territory: Whites, Native Americans and African Americans in Oklahoma, 1865–1907* (Baton Rouge: Louisiana State University Press, 2000), 85–88.

18. "Republican Politicians and Negroes," *Lawton Constitution,* March 30, 1905, 2.

19. "Tulsa's Professional Directory," *Tulsa World,* April 4, 1906, 6.

20. B. C. Franklin, *My Life and an Era: The Autobiography of Buck Colbert Franklin* (Baton Rouge: Louisiana State University Press, 1997), 200.

21. Wickett, *Contested Territory,* 88.

22. "Don't Stand Jim Crowism," *Muskogee Cimeter,* May 18, 1905, 4.

23. Richard Mize, "Sequoyah Convention," *Encyclopedia of Oklahoma History and Culture,* https://www.okhistory.org/publications/enc/entry.php?entry=SE021.

24. Mark Boxell, "From Native Sovereignty to an Oilman's State: Land, Race and Petroleum in Indian Territory and Oklahoma," *Journal of the Gilded Age and Progressive Era* 20, no. 2 (2021): 222.

25. Dianna Everett, "Enabling Act (1906)," *Encyclopedia of Oklahoma History and Culture,* https://www.okhistory.org/publications/enc/entry.php?entry=EN001.

26. Angie Debo, *And Still the Waters Run: The Betrayal of the Five Civilized Tribes* (Princeton, N.J.: Princeton University Press, 1968), 167; James R. Scales and Danny Goble, *Oklahoma Politics: A History* (Norman: University of Oklahoma Press, 1982), 19; Blue Clark, "Delegates to the Constitutional Convention," *Chronicles of Oklahoma* 48, no. 5 (Winter 1970): 413–14.

27. Keith L. Bryant, Jr., "Murray, William Henry David (1869–1956)," *Encyclopedia of Oklahoma History and Culture*, https://www.okhistory.org/publications/enc/entry?entry=MU014.

28. *Proceedings of the Constitutional Convention of the Proposed State of Oklahoma Held at Guthrie, Oklahoma, November 20, 1906 to November 16, 1907* (Muskogee, Okla.: Muskogee Printing Co., 1907), 21.

29. Danny M. Adkison, "Constitutional Convention," *Encyclopedia of Oklahoma History and Culture*, https://www.okhistory.org/publications/enc/entry.php?entry=CO047; Guthrie City Hall historical marker, 1980, Historical Marker Database, https://www.hmdb.org/m.asp?m=141688.

30. *Constitutional Convention, 1907*, photograph, No. 3832.A, Frederick S. Barde Collection, Oklahoma Historical Society, https://www.okhistory.org/publications/enc/viewer?entry=CO047&id=301.

31. *Proceedings of the Constitutional Convention*, 21.

32. "Negroes Meeting to Discuss Teddy," *Muskogee Times-Democrat*, December 5, 1906, 8; "Representative Negroes Assemble for Convention," *Muskogee Cimeter*, December 7, 1906, 5.

33. Wickett, *Contested Territory*, 195.

34. Danny M. Adkison, "Oklahoma Constitution," *Encyclopedia of Oklahoma History and Culture*, https://www.okhistory.org/publications/enc/entry.php?entry=OK036.

35. "Oklahoma Negro Issue Put Up to Roosevelt," *New York Times*, February 2, 1907, 4, https://www.nytimes.com/1907/02/02/archives/oklahoma-negro-issue-put-up-to-roosevelt-constitutional-convention.html.

36. *Oklahoma Enabling Act of 1906*, Pub. L. No. 59-234, 34 Stat. 267 (1906).

37. Ed J. Costello, "Convention Sidelights," *Norman Transcript*, February 21, 1907, 2.

38. "That Washington Trip," *Muskogee Cimeter*, November 1, 1907, 1.

39. "On the Wing," *Muskogee Cimeter*, March 2, 1905, 1; "President Inaugurated," *Muskogee Cimeter*, March 9, 1905, 1.

40. *Muskogee Cimeter*, November 1, 1907, 4.

41. Ibid.

42. James M. Smallwood, "Segregation," *Encyclopedia of Oklahoma History and Culture*, https://www.okhistory.org/publications/enc/entry.php?entryname=SEGREGATION.

43. "Small Comfort for Negroes," *Vinita Leader*, October 31, 1907, 2.

44. Adkison, "Oklahoma Constitution."

45. Larry O'Dell, "Senate Bill One," *Encyclopedia of Oklahoma History and Culture*, https://www.okhistory.org/publications/enc/entry.php?entry=SE017.

46. S. R. Cassius, "Jim Crow As I Saw It," *Western Age*, February 28, 1908, 4.

47. *John B. Stratford [sic] v. Midland Valley Railroad Co.*, 128 P. 98 (Okla. 1912), 33.

48. Ibid., 29.

49. Ibid.

50. " 'I Helped Elect You and You Asked Me to Do It,' Negro Boss Tells the Mayor—But Simmons Heard Him Not," *Tulsa Democrat*, August 8, 1916, 1.

51. Ibid.

52. "To Separate Whites and Negroes Monday," *Tulsa Democrat*, August 11, 1916, 1.

53. "Negroes Abiding by New City Ordinance," *Tulsa Democrat*, September 1, 1916, 3.

54. *Buchanan v. Warley*, 245 U.S. 60 (1917).

55. Mike Staniford, "Deja Vu: Attorney Feels Charter Lawsuit Reminiscent of 1916 Racist Law," *Oklahoma Eagle*, August 6, 1987, 1; Francis Dominic Burke, "A Survey of the Negro Community of Tulsa, Oklahoma," master's thesis, University of Tulsa, 1936, 110.

56. Tulsa County, Okla., Deed Book 73, 475, N. L. and Margaret Townsend and S. C. Stout, November 26, 1909.

57. Tulsa County, Okla., Deed Book 185, 161, C. C. and Kate C. Stebbins and O.K. Eysenbach, November 19, 1915.

58. "Lest We Forget," *Tulsa Star*, September 12, 1916, 12.

59. "G.O.P. Is Buried with Appropriate Exercises in Tulsa," *Tulsa Democrat*, November 15, 1916, 1.

60. "Old Glory Absent in Monday Parade?" *Tulsa World*, November 16, 1916, 10; Merritt J. Glass and Tate Brady, "Public Forum," *Tulsa Democrat*, November 20, 1916, 11.

61. "Tulsa Reunion Will Be Climactic Affair," *Tulsa Democrat*, June 13, 1917, 7.

62. Glass and Brady, "Public Forum."

63. Editorial, *Tulsa Star*, August 8, 1916, 4.

64. Andrew Jackson Smitherman, registration, Tulsa County, Okla., "U.S., World War I Draft Registration Cards, 1917–1918," https://www.ancestry.com/search/collections/6482/; "A.G.W. Sango Dies; Last of the Territorial Leaders," *Oklahoma Eagle*, July 14, 1949, 1.

65. "Wholesale Buying of Allotments," *Claremore Messenger*, July 22, 1904, 1; "Real Estate Man Arrested," *Woods County News*, October 27, 1905, 6; Tulsa County, Okla., Deed Book A, 11, Aaron Ross and Bradley Realty Bank and Trust Co., June 23, 1904.

66. U.S. Senate, *Report of the Select Committee to Investigate Matters Connected with Affairs in the Indian Territory* (Washington, D.C.: Government Printing Office, 1907), 1:651, 656.

67. Ibid., 1:654, 1041, 1117.

68. A. J. Smitherman, "Autobiography: The Negro Guardianship League," *Empire Star*, December 3, 1960.

69. "Bates Burnett Case Set for Trial," *Muskogee Daily Phoenix*, November 19, 1911, 7; *Hastain's Township Plats of the Creek Nation* (Muskogee, Okla.: Model Printing Co., 1910), 157; "Bailey Decision Against Burnett," *Vinita Daily Chieftain*, June 27, 1912, 1.

70. "The Guardianship Fight," *Tulsa Star*, November 13, 1915, 4.

71. A. J. Smitherman, "Autobiography: The Great Oil Boom," *Empire Star*, September 10, 1960.

72. "J. B. Stradford Civic Leader Is Taken in Death," *Chicago Defender*, January 4, 1936, 4; "Raided the House," *Star Press*, July 29, 1902, 5.

73. J.B.S., "Democracy Needed Here in Tulsa," *Tulsa Star*, January 26, 1918, 1.

74. J. B. Stradford, "My Life's Ambition," *Tulsa Star*, October 16, 1915, 1.

CHAPTER 5: THE WAR AT HOME AND ABROAD

1. "Pays Penalty for Her Brutal Crime," *Wagoner County Courier,* April 2, 1914, 1; "Marie Scott Is Lynched by Mob," *Cherokee County Democrat,* April 2, 1914, 4.
2. "Pays Penalty for Her Brutal Crime."
3. J. H. Coleman, letter to the editor, *Crisis,* June 1914, 76; Liz McMahan, "Lynchings Occurred in Wagoner," *Wagoner County American-Tribune,* August 3, 2013, https://tulsaworld.com/community/wagoner/news/lynchings -occurred-in-wagoner/article_aa205131-162a-5745-bd02-4f18dabf8c13 .html.
4. "Pays Penalty"; "Marie Scott."
5. "Six Women," *Crisis,* May 1914, 22.
6. "Locals and Otherwise," *Wagoner County Courier,* March 6, 1913, 5.
7. "Pays Penalty."
8. "Wagoner Lynching of Negro Woman," *Tulsa Democrat,* April 1, 1914, 1.
9. "Pays Penalty."
10. A. J. Smitherman, "One Hundred Men Lynched Negro Woman at Wagoner," *Tulsa Star,* April 4, 1914, 1.
11. "Hung by Mob," *McIntosh County Democrat,* August 6, 1914, 5.
12. "Another Man Lynched," *Tulsa Star,* August 8, 1914, 1.
13. "General War Is Now On," *Tulsa Star,* August 8, 1914, 1.
14. Editorial, *Tulsa Star,* November 13, 1915, 4.
15. "Editor Smitherman Attends Chicago Convention As Tulsa's Delegate," *Tulsa Star,* September 28, 1918, 2; "Colored Tulsans Take Active Part in Third Liberty Loan Drive," *Tulsa Star,* April 20, 1918, 1; "A Man Full of Push," *Tulsa Star,* November 23, 1918, 2.
16. "Soldier Boys Get Big Send Off," *Tulsa Star,* May 4, 1918, 1.
17. "Community Singing," *Tulsa Star,* August 30, 1918, 4; *Tulsa Star,* September 7, 1918, 2.
18. Monroe N. Work, *Negro Year Book: An Annual Encyclopedia of the Negro 1918–1919* (Tuskegee, Ala.: Negro Year Book Co., 1919), 216.
19. "What's Doing in Town?" *Tulsa Star,* April 27, 1918, 4; U.S. Army Transport Service Arriving and Departing Passenger Lists, 1910–1939, Willie Smitherman, https://www.ancestry.com/search/collections/61174/.
20. Oklahoma, U.S., County Marriage Records, 1890–1995, Travis and Goodwin, https://www.ancestry.com/search/collections/61379/.
21. "Thirty-Seven to Dental Reserve," *Daily Oklahoman,* November 18, 1917, 15; John M. Hyson, Jr., "American Dentists in the U.S. Army: The Origins," *Military Medicine* 161, no. 7 (July 1996): 378–80.
22. Arthur E. Barbeau and Florette Henri, *The Unknown Soldiers: African American Troops in World War I* (1974; reprint Cambridge, Mass.: Da Capo Press, 1996), 50, 99.
23. Norman Higgs, "Soldier Boy's Talk," *Tulsa Star,* October 19, 1918, 3; advertisement, *Tulsa Democrat,* August 26, 1916, 45; Norman Higgs, registration, Tulsa County, Okla., "U.S., World War I Draft Registration Cards, 1917–1918," https://www.ancestry.com/search/collections/6482/.

24. Gabriel Victor Cools, "The Negro in Typical Communities of Iowa," master's thesis, University of Iowa, 1918, 59.

25. Bill Douglas, "Wartime Illusions and Disillusionment: Camp Dodge and Racial Stereotyping, 1917–1918," *Annals of Iowa* 57, no. 2 (1998): 126.

26. Ibid., 126–28.

27. Ibid., 116–17.

28. Higgs, "Soldier Boy's Talk."

29. Addie W. Hunton and Kathryn M. Johnson, *Two Colored Women with the American Expeditionary Forces* (Brooklyn: Brooklyn Eagle Press, ca. 1920), 182–90.

30. Obadiah M. Foster to W.E.B. Du Bois, December 30, 1919, Du Bois Papers (MS 312), Special Collections and University Archives, University of Massachusetts Amherst Libraries; hereafter Du Bois Papers.

31. William A. Hewlett to W.E.B. Du Bois, August 26, 1919, Du Bois Papers.

32. W.E.B. Du Bois, "The Black Man in the Wounded World" (fragment), ca. 1936, Du Bois Papers; Hunton and Johnson, *Two Colored Women,* 186.

33. Barbeau and Henri, *Unknown Soldiers,* 168–69; Charles R. Isum to W.E.B. Du Bois, May 17, 1919, Du Bois Papers; Louis Pontlock to W.E.B. Du Bois, April 26, 1919, Du Bois Papers.

34. Louis Albert Linard, "Concerning Black American Troops," August 7, 1918, Du Bois Papers; W.E.B. Du Bois, "Documents of the War," *Crisis,* May 1919, 16.

35. Arlene Balkansky, "Harlem Hell Fighters: African-American Troops in World War I," Library of Congress blog, February 12, 2019, https://blogs.loc.gov/headlinesandheroes/2019/02/harlem-hell-fighters-african-american-troops/.

36. Barbeau and Henri, *Unknown Soldiers,* 107.

37. W.E.B. Du Bois, "Close Ranks," *Crisis,* July 1918, 111.

38. Higgs, "Soldier Boy's Talk."

39. Carlos F. Hurd, "Post-Dispatch Man, An Eye-Witness, Describes Massacre of Negroes," *St. Louis Post-Dispatch,* July 3, 1917, 1; Tony Rehagen, "Forgotten Lessons from the 1917 East St. Louis Race Riots," *St. Louis Magazine* (July 2017), https://web.archive.org/web/20210301153443/http://projects.stlmag.com/1917-stl-race-riots; Harper Barnes, *Never Been a Time: The 1917 Race Riot That Sparked the Civil Rights Movement* (New York: Walker & Co., 2008), 132–33.

40. C. Calvin Smith, "The Houston Riot of 1917, Revisited," *Houston Review* 13, no. 2 (1991): 89; Robert V. Haynes, "The Houston Mutiny and Riot of 1917," *Southwestern Historical Quarterly* 76, no. 4 (April 1973): 421–27.

41. Quintard Taylor, *In Search of the Racial Frontier* (New York: W.W. Norton, 1998), 179–81; Haynes, "Houston Mutiny," 428–31.

42. Haynes, "Houston Mutiny," 438; "Thirteen Negro Soldiers Hang for Houston Riot," *Scranton Times,* December 11, 1917, 1; "Five Get 'Death,' " *Topeka State Journal,* January 2, 1918, 1; "Six More Colored Soldiers to be Executed for the Houston Riot," *Richmond Planet* (Va.), September 14, 1918, 1.

43. "Wartime Illusions and Disillusionment," 123.

44. "Sign the Petition," *Tulsa Star,* February 2, 1918, 2.

45. "Bundy Convicted of Murder in the First Degree," *New York Age,* April 5, 1919, 1.

46. "Dyer Anti-Lynching Bill," NAACP, n.d., https://naacp.org/find-resources/history-explained/legislative-milestones/dyer-anti-lynching-bill; "Anti-Lynching Legislation Renewed," History, Art & Archives, U.S. House of Representatives, https://history.house.gov/Exhibitions-and-Publications/BAIC/Historical-Essays/Temporary-Farewell/Anti-Lynching-Legislation/.

47. "Dewey Police Head Is Shot by Negro," *Tulsa World,* August 13, 1918, 10.

48. "Colored People of Dewey Quit Town," *Tulsa World,* August 16, 1918, 3.

49. Michael S. Givel, "Sundown on the Prairie: The Extralegal Campaigns and Efforts from 1889 to 1967 to Exclude African Americans from Norman, Oklahoma," *Chronicles of Oklahoma* 96, no. 3 (2018); "Intimidation of Negroes," *Kingfisher Free Press,* June 16, 1904, 7; Arthur Tolson, *The Black Oklahomans: A History. 1541–1972* (New Orleans: Edwards Printing Co., 1974), 63–64; "Negroes Attacked Without Cause and Driven from Homes in Terror," *Daily Chieftain,* August 27, 1901, 1.

50. Mary Jones Parrish, *Events of the Tulsa Disaster* (Tulsa, ca. 1923), 77.

51. "Editor Is Appointed Justice of the Peace," *Tulsa Star,* March 23, 1918, 1; Melvin Ray Singleterry, "The Justice of the Peace Courts in Oklahoma: A Political Study," master's thesis, Oklahoma State University, 1968, 19–24.

52. "Editor Smitherman Asks Governor to Punish Dewey Mob," *Muskogee Cimeter,* August 17, 1918, 1.

53. "Gov. Williams Will Act," *Tulsa Star,* August 30, 1918, 1.

54. "Mayor of Dewey Indicted," *Caney News,* September 20, 1918, 2; "Grand Jury Returns 17 Dewey Riot Indictments," *Morning Examiner* (Bartlesville, Okla.), October 3, 1918, 2.

55. "Editor Smitherman Recipient of Many Letters of Admiration," *Tulsa Star,* August 30, 1918, 1.

56. "Whites Adopted Slavery Methods," *Tulsa Star,* October 19, 1918, 1.

57. William T. Lampe, *Tulsa County in the World War* (Tulsa, Okla.: Tulsa County Historical Society, 1919), 101.

58. "Editor Negro Paper Up to Council of Defense," *Tulsa World,* October 22, 1918, 10.

59. "Defense Council Named by Governor," *Tulsa Democrat,* May 13, 1917, 16.

60. Randy Hopkins, "Birthday of the Klan: The Tulsa Outrage of 1917," *Chronicles of Oklahoma* 97, no. 4 (Winter 2019–20), 412–49; James Henry Fowler II, "Extralegal Suppression of Civil Liberties in Oklahoma During the First World War and Its Causes," master's thesis, Oklahoma State University, 1974, 61–68.

61. "Get Out the Hemp," *Tulsa World,* November 9, 1917, 4; "I.W.W. Members Flogged, Tarred, and Feathered," *Tulsa World,* November 10, 1917, 1.

62. Hopkins, "Birthday of the Klan"; "Defense Board Holds Meeting," *Tulsa World,* August 5, 1917, 13.

63. Parrish, *Events of the Tulsa Disaster,* 78.

64. "A False Statement Nailed," *Tulsa Star,* October 26, 1918, 4.

65. "Their Little Stunt Wouldn't Go," *Tulsa Star,* September 7, 1918, 4.

66. Barbeau and Henri, *Unknown Soldiers,* 166.

67. "Community Service to Hold Home-Coming for Service Men Friday," *Tulsa Democrat*, August 24, 1919, 1; "Home-Coming to Be Held for Negroes," *Tulsa Democrat*, August 26, 1919, 12.

68. Vincent Mikkelsen, "Coming from Battle to Face a War: The Lynching of Black Soldiers in the World War I Era," Ph.D. diss., Florida State University, 2007, 145–46.

69. "Soldier in Uniform Is Beaten in Georgia Town," *Chicago Defender*, May 10, 1919, 10.

70. Jeff Wallenfeldt, "Wilmington Coup and Massacre," *Encyclopaedia Britannica*, February 3, 2022, https://www.britannica.com/event/Wilmington-coup -and-massacre; Clifford Kuhn and Gregory Mixon, "Atlanta Race Riot of 1906," *New Georgia Encyclopedia*, https://www.georgiaencyclopedia.org/ articles/history-archaeology/atlanta-race-riot-of-1906/; "Springfield Race Riot," *Encyclopaedia Britannica*, October 9, 2015, https://www.britannica .com/event/Springfield-Race-Riot.

71. W.E.B. Du Bois, "Let Us Reason Together," *Crisis*, September 1919, 231.

72. "For Action on Race Riot Peril," *New York Times*, October 5, 1919, https:// www.nytimes.com/1919/10/05/archives/for-action-on-race-riot-peril-radical -propaganda-among-negroes.html.

73. Chicago Commission on Race Relations, *The Negro in Chicago: A Study of Race Relations and a Race Riot* (Chicago: University of Chicago Press, 1922), 1.

74. McWhirter, *Red Summer*.

75. Francine Uenuma, "The Massacre of Black Sharecroppers That Led the Supreme Court to Curb the Racial Disparities of the Justice System," *Smithsonian Magazine*, August 2, 2018, https://www.smithsonianmag.com/history/ death-hundreds-elaine-massacre-led-supreme-court-take-major-step-toward -equal-justice-african-americans-180969863/.

76. McWhirter, *Red Summer*, 239.

77. J. G. Ellison, "Gives Millen Account of Recent Disorders," *Atlanta Constitution*, April 17, 1919, 5.

78. McWhirter, *Red Summer*, 239–41.

79. "Red Summer of '19," Woodrow Wilson Presidential Library and Museum, February 27, 2020, https://www.woodrowwilson.org/blog/2020/2/27/red -summer-of-19.

80. Lee Hawkins and Charity L. Scott, "The Dreams of Jack and Daisy Scott," *Wall Street Journal*, May 30, 2021; "Our Cartoonist," *Tulsa Star*, February 14, 1920, 1; "Mrs. Daisy J. Scott," *Tulsa Star*, February 15, 1919, 1.

81. Daisy Scott, "The Future," *Tulsa Star*, February 21, 1920, 1.

82. Bobby Dobbs, "Shedding Light on Painful Past," *Oklahoman*, February 21, 2016, 1A.

83. "Misguided Oklahoma Patriots," *Tulsa Star*, September 4, 1920, 4.

84. Randy Krehbiel, *Tulsa 1921: Reporting a Massacre* (Norman: University of Oklahoma Press, 2019), 36–37; "Mob Lynches Tom Owens," *Tulsa Daily World*, August 29, 1920, 1, 9.

85. "Probe Belton Lynching," *Tulsa World*, August 30, 1920, 3.

86. "An Indignant Protest," *Tulsa World*, August 30, 1920, 4.

87. "Gov. Invokes Law vs. Mobbists," *Tulsa Star,* September 4, 1920, 1.

88. A. J. Smitherman, "Smitherman Writes Governor, Says Brother John Was Democrat," *Black Dispatch,* March 23, 1922, 1.

89. "Judge Williams Appoint Delegates to the Inter-Racial Conference," *Tulsa Star,* November 13, 1920, 1.

90. Ann Ellis Pullen, "Commission on Interracial Cooperation," *New Georgia Encyclopedia,* https://www.georgiaencyclopedia.org/articles/history -archaeology/commission-on-interracial-cooperation/.

91. "Inter-Racial Conference Organized," *Tulsa Star,* November 27, 1920, 1.

92. "Citizens of Tulsa Tell of Conditions There Preceding the Race Riot," part 2, *St. Louis Post-Dispatch,* June 5, 1921, 1.

93. "Tulsa Negroes Ask City and County to Check Rampant Vice," *Tulsa Democrat,* August 19, 1919, 1.

94. Robert Fairchild, interview by Scott Ellsworth, June 8, 1978 (recording), Tulsa Race Massacre of 1921 Archive, University of Tulsa.

95. "Oklahoma," *Chicago Defender,* May 17, 1919, 18.

96. J. B. Stradford, "Memoir" (unpublished ms., ca. 1935), 191, Reel OHS-202, Tulsa Race Riot Commission Collection, Oklahoma Historical Society.

97. "Tulsa Colored Business Directory," *Tulsa Star,* February 7, 1920, 6; Mary Wisniewski Holden, "75 Years Later: Vindication in Tulsa," *Chicago Lawyer,* December 1996, 8.

98. Stradford, *Memoir,* 192.

99. Ibid., 189–90.

100. "Hubbard Dines at Big Negro Social Event," *Tulsa Morning Times,* June 18, 1919, 1.

101. Stradford, *Memoir,* 192.

102. "Democrats Only Possibilities in Coming Election," *Tulsa Tribune,* March 7, 1920, 11.

103. "Democracy Triumphs Over Aristocracy!" *Tulsa Star,* April 6, 1918, 1; Parrish, *Events of the Tulsa Disaster,* 77; "Simmons Hears His Fate in Tenth Precinct," *Tulsa Star,* March 30, 1918, 1.

104. "Split in Democratic Ranks Turns the Trick for Republicans," *Tulsa Star,* April 10, 1920, 1.

105. "Oklahoma, the Land of Opportunity for Negroes," *Topeka Plaindealer,* January 2, 1920, 1; W. D. Williams, interview by Ruth Sigler Avery, November 29, 1970, transcript, Box 7, Ruth Sigler Avery Collection, Oklahoma State University–Tulsa, hereafter Avery Collection.

106. Monroe N. Work, *Negro Year Book: An Annual Encyclopedia of the Negro 1921–1922* (Tuskegee, Ala.: Negro Year Book Co., 1922), 309.

107. Booker T. Washington High School Yearbook, 1921, National Museum of African American History and Culture, Smithsonian, Washington, D.C., https://collections.si.edu/search/record/edanmdm:nmaahc_2011.175.18.

108. "Dream Comes True," *Tulsa Tribune,* April 10, 1921, 3.

109. Mabel Little, *Fire on Mount Zion: My Life and History As a Black Woman in America* (Wilmington, Del.: Black Think Tank, 1992), 45; Mount Zion Baptist Church burning (Photo 1), 1921, photograph, Avery Collection.

110. Mabel Little, in *Goin' Back to T-Town,* PBS/American Experience, March 1, 1993; Little interview by Avery.

111. "Fisk Jubilee Group Gives Concert Here," *Tulsa Tribune,* March 29, 1931, 21.

112. Booker T. Washington High School Yearbook.

113. Scott Ellsworth, *Death in a Promised Land: The Tulsa Race Riot of 1921* (Baton Rouge: Louisiana State University Press, 1982), 14; *Tulsa Race Riot: A Report by the Oklahoma Commission to Study the Tulsa Race Riot of 1921* (Oklahoma City: Commission, 2001), 179 and map 8, https://www.okhistory .org/research/forms/freport.pdf; Black Wall Street Memorial, 1996, Greenwood Cultural Center, Tulsa.

114. U.S. Department of Commerce, Bureau of the Census, *Fourteenth Census of the United States: State Compendium: Oklahoma* (Washington, D.C.: Government Printing Office, 1924), tables 10 and 11.

115. Parrish, *Events of the Tulsa Disaster,* 7; "Free! Young Women! Young Men! Special Offer For 30 Days!," *Tulsa Star,* March 6, 1920, 5.

116. Parrish, *Events of the Tulsa Disaster,* 7.

117. Ibid.

CHAPTER 6: "GET A GUN AND GET BUSY"

1. Booker T. Washington High School Yearbook, 1921, National Museum of African American History and Culture, Smithsonian, Washington, D.C., https://collections.si.edu/search/record/edanmdm:nmaahc_2011.175.18.

2. W. D. Williams, interview by Scott Ellsworth, June 7, 1978 (recording), Tulsa Race Massacre of 1921 Archive, University of Tulsa.

3. Ed Goodwin, Sr., interview by Ruth Sigler Avery, November 21, 1976, transcript, Box 2, Ruth Sigler Avery Collection, Oklahoma State University–Tulsa; Booker T. Washington High School Yearbook.

4. Mabel Little, *Fire on Mount Zion: My Life and History as a Black Woman in America* (Wilmington, Del.: Black Think Tank, 1992), 9.

5. Mary Jones Parrish, *Events of the Tulsa Disaster* (Tulsa, ca. 1923), 8; *Tulsa Star,* March 6, 1920, 5.

6. Exhibit A, *Loula T. Williams v. Central States Fire Co. Insurance Dept.,* Case No. 19248 (Tulsa County District Court, 1922); *William Redfearn v. American Central Ins. Co.,* No. 15851 (Okla. 1926), 85.

7. J. B. Stradford, "Memoir" (unpublished ms., ca. 1935), 212, Reel OHS-202, Tulsa Race Riot Commission Collection, Oklahoma Historical Society.

8. Little, *Fire on Mount Zion,* 43; Annie Birdie, interview by Eddie Faye Gates (video), dik rowland, "Black Wall Street Survivors," https://www.youtube .com/watch?v=Q8_48DMON_A.

9. Gates, *They Came Searching,* 71.

10. Parrish, *Events of the Tulsa Disaster,* 8.

11. "Sheriff Says Telephone Call Started Riot," *Tulsa Tribune,* June 3, 1921, 1.

12. "Nab Negro for Attacking Girl in Elevator," *Tulsa Tribune,* May 31, 1921, 1, as reproduced in Loren Gill, "The Tulsa Race Riot," master's thesis, University of Tulsa, 1946, 22.

13. "Sheriff Says Telephone Call Started Riot."

14. Williams interview by Ellsworth.

15. Answer Brief of Defendant in Error, 99–100, *Redfearn v. American Central.*

16. "Tulsa Negroes Ask City and County to Check Rampant Vice," *Tulsa Democrat,* August 19, 1919, 1.

17. "Negro Tells How Others Mobilized," *Tulsa Tribune,* June 4, 1921, 1.

18. Answer Brief of Defendant in Error, 99–100, *Redfearn v. American Central.*

19. "Negro Tells How Others Mobilized"; Answer Brief of Defendant in Error, 100–1, *Redfearn v. American Central.*

20. Williams interview by Ellsworth; Henry C. Sowders, testimony, Answer Brief of Defendant in Error, 85–86, *Redfearn v. American Central.*

21. Williams interview by Ellsworth.

22. "Negro Tells How Others Mobilized"; "Grand Jurors' Probe Takes a New Angle," *Tulsa Tribune,* June 13, 1921, 1.

23. Stradford, "Memoir," 211.

24. "Misguided Oklahoma Patriots," *Tulsa Star,* September 4, 1920, 4.

25. Stradford, "Memoir," 212.

26. Ibid.; Parrish, *Events of the Tulsa Disaster,* 99.

27. Stradford, "Memoir," 212.

28. Williams interview by Ellsworth.

29. Robert Fairchild, interview by Scott Ellsworth, June 8, 1978 (recording), Tulsa Race Massacre of 1921 Archive, University of Tulsa.

30. Ibid.

31. "Nab Negro."

32. Scott Ellsworth, "The Tulsa Race Riot," in *Tulsa Race Riot: A Report by the Oklahoma Commission to Study the Tulsa Race Riot of 1921* (Oklahoma City: Commission, 2001), 56–57, https://www.okhistory.org/research/forms/freport.pdf.

33. "Story of Attack on Woman Denied," *Tulsa World,* June 2, 1921, 14; Walter F. White, "Tulsa Riot Based on Girl's Mistake," *New York Evening Post,* June 9, 1921, 5.

34. "Nab Negro."

35. *Tulsa Race Riot Report,* map 1; "Nab Negro."

36. Russell Cobb, " 'No Apology': Richard Lloyd Jones and the 1921 Race Massacre," *Tulsa People,* February 20, 2019, https://www.tulsapeople.com/no-apology/article_d76c97dd-6154-56bc-8d92-4c8a9139a7a4.html.

37. H. M. Stivers, "The Disinterested Spectator," *Tulsa Tribune,* June 23, 1920, 14.

38. William N. Randolph, "Freeling's Aid 'Shadowed' in Quiz of Crime," *Tulsa Tribune,* April 8, 1921, 1.

39. "Matron Bares Police Failures," *Tulsa Tribune,* May 21, 1921, 1.

40. "Nab Negro"; White, "Tulsa Riot Based on Girl's Mistake."

41. "Inefficiency of Police Is Denied," *Tulsa World,* July 19, 1921, 1.

42. John Gustafson testimony, 6, in *State of Oklahoma v. John A. Gustafson,* Civil Case No. 1062 (Tulsa County District Court, 1921), Box 25, Record Group 1–2, Oklahoma State Archives, Oklahoma City.

43. *Tulsa, Tulsa County, Oklahoma,* map (Sanborn Map Co., 1915), Image 26, Library of Congress.

44. "Sheriff Says Telephone Call Started Riot."

45. W. M. McCullough deposition, 15, in *J. B. Stradford v. American Central Ins. Co.,* Case No. 370,274 (Cook County Superior Court, 1921).

46. "Inefficiency of Police Is Denied."

47. Redmond S. Cole to Jas. G. Findley, June 6, 1921, Folder 32, Box 1, Series 1, Black American Military Experience Collection, Oklahoma State University Archives, Stillwater; "Charges Are Filed Against Cranfields," *Tulsa Tribune,* January 5, 1922, 1.

48. Randy Hopkins, "Racing to the Precipice, Tulsa's Last Lynching," Center for Public Secrets, https://www.centerforpublicsecrets.org/post/racing-to-the-precipice-tulsa-s-last-lynching.

49. Cole to Findley, June 6, 1921.

50. McCullough deposition, 15, *Stradford v. American Central.*

51. Gustafson testimony, 8–11, *Oklahoma v. Gustafson.*

52. Accusation, 12, ibid.

53. "New Battle Now in Progress," *Tulsa World,* June 1, 1921, 1.

54. McCullough deposition, 17, in *Stradford v. American Central.*

55. Answer Brief of Defendant in Error, 75, *Redfearn v. American Central.*

56. McCullough deposition, 17, in *Stradford v. American Central;* Stradford, "Memoir," 212–13.

57. "Sheriff Says Telephone Call Started Riot."

58. "Negro Tells How Others Mobilized"; Lee Hawkins and Charity L. Scott, "The Dreams of Jack and Daisy Scott," *Wall Street Journal,* May 30, 2021; Williams interview by Ellsworth; O. W. Gurley statement, 10, in *Oklahoma v. Gustafson;* "Much Interest by White Fans," *Muskogee Times-Democrat,* September 9, 1915, 7.

59. Stradford, "Memoir," 212.

60. Gustafson deposition, 28, in *Stradford v. American Central.*

61. Mabel Little, in *Goin' Back to T-Town,* PBS/American Experience, March 1, 1993.

62. Answer Brief of Defendant in Error, 92, *Redfearn v. American Central.*

63. William "Choc" Phillips, *Murder in the Streets* (Austin, Tex.: Eakin Press, 2021), 33.

64. Major Jas. A. Bell, *Report on Activities of the Natl. Gd. on the Night of May 31st and June 1st 1921,* July 2, 1921, Box 1, Series 1, Black American Military Experience Collection, Oklahoma State University Archives, Stillwater.

65. Ellsworth, "Tulsa Race Riot," 63.

66. White, "Tulsa Riot Based on Girl's Mistake"; Phillips, *Murder in the Streets,* 26.

67. *History of the Tulsa Street Railway Company,* n.d., 127, Box 6, Avery Collection.

68. Phillips, *Murder in the Streets,* 29.

69. Laurel Buck testimony, 33, in *Oklahoma v. Gustafson.*

70. Phillips, *Murder in the Streets,* 31–32; Ellsworth, "Tulsa Race Riot," 63; "Seven Battles Rage During War of Races," *Tulsa Tribune,* June 1, 1921, 3.

71. Buck testimony, 29–37, *Oklahoma v. Gustafson.*
72. "New Battle Now in Progress," *Tulsa World,* June 1, 1921, 1.
73. Buck testimony, 30, 35, *Oklahoma v. Gustafson.*
74. L. C. Clark, interview by Ruth Sigler Avery, June 25, 1975 (transcript), Box 1, Ruth Sigler Avery Collection, Oklahoma State University–Tulsa, hereafter Avery Collection; Maj. Byron Kirkpatrick to Lt. Col. L.J.F. Rooney, July 1, 1921, 2, Box 3, Folder 16, Oklahoma Governors' Papers, Oklahoma State Archives, Oklahoma City.
75. Attorney Notes of Witness Testimony, *Oklahoma v. Gustafson.*
76. Phillips, *Murder in the Streets,* 42; Gill, "Tulsa Race Riot," 28.
77. "Race War Rages for Hours After Courthouse Outbreak; Two Whites Dead Unknown," *Tulsa World,* June 1, 1921, 8.
78. Buck testimony, 38, *Oklahoma v. Gustafson.*
79. "Seven Battles Rage."
80. Phillips, *Murder in the Streets,* 33.
81. Helen Ingraham, interview by Ruth Sigler Avery, 1980 (transcript), Box 3, Avery Collection.
82. "Seven Battles Rage."
83. Clark interview by Avery; W. R. Holway, interview by Ruth Sigler Avery, September 9, 1974, transcript, Box 3, Avery Collection; *History of the Tulsa Street Railway Company,* 128, Avery Collection.
84. Phillips, *Murder in the Streets,* 39–40; Holway interview by Avery; George Miller, interview by Ruth Sigler Avery, August 1, 1971 (transcript), Box 5, Avery Collection.
85. Miscellaneous Witness List, 2[au: page no.?], in *Oklahoma v. Gustafson.*
86. Ellsworth, *Death in a Promised Land,* 53.
87. "Race War Rages."
88. Holway interview by Avery.
89. "Race War Rages"; Maj. C. W. Daley to Lt. Col. L.J.F. Rooney, July 6, 1921, 3, Box 3, Folder 16, Oklahoma Governors' Papers, Oklahoma State Archives, Oklahoma City.
90. "Race War Rages"; "Whites Advancing into 'Little Africa;' Negro Death List Is About 15," *Tulsa World,* June 1, 1921, 1; Stradford, "Memoir," 213.
91. Parrish, *Events of the Tulsa Disaster,* 8–9.
92. Stradford, "Memoir," 213–14.
93. Little, *Fire on Mount Zion,* 9.
94. David M. Breed, "A Look at the Life of E. L. Goodwin Sr.," *Oklahoma Eagle,* September 14, 1978, 10–11.
95. Ibid.
96. Maj. Byron Kirkpatrick to Lt. Col. L.J.F. Rooney, July 1, 1921, Box 1, Series 1, Black American Military Experience Collection, Oklahoma State University Archives, Stillwater; John A. Gustafson to James B. A. Robertson, telegram, June 1, 1921, Folder 16, Box 3, Record Group 8-D-1-3, Oklahoma State Archives, Oklahoma City.
97. "Whites Advancing into 'Little Africa.'"
98. Answer Brief of Defendant in Error, 133–34, *Redfearn v. American Central.*
99. Gustafson deposition, 29–30, *Stradford v. American Central.*

100. "Inefficiency of Police Is Denied," *Tulsa World,* July 19, 1921, 7.
101. Frank Van Voorhis to L.J.F. Rooney, July 30, 1921, Box 3, Folder 16, Record Group 8-D-1-3, Oklahoma State Archives, Oklahoma City.
102. Daley to Rooney, July 6, 1921; Ellsworth, "Tulsa Race Riot," 81.
103. Daley to Rooney, July 6, 1921.
104. Miscellaneous Witness Notes, 1, *Oklahoma v. Gustafson;* Stradford, "Memoir," 215.
105. Daley to Rooney, July 6, 1921.
106. Lt. Col. L.J.F. Rooney to Adjutant General, June 3, 1921, Folder 16, Box 3, Record Group 8-D-1-3, Oklahoma State Archives, Oklahoma City.
107. Ibid.
108. John A. Oliphant testimony, *State of Oklahoma v. John A. Gustafson,* 13; William T. Lampe, *Tulsa County in the World War* (Tulsa, Okla.: Tulsa County Historical Society, 1919), 73–77; Gill, "Tulsa Race Riot," 30.
109. Phillips, *Murder in the Streets,* 46.
110. Ibid., 50–51.
111. Ellsworth, "Tulsa Race Riot," 69.
112. Stradford, "Memoir," 215.
113. "Whites Advancing into 'Little Africa.'"
114. Stradford, "Memoir," 214.
115. Phillips, *Murder in the Streets,* 56–58.
116. Daley to Rooney, July 6, 1921; "Whites Advancing into 'Little Africa'"; "Mob Held Back by Major Daley for Two Hours," *Tulsa Tribune,* June 5, 1921, 7.
117. "Citizens Uphold Officers' Story," *Tulsa World,* July 21, 1921, 3.
118. "Mob Held Back."

CHAPTER 7: THE MASSACRE

1. W. D. Williams, interview by Scott Ellsworth, June 7, 1978 (recording), Tulsa Race Massacre of 1921 Archive, University of Tulsa.
2. Mary Jones Parrish, *Events of the Tulsa Disaster* (Tulsa, ca. 1923), 10; "Curriculum Resources–Meet the Survivors," John Hope Franklin Center for Reconciliation, https://www.jhfcenter.org/1921-race-massacre-survivors.
3. *Tulsa City Directory, 1921* (Polk-Hoffhine Directory Co.), 135, 175, 659; Williams interview by Ellsworth.
4. Parrish, *Events of the Tulsa Disaster,* 10; Bob Foresman, interview by Ruth Sigler Avery, April 9, 1975, transcript, Box 2, Ruth Sigler Avery Collection, Oklahoma State University–Tulsa, hereafter Avery Collection; *Tulsa City Directory, 1921,* 643.
5. "Observation Hill Has Always Loomed Up in a Figurative Way Before the City Council," *Tulsa Democrat,* February 18, 1917, 13.
6. Photograph of 500 Block, Greenwood, November 1921, No. 1984.002.003, Tulsa Race Massacre Collection, Tulsa Historical Society and Museum, https://www.tulsahistory.org/exhibit/1921-tulsa-race-massacre/photos/#gallery/79fff4159cc1ef156d2a88222449c2e5/1311, hereafter Tulsa Race Massacre Collection.

7. Parrish, *Events of the Tulsa Disaster,* 10–11.

8. Ibid.

9. Ibid., 8.

10. Ibid., 11.

11. Loren Gill, "The Tulsa Race Riot," master's thesis, University of Tulsa, 1946, 35; Green E. Smith, testimony in Answer Brief of Defendant in Error, 116, *William Redfearn v. American Central Insurance Co.,* No. 15851 (Okla. 1925); Parrish, *Events of the Tulsa Disaster,* 30, 34.

12. George Douglas Monroe, in Eddie Faye Gates, *They Came Searching: How Blacks Found the Promised Land in Oklahoma* (Austin, Tex.: Eakin Press, 1997), 152; George Douglas Monroe in Eddie Faye Gates, "Tulsa Race Riot (Massacre) Commission Interviews Tape 1" (video), April 16, 1999, Audio Archives, Oklahoma Historical Society, https://www.youtube.com/watch?v= 37NItC7AUJY.

13. Parrish, *Events of the Tulsa Disaster,* 43–47.

14. J. B. Stradford, "Memoir" (unpublished ms., ca. 1935), 215, Reel OHS-202, Tulsa Race Riot Commission Collection, Oklahoma Historical Society.

15. Richard Warner, "Airplanes and the Riot," in *Tulsa Race Riot: A Report by the Oklahoma Commission to Study the Tulsa Race Riot of 1921* (Oklahoma City: Commission, 2001), 104, https://www.okhistory.org/research/forms/ freport.pdf.

16. Gill, "Tulsa Race Riot," 40.

17. Parrish, *Events of the Tulsa Disaster,* 12, 33, 48; Mabel Little, *Fire on Mount Zion: My Life and History as a Black Woman in America* (Wilmington, Del.: Black Think Tank, 1992), 10; B. C. Franklin, "The Tulsa Race Riot and Three of Its Victims," August 22, 1931, 6–7, National Museum of African American History and Culture, Smithsonian; "Loot, Arson, Murder!," *Black Dispatch* (Oklahoma City), June 10, 1921, 1.

18. "Tulsa Man First to Transport Nitro by Means of Airplane," *Tulsa World,* April 20, 1921, 23.

19. "Use Airplanes in Big Red Hunt," *Tulsa Tribune,* May 1, 1920, 1.

20. Stradford, "Memoir," 217–18.

21. Miscellaneous Witness List, *State of Oklahoma v. John A. Gustafson,* Civil Case No. 1062 (Tulsa County District Court, 1921), Box 25, Record Group 1–2, Oklahoma State Archives, Oklahoma City.

22. Mr. and Mrs. I. S. Pittman, interview by Scott Ellsworth, July 26, 1978 (recording), Tulsa Race Massacre of 1921 Archive, University of Tulsa.

23. John Oliphant testimony, 6, in *Oklahoma v. Gustafson;* "Colorful Career of Judge John A. Oliphant, Soldier, Pioneer, Halted by Death," *Tulsa Tribune,* January 19, 1931, 5.

24. *Tulsa City Directory, 2021,* 280.

25. Parrish, *Events of the Tulsa Disaster,* 37.

26. Oliphant testimony, 3, 17, *Oklahoma v. Gustafson;* "Loot, Arson, Murder!"

27. Oliphant testimony, 4–11, *Oklahoma v. Gustafson;* "White Friends Tried to Save Dr. Jackson," *Black Dispatch,* June 10, 1921, 8; "Loot, Arson, Murder!"

28. Parrish, *Events of the Tulsa Disaster,* 26, 29–30; Ann E. Weisman, "Greenwood: Tulsa's Phoenix," *American Visions,* August 1987, 36.

29. Gates, "Tulsa Race Riot Commission Interviews."

30. Capt. John W. McCuen to Lt. Col. L.J.F. Rooney, n.d., Folder 32, Box 1, Series 1, Black American Military Experience Collection, Oklahoma State University Archives, Stillwater.

31. "74 Photos That Show the Impact of the Tulsa Race Massacre," *Oklahoman*, June 10, 1921, https://www.oklahoman.com/picture-gallery/news/2021/05/14/tulsa-race-massacre-photos-black-wall-street-1921-oklahoma-greenwood-district/7225459002.

32. Alice Andrews, in Gates, *They Came Searching*, 43.

33. Williams interview by Ellsworth.

34. Ibid.; "*Impact* Raps with W. D. Williams," *Oklahoma Impact Magazine*, June–July 1971, 35.

35. Williams interview by Ellsworth.

36. Stradford, "Memoir," 217.

37. B. C. Franklin, *My Life and an Era: The Autobiography of Buck Colbert Franklin* (Baton Rouge: Louisiana State University Press, 1997), 197.

38. Ibid., 30, 34, 41.

39. Oliphant testimony, 7, 22, *Oklahoma v. Gustafson*.

40. Williams interview by Ellsworth.

41. Ibid.

42. "Dead Estimated at 100; City Is Quiet," *Tulsa World*, June 2, 1921, 1.

43. "*Impact* Raps with Williams."

44. Ibid.; Parrish, *Events of the Tulsa Disaster*, 44; photographs no. A2440 and A2434, June 1, 1921, Tulsa Race Massacre Collection.

45. Parrish, *Events of the Tulsa Disaster*, 24; Eunice Cloman Jackson, interview by Ruth Sigler Avery, 1971, transcript, Box 3, Avery Collection.

46. "Blacks Carry Belongings as They Vacate," *Tulsa Tribune*, June 1, 1921, 6.

47. Charles F. Barrett, *Oklahoma After Fifty Years: A History of the Sooner State and Its People 1889–1939* (Oklahoma City: Historical Record Association, 1941), 212.

48. Photograph 1982.033.003, June 1, 1921, November 1921, Tulsa Race Massacre Collection.

49. "*Impact* Raps with Williams"; Williams interview by Ellsworth.

50. "Blacks Carry Belongings as They Vacate."

51. "Dead Estimated at 100"; Faith Heironymus [*sic*], "Negroes Gladly Accept Guards," *Tulsa Daily World*, June 2, 1921, 1.

52. Williams interview by Ellsworth; "Negroes Gladly Accept Guards."

53. Parrish, *Events of the Tulsa Disaster*, 17, 29; S. M. Jackson, interview by Ruth Sigler Avery, 1971, transcript, Box 3, Avery Collection.

54. Parrish, *Events of the Tulsa Disaster*, 38.

55. Ibid., 14, 34, 42; Fairchild interview by Ellsworth.

56. Williams interview by Ellsworth.

57. "*Impact* Raps with Williams"; Parrish, *Events of the Tulsa Disaster*, 25, 26, 47; "Negroes Gladly Accept Guards," 7.

58. Williams interview with Ellsworth; "*Impact* Raps with Williams"; Booker T. Washington High School Yearbook, 1921.

59. Williams interview by Ellsworth; *Tulsa City Directory*, 1921, 303.

60. "Vivid Contrast in Two Nights," *Tulsa World,* June 2, 1921, 1.

61. "Proclamation by Barrett," *Tulsa Tribune,* June 1, 1921, 1.

62. "All Blacks Must Wear Green Tags," *Tulsa Daily World,* June 7, 1921, 9; Mary E. Jones Parrish Identification Card, June 13, 1921, A2518, Tulsa Race Massacre Collection; Karlos K. Hill, *The 1921 Tulsa Race Massacre: A Photographic History* (Norman: University of Oklahoma Press, 2021), 139.

63. "Rescind Green Card Order," *Tulsa World,* July 8, 1921, 9.

64. W. D. Williams, oral history interview (audio recording), Tulsa Historical Society, Tulsa.

65. Williams interview by Ellsworth; "*Impact* Raps with Williams"; W. D. Williams, interview by Ruth Sigler Avery, November 29, 1970, transcript, Box 7, Avery Collection.

66. S. M. Jackson, interview by Ruth Sigler Avery, 4C; R. E. Maxey witness statement, *Oklahoma v. Gustafson.*

67. Otis Clark, *The 1921 Race War Survivors,* permanent exhibition, Greenwood Cultural Center.

68. Jackson interview by Avery.

69. Ibid; Joseph Jackson, *Die Jacksons* (Munich, Germany: Blanvalet, 2009), 11.

70. Jackson, *Die Jacksons,* 11; Parrish, *Events of the Tulsa Disaster,* 90; Ed Goodwin, Sr., interview by Carlie Goodwin.

71. Jackson interview by Avery.

72. Ibid.; "The Weather," *Tulsa Tribune,* June 1, 1921, 1.

73. Hill, *Race Massacre: Photographic History,* 43, 46, 47.

74. N. C. Williams, interview by Scott Ellsworth, June 20, 1978 (recording), Tulsa Race Massacre of 1921 Archive, University of Tulsa.

75. S. M. Jackson interview by Avery; Heironymus, "Negroes Gladly Accept."

76. *Tulsa City Directory, 1921,* 828; *Tulsa, Tulsa County, Oklahoma,* map (Sanborn Map Co., 1915), Image 26, Library of Congress.

77. Jackson interview by Avery; Clyde Collins Snow, "Confirmed Deaths: A Preliminary Report," in *Tulsa Race Riot: A Report by the Oklahoma Commission to Study the Tulsa Race Riot of 1921* (Oklahoma City: Commission, 2001), 118, https://www.okhistory.org/research/forms/freport.pdf; DeNeen L. Brown, "Tulsa Begins Search for 'Original 18' Black People Killed in 1921 Race Massacre," *Washington Post,* October 19, 2020, https://www.washingtonpost.com/history/2020/10/19/tulsa-orignal-18-race-massacre/.

78. Jackson interview by Avery; Andre Wilkes, interview by Ruth Sigler Avery, July 8, 1972, transcript, Box 7, Avery Collection; Henry Whitlow, interview by Scott Ellsworth, June 6, 1978 (recording), Tulsa Race Massacre of 1921 Archive, University of Tulsa.

79. Gill, "Tulsa Race Riot," 45; "5,000 Negro Refugees Guarded"; Walter White, "The Eruption of Tulsa," *Nation,* June 29, 1921; Snow, "Confirmed Deaths," 109–22.

80. "Bulletins," *Tulsa Tribune,* June 1, 1921, 1.

81. Surgeon, 3rd Infantry, to Adjutant General of Oklahoma, June 4, 1921, Box 3, Folder 16, Oklahoma Governors' Papers, Oklahoma State Archives, Oklahoma City.

82. Fairchild interview by Ellsworth; "J. B. Stradford Civil Leader Is Taken in

Death," *Chicago Defender,* January 4, 1946, 4; "Negroes from Tulsa Flee to Other Towns," *Tulsa Tribune,* June 2, 1921, 5.

83. Ernestine Gibbs, in Gates, *They Came Searching,* 86.
84. "Continue Riot Cases," *Tulsa Daily World,* September 29, 1921, 7; Randy Hopkins, "Recovering History: The Freeing of Dick Roland," Center for Public Secrets, https://www.centerforpublicsecrets.org/post/the-freeing-of-dick -roland.
85. "A Conspiracy of Silence," National Public Radio, Box 2, Avery Collection; Viola Fletcher, conversation with the author, May 2021.
86. Maurice Willows, "Full Social and Medical Relief Report Up To and Including December 31st, 1921," in Loula V. Watkins, ed., *Report: Tulsa Race Riot Disaster Relief,* American Red Cross, No. 1984.002.060, Tulsa Race Massacre Collection, https://www.tulsahistory.org/wp-content/uploads/2018/11/1984 .002.060_RedCrossReport-sm.pdf.
87. J. A. Gustafson deposition, in *J. B. Stradford v. American Central Ins. Co.,* Case No. 370,274 (Cook County Superior Court, 1921), 6.
88. *Black Wall Street Memorial,* 1996, Greenwood Cultural Center, Tulsa.
89. Parrish, *Events of the Tulsa Disaster,* 14–17, 19.
90. D. Jackson, S. Wiley, J. Simmons, and M. Jackson, "Faith Still Standing Membership," May 31, 2022, provided to the author.
91. Little, *Fire on Mount Zion,* 12.
92. Willows, "Full Social and Medical Relief Report."
93. Parrish, *Events of the Tulsa Disaster,* 17.
94. Ellsworth, *Death in a Promised Land,* 66–69; Snow, "Confirmed Deaths," 120–22.
95. Maurice Willows, "Narrative Report As of December 31st, 1921," 3, in Watkins, *Report: Tulsa Race Riot Disaster Relief.*

CHAPTER 8: A CONSPIRACY IN PLAIN SIGHT

1. Photograph of 100 Block of Greenwood Avenue, June 1921, No. 1984.002.025, Tulsa Race Massacre Collection, Tulsa Historical Society and Museum.
2. Photograph of Destroyed Dreamland Theatre, June 1921, No. 1984.002.024, ibid.
3. *C. M. Goodwin v. Camden Fire Ins. Co.,* No. 19235 (Tulsa County District Court, 1922).
4. "74 Photos That Show the Impact of the Tulsa Race Massacre," *Wisconsin Rapids Tribune,* June 10, 2021, https://www.wisconsinrapidstribune.com/ picture-gallery/news/2021/05/14/tulsa-race-massacre-photos-black-wall-street -1921-oklahoma-greenwood-district/7225459002/.
5. Mary Jones Parrish, *Events of the Tulsa Disaster* (Tulsa, ca. 1923), 8, 14.
6. Photograph of Burned Greenwood District, June 1921, No. 1984.480.001, Tulsa Race Massacre Collection.
7. Parrish, *Events of the Tulsa Disaster,* 14.
8. Randy Krehbiel, *Tulsa 1921: Reporting a Massacre* (Norman: University of Oklahoma Press, 2019), 98–99.

9. "Negroes Fear Winter, Build in Fire Zone," *Tulsa Tribune,* August 8, 1921, 8.

10. "85 Whites and Negroes Die in Tulsa Riots as 3,000 Armed Men Battle in Streets," *New York Times,* June 2, 1921, 1; "Tulsa Aflame; 85 Dead in Riot," *Chicago Defender,* June 4, 1921, 1.

11. Governor James B. A. Robertson to S. P. Freeling, in *State of Oklahoma v. John A. Gustafson,* Civil Case No. 1062 (Tulsa County District Court, 1921), Box 25, Record Group 1–2, Oklahoma State Archives, Oklahoma City.

12. "Tulsa Race Riot Is Conversation Topic in Eastern Cities," *Tulsa World,* June 2, 1921, 14.

13. James D. Robenalt, "The Republican President Who Called for Racial Justice in America After the Tulsa Massacre," *Washington Post,* June 21, 2020, https://www.washingtonpost.com/history/2020/06/21/warren-harding-tulsa -race-massacre-trump/.

14. "To Appraise All Loss by Negroes," *Tulsa World,* June 3, 1921, 1.

15. "Realtors Start Task of Listing All Losses," *Tulsa Tribune,* June 3, 1921, 11.

16. "Tulsa Real Estate Exchange," *Tulsa Daily World,* December 16, 1919, 15.

17. "Negro Leaders for New Site, Glass Claims," *Tulsa Tribune,* June 9, 1921, 3.

18. Ibid.; "Plan to Move Negroes into New District," *Tulsa Tribune,* June 3, 1921, 1; "Three Judges Hear Evidence in Negro Suit," *Tulsa Tribune,* August 25, 1921, 1.

19. "Merritt Julius Glass," *Chronicles of Oklahoma* 28, no. 3 (Autumn 1950): 366.

20. Merritt J. Glass and Tate Brady, "Public Forum," *Tulsa Democrat,* November 20, 1916, 11; Membership Roster, 1928–32, No. 1993.001.2-1, Tulsa, Ku Klux Klan Collection, McFarlin Library, University of Tulsa.

21. Andre Wilkes, interview by Ruth Sigler Avery, July 8, 1972, transcript, 52–54, Box 7, Ruth Sigler Avery Collection, Oklahoma State University–Tulsa; hereafter Avery Collection.

22. "Black Agitators Blamed for Riot," *Tulsa World,* June 6, 1921, 1.

23. "It Must Not Be Again," *Tulsa Tribune,* June 4, 1921, 8.

24. "Martin Blames Riots to Lax City Hall Rule," *Tulsa Tribune,* June 2, 1921, 1.

25. Maurice Willows, "Narrative Report As of December 31st, 1921," 19, in Loula V. Watkins, ed., *Report: Tulsa Race Riot Disaster Relief, American Red Cross,* No. 1984.002.060, Tulsa Race Massacre Collection, https://www .tulsahistory.org/wp-content/uploads/2018/11/1984.002.060_RedCrossReport -sm.pdf.

26. "Warning Against Further Trouble," *Tulsa World,* June 4, 1921, 1.

27. Loyal J. Martin unpublished biography excerpt, April 1940, Box 5, Avery Collection.

28. "City to Meet Demands Out of Own Purse," *Tulsa Tribune,* June 3, 1921, 1.

29. Willows, "Narrative Report," 20.

30. J.B.A. Robertson to Nick Chiles, June 3, 1921, Box 12, Avery Collection.

31. "Negro Section Abolished by City's Order," *Tulsa Tribune,* June 7, 1921, 1.

32. "Martin Blames Riots to Lax City Hall Rule."

33. "Public Welfare Board Vacated by Commission," *Tulsa Tribune,* June 14, 1921, 1–2.

34. Ibid.
35. "Want Wholesale Houses," *Tulsa World,* June 15, 1921, 2.
36. Lee Roy Chapman, "The Nightmare of Dreamland," *This Land,* April 18, 2012, https://thislandpress.com/2012/04/18/tate-brady-battle-greenwood/; "Fire Zone Area in Black Belt May Be Reduced," *Tulsa Tribune,* August 14, 1921, 3.
37. Meeting Minutes of the City of Tulsa Board of Commissioners, June 14, 1921, 26, City Clerk's Office, Tulsa.
38. "Public Welfare Board Resigns," *Tulsa Tribune,* June 15, 1921, 1.
39. "Favor Proposed New Depot Site," *Tulsa World,* June 30, 1921, 7.
40. "Barometer of Public Opinion," *Tulsa World,* June 15, 1921, 4; "Too Big for One Group," *Black Dispatch,* June 3, 1921, 4.
41. Randy Hopkins, "Birthday of the Klan: The Tulsa Outrage of 1917," *Chronicles of Oklahoma* 97, no. 4 (Winter 2019–20), 412–49.
42. "Police Say They Knew of 'War' Plans," *Tulsa Tribune,* June 3, 1921, 1.
43. Francis Burke, "A Survey of the Negro Community of Tulsa, Oklahoma," master's thesis, University of Tulsa, 1936, 1, 44–45; *Kiowa County Star,* August 9, 1934, 1.
44. "They Saved the Greenwood Area for Negroes," *Oklahoma Eagle,* November 2, 1950, 10; "To Rebuild Greenwood," *Black Dispatch,* June 24, 1921, 1; Hank Moore, "Highlights of 'Dimple L. Bush Day,' " *Oklahoma Eagle,* April 16, 1953, 1.
45. Parrish, *Events of the Tulsa Disaster,* 41.
46. "Members of Negro Baptist Church to Build Handsome Edifice in Tulsa Shortly," *Tulsa Democrat,* March 16, 1919, 9.
47. "Plan to Move Negroes into New District."
48. "Negro Leaders for New Site, Glass Claims."
49. "Ask Tramway Terminal in Burned Area," *Tulsa Tribune,* June 19, 1921, 1.
50. "Negro Leaders for New Site, Glass Claims."
51. "To Rebuild Greenwood"; *Tulsa City Directory,* 1921 (Polk-Hoffhine Directory Co.), 272.
52. "They Saved the Greenwood Area."
53. "Colored Citizens' Relief Committee Makes Appeal," *Topeka Plaindealer,* June 10, 1921, 1; "Finding Money Available to Rebuild Colored Tulsa, Okla.," *Southern Indicator,* August 13, 1921, 1.
54. "They Saved the Greenwood Area."
55. "Tulsa to Have New Negro Journal," *Black Dispatch,* March 26, 1920, 1; *Tulsa Star,* April 10, 1920, 12.
56. Parrish, *Events of the Tulsa Disaster,* 18.
57. "Negroes Publish New Daily Paper," *Tulsa World,* June 9, 1921, 7.
58. B. C. Franklin, *My Life and an Era: The Autobiography of Buck Colbert Franklin* (Baton Rouge: Louisiana State University Press, 1997), 150, 192–93.
59. Buck Colbert Franklin, photograph, 1901, Calvert Brothers Studio Glass Plate Negatives, Tennessee State Library and Archives, https://teva.contentdm.oclc.org/digital/collection/p15138coll24/id/114/; Buck Colbert Franklin, Sep. 12, 1918, U.S., World War I Draft Registration Cards, 1917–18, Ancestry.com.

60. Amended Petition for Injunction and Temporary Restraining Order, *Joe Lockard et al. v. City of Tulsa et al.*, No. 15730 (Tulsa County District Court, 1921).

61. Franklin, *My Life and an Era*, 198.

62. *Lockard v. Tulsa;* "Three Judges Hear Evidence in Negro Suit."

63. "Can Reconstruct Restricted Area," *Tulsa World*, August 26, 1921, 3.

64. "Negroes Build as City Passes New Ordinance," *Tulsa Tribune*, August 27, 1921, 1; "New Cases," *Tulsa Daily Legal News*, August 26, 1921, 1.

65. "Blacks Attack New Ordinance Passed by City," *Tulsa Tribune*, September 1, 1921, 1.

66. "City May Not Appeal Fire Zone Ruling," *Tulsa Tribune*, September 2, 1921, 1.

67. "Mayor to Keep Reconstruction Board on Job," *Tulsa Tribune*, September 3, 1921, 1.

68. Parrish, *Events of the Tulsa Disaster*, 20.

69. W.E.B. Du Bois, "Tulsa," *Crisis*, October 1921, 247.

70. "Seek Return of Alleged Rioter," *Tulsa World*, June 16, 1921, 1.

71. Indictment, *State of Oklahoma v. Will Robinson et al.*, No. 2227 (Tulsa County District Court, 1921); "Roundup of 64 Indicted Blacks Is On," *Tulsa Tribune*, June 17, 1921, 1; "Whites Named in New Batch of True Bills," *Tulsa Tribune*, June 18, 1921, 1.

72. "Bring Stratford Back for Trial," *Tulsa World*, June 7, 1921, 3.

73. Ann Letitia, "The Centennial of J. B. Stradford," n.d., 30, Woodford County Historical Society, Versailles, Ky.

74. "Seek Return of Alleged Rioter."

75. "Bring Stratford Back for Trial."

76. "Seek Return of Alleged Rioter."

77. "To Try Alleged Rioter," *Black Dispatch*, June 17, 1921, 2.

78. "Extradite Stradford," *Tulsa World*, June 17, 1921, 1.

79. Deton J. Brooks, Jr., "Stradford Saved Father from Lynchers' Noose," *Chicago Defender*, June 5, 1943, 13.

80. "Oklahoma Clears Black in Deadly 1921 Race Riot," *New York Times*, October 26, 1996, 8, https://www.nytimes.com/1996/10/26/us/oklahoma-clears-black-in-deadly-1921-race-riot.html.

81. "Roundup of 64 Indicted Blacks Is On," *Tulsa Tribune*, June 17, 1921, 1; "Whites Named in New Batch of True Bills."

82. Letitia, "Centennial of Stradford," 28.

83. "Police Seize 30 in Riot Wake," *Tulsa Tribune*, June 4, 1921, 1; A. J. Smitherman to Walter White, January 15, 1922, Box D-43, Group I, Papers of the NAACP, Auburn University, Auburn, Ala., hereafter NAACP Papers.

84. Moorfield Storey to Mary W. Ovington, January 17, 1922, Box D-43, Group I, NAACP Papers.

85. S. P. Freeling to James E. Markham, in *Oklahoma v. Gustafson*.

86. "'Go to Bottom' Courts Order to Grand Jury," *Tulsa Tribune*, June 9, 1921, 1.

87. "Peace Officers Give Testimony," *Tulsa World*, June 11, 1921, 3.

88. "Hundreds to Be Called in Probe," *Tulsa World,* June 10, 1921, 1; "Roundup of 64 Indicted Blacks Is On"; Ku Klux Klan Membership Roster.

89. "Grand Jury Blames Negroes for Inciting Race Rioting; Whites Clearly Exonerated," *Tulsa World,* June 26, 1921, 1.

90. Walter F. White, "The Eruption of Tulsa," *Nation,* June 29, 1921, https://www.thenation.com/article/society/tulsa-1921/.

91. A. J. Smitherman to Walter F. White, December 25, 1921, Box D-43, Group I, NAACP Papers.

92. "Urge Passing of Dyer Anti-Lynching Bill," *Boston Globe,* March 7, 1922, 5.

93. "Smitherman Writes Governor, Says Brother John Was Democrat," *Black Dispatch,* March 23, 1922, 1; Walter F. White to A. J. Smitherman, January 10, 1922, Box D-43, Group I, NAACP Papers.

94. "Candidates Now on Final Lap of Mayoralty Race," *Springfield Daily Republican,* November 28, 1924, 5.

95. Smitherman to White, December 25, 1921.

96. A. J. Smitherman, "Autobiography," *Empire Star,* October 15, 1960.

97. A. J. Smitherman, "The Tulsa Race Riot and Massacre," Box D-43, Group I, NAACP Papers.

98. Exhibit A, *Loula T. Williams v. Central States Fire Co. Insurance Dept.,* Case No. 19248 (Tulsa County District Court, 1922).

99. Exhibit B, ibid.

100. Williams interview by Avery; Photograph No. 1984.002.025, 1921, Tulsa Race Massacre Collection, Tulsa Historical Society and Museum, https://www.tulsahistory.org/exhibit/1921-tulsa-race-massacre/archive.

101. *Williams v. Central States Fire; Loula T. Williams v. London, Liverpool and Globe Insurance Co.,* No. 19249 (Tulsa County District Court, 1922); *Loula T. Williams v. Fire Association of Philadelphia,* No. 19250 (Tulsa County District Court, 1922).

102. Petition, *Williams v. Central States Fire.*

103. Answer, ibid.

104. Jared Council, "Insurance Exclusions Left Black Tulsans Footing the Bill for the Massacre," *Wall Street Journal,* May 29, 2021, https://www.wsj.com/articles/insurance-exclusions-left-black-tulsans-footing-the-bill-for-the-massacre-11622293201.

105. Answer, 3, *Williams v. Central States Fire.*

106. Ibid.; Clinton Orrin Bunn, ed., *Compiled Statutes of Oklahoma, 1921: Annotated* (Ardmore, Okla.: Bunn Publishing Co., 1922), 1:1063.

107. "Inefficiency of Police Is Denied," *Tulsa Daily World,* July 19, 1921, 7.

108. John Oliphant, testimony, 6, *State of Oklahoma v. John A. Gustafson,* Civil Case No. 1062 (Tulsa County District Court, 1921), Box 25, Record Group 1–2, Oklahoma State Archives, Oklahoma City; Green E. Smith, testimony, in Answer Brief of Defendant in Error, 115–16, *William Redfearn v. American Central Insurance Co.,* No. 15851 (Okla. 1926).

109. Alfred L. Brophy, *Reconstructing the Dreamland: The Tulsa Riot of 1921: Race, Reparations, and Reconciliation* (New York: Oxford University Press, 2002), 97–98; Answer, *Williams v. Central States Fire,* 5.

110. "New Cases," *Tulsa Daily Legal News,* June 1, 1923, 1.

111. Petition, *Mrs. J. H. Goodwin v. City of Tulsa et al.,* Case No. 23368 (Tulsa County District Court, 1923).

112. Larry O'Dell, "Riot Property Loss," in *Tulsa Race Riot: A Report by the Oklahoma Commission to Study the Tulsa Race Riot of 1921* (Oklahoma City: Commission, 2001), 145, https://www.okhistory.org/research/forms/freport.pdf.

113. *Tulsa City Directory, 1921,* 34, 632; Answer, 5–6, *Mabel Allen v. Continental Ins. Co.,* Case No. 16013 (Tulsa County District Court, 1922); Guardian's or Administrator's Report for Mabel Allen, Probate No. 7311, 1929, Oklahoma, U.S., Wills and Probate Records, 1801–2008, Ancestry.com.

114. Answer, *Allen v. Continental Insurance,* 5–6.

115. "New Cases."

116. Franklin, *My Life and an Era,* 31–32.

117. O'Dell, "Riot Property Loss," 145; "56 Damage Suits in Old Race Riot to Be Dismissed," July 1, 1937, 12.

118. *Redfearn v. American Central,* 929.

119. Jim Goodwin, conversation with the author, December 13, 2018.

120. "Building Permits," *Tulsa Daily Legal News,* July 26, 1921, 1.

121. Parrish, *Events of the Tulsa Disaster,* 42.

122. "The Opinion of the *Tulsa World* on Petition for Restraining Order," *Black Dispatch,* August 19, 1921, 1.

123. Franklin, *My Life and an Era,* 198; Photograph No. 1977.046.045, June 6, 1921, and No. 1977.046.045, Tulsa Race Massacre Collection.

124. George Buckner, "Second View of City of Ruins," *St. Louis Argus,* April 21, 1922 1; Henry Whitlow, "The History of the Greenwood Era in Tulsa," March 29, 1973 (transcript), 6, Box 2, Avery Collection.

125. W.E.B. Du Bois, "N.A.A.C.P. and Xmas," *Crisis,* January 1922, 105; W.E.B. Dubois, Diary of Journey typescript notes, ca. 1921, 3, MS 312, W.E.B. Du Bois Papers, Special Collections and University Archives, University of Massachusetts Amherst Libraries.

126. "American Woodman to Help Members," *Press-Forum Weekly,* November 26, 1921, 2.

127. Tulsa County, Okla., Deed Book 428, 538, Lula and J. W. Williams and Supreme Camp of the American Woodmen, October 17, 1922.

128. Williams interview by Ellsworth.

129. Willows, "Narrative Report"; "Willows Ends His Red Cross Work," *Tulsa World,* January 18, 1922, 15.

130. "Wash Tubs Given to Negro Women," *Tulsa World,* June 27, 1921, 10.

131. "Arsenal Fund Is Demanded by Red Cross," *Tulsa Tribune,* June 30, 1921, 1; Meeting Minutes of the City of Tulsa Board of Commissioners, June 29, 1921, 69, City Clerk's Office, Tulsa.

132. Parrish, *Events of the Tulsa Disaster,* 13.

133. Willows, "Narrative Report," 12.

134. Eddie Faye Gates, "Kav's Video: Tulsa Race Riot Survivors Speaks" (video), at https://www.youtube.com/watch?v=8652jvVcPWI.

135. Maurice Willows, "Condensed Report," 18, in Watkins, *Report: Tulsa Race Riot Disaster Relief*.

136. Gates, *They Came Searching*, 213.

137. "Sixth and Final Report Tulsa Relief Committee," *Black Dispatch*, May 11, 1922, 8; *Topeka Plaindealer*, October 7, 1921, 4; "Complete Report of the Donations Made the Colored Relief Committee of Tulsa," *Black Dispatch*, September 15, 1921, 7.

138. Mabel Little, interview by Ruth Sigler Avery, May 24, 1971, transcript, 128, Box 7, Avery Collection.

139. Parrish, *Events of the Tulsa Disaster*, 19.

140. Willows, "Narrative Report," 16–17.

141. East End Relief Committee, statement, December 24, 1921, in Watkins, *Report: Tulsa Race Riot Disaster Relief;* Tulsa Colored Hospital Association of Tulsa, Okla. Articles of Incorporation, December 22, 1921, No. 38005, Oklahoma Secretary of State, Oklahoma City.

142. Willows, "Narrative Report," 17; Tulsa Colored Hospital Articles of Incorporation.

143. Willows, "Condensed Report," 12.

144. "Opinion of the *Tulsa World* on Petition for Restraining Order."

145. William Pickens, "Tulsa in 1922," *Topeka Plaindealer*, November 24, 1922, 1.

146. East End Relief Committee statement.

147. Pickens, "Tulsa in 1922."

148. J. B. Stradford and J. W. Hamel quit claim deed record, November 21, 1921, Deed Book 357, Tulsa County Clerk, 527; *Stradford v. Wagner et al.*, 64 F.2d 749 (10th Cir. 1933).

149. "What the Editor Saw," *Topeka Plaindealer*, April 9, 1926, 1; "Mt. Zion Baptist Church Clears All Indebtedness," *Oklahoma Eagle*, November 7, 1942, 1; "A Monument to Patience," *Impact*, June 1971, 30.

150. *Tulsa City Directory, 1922*, 449; *Tulsa City Directory, 1923*, 466; "Becomes Editor of *Oklahoma Eagle*," *Topeka Plaindealer*, September 29, 1922, 1.

151. *Fisk University News*, August 1923, 14, Special Collections and Archives, Fisk University, Nashville, Tenn.

152. Booker T. Washington High School Yearbook, 1921, National Museum of African American History and Culture, Smithsonian, Washington, D.C., https://collections.si.edu/search/record/edanmdm:nmaahc_2011.175.18.

CHAPTER 9: FAR FROM HOME

1. "Registration at Fisk Is Heavy," *Nashville Banner*, September 30, 1922, 2; "Pledge Loyalty to Fisk President," *Tennessean*, September 26, 1917, 4.

2. "U.S., Social Security Death Index, 1935–2014" (digital image), Ancestry.com; "World War I Draft Registration Cards, 1917–1918" (digital image), Ancestry.com.

3. "Dress and Uniform Regulations," *Fisk University News*, August 1923, 8, Special Collections and Archives, Fisk University, Nashville, Tenn.; *Fisk University Bulletin of Information*, 1924, 17, 20, 26, W.E.B. Du Bois Papers

(MS 312), Special Collections and University Archives, University of Massachusetts Amherst Libraries.

4. "Register of Students, 1922–1923," *Fisk University News*, August 1923, 11–17.

5. "Pledge Loyalty to Fisk President."

6. Booker T. Washington, *The Story of My Life and Work* (Cincinnati: W.H. Ferguson, 1900), 141.

7. "Carnegie Gives $20,000 to Fisk," *Nashville Banner*, January 25, 1908, 13; "Fisk's Carnegie Library," *Tennessean*, July 25, 1908, 8.

8. "Campus and Buildings," *Fisk University News*, August 1923, 16.

9. U.S. Bureau of Education, *Negro Education: A Study of the Private and Higher Schools for Colored People in the United States* (Washington, D.C.: Government Printing Office, 1917), 537.

10. "Fisk University History," Fisk University, https://www.fisk.edu/about/history/.

11. "Fisk Gets Benefits Carnegie Foundation," *Tennessean*, November 17, 1921, 1.

12. "Fisk University," *New York Age*, June 29, 1911, 4; "Nashville Is the Nation's Center for Negro Educational Institutions," *Nashville Banner*, August 21, 1921, 45.

13. "General Information," *Fisk University News*, August 1923, 20.

14. "Registration at Fisk Is Heavy."

15. "President of Fisk University," *Nashville Banner*, January 19, 1915, 2.

16. Reavis L. Mitchell, Jr., "Fisk University," *Tennessee Encyclopedia*, October 8, 2017, https://tennesseeencyclopedia.net/entries/fisk-university/.

17. J. M. Stephen Peeps, "Northern Philanthropy and the Emergence of Black Higher Education," *Journal of Negro Education* 50, no. 3 (1981): 255.

18. Martin Summers, *Manliness and Its Discontents: The Black Middle Class and the Transformation of Masculinity, 1900–1930* (Chapel Hill: University of North Carolina Press, 2004), 246–47.

19. James D. Anderson, "Northern Philanthropy and the Training of the Black Leadership: Fisk University, a Case Study, 1915–1930," in Vincent P. Franklin and James D. Anderson, eds., *New Perspectives on Black Educational History* (Boston: G.K. Hall, 1978), 102–3.

20. Summers, *Manliness and Its Discontents*, 250.

21. "Register of Students, 1922–1923," *Fisk University News*, August 1923, 12.

22. Ibid., 15; Eddy Determeyer, *Rhythm Is Our Business: Jimmie Lunceford and the Harlem Express* (Ann Arbor: University of Michigan Press, 2006), 7.

23. "Department of Music," *Fisk University News*, August 1923, 76.

24. U.S. Bureau of Education, *Negro Education*, 536.

25. Reavis L. Mitchell, Jr., "Jubilee Singers of Fisk University," *Tennessee Encyclopedia*, https://tennesseeencyclopedia.net/entries/jubilee-singers-of-fisk-university/; Joe M. Richardson, *A History of Fisk University 1865–1946* (Tuscaloosa: University of Alabama Press, 2002), 33.

26. Joseph E. Roy, *Pilgrim's Letters: Bits of Current History: Picked up in the West and the South, During the Last Thirty Years, For the Independent, the Congregationalist, and the Advance* (Boston: Congregational Sunday-School

and Publishing Society, 1888), 178–79; "General Information," *Fisk University News*, August 1923, 20.

27. Jeanne Arradondo, conversation with the author, August 10, 2020.

28. J. H. Goodwin, "Why Not Use Your GI Rights?" *Oklahoma Eagle*, August 11, 1945, 8.

29. Jacoby Adeshei Carter and Corey Barnes, "Alain LeRoy Locke," *Stanford Encyclopedia of Philosophy* (Fall 2022), https://plato.stanford.edu/archives/fall2022/entries/alain-locke/.

30. Alain Locke, "Negro Education Bids for Par," *Survey* (1925), 592.

31. Muriel Miller Branch, "Maggie Lena Walker (1864–1934)," *Encyclopedia Virginia*, https://encyclopediavirginia.org/entries/walker-maggie-lena-1864 -1934/.

32. Walter B. Weare, *Black Business in the New South: A Social History of the North Carolina Mutual Life Insurance Company* (Durham, N.C.: Duke University Press, 1993), 116; advertisement, *Black Dispatch*, July 1, 1921, 4.

33. Bobby L. Lovett, *The African-American History of Nashville, Tennessee, 1780–1930* (Fayetteville: University of Arkansas Press, 1999), 120.

34. *Springfield City Directory, 1905* (R.L. Polk & Co.), 546.

35. "Jeanne Belle Osby Goodwin," in Julian Bond and Sondra K. Wilson, eds., *Lift Every Voice and Sing: A Celebration of the Negro National Anthem: 100 Years, 100 Voices* (New York: Random House, 2000), electronic ed.

36. *Springfield City Directory, 1905*, 546.

37. *Springfield City Directory, 1909*, 655; *Pictorial Souvenir: Central Illinois, 1912*, Internet Archive, https://archive.org/details/pictorialsouvenir1912/page/23/mode/2up.

38. "Congressman Selects New Washington Aide," *McHenry Plaindealer*, May 29, 1969, 13.

39. Eddie Faye Gates, "North Tulsa Project Tape 1" (video), Audio Archives, Oklahoma Historical Society, https://www.youtube.com/watch?v=OCdfvY45FLE.

40. "Congressman Selects New Washington Aide."

41. Bond and Wilson, *Lift Every Voice and Sing*.

42. Yvonne Nance, " 'God, I'm in Your Hands,' " *Abundant Life Magazine*, April 1970, 19–20.

43. "Community Leader, Educator, Jeanne. B. Goodwin, 102, Dies," *Tulsa World*, January 26, 2006, https://tulsaworld.com/archive/community-leader-educator -jeanne-b-goodwin-102-dies/article_2deb72da-ob5f-5c8e-902e-4bcec8ea2331 .html.

44. James L. Crouthamel, "The Springfield Race Riot of 1908," *Journal of Negro History* 48, no. 3 (July 1960): 165–73; Roberta Senechal, "Springfield Race Riot of 1908," Social Welfare History Project, Virginia Commonwealth University Libraries, https://socialwelfare.library.vcu.edu/eras/civil-war -reconstruction/springfield-race-riot-of-1908/.

45. Floyd Mansberger and Christopher Stratton, "The 1908 Springfield Race Riot: Burned Building Locations and Other Historic Photographic Views," *Fever River Research* (2016), 305, http://illinoisarchaeology.com/Papers/NAACP %20Freedom%20Dinner%202-2019.pdf.

46. Bond and Wilson, *Lift Every Voice and Sing.*

47. David Levering Lewis, *W.E.B. Du Bois: A Biography* (New York: Henry Holt & Co., 2009), 253.

48. "NAACP History: How the National NAACP Began," Springfield NAACP, n.d., http://springfieldnaacp.org/about-us/history/; Paula Giddings, "Missing in Action: Ida B. Wells, the NAACP, and the Historical Record" *Meridians* 1, no. 2 (Spring 2001): 5–6.

49. Fisk University Dean of Women, circular letter to unidentified correspondent, December 26, 1924, W.E.B. Du Bois Papers, Special Collections and University Archives, University of Massachusetts Amherst Libraries; hereafter Du Bois Papers.

50. "General Regulations," *Fisk University News*, August 1923, 6; Summers, *Manliness and Its Discontents*, 261.

51. "General Regulations"; Associated Fisk Clubs, *Fisk Herald*, 1925, 15, Du Bois Papers.

52. Lewis, *Du Bois: A Biography*, 50.

53. Peeps, "Northern Philanthropy and Black Higher Education," 256.

54. Anderson, "Northern Philanthropy and Black Leadership," 105.

55. Ibid.

56. Richardson, *History of Fisk University*, 89–90.

57. Lester C. Lamon, "The Black Community in Nashville and the Fisk University Student Strike of 1924–1925," *Journal of Southern History* 40, no. 2 (May 1974): 232.

58. Summers, *Manliness and Its Discontents*, 264.

59. Gerald L. Smith, *A Black Educator in the Segregated South* (Lexington: University Press of Kentucky, 2021).

60. J. T. Phillips, "What Do They Want at Fisk?," ca. March 7, 1925, Du Bois Papers.

61. Summers, *Manliness and Its Discontents*, 250.

62. W.E.B. Du Bois, "The Dilemma of the Negro," *American Mercury* 3 (1924), https://babel.hathitrust.org/cgi/pt?id=mdp.39015030748548&view=1up&seq =196&skin=2021&q1=fisk.

63. W.E.B. Du Bois, "Diuturni Silenti," in Herbert Aptheker, ed., *Education of Black People: Ten Critiques, 1906–1960* (New York: Monthly Review Press, 1973), 41–43.

64. W.E.B. Du Bois, "Diuturni Silenti," June 21, 1924, Du Bois Papers.

65. Fayette A. McKenzie to Paul D. Cravath, June 5, 1924, Du Bois Papers.

66. Edward Taylor, statement, 1925, Du Bois Papers.

67. Edward Goodwin, "Some Reasons Why We As Students Dislike Fisk," Du Bois Papers.

68. Jim Goodwin, conversation with the author, January 22, 2021; W.E.B. Du Bois to Anna Goodwin, August 2, 1928, Du Bois Papers.

69. Goodwin, "Some Reasons Why We As Students Dislike Fisk."

70. "Ohio Professor Discusses Race Problem in Founder's Day Address at Fisk," *Tennessean*, November 17, 1924, 6.

71. "Fisk University Given the First Million-Dollar Endowment for College Education of the Negro in the History of America," *Fisk University News*, Octo-

ber 1924, 1, Du Bois Papers; "Five Significant Press Comments on the Endowment," *Fisk University News,* October 1924, 7, Du Bois Papers.

72. Ralph Ellison, *Invisible Man* (New York: Random House, 1952), 42.

73. Taylor statement.

74. "Board of Trustees," *Fisk University News,* April 1924, 7.

75. Grievances and requests of the Student Body of Fisk University, 1924, Du Bois Papers.

76. Richardson, *History of Fisk University,* 96.

77. "50 Police Quell Demonstration of Fisk Students," *Tennessean,* February 5, 1925, 1; "Scene of Riot by Students at Fisk University," *Nashville Banner,* February 5, 1925, 9.

78. Taylor statement.

79. Ibid.; "50 Police Quell Demonstration."

80. "Things That Gave Rise to Demonstration of Feb. 4, 1925," ca. February 1925, Du Bois Papers.

81. Taylor statement.

82. Fisk University students' testimony, 1925, Du Bois Papers.

83. "Statements Give Various Angles of Trouble at Fisk," *Nashville Banner,* February 5, 1925, 1.

84. "50 Police Quell Demonstration."

85. Fisk students' testimony.

86. Fisk University and students, agreement, February 10, 1925, Du Bois Papers.

87. Taylor statement.

88. E. L. Goodwin to J. H. Goodwin, telegram, February 5, 1925, Susan Jordan (private collection).

89. "Fisk Students Stage Walkout," *Nashville Banner,* February 6, 1925, 1.

90. "Fisk Wrangle to Be Discussed at Meeting Tonight," *Tennessean,* February 9, 1925, 1.

91. "Fisk President's Offer Accepted with Amendment," *Tennessean,* February 10, 1925, 1.

92. W.E.B. Du Bois to Edward Taylor, October 2, 1924; George Streator to Du Bois, October 2, 1924; Du Bois to F. A. Stewart, February 5, 1925; Streator to Du Bois, February 5, 1925; Streator to Du Bois, February 12, 1925, all in Du Bois Papers.

93. W.E.B. Du Bois, "Fisk," *Crisis,* April 1925, 250.

94. Christopher Nicholson, "To Advance a Race: A Historical Analysis of the Intersection of Personal Belief, Industrial Philanthropy and Black Liberal Arts Higher Education in Fayette McKenzie's Presidency at Fisk University, 1915–1925," Ph.D. diss., Loyola, 2011, 289.

95. "Fisk Trustees Stand Behind Dr. M'Kenzie," *Nashville Banner,* February 12, 1921, 1.

96. "Fisk Seniors Give Books to Library," *Nashville Banner,* March 1, 1925, 20.

97. "Students Strike at Fisk University" (video), in *The Rise and Fall of Jim Crow,* PBS Learning Media, https://oeta.pbslearningmedia.org/resource/bf10.socst.us .indust.fiskstrike/students-strike-at-fisk-university/.

98. "M'Kenzie Will Leave Fisk," *Nashville Banner,* April 25, 1925, 7.

99. Du Bois, "Fisk."
100. "Graduates at Fisk Hear Rev. Chaffee," *Nashville Banner,* June 8, 1926, 12.
101. Anderson, "Northern Philanthropy and the Training of the Black Leadership," 109.
102. Lamon, "Black Community in Nashville," 243.
103. Eddie L. Madison, Jr., "Two Leaders at Peace," *Oklahoma Eagle,* February 2, 2006, 1.
104. *Atlanta City Directory, 1927* (Atlanta City Directory Co.), 960; U.S. National Park Service, 2022, "Martin Luther King, Jr., Birth Home," https://www.nps .gov/malu/planyourvisit/birth-home.htm.
105. Jeanne Osby to James Ballard Osby, September 16, 1926, Jeanne Osby Goodwin Arradondo Family Collection.
106. Ed Sr. interview by La Brie.
107. Bob Goodwin, conversation with the author, December 10, 2021.
108. Ibid.
109. Ed Sr. interview by La Brie.
110. Nance, " 'God I'm in Your Hands,' " 20.
111. Edward L. Goodwin and Jeanne B. Osby, marriage license, St. Louis County, September 3, 1927.
112. W.E.B. Du Bois, "Pilgrimage," *Crisis,* April 1926, 269.

CHAPTER 10: THE MYTH OF AN IMPERVIOUS PEOPLE

1. "New Dreamland Theater at Tulsa, Oklahoma," *Black Dispatch,* September 14, 1922, 8.
2. Scrapbook compiled by W. D. Williams while attending Hampton Institute, 1924–28, 18, 22, National Museum of African American History and Culture, Smithsonian, Washington, D.C., https://transcription.si.edu/project/37790.
3. Loula Williams to Dreamland Patrons, ca. 1924, Williams Dreamland LLC Collection, Dallas, Tex.
4. Tulsa County, Okla., Deed Book 428, 538, Loula and J. W. Williams and The Supreme Camp of the American Woodmen, October 27, 1922.
5. Tulsa County, Okla., Deed Book 396, 111, Lula and J. W. Williams and E. J. McJunkin, January 31, 1922; Tulsa County, Okla., Deed Book 396, 149, Lula and J. W. Williams and Carla McJunkin Conway, January 31, 1922; Tulsa County, Okla., Deed Book 358, 302, Lula and J. W. Williams and E. J. McJunkin, April 29, 1922.
6. Francis Dominic Burke, "A Survey of the Negro Community of Tulsa, Oklahoma," master's thesis, University of Tulsa, 1936, 45–46.
7. "Martha Jones into Movies?" *Muskogee Daily Phoenix,* October 18, 1921, 5.
8. "Delinquent Tax List for the Year 1921," *Okmulgee Daily Times,* September 7, 1922, 8.
9. Joseph J. McKeever testimony, Guardianship papers of Loula T. Williams, Probate no. 6696, 8, Ancestry.com.
10. Loula Williams to W. D. Williams, December 29, 1923, Williams Dreamland LLC Collection.

11. Loula Williams to W. D. Williams, January 26, 1924, Williams Dreamland LLC Collection; *Tulsa City Directory, 1924* (Polk-Hoffhine Directory Co.), 850.
12. Loula Williams to W. D. Williams, December 29, 1923, Williams Dreamland LLC Collection.
13. Loula Williams to W. D. Williams, April 17, 1924, Williams Dreamland LLC Collection.
14. "Race Woman Theatrical Magnate," *Topeka Plaindealer,* November 28, 1919, 1; Loula Williams to W. D. Williams, n.d., Williams Dreamland LLC Collection.
15. Loula Williams to W. D. Williams, n.d., Williams Dreamland LLC Collection.
16. William J. Greenleaf, *Self-Help for College Students* (Washington, D.C.: Government Printing Office, 1929), 131.
17. Scrapbook compiled by W. D. Williams, 40, 57.
18. W. D. Williams to Loula Williams, April 16, 1924, Williams Dreamland LLC Collection.
19. Loula Williams to W. D. Williams, April 18, 1924, Williams Dreamland LLC Collection.
20. "Mrs. Lulu T. 'Cotton' Williams: Williams Confectionery," *Tulsa Star,* August 19, 1914, 10.
21. Loula Williams to W. D. Williams, January 26, 1924, Williams Dreamland LLC Collection.
22. Loula Williams to W. D. Williams, February 26, 1924, Williams Dreamland LLC Collection.
23. Scrapbook compiled by W. D. Williams, 40.
24. Tulsa County, Okla., Deed Book 550, 481, Lula and J. W. Williams and Tulsa Building and Loan Association, March 16, 1925.
25. Tulsa County, Okla., Deed Book 517, 479, Lula and J. W. Williams and Security Life Insurance Company, October 15, 1924; Tulsa County, Okla., Deed Book 499, 41, Lula and J. W. Williams and E. J. McJunkin, October 27, 1924.
26. Charles Deal testimony, 210, in *Williams v. Deal,* 3 P. 867 (Okla. 1931).
27. William Redfearn testimony, 236, ibid.
28. Joseph J. McKeever, testimony, 8, Guardianship papers of Loula T. Williams, Probate no. 6696, Ancestry.com.
29. J. W. Williams testimony, 3, Guardianship papers of Williams.
30. Loula Williams to W. D. Williams, ca. 1924, Williams Dreamland LLC Collection.
31. "Negro Business League Held National Session," *New York Age,* August 29, 1925, 1; "Business League Meets in Tulsa," *Topeka Plaindealer,* August 28, 1925, 1.
32. Solomon Jones, "Film 20" (video), 1925, Yale Collection of Western Americana, Beinecke Rare Book and Manuscript Library, Yale University.
33. "Negro Business League Held National Session."
34. "Famous Military Band Is on Way to Negro Convention," *Tulsa Tribune,* August 16, 1925, 2.
35. "Negro Business League Held National Session"; Jones, "Film 20."

36. "Crack Cavalry Band Greets Dr. Moton," *Tulsa Tribune*, August 18, 1925, 3.

37. "Negro Business League Held National Session"; *Oklahoma Eagle*, August 20, 1925, 10.

38. *Tulsa City Directory, 1925*, 604.

39. "Negro Business League Held National Session."

40. "America's Way With Negroes to Prevail," *Tulsa Tribune*, August 19, 1925, 3; Albon L. Holsey, "Tulsa and the Business League," *Opportunity*, October 1925, 295.

41. "Negro Business League Held National Session"; *Tulsa City Directory, 1925*, 517; Mary Jones Parrish, *Events of the Tulsa Disaster* (Tulsa, ca. 1923), 90.

42. "Tulsa and the Business League."

43. "National Negro Business League Meets at Tulsa, Okla. in August," *Topeka Plaindealer*, July 10, 1925, 4.

44. Little, interview by Avery; Eddie Faye Gates, *They Came Searching: How Blacks Found the Promised Land in Oklahoma* (Austin, Tex.: Eakin Press, 1997), 181–82; "Tulsa and the Business League"; "New Bus Route," *Tulsa Tribune*, August 5, 1927, 7.

45. Berry in Gates, *They Came Searching*, 182.

46. "Crack Cavalry Band Greets Dr. Moton," *Tulsa Tribune*, August 18, 1925, 3.

47. Ibid.; Tulsa City Commission Minutes, June 7, 1921, 3, Tulsa City Clerk's Office.

48. "Tulsa and the Business League"; Ku Klux Klan Membership Roster, 1928–1932.

49. "Tulsa's Popular Mayor Welcomes the National Negro Business League," *Oklahoma Eagle*, August 20, 1925, 5; "Filling the Bill," *Oklahoma Eagle*, August 20, 1925, 8; "Our County Attorney," *Oklahoma Eagle*, August 20, 1925, 8.

50. Lorenzo J. Greene, *Selling Black History for Carter G. Woodson* (Columbia: University of Missouri Press, 1996), 154; "Negro Publisher Fought Battles of People, Says *Oklahoma Eagle*, Tulsa," *Sooner State Press*, July 17, 1937, 1.

51. "Tulsa's Popular Mayor."

52. Ibid.

53. "Go to Park Sanitarium, Guthrie, Okla.," *Black Dispatch*, August 20, 1925, sec. 2, 3.

54. "Big Sanitarium in Guthrie Is a Wonder," *Tulsa Star*, December 4, 1915, 1; Ivo Geikie Cobb, *A Manual of Neurasthenia (Nervous Exhaustion)* (United Kingdom: Baillière, Tindall and Cox, 1920), 14–22.

55. J. W. Williams testimony, 3, Guardianship papers.

56. "Go to Park Sanitarium."

57. "Big Sanitarium in Guthrie"; "Dr. Conrad's Sanitarium Has State-Wide Business," *Oklahoma State Register* (Guthrie, Okla.), September 2, 1920, 1; J. W. Williams testimony, 3–4, Guardianship papers.

58. Joseph J. McKeever, testimony, 8, Guardianship papers.

59. Joseph J. McKeever testimony, 7–9, Guardianship papers.

60. J. W. Williams testimony, 5, Guardianship papers.

61. "Have Violated Agreement," *Tulsa World*, May 26, 1922, 4; "Local Show

Houses Are Sold Today," *Holdenville Democrat*, March 31, 1927, 1; "Motion Picture Exhibitor's League, Oklahoma Convention," *Moving Picture World*, November 15, 1913, 740; Tulsa County, Okla., Deed Book 616, 84, Lula and J. W. Williams and J. W. Cotter, March 9, 1926.

62. Tulsa County, Okla., Deed Book 583, 190–93, Lula and J. W. Williams and J. W. Cotter, February 20, 1926.

63. A. B. Crews testimony, 95–96, *Williams v. Deal*.

64. Tulsa County, Okla., Deed Book 635, 166, J. W. Cotter and Helen Deal, October 12, 1926.

65. Crews testimony, 97, *Williams v. Deal*.

66. J. W. Williams testimony, 69–70, ibid.

67. Ibid., 183.

68. Ku Klux Klan Membership Roster, 1928–1932, Tulsa, Okla., Ku Klux Klan Collection, University of Tulsa; Rex F. Harlow, "The Hudson Statement Stirs Oklahoma," *Harlow's Weekly* (Oklahoma City), 12.

69. Journal Entry, 36, *Williams v. Deal*; Order, 38, *Williams v. Deal*; Ku Klux Klan Membership Roster, 1928–1932.

70. Supreme Court Ruling, *Williams v. Deal*.

71. Memorandum Brief in Support of Petition for Rehearing, 5, ibid.

72. Tulsa County, Okla., Deed Book 1239, 455, Tulsa County Sheriff and Trustees for the former stockholders of the Tulsa Building and Loan Association, July 26, 1937.

73. J. W. Williams testimony, 3, 5, Guardianship papers.

74. Joseph J. McKeever testimony, 9, Guardianship papers.

75. "Convention Time," *Chicago Defender*, August 29, 1925, A10.

76. Mabel Little, *Fire on Mount Zion: My Life and History As a Black Woman in America* (Wilmington, Del.: Black Think Tank, 1992), 41.

77. 1920 U.S. Census, Tulsa County, Okla., pop. sch., ED 256, sheet 4B, dwell. 92, fam. 111, Pressley Little; *Tulsa City Directory, 1921*, 61.

78. Little, *Fire on Mount Zion*, 45–46; Oklahoma State Department of Health, OK2EXPLORE - Vital Records, Pressley Little.

79. Burke, "Survey of the Negro Community," 23.

80. "Police Boss Puts Ban on Camera Men in Destroyed Area," *Tulsa Tribune*, June 14, 1921, 13.

81. "Tulsa Riot Victims Sue City for Millions," *Pittsburgh Courier*, June 23, 1923, 1.

82. J. M. Adkison, the police commissioner who banned photographers from the riot zone, and Mayor Newblock, who downplayed the massacre's impact during the Business League meeting, were both Klan members.

83. "Baptist Pastor, Klan Defender Tells Its Aims," *Tulsa Tribune*, August 11, 1921, 3.

84. Steve Gerkin, "Beno Hall: Tulsa's Den of Terror," *This Land*, September 3, 2011, https://thislandpress.com/2011/09/03/beno-hall-tulsas-den-of-terror/.

85. B. C. Franklin, *My Life and an Era: The Autobiography of Buck Colbert Franklin* (Baton Rouge: Louisiana State University Press, 1997), 201–2.

86. "Oklahoma's Welcome," *Black Dispatch*, August 20, 1925, 4; "The Smoking

Ruins of Tulsa After the Riots of June 1st, 1921," *Black Dispatch,* August 20, 1925, 2.

87. Victor Luckerson, "What a Florida Reparations Case Can Teach Us About Justice in America," *Time,* September 10, 2020, https://time.com/5887247/reparations-america-rosewood-massacre/.

88. "Moton Outlines Negro's Future," *Tulsa World,* August 20, 1925, 1.

89. Mabel Little, in *Goin' Back to T-Town,* PBS/American Experience, March 1, 1993, transcript, 14–15.

90. Parrish, *Events of the Tulsa Disaster,* 9.

91. Ibid., 18–19.

92. Ibid., 46, 54.

93. Ibid., 18.

94. S. M. Jackson, interview by Ruth Sigler Avery, transcript, Box 3, Ruth Sigler Avery Collection, Oklahoma State University–Tulsa.

95. "Race Riot 1921: Events of the Tulsa Disaster," *Oklahoma Eagle,* May 7, 1998, 1.

96. Parrish, *Events of the Tulsa Disaster,* 12, 33, 37.

97. Ibid., 8.

98. *Muskogee Times-Democrat,* November 29, 1922, 9.

99. "City Teacher Entertained Tuesday," *Tulsa Star,* September 23, 1916, 1.

100. "News Around Town," *Tulsa Star,* June 19, 1915, 4.

101. "The Parisienne Hat Shop," *Oklahoma Eagle,* August 20, 1925, 6.

102. "Prominent Society Woman Shot to Death by Husband," *Chicago Defender,* September 5, 1925, 3; "World Fellowship Vesper Service Sunday," *Oklahoma Eagle,* November 12, 1953, 1.

103. "Dentist Who Slew Pretty Wife Given Life Imprisonment," *Chicago World,* October 29, 1925, 1.

104. Itemized statement, *Dr. Plato Travis v. City of Tulsa,* No. 23344 (Tulsa County District Court, 1923); *Tulsa City Directory, 1921,* 659; "$2,500,000 of Negro Property Is Destroyed," *Black Dispatch,* June 3, 1921, 1.

105. Order of Dismissal, *Travis v. Tulsa; Tulsa City Directory, 1922* (Polk-Hoffhine Directory Co.), 242, 592; *Tulsa City Directory, 1923,* 261, 614; *Tulsa City Directory, 1924,* 329, 706.

106. "Tulsa Dentist Says Mind Blank When He Shot," *Black Dispatch,* October 22, 1925, 1.

107. Ibid.

108. "Crazed with Bad Whiskey, Slays Wife," *Black Dispatch,* August 27, 1925, 1.

109. Ibid.

110. "Dentist Who Slew Pretty Wife."

111. "Prominent Society Woman Shot to Death"; 1910 U.S. Census, Yalobusha County, Miss., pop. sch., ED 117, sheet 9B, dwell. 33, fam. 42, Lucille Goodwin.

112. "Prominent Society Woman Shot to Death."

113. "Did Enraged Husband Shoot Self?" *Black Dispatch* (Oklahoma City), September 10, 1925, 1.

114. "Tulsa Dentist Says Mind Blank."

115. "More Clemency Papers Signed," *Cushing Daily Citizen,* January 10, 1931, 4;

Plato Travis, World War II Draft Registration Cards, 1942, digital image, Ancestry.com.

116. *Tulsa City Directory, 1918,* 628; Ed Goodwin, World War II Draft Registration Cards, 1942, digital image, Ancestry.com; *Tulsa, Tulsa County, Oklahoma,* map (Sanborn Map Co., 1939), Image 4, Library of Congress.

117. Jo Ann Gilford, conversation with the author, July 30, 2019.

118. Ibid.

119. Regina Goodwin, conversations with the author, August 6, 2020, and August 17, 2022.

120. Scrapbook compiled by W. D. Williams, 50.

121. Ibid., 9, 16.

122. Ibid., 50.

123. Ibid., 44.

124. Ibid.

125. Polly Bowen, "Williams Tells Tulsa Past," *Oklahoma Eagle,* April 21, 1977, 1.

126. Scrapbook compiled by W. D. Williams, 18, 57.

127. Donation receipt for Anita Christopher, November 19, 2011, Williams Dreamland LLC Collection.

128. Charles Christopher, conversation with the author, August 17, 2022.

129. Loula Williams to W. D. Williams, March 22, 1924, and December 29, 1923, both in Williams Dreamland LLC Collection.

CHAPTER 11: SUGAR MAN

1. Ed Goodwin, Sr., interview by Henry La Brie, August 12, 1971, transcript, 4, Black Journalists Oral History Collection, Columbia University.

2. *Tulsa City Directory, 1929* (Polk-Hoffhine Directory Co.), 316; *Tulsa City Directory, 1916,* 193; *Tulsa, Tulsa County, Oklahoma,* map (Sanborn Map Co., 1939), Image 4, Library of Congress.

3. Yvonne Nance, "'God I'm in Your Hands,'" *Abundant Life Magazine,* April 1970, 20.

4. Jeanne Goodwin, interview by Jeanne Arradondo, n.d., Jeanne Osby Goodwin Arradondo Family Collection, Nashville, Tenn.

5. Ed Sr. interview by La Brie, 5.

6. Lorenzo J. Greene, *Selling Black History for Carter G. Woodson* (Columbia: University of Missouri Press, 1996), 156–57; *Tulsa, Tulsa County, Oklahoma,* map (Sanborn Map Co., 1939), Image 4, Library of Congress; ibid., 55.

7. Greene, *Selling Black History for Woodson,* 157–58.

8. Ed Sr. interview by La Brie, 4–5; *Tulsa City Directory, 1929,* 761.

9. *Tulsa City Directory,* 323; Ed Sr. interview by La Brie, 5; Photograph of Ed Sr. in Greenwood Haberdashery, ca. 1930, Jeanne Osby Goodwin Arradondo Family Collection.

10. Photograph of Ed Goodwin, Sr., in the Greenwood Haberdashery.

11. *Tulsa City Directory, 1929,* 760–61.

12. *Oklahoma Eagle,* August 20, 1925, 10; *Tulsa City Directory, 1933,* 92.

13. Ed Sr. interview by La Brie, 5.

14. Danney Goble, *Tulsa! Biography of the American City* (Tulsa: Council Oak Books, 1997), 140.
15. Francis Dominic Burke, "A Survey of the Negro Community of Tulsa, Oklahoma," master's thesis, University of Tulsa, 1936, 54.
16. Ibid., 56, 68.
17. Ibid., 69.
18. W. D. Williams, interview by Scott Ellsworth, June 7, 1978 (recording), Tulsa Race Massacre of 1921 Archive, University of Tulsa.
19. Mabel Little, in *Goin' Back to T-Town*, PBS/American Experience, March 1, 1993, transcript, 27–28.
20. B. C. Franklin, *My Life and an Era: The Autobiography of Buck Colbert Franklin* (Baton Rouge: Louisiana State University Press, 1997), 221.
21. Burke, "Survey of the Negro Community," 55.
22. Ibid., 78; Stephen R. Haynes, *Noah's Curse: The Biblical Justification of American Slavery* (New York: Oxford University Press, 2002), 66.
23. Burke, "Survey of the Negro Community," 80, 89–90, 78; Bobby Thomas Quinten, "The Social Impact of the Great Depression on Metropolitan Tulsa, 1929–1932," B.A. thesis, East Central State College, 1960, 56.
24. "CWA Program to Climax of Employment, 6,739 on Jobs," *Tulsa Tribune*, December 22, 1933, 13; Tanya Adele Davis, "New Deal Work Relief for Women: The Case for Oklahoma," master's thesis, Oklahoma State University, 1986, 44; "FERA Work and Relief at End Until Budget Is Set," *Tulsa Tribune,* January 2, 1934, 3.
25. Martha H. Swain, *Ellen S. Woodward: New Deal Advocate for Women* (Jackson: University Press of Mississippi, 1995), 92.
26. Burke, "Survey of the Negro Community," 67.
27. Ibid., 69; Davis, "New Deal Work Relief for Women," 50.
28. Davis, "New Deal Work Relief for Women," 87.
29. Juan F. Perea, "The Echoes of Slavery: Recognizing the Racist Origins of the Agricultural and Domestic Worker Exclusion from the National Labor Relations Act," *Ohio State Law Journal* 72, no. 1 (2011): 104–6.
30. Todd Michney and LaDale Winling, "New Perspectives on New Deal Housing Policy: Explicating and Mapping HOLC Loans to African Americans," *Journal of Urban History* 46, no. 1 (2020): 152.
31. Ibid., 171.
32. Franklin, *My Life and an Era,* 221.
33. Tulsa County, Okla., Deed Book 1104, 18, E. L. and Jeanne B. Goodwin and Home Owners' Loan Corporation, January 10, 1934.
34. David M. Breed, "A Look at the Life of E. L. Goodwin, Sr.," *Oklahoma Eagle,* September 14, 1978, 11; *Tulsa City Directory, 1934,* 224; 1940 U.S. Census, Tulsa County, Okla., pop. sch., ED 79–83, sheet 7B, Edwynna and Jo Ann Goodwin.
35. U.S. Bureau of the Census, *Sixteenth Census of the United States: 1940—Housing,* vol. 2: *General Characteristics,* pt. 1: *United States Summary* (Washington, D.C.: Government Printing Office, 1943), 115–17, 143–45; Michney and Winling, "New Perspectives on Housing Policy," 158.
36. U.S. Bureau of the Census, *Sixteenth Census of the United States:*

1940—Housing, vol. 4: *Mortgages on Owner-Occupied Nonfarm Homes,* pt. 3: *North Carolina—Wyoming* (Washington, D.C.: Government Printing Office, 1943), 170.

37. Ibid., 170, 180; U.S. Census Bureau, *Sixteenth Census, 1940—Housing,* 2:145.

38. Michney and Winling, "New Perspectives on Housing Policy," 159.

39. Ibid., 154–55.

40. Todd Michney, conversation with the author, August 24, 2022.

41. Todd Michney, "How the City Survey's Redlining Maps Were Made: A Closer Look at HOLC's Mortgagee Rehabilitation Division," *Journal of Planning History* 21, no. 4 (2021): 2.

42. Ibid., 2–3, 5–6.

43. Ibid., 9.

44. Ibid., 13.

45. Ibid., 7; R. L. Olson to Corwin A. Fergus, December 5, 1935, "[Region] 5B 17-Admin., Mortgages Rehab. Com.," Roll 296 [DSCF 3973], National Archives, Washington, D.C.

46. *Tulsa City Directory, 1935,* 251; "Glass Favors Excise Office," *Tulsa Tribune,* June 7, 1934, 8.

47. "Mapping Inequality: Redlining in New Deal America," in Robert K. Nelson and Edward L. Ayers, eds., *American Panorama: An Atlas of United States History,* https://dsl.richmond.edu/panorama/redlining/#loc=11/36.138/-96.128 &city=tulsa-ok.

48. Michney, "How the City Survey's Redlining Maps," 3.

49. Price V. Fishback et al., "New Evidence of Redlining by Federal Housing Programs in the 1930s," National Bureau of Economic Research, Working Paper No. 29244, 7, https://www.nber.org/papers/w29244.

50. Michney, "How the City Survey's Redlining Maps," 15.

51. LaDale C. Winling and Todd M. Michney, "The Roots of Redlining: Academic, Governmental and Professional Networks in the Making of the New Deal Lending Regime," *Journal of American History* 108, no. 1 (June 2021): 44.

52. "It Must Not Be Again," *Tulsa Tribune,* June 4, 1921, 8.

53. Richard Rothstein, *The Color of Law: A Forgotten History of How Our Government Segregated America* (New York: W.W. Norton, 2017), 64–66.

54. Andrew Wiese, *Places of Their Own: African American Suburbanization in the Twentieth Century* (Chicago: University of Chicago Press, 2004), 140.

55. Tulsa County, Okla., Deed Book 1952, 178, E. L. and Jeanne B. Goodwin and Home Owners' Loan Corporation, November 4, 1944.

56. Michney, "How the City Survey's Redlining Maps," 14.

57. Lynne Bayer Sagalyn, "Housing on the Installment Plan: An Economic and Institutional Analysis of Contract Buying in Chicago," Ph.D. diss., Massachusetts Institute of Technology, 1980, 113, 297.

58. "Death Takes Retired Newspaper Publisher," *Tulsa World,* September 12, 1978, A1.

59. Ed Sr. interview by La Brie, 6.

60. Burke, "Survey of the Negro Community," 98–100.

61. Ibid., 99.
62. Ralph Martin, "Hitting the High Spots," *Tulsa World,* July 21, 1937, 5.
63. Ibid.
64. Ivan Light, "Numbers Gambling Among Blacks: A Financial Institution," *American Sociological Review* 42, no. 6 (December 1977): 896–97.
65. Burke, "Survey of the Negro Community," 99; Martin, "Hitting the High Spots," July 21, 1937.
66. Ralph Martin, "Hitting the High Spots," *Tulsa World,* July 23, 1937, 6.
67. Martin, "Hitting the High Spots," July 21, 1937.
68. "Downtown Gaming House Is Raided," *Tulsa World,* August 7, 1937, 1.
69. Burke, "Survey of the Negro Community," 99.
70. Ibid., 100.
71. Ibid.
72. Ibid.
73. Ibid., 98.
74. Julian B. Roebuck, "The Negro Numbers Man as a Criminal Type: The Construction and Application of a Typology," *Journal of Criminal Law and Criminology* 54, no. 1 (Spring 1963): 56.
75. Ibid., 52; Matthew Vaz, *Running the Numbers: Race, Police and the History of Urban Gambling* (Chicago: University of Chicago Press, 2020), 24; LaShawn Harris, "Playing the Numbers: Madame Stephanie St. Clair and African American Policy Culture in Harlem," *Black Women, Gender + Families* 2, no. 2 (Fall 2008): 58.
76. Roebuck, "Negro Numbers Man," 55.
77. Nance, " 'God I'm in Your Hands,' " 20.
78. Ed Sr. interview by La Brie, 6.
79. O. C. Foster, World War I Draft Registration Cards, 1917–18, digital image, Ancestry.com; *Tulsa City Directory, 1927,* 629.
80. Mike Staniford, "Looking Back with Atty. Jones," *Oklahoma Eagle,* February 19, 1987, 1.
81. James Hollis testimony, 67, 21, 130–31, *State of Oklahoma v. O. C. Foster,* A-8693 (Tulsa County District Court, 1934).
82. Staniford, "Looking Back with Atty. Jones."
83. *Tulsa City Directory, 1933,* 568.
84. Ibid., 217; "Slaying of Tulsan Mystifies Police," *Tulsa World,* August 19, 1933, 10; "One Dies Here in 'Policy War,' " *Tulsa Tribune,* August 19, 1933, 2.
85. Ed Sr. interview by La Brie, 6.
86. Burke, "Survey of the Negro Community," 98.
87. Harris, "Playing the Numbers," 54, 63.
88. Vaz, *Running the Numbers,* 24.
89. Robert M. Lombardo, *Organized Crime in Chicago: Beyond the Mafia* (Urbana: University of Illinois Press, 2013), 120–22; Ron Grossman, "When Policy Kings Ruled," *Chicago Tribune,* March 10, 2013, https://www .chicagotribune.com/news/ct-per-flash-policy-kings-0303-20130310-story .html; Ronald J. Stephens, *Idlewild: The Rise, Decline, and Rebirth of a*

Unique African American Resort Town (Ann Arbor: University of Michigan Press, 2013), 81.

90. "Negro Druggist Murder Suspect," *Tulsa Tribune*, October 24, 1933, 9.
91. *Tulsa City Directory, 1933*, 371; "Slaying of Tulsan Mystifies Police."
92. Hollis testimony, 133, *Oklahoma v. Foster.*
93. "Slaying of Tulsan Mystifies Police."
94. Hollis testimony, 77–81.
95. Motion to Advance, *Oklahoma v. Foster.*
96. "Slaying of Tulsan Mystifies Police."
97. "Hurt Suspect Denies Killing," *Tulsa Tribune*, August 20, 1933, 6.
98. "Negro Druggist Murder Suspect."
99. Hollis testimony, 3, 63, *Oklahoma v. Foster.*
100. Ibid., 67.
101. Defendant in Error Answer Brief, *Oklahoma v. Foster.*
102. Franklin, *My Life and an Era*, 224.
103. "Foster Freed by Jury Here," *Tulsa Tribune*, February 4, 1934, 6.
104. Franklin, *My Life and an Era*, 226.
105. Staniford, "Looking Back with Atty. Jones."
106. Jimmie Lewis Franklin, *Born Sober: Prohibition in Oklahoma 1907–1959* (Norman: University of Oklahoma Press, 1971), 94.
107. Ed Sr. interview by La Brie, 6.
108. "Publisher of *Oklahoma Eagle*, Noted Businessman, Is Buried," *Atlanta Daily World*, October 5, 1978, 5; David M. Breed, "A Look at the Life of E. L. Goodwin, Sr." *Oklahoma Eagle*, September 14, 1978.
109. Inter-racial Committee of YWCA, "Study of Conditions Among the Negro Population of Tulsa," April 1938, 10, Digital Collection, Tulsa City-County Library.
110. Cleora Butler, *Cleora's Kitchens: The Memoir of a Cook* (Tulsa: Council Oak Books, 1985), 41–42.
111. "Tulsa's 'Goode-Goodie' Club Raided by Police; Night Lifers Draw Jail Sentences," *Black Dispatch*, February 25, 1939, 2.
112. Walter Barnes, "'Tulsa Has Plenty of Niteries,' Says Dapper Walter Barnes," *Chicago Defender*, December 5, 1936, 20; Preston Lauterbach, *The Chitlin' Circuit: And the Road to Rock 'n' Roll* (New York: W.W. Norton, 2011), 51–52.
113. Ed Sr. interview by La Brie, 6.
114. "Negroes Ready to Cast Heavy 'No' Vote Again," *Tulsa Tribune*, May 14, 1937, 1.
115. Ibid., 12; "Honest Government Is Cheap Government," *Tulsa Tribune*, May 16, 1937.
116. "Negroes Ready to Cast Heavy 'No' Vote."
117. Ralph Martin, "Hitting the High Spots," *Tulsa World*, August 3, 1937, 14, and July 28, 1937, 16.
118. "Gambling Edict Issued by Mayor," *Tulsa World*, August 8, 1937, 1.
119. Martin, "Hitting the High Spots," July 22, 1937, 3.
120. Ibid.; Martin, "Hitting the High Spots," July 23, 1937.
121. "Graduates at Fisk Hear Rev. Chaffee," *Nashville Banner*, June 8, 1926, 12.

122. "Keeper of Greenwood's Torch Remembered," *Oklahoma Eagle,* July 31, 2014, 1.

123. Martin, "Hitting the High Spots," July 22, 1937.

124. "Angel Promises Lowe Resignation Soon," *Tulsa World,* May 12, 1937; Kerry Segrave, *Jukeboxes: An American Social History* (Jefferson, N.C.: McFarland & Co., 2002), 47.

125. Martin, "Hitting the High Spots," July 22, 1937.

126. Burke, "Survey of the Negro Community," 96.

127. Martin, "Hitting the High Spots," July 22, 1937.

128. Ibid.

129. Ed Sr. interview by La Brie, 6.

130. Ibid., 10.

131. Ibid., 7.

132. Inter-racial Committee of YWCA, "Study of Conditions Among the Negro Population," 9; *Tulsa City Directory, 1935,* 652.

133. "Becomes Editor of *Oklahoma Eagle,*" *Topeka Plaindealer,* September 29, 1922, 1.

134. Greene, *Selling Black History for Woodson,* 154.

135. Ed Sr. interview by La Brie, 7.

136. "The *Oklahoma Eagle*—Then and Now," *Oklahoma Eagle,* March 21, 1963, 13; Solomon Jones, "Film 2" (video), 1927, Yale Collection of Western Americana, Beinecke Rare Book and Manuscript Library, Yale University.

137. Greene, *Selling Black History for Woodson,* 154; 1930 U.S. Census, Tulsa County, Okla., pop. sch., ED 72–60, sheet 12A, dwell. 252, fam. 339, Theo Baughman.

138. Ed Sr. interview by La Brie, 7.

139. "Shop Talk," *Sooner State Press,* May 15, 1937, 2; Jim Goodwin conversation, December 13, 2018.

140. "Tulsa Negro Publisher Dies in City Hospital," *Sooner State Press,* July 10, 1937, 3.

141. Bill Dillard, "O. B. Graham Dies Suddenly," *Oklahoma Eagle,* February 28, 1952, 1; Petition to Dissolve a Partnership, *O. B. Graham v. Charles Roberts and Ed Goodwin,* Case No. 65354 (Tulsa County District Court, 1937); "Receivership for *Oklahoma Eagle* Is Aired in Court," *Black Dispatch,* January 8, 1938, 1.

142. "The *Oklahoma Eagle*—Then and Now"; "Shop Talk," *Sooner State Press,* June 1, 1935, 2.

143. Articles of Incorporation, Greenwood Chamber of Commerce, May 1938, Oklahoma Secretary of State Archives.

144. Mary McLeod Bethune, "From Day to Day with Mary McLeod Bethune," *Pittsburgh Courier,* May 28, 1938, 14.

145. "Mary McLeod Bethune Speaks to Tulsa Citizen on Program, of Negro Youth Administ'n," *Oklahoma Eagle,* May 21, 1938.

146. "Greenwood Mayor Fete Has Earmarks of Political Rally," *Tulsa Tribune,* September 17, 1937, 12.

147. Ibid.; "And So the 'Mayor' of Greenwood Is Winner," *Tulsa Tribune,* November 9, 1937, 2.

148. Ed Sr. interview by La Brie, 10.
149. Burke, "Survey of the Negro Community," 73.
150. Ibid., 60.
151. Ed Sr. interview by La Brie, 7.

CHAPTER 12: FAMILY BUSINESS

1. "We Wish You a Very Merry Christmas and Happiness Throughout the New Year," *Oklahoma Eagle,* December 25, 1941, 1; "Goodwinettes Growing Rapidly," *Oklahoma Eagle,* December 25, 1941, 2.
2. Edwyna L. Goodwin Dones Anderson funeral program, Jeanne Osby Goodwin Arradondo Family Collection, Nashville, Tenn.
3. E. L. Goodwin, Jr., "There Must Be a God Somewhere" (unpublished manuscript, n.d.), 3.
4. "Goodwinettes Growing Rapidly"; "Carver Junior High Organizes First Honor Society," *Oklahoma Eagle,* November 19, 1941, 7.
5. "Goodwinettes Growing Rapidly"; "Kiddies Enjoy Lessons in French," *Oklahoma Eagle,* December 9, 1939, 7.
6. "Goodwinettes Growing Rapidly."
7. Ibid.; "We Wish You a Very Merry Christmas."
8. Jeanne Arradondo, conversation with the author, August 24, 2020.
9. Jo Ann Gilford, conversation with the author, September 11, 2019.
10. "Goodwinettes Growing Rapidly."
11. Ibid.; Goodwin Jr., "There Must Be a God," 3.
12. "Goodwinettes Growing Rapidly."
13. "Famous Hot Spot Wrecked By Law as 2,000 Look On," *Black Dispatch,* July 15, 1939, 1.
14. "NAACP Outlines Program for the Year," *Oklahoma Eagle,* January 23, 1943, 1; "To Address Church Federation," *Oklahoma Eagle,* August 30, 1941, 1.
15. Yvonne Nance, " 'God I'm in Your Hands,' " *Abundant Life Magazine,* April 1970, 20.
16. Goodwin Jr., "There Must Be a God," 3–5.
17. "Mrs. Goodwin to Address Youth on Saturday Night," *Oklahoma Eagle,* March 15, 1941, 1.
18. Jeanne Goodwin to Jeanne Arradondo, ca. 1982, Jeanne Osby Goodwin Arradondo Family Collection.
19. "Entertainment," *Oklahoma Eagle,* December 25, 1941, 2.
20. Rob Citino, "Remembering Pearl Harbor," National WWII Museum, https://www.nationalww2museum.org/war/topics/pearl-harbor-december-7-1941.
21. "President Tells Nation War Will Be Hard, Long," *Oklahoma Eagle,* December 13, 1941, 1; H. S. Hughes, "The 'Tenth Man' Speaks to America," *Oklahoma Eagle,* December 13, 1941, 1.
22. George Douglas Monroe, in Eddie Faye Gates, *They Came Searching: How Blacks Found the Promised Land in Oklahoma* (Austin, Tex.: Eakin Press, 1997), 153; Mark Schlachtenhaufen, "100-plus Veterans See National World War II Memorial," *Enid News & Eagle,* October 27, 2012, https://www

.enidnews.com/news/local_news/100-plus-veterans-see-national-world-war-ii
-memorial/article_1f2ab872-d256-5a4d-9d8b-7b035136afd7.html.

23. "BTW Elementary School News," *Oklahoma Eagle,* March 28, 1942, 3; Ann
Brown (pseud. for Jeanne Goodwin), "Scoopin' the Scoop," *Oklahoma Eagle,*
January 3, 1942, 3.

24. Jill Watts, *The Black Cabinet: The Untold Story of African Americans and
Politics During the Age of Roosevelt* (New York: Grove Press, 2020), 375.

25. Neil A. Wynn, *The African American Experience During World War II* (Lanham, Md.: Rowman & Littlefield, 2010), 51–52.

26. Ibid., 47, 85–86.

27. Caesar Latimer in Gates, *They Came Searching,* 137.

28. " 'All Negroes Are Undependable,' " *Oklahoma Eagle,* November 28, 1942, 8;
"Tulsa's Problem," *Oklahoma Eagle,* March 21, 1942, 8.

29. Arley Ward, "The *Oklahoma Eagle* in World War II: Agitation, Advocacy and
Invisibility," master's thesis, University of Tulsa, 2014, 23–24.

30. Doretha McMillon, "The *Oklahoma Eagle,*" March 10, 1960, 1; "Horace S.
Hughes, Noted Educator Killed by Train," *Oklahoma Eagle,* August 28,
1952, 1.

31. "NAACP Fights for More Jobs for Negroes," *Oklahoma Eagle,* January 18,
1941, 1.

32. "Judge Hall Hits 75th Milestone," *Oklahoma Eagle,* October 7, 1971, 1;
Tulsa City Directory, 1921 (Polk-Hoffhine Directory Co.), 232; *Tulsa City Di-
rectory, 1922,* 257; "Amos T. Hall, Found Dead in Automobile," *Oklahoma
Eagle,* November 18, 1971, 1. [au: page no.?].

33. *Tulsa City Directory, 1923,* 276; "Judge Hall Hits 75th Milestone."

34. Kent A. Schell, "Tulsa Bomber Plant," *Encyclopedia of Oklahoma History
and Culture,* https://www.okhistory.org/publications/enc/entry.php?entry
=TU006.

35. "Don't Fail to Vote," *Oklahoma Eagle,* March 22, 1941, 8; "What to Do If
You Want a Job at the Bomber Plant," *Oklahoma Eagle,* March 22, 1941, 1.

36. "Ban Lifted; Negroes Employed at Tulsa Bomber Plant," *Oklahoma Eagle,*
November 22, 1941, 1.

37. Bruce Nelson, "Organized Labor and the Struggle for Black Equality in Mobile During World War II," *Journal of American History* 80, no. 3 (December
1993): 970.

38. "Ban Lifted."

39. "NAACP Fights for More Jobs for Negroes"; "Hundreds Attend NAACP
Mass Meeting Sunday," *Oklahoma Eagle,* February 1, 1941, 1.

40. "March on Washington Is Postponed," *Minneapolis Spokesman,* July 4, 1941, 1.

41. Watts, *Black Cabinet,* 339–41.

42. "Ban Lifted."

43. "Local Branch of NAACP Lands These Carpenters Jobs," *Oklahoma Eagle,*
November 22, 1941, 1.

44. Ed Goodwin, Sr., interview by Henry La Brie, August 12, 1971, transcript, 7,
Black Journalists Oral History Collection, Columbia University.

45. Arley Ward, "[Dis]Assembling Race: The FEPC in Oklahoma, 1941–1946,"
Ph.D. diss., University of Arkansas, 2021, 90–91, 97; "Amos Hall Bares Facts

in Effort to Secure Employment for Negroes in Local War Plants," *Oklahoma Eagle*, April 3, 1943, 1.

46. "Vocational Training for War Workers," *Oklahoma Eagle*, July 10, 1943, 1.
47. "Washington Promises NAACP Appropriation for National Defense Shop in Next Few Days," *Oklahoma Eagle*, January 24, 1942, 1.
48. "Vocational Training for War Workers."
49. Mabel Little, in *Goin' Back to T-Town*, PBS/American Experience, March 1, 1993, transcript, 5.
50. "Skilled Negro Labor Taboo at Douglas Bomber Plant," *Oklahoma Eagle*, November 21, 1942, 1.
51. Ward, "[Dis]Assembling Race," 95–96.
52. "Skilled Negro Labor Taboo at Douglas Bomber Plant"; "Negroes Employed at Douglas Aircraft Plant Dissatisfied with Company's Discriminatory Practices," *Oklahoma Eagle*, March 6, 1943, 1.
53. "We Want a Break at Home," *Oklahoma Eagle*, November 21, 1942, 8.
54. "Skilled Negro Labor Taboo at Douglas Bomber Plant."
55. "Tulsa's Problem," *Oklahoma Eagle*, March 21, 1942, 8.
56. "One Hundred Years of Price Change: The Consumer Price Index and the American Inflation Experience," U.S. Bureau of Labor Statistics, April 2014, https://www.bls.gov/opub/mlr/2014/article/one-hundred-years-of-price-change -the-consumer-price-index-and-the-american-inflation-experience.htm.
57. Watts, *Black Cabinet*, 276, 350.
58. "Mounting Living Costs Threaten Existence of Tulsa Negroes Barred from More Lucrative Jobs," *Oklahoma Eagle*, March 21, 1942, 1.
59. Ward, "[Dis]Assembling Race," 59.
60. Watts, *Black Cabinet*, 343–44, 368.
61. "Amos Hall Bares Facts in Effort to Secure Employment for Negroes in Local War Plants," *Oklahoma Eagle*, April 3, 1943, 1; "OCD Authorizes Interracial Comm.," *Oklahoma Eagle*, April 17, 1943, 1.
62. Ward, "[Dis]Assembling Race," 101.
63. Ibid., 102.
64. Ibid.
65. "Amos Hall Bares Facts."
66. "Tulsa Council for FEPC Organized Thursday," *Oklahoma Eagle*, August 4, 1945, 1.
67. Eileen Boris, "Fair Employment and the Origins of Affirmative Action in the 1940s," *NWSA Journal* 10, no. 3 (Autumn 1998): 143.
68. Ed Sr. interview by La Brie, 20.
69. Beezee Littles, "Town Talk," *Oklahoma Eagle*, June 13, 1942, 6.
70. "NNPA History," National Newspaper Publishers Association, https://nnpa .org/nnpa-history/.
71. "The Press: Negro Publishers," *Time*, June 15, 1942, https://content.time.com/ time/subscriber/article/0,33009,795878,00.html; "Wabash Avenue YMCA," Chicago Landmarks, City of Chicago, https://webapps1.chicago.gov/ landmarksweb/web/landmarkdetails.htm?lanId=1446.
72. "Publishers to Absorb Associated Negro Press," *Chicago Defender*, June 13, 1942, 1.

73. E. Franklin Frazier, *Black Bourgeoisie* (New York: Collier Books, 1957), 148.

74. E. L. Goodwin, Sr., "Taft Orphanage in Sad Plight Under Political Set-Up," *Oklahoma Eagle,* April 12, 1941, 1; "Representatives Norman, Mountcastle, Rogers, Ask Special Committee to Probe State Institutions," *Oklahoma Eagle,* April 26, 1941, 1; "Legislators Order Probe of Taft Institutions," *Oklahoma Eagle,* May 3, 1941, 1.

75. "Publishers Take Over ANP Setup," *Pittsburgh Courier,* June 13, 1942, 1; Frazier, *Black Bourgeoisie,* 149.

76. 1940 U.S. Census, Tulsa County, Okla., pop. sch., ED 79-80, sheet 9B, dwell. 180, Bernzetta Littles.

77. Littles, "Town Talk."

78. "The Press: Negro Publishers."

79. Ed Sr. interview by La Brie, 18.

80. William J. Broad, "The Black Reporter Who Exposed a Lie About the Atom Bomb," *New York Times,* August 9, 2021, https://www.nytimes.com/2021/08/09/science/charles-loeb-atomic-bomb.html; Charles H. Loeb, "Loeb Reflects on Atomic Bombed Area," *Atlanta Daily World,* October 5, 1945, 1.

81. Charles H. Loeb, interview by Henry La Brie, June 12, 1971, transcript, 25, Black Journalists Oral History Collection, Columbia University.

82. "The Press: Mister Pegler," *Time,* October 10, 1938, https://content.time.com/time/subscriber/article/0,33009,883713,00.html.

83. Westbrook Pegler, "Fair Enough," *Tribune* (Scranton, Penn.), April 29, 1942, 6; Westbrook Pegler, "The State of the Nation," *Greenville News* (S.C.), May 12, 1942, 12.

84. Westbrook Pegler, "The State of the Nation," *Greenville News,* May 18, 1942, 10; Pegler, "Fair Enough."

85. Westbrook Pegler, "Fair Enough," *Santa Cruz Sentinel,* June 18, 1942, 4.

86. Horace S. Hughes, "Westbrook Pegler Miscues," *Oklahoma Eagle,* May 9, 1942, 8.

87. Ed Sr. interview by La Brie, 22.

88. "Westbrook Pegler Visits *Eagle,*" *Oklahoma Eagle,* June 6, 1942, 2.

89. "Buy Stamps and Boost Tulsa," *Oklahoma Eagle,* June 27, 1942, 1; "Tulsa Gives Draftees Big Send Off," *Oklahoma Eagle,* April 25, 1942, 2.

90. Beezee Littles, "Town Talk," June 6, 1942, 6.

91. Horace S. Hughes, "Mr. Pegler Pays Us a Visit," *Oklahoma Eagle,* June 6, 1942, 8.

92. Diane McWhorter, "Dangerous Minds," *Slate,* March 4, 2004, https://slate.com/culture/2004/03/revisiting-the-controversial-career-of-westbrook-pegler.html; David Witwer, "Who Was Westbrook Pegler?" *Humanities* 33, no. 2 (March–April 2012), https://www.neh.gov/humanities/2012/marchapril/feature/who-was-westbrook-pegler; Oliver Pilat, *Pegler: Angry Man of the Press* (Boston: Beacon Press, 1963), 276–78.

93. Jim Goodwin, conversations with the author, January 22 and February 1, 2021.

94. Jim Goodwin, conversation with the author, December 13, 2018.

95. "Know Your Tulsans," *Oklahoma Eagle,* August 22, 1942, 6.

96. *Tulsa City Directory, 1948,* 887.

97. "Know Your Tulsans."

98. Eddie Faye Gates, *Miz Lucy's Cookies: And Other Links in My Black Family Support System* (Tulsa: Coman & Associates, 1999), 148; "Interviews Satchel Paige at Famous Small Hotel," *Oklahoma Eagle,* July 27, 1961.

99. "Greenwood District, Tulsa, Oklahoma, 1948–1952" (video), Harold M. Anderson Black Wall Street Film Collection, National Museum of American History, https://www.youtube.com/watch?v=eXlL_97fbvg&t.

100. Ibid.

101. Ibid.

102. Daisy Rogers, conversation with the author, September 9, 2021.

103. "Light of Truth Spiritualist," *Oklahoma Eagle,* May 9, 1942, 6.

104. *Tulsa City Directory, 1948,* 36.

105. Therese Alduni, conversation with the author, August 16, 2021.

106. "Greenwood Tour" series, *Oklahoma Eagle,* September 13, 1951–December 18, 1952.

107. J. Goodwin conversation, January 22, 2021.

108. *Oklahoma Eagle,* February 12, 1948, 3; *Oklahoma Eagle,* May 18, 1946, 3.

109. J. Goodwin conversation, February 1, 2021.

110. Goodwin Jr., "There Must Be a God."

111. Jo Ann Gilford, conversation with the author, August 30, 2022.

112. Wesley Brown, "The Full History: Black Pioneers Had a Big Role in Shaping Tulsa," *Tulsa World,* February 2, 1997, A1, https://tulsaworld.com/archive/the -full-history-black-pioneers-had-a-big-role-in-shaping-tulsa/article_5efba130 -d66c-567b-8d1a-3a5d02f7f944.html.

113. "Statement of Management of the *Oklahoma Eagle,*" *Oklahoma Eagle,* October 2, 1943, 7.

114. Doretha McMillon, "The *Oklahoma Eagle,*" *Oklahoma Eagle,* March 10, 1960, 1; "Mother of Tulsa Negro Newspaper Publisher Dies," *Tulsa Tribune,* July 27, 1938, 18.

115. Ann Brown (pseud. for Jeanne Goodwin), "Scoopin' the Scoop," *Oklahoma Eagle,* December 11, 1943, 3; J. B. Goodwin, "At Last One Claim Is Settled," *Oklahoma Eagle,* June 5, 1947, 1; "The *Oklahoma Eagle*—Then and Now," *Oklahoma Eagle,* March 21, 1963, 13; "Statement of the Ownership, Management, Circulation, etc. Required by Acts of Congress of August 4, 1912, and March 3, 1933," *Oklahoma Eagle,* October 14, 1944, 8.

116. "Community Leader, Educator, Jeanne B. Goodwin, Dies," *Tulsa World,* January 26, 2006, https://tulsaworld.com/archive/community-leader-educator -jeanne-b-goodwin-102-dies/article_2deb72da-0b5f-5c8e-902e-4bcec8ea2331 .html.

117. Goodwin Jr., "There Must Be a God."

118. "James 'Red' Williams Marches Off to Heaven," *Oklahoma Eagle,* January 24, 1991, 4.

119. Goodwin Jr., "There Must Be a God."

120. J. Goodwin conversation, January 22, 2021; Jeanne Arradondo, conversation with the author, August 10, 2020.

121. "The *Oklahoma Eagle*."
122. "James Madden Gets Appointment as Mail Carrier," *Oklahoma Eagle*, February 7, 1942, 1.
123. "Frank Decatur White Is Flying Here for School," *Oklahoma Eagle*, December 9, 1939, 1; "Negro City Directory a Great Success," *Oklahoma Eagle*, May 17, 1941, 2.
124. Ed Sr. interview by La Brie, 16, 25.
125. "Spring Newsboy Contest," *Oklahoma Eagle*, March 14, 1942, 2.
126. "The *Eagle* Staff," *Oklahoma Eagle*, August 7, 1947, 8; J. Goodwin conversation, December 13, 2018; Goodwin Jr., "There Must Be a God."
127. J. Goodwin conversation, January 22, 2021.
128. "Eagle Newsboys Feted with Party," *Oklahoma Eagle*, October 29, 1959, 7.
129. "53 Eagle Newsboys Attend Meeting of Club Tuesday," *Oklahoma Eagle*, July 18, 1957, 1; "4 Days Are Left in Newsboy's Contest," *Oklahoma Eagle*, May 17, 1956, 9.
130. "Our Story," *Oklahoma Eagle*, n.d., http://theoklahomaeagle.net/about-us/.

CHAPTER 13: A WORLD APART

1. Kim Jones (Oklahoma aviation expert), conversation with the author, September 22, 2021; Ed Goodwin, Sr., interview by Carlie Goodwin, ca. 1970s, Jeanne Osby Goodwin Arradondo Family Collection, Nashville, Tenn. What Ed would have seen from his plane is surmised from satellite imagery of the route between Alsuma and Taft.
2. Jeanne Arradondo, conversation with the author, August 10, 2020.
3. Jones conversation.
4. Ed Sr. interview by Carlie Goodwin.
5. "*Eagle* Publisher to Superintendency of Taft Institutions," *Oklahoma Eagle*, July 3, 1943, 1.
6. Joseph E. Howell, "Ed Goodwin, Publisher, to Be Manager of Taft Institutions," *Tulsa Tribune*, May 26, 1943; " 'We Accept Your Challenge,' " *Oklahoma Eagle*, June 27, 1942, 1.
7. "A Flying Publisher," *Oklahoma Eagle*, August 31, 1946, 1.
8. Ed Sr. interview by Carlie Goodwin.
9. "Tulsan Sues to Get in Army Corps," *Oklahoma Eagle*, February 1, 1941, 2.
10. J. Todd Moye, *Freedom Flyers: The Tuskegee Airmen of World War II* (New York: Oxford University Press, 2010), 37–38.
11. "Tuskegee Airmen," *Encyclopaedia Britannica*, June 20, 2022, https://www.britannica.com/topic/Tuskegee-Airmen.
12. "Eastern Oklahoma Gets Flying School," *Oklahoma Eagle*, March 27, 1947, 1.
13. "Flying Publisher."
14. "The *Oklahoma Eagle*—Then and Now," *Oklahoma Eagle*, March 21, 1963.
15. Jo Ann Gilford, conversation with the author, August 30, 2022; E. L. Goodwin, Jr., "There Must Be a God Somewhere" (unpublished manuscript, n.d.); advertisement, *Oklahoma Eagle*, February 22, 1951, 5; "Edwyna Goodwin," *Oklahoma Eagle*, August 7, 1947, 8.
16. Goodwin Jr., "There Must Be a God."

17. "Ed Goodwin to Be Manager of Taft."

18. Jim Goodwin, conversation with the author, January 22, 2021.

19. Jo Ann Gilford, conversation with the author, July 30, 2019.

20. J. Goodwin conversation, January 22, 2021; Matthew Vaz, *Running the Numbers: Race, Police and the History of Urban Gambling* (Chicago: University of Chicago Press, 2020), 97–100.

21. Jo Ann Gilford, conversation with the author, September 11, 2019.

22. J. Goodwin conversation, January 22, 2021.

23. Jeanne Arradondo, conversation with the author, September 11, 2020.

24. National Urban League, "A Study of the Social and Economic Conditions of the Negro Population of Tulsa, Oklahoma" (1946), 37–39, 44–45.

25. Tulsa County, Okla., Deed Book 1654, 208, Caroline Herbig and E. A. Herbig and J. H. Goodwin, June 19, 1945.

26. Tulsa County, Okla., Deed Book 1946, 336, J. H. Goodwin and E. L. Goodwin, November 1, 1948.

27. Jim Goodwin, conversation with the author, February 1, 2021; Goodwin Jr., "There Must Be a God."

28. Jim Goodwin, conversation with the author, January 22, 2021.

29. Goodwin Jr., "There Must Be a God."

30. Edwyna Anderson résumé, n.d., Jeanne Osby Goodwin Arradondo Family Collection.

31. Ann E. Weisman, "Greenwood: Tulsa's Phoenix," *American Visions,* August 1987, 37.

32. Ed Sr. interview by Carlie Goodwin.

33. J. Goodwin conversation, February 1, 2021.

34. Ibid.; Jeanne Arradondo, conversation with the author, September 7, 2020.

35. J. Goodwin conversation, February 1, 2021.

36. Greg Goodwin, conversation with the author, July 30, 2019; Ann Brown (pseud. for Jeanne Goodwin), "Scoopin' the Scoop," *Oklahoma Eagle,* June 19, 1958, 3.

37. "Children Feted at Egg Hunt," *Oklahoma Eagle,* April 10, 1947, 8; David Arnett, "Alsuma: The Town That Disappeared from Southeast Tulsa," *Greater Tulsa Reporter,* March 1993, https://gtrnews.com/alsumathetownthatdisappearedfromsoutheasttulsa-d1/; J. Goodwin conversation, January 22, 2021.

38. Jeanne Arradondo, conversation with the author, August 10, 2020; Brown, "Scoopin' the Scoop," June 19, 1958.

39. Washington Rucker, conversation with the author, August 25, 2021.

40. Ibid.

41. *Business Directory of North Tulsa, Oklahoma,* Greenwood Chamber of Commerce, ca. 1948, 1; Washington Rucker, conversation with the author, August 25, 2021.

42. Rucker conversation, August 25, 2021.

43. Washington Rucker, conversation with the author, September 4, 2022.

44. U.S. Bureau of the Census, *Supplement to the First Series Housing Bulletin for Oklahoma—Tulsa Block Statistics* (Washington, D.C.: Government Printing Office, 1942), 3–4, 22.

45. U.S. Bureau of the Census, *Sixteenth Census of the United States: 1940—Housing*, vol. 2: *General Characteristics*, pt. 4: *Nebraska–Pennsylvania* (Washington, D.C.: Government Printing Office, 1943), 721.

46. Urban League, "Study of the Social and Economic Conditions," 38.

47. *Business Directory of North Tulsa*, 1.

48. Burke, "Survey of the Negro Community," 35.

49. Census Bureau, *Supplement to the First Series Housing Bulletin*, 20–22.

50. Urban League, "Study of the Social and Economic Conditions," 38.

51. Ibid., 5.

52. Ibid., 38.

53. Tulsa County, Okla., Deed Book 301, 80, Mary P. Davis and W. M. Wilson and Peter and Rebecca Moran, August 27, 1919.

54. Tulsa County, Okla., Deed Book 175, 356, John T. and Amelia Kramer and Peter and Dencie E. Darnell, April 8, 1915; "Trouble Flares in Land Rulings," *Oklahoma Eagle*, November 3, 1945, 1.

55. City of Tulsa Preservation Commission, "A Neighborhood History of Tulsa's Historic White City" (September 1998), 4; White City Addition plat, December 30, 1925, Tulsa County Clerk's Office.

56. Urban League, "Study of the Social and Economic Conditions," 45.

57. *Shelley v. Kraemer*, 334 U.S. 1 (1948).

58. Richard Rothstein, *The Color of Law: A Forgotten History of How Our Government Segregated America* (New York: W.W. Norton, 2017), 90; *Correll v. Earley*, 237 P. 2d 1017 Okla. (1951).

59. Washington Rucker and Jim Goodwin, conversation with the author, August 25, 2021.

60. Rucker conversation, August 25, 2021; Washington Rucker, *Jazz Road* (self-published), 6–8.

61. Rucker conversation, August 25, 2021.

62. Ibid.

63. Rucker, *Jazz Road*, 17–18.

64. Ibid., 59.

65. Ibid., 71–72, 89.

66. Rucker conversation, August 25, 2021.

67. Francis Dominic Burke, "A Survey of the Negro Community of Tulsa, Oklahoma," master's thesis, University of Tulsa, 1936, 29.

68. Herbert Scott, "Race, Class and Politics in Mid 20th Century North Tulsa," *Embers*, Spring 2021, 6.

69. Burke, "Survey of the Negro Community," 31–32.

70. Rucker conversation, August 25, 2021.

71. Rucker, *Jazz Road*, 104–5.

72. Rucker conversation, August 25, 2021.

73. Early, conversation with the author, August 25, 2020.

74. J. Goodwin conversation, February 1, 2021; Arradondo conversation, September 11, 2021; Goodwin Jr., "There Must Be a God."

75. Gilford conversation, July 30, 2019.

76. "Cub Scout Hosts," *Oklahoma Eagle*, January 5, 1946, 6; Jim Goodwin, conversation with the author, September 4, 2022.

77. Jeanne Arradondo, conversations with the author, August 3 and September 7, 2020.
78. Bob Goodwin, conversation with the author, December 10, 2021.
79. "Couple Wed in Ceremony at Alsuma," *Oklahoma Eagle,* June 28, 1951, 5.
80. Cal Tinney, "Robeson! Listen to a Woman Who Loves Oklahoma," *Tulsa Tribune,* October 19, 1949.
81. J. Goodwin conversation, January 22, 2021; Gilford conversation, September 11, 2019.
82. Jo Ann Gilford, conversation with the author, July 30, 2019.
83. Ibid.
84. "Carlie Shares Concerns," *Oklahoma Eagle,* July 5, 1973, 6.
85. *Tulsa City Directory, 1960* (Polk-Hoffhine Directory Co.), 649.
86. Susan Goodwin Jordan, conversation with the author, September 18, 2021.
87. "Eddie Warrior to Manage Taft State Institutions," *Oklahoma Eagle,* December 11, 1947, 1; *Oklahoma Eagle,* August 8, 1963, 7.
88. Bob Goodwin, conversation with the author, December 17, 2021.
89. Jeanne Arradondo, conversation with the author, September 14, 2020.
90. B. Goodwin conversation, December 17, 2021.
91. Gilford conversation, September 11, 2019.
92. Jordan conversation, September 18, 2021.
93. Tinney, "Robeson! Listen to a Woman"; Cal Tinney, "Jim Goodwin Is All Man, Says Friend," *Oklahoma Eagle,* September 29, 1949, 1.
94. Arradondo conversation, September 7, 2020.
95. Ed Goodwin, Sr., interview by Henry La Brie, August 12, 1971, transcript, 25, Black Journalists Oral History Collection, Columbia University; National Advisory Commission on Civil Disorders, *Report of the National Advisory Commission on Civil Disorders* (Washington, D.C.: Government Printing Office, 1968), 210–11.
96. Tinney, "Robeson! Listen to a Woman."
97. Gilbert King, "What Paul Robeson Said," *Smithsonian Magazine,* September 13, 2011.
98. Ibid.; Mark Alan Rhodes II, "Placing Paul Robeson in History: Understanding His Philosophical Framework," *Journal of Black Studies* 47, no. 3 (April 2016): 244–45.
99. King, "What Robeson Said."
100. Tinney, "Robeson! Listen to a Woman."
101. "Robinson Quoted in Attack on Paul Robeson," *Oklahoma Eagle,* July 21, 1949, 1; Johnny Smith, "Jackie Robinson Was Asked to Denounce Paul Robeson. Instead, He Went After Jim Crow," *Andscape,* April 15, 2019, https://andscape.com/features/jackie-robinson-was-asked-to-denounce-paul-robeson-before-huac-instead-he-went-after-jim-crow/.
102. "Dunbar Nursery School," *Oklahoma Eagle,* February 14, 1942, 10; "The Nursery School," *Oklahoma Eagle,* August 7, 1947, 12.
103. Jeanne B. Goodwin, "A Negro Mother's Urgent Request," *Tulsa Tribune,* December 17, 1946, 18.
104. Jeanne Goodwin, in Eddie Faye Gates, *They Came Searching: How Blacks Found the Promised Land in Oklahoma* (Austin, Tex.: Eakin Press, 1997), 87.

105. Tinney, "Robeson! Listen to a Woman."

106. "We Prefer America," *Oklahoma Eagle*, August 17, 1950, 1.

107. W.E.B. Du Bois, *In Battle for Peace: The Story of My 83rd Birthday* (Oxford: Oxford University Press, 2007), 107.

108. W.E.B. Du Bois, "What Is Wrong with the NAACP," May 18, 1932, W.E.B. Du Bois Papers (MS 312), Special Collections and University Archives, University of Massachusetts Amherst Libraries; hereafter Du Bois Papers.

109. Thomas C. Holt, "Du Bois, W.E.B.," *African American National Biography*, ed. Henry Louis Gates, Jr., and Evelyn Brooks Higginbotham (New York: Oxford University Press, 2008).

110. W.E.B. Du Bois to Communist Party of the U.S.A., October 1, 1961, Du Bois Papers.

111. "We Prefer America."

112. E. Franklin Frazier, *Black Bourgeoisie* (New York: Collier Books, 1957), 126.

113. Ibid., 151–52.

114. Ibid., 10.

115. Ibid., 149.

116. Horace S. Hughes, "A House Divided," *Oklahoma Eagle*, July 26, 1941, 8.

117. Goodwin Jr., "There Must Be a God."

118. Tinney, "Robeson! Listen to a Woman."

119. Ibid.

120. J. Goodwin conversation, February 1, 2021.

121. "Jim Goodwin Is All Man, Says Friend."

122. J. Goodwin conversation, February 1, 2021.

123. "Jim Goodwin Is All Man, Says Friend."

124. J. Goodwin conversation, February 1, 2021.

125. Urban League, "Study of the Social and Economic Conditions," 36.

126. Ibid.; Jo Ann Gilford, conversation with the author, September 3, 2021.

127. Brown, "Scoopin' the Scoop," October 6, 1949.

128. Tinney, "Robeson! Listen to a Woman."

129. Jordan conversation, September 18, 2021.

CHAPTER 14: SEPARATE BUT EQUAL

1. "'Prof' Williams Succumbs," *Oklahoma Eagle*, January 4, 1979, 1; "Noted Educator 'Mr. W. D.' Dies," *Oklahoma Eagle*, January 5, 1984, 1.

2. "About Us," Booker T. Washington High School, https://btw.tulsaschools.org/about-us.

3. Hannah Atkins, "Franklin, John Hope (1915–2009)," *Encyclopedia of Oklahoma History and Culture*, https://www.okhistory.org/publications/enc/entry.php?entry=FR003; V. P. Franklin, "From Slavery to Freedom: The Journey from Our Known Past to Our Unknown Future," *Journal of Negro History* 85, no. 1–2 (2000): 6–12.

4. Eva K. Turner, "Outstanding Graduates of BTW High," *Oklahoma Eagle*, November 2, 1950, 4; *Tulsa City Directory, 1935* (Polk-Hoffhine Directory Co.), 361; Emily McConville, "At Father's Alma Mater, 'Real American' Au-

thor Discusses Growing Up Black and Biracial," Bates College, September 21, 2018, https://www.bates.edu/news/2018/09/21/118645/.

5. Turner, "Outstanding Graduates"; "Husband and Wife First Optometrists to Practice Here," *Oklahoma Eagle*, August 23, 1951, 1.

6. Tim Stanley, "Late North Tulsa Optometrist, Daughter of Race Massacre Survivor, Honored as Pioneer in Her Field by State Association," *Tulsa World*, November 19, 2021, https://tulsaworld.com/news/local/racemassacre/late -north-tulsa-optometrist-daughter-of-race-massacre-survivor-honored-as -pioneer-in-her-field/article_a1d13f22-4732-11ec-90c3-57b13aa80213.html.

7. "Big Issue of Permits Made," *Tulsa Weekly Democrat*, May 23, 1918, 2.

8. Editorial, "Tulsa Bond Situation," *Oklahoma Eagle*, October 20, 1945, 8.

9. John Hope Franklin, in *Goin' Back to T-Town*, PBS/American Experience, March 1, 1993.

10. R. L. Williams, *The Constitution and Enabling Act of Oklahoma: Annotated with References to the Constitution, Statues, and Decisions of Other States of the United States* (Kansas City: Pipes-Reed Book Company, 1912), 161.

11. Mary C. Moon, "Frederick Douglas Moon: A Study of Black Education in Oklahoma," Ph.D. diss., University of Oklahoma, 1978, 18; "State Educators Seek Better Schools," *Black Dispatch*, December 28, 1940, 1.

12. Oklahoma Department of Education, *The Seventeenth Biennial Report of the State Superintendent of Public Instruction*, 1938, 4–5.

13. Moon, "Frederick Douglas Moon," 158–59.

14. "Spirit of Fair Play," *Oklahoma Eagle*, November 3, 1945, 8; "A New High School Will Mean Better Jobs for Young People," *Oklahoma Eagle*, November 10, 1945, 8.

15. "Citizens Vote Bonds by 3 to 1 Margin," *Oklahoma Eagle*, November 24, 1945; Evelyn Strong, "Historical Development of the Oklahoma Association of Negro Teachers: A Study in Social Change, 1893–1958," Ph.D. diss., University of Oklahoma, 1961, 180–81.

16. "The New Booker T. Washington High School," *Oklahoma Eagle*, November 2, 1950, 9.

17. Ibid.; "Plan BTW Open House September 3," *Oklahoma Eagle*, August 24, 1950, 1; Gilford conversation, September 30, 2021.

18. "Lifting the Veil," National Park Service, February 26, 2015, https://www.nps .gov/bowa/learn/education/liftingtheveil.htm; *The Hornet*, 1961, Tulsa City-County Public Library.

19. "The New Booker T."; "First High School Building," *Oklahoma Eagle*, November 2, 1950, 9; "The First High School, the First Faculty, the First Graduates," *Oklahoma Eagle*, November 2, 1950, 9.

20. Bate, "Homes of North Tulsa"; Alma Rickey Marsh, "What North Tulsa Owes to Its Women," *Oklahoma Eagle*, November 2, 1950, 13.

21. "North Tulsa Negroes Play a Part in Law Enforcement," *Oklahoma Eagle*, November 2, 1950, 12; Reginald Thair, "Mail Man," *Oklahoma Eagle*, November 2, 1950, 14; Lawrence Heatley, "Bus Driver," *Oklahoma Eagle*, November 2, 1950, 15.

22. Edna Jordan, "Principal Woods As I Remember Him," *Oklahoma Eagle*, No-

vember 2, 1950, 9; C. L. Cole, "New School Increases Problems," *Oklahoma Eagle*, November 2, 1950, 9.

23. "They Saved the Greenwood Area for Negroes," *Oklahoma Eagle*, November 2, 1950, 10.

24. Jim Goodwin, conversation with the author, September 2, 2021.

25. James Bolton, conversation with the author, October 6, 2022.

26. Eddie Faye Gates, "Tulsa Race Riot (Massacre) Commission Interviews Tape 1" (video), Audio Archives, Oklahoma Historical Society, https://www .youtube.com/watch?v=37NItC7AUJY.

27. "They Saved the Greenwood Area for Negroes."

28. Jo Ann Goodwin, "Teen Tattle," *Oklahoma Eagle*, January 18, 1951, 7.

29. Ibid., November 16, 1950, 7; ibid., January 11, 1951, 7.

30. Ibid., February 8, 1951, 7.

31. Ibid., January 18, 1951, 7; ibid., April 26, 1951, 7.

32. Ibid., February 15, 1951, 7.

33. Jo Ann Gilford, conversation with the author, October 7, 2021.

34. Jo Ann Goodwin, "Teen Tattle," *Oklahoma Eagle*, April 19, 1951, 7.

35. *The Comet* (Tulsa: Booker T. Washington High School, 1948).

36. Gilford conversation, October 7, 2021.

37. Bill Boulware, conversation with the author, August 8, 2022.

38. Polly Bowen, "Williams Tells Tulsa Past," *Oklahoma Eagle*, April 21, 1977, 1.

39. Donald Ross, *Pillage of Hope: A Family History from the Trail of Tears, Slavery, Segregation, the 1921 Race Massacre and Beyond* (Mission Critical Consulting Group, 2021), 58.

40. Washington Rucker, conversation with the author, August 25, 2021.

41. Gilford conversation, October 7, 2021.

42. Bill Boulware, conversion with the author, August 5, 2022.

43. Ross, *Pillage of Hope,* 58.

44. Victor Luckerson, "Watching 'Watchmen' as a Descendant of the Tulsa Race Massacre," September 20, 2020, https://www.newyorker.com/news/news-desk/ watching-watchmen-as-a-descendant-of-the-tulsa-race-massacre.

45. Ross, *Pillage of Hope,* 58.

46. Ibid., 58, 60.

47. Ibid., 52–53.

48. Ibid., 58–62.

49. Karlos K. Hill, "Where Did Images of the Tulsa Race Massacre Come From?" PBS/American Experience, May 27, 2021, https://www.pbs.org/wgbh/ americanexperience/features/t-town-tulsa-race-massacre-photographs/.

50. Ross, *Pillage of Hope,* 61–62.

51. "State NAACP Conference Plans Bold Attack Upon Educational Inequalities in Sooner State," *Black Dispatch*, November 10, 1945.

52. Ibid.

53. David W. Levy, *Breaking Down Barriers: George McLaurin and the Struggle to End Segregated Education* (Norman: University of Oklahoma Press, 2020), 154.

54. Melvin C. Hall, "Fisher, Ada Lois Sipuel (1924–1995)," *Encyclopedia of*

Oklahoma History and Culture, https://www.okhistory.org/publications/enc/ entry.php?entry=FI009.

55. Ada Lois Sipuel Fisher, *A Matter of Black and White: The Autobiography of Ada Lois Sipuel Fisher* (Norman: University of Oklahoma Press, 1996), 12, 46–47.

56. Ibid., xviii.

57. Levy, *Breaking Down Barriers,* 49–51.

58. Fisher, *Matter of Black and White,* 96, 100.

59. Levy, *Breaking Down Barriers,* 54.

60. Ibid., 97.

61. Don Ross, "Amos T. Hall Named 2nd Negro Judge," *Oklahoma Eagle,* December 5, 1968, 1.

62. Michael S. Givel, "Sundown on the Prairie: The Extralegal Campaigns and Efforts from 1889 to 1967 to Exclude African Americans from Norman, Oklahoma," *Chronicles of Oklahoma* 96, no. 3 (2018): 260–79.

63. Ross, "Amos T. Hall Named 2nd Negro Judge."

64. Fisher, *Matter of Black and White,* 101.

65. "Tulsa Negro Police Suspended," *Oklahoma Eagle,* September 19, 1942, 1.

66. Hannah D. Atkins, "Hall, Amos T. (1896–1971)," *Encyclopedia of Oklahoma History and Culture,* https://www.okhistory.org/publications/enc/entry.php ?entry=HA006.

67. "Court Says O.U. Does Not Have to Enroll Negro," *Oklahoma Eagle,* July 13, 1946, 1.

68. Ibid.

69. Levy, *Breaking Down Barriers,* 56–57.

70. Ibid., 93–94.

71. Ibid., 67–69.

72. Alfred L. Brophy, "*McLaurin v. Oklahoma State Regents* (1950)," *Encyclopedia of Oklahoma History and Culture,* https://www.okhistory.org/ publications/enc/entry.php?entry=MC034; Eric Lomazoff and Baile Gregory, "Thurgood Marshall's 'Broom Closet': The Structure of Segregation in *McLaurin v. Oklahoma State Regents,*" *Chronicles of Oklahoma* 97, no. 1 (2019): 31.

73. Levy, *Breaking Down Barriers,* 174, 187–88.

74. "Admission to T.U. Sought by Two Applicants," *Oklahoma Eagle,* February 2, 1950, 1.

75. "Negro Branch of T.U. Still Available," *Oklahoma Eagle,* May 25, 1950, 1.

76. Violet Bate, "Looking at Life," *Oklahoma Eagle,* September 28, 1950, 4.

77. "Segregated Branch of T.U. Opens," *Oklahoma Eagle,* September 28, 1950, 1.

78. "Tulsa U. Offers Graduate Courses," *Oklahoma Eagle,* February 1, 1951, 1.

79. "Segregated Branch of T.U. Opens."

80. Anita Hairston, in Eddie Faye Gates, *They Came Searching: How Blacks Found the Promised Land in Oklahoma* (Austin, Tex.: Eakin Press, 1997), 98–99.

81. Monica Davey, "The Cases; The Reluctant Icons," *New York Times,* January 18, 2004, https://www.nytimes.com/2004/01/18/education/the-cases-the

-reluctant-icons.html; Michael Carlson, "Linda Brown obituary," *Guardian,* March 28, 2018, https://www.theguardian.com/education/2018/mar/28/linda-brown-obituary.

82. "What's the Most Important Supreme Court Case No One's Ever Heard Of?" *Atlantic,* May 2013, https://www.theatlantic.com/magazine/archive/2013/05/the-big-question/309290/; Jere Roberson, "McCabe, Edward P. (1850–1920)," *Encyclopedia of Oklahoma History and Culture,* https://www.okhistory.org/publications/enc/entry.php?entry=MC006; *McCabe v. Atchison, T. & S.F. Ry. Co.,* 235 U.S. 151 (1914).

83. Leon Friedman, *Brown v. Board: The Landmark Oral Argument Before the Supreme Court* (New York: New Press, 2004), 240.

84. *Brown v. Board of Education of Topeka,* 347 U.S. 483 (1954).

85. John Hope Franklin, "To and From *Brown v. Board of Education,*" *Washington History* 16, no. 2 (Fall–Winter 2004–5): 11–13.

86. *Oklahoma Eagle,* May 20, 1954, 1.

87. "Educators Reactions to Supreme Court Decision Show Faith in Democracy," *Oklahoma Eagle,* May 20, 1954, 6.

88. "A New Birth of Freedom," *Oklahoma Eagle,* May 24, 1957, 10.

89. Bill Boulware, conversation with the author, August 8, 2022.

CHAPTER 15: CROSSING THE LINE

1. "Anti-Segregation Fight Mapped," *Oklahoma Eagle,* May 27, 1954, 1.

2. "White Citizens' Councils," PBS/American Experience, n.d., https://www.pbs.org/wgbh/americanexperience/features/emmett-citizens-council/.

3. "When Offended, Tell the Eagle," *Oklahoma Eagle,* February 9, 1946, 8; "Discrimination Charged to 4 Large Department Stores," *Oklahoma Eagle,* May 25, 1950, 1.

4. "New Manager Named for *Oklahoma Eagle,*" *Oklahoma Eagle,* February 2, 1950, 1.

5. "Obituary: Eddie L. Madison, Jr., Former *Oklahoma Eagle* Editor, Pioneering Black Journalist," *Tulsa World,* August 19, 2016, https://tulsaworld.com/obituaries/localobituaries/obituary-eddie-l-madison-jr-former-oklahoma-eagle-editor-pioneering-black-journalist/article_4f230a50-3dc2-59e8-ba7c-a4711b850bf6.htm; "Madison Joins *Eagle* Staff," *Oklahoma Eagle,* June 19, 1952.

6. Ben H. Hill, "The Truth Must Come Out," *Oklahoma Eagle,* June 10, 1954, 10.

7. Ben H. Hill, "The Truth Must Come Out," *Oklahoma Eagle,* May 26, 1955, 2A.

8. Washington Rucker, conversation with the author, September 6, 2022.

9. Luix Virgil Overbea, "Sportopics," *Oklahoma Eagle,* September 2, 1954, 11.

10. Oklahoma Advisory Committee to the U.S. Commission on Civil Rights, *School Desegregation in Tulsa, Oklahoma* (1977), 62.

11. Overbea, "Sportopics"; Tulsa City Directory, 1955, 703.

12. Bryan Marquard, "Luix Overbea, Groundbreaking Reporter, Inspired Young Journalists," *Boston Globe,* July 15, 2010, B14; Commission on Human Relations, "Non-White Population Changes 1950–1960," *Human Relations News*

of Chicago 3, no. 3 (July 1961), https://www.nlm.nih.gov/exhibition/forallthepeople/img/1234.pdf; Chicago Commission on Race Relations, *The Negro in Chicago: A Study of Race Relations and a Race Riot* (Chicago: University of Chicago Press, ca. 1922), 299.

13. Marquard, "Overbea, Groundbreaking Reporter"; "Celebrating the Earliest Black Alumni of Northwestern," Northwestern Alumni, n.d., https://www.alumni.northwestern.edu/s/1479/02-naa/16/interior.aspx?pgid=30883&gid=2&cid=33514#:~:text=Charla%20Wilson%2C%20the%20university%20archivist,She%20graduated%20in%201905; "De Priest, Oscar Stanton, 1871–1951," U.S. House of Representatives, History, Art, and Archives, https://history.house.gov/People/Detail/12155.

14. U.S. Bureau of the Census, "Race of the Population of the United States by State: 1960," *1960 Census of the U.S. Population: Supplementary Reports* (Washington, D.C.: Government Printing Office, 1961), 3.

15. "We Endorse Bob Kerr for Governor," *Oklahoma Eagle*, May 21, 1942, 8; "Forward, Oklahoma, With Democratic Party," *Oklahoma Eagle*, November 2, 1946, 8; "Mr. Voter, Are You Ready for the Question," *Oklahoma Eagle*, November 2, 1950, 1.

16. Luix Virgil Overbea, "The Ringside," *Oklahoma Eagle*, October 30, 1952, 8; Luix Virgil Overbea, "At the Ringside," *Oklahoma Eagle*, October 6, 1952, 10.

17. Karen F. Brown, "The *Oklahoma Eagle*: A Study of Black Press Survival," *Howard Journal of Communications* 1, no. 2 (1988), 7; "Professor Gorham: Goodbye to a Pioneer Journalist," *Tallahassee Democrat*, January 9, 1992, 5.

18. Overbea, "Sportopics," *Oklahoma Eagle*, September 2, 1954.

19. Ibid., September 9, 1954, 11.

20. Ibid., October 7, 1954, 11.

21. Luix Virgil Overbea, "Mann Brothers' Super Market Located on Site of Tulsa Landmark, on Same Corner Since 1918," *Oklahoma Eagle*, February 3, 1955, 9.

22. *J. D. Mann v. Continental Ins. Co.*, No. 16764 (Tulsa County District Court, 1921).

23. Overbea, "Mann Brothers' Super Market."

24. Daisy Rogers, conversation with the author, September 9, 2021.

25. "Greenwood Tour: Man Behind the T-Town Clowns," *Oklahoma Eagle*, November 22, 1951, 4; Jon Lawrence, "Bets Racket Details Told in Tax Trial," *Tulsa World*, September 30, 1964.

26. Princetta Rudd-Newman, conversation with the author, August 26, 2022.

27. "No Negroes Served, Restaurant Says," *Oklahoma Eagle*, April 28, 1955, 1.

28. Luix Virgil Overbea, "Jimcrow Policy in Oklahoma Is Not the Law," *Oklahoma Eagle*, April 28, 1955, 9.

29. Ibid.

30. *Oklahoma Eagle*, April 1, 1954, 10.

31. "Human Rights Day Observance Planned," *Tallahassee Democrat*, December 7, 1974, 17.

32. Thelma Thurston Gorham, "Parents, Teachers Charged with Stressing Right Values," *Oklahoma Eagle*, October 21, 1954, 1.

33. Thelma Thurston Gorham, "Whites as Well as Negroes Must Help Smooth Path to Integration," September 23, 1954, 1.

34. "The Street," *Oklahoma Eagle,* August 20, 1959, 2.

35. Ginnie Graham, "Renovation of Big 10 Ballroom a Decade in the Making," *Tulsa World,* October 25, 2017, https://tulsaworld.com/news/ginnie-graham -renovation-of-big-10-ballroom-a-decade-in-the-making/article_9abc52e3 -3a97-5e81-a8ee-924dbe017dc2.html.

36. Luix Virgil Overbea, " 'Big Rock and Roll Show' Slated for Big Ten Ballroom Saturday Night, October 1," *Oklahoma Eagle,* September 29, 1955, 4A; Overbea, "The Night Beat," *Oklahoma Eagle,* May 26, 1955, 4A.

37. Luix Virgil Overbea, "Big '10' Rocks with R&B Show Saturday Night," *Oklahoma Eagle,* February 24, 1955, 4A.

38. Luix Virgil Overbea, "B.B. King Plays, Sings the Blues at Big '10,' Adds Mambo and Girl Singer," *Oklahoma Eagle,* March 31, 1955, 5A.

39. Luix Virgil Overbea, "Fats Domino Brings New Orleans Style Blues to Tulsa," *Oklahoma Eagle,* April 21, 1955, 6A.

40. Luix Virgil Overbea, "The Night Beat," *Oklahoma Eagle,* May 5, 1955, 6A.

41. Peter Guralnick, *Last Train to Memphis: The Rise of Elvis Presley* (Boston: Little, Brown, 1994), 311–12; Louis Menand, "The Elvic Oracle," *New Yorker,* November 8, 2015, https://www.newyorker.com/magazine/2015/11/ 16/the-elvic-oracle; Joyce Halasa, "Rock 'N Roll," *Encyclopedia of Cleveland History,* https://case.edu/ech/articles/r/rock-n-roll.

42. Luix Virgil Overbea, "Bo Diddley Is 'Cat'; Facts on Etta James, Gene & Eunice," *Oklahoma Eagle,* September 22, 1955, 3A.

43. Ibid.

44. Ed Komara, " 'Bo Diddley' and 'I'm a Man' (1955)," National Recording Registry, Library of Congress, 2011, https://www.loc.gov/static/programs/national -recording-preservation-board/documents/BoDiddley.pdf; "Slash Remembers Bo Diddley," NME, June 3, 2008, https://www.nme.com/news/music/bo -diddley-9-1333402.

45. Overbea, "Bo Diddley Is 'Cat.' "

46. Luix Virgil Overbea, "The Night Beat," *Oklahoma Eagle,* May 26, 1955, 6A.

47. Ibid., April 28, 1955, 7A, and April 21, 1955, 6A.

48. Ibid., July 14, 1955, 4B.

49. Ibid., March 24, 1955, 4A.

50. Ibid., June 23, 1955, 5A; Martie, "Personally Speaking," *Oklahoma Eagle,* August 5, 1954, 5.

51. Luix Virgil Overbea, "The Night Beat," *Oklahoma Eagle,* November 4, 1954, 4A.

52. Luix Virgil Overbea, "Jimmy (Cry) Hawkins Band to Head Weekend Floor Shows at Flamingo," *Oklahoma Eagle,* October 28, 1954, 3A; Washington Rucker, conversation with the author, August 25, 2021.

53. Luix Virgil Overbea, "The Night Beat," *Oklahoma Eagle,* March 10, 1955, 5A.

54. Rucker conversation, August 25, 2021; Washington Rucker, interview by John Erling, in "Washington Rucker: Legendary Jazz Drummer," July 2, 2015,

Voices of Oklahoma, Oklahoma Historical Society, https://www
.voicesofoklahoma.com/interviews/rucker-washington.

55. Luix Virgil Overbea, "The Night Beat," *Oklahoma Eagle,* June 9, 1955, 3A;
"The Night Beat," *Oklahoma Eagle,* April 28, 1955, 7A.

56. Luix Virgil Overbea, "The *Eagle* Presents Pictorial Highlights of '54," *Oklahoma Eagle,* December 30, 1954, 1A.

57. Luix Virgil Overbea, "The Night Beat," *Oklahoma Eagle,* June 9, 1955, 11,
and May 19, 1955, 3A.

58. Leon Rollerson, conversation with the author, July 20, 2020.

59. "Night Club Segregation," *Oklahoma Eagle,* February 8, 1951, 4.

60. Jerry Wofford, "Tulsa's Blues Roots Explored Ahead of Blues Challenge, Festivals," *Tulsa World,* August 13, 2014, https://tulsaworld.com/entertainment/
music/tulsas-blues-roots-explored-ahead-of-blues-challenge-festivals/article
_eab170ac-0bf5-5704-a443-a1b268a573f8.html.

61. "Songwriter, Tulsa Sound Innovator J. J. Cale Dies at 74," *Tulsa World,* July
28, 2013, https://tulsaworld.com/news/local/songwriter-tulsa-sound-innovator
-jj-cale-dies-at-74/article_687a115f-3cca-53a6-86fa-778bfd0e4d33.html; Neil
Young, *Waging Heavy Peace: A Hippie Dream* (New York: Blue Rider Press,
2012), 10.

62. David Cook, "Longtime *Monitor* Writer Luix V. Overbea: An Appreciation,"
Christian Science Monitor, July 14, 2010, https://www.csmonitor.com/USA/
2010/0714/Longtime-Monitor-writer-Luix-V.-Overbea-an-appreciation.

63. Bob Goldsborough, "*Tribune*'s 1st Local Black Writer Also Covered Mussolini's Execution, Interviewed Pope Pius XII: 'Roi Was a Pioneer,'" *Chicago
Tribune,* February 18, 2021, https://www.chicagotribune.com/lifestyles/ct-life
-roi-ottley-chicago-tribune-first-black-local-writer-20210218
-vfz4nij4xvbmzcaml3ud3knly4-story.html.

64. "*Eagle*'s City Editor Resigns for Post with NY Company," *Oklahoma Eagle,*
March 28, 1957, 1.

65. "NABJ Mourns the Loss of Founder Luix Overbea," National Association of
Black Journalists, July 11, 2010.

66. "Terror in Miss. Takes New High," *Oklahoma Eagle,* September 8, 1955, 1.

67. "Victim's Mother to Attend Trial," *Oklahoma Eagle,* September 15, 1955, 1.

68. "Murder Made Easy," *Oklahoma Eagle,* September 8, 1955, 8.

69. Ibid.

70. "Remembering Emmett Till," U.S. Civil Rights Trail, https://civilrightstrail
.com/experience/sumner/#:~:text=the%20American%20South.-,Trial
,spectators%20who%20filled%20the%20courtroom; "Getting Away with
Murder," PBS/American Experience, https://www.pbs.org/wgbh/american
experience/features/emmett-biography-roy-carolyn-bryant-and-jw-milam/.

71. "Tulsans Comment on Till Trial Held in Sumner, Miss.," *Oklahoma Eagle,*
September 29, 1955, 1.

72. "Tulsans Comment on Till Trial Held in Sumner, Miss.," *Oklahoma Eagle,*
October 6, 1955, 6A.

73. "Biographical Note," Dr. T.R.M. Howard Papers, Chicago Public Library,
https://www.chipublib.org/fa-t-r-m-howard-papers/.

74. Michael Klarman, *From Jim Crow to Civil Rights: The Supreme Court and the Struggle for Racial Equality* (New York: Oxford University Press, 2004), 424–25.

75. Bill Dillard, "Till's Last Words: 'Mama . . . Save Me,'" *Oklahoma Eagle*, February 9, 1956, 1.

76. Ibid.

77. Neil J. McMillen, *The Citizens' Councils: Organized Resistance to the Second Reconstruction* (Urbana: University of Illinois Press, 1971).

78. "The White Citizens' Council," Mississippi Civil Rights Project, n.d., https://mscivilrightsproject.org/hinds/organization-hinds/the-white-citizens-council/.

79. "Citizens Councils Get Setback in Major Ruling," *Oklahoma Eagle*, September 1, 1955, 8; Dillard, "Till's Last Words."

80. Neil R. McMillen, "The White Citizens' Council and Resistance to School Desegregation in Arkansas," *Arkansas Historical Quarterly* 66, no. 2 (2007): 132–35.

81. Relman Morin, "AP Was There: Mob Protests Little Rock Central Desegregation," Associated Press, September 23, 2017, https://apnews.com/article/north-america-us-news-race-and-ethnicity-ar-state-wire-arkansas-bf969c36a3c44571a8d1e3285e5e7b5e.

82. E. L. Madison, Jr., "*Eagle* Publisher Wires Faubus," *Oklahoma Eagle*, September 26, 1957, 1.

83. E. L. Madison, Jr., "Chest Attack Called Lie-Hate Campaign," *Oklahoma Eagle*, October 10, 1957, 1.

84. E. L. Madison, Jr., "Thurgood Marshall Says Problem Faces the South," *Oklahoma Eagle*, June 6, 1957, 1.

85. Peggi Gamble, conversation with the author, February 24, 2021.

86. Eddie L. Madison, Jr., and Claude Taylor, "Bombing of Gamble's Home Alerts Officials," *Oklahoma Eagle*, January 23, 1958, 1; E. L. Madison, Jr., "4-ft. Cross Burned; Negro Seeks Peace," *Oklahoma Eagle*, May 16, 1957, 1.

87. Citizens Councils Report, May 14, 1957, Oklahoma City Division, FBI, https://archive.org/details/foia_CitCouncils-OKC.PDF/page/n11/mode/2up.

88. Citizens Councils Report, May 24, 1957, Oklahoma City Division, FBI, https://archive.org/details/foia_CitCouncils-OKC.PDF/page/n11/mode/2up.

89. Gamble conversation.

90. Karl Thiele, "The Racially Changing Community," master's thesis, University of Oklahoma, 1962, 25.

91. Jim Seaver, "Dynamite Blast Jars Negro Home in Mixed-Race Area; Three Occupants Uninjured," *Tulsa World*, January 20, 1958.

92. Seaver, "Dynamite Blast"; Gamble conversation.

93. Gamble conversation.

94. Ibid.; Seaver, "Dynamite Blast Jars Negro Home."

95. Seaver, "Dynamite Blast Jars Negro Home."

96. Gamble conversation.

97. Seaver, "Dynamite Blast Jars Negro Home."

98. Gamble conversation.

99. Seaver, "Dynamite Blast Jars Negro Home."

100. FBI correspondence Concerning Citizens' Council, May 13, 1957, Oklahoma

City Division, FBI, https://archive.org/details/foia_CitCouncils-OKC.PDF/
page/n13/mode/2up; "The Citizens' Council" (pamphlet), ibid.

101. Thiele, "Racially Changing Community," 25.

102. Gamble conversation.

103. Ibid.; Madison and Taylor, "Bombing of Gamble's Home Alerts Officials."

104. Gamble conversation.

CHAPTER 16: YOU'LL BE A MAN, MY SON

1. "Son of *Eagle* Publisher Gets B.S. Degree," *Oklahoma Eagle*, May 31, 1956, 1.

2. E. L. Goodwin, Jr., "The Party Is Over . . . Further on Down the Road," *Oklahoma Eagle*, August 29, 1985, 16.

3. E. L. Goodwin, Jr., interview by Henry G. La Brie III, August 12, 1971, transcript, 9, 13, Black Journalists Oral History Collection, Columbia University.

4. "Rites Set for Alquita Goodwin, Former *Oklahoma Eagle* Operations Manager," *Tulsa World*, December 17, 2015, https://tulsaworld.com/obituaries/localobituaries/rites-set-for-alquita-goodwin-former-oklahoma-eagle-operations-manager/article_79a0bcac-b693-5221-b988-feed5dd2cd65.html.

5. Greg Goodwin, conversation with the author, December 8, 2022.

6. E. L. Goodwin, Jr., "There Must Be a God Somewhere" (unpublished manuscript, n.d.).

7. Regina Goodwin, conversation with the author, August 14, 2020.

8. Goodwin Jr., "There Must Be a God."

9. "Atty. Dones to Open Offices in Tulsa; Admitted to Bar Tues.," *Oklahoma Eagle*, March 22, 1956, 1.

10. Edwyna Goodwin Anderson, résumé, Jeanne Osby Goodwin Arradondo Family Collection, Nashville, Tenn.; Ken Palmer, "Tenacity Finally Broke Color Barrier for Reporter," *Flint Journal*.

11. Jeanne Arradondo, conversation with the author, August 10, 2020; Susan Goodwin Jordan, conversation with the author, September 7, 2021; Carlie M. Goodwin, "Knowledge Is Power: Drugs Are Sickening," *Oklahoma Eagle*, February 10, 1972, 8B.

12. Jo Ann Gilford, conversation with the author, July 30, 2019; Bob Goodwin, conversation with the author, December 10, 2021.

13. Alquita Goodwin, "What Kind of People Publish a Newspaper?" *Oklahoma Eagle*, April 14, 1966, 8A.

14. Princetta Rudd-Newman, conversation with the author, August 26, 2022.

15. Viola Sue Drew, "33 Negro Children Victorious in OC Effort to Gain Service," *Oklahoma Eagle*, August 28, 1958, 1.

16. Emma Brown, "Okla. Civil Rights Activist Clara Luper, Who Led One of First Sit-in Protests, Dies at 88," *Washington Post*, June 13, 2011, https://www.washingtonpost.com/local/obituaries/okla-civil-rights-activist-clara-luper-who-led-one-of-first-sit-in-protests-dies-at-88/2011/06/12/AGHIMiTH_story.html; "Negro Youths 'Store Sitting' in Fourth Day," *Daily Oklahoman*, August 23, 1958, 31.

17. Clara Luper, *Behold the Walls* (Jim Wire, 1979), 10.

18. "Negro Youths 'Store Sitting.' "

19. Drew, "33 Negro Children Victorious."

20. Alexander R. Stoesen, "Greensboro Sit-Ins," *Encyclopedia of North Carolina*, https://www.ncpedia.org/greensboro-sit-ins/.

21. "Street Department Bias Investigated," *Oklahoma Eagle*, September 9, 1965, 1; E. L. Goodwin, Jr., "Superintendent Anderson Under Fire," *Oklahoma Eagle*, October 7, 1965, 1.

22. E. L. Goodwin, Jr., "It's from Cradle to Kindergarten at Crenshaw's Childcare Center," *Oklahoma Eagle*, January 14, 1960, 1A; E. L. Goodwin, Jr., "Five-Year-Old Black's Nursing Home Now Largest in State for Negroes," *Oklahoma Eagle*, September 17, 1959, 1A.

23. E. L. Goodwin, Jr., "Torch Victim Dying from Severe Burns," *Oklahoma Eagle*, September 25, 1958, 1; E. L. Goodwin, Jr., "Act Now, Don't Sleep Your Rights Away," *Oklahoma Eagle*, August 6, 1959, 1.

24. Ed Jr. interview by La Brie.

25. E. L. Goodwin, Jr., " 'Am I My Brother's Keeper?' The Answer Must Be Yes," *Oklahoma Eagle*, July 23, 1959, 1A.

26. E. L. Goodwin, Jr., "Richardson Family Expresses Appreciation to Oklahomans," *Oklahoma Eagle*, July 30, 1959, 1.

27. "Letters to the Editor," *Oklahoma Eagle*, August 13, 1959, 3.

28. Jim Goodwin, conversation with the author, September 2, 2021.

29. E. L. Goodwin, Jr., "The Party Is Over," *Oklahoma Eagle*, August 29, 1985, 16.

30. Jim Goodwin, conversation with the author, February 1, 2021.

31. Jim Goodwin, conversation with the author, January 22, 2021.

32. J. Goodwin conversation, February 1, 2021.

33. Jo Ann Gilford, conversation with the author, September 11, 2019.

34. Jeanne Arradondo, conversation with the author, August 17, 2020.

35. Jim Goodwin, conversation with the author, January 22, 2021.

36. "Sophomore Talent Numbers Spice Second BTW Assembly as Citizenship Day Is Held," *Oklahoma Eagle*, September 23, 1954, 7.

37. "Booker T. Presents 'Crewcuts and Longhairs,' " *Oklahoma Eagle*, April 14, 1955, 8A.

38. Jim Goodwin, conversation with the author, October 19, 2021.

39. "Tulsa Buses Are Completely Desegregated—A. Hauer," *Oklahoma Eagle*, August 30, 1956, 1A.

40. Jim Goodwin, conversation with the author, December 13, 2018.

41. J. Goodwin conversation, October 19, 2021; "Waldo E. Jones II," Biglow Funerals, 2006, https://www.biglowfunerals.com/obituary/2850826.

42. Goodwin Jr., "There Must Be a God."

43. E. L. Goodwin, Jr., "The Party's Over . . . Can I Make a Phone Call?" *Oklahoma Eagle*, October 31, 1985, 5B.

44. E. L. Goodwin, Jr., "The Party Is Over . . . We Had a Barrel of Fun," *Oklahoma Eagle*, August 22, 1985, 6.

45. Goodwin Jr., "Party Is Over . . . Further On Down."

46. J. Goodwin conversation, September 2, 2021.

47. E. L. Goodwin, Jr., "The Party's Over . . . Whiskey In—Sense Out," *Oklahoma Eagle*, January 23, 1986, 8.

48. Goodwin Jr., "Party Is Over . . . Barrel of Fun."

49. E. L. Goodwin, Jr., "The Party's Over . . . Bottoms Up," *Oklahoma Eagle*, February 20, 1986, 14.

50. Jeanne Arradondo, conversation with the author, September 7, 2020.

51. J. Goodwin conversation, September 2, 2021; B. Goodwin conversation, December 10, 2021.

52. E. L. Goodwin, Jr., "The Party's Over . . . You Don't Have to Be a Star," *Oklahoma Eagle*, April 17, 1986, 12.

53. Arradondo conversation, September 7, 2020.

54. Gilford conversation, September 11, 2019; Bob Goodwin, conversation with the author, January 22, 2022.

55. Goodwin Jr., "Party's Over . . . Make a Phone Call?"

56. "New White Way Lights on Greenwood Turned Over to Mayor in Ceremony," *Oklahoma Eagle*, January 27, 1955, 1.

57. Ibid.

58. "Ponca City Cagers Receive Program-Banquet Honors," *Oklahoma Eagle*, April 8, 1954, 1A; "*Eagle* Publisher Speaks to Group on Brotherhood," *Oklahoma Eagle*, March 14, 1957, 1; "*Eagle* Publisher Addresses Y's Hungry Club Forum," *Oklahoma Eagle*, May 19, 1955, 2.

59. E. L. Madison, Jr., "*Eagle* Publisher Tells Democrats of Negroes' Needs," *Oklahoma Eagle*, November 1, 1956, 1.

60. "*Eagle* Publisher Speaks at Red Bird," *Oklahoma Eagle*, June 25, 1959, 1.

61. Jim Goodwin, conversation with the author, January 22, 2021.

62. Arradondo conversation, August 10, 2020.

63. Ibid.

64. J. Goodwin conversation, January 22, 2021.

65. Ibid.

66. Jeanne Arradondo, conversation with the author, September 5, 2022.

67. "Atty. E. L. Goodwin Begins Law Practice," *Oklahoma Eagle*, August 25, 1960, 1.

68. J. Goodwin conversation, October 19, 2021.

69. Ed Goodwin, Sr., interview by Henry La Brie, August 12, 1971, transcript, 9, Black Journalists Oral History Collection, Columbia University.

70. Ibid.

71. "Hall and Goodwin Deny Arson Count at Okemah," *Tulsa Tribune*, October 24, 1957.

72. Lit Roper, "Hall, Goodwin to Try to Block Bank Records," *Tulsa Tribune*, November 8, 1957, 22.

73. "Plead Innocent in Arson Case," *Oklahoma Eagle*, October 31, 1957, 1.

74. Yvonne Nance, " 'God, I'm in Your Hands' '"; *Abundant Life Magazine*, April 1970, 20.

75. Gilford conversation, September 11, 2019.

76. "Law Wives Get (P)utting (H)usbands (T)hru Degrees," *Oklahoma Eagle*, May 19, 1957, 1A.

77. Jeanne B. Goodwin, "Greenwood . . . The Best of the Story," *Oklahoma Eagle,* July 28, 1988, 1; "Alsuma: The Town That Disappeared from Southeast Tulsa," *Oklahoma Eagle,* September 12, 2019; "Moto Hospital Gets Elevator, Gas Machine; Mayor Is Guest," *Oklahoma Eagle,* March 7, 1957, 1.

78. "Law Wives Get (P)utting (H)usbands (T)hru Degrees."

79. Nance, " 'God, I'm in Your Hands,' " 20.

80. "Atty. E. L. Goodwin Begins Law Practice."

81. "Negro Freed in Fire Case," *Tulsa World,* September 9, 1959.

82. J. Goodwin conversation, October 19, 2021.

83. "Atty. E. L. Goodwin Begins Law Practice."

84. Jim Goodwin, "Equality Reconsidered," *Notre Dame Scholastic,* April 8, 1960, 15.

85. "*Browder v. Gayle,* 352 U.S. 903," *King Encyclopedia,* https://kinginstitute.stanford.edu/encyclopedia/browder-v-gayle-352-us-903.

86. "Tulsa Buses Are Completely Desegregated—A. Hauer."

87. J. Goodwin conversation, October 19, 2021.

88. J. Goodwin conversation, February 1, 2021.

89. "Class Listings, Black Alumni of Notre Dame," *Black Alumni Directory: University of Notre Dame* (2001), 63; "6,000 Students Begin Fall Term Classes," *Notre Dame Alumnus,* October–November 1957, 3.

90. Dennis Brown, "Black Alumni of Notre Dame Expands Scope of Frazier Thompson Scholarship," *Notre Dame News,* April 8, 2021, https://news.nd.edu/news/black-alumni-of-notre-dame-expands-scope-of-frazier-thompson-scholarship/; Margaret Fosmoe, "At 50 Years," *Notre Dame Magazine,* Summer 2022, https://magazine.nd.edu/stories/at-50-years/.

91. Jim Goodwin, "Repercussions," *Notre Dame Scholastic,* October 7, 1960, 37.

92. Goodwin, "Equality Reconsidered."

93. Jim Goodwin, conversation with the author, August 25, 2021.

94. Mel Watkins, "What Was It About Amos 'n' Andy?" *New York Times,* July 7, 1991, https://www.nytimes.com/1991/07/07/books/what-was-it-about-amos-n-andy.html.

95. J. Goodwin conversation, August 25, 2021.

96. J. Goodwin conversation, February 1, 2021.

97. Ibid.; General Program Basic Reading List, 1957, University Archives, University of Notre Dame, South Bend, Ind.

98. J. Goodwin conversation, February 1, 2021.

99. Jim Goodwin, "Atty. Thurgood Marshall Says 'Negroes Are Too Satisfied,' " *Oklahoma Eagle,* June 9, 1960, 1; J. Goodwin conversation, October 19, 2021.

100. Jim Goodwin, "Negroes and Downtown Tulsa," *Oklahoma Eagle,* June 23, 1960, 1; Jim Goodwin, "Negroes and . . . Downtown Tulsa," *Oklahoma Eagle,* July 14, 1960, 1.

101. Jeanne-Marguerite Goodwin, conversation with the author, May 27, 2021.

102. James O. Goodwin, "Action for Better Employment," senior essay, University of Notre Dame, June 1961, 3–4.

103. J. Goodwin conversation, February 1, 2021.

104. Ibid.

105. Rucker, *Jazz Road,* 309–50; Bill Boulware, conversation with the author, August 3, 2022.

106. J. Goodwin conversation, February 1, 2021.

107. E. L. Goodwin, Jr., Regina Goodwin funeral program, 2014, private collection.

108. Princetta Rudd-Newman, conversation with the author, August 26, 2022.

109. E. L. Goodwin, Jr., "I'm Telling It, Like It IZZ!" *Oklahoma Eagle,* July 17, 2003, B4.

110. J. Goodwin conversation, September 2, 2021.

111. Ed Sr. interview by La Brie, 9.

112. Ed Sr.'s brother James Jr. was a wayward son and was possibly murdered under mysterious circumstances in the early 1930s, according to family oral history.

113. Jeanne Arradondo, conversation with the author, August 3, 2020.

114. Ibid.; Greg Goodwin, conversation with the author, July 30, 2019.

115. Charles Loeb, "Finds Tulsa Is a City of Racial Paradoxes," *Chicago Defender,* July 3, 1954, 4.

116. "Gurley Leaves Tulsa," *Chicago Defender,* March 10, 1923, 1.

117. *California Eagle,* April 7, 1923, 2.

118. "Official Death List," *Los Angeles Times,* August 11, 1935, 34.

119. "The Stradford Hotel and Theater Company," *Broad Ax,* September 16, 1922, 1.

120. "J. B. Stradford Civic Leader Is Taken in Death," *Chicago Defender,* January 4, 1936, 4.

121. John Wesley Williams funeral program, January 31, 1939, Williams Dreamland LLC; Mary S. Williams, "Personal History: John Wesley Williams," n.d., Williams Dreamland LLC.

122. "$6,000 of Drugs Seized in Arkansas," *Pine Bluff Daily News,* January 24, 1920, 6; "A.G.W. Sango Now Head Barber at Pen," *Muskogee Times-Democrat,* February 2, 1922, 1.

123. "Sango Leads Scott for Justice of Peace Post," *Oklahoma Eagle,* November 9, 1946, 1.

124. "Creek Freedmen Hold Annual Meet at Tulsa," *Pittsburgh Courier,* August 18, 1934, 5.

125. "A.G.W. Sango Dies; Last of the Territorial Leaders," *Oklahoma Eagle,* July 14, 1949, 1.

126. B. C. Franklin, "My New Years Message," *Oklahoma Eagle,* January 14, 1960, 1A.

127. "Buck C. Franklin Dies; Rites Held," *Oklahoma Eagle,* September 29, 1960, 1.

128. "Publisher of Nation's First Negro Daily Paper Is Dead," *Buffalo Evening News,* June 22, 1961, 38.

129. "*Black Dispatch* Officials Name Woman Editor," *Black Dispatch,* June 25, 1955, 1.

130. A. J. Smitherman, "A Biography," *Empire Star,* September 3, 1960, 8.

131. Ibid.

132. "Publisher of Nation's First Negro Daily Paper Is Dead."

133. A. J. Smitherman, "Autobiography: Meeting the Democratic Chairman," *Empire Star,* June 17, 1961, 10.
134. "Publisher of Nation's First Negro Daily Paper Is Dead."
135. Arradondo conversation, August 3, 2020.
136. Ibid.
137. Martie, "J. H. Goodwin, Pioneer, Man of Goodwill, Dies," *Oklahoma Eagle,* March 13, 1958, 1; Charles James Bate, *"It's Been a Long Time" and We've Come a Long Way* (Tulsa: Acorn Printing Co., 1986), 208.
138. "So Long, Papa," *Oklahoma Eagle,* March 13, 1958, 1.

CHAPTER 17: SOMEWHERE BETWEEN HOPE AND EXPECTATION

1. *Oklahoma Eagle,* August 4, 1960, 9.
2. "Martin L. King to Appear at Freedom Rally July 28," *Oklahoma Eagle,* July 21, 1960, 1.
3. "Attended by 1,500 King Urges Sit-Ins," *Oklahoma Eagle,* August 4, 1960, 1.
4. Jeanne Arradondo, conversation with the author, August 3, 2020.
5. Tim Stanley, "Martin Luther King, Jr., Spoke in Tulsa Only Once. But Sixty Years Later, His 'Inspiring and Electrifying' Presence Has Not Been Forgotten," *Tulsa World,* January 19, 2020, https://tulsaworld.com/news/local/martin-luther-king-jr-spoke-in-tulsa-only-once-but-60-years-later-his-inspiring/article_d2dfd884-c84a-5fdb-a377-93d8c796946e.html.
6. Arradondo conversation, August 3, 2020.
7. Ronald Powell, " 'Live Together as Brothers or Die Together as Fools,' " *Oklahoma Eagle,* August 4, 1960, 1A.
8. "Attended By 1,500 King Urges Sit-Ins."
9. Powell, " 'Live Together as Brothers.' "
10. Eddie Faye Gates, *They Came Searching: How Blacks Found the Promised Land in Oklahoma* (Austin, Tex.: Eakin Press, 1997), 190.
11. Jim Goodwin, conversation with the author, October 19, 2021.
12. *Oklahoma Eagle,* August 4, 1960, 1A.
13. General Studies Curriculum, 1957, University Archives, University of Notre Dame, South Bend, Ind.; Martin Luther King, Jr., "Pilgrimage to Nonviolence," *Christian Century,* April 13, 1960, 439–41; Martin Luther King, Jr., "A Walk Through the Holy Land," Easter Sunday Sermon, Dexter Avenue Baptist Church, March 29, 1959, Montgomery, Ala., transcript, Martin Luther King, Jr. Papers (Series I-IV), Martin Luther King, Jr., Center for Nonviolent Social Change, Atlanta.
14. J. Goodwin conversation, October 19, 2021.
15. Ibid.
16. " 'Negro Wants Freedom Now,' Says King," *Black Dispatch,* August 5, 1960, 1; "King Preaches 'Making the Most of a Difficult Situation' at Ebenezer," Chronology, Martin Luther King, Jr. Research and Education Institute, https://kinginstitute.stanford.edu/encyclopedia/king-preaches-making-most-difficult-situation-ebenezer-reports-baptist-world-alliance.
17. "Seminole Hills Forum Slated," *Oklahoma Eagle,* November 30, 1961, 1.

18. "300 Residents Urged to Aid UR Project," *Tulsa World,* April 14, 1961, 13; "Urban Renewal Housing Forum Is Successful," *Oklahoma Eagle,* April 20, 1961, 1.

19. "Urban Renewal Housing Forum Is Successful."

20. Erin Blakemore, "How the GI Bill's Promise Was Denied to a Million Black WWII Veterans," History Channel, June 21, 2019, https://www.history.com/news/gi-bill-black-wwii-veterans-benefits.

21. Alexander von Hoffman, "A Study in Contradictions: The Origins and Legacy of the Housing Act of 1949," *Housing Policy Debate* 11, no. 2 (2000): 303.

22. Housing Act of 1949, Pub. L. No. 81-171, 63 Stat. 432 (1949).

23. Hoffman, "Study in Contradictions," 310–13.

24. Dan Fitzpatrick, "The Story of Urban Renewal," *Pittsburgh Post-Gazette,* May 21, 2000, https://old.post-gazette.com/businessnews/20000521eastliberty1.asp.

25. "Urban Renewal Drive Strategy Mapped Here," *Tulsa Tribune,* March 4, 1959, 33.

26. T. R. Gustafson, "Protect Our Beloved America," *Tulsa Tribune,* April 21, 1958, 36.

27. Tulsa Urban Renewal Authority, *First Annual Report,* 1961, PartnerTulsa Archives, Tulsa.

28. Edgar T. Rouzeau, "Large Area Undergoes Disadvantage Because of Industrial Classification," *Oklahoma Eagle,* November 1, 1951, 1.

29. Amanda K. Coleman, "A Socioeconomic Analysis of the Greenwood District of Tulsa, Oklahoma: 1940–1980," master's thesis, Oklahoma State University, 2001, 68.

30. Tulsa Urban League, "A Concise Review of Housing Problems Affecting Negroes in Tulsa," October 1958, Tulsa and Oklahoma History Collection, Tulsa City-County Library, http://digitalcollections.tulsalibrary.org/digital/collection/p16063coll1/id/5358.

31. "'Little Harlem': That's Tulsa's Progressive Negro District," *Oklahoma Eagle,* August 7, 1943, 12.

32. "Urban Renewal? When?" *Oklahoma Eagle,* June 25, 1959, 8.

33. Bill Ellis, "Slum Areas Big Roadblock in Path of Tulsa Progress," *Tulsa World,* June 25, 1959, 47.

34. Tulsa Urban Renewal Authority, *Third Annual Report,* 1963.

35. "Vanished: Slum Clearance and Segregation in Little Rock," 2020, Mapping Renewal, Center for Arkansas History and Culture, University of Arkansas at Little Rock, draft text provided to the author; Acadia Roher, "Urban Renewal in Little Rock's Dunbar Historic Neighborhood: A Walking Tour," master's thesis, University of Arkansas at Little Rock, 2021, 17, 23–32.

36. "Urban Renewal Housing Forum Is Successful."

37. Tulsa Urban Renewal Authority, *Seventh Annual Report,* 1967, PartnerTulsa Archives, Tulsa.

38. "Urban Renewal Aired in Forum," *Oklahoma Eagle,* December 7, 1961, 1.

39. Don Bachelder, "Tulsa OK's Urban Renewal," *Tulsa World,* October 20, 1962, sec. 2, 1.

40. Tom Birmingham, "Urban Renewal Has Human Side," *Tulsa Tribune,* July 30, 1966, 13; "TURA Gets First Check for Buying," *Tulsa World,* February 28, 1963, 49.

41. Windsor Ridenour, "Seminole Hills: Good or Bad?" *Tulsa Tribune,* March 12, 1969, 1C.

42. Elizabeth M. Burton, "Tulsa Wealth Disparity: The Political Legacy of the 1921 Race Massacre," undergraduate thesis, Macalester College, 2021, 30–31, https://digitalcommons.macalester.edu/poli_honors/91.

43. "What Urban Renewal Unveils," *Oklahoma Eagle,* December 14, 1961, 9.

44. Nora Froeschle, "School Integration, Magnet Plan/Forced Busing: Tulsa Used a Managed Approach," *Tulsa World,* July 15, 2007, https://tulsaworld.com/archive/school-integration-magnet-plan-forced-busing-tulsa-used-a-magnet-approach/article_f98b4ef8-2846-5f62-8134-527c368cd530.html; "Jo Ann Goodwin Weds Ernie Fields in Home of Parents," *Oklahoma Eagle,* January 3, 1957, 2.

45. "Goodwin Birthdays," David Goodwin private collection; Jo Ann Gilford, conversation with the author, September 11, 2019.

46. Jo Ann Gilford, conversation with the author, July 30, 2019.

47. Ibid.

48. Cathy Ambler, "Historic Resources Survey of the Cliff Dweller Houses on Reservoir Hill," August 24, 2012, 6–9, City of Tulsa, https://www.okhistory.org/shpo/docs/HRSofOakCliff.pdf/.

49. "Oak Cliff: Tulsa's Sub-Division Deluxe," *Tulsa World,* December 17, 1922, 31.

50. Tulsa County, Okla., Deed Book 497, 159, Oak Cliff Realty Company and Robert F. Fitzgerald, April 3, 1923.

51. Gilford conversation, September 11, 2019; Francis Dominic Burke, "A Survey of the Negro Community of Tulsa, Oklahoma," master's thesis, University of Tulsa, 1936.

52. Burke, "Survey of the Negro Community," 111.

53. Danney Goble, *Tulsa! Biography of an American City* (Tulsa: Council Oak Books, 1997), 210–13.

54. Coleman, "Socioeconomic Analysis," 47.

55. Goble, *Tulsa! Biography,* 213–15; Froeschle, "School Integration, Magnet Plan/Forced Busing."

56. "Sabotage at Burroughs School," *Oklahoma Eagle,* September 21, 1961, 7.

57. "Publishers Daughter at Work," *Oklahoma Eagle,* October 6, 1955, 7.

58. Jo Ann Gilford, conversation with the author, September 11, 2019.

59. Jo Ann Gilford, conversation with the author, August 30, 2022.

60. Gilford conversation, September 11, 2019.

61. "Salute the Transferred-In," *Oklahoma Eagle,* September 13, 1962, 7.

62. "Local Youth Join March to D.C. After Rousing Rally," *Oklahoma Eagle,* August 29, 1963, 6; Pat Lark, "Freedom Now!" *Oklahoma Eagle,* September 5, 1963, 1.

63. Pat Lark, "The Street," *Oklahoma Eagle,* August 15, 1963, 2; Doretha McMillon, "The Street," *Oklahoma Eagle,* August 22, 1963.

64. Pat Bell, conversation with the author, November 16, 2021.

65. Ibid.
66. "March on Washington for Jobs and Freedom," *King Encyclopedia,* https:// kinginstitute.stanford.edu/encyclopedia/march-washington-jobs-and-freedom; Martin Arnold, "Rights March on Washington Reported Growing," *New York Times,* August 4, 1963, 57, https://www.nytimes.com/1963/08/04/ archives/rights-march-on-washington-reported-growing-many-more-than -100000.html; Alex Haley and Malcolm X, *The Autobiography of Malcolm X* (New York: Ballantine Books, 1964), 280.
67. Bell conversation, November 16, 2021.
68. Pat Lark, "Prelude to History," *Oklahoma Eagle,* August 29, 1963, 1.
69. "Birmingham Campaign," *King Encyclopedia,* https://kinginstitute.stanford .edu/encyclopedia/birmingham-campaign.
70. P. L. Prattis, "Issues: Good and Bad," *Oklahoma Eagle,* August 1, 1963, 7.
71. Bell conversation, November 16, 2021.
72. Lark, "Freedom Now!"
73. Bell conversation, November 16, 2021.
74. Don Lipman, "A Day to Remember: August 28, 1963—What Was Weather Like for MLK Dream Speech?" *Washington Post,* August 24, 2011, https:// www.washingtonpost.com/blogs/capital-weather-gang/post/a-day-to-remember -august-28-1963/2011/08/24/gIQADeZZbJ_blog.html; Nina Bassuk et al., "The State of the Elms on the National Mall in Washington, D.C.," April 2018, 7, http://www.hort.cornell.edu/uhi/research/articles/National%20Mall %20Elms_2018.04.07.pdf.
75. Bell conversation, November 16, 2021.
76. Charles Euchner, *Nobody Turn Me Around: A People's History of the 1963 March on Washington* (Boston: Beacon Press, 2010), 194.
77. John Lewis, "Speech at the March on Washington," August 28, 1963, Voices of Democracy: U.S. Oratory Project, University of Maryland, https:// voicesofdemocracy.umd.edu/lewis-speech-at-the-march-on-washington-speech -text/.
78. Mahalia Jackson singing "How I Got Over" at the March on Washington, August 28, 1963, video, https://www.youtube.com/watch?v=t9iQUIwAgus.
79. Bell conversation, November 16, 2021.
80. Emily Crockett, "The Woman Who Inspired Martin Luther King's 'I Have a Dream' Speech," *Vox,* January 16, 2017, https://www.vox.com/2016/1/18/ 10785882/martin-luther-king-dream-mahalia-jackson.
81. Bell conversation, November 16, 2021.
82. "Borden's Justice," *Oklahoma Eagle,* October 10, 1963, 7.
83. "Two Rights Sections Hit," *Daily Oklahoman,* February 6, 1964, 3; Don Thompson, "Air Accommodations Views at City Hall Public Hearing," *Oklahoma Eagle,* December 12, 1963, 1.
84. "Mayor Gets 47 Anti Letters to Ordinance," *Oklahoma Eagle,* August 8, 1963, 1.
85. "Protest March Scheduled Here Mon.," *Oklahoma Eagle,* March 26, 1964, 1.
86. "Clara Luper, Militant Fighter and OC Youths Join March," *Oklahoma Eagle,* April 2, 1964, 1.
87. Ibid.; Luper, *Behold the Walls,* 184.

88. "Zetas to Observe Womanhood Sun. at Mt. Zion," *Oklahoma Eagle*, February 21, 1963, 3; Elmer L. Davis, "NAACP, Tulsans Celebrate Anniv. of Emancipation Proclamation Day," *Oklahoma Eagle*, June 20, 1963, 1; "Dynamic Integration Leader Addresses Youth Group Sun," *Oklahoma Eagle*, September 12, 1963, 1.

89. Rev. Benjamin S. Roberts, in Eddie Faye Gates, *They Came Searching: How Blacks Found the Promised Land in Oklahoma* (Austin, Tex.: Eakin Press, 1997), 165.

90. "Clara Luper, Militant Fighter."

91. Luper, *Behold the Walls*, 185.

92. Ibid.; "Tulsa Arrests 33 in Demonstration," *Daily Oklahoman*, March 31, 1964, 13.

93. Luper, *Behold the Walls*, 186; Neil R. McMillen, *The Citizens' Council: Organized Resistance to the Second Reconstruction, 1954–64* (Urbana: University of Illinois Press, 1994), xii; "Tulsa Arrests 33 in Demonstration."

94. "Tulsa Arrests 33."

95. Luper, *Behold the Walls*, 186.

96. Ibid.

97. "Arrests Follow Tulsa's 1st Rights Demonstration," *Oklahoma Eagle*, April 2, 1964, 1; "Tulsa Arrests 33."

98. "Arrests Follow."

99. Luper, *Behold the Walls*, 187.

100. E. L. Goodwin, Sr., interview by Henry G. LaBrie III, August 12, 1971, transcript, 9, 19–20, Black Journalists Oral History Project, Columbia Center for Oral History.

101. "CORE Hits Piccadilly, Apache Circle in Drenching Rain; May Hit Tonight," *Oklahoma Eagle*, April 9, 1964.

102. "Non-Jury Trials Due in Sit-In," *Tulsa Tribune*, April 13, 1964, 2; "29 Arrested in New Sit-In Deny Charges," *Tulsa Tribune*, April 2, 1964, 35.

103. *Oklahoma Eagle*, April 30, 1964, 1.

104. Ed Goodwin, Jr., "Seeing Is Believing," *Oklahoma Eagle*, June 11, 1964, 1.

105. "City Commission Passes Ordinance," *Oklahoma Eagle*, July 2, 1964, 1.

106. "Civil Rights Act (1964)," Milestone Documents, National Archives, https://www.archives.gov/milestone-documents/civil-rights-act.

107. Ed Goodwin, Jr., "With Reservations," *Oklahoma Eagle*, July 2, 1964, 1.

108. Bell conversation, November 16, 2021.

109. Lark, "Freedom Now!"

110. Bell conversation, November 16, 2021.

111. Joe Looney, "An Old Tulsa Street Is Slowly Dying," *Tulsa Tribune*, May 4, 1967.

112. E. L. Goodwin, Jr., "Citizens Concerned over Debris, Parking Meters on Greenwood," *Oklahoma Eagle*, July 27, 1967, 1.

113. Oklahoma State Highway Department, *Comprehensive Functional Plans for the Long Range Highway Needs for Tulsa, Oklahoma* (Tulsa: Associated Expressway Engineers, 1961), 3–4.

114. William Paul Corbett, "Oklahoma's Highways: Indian Trails to Urban Expressways," Ph.D. diss., Oklahoma State University, 1982, 307.

115. Mark H. Rose, *Interstate: Highway Politics and Policy Since 1939*, 3rd ed. (Knoxville: University of Tennessee Press, 2012), 92.

116. Highway Department, *Comprehensive Functional Plans*, 4.

117. Claude Taylor, "Progress Hinges on Expressway Voting," *Oklahoma Eagle*, October 17, 1957, 1.

118. "Record Vote Passes Tulsa Bond Issues," *Oklahoma Eagle*, October 24, 1957, 1.

119. Gary T. Schwartz, "Urban Freeways and the Interstate System," *Transportation Law Journal* 8 (1976): 185.

120. Bureau of Public Roads, *General Location of National System of Interstate Highways* (Washington, D.C.: Government Printing Office, 1955), 55, https://commons.wikimedia.org/wiki/File:Tulsa,_Oklahoma_1955_Yellow_Book.jpg.

121. Jeffrey Brinkman and Jeffrey Lin, "Freeway Revolts!: The Quality of Life Effects of Highways," August 2022, Federal Reserve Bank of Philadelphia Research Department, 53, https://jlin.org/papers/BL-FR.pdf.

122. Highway Department, *Comprehensive Functional Plans*, 1.

123. " 'The Monster': Claiborne Avenue Before and After the Interstate," Tripod: New Orleans at 300, WWNO, https://www.wwno.org/podcast/tripod-new-orleans-at-300/2016-05-05/the-monster-claiborne-avenue-before-and-after-the-interstate.

124. Corbett, "Oklahoma's Highways," 301.

125. Michael Overall, "For Better or Worse, Riverside Expressway Would Have Reshaped Tulsa Forever," *Tulsa World*, May 27, 2019, https://tulsaworld.com/news/local/michael-overall-for-better-or-worse-riverside-expressway-would-have-reshaped-tulsa-forever/article_ef64d519-1e7f-5668-9db8-dfb342eb45dc.html.

126. William M. Dane, *Proceedings of the First Annual Highway and Street Conference*, February 27, 1962, 3, Oklahoma State Archives, Oklahoma City.

127. Amos T. Hall and Ella Hall, Land Acquisition File, Parcel No. 461, December 7, 1965; and Josephine Villareal, Land Acquisition File, Parcel No. 404, October 21, 1965; both in Oklahoma Department of Transportation Archives, Oklahoma City.

128. Alex Spann and A. G. Bacoats, Land Acquisition File, Parcel No. 459, October 15, 1968, Oklahoma Department of Transportation.

129. Land acquisition files, 1965–68, Oklahoma Department of Transportation Archives, Oklahoma City.

130. "Maybe We Need to Think South," *Oklahoma Eagle*, May 18, 1967, 14.

131. Martin Luther King, Jr., "Keep Moving from This Mountain," April 10, 1960, Martin Luther King, Jr., Research and Education Institute, https://kinginstitute.stanford.edu/king-papers/documents/keep-moving-mountain-address-spelman-college-10-april-1960.

132. "Maybe We Need to Think South."

133. Doretha McMillon, "The Street," *Oklahoma Eagle*, March 2, 1967, 4.

134. Jim Goodwin, conversation with the author, November 9, 2021.

135. Don Thompson, conversation with the author, October 19, 2022.

136. Looney, "Old Tulsa Street"; "Greenwood Tour," *Oklahoma Eagle*, July 26, 1951, 4.

137. E. L. Goodwin, Sr., Land Acquisition File, Parcel No. 460, January 4, 1966, Oklahoma Department of Transportation.

138. Looney, "Old Tulsa Street."

139. Tulsa County, Okla., Deed Book 1677, 105, Bijou-Tulsa Corporation and J. H. Goodwin, July 19, 1945.

140. "$75,000 Fire Guts Greenwood," *Oklahoma Eagle,* January 15, 1944, 1.

141. Looney, "Old Tulsa Street."

142. Ibid.

143. "History of *Eagle* Existence Cited on Eve of G. Opening," *Oklahoma Eagle,* April 14, 1966, 12.

144. Mary Ellen Walton, "Arched Doorway Graces the Luxurious *Eagle* Home," *Oklahoma Eagle,* April 14, 1966, 18; Looney, "Old Tulsa Street."

145. Regina Goodwin, conversation with the author, August 6, 2020.

146. Author analysis of 1960s Tulsa city directories.

147. Jim Henderson, "What Builds a Ghetto? How Do You Flee?" *Tulsa World,* June 21, 1967.

148. R. Goodwin conversation, August 6, 2020.

149. Bob Goodwin, conversation with the author, January 22, 2022.

150. Looney, "Old Tulsa Street."

151. Jim Goodwin, conversation with the author, December 1, 2021.

152. Robert F. Darden, "MLK Requested a Song Minutes Before His Assassination, and That Tune Comforted Millions," *Dallas Morning News,* March 28, 2018, https://www.dallasnews.com/opinion/commentary/2018/03/28/mlk-requested -a-song-minutes-before-his-assassination-and-that-tune-comforted-millions/.

153. J. Goodwin conversation, December 1, 2021.

154. "Tulsa and State Join in Mourning Death of King," *Tulsa Tribune,* April 5, 1968, 39.

155. J. Goodwin conversation, December 1, 2021; "City Commission Passes Ordinance."

156. Norvell Coots, conversation with the author, February 27, 2021.

157. "'Racial' Rumors Spread in Tulsa," *Tulsa Tribune,* April 6, 1968, 13.

158. Coots conversation, February 27, 2021.

159. Kyle Goddard, "Memorial Service Fills Church," *Tulsa Tribune,* April 6, 1968, 13.

160. J. Goodwin conversation, December 1, 2021.

161. Rebecca Burns, *Burial for a King* (New York: Scribner, 2011), 149–53, 156.

162. E. L. Goodwin, Jr., "Thousands Attend Rites for Martyred Leader," *Oklahoma Eagle,* April 11, 1968, 1.

163. "Mules Symbolize Plight of Poor," *Oklahoma Eagle,* April 11, 1968, 1; "New Violence Hits Washington," *Tulsa Tribune,* April 5, 1968, 1; "Race Violence Strikes 46 Cities; Troops Struggle to Hold Down Marauders," *Tulsa World,* April 6, 1968, 1.

164. Greg Goodwin, "Martin Luther King," *Oklahoma Eagle,* April 11, 1968, 4B; Eric Goodwin, "Martin Luther King," *Oklahoma Eagle,* April 11, 1968, 4B.

165. "Gangland Bemoans Its Victims," *Oklahoma Eagle,* April 11, 1968, 1B.

166. Samir Meghelli, "Smithsonian's Anacostia Community Museum: 'Prepare to Participate'—When Dr. King Urged for Community-Led Development in

D.C.," *Washington Informer,* January 9, 2020, https://www
.washingtoninformer.com/prepare-to-participate-when-dr-king-urged-for
-community-led-development-in-d-c/.

CHAPTER 18: A SLOWER BURN

1. Mabel Little, interview by Ruth Sigler Avery, May 24, 1971, transcript, Box 7, Ruth Sigler Avery Collection, Oklahoma State University–Tulsa; Presley [*sic*] Little and Cyrus S. Avery deed, March 17, 1921, Deed Book 363, 205, Tulsa County Clerk, Tulsa.

2. Ibid.; *Tulsa City Directory, 1930* (Polk-Hoffhine Directory Co.), 796; Mabel Little, *Fire on Mount Zion: My Life and History As a Black Woman in America* (Wilmington, Del.: Black Think Tank, 1992), 42, 60.

3. Mabel Little, in *Goin' Back to T-Town,* PBS/American Experience, March 1, 1993, transcript, 14–15.

4. "Mabel Little, Survivor of Riot, Dead at 104," *Tulsa World,* January 19, 2001, https://tulsaworld.com/archive/mabel-little-survivor-of-riot-dead-at-104/article_b137d7d7-6b9c-5f39-ab1a-d38da294a62e.html.

5. Tulsa County, Okla., Deed Book 972, 174, Mabel Little and Katie Williams, February 12, 1931; Little, *Goin' Back to T-Town,* 27–28; "Mabel Little in Business Forty-One Years," *Oklahoma Eagle,* October 15, 1953, 1.

6. Ann Patton, "Moratorium on Renewal Work Eyed," *Tulsa World,* April 11, 1970, B1.

7. Joe Looney, "An Old Tulsa Street Is Slowly Dying," *Tulsa Tribune,* May 14, 1967; Right-of-way Acquisition Files, 1965–68, Oklahoma Department of Transportation, Oklahoma City; Florence Simons, Land Acquisition File, Parcel No. 405, October 12, 1965, Oklahoma Department of Transportation; Clemmie Thompson, Land Acquisition File, Parcel No. 451, November 16, 1965, Oklahoma Department of Transportation.

8. Bret A. Weber and Amanda Wallace, "Revealing the Empowerment Revolution: A Literature Review of the Model Cities Program," *Journal of Urban History* 38, no. 1 (2012): 174; D. Bradford Hunt, "Model Cities," *Encyclopedia of Chicago,* http://www.encyclopedia.chicagohistory.org/pages/832.html; "Conversation with James Baldwin, A; James Baldwin Interview," June 24, 1963, WGBH Archives, http://openvault.wgbh.org/catalog/V_C03ED1927 DCF46B5A8C82275DF4239F9.

9. Tonette England, ed., *Tulsa Model Cities* (Tulsa: Tulsa Model Cities Program, 1971), 7.

10. Bernard J. Frieden and Martin Kaplan, *The Politics of Neglect: Urban Aid from Model Cities to Revenue Sharing* (Cambridge, Mass.: MIT Press, 1975), 69.

11. J. Bob Lucas, "Referendum Suggested on Model Cities," *Tulsa Tribune,* April 9, 1970.

12. *Tulsa City Directory, 1971,* 418.

13. Hannah D. Atkins, "Hall, Amos T. (1896–1971)," *Encyclopedia of Oklahoma History and Culture,* https://www.okhistory.org/publications/enc/entry.php ?entry=HA006.

14. Greg Goodwin, conversation with the author, December 7, 2021.

15. "Black Panther Leader Says People Misinformed on Party," *Oklahoma Eagle,* February 5, 1970, 9.

16. "Crisis and Commitment," *New York Times,* October 14, 1966, 35.

17. Don Ross, "Amos T. Hall Named 2nd Negro Judge," *Oklahoma Eagle,* December 5, 1968, 1.

18. Tulsa Urban Renewal Authority, *Fourteenth Annual Report,* 1974, 6, Tulsa Urban Renewal Authority Library.

19. "Homegoing Service for J. Homer Johnson, Jr." (obituary), October 8, 2005, Francine Campbell private collection; "Pioneer City Worker Dies," *Oklahoma Eagle,* March 22, 1984, 1; James H. Johnson, March 2, 1946, U.S. World War II Army Enlistment Records, 1938–46, Ancestry.com.

20. "Homegoing Service for Johnson, Jr."

21. Education Committee Final Statement, *Tulsa Model Cities Program: A Comprehensive Demonstration Program to Improve the Quality of Urban Life* (Tulsa: City Demonstration Agency, 1969), 11; "Model Cities Program Cost Put at $3.1 Million," *Tulsa World,* April 20, 1970, 3.

22. "TAAG to Evaluate Programs," *Oklahoma Eagle,* November 20, 1969, 1.

23. Dale Speer, "TURA OKs Greenwood Plan," *Tulsa World,* May 23, 1969.

24. Frieden and Kaplan, *Politics of Neglect,* 23.

25. "TURA OKs Greenwood Plan."

26. England, *Tulsa Model Cities,* 10.

27. Frieden and Kaplan, *Politics of Neglect,* 76–78.

28. Education Committee Final Statement, *Tulsa Model Cities Program,* 10.

29. Housing Committee Project #701, ibid., 22.

30. Lucas, "Referendum Suggested on Model Cities"; "Moratorium on Renewal Work Eyed."

31. Lucas, "Referendum Suggested on Model Cities."

32. Tulsa Urban Renewal Authority, *Seventh Annual Report,* 1967, Tulsa Urban Renewal Authority Library.

33. Ibid.; Tulsa Urban Renewal Authority, *Eighth Annual Report,* 1968, Tulsa Urban Renewal Authority Library.

34. Lucas, "Referendum Suggested on Model Cities."

35. Cathy Ambler, Mount Zion Baptist Church National Register of Historic Places Registration, April 2008, section 8, 10, http://nr2_shpo.okstate.edu/pdfs/8000847.pdf; "North Side of IDL to Open," *Oklahoma Eagle,* April 12, 1973, 8.

36. David M. Breed, "'The First Lady of Greenwood,'" *Oklahoma Eagle,* December 4, 1975, 1; Tulsa Urban Renewal Authority, *Seventh Annual Report,* 15.

37. Lucas, "Referendum Suggested on Model Cities."

38. "Golden Anniversary of the Riot" (recording), Mt. Zion Baptist Church, June 1, 1971, Ruth Sigler Avery Collection, Oklahoma State University–Tulsa; hereafter Avery Collection.

39. "Riot Committee Meeting Slated April 22nd," *Oklahoma Eagle,* April 15, 1971, 1.

40. "North Tulsans Gear for Riot Commemoration," *Oklahoma Eagle,* May 27, 1971, 1.

41. W. D. Williams, interview by Scott Ellsworth, June 7, 1978 (recording), Tulsa Race Massacre of 1921 Archive, University of Tulsa.
42. "North Tulsans Gear for Riot Commemoration."
43. Ed Goodwin, Sr., in "Golden Anniversary of the Riot."
44. "North Tulsans Gear for Riot Commemoration."
45. "Riot of '21 Retold at Commemoration Program," *Oklahoma Eagle,* June 3, 1971, 1; "Negro Baptist Church, Destroyed at Tulsa, Was Arsenal of Black Bolshevists, Charge," *Daily Oklahoman* (Oklahoma City), June 5, 1921, 34.
46. Hill, *1921 Tulsa Race Massacre,* 66.
47. Avery, "Golden Anniversary of the Riot," recording; S. M. Jackson, interview by Ruth Sigler Avery, 1971, transcript, Box 23 Avery Collection.
48. "Riot Material Needed for Book," *Oklahoma Eagle,* February 11, 1971, 1; Finding Aid, Tulsa Race Massacre of 1921, Ruth Sigler Avery Collection, Oklahoma State University at Tulsa, 12–16, 49–56, https://tulsa.okstate.edu/ sites/default/files/library/archives/Series_1_TulsaRaceMassacre.pdf.
49. Tim Stanley, "50 Years Ago, the 1921 Tulsa Race Massacre Was a Taboo Subject When Tulsan Ed Wheeler Set Out to Write an Article to 'Find Out What Happened,'" *Tulsa World,* April 12, 2021, https://tulsaworld.com/news/local/ racemassacre/50-years-ago-the-1921-tulsa-race-massacre-was-a-taboo-subject -when-tulsan-ed/article_58c4ad0c-918c-11eb-a5f5-8bb30424d29b.html.
50. Ed Wheeler, "Profile of a Race Riot," *Impact,* June–July 1971, https://www.si .edu/object/nmaahc_2011.60.18.
51. David Goodwin, conversation with the author, May 30, 2021; Victor Luckerson, "Black Wall Street: The African American Haven That Burned and Then Rose From the Ashes," *Ringer,* June 28, 2018, https://www.theringer.com/ 2018/6/28/17511818/black-wall-street-oklahoma-greenwood-destruction -tulsa.
52. Polly Bowen, "Williams Tells Tulsa Past," *Oklahoma Eagle,* April 21, 1977, 1; W. D. Williams funeral program, 1984, National Museum of African American History and Culture, https://transcription.si.edu/view/37748/NMAAHC -2011_60_3_003.
53. W. D. Williams, in "Golden Anniversary of the Riot."
54. Ibid.
55. Ibid.
56. Ibid.
57. Mabel Little, in "Golden Anniversary of the Riot."
58. Ibid.
59. Mabel Little, in *Goin' Back to T-Town,* PBS/American Experience, March 1, 1993.
60. Little, in "Golden Anniversary of the Riot."
61. Little, in *Goin' Back to T-Town.*
62. Little, in "Golden Anniversary of the Riot."
63. "With All Deliberate Speed," "Separate Is Not Equal: *Brown v. Board of Education,*" Smithsonian National Museum of American History, https:// americanhistory.si.edu/brown/history/6-legacy/deliberate-speed.html; Oklahoma Advisory Committee to the U.S. Commission on Civil Rights, *School Desegregation in Tulsa, Oklahoma,* August 1977, 37–48.

64. Nell Jean Boggs, "Abuse of Schools' Transfer Policies by Parents Claimed," *Tulsa Tribune*, January 21, 1970.

65. Jim Sellars, "School Dispute Fatal to Father," *Tulsa Tribune*, December 11, 1970.

66. Oklahoma Advisory Committee to the U.S. Commission on Civil Rights, *School Desegregation in Tulsa, Oklahoma* (1977), 39.

67. Ibid., 47–48.

68. "Peaceful Solution," *Oklahoma Eagle*, August 5, 1971, 1.

69. "TAAG Should Be Given Chance Says Evaluators," *Oklahoma Eagle*, December 24, 1970, 1; Central High School Yearbook, 1971, Tulsa, U.S., School Yearbooks, 1900–2016, Ancestry.com.

70. "Role of Tulsans for Quality Education Refuted by Board," *Oklahoma Eagle*, October 7, 1971, 1.

71. "Tulsa School Board Approves Changes at Washington Carver," *Oklahoma Eagle*, July 22, 1971, 1.

72. Jeanne Arradondo, "Mass Rally for Re-Opening of Carver Reveals Concern," August 5, 1971, 1.

73. Beth Macklin, "Blacks Pledge to Operate Carver 'Liberation School,'" *Tulsa World*, August 2, 1971.

74. "Blacks Plan to Boycott All Tulsa Schools," *Oklahoma Eagle*, August 12, 1971, 1.

75. "U.S. OKs One Black Group in School Suit," *Tulsa World*, October 27, 1971, B7.

76. Macklin, "Blacks Pledge to Operate Carver."

77. Rev. Ben H. Hill, "Black Power Movement Due for Fall!" *Oklahoma Eagle*, August 10, 1967, 12.

78. E. L. Goodwin, Jr., "Can You Dig It?" *Oklahoma Eagle*, August 5, 1971, 15.

79. "Panelist Claims Ravish of Black Community," *Tulsa World*, October 23, 1971, 16.

80. Little, in *Goin' Back to T-Town*, 40.

81. Arradondo, "Mass Rally for Re-Opening"; Mabel Little, *Fire on Mount Zion*, 80; "Carver Captivates Tulsans During Dedication of New School," *Black Dispatch*, May 9, 1929, 1.

82. Peter Duncan Burchard, *Carver: A Great Soul* (Fairfax, Calif.: Serpent Wise, 1998), 65.

83. Little, *Fire on Mount Zion*, 81.

84. "Freedom Class Facility Named," *Tulsa Tribune*, August 30, 1971, 1B.

85. "Freedom Schools," March on Milwaukee, University of Wisconsin–Milwaukee Libraries, https://uwm.edu/marchonmilwaukee/keyterms/freedom-schools/.

86. "Pegues Thinks Money Pinch to Aid Blacks," *Tulsa World*, September 19, 1971, B1.

87. "Tulsa Race Mix Slight in Schools," *Tulsa Tribune*, April 21, 1970; "Freedom School Opens with 238 Attendance, Needs Funds," *Oklahoma Eagle*, September 16, 1971, 1.

88. Carol Langston, "Freedom School Is Opened," *Tulsa Tribune*, September 1971.

89. Ibid.

90. "Rummage Sale," *Oklahoma Eagle,* November 4, 1971, 7; "Freedom School Candy Sale," *Oklahoma Eagle,* January 13, 1972, 1.

91. "Huge Crowd Warmly Receives Celebrated Actor at Rally," *Oklahoma Eagle,* September 9, 1971, 1.

92. E. L. Goodwin, Jr., "Freedom School Dubbed a Community Must," *Oklahoma Eagle,* December 9, 1971, 1.

93. Langston, "Freedom School Is Open"; "YWCA," *Oklahoma Eagle,* October 14, 1971, 16.

94. "Reopening of Carver Wanted By Any Means," *Oklahoma Eagle,* November 25, 1971, 1; E. L. Goodwin, Jr., "Carver Protesters Jailed; Released," *Oklahoma Eagle,* December 2, 1971, 1.

95. Little, *Fire on Mount Zion,* 83.

96. Ibid., 91.

97. "Board of Education Moves to Reopen Carver, Maybe," *Oklahoma Eagle,* February 10, 1972, 1; "A Sensible Approach," *Oklahoma Eagle,* February 3, 1972, 1.

98. "School Desegregation Plans Aired at Hearing," *Lawton Constitution,* September 23, 1971, 3.

99. *Oklahoma Eagle,* January 27, 1983, 1.

100. "Names, Faces and Interesting Places," *Oklahoma Eagle,* November 11, 1971, 22.

101. "Heroes of Freedom," *Oklahoma Eagle,* February 17, 1972, 1.

102. Mary Garrison to Mabel Little, Notice of Intent to Acquire, October 13, 1975, Parcel No. 10-12-17, Tulsa Urban Renewal Authority Library.

103. Ron Cash to Maria Latimer, Notice of Intent to Acquire, February 6, 1974, Parcel No. 6-55-11 and 6-55-12, Tulsa Urban Renewal Authority Library.

104. "Acquisition and Disposition," *Tulsa Urban Renewal Authority 1975,* 4, Tulsa Urban Renewal Authority Library.

105. Evelyn Lawson, Acquisition Report, October 7, 1970, Parcel No. 10-5-2, Tulsa Urban Renewal Authority Library.

106. Ola Mae Pierro, Acquisition Report, January 8, 1975, Parcel No. 10-2-25, Tulsa Urban Renewal Authority Library.

107. "The Other Side of the Williams Brothers," *Oklahoma Eagle,* December 16, 1971, 15.

108. David M. Breed, "A Sense of Place—North Tulsa Homes," *Oklahoma Eagle,* February 19, 1976, 6.

109. Mabel Little and Tulsa Urban Renewal Authority deed, November 11, 1975, Parcel No. 10-12-1, PartnerTulsa Archives.

110. Breed, "Sense of Place."

111. Little, in *Goin' Back to T-Town.*

112. Hank Moore, "Views on Public Housing, Police," *Oklahoma Eagle,* August 22, 1968, 1.

113. Little, in *Goin' Back to T-Town;* "TURA OKs Greenwood Plan."

114. Paul D. Chapman to Mabel Little, November 11, 1975, Parcel No. 10-12-1, PartnerTulsa Archives.

115. David M. Breed, "An Outstanding Example of Model Cities Methodology on the City," *Oklahoma Eagle*, November 2, 1978, G-11.

116. Catherine Thomas to Model Cities Program, n.d., *Tulsa Model Cities Program*.

117. David M. Breed, "In North Tulsa, at Least, TURA's Not a Dirty Word," *Oklahoma Eagle*, June 13, 1974, 7.

118. Bob Goodwin, conversation with the author, December 18, 2021.

119. R. Allen Hays, *The Federal Government and Urban Housing*, 3rd ed. (Albany: State University of New York Press, 2012), 135.

120. Tulsa Urban Renewal Authority, "Redevelopment," *Tulsa Urban Renewal Authority 1975*, 10, Tulsa Urban Renewal Authority Library.

121. "TURA OKs Greenwood Plan."

122. Tulsa Urban Renewal Authority, "Acquisition and Disposition," *Sixteenth Annual Report*, 1976, 4, Tulsa Urban Renewal Authority Library.

123. Jim Goodwin, conversation with the author, November 9, 2021.

124. Wilbur D. Campbell (Government Accountability Office) to David O. Meeker, Jr., March 28, 1974, https://www.gao.gov/assets/089480.pdf.

125. "TAAG Faces Budget Approval," *Oklahoma Eagle*, June 11, 1970, 1.

126. Frieden and Kaplan, *Politics of Neglect*, 59.

127. Community Planning Associates, *Urban Renewal Handbook* (Tulsa: Tulsa Urban Renewal Authority, ca. 1970), 47.

128. Tulsa Urban Renewal Authority, "Redevelopment," *Tulsa Urban Renewal Authority 1975*, 10; Tulsa Urban Renewal Authority, "Relocation," *Tulsa Urban Renewal Authority 1975*, 6; both in Tulsa Urban Renewal Authority Library.

129. Brian Ford, "State Regents Give Administrative Control to University Center Execs," *Tulsa World*, June 29, 1988, 2.

130. Little, *Fire on Mount Zion*, 98.

131. David M. Breed, "'The First Lady of Greenwood,'" *Oklahoma Eagle*, December 4, 1975, 1.

132. Ibid.

CHAPTER 19: HANDOFFS

1. Bob Goodwin, conversation with the author, December 10, 2021.

2. Regina Goodwin, conversation with the author, August 6, 2020.

3. *Wilbert Montell Brown v. State of Oklahoma*, No. A-16,269 (Okla. Crim. App. 1971); "U.S. Will Fall, Says Speaker," *Daily Oklahoman*, October 16, 1969, 79.

4. "The Goal Is Tragic," *Oklahoma Eagle*, July 7, 1966, 10; Ben H. Hill, "Black Power Movement Due for Fall!" *Oklahoma Eagle*, August 10, 1967, 12.

5. Jim Goodwin, conversation with the author, December 14, 2018.

6. "Defense Ready in Panther Trial," *Lawton Constitution*, February 24, 1970, 2.

7. "Black Panther Given 30 Days, Fine for Speech Made at TU," *Oklahoma Eagle*, February 26, 1970, 1; J. Goodwin conversation.

8. J. Goodwin conversation; *Wilbert Montell Brown v. State of Oklahoma*, 408 U.S. 914 (1972).

9. J. Goodwin conversation.

10. Edwyna Goodwin Anderson, résumé, Jeanne Osby Goodwin Arradondo Family Collection, Nashville, Tenn.; "Service Planned for Longtime Tulsa Teacher," *Tulsa World,* September 28, 2006, https://tulsaworld.com/archive/service-planned-for-longtime-tulsa-teacher/article_912160c1-b11a-5980-a2dc-8b807d66a9d2.html; Jeanne Arradondo, conversation with the author, August 10, 2020; "Carlie Shares Concerns," *Oklahoma Eagle,* July 5, 1973, 6A.

11. B. Goodwin conversation.

12. Ibid.

13. "Golden Anniversary of the Riot" (recording), Mt. Zion Baptist Church, June 1, 1971, Ruth Sigler Avery Collection, Oklahoma State University–Tulsa.

14. B. Goodwin conversation.

15. Ibid.

16. Ibid.

17. Lenore McAllister, "Fish Farm Makes Third Career," *Tulsa World,* November 17, 1974.

18. Chuck Tryon, "Goodwin Katt Farm: 'Haven' for City Fishermen," *Oklahoma Eagle,* July 6, 1978, 2B.

19. McAllister, "Fish Farm Makes Third Career"; Bob Parkhurst, "Goodwin Raises Catfish in Retirement," *Tulsa Tribune,* July 19, 1974, 6C.

20. Regina Goodwin, conversation with the author, August 14, 2020.

21. R. Goodwin conversation, August 6, 2020.

22. R. Goodwin conversation, August 14, 2020.

23. Ibid.; Greg Goodwin, conversation with the author, December 7, 2021.

24. R. Goodwin conversation, August 14, 2020.

25. Greg Goodwin, conversation with the author, July 30, 2019.

26. G. Goodwin conversation, May 30 and December 7, 2021.

27. R. Goodwin conversation, August 6 and 14, 2020.

28. Sabrina Goodwin Monday, conversation with the author, October 11, 2022; Regina Goodwin, conversation with the author, October 23, 2022.

29. R. Goodwin conversation, August 14, 2020.

30. Bob Goodwin, conversation with the author, December 18, 2021; R. Goodwin conversation, October 23, 2022.

31. B. Goodwin conversation, December 18, 2021; G. Goodwin conversation, December 7, 2021.

32. David M. Breed, "A Look at the Life of E. L. Goodwin Sr.," *Oklahoma Eagle,* September 14, 1978, 11.

33. Anna Goodwin, undated recollections of childhood, David Goodwin private collection.

34. "Hundreds Attend Final Rites for Judge Hall," *Oklahoma Eagle,* November 25, 1971, 1; Gene Curtis, "Only in Oklahoma: Judge Led Battle for Desegregation," *Tulsa World,* March 18, 2007, https://tulsaworld.com/archive/only-in-oklahoma-judge-led-battle-for-desegregation/article_7311459c-d351-5413-9acf-64eefe824596.html.

35. Tim Stanley, "Black History Month: Pastor Ben Hill Assumed Leading Role in Tulsa Activism," *Tulsa World,* February 3, 2020, https://tulsaworld.com/news/

local/black-history-month-pastor-ben-hill-assumed-leading-role-in-tulsa
-activism/article_d966e43a-fa40-5c3d-88df-eed12a8330 85.html.

36. Charles J. Jeffrey, Jr., "3000 Mourn Ben Hill," *Oklahoma Eagle,* September 23, 1971, 1.

37. Anna Goodwin, undated recollections of childhood.

38. Ed Goodwin, Sr., interview by Ruth Sigler Avery, November 21, 1976, transcript, Box 2, Ruth Sigler Avery Collection, Oklahoma State University–Tulsa.

39. Ibid.

40. "Carter Stresses Jobs, Bureaucracy Overhaul," *Tulsa World,* January 30, 1976, 4D.

41. "Airplane Leads Klan Procession in Quiet Parade," *Tulsa Daily World,* April 2, 1922, 1.

42. "Best Seller List," *New York Times Book Review,* November 21, 1976, 77.

43. Les Brown, "ABC Took a Gamble with 'Roots' and Is Hitting Paydirt," *New York Times,* January 28, 1977, https://www.nytimes.com/1977/01/28/archives/long-island-opinion-abc-took-a-gamble-with-roots-and-is-hitting.html.

44. Jonathan Franklin, "Here's the Story Behind Black History Month—And Why It's Celebrated in February," NPR, February 1, 2022, https://www.npr.org/2022/02/01/1075623826/why-is-february-black-history-month.

45. Sudeepto Chakraborty, "Dr. Nathan Hare," *Changemakers: Biographies of African Americans in San Francisco Who Made a Difference,* University of San Francisco Blogs, July 3, 2020, https://usfblogs.usfca.edu/sfchangemakers/2020/07/03/dr-nathan-hare/; *Oklahoma Eagle,* September 9, 1971, 10.

46. Rebecca Sharpless, "The History of Oral History," in Thomas L. Charlton, Lois E. Myers, and Rebecca Sharpless, eds., *History of Oral History: Foundations and Methodology* (Lanham, Md.: AltaMira Press, 2007), 13–14.

47. Scrapbook compiled by W. D. Williams, 1924–28, National Museum of African American History and Culture, https://transcription.si.edu/project/37790; Victor Luckerson, "Watching 'Watchmen' as a Descendant of the Tulsa Race Massacre," *New Yorker,* September 20, 2020, https://www.newyorker.com/news/news-desk/watching-watchmen-as-a-descendant-of-the-tulsa-race-massacre.

48. Ibid.

49. Scott Ellsworth, conversation with the author, January 7, 2021.

50. David M. Breed, "Only Whites Make History?" *Oklahoma Eagle,* March 6, 1975, 2.

51. John Hope Franklin and Scott Ellsworth, "History Knows No Fences: An Overview," in *Tulsa Race Riot: A Report by the Oklahoma Commission to Study the Tulsa Race Riot of 1921* (Oklahoma City: Commission, 2001), 26, https://www.okhistory.org/research/forms/freport.pdf.

52. Ellsworth conversation.

53. Ibid.

54. W. D. Williams, interview by Scott Ellsworth, June 7, 1978 (recording), Tulsa Race Massacre of 1921 Archive, University of Tulsa.

55. John Hope Franklin, *Death in a Promised Land: The Tulsa Race Riot of 1921* (Baton Rouge: Louisiana State University Press, 1982), foreword.

56. Luckerson, "Watching 'Watchmen' as a Descendant."

57. Polly Bowen, "Williams Tells Tulsa Past," *Oklahoma Eagle,* April 21, 1977, 1.

58. *Tulsa City Directory, 1979* (Polk-Hoffhine Directory Co.), 324; "North Side of IDL to Open," *Oklahoma Eagle,* April 12, 1973, 8.

59. *Oklahoma Eagle,* August 11, 1977, 3; "Long-time Restaurateur Dies," *Oklahoma Eagle,* September 16, 1982, 1.

60. West Side of 100-Block of Greenwood Avenue, Acquisition Report, April 14, 1977, Parcel No. 25-45-9; East Side of 100-Block of Greenwood Avenue, Acquisition Report, December 14, 1977, Parcel No. 25-46-3; both in Tulsa Urban Renewal Authority Library.

61. Sabrina Goodwin Monday, conversation with the author, October 11, 2022.

62. Holloway, Watkins, & Graham, Inc., *Greenwood Market: Feasibility Analysis* (1979), 5, Tulsa Urban Renewal Authority Library.

63. "Citizens Work While State Loafs," *Oklahoma Eagle,* March 29, 1973, 5B.

64. *Tulsa Urban Renewal Authority 1976,* 6, PartnerTulsa Archives.

65. Don Thompson, conversation with the author, October 19, 2022.

66. Regina Goodwin, conversation with the author, September 3, 2020.

67. Monday conversation; G. Goodwin conversation, December 7, 2021.

68. Greg Goodwin, conversation with the author, December 8, 2022.

69. G. Goodwin conversation, December 7, 2021.

70. R. Goodwin conversation, August 6, 2020.

71. Jeanne B. Goodwin, Acquisition Report, April 19, 1974, Parcel No. 10-5-1, Tulsa Urban Renewal Authority Library.

72. Jimmie Trammel, "Turning the Page: Former Brady Mansion, Now Owned by Retired NFL Player, to Host 'Born on Black Wall Street' Concert, *Tulsa World,* February 8, 2020, https://tulsaworld.com/entertainment/music/turning-the-page-former-brady-mansion-now-owned-by-retired-nfl-player-to-host-born/article_15663f9f-333b-5f82-b368-4e18d6db54f5.html.

73. R. Goodwin conversation, September 3, 2020.

74. "Target Store Grand Opening Sun., April 12," *Oklahoma Eagle,* April 9, 1970, 1; Tim Chavez, "Wal-Mart Readies First Store in City," *Daily Oklahoman,* July 21, 1983, https://www.oklahoman.com/story/news/1983/07/21/wal-mart-readies-first-store-in-city/62837923007/.

75. "Our History," Morton Comprehensive Health Services, https://www.mortonhealth.com/about-us/our-history/.

76. Shalini Ramachandran, "A Century After the Tulsa Massacre, Inequities in Medical Infrastructure Drive Health Gap," *Wall Street Journal,* May 29, 2021, https://www.wsj.com/articles/in-north-tulsa-inequities-in-medical-infrastructure-drive-health-gap-11622293203.

77. James Adrian Ferrell, "A Magnet School and Desegregation: A Case Study of Booker T. Washington High School, 1975–1980," Ph.D. diss., Oklahoma State University, 2008, 25–26.

78. Caleigh Bartash, " 'It's Up to Us to Keep the Flame Burning,' " *Oklahoma Eagle,* July 22, 2022, https://theokeagle.com/2022/07/22/its-up-to-us-to-keep-the-flame-burning/.

79. *Tulsa Urban Renewal Authority 1975,* 6.

80. "A Northside Rebirth: Challenge of the '80s," *Oklahoma Eagle,* January 3, 1980, 1.

81. "Urban Renewal Project," *Oklahoma Eagle,* October 1, 1959, 1.
82. David M. Breed, "City Moves to Close the Books on TAAG," *Oklahoma Eagle,* August 3, 1978, 1.
83. "Protests Mark Allocation of CD Funds," *Oklahoma Eagle,* May 21, 1979, 1.
84. C. E. Christopher, "A Questionable Gift," *Oklahoma Eagle,* January 17, 1980, 8B.
85. Tulsa County, Okla., Deed Book 663, 145, Sheriff's Deed, December 22, 1926.
86. B. L. Robinson, Acquisition Report, June 6, 1977, Parcel No. 25-45-10, Tulsa Urban Renewal Authority Library.
87. David M. Breed, "Goodwin Urges Unity for North Tulsans," *Oklahoma Eagle,* October 11, 1973, 1.
88. "Former Newspaper Chief Is Hospitalized," *Tulsa Tribune,* January 21, 1977.

CHAPTER 20: IN FLESH AND STONE

1. Ed Goodwin, Sr., in "Golden Anniversary of the Riot" (recording), Mt. Zion Baptist Church, June 1, 1971, Ruth Sigler Avery Collection, Oklahoma State University–Tulsa.
2. Jeanne Arradondo, conversation with the author, August 10, 2020.
3. Regina Goodwin, conversation with the author, June 1, 2018.
4. "James Henri Goodwin Among the Black Wall Street's Pioneering Souls," Greenwood Cultural Center, https://www.greenwoodculturalcenter.org/goodwin.
5. Arradondo conversation.
6. Ed Sr. in "Golden Anniversary of the Riot."
7. Carlie M. Goodwin, "A Golden Bond From Heaven," *Oklahoma Eagle,* September 1, 1977, 1; Ann Brown (pseud. for Jeanne Goodwin), "Scoopin' the Scoop," *Oklahoma Eagle,* September 8, 1977, 3.
8. Jim Goodwin, conversation with the author, January 22, 2021.
9. Jo Ann Gilford, conversation with the author, September 11, 2019.
10. Yvonne Nance, " 'God, I'm in Your Hands,' " *Abundant Life Magazine,* April 1970, 20; Bob Goodwin, conversation with the author, December 10, 2021.
11. Nance, " 'God, I'm in Your Hands,' " 23; David Edwin Harrell, Jr., *Oral Roberts: An American Life* (Bloomington: Indiana University Press, 1985), 446–47.
12. Ibid.
13. Arradondo conversation.
14. B. Goodwin conversation; Ed Goodwin, Sr., funeral program, David Goodwin private collection.
15. Arradondo conversation.
16. Bob Goodwin, conversation with the author, January 22, 2022.
17. B. Goodwin conversation, December 10, 2021.
18. Bob Goodwin, in "Golden Anniversary of the Riot."
19. Robert K. Goodwin, "Eulogy, Edward L. Goodwin, Sr.," funeral of Ed Goodwin, Sr., Alsuma, Okla., September 14, 1978.

20. Ed Sr. funeral program.
21. Charles J. Jeffrey Jr., "Humanity of a Leader," *Oklahoma Eagle,* September 14, 1978, 1.
22. David M. Breed, "Caution Urged in Greenwood Renovation Study," *Oklahoma Eagle,* September 14, 1978, 1B.
23. David M. Breed, "Greenwood Clearance Proposed," *Oklahoma Eagle,* July 12, 1979, 1.
24. "N'siders Lambast Renewal Efforts," *Oklahoma Eagle,* May 21, 1979, 8.
25. Homer Johnson and Gerald Wilhite, interview by Clayton Vaughn, KOTV, 1980, Box 3, Ruth Sigler Avery Collection, Oklahoma State University–Tulsa.
26. Holloway, Watkins, and, Graham, Inc., *Greenwood Market: Feasibility Analysis* (1979), 1, Tulsa Urban Renewal Authority Library.
27. Ibid., 42–43.
28. Ibid., iii, 42.
29. Ibid., i.
30. *Tulsa Urban Renewal Authority 1975,* 16–17, Tulsa Urban Renewal Authority Library; Michael Bates, "Forgotten West Tulsa Lives On in Book Form," BatesLine, October 15, 2009, http://www.batesline.com/archives/2009/10/forgotten-west-tulsa-lives-on-in.html; "Tulsa Hotel Sale Near," *Daily Oklahoman,* November 11, 1972, 54.
31. David M. Breed, "Greenwood Project Called 'Feasible,' Faces Uphill Road," *Oklahoma Eagle,* July 19, 1979, 1.
32. Jim Goodwin, conversation with the author, December 13, 2018.
33. James O. Goodwin to Milton Goodwin, October 9, 1979; "Extract from Minutes of TURA Board Meeting Held October 25, 1979"; both in Tulsa Urban Renewal Authority Library.
34. "Greenwood Enterprises, Ltd. Equity Subscriptions," Greenwood Chamber of Commerce, Tulsa Urban Renewal Authority Library.
35. Waldo E. Jones II to Paul Chapman, January 7, 1981; Jerry E. Sutton to Ralph McIntosh, Sr., May 6, 1982; both in Tulsa Urban Renewal Authority Library.
36. Sidney I. Shupack to Ralph McIntosh, October 13, 1981, Tulsa Urban Renewal Authority Library; "The Untold Story: Why the Greenwood Market Fuss," *Oklahoma Eagle,* May 13, 1982, 1.
37. "The Untold Story: Why the Greenwood Market Fuss"; "Black Project Okay, If Blacks Don't Run It," *Oklahoma Eagle,* January 14, 1982.
38. "The Untold Story."
39. "Speech to City Commissioners," *Oklahoma Eagle,* March 4, 1982, 1.
40. Henry Louis Gates, Jr., "What Is Juneteenth?" PBS/African Americans, n.d., https://www.pbs.org/wnet/african-americans-many-rivers-to-cross/history/what-is-juneteenth/.
41. "Big Picnic Week," *Tulsa Star,* June 13, 1913, 1.
42. "Young Negro Democratic Organization," *Oklahoma Eagle,* June 13, 1942, 4.
43. "Greenwood Jubilee," *Oklahoma Eagle,* May 13, 1982, 1.
44. Don Ross, "Pilgrimage to Greenwood Brings 30,000," *Oklahoma Eagle,* June 24, 1982, 1.

45. Regina Goodwin and Sabrina Goodwin, "Volunteers Help Make Greenwood Jubilant," *Oklahoma Eagle,* June 24, 1982, 1.

46. "Black Enrollment at State Universities," *Wichita Eagle,* January 20, 1988, 4D.

47. Regina Goodwin, conversation with the author, September 3, 2020.

48. Goodwin and Goodwin, "Volunteers Help Make Greenwood Jubilant."

49. RaMona Carlin, " 'Mums the Word No More,' " *Oklahoma Eagle,* June 24, 1982, 1.

50. James O. Goodwin, "The Heart of Greenwood," *Oklahoma Eagle,* June 24, 1982, 16.

51. Goodwin and Goodwin, "Volunteers Help Make Greenwood Jubilant."

52. Ross, "Pilgrimage to Greenwood Brings 30,000."

53. Goodwin and Goodwin, "Volunteers Help Make Greenwood Jubilant."

CHAPTER 21: RECONCILIATION DAY

1. Phetote Mshairi, "I Am the Line," *An Old Fart and a Thousand Sentiments* (Tulsa, Okla.: New Greenwood, 2022).

2. Victor Luckerson, "Black Wall Street: The African American Haven That Burned and Then Rose from the Ashes," *Ringer,* June 28, 2018, https://www .theringer.com/2018/6/28/17511818/black-wall-street-oklahoma-greenwood -destruction-tulsa.

3. Joseph Rushmore, "Photo Gallery: Marchers Head from Black Wall Street to Reconciliation Park on 97th Anniversary of Tulsa Race Massacre," *Tulsa World,* May 31, 2018, https://tulsaworld.com/news/photo-gallery-marchers -head-from-black-wall-street-to-reconciliation-park-on-97th-anniversary-of/ collection_ea177858-d0e1-51e0-a325-4d3cae4793d8.html.

4. "Welcome to the 2020 Reconciliation in America National Virtual Sympo- sium," John Hope Franklin Center for Reconciliation, https://www.jhfcenter .org/national-symposium.

5. Harrison Grimwood, "John Hope Franklin Reconciliation Park Dedicated as National Literary Landmark," *Tulsa World,* May 31, 2018; Kevin Can- field, "Five Years Later, City Council Votes to Change M.B. Brady Street to Reconciliation Way," *Tulsa World,* November 28, 2018, https://tulsaworld .com/news/local/five-years-later-city-council-votes-to-change-m-b-brady -street-to-reconciliation-way/article_fd79594b-66c3-53f6-93f0-95fcd29 fba35.html.

6. Center for Poets and Writers at OSU-Tulsa, "We Are Live" (video), Facebook, May 31, 2018, https://www.facebook.com/cpwosutulsa/videos/1883181525 036868/.

7. Mshairi, "I Am the Line."

8. John Hope Franklin Center for Reconciliation, "The DNA of Reconciliation: 2018 John Hope Franklin National Symposium (3 Day Event)," Facebook, May 30–June 1, 2018, https://www.facebook.com/events/170621860248883.

9. Luckerson, "Black Wall Street."

10. "Greenwood Centre Officially Opened," *Oklahoma Eagle,* February 7, 1985, 1.

11. Kesean Cleveland, "Wanda J's Next Generation Restaurant: Fried Flavor on Black Wall Street," *Black Wall Street Times,* June 3, 2022, https://theblackwallsttimes.com/2022/06/03/wanda-js-next-generation-restaurant-fried-flavor-on-black-wall-street/; Mike Simons, "Two Years Ago Today: Black Lives Matter Mural on Greenwood Avenue Removed," *Tulsa World,* October 5, 2022, https://tulsaworld.com/news/local/history/two-years-ago-today-black-lives-matter-mural-on-greenwood-avenue-removed/collection_493f109e-1633-11ec-a217-9f6c107b1ac7.html#19; Tee's: Taryn Johnson, "A Barber and His Place in Greenwood," KOSU, June 14, 2021, https://www.kosu.org/business/2021-06-14/a-barber-and-his-place-in-greenwood.

12. Jim Goodwin, conversation with the author, December 13, 2018; David Goodwin, conversation with the author, November 23, 2022.

13. Albert Lee, "200 Acres Donated for UCT Building Site," *Oklahoma Eagle,* July 24, 1986, 1; "Land Given for Tulsa Campus," *Daily Oklahoman,* May 7, 1986, 14.

14. Jim Killackey, "Tulsa's University Center Hopes It Has 20,000 Students by 2000," *Daily Oklahoman,* July 22, 1984, 18; Robert Lee, "Panelists View Langston's Role," *Oklahoma Eagle,* July 18, 1985, 1; "Why Langston?" Langston University, https://www.langston.edu/.

15. "Group Offers Alternative UCT Land Use Plan," *Oklahoma Eagle,* June 13, 1985, 1.

16. Kevin Canfield, "Tulsa Development Authority Wants Undeveloped UCAT Property to Revert to City," *Tulsa World,* February 3, 2018, https://tulsaworld.com/news/local/education/tulsa-development-authority-wants-undeveloped-ucat-property-to-revert-to-city/article_26d8abec-eed1-5141-a0fb-37e663e86058.html.

17. United States Geological Survey, "High Altitude Aerial Photograph Facing Over North Tulsa, OK" (photograph), September 10, 1967, Tulsa City-County Library.

18. "Big Changes Could Be Coming to OSU-Tulsa, Langston Campus North of Downtown," *Frontier,* April 28, 2016, https://www.readfrontier.org/stories/the-university-center-at-tulsa-was-created-30-years-ago/.

19. Michael D. Bates, "Steps to Nowhere," *This Land,* June 8, 2014, https://thislandpress.com/2014/06/18/steps-to-nowhere/.

20. Brian Barber, "Greenwood Plan Advances," *Tulsa World,* January 22, 2008, https://tulsaworld.com/archive/greenwood-plan-advances/article_0252909b-e7ec-5ae0-8634-b022f20a86db.html.

21. P. J. Lassek, "Drillers Site: Greenwood," *Tulsa World,* June 26, 2008, https://tulsaworld.com/news/local/govt-and-politics/drillers-site-greenwood/article_7b950844-3e2c-56da-adff-8e4c2a4e6884.html; Chris Bouldin, "Drillers Could Anchor $1B Project," *Tulsa World,* September 3, 2007, https://tulsaworld.com/archive/drillers-could-anchor-1b-project/article_53b54983-c20e-58a1-86a8-b6ce2c3e59d8.html.

22. Lassek, "Drillers Site: Greenwood."

23. "About TCF," Tulsa Community Foundation, https://tulsacf.org/about-tcf/then-and-now/; P. J. Lassek, "City Council Has Few Options on Assessment Fees," *Tulsa World,* April 12, 2009, https://tulsaworld.com/news/local/govt-and

-politics/city-council-has-few-options-on-assessment-fees/article_a53cce4c
-aa9b-527e-9f1c-3204ff7e6cb2.html.

24. P. J. Lassek, "Area Around Stadium Key, Aide Says," *Tulsa World,* July 13, 2008, https://tulsaworld.com/news/local/govt-and-politics/area-around -stadium-key-aide-says/article_0b218d70-1cb8-53b8-834a-ae5ba64e7387 .html.

25. George Kaiser Family Foundation, 2019 Form 990 tax filing, November 13, 2020, 2.

26. "It's Official, the *Oklahoma Eagle* Is 100 Years Old," *Oklahoma Eagle,* October 24, 2022, https://theokeagle.com/2022/10/24/its-official-the-oklahoma -eagle-is-100-years-old/.

27. P. J. Lassek, "Councilors May Delay Vote on Financing," *Tulsa World,* July 10, 2008, https://tulsaworld.com/news/local/govt-and-politics/councilors-may -delay-vote-on-financing/article_a101f180-f8c7-5ec9-8768-2cbfa73502eb .html.

28. James O. Goodwin, "Thoughts on the Proposed Baseball Stadium," *Oklahoma Eagle,* July 4, 2008, 1.

29. Lassek, "Drillers Site: Greenwood."

30. Reuben Gant, conversation with the author, December 14, 2018.

31. Jim Goodwin, conversation with the author, December 11, 2022; P. J. Lassek, "Tulsa Drillers Stadium Coming Downtown to Greenwood District," *Tulsa World,* June 25, 2008, https://tulsaworld.com/archive/tulsa-drillers-stadium -coming-downtown-to-greenwood-district/article_c636127b-0d80-587c-a750 -2ce596190597.html.

32. "We Support the Baseball Stadium at Greenwood but Will Tulsa North Be Thrown a Bean Ball?" *Oklahoma Eagle,* July 11, 2008, 4.

33. Tulsa City Council Minutes, July 10, 2008, 5717, Tulsa City Clerk's Office.

34. Joseph Goodwin, "The City of Tulsa's Changing Face—From a Younger Tulsan's Point of View," *Oklahoma Eagle,* July 11, 2018, 4; "Goodwin Birthdays," n.d., David Goodwin personal collection.

35. Kevin Canfield, "Tulsans of the Year: Kajeer Yar and Maggie Yar Dedicated to Seeing Greenwood Flourish," *Tulsa World,* December 5, 2021, https:// tulsaworld.com/lifestyles/magazine/tulsans-of-the-year-kajeer-and-maggie-yar -dedicated-to-seeing-greenwood-flourish/article_eef4f3e2-271c-11ec-be9c -dfec39960089.html; David Harper, "Greenwood Chamber Sues City of Tulsa over Alleged 'Blackballing,' " *Tulsa World,* June 7, 2013, https://tulsaworld .com/archive/greenwood-chamber-sues-city-of-tulsa-over-alleged-blackballing/ article_81a2094f-4565-5ba0-88e5-01b7e199c215.html.

36. Rhett Morgan, "Tulsa Development Authority OKs Ross Group's Mixed-Use Proposal in Greenwood District," *Tulsa World,* February 3, 2017, https:// tulsaworld.com/business/tulsa-development-authority-oks-ross-groups-mixed -used-proposal-in-greenwood-district/article_e772896b-1fa8-5a40-9746 -239e279dff7d.html.

37. Rhett Morgan, "Future Headquarters of Vast Bank Attains Elevated Status with Construction Ceremony," *Tulsa World,* March 1, 2019, https:// tulsaworld.com/business/future-headquarters-of-vast-bank-attains-elevated

-status-with-construction/article_3f58aa44-a9b5-5c34-a8f8-09663b5a8d68
.html.

38. Dylan Goforth, "Missing Markers: As Tulsa Race Massacre Centennial Nears,
Plaques Memorializing Destroyed Businesses Disappear," *Frontier,* February
27, 2019, https://www.readfrontier.org/stories/missing-markers-as-tulsa-race
-massacre-centennial-nears-plaques-memorializing-destroyed-businesses
-disappear/.

39. Rushmore, "Photo Gallery: Marchers Head from Black Wall Street."

40. "John Hope Franklin Reconciliation Park," John Hope Franklin Center for
Reconciliation, https://www.jhfcenter.org/reconciliation-park.

41. Grimwood, "Franklin Reconciliation Park Dedicated."

42. Center for Poets and Writers at OSU-Tulsa, "We Are Live."

43. Nehemiah Frank, "Tulsa Race 'Riot' Commission Is Causing Division in
Tulsa," *Black Wall Street Times,* February 26, 2018, https://
theblackwallsttimes.com/2018/02/26/tulsa-race-riot-commission-is-causing
-division-in-tulsa/.

44. Ibid.

45. "Representative Regina Goodwin," Oklahoma House of Representatives,
https://www.okhouse.gov/members/District.aspx?District=73; "Oklahoma
House of Representatives District 73," Ballotpedia, https://ballotpedia.org/
Oklahoma_House_of_Representatives_District_73.

46. Center for Poets and Writers at OSU-Tulsa, "We Are Live."

47. Regina Goodwin, conversation with the author, September 3, 2020.

48. Regina Goodwin, conversation with the author, August 6, 2020.

49. *Oklahoma Eagle,* April 12, 1979, 1.

50. Regina Goodwin, conversations with the author, February 11, 2019, and November 10, 2020.

51. R. Goodwin conversation, November 10, 2020.

52. R. Goodwin conversation, February 11, 2019.

53. Tulsa County, Okla., Deed Book 4607, 196, Jeanne B. Goodwin and Bob D.
Hale, Robert L. Triplett, Jr., and William J. McPartland, April 9, 1982.

54. Jo Ann Gilford, conversation with the author, August 30, 2022.

55. Carrie Teresa, "The Jim Crow Era Black Press: Of and For Its Readership,"
Organization of American Historians, n.d., https://www.oah.org/tah/issues/
2018/august/the-jim-crow-era-black-press-of-and-for-its-readership/.

56. Karen F. Brown, "The *Oklahoma Eagle*: A Study of Black Press Survival,"
Howard Journal of Communications 1, no. 4 (1988).

57. *Oklahoma Eagle,* May 11, 1978; *Oklahoma Eagle,* December 13, 2001.

58. "The Eagle to Remain Black-Owned," *Oklahoma Eagle,* November 14, 1996,
1; Laurie Winslow, "*Oklahoma Eagle* Files Chapter 11," *Tulsa World,* July 4,
2003, https://tulsaworld.com/archive/oklahoma-eagle-files-chapter-11/article
_aaf0230a-2c7c-5b5b-8a7b-75141e3d1052.html.

59. J. Goodwin conversation, December 13, 2018.

60. Jeanne Arradondo, conversation with the author, August 17, 2020; Sisters Sip-
pin' Tea Reunion Program, April 2005, Jeanne Osby Goodwin Arradondo
Family Collection, Nashville, Tenn.

61. R. Goodwin conversation, November 10, 2020.

62. "Safeway Closing," *Oklahoma Eagle*, January 17, 1980, 20; Michael Overall, "How Did the Crown Jewel of Tulsa Shopping Centers End Up Mostly Empty?" *Tulsa World*, June 13, 2021, https://tulsaworld.com/news/local/ michael-overall-how-did-the-crown-jewel-of-tulsa-shopping-centers-end-up -mostly-empty/article_26704caa-cabf-11eb-8187-d33a7eb5e53a.html; Deon Hampton, "North Tulsa Albertsons Closing," *Tulsa World*, July 4, 2007, https://tulsaworld.com/archive/north-tulsa-albertsons-closing-unsettled -stomachs-some-believe-perception-prices-to-blame/article_dccdbb30-675a -5boe-b29e-9f5ff3b6b4be.html.

63. Karen Shade, "Bringing Back the Big 10," *Tulsa World*, August 17, 2008, https://tulsaworld.com/archive/bringing-back-the-big-10/article_37e627a9 -d188-5a63-962d-e1addcec49a5.html.

64. Greg Goodwin, conversation with the author, July 30, 2019.

65. R. Goodwin conversation, November 10, 2020; Regina Goodwin, conversation with the author, December 10, 2022.

66. Sabrina Goodwin Monday, conversation with the author, October 11, 2022.

67. Regina Goodwin, conversation with the author, February 11, 2019; Kristin Lam and Joshua Bote, "How Did Martin Luther King, Jr. Day Become a Federal Holiday? Here's the History," *USA Today*, January 16, 2020, https://www .usatoday.com/story/news/nation/2020/01/16/mlk-day-martin-luther-king-jr -holiday-monday/2838025001/.

68. Regina Goodwin, conversation with the author, November 19, 2020.

69. Ibid.; R. Goodwin conversation, December 10, 2022.

70. R. Goodwin conversation, February 11, 2019.

71. "Regina Goodwin for State Senate District 11" (video), candidacy announcement, January 30, 2015, https://www.youtube.com/watch?v=WGoOVpTO 9AE.

72. "Regina Goodwin for State Senate District 11 Speaking at Paradise Baptist Church" (video), February 25, 2015, https://www.youtube.com/watch?v= WxpMLDGbA8E; "Regina Goodwin for State Senate District 11 Speaking at Deborah Brown School Black History Program" (video), February 18, 2015, https://www.youtube.com/watch?v=6g3uCQjviP8.

73. "Regina Goodwin for State Senate District 11 speaking at Deborah Brown School Black History Program," video, https://www.youtube.com/watch?v =6g3uCQjviP8&t.

74. "Jo Ann Wins Seat, Sanders Loses 2 to 1," *Oklahoma Eagle*, January 27, 1977, 1; "Achievers," *Oklahoman*, January 7, 2017, https://www.oklahoman .com/story/news/religion/2017/01/07/achievers/60626474007/; "Edwyna Anderson Scored Many 'Firsts' with Grace," *Flint Journal*, n.d., Jeanne Osby Goodwin Arradondo Family Collection.

75. "Jayne Reed and Attorney Jim Goodwin Speaking About Regina Goodwin" (video), March 7, 2015, https://www.youtube.com/watch?v=Jy11vjYba_g.

76. "Kevin Matthews," Ballotpedia, https://ballotpedia.org/Kevin_Matthews.

77. "Regina Goodwin," Ballotpedia, https://ballotpedia.org/Regina_Goodwin.

78. "Historic Members," Oklahoma House of Representatives, https://www .okhouse.gov/Members/Historic.aspx; Robert H. Henry, "Civil Rights Move-

ment," *Encyclopedia of Oklahoma History and Culture,* https://www
.okhistory.org/publications/enc/entry.php?entry=CI010.

79. R. Goodwin, conversation, December 10, 2022.

80. Regina Goodwin, "A Remembrance," *Oklahoma Eagle,* December 17, 2015, 2.

81. J. Kavin Ross, "A Walking, Breathing History Book: Edward Goodwin, Jr., Keeper of Greenwood's Torch Remembered," *Oklahoma Eagle,* July 31, 2014, 2.

82. Regina Goodwin, conversation with the author, August 14, 2020.

83. HB 2383, Oklahoma House of Representatives, 55th Leg., 2nd sess., introduced January 19, 2016, http://webserver1.lsb.state.ok.us/cf_pdf/2015-16 %20INT/hB/HB2383%20INT.PDF; HB 2385, Oklahoma House of Representatives, 55th Leg., 2nd sess., introduced January 19, 2016, http://webserver1 .lsb.state.ok.us/cf_pdf/2015-16%20INT/hB/HB2385%20INT.PDF; HB 2386, Oklahoma House of Representatives, 55th Leg., 2nd sess., introduced January 19, 2016, http://webserver1.lsb.state.ok.us/cf_pdf/2015-16%20INT/hB/ HB2386%20INT.PDF.

84. Oklahoma Policy Institute, *2017 Legislative Primer,* 14.

85. Trevor Brown, "Hundreds of Bills Passed the Legislature. Just a Dozen Were Authored by Democrats," *Oklahoma Watch,* June 2, 2022, https:// oklahomawatch.org/2022/06/02/hundreds-of-bills-passed-the-legislature-just-a -dozen-were-authored-by-democrats/.

86. Oklahoma Policy Institute, *2016 Legislative Primer,* 18–22.

87. Regina Goodwin, conversation with the author, January 18, 2020.

88. Tres Savage, "End of #okleg Session: Lessons Learned on Twitter, Race," NonDoc, May 26, 2017, https://nondoc.com/2017/05/26/okleg-session-lessons -learned/.

89. "Repulsive Racism and Sexism Alive in the State House of Representatives," Oklahoma Democratic Party, May 26, 2017, https://okdemocrats.org/release -odp-repulsive-racism-and-sexism-alive-in-the-state-house-of-representatives/.

90. Savage, "End of #okleg Session."

91. Sarah Stillman, "America's Other Family-Separation Crisis," *New Yorker,* October 29, 2018, https://www.newyorker.com/magazine/2018/11/05/americas -other-family-separation-crisis.

92. "Once Imprisoned, An OSU-Tulsa Graduate Takes on Oklahoma's Female Incarceration Problem," Oklahoma State University–Tulsa, November 25, 2019, https://tulsa.okstate.edu/news/once-imprisoned-osu-tulsa-graduate-takes -oklahoma%E2%80%99s-female-incarceration-problem.

93. Stillman, "America's Other Family-Separation Crisis."

94. Regina Goodwin, conversation with the author, November 24, 2020.

95. Crystal Patrick, *Focus: Black Oklahoma,* Episode 1, Public Radio Tulsa, February 24, 2020, https://www.publicradiotulsa.org/podcast/2020-02-24/focus -black-oklahoma-episode-1.

96. HB 3393, Oklahoma House of Representatives, 56th Leg., 2nd sess., introduced January 18, 2018, http://webserver1.lsb.state.ok.us/cf_pdf/2017-18 %20INT/hB/HB3393%20INT.PDF.

97. Ashley Southall, "She Was Forced to Give Birth in Handcuffs. Now Her Case

Is Changing Police Rules," *New York Times,* July 3, 2019, https://www
.nytimes.com/2019/07/03/nyregion/nypd-pregnant-women-handcuffs.html.

98. Harrison Grimwood and Kyle Lichney, " 'Recipe for Disaster': Oklahoma's Incarceration Rate Now No. 1 in U.S., Study Finds," *Tulsa World,* June 7, 2018,
https://tulsaworld.com/news/local/recipe-for-disaster-oklahomas-incarceration
-rate-now-no-1-in-u-s-study-finds/article_0561c981-5e48-51a0-812e
-19c22b33f55d.html#:~:text=Oklahoma's%20incarceration%20rate%20is
%201%2C079,to%20the%20Prison%20Policy%20Initiative.

99. "Oklahoma No. 2 in the Nation in Overall Incarceration Rate in 2016; No. 1
in Female Incarceration," Oklahoma Department of Corrections, January 13,
2018, https://oklahoma.gov/doc/newsroom/2018/oklahoma-no-2-in-the-nation
-in-incarceration-in-2016.html.

100. R. Goodwin, conversation, December 10, 2022.

101. Randy Krehbiel, "Tulsa Lawmaker Praises New Law That Bars Shackling of
Women Inmates During Childbirth," *Tulsa World,* May 11, 2018, https://
tulsaworld.com/news/local/tulsa-lawmaker-praises-new-law-that-bars
-shackling-of-women-inmates-during-childbirth/article_aa63f037-c407-5aa0
-a4ec-3d874ef3d59d.html.

102. HB 1357, Oklahoma House of Representatives, 56th Leg., 1st sess., introduced January 18, 2017, http://webserver1.lsb.state.ok.us/cf_pdf/2017-18
%20INT/hB/HB1357%20INT.PDF.

103. HB 2253, Oklahoma House of Representatives, 57th Leg., 1st sess., introduced January 17, 2019, http://webserver1.lsb.state.ok.us/cf_pdf/2019-20
%20INT/hB/HB2253%20INT.PDF.

104. State Legislative Effectiveness Scores spreadsheet, Oklahoma, 1993–2018,
Center for Effective Lawmaking; Peter Bucchianeri, Craig Volden, and Alan E.
Weisman, "Legislative Effectiveness in the American States" (working paper),
Center for Effective Lawmaking, September 2020.

105. "Greenwood District License Plates Signed Into Law," *Oklahoma Eagle,*
May 30, 2019.

106. Regina Goodwin, speech at the Black Wall Street Mural dedication ceremony,
Greenwood Cultural Center, June 1, 2018.

107. "Dignitaries to Break Ground for $1.2 Million Greenwood Center," *Okla-
homa Eagle,* August 22, 1985, 1.

108. Ross, *Pillage of Hope,* 135–36; Michelle Brown-Burdex, conversation with the
author, October 12, 2022.

109. *A Century of African American Experience, Greenwood: Ruins, Resilience
and Renaissance,* Greenwood Cultural Center.

110. Samantha Vicent, "Mural Near Greenwood Cultural Center Honors Black
Wall Street," *Tulsa World,* June 1, 2018, https://tulsaworld.com/news/local/
mural-near-greenwood-cultural-center-honors-black-wall-street/article_589ad151
-5847-502a-9dae-b22583fdd352.html.

111. Luckerson, "Black Wall Street."

112. Tiffany Crutcher, conversation with the author, June 1, 2018.

113. Hailey Ferguson, "Community Policing Missteps and the Culture of Superior-
ity Within the Fraternal Order of Police," *Black Wall Street Times,* Decem-

ber 31, 2017, https://theblackwallsttimes.com/2017/12/31/community-policing -missteps-and-the-culture-of-superiority-within-the-fraternal-order-of-police/; Arianna Pickard and Paris Burris, "Rev. Al Sharpton Rallies with Hundreds for Terence Crutcher in Downtown Tulsa," *Tulsa World,* September 28, 2016, https://tulsaworld.com/news/local/rev-al-sharpton-rallies-with-hundreds-for -terence-crutcher-in-downtown-tulsa/article_b4c3fbfe-622b-5a5e-b3f1 -0a71760d551b.html.

114. Samantha Vicent, "Crutcher Family Files Second Wrongful Death Lawsuit Against City of Tulsa," *Tulsa World,* April 5, 2018, https://tulsaworld.com/ news/local/crime-and-courts/crutcher-family-files-second-wrongful-death -lawsuit-against-city-of-tulsa/article_occ37e5c-80b8-5b8b-b732 -1b690510a2b1.html.

115. NAACP Legal Defense and Educational Fund to G. T. Bynum and David Patrick, May 31, 2018.

116. Victor Luckerson, "Tulsa's Hopeful Anger," *New Yorker,* June 16, 2020, https://www.newyorker.com/news/us-journal/tulsas-hopeful-anger.

117. Crutcher conversation.

118. Maxine and Jack Zarrow Family Foundation Gallery of Distinguished Citizens, *The 1921 Race War Survivors,* permanent exhibition, Greenwood Cultural Center.

119. Regina Goodwin, conversation with the author, June 1, 2018.

120. Kelly Kerr, "Suit Filed for Riot Survivors," *Tulsa World,* February 5, 2003, https://tulsaworld.com/archive/suit-filed-for-riot-survivors/article_4134547f -8239-5c91-a1a9-febd9ddd756a.html. Loula Williams's granddaughter Anita Christopher was also a plaintiff in the case.

121. *Alexander v. Oklahoma,* 82 F.3d 1206 (2004).

122. "Judge Nixes Tulsa Race Riot Reparations," Associated Press, March 23, 2004, https://www.nbcnews.com/id/wbna45888836.

123. Brian Ford, "Memories of Riot Evoked as Survivors Win Medals," *Tulsa World,* April 25, 2001, https://tulsaworld.com/archive/memories-of-riot -evoked-as-survivors-win-medals/article_4a6e61e5-2c53-536f-b96b -15652da17ec4.html.

124. R. Goodwin conversation, November 19, 2020.

CHAPTER 22: "TRUST THE SYSTEM"

1. Caleb Gayle, "100 Years After the Tulsa Massacre, What Does Justice Look Like?" *New York Times,* May 25, 2021, https://www.nytimes.com/2021/05/ 25/magazine/tulsa-race-massacre-1921-greenwood.html.

2. Tiffany Crutcher, conversation with the author, June 7, 2020.

3. "Terence Crutcher Was Turning Life Around Before Fatal Tulsa Police Shooting, Family Says," *Chicago Tribune,* September 21, 2016, https://www .chicagotribune.com/nation-world/ct-tulsa-police-shooting-20160921-story .html.

4. Crutcher conversation.

5. Tiffany Crutcher, conversation with the author, June 5, 2020.

6. Kimberly Jackson, "Crutcher Family Finds Peace with Church Family as Betty Shelby Heads to Trial," KTUL, May 9, 2017, https://ktul.com/news/local/crutcher-family-finds-peace-with-church-family-as-betty-shelby-heads-to-trial.

7. Tim Stanley, "Faces of COVID: Leanna Crutcher's 'Quiet Strength' Helped Family Through Loss of Son Terence, Fight for Change That Followed," *Tulsa World,* January 31, 2021, https://tulsaworld.com/news/local/faces-of-covid-leanna-crutchers-quiet-strength-helped-family-through-loss-of-son-terence-fight/article_5ecc6984-6012-11eb-a015-23642ee76a08.html#tncms-source=login.

8. Crutcher conversation, June 7, 2020.

9. "Terence Crutcher Was Turning Life Around."

10. "Tulsa Police Release Audio of 911 Calls Involving the Abandoned Vehicle of Terence Crutcher," KJRH, September 19, 2016, https://www.kjrh.com/news/local-news/tulsa-police-release-audio-of-911-calls-involving-the-abandoned-vehicle-of-terence-crutcher.

11. Liam Stack, "Video Released in Terence Crutcher's Killing by Tulsa Police," *New York Times,* September 19, 2016, https://www.nytimes.com/2016/09/20/us/video-released-in-terence-crutchers-killing-by-tulsa-police.html.

12. "Police Supervisor Told Officer to Say Nothing After Shooting," WTVQ, May 11, 2017, https://www.wtvq.com/police-supervisor-told-officer-to-say-nothing-after-shooting/.

13. "Video Released in Terence Crutcher's Killing."

14. "Protests Underway in Tulsa Over Killing of Terence Crutcher," WBUR, September 20, 2016, https://www.wbur.org/hereandnow/2016/09/20/terence-crutcher-tulsa.

15. Tiffany Crutcher, conversation with the author, June 7, 2020.

16. Francis Dominic Burke, "A Survey of the Negro Community of Tulsa, Oklahoma," master's thesis, University of Tulsa, 1936, 111.

17. Charles J. Jeffrey, "Cops Don't Always Use Brains in Making Arrests," *Oklahoma Eagle,* August 19, 1971, 1.

18. Don Thompson, "Not Enough Officers to Give Citizens Necessary Protection," *Oklahoma Eagle,* October 17, 1963, 1; Hank Moore, "Views on Public Housing, Police," *Oklahoma Eagle,* August 22, 1968, 1.

19. Clayton Bellamy, "Tulsa Settles 1994 Police Discrimination Lawsuit," *Oklahoman,* April 2002, https://www.oklahoman.com/story/news/2002/04/07/tulsa-settles-1994-police-discrimination-lawsuit/62099945007/.

20. Tulsa Equity Indicators, *Annual Report 2018,* 26, https://www.csctulsa.org/wp-content/uploads/2020/10/Tulsa_Equality_Indicators_Annual_Report_2018_Web.pdf.

21. "Video: The Rev. Al Sharpton Speaks at Rally with Terence Crutcher Family," *Tulsa World,* September 26, 2017, https://tulsaworld.com/news/local/video-the-rev-al-sharpton-speaks-at-rally-with-terence-crutcher-family/article_3469ce21-4868-599a-ab36-c14f51f7aa96.html.

22. "Al Sharpton, Benjamin Crump Talk About Terence Crutcher Fatal Shooting" (video), KJRH-TV, https://www.youtube.com/watch?v=UMo5iDJQEH8.

23. Bill Chappell, "Tulsa Police Officer Will Face Manslaughter Charge in Unarmed Man's Death," NPR, September 22, 2016, https://www.npr.org/

sections/thetwo-way/2016/09/22/495079263/tulsa-police-officer-will-face -manslaughter-charge-in-unarmed-mans-death.

24. "From the 60 Minutes Archives: The Terence Crutcher Shooting," *60 Minutes* (video), https://www.youtube.com/watch?v=qVRNmGpjqc8.

25. Dylan Goforth, "Update: Increasingly Emotional Betty Shelby Shown in Dramatic Video Interview with Investigators," *Frontier,* May 11, 2017, https:// www.readfrontier.org/stories/officer-testifies-told-shelby-not-speak-following -shooting1/.

26. Clayton Sandell and Enjoli Francis, "Terence Crutcher Had PCP in System at Time of Fatal Shooting by Tulsa Police, Autopsy Says," ABC News, October 11, 2016, https://abcnews.go.com/US/terence-crutcher-pcp-system-time -fatal-shooting-tulsa/story?id=42735049#:~:text=The%20report%20shows %20that%20Terence,just%2Dreleased%20medical%20examiner's %20report.

27. Goforth, "Increasingly Emotional Shelby."

28. Paris Burris, "Betty Shelby on '60 Minutes': 'I Never Wanted to Kill Anyone,'" *Tulsa World,* April 2, 2017, https://tulsaworld.com/news/local/betty -shelby-on-minutes-i-never-wanted-to-kill-anyone/article_fa3ea361-d4b4-5bc5 -8d67-b2b49ba60499.html.

29. Karma Allen, "Tulsa Police Officer Acquitted in Death of Unarmed African-American Man," ABC News, May 18, 2017, https://abcnews.go.com/US/tulsa -police-officer-acquitted-death-unarmed-african-american/story?id=47480144.

30. Samantha Vicent, "Not Guilty: Betty Shelby Acquitted; Jurors in Tears; Crutcher's Sister Says Police Tried to Cover Up Her Brother's 'Murder,'" *Tulsa World,* May 17, 2017, https://tulsaworld.com/news/local/not-guilty-betty -shelby-acquitted-jurors-in-tears-crutchers-sister-says-police-tried-to-cover/ article_cfdc970b-2b10-5f15-b4c1-711c5da4cc03.html.

31. Aaron Morrison, "Read the Public Letter Jurors Wrote After Acquitting the Tulsa Officer Who Killed Terence Crutcher," *Business Insider,* May 23, 2017, https://www.businessinsider.com/public-letter-from-jurors-betty-shelby-not -guilty-of-manslaughter-terence-crutcher-2017-5.

32. Vicent, "Not Guilty: Shelby Acquitted"; Rhiannon Poolaw, "As Officer Betty Shelby Prepares to Return to Duty, Jurors Express Regret About the Verdict," KSWO, May 19, 2017, https://www.kswo.com/story/35472722/as-officer -betty-shelby-prepares-to-return-to-duty-jurors-express-regret-about-the -verdict/.

33. Vicent, "Not Guilty: Shelby Acquitted."

34. Erik Ortiz and Phil Helsel, "Jury Acquits Tulsa Officer Betty Shelby in Shooting Death of Terence Crutcher," NBC News, May 17, 2017, https://www .nbcnews.com/news/us-news/jury-acquits-tulsa-officer-shooting-death-terence -crutcher-n761206.

35. Dylan Goforth, Kassie McClung, and Kevin Canfield, "Contentious Trial Ends with Acquittal of Embattled Tulsa Police Officer," *Frontier,* May 18, 2017, https://www.readfrontier.org/stories/contentious-trial-ends-acquittal-embattled -tulsa-police-officer/.

36. Terence Crutcher Foundation, *Our Generational Vision for Justice and Liberation,* August 17, 2021, https://www.terencecrutcherfoundation.org/thereport;

Ginnie Graham, "Launch of Terence Crutcher Foundation Coincides with Birthday and Anniversary of His Death," *Tulsa World,* August 14, 2017, https://tulsaworld.com/news/launch-of-terence-crutcher-foundation-coincides -with-birthday-and-anniversary-of-his-death/article_4780ce9b-9577-5a40 -b6de-a78b93eeaba7.html.

37. Harrison Grimwood, " 'The Situation Is Very Ugly': Protest Targets Betty Shelby's Teaching Law Enforcement Training Class," *Tulsa World,* August 27, 2018, https://tulsaworld.com/news/local/the-situation-is-very-ugly-protest -targets-betty-shelbys-teaching-law-enforcement-training-class/article _ef592b5c-4fb9-5ee1-9f4a-543cb21ac559.html.

38. Burt Mummolo, "Citation for Crutcher Legacy Draws Controversy," KTUL, October 30, 2017, https://ktul.com/news/local/citation-for-crutcher-legacy -draws-controversy.

39. Bill Hutchinson and Sabina Ghebremedhin, "Officer Who Killed Unarmed Black Man Responds to Critics of Her 'Critical Incident' Course," ABC News, August 29, 2018, https://abcnews.go.com/US/protest-erupts-critical-incident -class-taught-oklahoma-officer/story?id=57448147.

40. HB 2381, Oklahoma House of Representatives, 55th Leg., 2nd sess., introduced January 19, 2016, http://webserver1.lsb.state.ok.us/cf_pdf/2015-16 %20INT/hB/HB2383%20INT.PDF; HB 2380, Oklahoma House of Representatives, 55th Leg., 2nd sess., introduced January 19, 2016, http://webserver1 .lsb.state.ok.us/cf_pdf/2015-16%20INT/hB/HB2380%20INT.PDF; HB 1361, Oklahoma House of Representatives, 56th Leg., 1st sess., introduced January 18, 2017, http://webserver1.lsb.state.ok.us/cf_pdf/2017-18%20INT/hB/ HB1361%20INT.PDF.

41. Victor Luckerson, "Tulsa's Hopeful Anger," *New Yorker,* June 16, 2020, https://www.newyorker.com/news/us-journal/tulsas-hopeful-anger.

42. *Oversight Agency Directory,* National Association for Civilian Oversight of Law Enforcement, n.d., https://www.nacole.org/oversight_agency_directory.

43. Goforth, "Increasingly Emotional Betty Shelby."

44. Luckerson, "Tulsa's Hopeful Anger."

45. "Bynum Takes Office as Tulsa Mayor," *Journal Record,* December 5, 2016, https://journalrecord.com/2016/12/05/bynum-takes-office-as-tulsa-mayor/; Rick Maranon, "Bynum Announces New Tulsa Community Policing Commission," *Fox 23 News,* December 16, 2016, https://www.fox23.com/news/ bynum-announces-new-tulsa-community-policing-commission/476704206/.

46. G. T. Bynum, "A Republican Mayor's Plan to Replace Partisanship with Policy" (video), TED Talk, https://www.youtube.com/watch?v=CiLn-GrcuEs.

47. Jarrel Wade, "Who Is G. T. Bynum? A Man with Deep Family Roots in Tulsa Politics," *Tulsa World,* May 22, 2016, https://tulsaworld.com/news/local/who -is-g-t-bynum-a-man-with-deep-family-roots-in-tulsa-politics/article_51752dab -21c7-53c1-86dd-1b9218d5cb5e.html; "Throwback Tulsa: Get to Know Our First Mayor Bynum," *Tulsa World,* August 26, 2020, https://tulsaworld.com/ news/local/history/throwback-tulsa-get-to-know-our-first-mayor-bynum/ collection_ee641e99-d324-52cf-bc56-1b699ad48ea0.html#1.

48. DeNeen L. Brown, "Tulsa Mayor Reopens Investigation into Possible Mass Graves from 1921 Race Massacre," *Washington Post,* October 3, 2018,

https://www.washingtonpost.com/local/tulsa-mayor-reopens-investigation-into
-possible-mass-graves-from-1921-race-massacre/2018/10/02/df713c96-c68f
-11e8-b2b5-79270f9cce17_story.html.

49. Tulsa Health Department, *Narrowing the Gap,* May 26, 2015, https://www
.tulsa-health.org/sites/default/files/page_attachments/Life%20Expectancy
%20Report.pdf.

50. Kevin Canfield, "Tulsa Officials Look to Denver as Example of Effective Independent Police Monitoring Program," *Tulsa World,* January 27, 2019, https://
tulsaworld.com/news/local/tulsa-officials-look-to-denver-as-example-of
-effective-independent/article_6bb331eb-6d8a-5e27-966e-f1b32c42a7e2.html.

51. Associated Press, "Mayor Setting Up Office to Monitor Police Force," *Journal
Record,* January 21, 2019, https://journalrecord.com/2019/01/21/mayor
-setting-up-office-to-monitor-police-force/.

52. Kevin Canfield, "Police Use-of-Force Incidents Need Outside Scrutiny, Mayor
Says in Proposing Independent Monitor," *Tulsa World,* January 17, 2019,
https://tulsaworld.com/news/local/police-use-of-force-incidents-need-outside
-scrutiny-mayor-says-in-proposing-independent-monitor/article_652210a1
-df63-5ed1-9866-2db2d24dd5df.html.

53. Tiffany Crutcher, conversation with the author, June 7, 2020.

54. Tim Talley, "Oklahoma Dedicates Capitol Dome," *Edwardsville Intelligencer*
(Ill.), November 15, 2002, https://www.theintelligencer.com/news/article/
Oklahoma-Dedicates-Capitol-Dome-10549195.php; "Dome Donors Recognized in Ring of Honor," *News on 6,* September 29, 2002, https://www
.newson6.com/story/5e3682212f69d76f620969de/dome-donors-recognized-in
-ring-of-honor; Tom Lindley, "Capitol's Dome Turns Heads," *Oklahoman,*
February 15, 2004, https://www.oklahoman.com/story/news/2004/02/15/
capitols-dome-turns-heads/62002715007/.

55. Janice Francis-Smith, "Petunia #1 Will Remain at Oklahoma Capitol; Empty
Tanks Gone," *Journal Record,* September 30, 2021, https://journalrecord.com/
2021/09/30/petunia-1-will-remain-at-oklahoma-capitol-empty-tanks-gone/.

56. Michael L. Bruce, "Hamlin, Albert Comstock (1881–1912)," *Encyclopedia of
Oklahoma History and Culture,* https://www.okhistory.org/publications/enc/
entry.php?entry=HA015.

57. Robert H. Henry, "Civil Rights Movement," *Encyclopedia of Oklahoma History and Culture,* https://www.okhistory.org/publications/enc/entry.php?entry
=CI010; "Baker v. Carr," *Encyclopaedia Britannica,* July 20, 1998, https://
www.britannica.com/event/Baker-v-Carr; Mick Hinton, "Young, Minority
Lawmakers Highlight Changes," *Tulsa World,* February 4, 2007, https://
tulsaworld.com/archive/young-minority-lawmakers-highlight-changes/article
_ea5d3140-3eb5-5360-8967-8ebc6e034b34.html.

58. Chris Brown during Interim Study on Law Enforcement Reform, Oklahoma
Legislature, House, 58th Leg., 2nd sess., October 6, 2020.

59. Ibid.

60. HB 3515, Oklahoma House of Representatives, 55th Leg., 2nd sess., introduced January 16, 2020, http://webserver1.lsb.state.ok.us/cf_pdf/2019-20
%20INT/hB/HB3515%20INT.PDF.

61. "New Law Enforcement Body Camera Bill Sparks Debate," KJRH, January

21, 2020, https://www.kjrh.com/news/local-news/new-law-enforcement-body
-camera-bill-sparks-debate.

62. Jonathan Cooper, "Proposed Oklahoma Bill Would Require Officer Body
Cams On at All Times," *News 9*, January 27, 2020, https://www.news9.com/
story/5e370be273ed4c0f33ed9705/proposed-oklahoma-bill-would-require
-officer-body-cams-on-at-all-times.

63. "Public Safety Committee, Oklahoma House of Representatives," Ballotpedia,
updated March 2021, https://ballotpedia.org/Public_Safety_Committee,
_Oklahoma_House_of_Representatives. The following sources all come from
the Oklahoma Ethics Commission: Toni Hasenbeck Contributions and Expenditures Report for Q4 2019, January 31, 2020; Jay Steagall Contributions and
Expenditures Report for 2020 Pre-General, October 26, 2020; Tammy Town-
ley Contributions and Expenditures Report for Q4 2019, January 8, 2020;
Ben Loring Contributions and Expenditures Report for Q1 2017, April 15,
2017; Robert Manger, Contributions and Expenditures Report for Q1 2020,
April 30, 2020; Justin Humphrey, Contributions and Expenditures Report for
Q4 2019, January 31, 2020.

64. Justin Humphrey Contributions and Expenditures Report for Q1 2020, Oklahoma Ethics Commission, April 30, 2020.

65. Regina Goodwin, conversation with the author, November 24, 2020; Tulsa
Fraternal Order of Police Political Action Committee Contribution and Expenditures Report, Oklahoma Ethics Commission, April 21, 2016.

66. Regina Goodwin, conversation with the author, ca. February 2022.

67. Deliberation on HB 3515 Before the Public Safety Committee, Oklahoma
House of Representatives, 58th Leg., 2nd sess., February 20, 2020.

68. Randy Krehbiel, "Oklahoma House Committee Expands Stand-Your-Ground
Law, Preserves Permitless Carry," *Tulsa World*, February 20, 2020, https://
tulsaworld.com/news/oklahoma-house-committee-expands-stand-your-ground
-law-preserves-permitless-carry/article_89706720-e73d-5ba3-aea6-434fb0ad
283c.html.

69. Deliberation on HB 3515 Before the Public Safety Committee.

70. Ibid.

71. Regina Goodwin, conversation with the author, February 20, 2020.

72. Adriana Laws, conversation with the author, February 20, 2020.

73. HB 3548, Oklahoma House of Representatives, 57th Leg., 2nd sess., introduced January 16, 2020, http://webserver1.lsb.state.ok.us/cf_pdf/2019-20
%20INT/hB/HB3548%20INT.PDF.

74. Regina Goodwin, conversation with Rose State College students (recording),
Oklahoma State Capitol, February 20, 2020.

75. Ibid.

76. Laws conversation.

77. R. Goodwin conversation with Rose State students.

78. Laws conversation.

79. Ibid.

80. Kevin Canfield, "Police Union to Bynum: Negotiate with FOP to Create Independent Monitor or Face Lawsuit," *Tulsa World*, January 26, 2019, https://

tulsaworld.com/news/local/police-union-to-bynum-negotiate-with-fop-to
-create-independent/article_dabcc070-65f2-5e86-a3d7-96a87eed2127.html.

81. Noam Scheiber, Farah Stockman, and J. David Goodman, "How Police
Unions Became Such Powerful Opponents to Reform Efforts," *New York
Times,* June 6, 2020, https://www.nytimes.com/2020/06/06/us/police-unions
-minneapolis-kroll.html.

82. Kevin Canfield, "Mayor Unveils Ordinance to Create Independent Office to
Review Police Use-of-Force Incidents," *Tulsa World,* July 31, 2019, https://
tulsaworld.com/news/mayor-unveils-ordinance-to-create-independent-office-to
-review-police-use-of-force-incidents/article_a3060f91-9f6f-5400-9c5a-c8d
1ca5b3b86.html.

83. Meeting between Mayor G. T. Bynum and North Tulsa community leaders,
June 1, 2020, City Hall, Tulsa.

84. Crutcher conversation, June 7, 2020.

85. Ibid.; "Mayor G. T. Bynum Pulls Plans for an Office of Independent Monitor,"
KJRH, September 7, 2019, https://www.kjrh.com/news/local-news/mayor-g-t
-bynum-pulls-plans-for-an-office-of-independent-monitor; meeting between
Mayor Bynum and North Tulsa community leaders.

86. Kevin Canfield, "Majority of Councilors Support Putting Police Oversight
Monitor to a Vote of the People," *Tulsa World,* February 28, 2020, https://
tulsaworld.com/news/local/majority-of-councilors-support-putting-police
-oversight-monitor-to-a/article_8c8d6d08-ae16-5ef5-a20b-4ab54c54dfd8
.html.

87. Tulsa Fraternal Order of Police 93 PAC Contributions and Expenditures Report for Q3 2018, Oklahoma Ethics Commission, October 23, 2018.

88. Kevin Canfield, "How Tulsa's Police Union Tries to Win Elections and Influence People," *Tulsa World,* December 7, 2020, https://tulsaworld.com/news/
local/how-tulsas-police-union-tries-to-win-elections-and-influence-people/
article_1ac034c0-34c8-11eb-bda1-9f3c691e8857.html.

89. Kevin Canfield, "Police Union Leader Explains How Organization 'Flipped
the Vote' on City Council's Oversight Proposal," *Tulsa World,* June 14, 2020,
https://tulsaworld.com/news/local/government-and-politics/police-union-leader
-explains-how-organization-flipped-the-vote-on-city-councils-oversight
-proposal/article_55b65dd9-2856-5008-9180-6b1783d73053.html.

90. Kevin Canfield, "Latest Proposal for Tulsa Police Oversight Dies in City
Council Procedural Vote," *Tulsa World,* March 5, 2020, https://tulsaworld
.com/news/local/govt-and-politics/latest-proposal-for-tulsa-police-oversight
-dies-in-city-council-procedural-vote/article_6cca9665-1495-5c99-9e2d
-de85e91fe311.html.

91. Hannah Jarman, "Dr. Crutcher's Personal Journey Toward Justice & Reconciliation," Terence Crutcher Foundation, https://www.terencecrutcherfoundation
.org/news/https-terencecrutcherfoundation-org-news-f-dr-crutcher-e2-80-99s
-personal-journey-towards-justice-reconciliation.

92. Crutcher conversation, June 5, 2020.

CHAPTER 23: THIS IS OUR TIME

1. Tiffany Crutcher, conversation with the author, June 5, 2020.

2. Ibid.

3. Tiffany Crutcher, "Rioting Is the Language of the Unheard" (post), Facebook, May 28, 2020, https://www.facebook.com/tiffany.crutcher.73/posts/102226 46769543047; Tiffany Crutcher, "For Those Reaching Out to Me" (post), Facebook, May 27, 2020, https://www.facebook.com/tiffany.crutcher.73/posts/ 10222630551137597.

4. Derrick Bryson Taylor, "George Floyd Protests: A Timeline," *New York Times,* November 21, 2021, https://www.nytimes.com/article/george-floyd -protests-timeline.html.

5. Debbie Elliott, "Brunswick, Georgia Prepares for the Trial in the Killing of Ahmaud Arbery," NPR, October 25, 2021, https://www.npr.org/2021/10/15/ 1046279399/brunswick-georgia-prepares-for-the-trial-in-the-killing-of-ahmaud -arbery; Sudhin Thanawala, "Protests, Some Violent, Spread in Wake of George Floyd Death," Associated Press, May 30, 2020, https://apnews.com/ article/nv-state-wire-az-state-wire-co-state-wire-fl-state-wire-virus-outbreak -baf3b29612527b8e9a841cb34f6f5789.

6. Mike Baker, "7 People Shot at Louisville Protest Over the Death of Breonna Taylor," *New York Times,* May 29, 2020, https://www.nytimes.com/2020/05/ 29/us/louisville-protest-shooting-breonna-taylor.html.

7. Norvell Coots, conversation with the author, February 27, 2021.

8. Jarrel Wade, "President Obama Calls Tulsa Mayor Dewey Bartlett to Discuss City's Response To Fatal Police Shooting," *Tulsa World,* September 22, 2016, https://tulsaworld.com/news/local/president-obama-calls-tulsa-mayor-dewey -bartlett-to-discuss-citys-response-to-fatal-police-shooting/article_32ea6816 -8929-56e2-961a-b86c585838fa.html.

9. North Tulsa ministers and community leaders, press conference, North Peoria Church of Christ, May 28, 2020.

10. Crutcher conversation.

11. Nehemiah Frank, "Tulsa Race 'Riot' Commission Is Causing Division in Tulsa," *Black Wall Street Times,* February 26, 2018; Kendrick Marshall, "Tulsa Race Massacre: For Years It Was Called a Riot. Not Anymore. Here's How It Changed," *Tulsa World,* May 31, 2020, https://tulsaworld.com/news/ local/racemassacre/tulsa-race-massacre-for-years-it-was-called-a-riot-not -anymore-heres-how-it/article_47d28f77-2a7e-5b79-bf5f-bdfc4d6f976f.html.

12. Mary Jones Parrish, *Events of the Tulsa Disaster* (Tulsa, ca. 1923), 98.

13. Nehemiah Frank, conversation with the author, May 31, 2018.

14. *Black Wall Street Times* et al., "We Can't Breathe—Peaceful Protest" (post), Facebook, https://www.facebook.com/events/480807889354857.

15. Crutcher conversation.

16. Victor Luckerson, "Tulsa's Hopeful Anger," *New Yorker,* June 16, 2020, https://www.newyorker.com/news/us-journal/tulsas-hopeful-anger.

17. Tiffany Crutcher, "Tulsa Has Shut Down South Peoria at Brookside" (video post), Facebook, May 30, 2020, https://www.facebook.com/tiffany.crutcher .73/videos/10222661902961373/.

18. Luckerson, "Tulsa's Hopeful Anger."
19. Ibid.
20. Crutcher, "Tulsa Has Shut Down South Peoria."
21. Greg Robinson, conversation with the author, June 3, 2020.
22. "Activist, Ex-candidate Greg Robinson Dies," *Tulsa World,* January 24, 2003, https://tulsaworld.com/archive/activist-ex-candidate-greg-robinson-dies/article_b8047be5-ff00-5aeb-af53-327c345da12c.html.
23. Greg Robinson, conversation with the author, June 3, 2020.
24. Luckerson, "Tulsa's Hopeful Anger."
25. Crutcher conversation.
26. "Albany Movement," Martin Luther King, Jr., Research and Education Institute, November 17, 1961, https://kinginstitute.stanford.edu/encyclopedia/albany-movement.
27. Crutcher, "Tulsa Has Shut Down South Peoria."
28. Hicham Raache, "Protester Hit by Vehicle During Protest in Tulsa over George Floyd's Death," KFOR, May 30, 2020, https://kfor.com/news/local/protester-hit-by-vehicle-during-protest-in-tulsa-over-george-floyds-death/.
29. Luckerson, "Tulsa's Hopeful Anger."
30. Ibid.
31. Mayor G. T. Bynum, "I Ran for Mayor Because" (post), Facebook, May 30, 2020, https://www.facebook.com/gtbynumfortulsamayor/posts/pfbid02sowo8owrACfmK7V3pQh4f4ZgYGjgmdhsjQ4zfDMKwNNCWFgZTkHFfed9rkxx9QLTl.
32. Luckerson, "Tulsa's Hopeful Anger."
33. Tim Landes, "Scenes from Sunday's Black Lives Matter Rally and Protests," June 1, 2020, https://www.tulsapeople.com/the-voice/scenes-from-sundays-black-lives-matter-rally-and-protests/collection_03e2e156-a41a-11ea-a0a5-ab6bab37ee38.html.
34. Nkem Ike, conversation with the author, July 24, 2020.
35. Ian Maule and Mike Simons, "Photos: 2020 Protests in Tulsa End with Tear Gas, Pepper Balls After Truck Drove Through Crowd," *Tulsa World,* June 1, 2020, https://tulsaworld.com/news/photos-2020-protests-in-tulsa-end-with-tear-gas-pepper-balls-after-truck-drove-through/collection_83e1959f-2ee1-5397-bc13-dcd09b1be4ee.html#1.
36. "More National Guard Troops Heading to Seattle, Governor Says," *Honolulu Star-Advertiser,* May 31, 2020, https://www.staradvertiser.com/2020/05/31/breaking-news/more-national-guard-troops-heading-to-seattle-governor-says/.
37. Rose Semenov, "1 Year Since Third Precinct Building Burned in Minneapolis," *Fox9,* May 28, 2021, https://www.fox9.com/news/1-year-since-the-fall-of-third-precinct-in-minneapolis; Phil Helsel, "Large Truck Drives Through Crowd of Protesters in Minneapolis," NBC News, May 31, 2020, https://www.nbcnews.com/news/us-news/large-truck-drives-through-crowd-protesters-minneapolis-n1220586.
38. Tom Gjelten, "Peaceful Protesters Tear-Gassed to Clear Way for Trump Church Photo-Op," NPR, June 1, 2020, https://www.npr.org/2020/06/01/867532070/trumps-unannounced-church-visit-angers-church-officials.
39. Nolan Clay, "Black Lives Matter Protest over Criminal Charges Planned in

OKC," *Oklahoman*, July 2, 2020, https://www.oklahoman.com/story/news/columns/2020/07/02/protest-over-criminal-charges-planned/60393716007/.

40. Jarrel Wade, "Tulsa City Hall Down to Last 5 Percent of Unleased Space," *Tulsa World*, August 31, 2020, https://tulsaworld.com/news/local/tulsa-city-hall-down-to-last-5-percent-of-unleased-space/article_2d6bde6b-2ed3-58ec-8f5c-67f9e9ddbe6b.html; Kendra Blevins, "A Greener City Hall," *Tulsa People*, May 24, 2010, https://www.tulsapeople.com/a-greener-city-hall/article_4a7a941a-4929-5ed0-afbe-c882acee3609.html.

41. Meeting between Mayor G. T. Bynum and North Tulsa community leaders, June 1, 2020, City Hall, Tulsa.

42. Ibid.; "Tulsa Mayor Agrees to Not Renew Live PD Contract After Meeting with Protest Organizers," *News on 6*, June 1, 2020, https://www.newson6.com/story/5ed56521311afe409f0454b9/tulsa-mayor-agrees-to-not-renew-live-pd-contract-after-meeting-with-protest-organizers; Sarah Whitten, " 'Live P.D.' Canceled by A&E Following Report That the Reality Show Filmed Police Custody Death," CNBC, June 11, 2020, https://www.cnbc.com/2020/06/11/live-pd-canceled-over-report-that-show-filmed-police-custody-death.html.

43. Luckerson, "Tulsa's Hopeful Anger."

44. Mary Raffalli, "How an Act of Racial Violence Reverberates Across Generations," CBS News, June 7, 2020, https://www.cbsnews.com/news/tulsa-1921-how-an-act-of-racial-violence-reverberates-across-generations/.

45. Bynum, "I Ran for Mayor Because."

46. David K. Li, "African Americans 'Probably Ought to Be' Shot More by Police, a Top Tulsa Officer Said," NBC News, June 11, 2020, https://www.nbcnews.com/news/us-news/african-americans-probably-ought-be-shot-more-police-top-tulsa-n1229981.

47. Aya Elamroussi, "Jaywalking Arrest of 2 Black Teens in Oklahoma Under Review," Associated Press, June 10, 2020, https://apnews.com/article/343acad7175ba4be4e300e56d099f8ca.

48. *Black Wall Street Times*, "Greg Robinson II Announces Historic Candidacy for Mayor of Tulsa" (video post), Facebook, June 10, 2020, https://tinyurl.com/bddmxvws.

49. Tiffany Crutcher, conversation with the author, June 12, 2020.

50. "Trump Picks Tulsa on Juneteenth for Return to Campaign Rallies," NBC News, June 10, 2020, https://www.nbcnews.com/politics/donald-trump/trump-picks-tulsa-juneteenth-return-campaign-rallies-n1229681.

51. Ibid.

52. Audra D. S. Burch et al., "How Black Lives Matter Reached Every Corner of America," *New York Times*, June 13, 2020, https://www.nytimes.com/interactive/2020/06/13/us/george-floyd-protests-cities-photos.html.

53. Maggie Haberman, *Confidence Man: The Making of Donald Trump and the Breaking of America* (New York: Penguin, 2022), 443–49.

54. Glenn Kessler, "The 'Very Fine People' at Charlottesville: Who Were They?" *Washington Post*, May 8, 2020, https://www.washingtonpost.com/politics/2020/05/08/very-fine-people-charlottesville-who-were-they-2/; Isabel Soisson, "LeBron James Fires Back at Trump After Insult: 'You Really Got This Much Time That You Can Comment on Me?' " CNBC, September 18, 2018, https://

www.cnbc.com/2018/09/20/lebron-james-fires-back-at-president-trump-after
-insult.html; John Raphling, "Is Trump Protecting Police from Harm or Oversight?" *Hill,* February 16, 2017, https://thehill.com/blogs/pundits-blog/crime/
319889-is-trump-protecting-us-police-from-harm-or-oversight/.

55. "Charlottesville Mourns Woman Killed in Rally That Turned Violent," *Washington Post,* August 16, 2017, https://www.washingtonpost.com/lifestyle/
kidspost/charlottesville-mourns-woman-killed-in-rally-that-turned-violent/
2017/08/16/29975362-8296-11e7-902a-2a9f2d808496_story.html.

56. Tiffany Crutcher, conversation with the author, July 26, 2020.

57. Astead W. Herndon, "Black Tulsans, with a Defiant Juneteenth Celebration,
Send a Message to Trump," *New York Times,* June 19, 2020, https://www
.nytimes.com/2020/06/19/us/politics/juneteenth-tulsa-trump-rally.html.

58. Tiffany Crutcher, conversation with author, July 26, 2020.

59. Victor Luckerson, "In Tulsa, an Energized Juneteenth Celebration Focusses on
Change, Not Trump," *New Yorker,* June 20, 2020, https://www.newyorker
.com/news/dispatch/in-tulsa-an-energized-juneteenth-celebration-focusses-on
-change-not-trump.

60. Ryan Rhoades, conversation with the author, July 31, 2020; Fenit Nirappil,
Julie Zauzmer Weil, and Rachel Chason, " 'Black Lives Matter': In Giant Yellow Letters, D.C. Mayor Sends Message to Trump," *Washington Post,* June 5,
2020; https://www.washingtonpost.com/local/dc-politics/bowser-black-lives
-matter-street/2020/06/05/eb44ff4a-a733-11ea-bb20-ebf0921f3bbd_story
.html; Michael Tomberlin, "Black Lives Matter Street Painting Complete at
Birmingham Railroad Park," *Alabama NewsCenter,* June 18, 2020, https://
alabamanewscenter.com/2020/06/18/black-lives-matter-street-painting
-complete-at-birmingham-railroad-park/; Roz Plater and Brendan Weber,
"Black Lives Matter Mural Painted on San Francisco Street," *NBC Bay Area,*
June 12, 2020, https://www.nbcbayarea.com/news/local/black-lives-matter
-mural-painted-on-san-francisco-street/2308590/.

61. Luckerson, "In Tulsa, an Energized Juneteenth."

62. Nehemiah Frank, conversation with the author, July 22, 2020.

63. *Black Wall Street Times,* June 19, 2020, 1.

64. Frank conversation, July 22, 2020.

65. Erik Byrd, conversation with the author, June 19, 2020.

66. Cherrelle Swain, conversation with the author, June 19, 2020.

67. Luckerson, "In Tulsa, an Energized Juneteenth."

68. Kevin Canfield, "Bynum Says He Told BOK Center Officials He Would Back
Decision Not to Hold Trump's Rally," *Tulsa World,* June 23, 2020, https://
tulsaworld.com/news/bynum-says-he-told-bok-center-officials-he-would-back
-decision-to-not-hold-trump/article_49fc5f89-eb16-5c71-96c1-9d5158056e6f
.html.

69. Luckerson, "In Tulsa, an Energized Juneteenth."

70. Adriana Laws, conversation with the author, July 22, 2020; Bryan Terry,
"Trump in Tulsa: Protester Arrested Outside BOK Center: Article Photos,"
Daily Oklahoman, https://web.archive.org/web/20210116121401/https://
oklahoman.com/gallery/articleid/5665052.

71. Laws conversation.

72. "Trump Warns Protesters to Face 'Different Scene' at His Oklahoma Rally," Reuters, June 19, 2020.
73. Laws conversation.
74. "Trump in Tulsa: Protester Arrested: Article Photos."
75. Laws conversation.
76. Black Wall Street Times, "Descendants of the Greenwood Community and Allies" (video post), Facebook, June 20, 2020, https://www.facebook.com/TheBWSTimes/videos/845421139315499/.
77. Frank conversation, July 22, 2020; Crutcher conversation, July 26, 2020.
78. Victor Luckerson, photograph of Black Wall Street memorial, June 20, 2020.
79. Tyrance Billingsley, conversation with the author, August 28, 2020.
80. Greg Robinson, conversation with the author, June 20, 2020.
81. "Oklahoma State Rep. Regina Goodwin on Trump's Visit to Tulsa," NPR, June 20, 2020, https://www.npr.org/2020/06/20/881285814/oklahoma-state-rep-regina-goodwin-on-trumps-visit-to-tulsa.
82. Jim Goodwin, conversation with the author, July 18, 2020.
83. Regina Goodwin, conversation with the author, June 20, 2020.
84. Victor Luckerson, "The Story of Black Wall Street #012: Black Patriots," Run It Back, June 25, 2020, https://runitback.substack.com/p/012-black-patriots.
85. Laws conversation.
86. Luckerson, "Story of Black Wall Street #012."
87. "Trump in Tulsa: Protester Arrested: Article Photos."
88. Ibid.
89. Laws conversation.
90. Yatika Starr Fields, conversation with the author, August 11, 2020.
91. Billingsley conversation.
92. Giovanni Russonello, "Trump's Tulsa Rally Attendance: 6,200, Fire Dept. Says," New York Times, June 22, 2020, https://www.nytimes.com/2020/06/22/us/politics/trump-rally-coronavirus.html.
93. Black Wall Street Times, untitled (video post), Facebook, June 20, 2020, https://www.facebook.com/TheBWSTimes/videos/296773664689793/.
94. Randy R. Potts and Victor Luckerson, "A Trump Visit Lays Bare Two Tulsas, a Mile and a Universe Apart," New Yorker, June 21, 2020, https://www.newyorker.com/news/dispatch/a-trump-visit-lays-bare-two-tulsas-a-mile-and-a-universe-apart.
95. Laws conversation.
96. Billingsley conversation.
97. Ibid.
98. "Donald Trump Tulsa, Oklahoma Rally Speech Transcript," Rev, June 21, 2020, https://www.rev.com/blog/transcripts/donald-trump-tulsa-oklahoma-rally-speech-transcript.
99. Jonathan Karl, "Lawsuit Threats, Empty Seats, and a 'COVID Mobile': Trump's Disastrous Tulsa Rally Was Even More of a Train Wreck than Originally Thought," Vanity Fair, November 11, 2021, https://www.vanityfair.com/news/2021/11/trumps-disastrous-tulsa-rally-was-even-more-of-a-train-wreck-than-originally-thought.
100. Laws conversation.

101. Potts and Luckerson, "Trump Visit Lays Bare Two Tulsas."
102. Ibid.
103. Billingsley conversation.
104. Greg Robinson, conversation with the author, June 3, 2020.
105. Billingsley conversation.

CHAPTER 24: DISSOLUTION

1. "Greenwood Rising Groundbreaking" (video), *Tulsa World*, August 22, 2020, https://tulsaworld.com/greenwood-rising-groundbreaking/video_f302e5c2 -5758-5a1c-a5ae-2d75d933ebbc.html.
2. Brandy McDonnell, "101 Years After Tulsa Race Massacre, Crowds Flock to Black Wall Street History Center," *Oklahoman*, May 30, 2022, https://www .oklahoman.com/story/entertainment/2022/05/30/greenwood-rising-teaches -tulsa-race-massacre-oklahomas-black-history/9651603002/?gnt-cfr=1.
3. Amy Hybels, "New Greenwood Development Set to Open Its Doors in June," *Fox 23 News*, March 10, 2022, https://www.fox23.com/news/21-n-greenwood -development-set-open-its-doors-june/UADKDRYF2FEUBOLR67RFQ6RL7I/; Matt Hickman, "Up From the Ashes," *Architect's Newspaper*, May 4, 2021, https://www.archpaper.com/2021/05/new-history-center-in-tulsa-greenwood -recounts-a-grievous-past/.
4. 1921 Tulsa Race Massacre Centennial Commission, *Greenwood Rising*, https://www.greenwoodrisingxr.com/about.html; Randy Krehbiel, "Tulsa Race Riot Centennial Commission Announced," *Tulsa World*, February 25, 2017, https://tulsaworld.com/news/local/tulsa-race-riot-centennial-commission -announced/article_0d2b43c2-1ef4-59f3-a21a-d9c0a6b90d8a.html.
5. Kevin Matthews, conversation with the author, December 13, 2018.
6. Krehbiel, "Tulsa Race Riot Centennial Commission"; Michael Mason, "The Kaiser System," *Medium*, https://michaelpaulmason.medium.com/the-kaiser -system-e8c14bca395.
7. Kevin Canfield, " 'One of Our Greatest Gifts If We Just Tell the Story': Fund-raising Campaign Aims to Expand, Remodel Greenwood Cultural Center," *Tulsa World*, April 1, 2019, https://tulsaworld.com/news/local/one-of-our -greatest-gifts-if-we-just-tell-the-story-fundraising-campaign-aims-to/article _b7cddod2-9756-57fb-a898-a7939c681b52.html.
8. Kevin Canfield, "Greenwood Investors Happy to Help City Find New Home for Greenwood Rising History Center," *Tulsa World*, May 2, 2020, https:// tulsaworld.com/news/local/greenwood-investors-happy-to-help-city-find-new -home-for-greenwood-rising-history-center/article_d29e9b5b-5b5c-51af-9193 -fda16364b77a.html.
9. Tulsa County, Oklahoma, Memorandum of Development Agreement Between 21 NG Developer and TCF Developer, Document No. 2020041243, May 7, 2020.
10. Campbell Robertson and Audra D. S. Burch, "Anniversary Event for Tulsa Race Massacre Unraveled over Reparations," *New York Times*, May 28, 2021, https://www.nytimes.com/2021/05/28/us/tulsa-race-massacre -commission.html; Grant Stephens, "Boeing Donates $500,000 to Greenwood

Rising History Center," *Newson6,* May 26, 2021, https://www.newson6.com/
story/60afo5b4d6dac10bf93ede74/boeing-donates-500000-to-greenwood
-rising-history-center-; Rhett Morgan, "JPMorgan Chase Gives Quarter-
Million Dollars to 1921 Tulsa Race Massacre Centennial Commission," *Tulsa
World,* May 19, 2021, https://tulsaworld.com/business/local/jpmorgan-chase
-gives-quarter-million-dollars-to-1921-tulsa-race-massacre-centennial
-commission/article_befoaf18-b810-11eb-8b5c-d7190dd40ac5.html; Randy
Krehbiel, "Bank of America Pledges $1 Million for Greenwood Rising Proj-
ect," *Tulsa World,* October 29, 2020, https://tulsaworld.com/business/local/
jpmorgan-chase-gives-quarter-million-dollars-to-1921-tulsa-race-massacre
-centennial-commission/article_befoaf18-b810-11eb-8b5c-d7190dd40ac5
.html.

11. Randy Krehbiel, "Appropriations Bill Includes $1.5 Million for Race Massa-
cre Centennial," *Tulsa World,* May 17, 2019, https://tulsaworld.com/news/
appropriations-bill-includes-1-5-million-for-race-massacre-centennial/article
_f60dc604-05ce-559a-95d1-86652fd58994.html.

12. Phil Armstrong, conversation with author, December 14, 2022; Matt Trot-
ter, "1921 Tulsa Race Massacre Centennial Commission Donates $200K
to Vernon AME Church Renovations," Public Radio Tulsa, April 5, 2021,
https://www.publicradiotulsa.org/local-regional/2021-04-05/1921-tulsa
-race-massacre-centennial-commission-donates-200k-to-vernon-ame-church
-renovations.

13. Tulsa Race Massacre Centennial Commission, *Greenwood Rising;* "US: Failed
Justice 100 Years After the Tulsa Race Massacre," Human Rights Watch,
May 21, 2021, https://www.hrw.org/news/2021/05/21/us-failed-justice-100
-years-after-tulsa-race-massacre.

14. Armstrong conversation.

15. Randy Krehbiel, "Tulsa Race Massacre: Struggle for Reparations from 1921
Massacre Continue, and So Do the Disagreements," *Tulsa World,* May 24,
2021, https://tulsaworld.com/news/local/racemassacre/tulsa-race-massacre
-struggle-for-reparations-from-1921-massacre-continue-and-so-do-the
-disagreements/article_ofc18086-b4f9-11eb-8620-4feb28d687do.html.

16. Adrian Brune, "The Fight for Tulsa's Soul," *Air Mail,* May 29, 2021, https://
airmail.news/issues/2021-5-29/the-fight-for-tulsas-soul.

17. *Tulsa Race Riot: A Report by the Oklahoma Commission to Study the Tulsa
Race Riot of 1921* (Oklahoma City: Commission, 2001), https://www
.okhistory.org/research/forms/freport.pdf.

18. Regina Goodwin, conversation with the author, September 3, 2020.

19. Krehbiel, "Tulsa Race Riot Centennial Commission"; "US: Failed Justice
100 Years After the Tulsa Race Massacre"; Regina Goodwin, conversation
with the author, October 1, 2020.

20. Greenwood Rising, "Greenwood Rising—Ground Breaking Event" (video
post), Facebook, August 21, 2020, https://www.facebook.com/watch/live/?ref=
watch_permalink&v=583745252293214.

21. "Commission Members," Tulsa Race Massacre Centennial Commission,
https://web.archive.org/web/20200412221314/https://www.tulsa2021.org/

members; "Founding Board of Directors," 1921 Tulsa Race Massacre Centennial Commission, https://www.greenwoodrisingxr.com/about.html.

22. Rhett Morgan, "'A Beacon for People': New 21 North Greenwood Building Opening with Law Firm," *Tulsa World*, April 17, 2022, https://tulsaworld .com/business/local/a-beacon-for-people-new-21-north-greenwood-building -opening-with-law-firm/article_a091cee4-b68e-11ec-b7a4-c76a80343907 .html.

23. Greenwood Rising, "Greenwood Rising—Ground Breaking Event."

24. "Public Welfare Board Vacated by Commission," *Tulsa Tribune*, June 14, 1921, 1.

25. Greenwood Rising, "Greenwood Rising—Ground Breaking Event."

26. Kendrick Marshall, "Apparel Line Named in Honor of Black Wall Street Pioneers Launches with Online Shop," *Tulsa World*, April 25, 2020, https:// tulsaworld.com/business/apparel-line-named-in-honor-of-black-wall-street -pioneers-launches-with-online-shop/article_ed49aa61-ff1f-582c-99c5 -a87e531580ac.html.

27. Brett Pulley and Jordyn Holman, "How Greenwood Became the Most Hyped Startup in Black America," *Bloomberg*, April 8, 2022, https://www.bloomberg .com/news/features/2022-04-08/greenwood-banking-app-wants-to-undo-racist -financing.

28. Victor Luckerson, "Watching 'Watchmen' as a Descendant of the Tulsa Race Massacre," *New Yorker*, September 20, 2020, https://www.newyorker.com/ news/news-desk/watching-watchmen-as-a-descendant-of-the-tulsa-race -massacre.

29. Ibid.

30. Marilyn Christopher, conversation with the author, August 24, 2020.

31. Craig Elvy, "*Watchmen* Series Ratings Not as Big a Hit for HBO as You May Think," *Screenrant*, March 5, 2020, https://screenrant.com/watchmen-hbo -series-low-viewership-popularity/; Adam B. Vary, "'Watchmen' Makes History as First Comic-Book Adaptation to Earn Top Emmy," *Variety*, September 20, 2020, https://variety.com/2020/tv/news/watchmen-emmys-best-limited -series-1234775407/.

32. Damon Lindelof, conversation with the author, September 17, 2020.

33. Luckerson, "Watching 'Watchmen.'"

34. Ibid.

35. Ibid.

36. Ibid.

37. Greg Robinson, conversation with the author, August 11, 2020; Contributions and Expenditures Report for Mayoral Campaign of Greg Robinson, January 31, 2021; Monetary Contributions Report for Mayoral Campaign of Greg Robinson, April 1–June 30, 2020; Monetary Contributions Report for Mayoral Campaign of Greg Robinson, August 11–September 30, 2020; Monetary Contributions Report for Mayoral Campaign of Greg Robinson, July 1– August 10, 2020; Contributions and Expenditures Report for Mayoral Campaign of Greg Robinson, October 1–December 31, 2020; the last five in Tulsa Clerk's Office.

38. Tori Tyson, conversation with the author, October 16, 2020.
39. "Rep. Goodwin to Hold Capitol Hearing on Law Enforcement Reform," *Oklahoma Eagle,* October 5, 2020, http://theoklahomaeagle.net/2020/10/05/rep-goodwin-to-hold-capitol-hearing-on-law-enforcement-reform/.
40. Curtis Killman, "Bynum Won 8 in 10 Tulsa Precincts to Capture Second Term but Support Waned North of 21st Street, Voting Data Shows," *Tulsa World,* August 31, 2020, https://tulsaworld.com/news/bynum-won-8-in-10-tulsa-precincts-to-capture-second-term-but-support-waned-north/article_cee1ad2e-e8a8-11ea-b32d-67f6294d5f9b.html; Robinson conversation.
41. "Greg's Proactive Plans for Building a Better Tulsa," Greg for Mayor, https://web.archive.org/web/20200821075433/https://www.gregfortulsa.com/his-vision/.
42. Robinson conversation.
43. "City of Tulsa Creates Citizen Advisory Board and Action Groups as Part of Community Policing Initiative," *City of Tulsa,* November 8, 2017, https://www.cityoftulsa.org/press-room/city-of-tulsa-creates-citizen-advisory-board-and-action-groups-as-part-of-community-policing-initiative/.
44. Monetary Contributions Report for Mayoral Campaign of G. T. Bynum, August 11–October 19, 2020, Tulsa Clerk's Office; Kevin Canfield, "Bynum Campaign Has Big Fundraising Edge in Mayor's Race, Latest Campaign Finance Reports Show," *Tulsa World,* August 7, 2020, https://tulsaworld.com/news/bynum-campaign-has-big-fundraising-edge-in-mayors-race-latest-campaign-finance-reports-show/article_a277da57-9fa9-528b-98d1-419bddf863ba.html; Lobbying by George Kaiser Family Foundation, *ProPublica,* https://projects.propublica.org/represent/lobbying/300948102; Contributions and Expenditures Report for Mayoral Campaign of G. T. Bynum, October 20–December 31, 2020, Tulsa Clerk's Office.
45. Contributions and Expenditures Report for Mayoral Campaign of G. T. Bynum, August 11–October 19, 2020, Tulsa Clerk's Office.
46. Kelsy Schlotthauer, "Nearly 3 Years After Mayor's Proposal, Where Is Tulsa on Police Oversight?" *Tulsa World,* September 5, 2021, https://tulsaworld.com/news/local/govt-and-politics/nearly-3-years-after-mayors-proposal-where-is-tulsa-on-police-oversight/article_e3e17436-0754-11ec-86b0-67ef1e2d8cab.html.
47. Dylan Goforth, "Ally or Adversary: Following Mayoral Election, Bynum, Robinson Likely to Face Each Other Off the Campaign Trail," *Frontier,* August 28, 2020, https://www.readfrontier.org/stories/ally-or-adversary-following-mayoral-election-bynum-robinson-likely-to-face-each-other-off-the-campaign-trail/.
48. Kevin Canfield, "Watch Now: City Removes Black Lives Matter Mural from Site of Tulsa Race Massacre," *Tulsa World,* October 6, 2020, https://tulsaworld.com/news/local/watch-now-city-removes-black-lives-matter-mural-from-site-of-tulsa-race-massacre/article_b6eec872-06f9-11eb-84fe-bf740edf06da.html.
49. Victor Luckerson, "The Defacement and Destruction of Black Lives Matter Murals," *New Yorker,* November 19, 2020, https://www.newyorker.com/news/us-journal/the-defacement-and-destruction-of-black-lives-matter-murals.

50. Sean Murphy, "Attorneys File Lawsuit Seeking Redress for Tulsa Massacre," Associated Press, September 1, 2020, https://apnews.com/article/78853965caa9a4956bed52391a358915.

51. *Lessie Benningfield Randle v. City of Tulsa,* Case No. CV 2020-1179 (Tulsa County District Court, 2020).

52. Victor Luckerson, "What a Florida Reparations Case Can Teach Us About Justice in America," *Time,* September 10, 2020, https://time.com/5887247/reparations-america-rosewood-massacre/.

53. Matt Reynolds, "Tulsa Reckoning: An Ongoing Lawsuit Seeks Justice for Massacre Victims," *ABA Journal,* October 1, 2022, https://www.abajournal.com/magazine/article/tulsa-reckoning.

54. *Black Wall Street Times,* "Justice for Greenwood Prayer Rally for Justice" (video post), Facebook, May 1, 2022, https://www.facebook.com/watch/live/?ref=watch_permalink&v=1017243375582242.

55. Hearings on HR 40 and the Path to Restorative Justice, House Judiciary Committee, 116th Cong., 1st sess. (June 19, 2019).

56. Tim Stanley, "Success of New Tulsa Race Massacre Reparations Lawsuit Hinges on State's Nuisance Law, Attorney Says," *Tulsa World,* September 2, 2020, https://tulsaworld.com/news/local/racemassacre/success-of-new-tulsa-race-massacre-reparations-lawsuit-hinges-on-states-nuisance-law-attorneys-say/article_772c2424-ebdc-11ea-a921-a7223bb10ffb.html; Sara Aridi, "Hal Singer, Influential Saxophonist, Is Dead at 100," *New York Times,* September 11, 2020, https://www.nytimes.com/2020/09/11/arts/music/hal-singer-dead.html.

57. L. Mark Walker and Dale E. Cottingham, "An Abridged Primer on the Law of Public Nuisance," *Tulsa Law Review* 30, no. 2 (Winter 1994), https://core.ac.uk/download/pdf/232679428.pdf.

58. Jan Hoffman, "Johnson & Johnson Ordered to Pay $572 Million in Landmark Opioid Trial," *New York Times,* August 26, 2019, https://www.nytimes.com/2019/08/26/health/oklahoma-opioids-johnson-and-johnson.html.

59. Amir Vera, Omar Jimenez, Ashley Killough, and Leonel Mendez, "Tulsa Race Massacre Reparations Lawsuit Survives Motion to Deny and Will Move Forward, Judge Rules," CNN, May 3, 2022, https://lite.cnn.com/en/article/h_3af60de99fba2775d7b9d9a29e8d72a8.

60. *Randle v. Tulsa.*

61. "Rep. Goodwin to Hold Hearing on Law Enforcement Reform."

62. HB 1674, Oklahoma House of Representatives, 58th Leg., 1st sess., introduced January 19, 2021, http://webserver1.lsb.state.ok.us/cf_pdf/2021-22%20INT/hB/HB1674%20INT.PDF.

63. "Oklahoma House Passes Bill to Protect Drivers Who Hit Protesters" (video), https://www.youtube.com/watch?v=F9gBW1rycs4.

64. HB 1775, Oklahoma House of Representatives, 58th Leg., 1st sess., introduced January 20, 2021, http://webserver1.lsb.state.ok.us/cf_pdf/2021-22%20INT/hB/HB1775%20INT.PDF.

65. Deliberation on HB 1775, Oklahoma House of Representatives, 58th Leg., 2nd sess., April 29, 2021.

66. Ibid.

67. *Black Emergency Response Team v. John O'Connor,* Case No. 5:21-cv-1022-G (U.S. District Court, Western Oklahoma, 2021).

68. Kiara Alfonseca, "Map: Where Anti-Critical Race Theory Efforts Have Reached," ABC News, March 24, 2022, https://abcnews.go.com/Politics/map -anti-critical-race-theory-efforts-reached/story?id=83619715.

69. Danika Ellis, "Here Are the Top 10 Most Banned and Challenged Books of 2021," *Book Riot,* April 5, 2022, https://bookriot.com/most-challenged-books -of-2021/; Andrew Jeong, "Holocaust Graphic Novel 'Maus' Banned in Tennessee County Schools over Nudity and Profanity," *Washington Post,* January 27, 2022, https://www.washingtonpost.com/education/2022/01/27/maus-ban -tennessee-mcminn-county-holocaust/.

70. Randy Krehbiel, "Tulsa Race Massacre Centennial Commission Formally Severs Ties with Gov. Kevin Stitt," *Tulsa World,* May 15, 2021, https://tulsaworld .com/news/local/racemassacre/tulsa-race-massacre-centennial-commission -formally-severs-ties-with-gov-kevin-stitt/article_efc4d76c-b4f6-11eb-b405 -bbf3f0572bc7.html; Randy Krehbiel, "Lankford Steps Down from Race Massacre Centennial Commission, Citing Partisan Shift in Goals," *Tulsa World,* May 28, 2021, https://tulsaworld.com/news/local/racemassacre/lankford-steps -down-from-race-massacre-centennial-commission-citing-partisan-shift-in -goals/article_7d65fff4-bfe9-11eb-9d4c-c3b1cc86e083.html.

71. Greenwood Rising, "Thank You to Lauren Snedden at Visittulsa.com and Our Dynamic Marketing Committee" (photo post), Instagram, February 15, 2021, https://www.instagram.com/p/CLUqMowrLaH/.

CHAPTER 25: THE RITUALS OF REMEMBRANCE

1. *Oklahoma Sun,* August 3, 1921.

2. "Southwest Mourns Passing of Editor," *Chicago Defender,* July 24, 1937, 7.

3. David Goodwin, conversation with the author, May 27, 2021.

4. David Goodwin, *Eagle* critique, Benedictine College.

5. Ibid.

6. D. Goodwin conversation.

7. Jaden Janak, "Digital Archive—Rising from the Ashes: The *Oklahoma Eagle* and Its Long Road to Preservation," *Not Even Past,* n.d., https://notevenpast .org/rising-from-the-ashes-the-oklahoma-eagle-and-its-long-road-to -preservation/.

8. "The *Oklahoma Eagle* Second Century Campaign," *Oklahoma Eagle,* n.d., http://theoklahomaeagle.net/liberty-mutual-2021/.

9. D. Goodwin conversation.

10. Jeanne-Marguerite Goodwin, conversation with the author, May 27, 2021.

11. *Oklahoma Eagle* 2021 distribution route spreadsheet.

12. Ibid.; J.-M. Goodwin conversation.

13. "1921 Tulsa Race Massacre: Day 0," *Oklahoma Eagle,* May 28, 2021, C1.

14. "Impact Magazine 1971: 'Profile of a Race Riot,'" *Oklahoma Eagle,* May 28, 2021, C2.

15. "They Saved the Greenwood Area for Negroes," *Oklahoma Eagle,* May 28, 2021, C6.

16. "After One Year, Will We See Real Police Reform," *Oklahoma Eagle*, May 28, 2021, A5.

17. J. Kavin Ross, "Mass Graves Investigation Resumes Tuesday," *Oklahoma Eagle*, May 28, 2021, A3.

18. "The Oklahoma Eagle Church Directory," *Oklahoma Eagle*, May 28, 2021, A6.

19. *Oklahoma Eagle*, May 28, 2021, A1.

20. D. Goodwin conversation.

21. Lauren Elizabeth Palmer, conversation with the author, July 12, 2022; "Epilogue: SendFlowersToGreenwood," Wild Mother, https://www.thewildmother .com/sendflowerstoresources/epilogue.

22. Lauren Elizabeth Palmer, conversation with the author, July 5, 2022.

23. KJRH, "Black Wall Street Legacy Festival's Closing Remembrance Ceremony Is Hosted by Tulsa's Community Remembrance Coalition in Partnership with the Equal Justice Initiative" (video post), Facebook, https://www.facebook .com/kjrhtv/videos/1596333382802153/.

24. Noa Yachot, " 'The Loss Is Incalculable': Descendants of the Tulsa Massacre on What Was Stolen from Them," *Guardian*, May 31, 2021, https://www .theguardian.com/us-news/2021/may/31/tulsa-massacre-descendants-callout -stories.

25. KJRH, "Black Wall Street Legacy Festival's Closing Ceremony."

26. Ibid.

27. "Community Remembrance Project," Equal Justice Institute, n.d., https://eji .org/projects/community-remembrance-project/.

28. Kendrick Marshall, "McLain Students, Community Members Collect Soil in Remembrance of 1921 Tulsa Race Massacre Victims," *Tulsa World*, November 7, 2019, https://tulsaworld.com/news/local/racemassacre/mclain-students -community-members-collect-soil-in-remembrance-of-1921-tulsa-race -massacre-victims/article_ddb658b8-b1b2-5b29-bd56-eae6b3319edc.html; "The Tulsa Community Remembrance Project Soil Collection Event Today to Honor Rosa Morrison," *Oklahoma Eagle*, November 8, 2019, http:// theoklahomaeagle.net/2019/11/08/the-tulsa-community-remembrance-project -soil-collection-event-today/; "Soil Collection Ceremony to Begin for Lynched Victims of Tulsa's Race Massacre," *Black Wall Street Times*, May 24, 2019, https://theblackwallsttimes.com/2019/05/24/soil-collection-ceremony-to-begin -for-lynched-victims-of-tulsas-race-massacre/; Carla Hinton, "Tulsa Race Massacre Victim Honored with Soil Collection Ceremony," *Oklahoman*, November 9, 2020, https://www.oklahoman.com/story/news/religion/2020/11/09/ tulsa-race-massacre-victim-honored-with-soil-collection-ceremony/3115 00007/.

29. Victor Luckerson, "What the Tulsa Race Massacre Survivors Want," *Run It Back*, May 25, 2021, https://runitback.substack.com/p/what-the-tulsa-race -massacre-survivors; DeNeen L. Brown, "One of the Last Survivors of the 1921 Tulsa Race Massacre, 107 Years Old, Wants Justice," *Washington Post*, May 19, 2021, https://www.washingtonpost.com/history/2021/05/19/viola -fletcher-tulsa-race-massacre-survivor/.

30. Brown, "One of the Last Survivors."

31. Luckerson, "What the Massacre Survivors Want."
32. KJRH, "Black Wall Street Legacy Festival's Closing Ceremony."
33. HR 40, Commission to Study and Develop Reparation Proposals for African-Americans Act, 116th Cong., 1st sess. (2019).
34. KJRH, "Black Wall Street Legacy Festival's Closing Ceremony."
35. Ibid.
36. "Pioneer Teacher Expires," *Oklahoma Eagle*, May 27, 1965, 1; "Dr. J. J. McKeever Dies; Rites Slated," *Oklahoma Eagle*, September 7, 1961, 1.
37. "Longtime Social Worker, Mrs. Mary Williams, Dies," *Oklahoma Eagle*, July 2, 1970, 1.
38. "Community Activist and Philanthropist Dr. Anita Christopher Succumbs," *Oklahoma Eagle*, January 10, 2019, http://theoklahomaeagle.net/2019/01/10/community-activist-and-philanthropist-dr-anita-christopher-succumbs/; "Tulsans Agree That Public Service Was Christopher's Passion," *Oklahoma Eagle*, January 5, 2006, 4.
39. Charles Christopher, Jr., conversation with the author, May 31, 2021.
40. Allyn Baccus, conversation with the author, May 31, 2021.
41. "Critics Say Changing Cemetery's Name Buries Black History," *Tulsa World*, April 30, 1997, https://tulsaworld.com/archive/critics-say-changing-cemeterys-name-buries-black-history/article_8b825912-e4f2-5d0e-b299-e93145aa4699.html.
42. Gabrielle Sorto, "Tulsa Searches for Mass Graves from 1921 Tulsa Race Massacre," CNN, October 8, 2019, https://www.cnn.com/2019/10/08/us/tulsa-mass-graves-search-race-massacre-trnd.
43. Scrapbook compiled by W. D. Williams while attending Hampton Institute, 1924–28, 44, National Museum of African American History and Culture, Smithsonian, Washington, D.C., https://transcription.si.edu/project/37790.
44. Byron Crenshaw, conversation with the author, June 8, 2021.
45. Byron Crenshaw, conversation with the author, January 18, 2021.
46. Crenshaw conversation, June 8, 2021.
47. Victor Luckerson, "The Rituals of Remembrance," *Run It Back*, June 5, 1921, https://runitback.substack.com/p/the-rituals-of-remembrance.
48. Charles Christopher III, conversation with the author, May 31, 2021.
49. Baccus conversation.
50. Milton Washington, conversation with the author, May 31, 2021.
51. Byron Crenshaw, conversation with the author, May 31, 2021.
52. Charles Christopher, Jr., and Jan Christopher, conversation with the author, September 4, 2022.
53. Carla Hinton, "Attorneys Requested Funds to Go to Tulsa Race Massacre Survivors for Involvement in 'Remember + Rise,'" *Oklahoman*, May 28, 2021, https://www.oklahoman.com/story/news/2021/05/28/remember-rise-tulsa-race-massacre-survivors-reparations-centennial-events-greenwood/5246215001/.
54. Victor Luckerson, "The Women Who Preserved the Story of the Tulsa Race Massacre," *New Yorker*, May 28, 2021, https://www.newyorker.com/news/us-journal/the-women-who-preserved-the-story-of-the-tulsa-race-massacre.

55. Anneliese Bruner, Portia Hurtt, and Kevin Hurtt, conversation with the author, May 30, 2021.
56. Lauren Usher, conversation with the author, June 1, 2021.
57. Lauren Usher, introduction of President Joe Biden, Greenwood Cultural Center, June 1, 2021.
58. Ibid.
59. Randy Krehbiel, "Watch Now: 'Hate Is Never Defeated,' Biden Says on Race Massacre Centennial," *Tulsa World,* June 2, 2021, https://tulsaworld.com/news/local/racemassacre/watch-now-hate-is-never-defeated-biden-says-on-race-massacre-centennial/article_5e141afo-c246-11eb-b815-6ff32af829b4.html.
60. Ibid.
61. "Remarks by President Biden Commemorating the 100th Anniversary of the Tulsa Race Massacre," White House, June 1, 2021, https://www.whitehouse.gov/briefing-room/speeches-remarks/2021/06/02/remarks-by-president-biden-commemorating-the-100th-anniversary-of-the-tulsa-race-massacre/.
62. Lauren Usher and Karen Usher, conversation with the author, June 1, 2021.
63. Taylor Borden, "The Hyatt Story: How a Packed LAX Motel and a $2.2 Million Offer Scribbled on a Napkin Spawned One of The World's Biggest Hotel Empires," *Business Insider,* February 13, 2020, https://www.businessinsider.com/how-hyatt-hotel-empire-was-created-pritzker-family.
64. Usher and Usher conversation.
65. Palmer conversation, July 5, 2022.

CHAPTER 26: BEYOND CEREMONY

1. Regina Goodwin, conversation with the author, February 7, 2022.
2. Ibid.
3. Dianna Everett, "Turnpikes and Toll Bridges," *Encyclopedia of Oklahoma History and Culture,* https://www.okhistory.org/publications/enc/entry.php?entry=TU022.
4. R. Goodwin conversation.
5. HB 4152, Oklahoma House of Representatives, 58th Leg., 2nd sess., introduced January 20, 2022, http://webserver1.lsb.state.ok.us/cf_pdf/2021-22%20INT/hB/HB4152%20INT.PDF.
6. Larry O'Dell, "Riot Property Loss," in *Tulsa Race Riot: A Report by the Oklahoma Commission to Study the Tulsa Race Riot of 1921* (Oklahoma City: Commission, 2001), 145, https://www.okhistory.org/research/forms/freport.pdf.
7. "Tulsa, OK Housing Market," Realtor.com, https://www.realtor.com/realestateandhomes-search/Tulsa_OK/overview.
8. R. Goodwin conversation.
9. David Blatt, "Increased Gross Production Taxes Are Fueling State's Revenue Boom," Oklahoma Policy Institute, June 5, 2019, https://okpolicy.org/increased-gross-production-taxes-are-fueling-states-revenue-boom/; Tres Savage, "State Savings Accounts Rise, Huge Turnpike Plan Unveiled," *NonDoc,* February 22, 2022, https://nondoc.com/2022/02/22/state-savings-accounts-rise-huge-turnpike-plan-unveiled/.

10. HB 4153, Oklahoma House of Representatives, 58th Leg., 2nd sess., introduced January 20, 2022, http://webserver1.lsb.state.ok.us/cf_pdf/2021-22%20INT/hB/HB4153%20INT.PDF.

11. David Sherfinski, "Feature: Biden Infrastructure Bill Aims to Heal Black Areas Split by Highways," Reuters, February 24, 2022, https://www.reuters.com/article/usa-highways-race/feature-biden-infrastructure-bill-aims-to-heal-black-areas-split-by-highways-idUSL8N2UI65H.

12. "State Rep. Goodwin Holds Study, Looks to Remove IDL Running Through Greenwood District," KJRH, September 28, 2021, https://www.kjrh.com/local-news/state-rep-goodwin-holds-study-looks-to-remove-idl-running-through-greenwood-district; Nadja Popovich, Josh Williams, and Denise Lu, "Can Removing Highways Fix America's Cities?," New York Times, May 27, 2021, https://www.nytimes.com/interactive/2021/05/27/climate/us-cities-highway-removal.htm.

13. Stephen Dolman, "Panel Legislators Say Proposal Is Doomed to Rejection," Tulsa World, February 5, 2000, https://tulsaworld.com/archive/panel-legislators-say-proposal-is-doomed-to-rejection/article_3b417b29-7b19-5b2d-9296-c614600d6a9b.html.

14. Trevor Brown, "Hundreds of Bills Passed the Legislature. Just a Dozen Were Authored by Democrats," Oklahoma Watch, June 2, 2022, https://oklahomawatch.org/2022/06/02/hundreds-of-bills-passed-the-legislature-just-a-dozen-were-authored-by-democrats/.

15. HB 2988, Oklahoma House of Representatives, 58th Leg., 2nd sess., introduced December 2, 2022, http://webserver1.lsb.state.ok.us/cf_pdf/2021-22%20INT/hB/HB2988%20INT.PDF; SB 1142, Oklahoma Senate, 58th Leg., 2nd session, introduced December 16, 2021, http://webserver1.lsb.state.ok.us/cf_pdf/2021-22%20INT/SB/SB1142%20INT.PDF.

16. Caroline Kitchener, "Okla. Legislature Approves Bill Banning Abortions After 6 Weeks of Pregnancy," Washington Post, April 28, 2022, https://www.washingtonpost.com/politics/2022/04/28/abortion-oklahoma-republicans/.

17. R. Goodwin conversation.

18. Garrett Yalch, "After More Than 20 Years, a Scholarship to Help Students Harmed by the Tulsa Race Massacre Has New Funding," Frontier, June 23, 2022, https://www.readfrontier.org/stories/after-more-than-20-years-a-scholarship-to-help-students-harmed-by-the-tulsa-race-massacre-has-new-funding/; Regina Goodwin, conversation with the author, January 26, 2022.

19. Victor Luckerson, "What a Florida Reparations Case Can Teach Us About Justice in America," Time, September 10, 2020, https://time.com/5887247/reparations-america-rosewood-massacre/.

20. HB 4154, Oklahoma House of Representatives, 58th Leg., 2nd sess., introduced January 20, 2022, http://webserver1.lsb.state.ok.us/cf_pdf/2021-22%20INT/hB/HB4154%20INT.PDF.

21. R. Goodwin conversation, February 7, 2022.

22. Ibid.

23. Ibid.

24. "Appropriations and Budget, Education," House Committee Members, Okla-

homa House of Representatives, https://www.okhouse.gov/committees/CommitteeMembers.aspx?CommID=101&SubCommID=50.

25. Regina Goodwin, conversation with the author, February 21, 2022.

26. Regina Goodwin, conversation with the author, July 6, 2022.

27. R. Goodwin conversation, February 21, 2022.

28. Deliberation on HB 4154 Before the Appropriations and Budget Education Subcommittee, Oklahoma House of Representatives, 58th Leg., 2nd sess., February 21, 2022.

29. Deliberation on HB 4154.

30. Deliberation on HB 4154.

31. HB 4154, Oklahoma House of Representatives, 58th Leg.

32. Ibid.

33. Ibid.

34. R. Goodwin conversation, February 21, 2022.

35. Deliberation on HB 4154.

36. Deliberation on HB 3720 before the Appropriations and Budget Education Subcommittee, Oklahoma House of Representatives, 58th Leg., 2nd sess., February 21, 2022.

37. R. Goodwin conversation, February 21, 2022.

38. Victor Luckerson, "Celebrations in the Courthouse as Race Massacre Lawsuit Moves Forward," *Oklahoma Eagle,* May 6, 2022, 1.

39. Ashlyn Brothers, "Prayer Rally Held by Justice for Greenwood Movement," *News on 6,* May 1, 2022, https://www.newson6.com/story/626f52990 5f9fc072d56688a/prayer-rally-held-by-justice-for-greenwood-movement.

40. Luckerson, "Celebrations in the Courthouse."

41. Ibid.; Caleb Gayle, "100 Years After the Tulsa Massacre, What Does Justice Look Like?" *New York Times,* May 25, 2022, https://www.nytimes.com/2021/05/25/magazine/tulsa-race-massacre-1921-greenwood.html.

42. Ken Miller, "Judge Lets Tulsa Race Massacre Reparations Lawsuit Proceed," *Hill,* May 2, 2022, https://thehill.com/homenews/state-watch/3474631-judge-lets-tulsa-race-massacre-reparations-lawsuit-proceed/.

43. Luckerson, "Celebrations in the Courthouse."

44. *Oklahoma ex rel. Attorney General of Oklahoma v. Johnson & Johnson,* OK 54 (2021).

45. Ibid.

46. Luckerson, "Celebrations in the Courthouse."

47. *Lessie Benningfield Randle v. City of Tulsa,* Case No. CV 2020-1179 (Tulsa County District Court, 2020).

48. Luckerson, "Celebrations in the Courthouse."

49. Vote record for HB 4146, Oklahoma House of Representatives, 58th Leg., 2nd sess., 2022; Vote record for HB 4146, Oklahoma Senate, 58th Leg., 2nd sess., 2022.

50. Regina Goodwin, conversation with the author, April 28, 2022.

51. Nuria Martinez-Keel, "Charter School Reform Bill Passes Oklahoma House," *Oklahoman,* April 28, 2022, https://www.oklahoman.com/story/news/education/2022/04/28/charter-school-reform-bill-passes-oklahoma-house/9561854002/?gnt-cfr=1.

52. R. Goodwin conversation, April 28, 2022.
53. HB 3564, Oklahoma House of Representatives, 58th Leg., 2nd sess., introduced January 20, 2022, http://webserver1.lsb.state.ok.us/cf_pdf/2021-22%20INT/hB/HB3564%20INT.PDF.
54. R. Goodwin conversation, April 28, 2022.
55. Regina Goodwin, conversation with the author, July 6, 2022.
56. Yalch, "After More Than Twenty Years."
57. HB 4154, Oklahoma House of Representatives, 58th Leg., 2nd sess., introduced January 20, 2022, http://webserver1.lsb.state.ok.us/cf_pdf/2021-22%20INT/hB/HB4154%20INT.PDF.
58. Regina Goodwin, conversation with the author, July 6, 2022.
59. Yalch, "After More Than Twenty Years."
60. Regina Goodwin, conversation with the author, January 26, 2022.
61. Terence Crutcher Foundation, *Our Generational Vision for Justice and Liberation,* August 17, 2021, https://www.terencecrutcherfoundation.org/thereport.
62. "Terence Crutcher Foundation Hosts Annual Day of Service," KJRH, September 28, 2021, https://www.kjrh.com/news/local-news/terence-crutcher-foundation-hosts-annual-day-of-service.
63. Tiffany Crutcher, Terence Crutcher Foundation Day of Service, speech, September 17, 2022, 36th Street North Event Center, Tulsa.
64. Tyrance Billingsley, Terence Crutcher Foundation Day of Service, speech, September 17, 2022, 36th Street North Event Center, Tulsa.
65. Tiffany Crutcher, Terence Crutcher Foundation Day speech.
66. Martin Kaste, "Minneapolis Voters Reject a Measure to Replace the City's Police Department," NPR, November 3, 2021, https://www.npr.org/2021/11/02/1051617581/minneapolis-police-vote.
67. Daniela Ibarra, "Tulsa City Council Rejects Proposal for Police Oversight Monitor, for Now," KTUL, March 31, 2022, https://ktul.com/news/local/tulsa-city-council-rejects-proposal-for-police-oversight-monitor-for-now-2019-accountable-shot-killed-ladonna-paris-terence-crutcher-office-of-independent-monitors.
68. "Editorial: External Police Liaison Good First Step for Creating Tulsa Solution," *Tulsa World,* July 8, 2022, https://tulsaworld.com/opinion/editorial/editorial-external-police-liaison-good-first-step-for-creating-tulsa-solution/article_a6ce4956-fc9b-11ec-afe3-7f6653c1b4bf.html.
69. Eric Levenson, "The Charges Against Derek Chauvin in the Death of George Floyd, Explained," CNN, April 20, 2021, https://www.cnn.com/2021/04/19/us/derek-chauvin-charges-explain/index.html.
70. Philip Bump, "How the First Statement from Minneapolis Police Made George Floyd's Murder Seem Like George Floyd's Fault," *Washington Post,* April 20, 2021, https://www.washingtonpost.com/politics/2021/04/20/how-first-statement-minneapolis-police-made-george-floyds-murder-seem-like-george-floyds-fault/.
71. "Dr. Tiffany Crutcher Witnessed Pres. Biden Sign Policing Reform Order," KJRH, May 25, 2022, https://www.kjrh.com/news/local-news/dr-tiffany-crutcher-traveled-to-white-house-at-invitation-of-president-biden.
72. Zolan Kanno-Youngs and Charlie Savage, "Biden Set to Issue Policing Order on

Anniversary of Floyd Killing," *New York Times*, May 24, 2022, https://www
.nytimes.com/2022/05/24/us/politics/police-executive-order-george-floyd.html.

73. Tiffany Crutcher, conversation with the author, December 4, 2022.

74. Kode Ransom, Greenwood tour, June 4, 2022, Black Wall Street Liquid Lounge, Tulsa.

75. Ibid.

76. Chief Amusan, conversation with the author, June 4, 2022.

77. Sydney Anderson, "Nikole Hannah-Jones Takes 1619 Project to Trump Country in Oklahoma," *Black Wall Street Times*, June 1, 2022, https://theblack wallsttimes.com/2022/06/01/nikole-hannah-jones-takes-1619-project-to-trump -country-in-oklahoma/.

78. Emily Farris, "Greenwood Rising Hosts Candlelight Vigil to Commemorate Tulsa Race Massacre," KJRH, May 31, 2022, https://www.kjrh.com/news/ local-news/greenwood-rising-hosts-candlelight-vigil-to-commemorate-tulsa -race-massacre.

79. Tiffany Crutcher, conversation with the author, June 4, 2022.

80. Victor Luckerson, "U.S. Senior Biden Administration Official Visits Greenwood, Discusses Removal of Highway," *Oklahoma Eagle*, May 27–June 9, 2022, 1.

81. Ahrray Young, conversation with the author, June 4, 2022.

EPILOGUE

1. B. C. Franklin, *My Life and an Era: The Autobiography of Buck Colbert Franklin* (Baton Rouge: Louisiana State University Press, 1997), 246.

2. Regina Goodwin, conversation with the author, January 26, 2022.

3. DeNeen L. Brown, "'They Was Killing Black People,'" *Washington Post*, September 28, 2018, https://www.washingtonpost.com/news/local/wp/2018/09/ 28/feature/they-was-killing-black-people/?itid=ap_deneenl.brown; DeNeen L. Brown, "Tulsa Mayor Reopens Investigation into Possible Mass Graves from 1921 Race Massacre," *Washington Post*, October 3, 2018, https://www .washingtonpost.com/local/tulsa-mayor-reopens-investigation-into-possible -mass-graves-from-1921-race-massacre/2018/10/02/df713c96-c68f-11e8-b2b5 -79270f9cce17_story.html.

4. 1921 Graves, "1921 Graves Investigation Update—November 18, 2022," Facebook (video post), https://www.facebook.com/1921Graves/videos/ 650892003432297.

5. *Oaklawn*, documentary screening, Center for Public Secrets, November 11, 2022.

6. Kendrick Marshall, "Tulsa Mass Graves Investigation Public Oversight Committee Sets Rules for Physical Process," *Tulsa World*, August 23, 2019, https:// tulsaworld.com/news/local/racemassacre/tulsa-mass-graves-investigation -public-oversight-committee-sets-rules-for-physical-process/article_be8a83d4 -33a4-5961-96c2-da90cfbf2c87.html; Randy Hopkins, "An Open Letter to the Tulsa City Council," *Center for Public Secrets*, March 2022, https://www .centerforpublicsecrets.org/post/an-open-letter-to-the-tulsa-city-council.

7. Randy Krehbiel, "Watch Now: Exhumed Remains Reburied at Oaklawn amid Protests from Greenwood Descendants," *Tulsa World*, July 30, 2021, https://

tulsaworld.com/news/local/racemassacre/watch-now-exhumed-remains
-reburied-at-oaklawn-amid-protests-from-greenwood-descendants/article
_3b04fb58-f08e-11eb-95c1-d78bc2d50b27.html.

8. Raja Razek, "In Search for Unidentified Victims of 1921 Tulsa Race Massacre, Remains Were Found of a Man with a Gunshot Wound," CNN, November 12, 2022, https://www.cnn.com/2022/11/12/us/tulsa-massacre-burial -excavation-victim-gunshot-wound-reaj/index.html.

9. Associated Press, "Tulsa Race Massacre: 19 Bodies Reinterred as Protesters Demand Investigation," *Guardian,* July 31, 2021, https://www.theguardian .com/us-news/2021/jul/31/bodies-tulsa-race-massacre-oklahoma-reinterred.

10. Order on Defendants' Motion to Dismiss, *Lessie Benningfield Randle v. City of Tulsa,* August 3, 2022, 3–4.

11. Mike Creef, "Transformation Church Gifts over $1 Million to Tulsa Race Massacre Survivors, Nonprofits," *Black Wall Street Times,* June 22, 2021, https://theblackwallsttimes.com/2021/06/22/transformation-church-gifts-over -1-million-to-tulsa-race-massacre-survivors-nonprofits/; DeNeen L. Brown, "Three Survivors of Tulsa Race Massacre Receive $1 Million Donation," *Washington Post,* May 18, 2022, https://www.washingtonpost.com/history/ 2022/05/18/tulsa-massacre-survivors-donation/.

12. Ken Miller, "Judge: Tulsa Race Massacre Victims Descendants Can't Sue," Associated Press, August 4, 2022, https://apnews.com/article/lawsuits-race-and -ethnicity-tulsa-oklahoma-massacres-61e4a271a584c40483e1ba0709699159.

13. Victor Luckerson, "Can Buttigieg's $1B Plan Help Remove I-244 from the Historic Greenwood District's 'Black Wall Street'?" *Oklahoma Eagle,* September 3, 2022, https://theokeagle.com/2022/09/03/can-buttigiegs-1b-plan-help -remove-i-244-from-greenwood/.

14. Tulsa Greenwood Reconnecting Communities Pilot (RCP) Planning Grant Application, October 13, 2022.

15. Oklahoma Department of Transportation, "Enhancing Community Connectivity in Tulsa: I-244 Planning Study," https://tinyurl.com/vfu67mvh.

16. U.S. Department of Transportation, "Reconnecting Communities Pilot Program FY 2022: Award Fact Sheets," February 28, 2023, https://www.transportation.gov/sites/dot.gov/files/2023-02/RCP%20Fact%20Sheets%202022.pdf.

17. R. Goodwin conversation, March 5, 2023.

18. Nuria Martinez-Keel, "Tulsa, Mustang Schools' Accreditation Demoted for HB 1775 Violations," *Oklahoman,* July 28, 2022, https://www.oklahoman .com/story/news/education/2022/07/28/tulsa-ok-mustang-schools-demoted-hb -1775-violations/65385030007/.

19. Lenzy Krehbiel-Burton, "Watch Now: Tulsa Public Schools Accredited with a Warning over HB 1775 Violation," *Tulsa World,* July 29, 2022, https:// tulsaworld.com/news/local/education/watch-now-tulsa-public-schools -accredited-with-a-warning-over-hb1775-violation/article_e2aa9fa2-0dd9 -11ed-aca4-4bfac4fed0ef.html.

20. Nuria Martinez-Keel, "Oklahoma Teachers on Notice After 'Watershed' Vote on Tulsa, Mustang HB 1775 Violations," *Oklahoman,* August 10, 2022, https://www.oklahoman.com/story/news/education/2022/08/10/tulsa-mustang -race-gender-curriculum-violation-vote-oklahoma-teachers/65393793007/.

21. Ryan Walters, "We Will Reject," Twitter, August 8, 2022, https://twitter.com/sec_walters/status/1556742939547783169?lang=en.

22. Ryan Walters, "Opinion: Oklahoma House Bill 1775 Says We Must Teach History Without Prejudicing the Future," *Tulsa World,* May 11, 2021, https://tulsaworld.com/opinion/columnists/opinion-okalahoma-house-bill-1775-says-we-must-teach-history-without-prejudicing-the-future/article_8b417018-b184-11eb-a06b-c73f425d3e8a.html#tncms-source=login; James Bickerton, "Oklahoma School Book Ban Blocks Works from Eight Black Authors—Full List," *Newsweek,* September 6, 2022, https://www.newsweek.com/oklahoma-school-book-ban-blocks-works-eight-black-authorsfull-list-1740301.

23. Oklahoma State Board of Education, deliberation, July 28, 2022.

24. Cal Day, "Tulsa City Leaders Project 2022 to Be Big Year for Tourism," *News on 6,* January 17, 2022, https://www.newson6.com/story/61e577734ec3oeoco4a1a251/tulsa-city-leaders-project-2022-to-be-big-year-for-tourism.

25. Meredith McCown, "Greenwood Rising Reopens to the Public with Exhibit Updates," *News on 6,* August 31, 2022, https://www.newson6.com/story/630f62f1ce1b15072b876a1f/greenwood-rising-reopens-to-the-public-with-exhibit-updates/.

26. "Alaskans Receive over $3,000 in Wealth Payment Checks," CBS News, September 21, 2022, https://www.cbsnews.com/news/alaska-oil-wealth-payments-2022/.

27. Mike Wendling, "Reparations: The U.S. Town Paying Its Black Residents," BBC News, October 12, 2022, https://www.bbc.com/news/world-us-canada-63165668.

28. "Bruce's Beach Being Returned to Black Family 100 Years After City 'Used the Law to Steal It,'" *Guardian,* October 1, 2021, https://www.theguardian.com/us-news/2021/oct/01/bruces-beach-returned-100-years-california.

29. "Middleton Scholars Education Assistance Fund," *Middleton Place,* https://www.middletonplace.org/news-and-events/wp-content/uploads/2021/10/MPF-endowed-scholarship.pdf.

30. "About Transitional Justice and Human Rights," United Nations, Office of the High Commissioner for Human Rights, https://www.ohchr.org/en/transitional-justice/about-transitional-justice-and-human-rights.

31. Kevin Canfield, "Terence Crutcher Foundation Buys North Pointe Shopping Center," *Tulsa World,* December 20, 2022, https://tulsaworld.com/news/local/terence-crutcher-foundation-buys-north-pointe-shopping-center/article_a8df9dd2-7fco-11ed-9912-5f6931900b8e.html.

32. Luckerson, "Can Buttigieg's $1B Plan Help."

33. Princetta Rudd-Newman, conversation with the author, August 26, 2022.

34. "It's Official, the *Oklahoma Eagle* Is 100 Years Old," *Oklahoma Eagle,* October 24, 2022, https://theokeagle.com/2022/10/24/its-official-the-oklahoma-eagle-is-100-years-old/.

35. Caleigh Bartash, "'It's Up to Us to Keep the Flame Burning,'" *Oklahoma Eagle,* July 22, 2022, https://theokeagle.com/2022/07/22/its-up-to-us-to-keep-the-flame-burning/.

36. David Goodwin, conversation with the author, November 6, 2022.

PHOTOGRAPH CREDITS

3. Water Valley Casey Jones Railroad Museum

6. *Oklahoma Eagle*

16. Williams Dreamland LLC

23. Williams Dreamland LLC

29. Tulsa Historical Society & Museum

46. Courtesy of the Oklahoma Historical Society

52. Library of Congress, Prints & Photographs Division, LC-DIG-ggbain-08334 (digital file from original neg.)

62. Tulsa Historical Society & Museum

75. **Top:** Courtesy of the Greenwood Cultural Center

75. **Bottom:** Tulsa Historical Society & Museum

77. Tulsa Historical Society & Museum

90. Tulsa Historical Society & Museum

93. Tulsa Historical Society & Museum

95. Collection of the Smithsonian National Museum of African American History and Culture, Gift of Cassandra P. Johnson Smith

97. Houses on fire during looting, 1921-06-01, 1989.004.5.43. Tulsa Race Massacre of 1921 archive, 1989-004. The University of Tulsa, McFarlin Library, Department of Special Collections & University Archives. [McFarlin Library, University of Tulsa]

103. Tulsa Historical Society & Museum

105. Collection of the Smithsonian National Museum of African American History and Culture, Gift of Princetta R. Newman

106. Tulsa Historical Society & Museum

109. **Top Left:** African-American family standing by truck, 1921-06-01,

1989.004.5.21. Tulsa Race Massacre of 1921 archive, 1989-004. The University of Tulsa, McFarlin Library, Department of Special Collections & University Archives. [McFarlin Library]

109. **Top:** Tulsa Historical Society & Museum

109. **Bottom left:** Ruth Sigler Avery Collection—Tulsa Race Massacre of 1921, Department of Special Collections and Archives, Oklahoma State University–Tulsa

109. **Bottom right:** Tulsa Historical Society & Museum

110–111. Corner of Greenwood and Archer devastated, 1921-06-01, 1989.004.5.W14. Tulsa Race Massacre of 1921 archive, 1989-004. The University of Tulsa, McFarlin Library, Department of Special Collections & University Archives. [McFarlin Library]

113. Tulsa Historical Society & Museum

116. Tulsa Historical Society & Museum

121. Collection of the Smithsonian National Museum of African American History and Culture, Gift from Tulsa Friends and John W. and Karen R. Franklin

122. Tulsa Historical Society & Museum

131. Tulsa Historical Society & Museum

137. Library of Congress Prints and Photographs Division, LC-USZ62-38623 (b&w film copy neg.)

140. Jeanne Osby Goodwin Arradondo Family Collection

142. Jeanne Osby Goodwin Arradondo Family Collection

153. Tulsa Historical Society &
Museum
154. Williams Dreamland LLC
162. Tulsa Historical Society &
Museum
168. Williams Dreamland LLC
170. Jeanne Osby Goodwin Arradondo
Family Collection
188. *Oklahoma Eagle*
194. Tulsa Historical Society &
Museum
197. **Left:** Williams Dreamland LLC
197. **Right:** Tulsa Historical Society &
Museum
202. Courtesy of the Greenwood
Cultural Center
204. *Oklahoma Eagle*
207. Jeanne Osby Goodwin Arradondo
Family Collection
215. Susan Jordan
218. Jeanne Osby Goodwin Arradondo
Family Collection
219. Jeanne Osby Goodwin Arradondo
Family Collection
226. Tulsa Historical Society &
Museum
232. Williams Dreamland LLC
236. Courtesy of the Greenwood
Cultural Center
240. Courtesy of the Oklahoma
Historical Society
255. Jeanne Osby Goodwin Arradondo
Family Collection
258. Jeanne Osby Goodwin Arradondo
Family Collection
260. Jeanne Osby Goodwin Arradondo
Family Collection
276. Jeanne Osby Goodwin Arradondo
Family Collection
298. Jo Ann Gilford Collection
304. Courtesy of the Oklahoma
Historical Society
307. *Tulsa World*
312. Tulsa Historical Society &
Museum

319. Jeanne Osby Goodwin Arradondo
Family Collection
323. Victor Luckerson
329. Jeanne Osby Goodwin Arradondo
Family Collection
332. Jeanne Osby Goodwin Arradondo
Family Collection
335. Jeanne Osby Goodwin Arradondo
Family Collection
343. Photograph by Don Thompson—
Baltimore Barbershop © 1970
348. Jeanne Osby Goodwin Arradondo
Family Collection
361. Theatre North
365. Victor Luckerson
367. Victor Luckerson
371. Joseph Rushmore
373. Jeanne Osby Goodwin Arradondo
Family Collection
383. Victor Luckerson
385. Joseph Rushmore
386. Tiffany Crutcher Family Photo
Album
390. *Tulsa World*
400. Christopher Creese
403. Victor Luckerson
406. Victor Luckerson
416. DeRico M. Green
417. Joseph Rushmore
421. Victor Luckerson
422. Victor Luckerson
433. State of Oklahoma Legislative
Service Bureau: Photo Division
435. Christopher Creese
437. Victor Luckerson
440. Christopher Creese
443. Christopher Creese
445. Victor Luckerson
447 Williams Dreamland LLC
451. Victor Luckerson
454. Victor Luckerson
460. Victor Luckerson
464. Victor Luckerson
468. Victor Luckerson
474. Victor Luckerson

INDEX

Page numbers of photographs appear in italics.
Key to abbreviations: Ed Jr. = Edward Goodwin, Jr.; Ed Sr. = Edward Goodwin, Sr.;
FEPC = Fair Employment Practices Committee; HOLC = Home Owners Loan
Corporation; MLK = Martin Luther King, Jr.; TAAG = Target Area Action Group;
TURA = Tulsa Urban Renewal Authority

ABOUT THE AUTHOR

VICTOR LUCKERSON is a journalist and author based in Tulsa who works to bring neglected black history to light. He is a former staff writer at *The Ringer* and business reporter for *Time* magazine. His writing and research have appeared in *The New Yorker*, *The New York Times*, *Wired*, and *Smithsonian Magazine*. He was nominated for a National Magazine Award for his reporting in *Time* on the 1923 Rosewood Massacre. He also manages an email newsletter about underexplored aspects of black history called *Run It Back*.

vicluckerson.com
Twitter: @VLuck
Instagram: @vluck89